Understanding Human Development

Biological, Social and Psychological Processes from Conception to Adult Life

Stephanie Thornton

palgrave
macmillan

First published 2008 by
PALGRAVE MACMILLAN
Houndmills, Basingstoke, Hampshire RG21 6XS and
175 Fifth Avenue, New York, N.Y. 10010
Companies and representatives throughout the world

PALGRAVE MACMILLAN is the global academic imprint of the Palgrave Macmillan division of St. Martin's Press, LLC and of Palgrave Macmillan Ltd. Macmillan® is a registered trademark in the United States, United Kingdom and other countries. Palgrave is a registered trademark in the European Union and other countries.

ISBN-13: 978-1-4039-3305-8   hardback
ISBN-10: 1-4039-3305-7   hardback
ISBN-13: 978-1-4039-3306-5   paperback
ISBN-10: 1-4039-3306-5   paperback

This book is printed on paper suitable for recycling and made from fully managed and sustained forest sources. Logging, pulping and manufacturing processes are expected to conform to the environmental regulations of the country of origin.

A catalogue record for this book is available from the British Library.

A catalog record for this book is available from the Library of Congress.

10   9   8   7   6   5   4   3   2   1
17   16   15   14   13   12   11   10   09   08

Printed and bound in China

For Simon, and for Michael

contents

figures

tables

boxes

studying
human
development

You and I are members of an extraordinary species: a species that has a capacity far beyond any other to create and use tools and technologies, to think in abstract and hypothetical ways, to analyse and communicate our thoughts, to plot and plan, fall in and out of love and reflect on our experience in music, painting, poetry.

And yet like every other species, we are biological organisms. Like every other creature, we began life as a single cell: a fertilized ovum. How is it possible for all the complexity of the human mind to develop from such a humble beginning? What unique biological endowment does the human conception carry, that our young develop so differently from those of other species? What human experience is necessary, to bring that biological promise to fruition? And how can it be that a process that universally generates the characteristic intelligence that marks us as human also creates the rich diversity of ability and personality we see across individuals? Questions such as these are at the heart of developmental psychology. They are what this book is about.

Why study human development?

For me, unraveling the puzzle of human development is the most intriguing and exciting challenge that science can possibly tackle. We take the changes that occur through childhood for granted. Actually, these changes are as remarkable as anything else in nature! Where else can we see the rise of intelligence and individuality before our very eyes, as we do in watching a newborn baby grow into a toddler, a child, an adolescent, an adult?

The phenomena of childhood are intrinsically interesting. But developmental psychology has a far greater significance: it enriches our understanding of human nature as a whole. If you follow a sequence of events through, as we do in studying childhood development, you end up with a far richer understanding of a given state of affairs than you would had you only seen that one state. **Figure 1.1** illustrates the point. If you saw only picture C, you would probably infer that the big dog had stolen pie from the plate, while the small dog innocently slept. But if you had seen the sequence of events leading up to picture C (pictures A and B) you would realize that the big dog is innocent, where the small dog was not only the thief, but also sneaky and deceptive! Understanding how events unfold can radically change your interpretation of the end state.

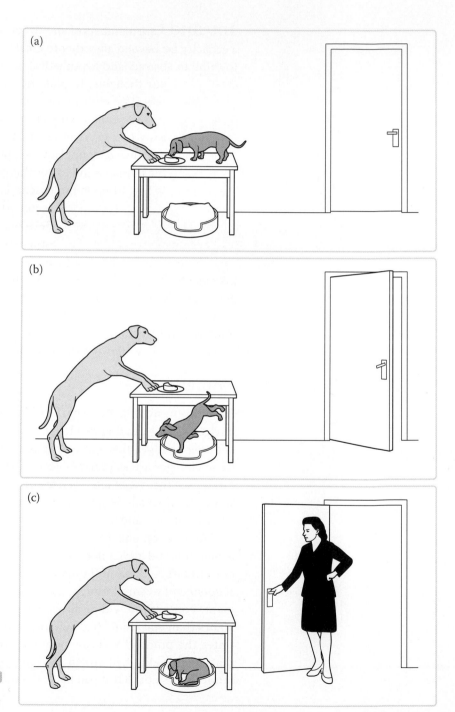

figure **1.1**

Seeing the bigger picture

Understanding how children develop into adults can radically alter our understanding of human nature, and this is an important goal in itself. For instance: are we, as a species, *inevitably* doomed to all the bigotry, paranoia, racism, murderous intent and thoughtlessness that presently blight lives and despoil our planet? Are we born biologically predisposed to such things, or are they by-products of the contexts in which children develop, the ways that children are treated? Could deeper understanding of human development open up ways to change things for the better?

Developmental psychology has a strong and continuing commitment to child welfare, and to fostering the full potential of individual development. In fact, our discipline has already changed children's lives in many ways, both through altering our understanding of childhood, and through influencing social policy (some examples of this are listed in Table 1.1). For example, disorders such as ADHD (attention deficit hyperactivity disorder) have only recently been recognized. A child with such a disorder (illustrated in Box 1.1) is difficult to cope with, and would, a generation ago, have been dismissed as unteachable, unintelligent, naughty. He (it is usually a boy) would probably have been punished and excluded from ordinary education. Today, he would be diagnosed, treated, supported: the outlook for his future is much better.

A second example is the change in policy for dealing with child witnesses: young children are easily intimidated and confused in courts, so that their experience of being witnesses used often to be very distressing,

table **1.1**

Some ways developmental psychology has changed children's lives

Intelligence tests	Have replaced subjective and sometimes prejudiced opinions about a child's potential and thus opened up access to education
Studies of intelligence over time	Have shown that individual IQ scores vary far more over time than is popularly thought and thus reduced 'once for all' labelling of children's abilities
The discovery of developmental problems such as dyslexia, ADHD, autism	Have created tolerance and support for children who were once dismissed as irredeemably stupid or naughty
The discovery that reward works far better than punishment	Has shifted education and parenting away from *'spare the rod and spoil the child'* toward more constructive emphasis on encouraging the child's confidence and self-esteem
Studies of sex differences in development	Have changed our perception of both girls and boys, the ways we treat them and what we allow or expect girls and boys to be like
Research on how children's minds and skills develop	Has changed how we view learning and education: less rote learning, more activity-based learning

and their testimony disregarded. Research showed that children are easily led to remember things that didn't happen – even very bizarre things – especially if they are asked the same questions over and over, or the questioner suggests things they might 'remember' (Ceci, Leichman and White, 1999). But questioned less aggressively and without leading questions, even the very young can recall things quite well, and do not usually invent or embroider stories (Howe and Courage, 1997). Such discoveries have changed how child witnesses are handled during enquiries and in courts, making it possible to secure better justice both for child victims (of abuse, say) and for adults who might have been wrongly accused.

box **1.1**

An example of attention deficit hyperactivity disorder

Source: Wallis (1994).

Seven-year-old Dusty awoke at 5.00 one recent morning in his Chicago home. Every muscle in his 50 lb body flew in furious motion as he headed downstairs for breakfast. After pulling a box of cereal from the cupboard, Dusty started grabbing cereal with his hands and kicking the box, scattering the cereal across the room. Next he began peeling the decorative paper covering off the TV table. Then he started stomping the spilled cereal to bits. After dismantling the plastic dustpan he had gotten to clean up the cereal, he moved onto his next project: grabbing three rolls of toilet paper from the bathroom and unravelling them around the house.

A short history of developmental psychology

People have been interested in child development for a very long time. Both Plato and Aristotle, for example, had theories about child development and child rearing, and many subsequent philosophers, including Locke and Rousseau, put forward theories on these topics. But their work was based on intelligent speculation rather than evidence or scientific test. Developmental psychology as a separate discipline began only about 150 years ago. Three crucial things made developmental psychology possible in the middle of the 19th century:

■ The industrial revolution created a need for a new, urban workforce with skills (such as literacy and numeracy) that required mass education. Thus there was a new economic need to understand the process of learning and the development of the mind.

■ Social reformers became concerned at the brutalizing effects of sending small children to work long hours (7-year-olds doing shifts of 10 hours a day were common) in coalmines and factories. This created a new interest in understanding the effects of childhood experience on individual disposition and behaviour.

■ Darwin's book *The Origin of Species by Means of Natural Selection* (1859/2003) changed our perception of human beings from almost celestial beings 'made in the image of God' to biological beings shaped by natural selection just like every other living creature. In so doing it changed where we would look to understand human nature and development: to biology and science rather than to theology and religion. For the first time, Darwin's theory moved human beings into the realm of phenomena that might be studied and understood through science as part of the natural world.

Darwin's book was published in 1859, creating a level of excitement (and outrage) that is almost impossible to imagine today. It triggered the birth of developmental psychology as a scientific discipline. By 1888 there were about 50 published empirical studies of child development across Europe and America. In the 1890s specialist academic journals began to be published, and institutes for research in child development began to appear. By the early years of the 20th century developmental psychology was a going concern.

Although developmental psychology has a single overall focus (understanding human development) it's a mistake to think of it as a single, monolithic enterprise. There are a number of things on which almost all developmental psychologists would agree. But different researchers have focused on different issues, or come to different conclusions on the same issue. This has been true since the earliest days of research: it's how science works, and is just as true in any other science (not all medical researchers agree that HIV causes AIDS, for example). One thing that all developmental psychologists share, however, is history: a familiarity with the ideas that have gone before. Knowing this history enriches our understanding of modern research (just as knowing the sequence of events in Figure 1.1 enriches our understanding of the canine characters involved). So let's briefly review that history before reviewing modern psychology.

Darwin and the theory of evolution

It would be impossible to exaggerate the importance of Darwin's work for psychology and for biology as a whole. Nothing has ever revolutionized our understanding of human nature and development so much. Almost all work in developmental psychology is influenced by Darwin in one way or another.

The heart of Darwin's insight was that the physical features of living organisms have been selected, over many generations, because they are particularly successful (*adaptive*) in ensuring survival in the environment the creature inhabits. For instance, in environments where a long thin beak is best suited for getting food, the individual birds within a species who have longer thinner beaks will survive better than those with shorter stubbier ones. Because they survive better, the thin-beaked individuals will be more likely to mate and rear young successfully. They pass on their thin-beak genes, and so gradually the species shifts towards thin-beakedness.

Of course, this process of *natural selection* applies just as much to behaviour as to body shapes. Behaviours associated with survival and reproductive success will be selected for, just as body types associated with success are selected for. In fact, evolution must work first at the level of behaviour rather than body shape: after all, thin-beakedness is only adaptive if you're already trying to suck food from long thin apertures. Shifting from gills to lungs is only adaptive if you're already trying to leave the water and live on the land.

Darwin's work posed fundamental questions about the origins of human behaviour. What role has evolution played in shaping our minds and how we behave? What role does it play in shaping our individual development? How much of who we are, how we develop, is innate, set by our biological history? Darwin began the work on these questions. For example, in 1877 he published 'A biographical sketch of an infant': a detailed diary recording his baby son Doddy's emotional expressions, to explore whether these were innate or not. This 'baby diary' was a milestone for developmental psychology. It was the first attempt to make rigorous and systematic observations of child development. Baby diaries became an important early methodology, and are still in use for some kinds of research today.

Comparative psychology and ethology

figure 1.2

The grebe courtship ritual

Source: A. Manning: *An Introduction to Animal Behavior.* (Edward Arnold). © 1972. Reproduced with permission from Hodder Education.

One consequence of Darwin's work was that researchers began to ask: can we understand human behaviour and development in the same terms as we explain animal behaviour and development? What can we discover about human development by comparison with other species?

Quite a lot of key animal behaviours are rigid, ritualized or stereotyped, and very typical of a particular species. Well-known examples are the courtship dances of birds (**Figure 1.2**), and the kill behaviours of lions or crocodiles. Ethologists such as Niko Timbergen argued that these rigidly stereotyped *species typical* patterns of behaviour (which he called *fixed action patterns*, or FAPs) are instinctive: that is to say, these behaviours are innate, programmed into the animal rather than learned. Each FAP is triggered by a *sign stimulus* in the environment, to which the animal is innately programmed to respond. For example, a certain silhouette is a sign stimulus triggering fighting in the male stickleback fish. The silhouette is that of a rival – but in fact, a piece of cardboard of the right shape will also trigger or *release* FAPs protecting territorial rights.

Some instinctive behaviours identified by Timbergen and others seem to be present from birth: for example, the tendency of young birds to gape at the sight of a parent (or a parent-shaped piece of cardboard), thus making it easy to be fed. Other FAPs seem to emerge later, as the animal matures: sexual or courtship FAPs, for example, might occur only as the animal reaches sexual maturity. Just as animals' bodies are programmed to change at adolescence, so their behaviour may be pre-programmed to change as they mature. Like FAPs present from birth, these later occurring behaviours were thought to be largely independent of the environment, and to reflect a process of *maturation* rather than learning.

Innate behaviours such as fixed action patterns exist, according to ethology, because they are adaptive and enhance the chances of survival for the individual and hence for the species. Such patterns of behaviour have been shaped up by the process of natural selection identified by Darwin, through the evolutionary history of the species. Individual development then reflects the unfolding of these innate behaviours through a process of maturation.

Do human beings also have instinctive behaviours, FAPs? Is our development characterized by maturation? Ethologists such as Timbergen and Irenaus Eibl-Eibesfeldt argued that some human behaviour, too, can be understood in these terms. Indeed, it would be surprising if we alone of all the species were not pre-programmed to develop in certain ways. But the concepts of fixed action patterns and sign stimuli have not been very helpful in understanding human behaviour or development. Human behaviour is extremely flexible and variable. Almost no human behaviours have the universal, rigid, ritualized characteristics of a fixed action pattern. In fact, the only instances of human behaviour that look at all like a fixed action pattern are quite minor: for example, certain social gestures that seem to be universal to all human beings (Eibl-Eibesfeldt, 1971), such as the open palm wave when we greet someone (**Figure 1.3**).

Nor does there seem to be much evidence for the idea of maturation as a key factor in human development, although at one time this idea was advocated by some researchers. For example, Arnold Gesell studied children's developing physical coordination and control over their bodies (*motor development*), and found that the sequence of development did not vary between children. Motor control develops from the head down (head first, then the trunk, last the legs) and from the central to the peripheral elements (head and trunk first, then a progressive mastery of the limbs from elbow to wrist to fingers, and from knee to ankle to toes). Furthermore, children achieve milestones (such as head control, sitting, crawling) at very similar ages. On the basis of such data, Gesell concluded that motor development is importantly controlled by maturation, in other words by the unfolding of a biological programme (Gesell and Ames, 1940).

However, the evidence is that Gesell was wrong. For instance, the speed of a child's mastery of motor control can be increased by training (McGraw, 1945). This should not be the case, if motor development reflects the maturation of a pre-set biological programme. Furthermore, modern work shows that the consistent order of events which Gesell noticed need not reflect a biological programme maturing so much as the basic dynamics of the situation. It would be hard, for example, to learn to walk before you had learned to stand up! Standing up comes first because it is a necessary subskill of walking, not because it is 'programmed' to mature first. If even so basic a thing as motor development is not controlled by maturation, it seems most unlikely that more complex human behaviours could develop in this way. Maturation is not now regarded as important in understanding human development.

In fact, the concepts of maturation and of instinctive behaviours of the kind described as FAPs have been problematic as a whole, even in describing animal behaviour: more is learned, more is affected by the environment than these concepts allow. Nonetheless, the basic idea that evolution may prime us to behave or to develop in certain ways remains a plausible hypothesis, and other conceptualizations of how this may work have had interesting implications for developmental psychology.

Imprinting and attachment

For instance, Konrad Lorenz (1981) argued that the young of many species are biologically programmed to *imprint* on (in other words, to become attached to) their parent. According to Lorenz, a gosling is programmed to imprint on the first moving object it sees, during a *critical period* a few hours after hatching. Normally this is the mother, and the result has huge advantages for survival: the 'imprinted' gosling stays close to the object of its attachment (the mother) and is therefore to hand for feeding and protection. Furthermore, this early imprinting sets the gosling's later orientation when it comes to mating: it will mate with something reminiscent of the mother – another goose, rather than, say, a chicken or a dog. But if the mother is absent at the crucial time, then either the gosling does not imprint at all, or it may imprint on some other creature or object. Lorenz demonstrated that goslings would imprint on him, would attach themselves to him as they would to their mother: they would follow him as they followed their mother, and in later life would even try to mate with him rather than with another goose.

Lorenz's idea of imprinting very much impressed the psychologist John Bowlby. Bowlby suggested that human babies are born with an innate drive to become attached to the mother, just as a gosling is (Bowlby, 1953, 1969). At the time, this was a revolutionary idea. The general assumption had been that babies became attached to people for entirely instrumental reasons: because they were fed, for instance. Bowlby's suggestion was that we become attached to our mothers because we are biologically programmed to need attachment and love every bit as much as we need food.

Bowlby's conclusion was supported by experiments by Harry Harlow (Harlow and Zimmerman, 1959), who reared baby monkeys with two surrogate 'mothers', one made of wire, cold and uncuddly but with a nipple through which the baby monkey was fed, and the other made of soft, cuddly cloth but with no nipple. The baby monkeys preferred the soft cuddly 'mother', choosing to run to 'her' when frightened, rather than to the cold food-giver. If monkeys attach for comfort rather than food, surely humans do too?

Bowlby's theories about infant attachment have been hugely influential, and are of lasting importance. His conclusions were not right in every respect, as we shall see later in this book: babies do not necessarily attach to just one person as he thought, and do not necessarily prefer the mother. But the basic idea that human development and feeling might reflect biological need is a continuing theme for research.

Sociobiology and evolutionary psychology

Today, probably the best-known supporters of the idea that human behaviour and development can be understood by reference to our evolutionary history are the adherents of sociobiology and evolutionary psychology. Both of these disciplines argue that many human behaviours are importantly shaped by innate tendencies which have evolved to enhance our survival and reproductive success, even if we don't inherit instinctive fixed action patterns.

A key area where this sort of idea has been explored is social interaction. For example: why do individuals sometimes behave altruistically? Darwin's theory as originally conceptualized seemed to imply that organisms should be selfishly focused on their own survival, or on the survival of their own direct offspring. If they helped others, it should only be for direct mutual advantage. But in fact people aren't like that – and nor are other creatures.

Take the bee: one individual, the queen, breeds. Hundreds of others serve her, never breeding themselves, apparently sacrificing themselves for her offspring. How is this *altruism* adaptive for them? A British biologist suggested an explanation based on the concept of *kin selection* (Hamilton, 1964). In brief, male bees derive from unfertilized eggs, and therefore have only one set of chromosomes. Queen bees mate but once in a lifetime: so all their offspring share the chromosomes of the male mate, plus a melange of the chromosomes from the queen herself. The bees who serve the queen are her daughters. They share all their father's chromosomes, plus some percentage of the mother's. This means that they share more chromosomes with their sisters than they would share with their own offspring, were they to mate with a male other than their own father. By serving their mother's daughters, including the new queens she will create, they secure the best future for their own genes. Thus their 'altruistic' behaviour is in fact adaptive – *for their genes*. This is a natural extension of Darwin's theory. It offers an explanation of all sorts of behaviour in the animal world that seems otherwise to fly in the face of a simple view of natural selection.

Hamilton's ideas have been taken further by naturalists such as E. O. Wilson (1980), who proposed the new discipline of *sociobiology*. Sociobiologists assume that human behaviour has evolved to optimize the survival of what Richard Dawkins has famously called our 'selfish genes'. This theory predicts that, just like bees, human beings will show 'kin selection' – in other words, will be helpful and altruistic to the kinfolk who share their genes (offspring, siblings, cousins, in that order) rather than to unrelated strangers. There is much evidence to support this idea. But not all altruistic behaviour can be explained by kin selection. In fact, we are often altruistic to individuals unrelated to us.

Sociobiology has proposed the notion of *reciprocal altruism* (Trivers, 1971) to explain why we help those who don't share our genes: an individual will help another if the cost is not too great, and if he or she expects the other to reciprocate, in a sort of 'tit for tat' universe that helps everyone survive. Interestingly, this hypothesis suggests that there is important adaptive value in the ability to recognize one another, so that we can know the reputation of different individuals (who is reliably helpful and who is not). Does this explain the endless social fascination with gossip in our species?

Sociobiologists have identified many parallels between human behaviour and that of animals, particularly our nearest relations, the apes. Their claim that these behaviours must be adaptive and must have evolved because they have survival value is intriguing. However, this approach is very controversial. Critics object that, though the theories offered by sociobiologists may be plausible and seductive, they are not backed by convincing evidence. It may be true that the predictions of sociobiology fit the data, but this scarcely constitutes an independent test of the ideas, since the theory was developed to explain those data in the first place! For example, the fact that individuals help siblings and cousins as well as their offspring was the reason that Hamilton proposed his hypothesis about kin selection. So a new demonstration that individuals are altruistic to their kin is not an independent test of the theory of kin selection.

In fact, the theories of kin selection and reciprocal altruism don't fit the data very well, if you take a broader look. Altruism happens where it shouldn't, according to sociobiological accounts: people sacrifice time, effort, even their lives to help unrelated strangers who cannot possibly reciprocate (this is the basis not only of outstanding human lives such as that of Mother Theresa, or of heroic military acts, but of all voluntary work, and of career choices to pursue 'caring professions' rather than power or wealth). Equally, and depressingly often, altruism doesn't happen where it should, according to sociobiology, as the many children abused, abandoned or killed by their families testify.

Many critics argue that there is just too much variability in human behaviour to be captured by the precepts of sociobiology. Other factors must be involved, and may in fact provide a far better explanation for our behaviour. Many believe that sociobiology has not yet made a convincing case for its thesis. Some do not even accept that sociobiology amounts to science (Maddox, 1998).

Learning theory and behaviourism

A radically different application of Darwin's principles of natural selection comes from *learning theory* and *behaviourism*, which dominated psychology as a whole for the first half of the 20th century. Natural selection implies that things that are adaptive and successful in serving survival will tend to prosper and become more frequent, whereas things that are maladaptive will die out. Through evolutionary time, this principle will shape physiology and innate tendencies. But in an individual life, it will be a potent force for shaping specific behaviours, specific *learning*.

The Russian physiologist Ivan Pavlov (1927) observed that dogs can learn to associate a bell with the arrival of food. Dogs naturally salivate at the sight or smell of food, making ready to digest more easily. If a bell was rung systematically before the food was offered, the dog would begin to salivate whenever the bell was rung, even though there was no food present. This reaction was called a *conditioned response*. This sort of *learning by association* to respond to one stimulus (here, a bell) as if it were another (here, food) is called *classical conditioning*, and occurs in human beings just as it does in animals. You can probably think of examples of such associations in your own life (just as certain little cakes evoked particular feelings for the writer Marcel Proust).

A second principle of conditioning was articulated by Thorndike (1911) as the *law of effect*. This simply states that an action is more likely to be repeated if it leads to reward, and less likely to be repeated if it does not (or worse, leads to punishment). For example, a rat will learn to press a lever if doing that is associated with the arrival of food, but not if it isn't, and will learn to avoid the lever if pressing it is associated with getting an electric shock. Again, human beings are much the same!

This type of process was most powerfully explored by Burrhus Frederic (B. F.) Skinner, who pointed out that animals are not simply led passively into this or that behaviour by the presence or absence of stimuli for reward or punishment in their environment. Rather, they actively operate on the environment to create reward or punishment. For example, a dog that is rewarded with a biscuit for cute begging behaviour will do his party piece when he wants to get a biscuit. The dog thus controls the owner as much as the owner is controlling the dog (a thing many dog owners have long suspected!). This is *operant conditioning*. Skinner's account of operant conditioning extends the law of effect, providing a more dynamic interpretation of the relationship between behaviour and environmental stimuli. The effects of operant conditioning are, of course, as clearly visible in human beings as in animals.

Many psychologists saw these principles of learning as the basis for a new and more rigorous way of explaining human behaviour and development. At last, we could explain why an individual behaves as he or she does, not by inferring invisible thoughts in the mind or hypothetical innate tendencies, but by referring to external, highly visible stimuli and the equally visible overt responses associated with them. Like physicists or biologists, psychologists could study things in the external world, rather than introspections or speculations. Thus this *stimulus–response* or *S–R* approach seemed to provide an objective and scientific basis for psychology. This way of thinking was called *behaviourism*.

Some early behaviourists were so taken with the power of S–R explanations of behaviour that they saw no role at all for the mind or any other type of thought process in psychological theories. All behaviour, including verbal behaviour, could be explained in terms of chains of associations between stimuli and responses. That being the case, it seemed natural to further suppose that human behaviour was entirely learned, rather than having any innate component. So although the law of effect is very much in line with Darwin's theory of natural selection, behaviourism moved strongly away from the notion that behaviour is inherited after having been shaped through evolutionary history. Evolution and development might use the same *process* (natural selection) but were not continuous with one another, as those who believed in innate behaviours as an important factor in development (for example, ethologists, and later sociobiologists) thought. Instinct was 'out', and learning was 'in'. And this put new emphasis on child development.

Many prominent behaviourists focused on childhood. For example, John Watson, an early and very radical behaviourist, believed that behaviourism could explain everything about a child's development, and indeed could *control* that development, shaping a child to be whatever you wanted him or her to be. He famously wrote:

Give me a dozen healthy infants, well formed, and my own specified world to bring them up in and I'll guarantee to take any one at random and train him to become any type of specialist I might select – doctor, lawyer, artist, merchant-in-chief and yes, even beggar man and thief, regardless of his talents, penchants, tendencies, abilities, vocations and race of his ancestors.

(Watson, 1930)

Watson's most famous (or possibly infamous) studies involved demonstrating that babies' irrational fears can be explained by classical conditioning. For instance, after a baby known as 'Little Albert' had been frightened while playing with a furry toy he became frightened of the toy and of other similar-looking furry things, including beards (Watson and Rayner, 1920).

Skinner too believed that child development could be entirely explained in behaviourist S–R terms. He designed whole programmes of childrearing based on behaviourist principles, and wrote a novel advocating the principles of learning theory as a means of creating Utopia (*Walden Two*). Every aspect of development was covered by Skinner's behaviourism, including language (which Skinner saw as 'verbal behaviour' – Skinner, 1957) and thought (which Skinner believed was sub-vocal verbal behaviour).

It is fashionable today to decry behaviourism as a deeply misguided approach to psychology and development. Indeed, the approach ran into some very severe problems. One problem was that behaviourism supposed that, since there are no innate behaviours or tendencies, one can condition (in other words, train) any animal to associate any stimulus with any response. This is not the case. It's very easy, for example, to condition a dog to run away or to freeze to end a painful experience (such as an electric shock), but it's very nearly impossible to condition it to salivate or eat a biscuit to end the shock. It turns out that animals (including human beings) have innate predispositions to learn some S–R associations rather than others. Typically, animals confronted by something dangerous, painful or threatening will fight, flee or freeze, and are genetically 'prepared' to learn to associate these responses with escaping particular noxious events. Thus the concept of *preparedness to learn* reintroduced innate tendencies carried over from evolutionary history into S–R theories of how behaviour develops.

A worse problem for learning theory comes from the fact that S–R chains cannot in fact explain the creativity and diversity of behaviour – certainly not in human beings. The best example of this is human language. We are obviously capable of constructing new sentences, sentences that carry new ideas, or refer to non-existent fantasy things: sentences that cannot, therefore, be explained in terms of any simple S–R chain of events. Such phenomena suggest that in fact, something other than S–R chains (such as mental processes) must be involved in the generation of behaviour – a conclusion that radically undermines the power of behaviourism to explain human psychology.

Problems such as preparedness to learn and creativity showed that behaviourism and S–R theory could not provide a complete account of human behaviour or development. Nonetheless, it is quite clear that human behaviour is shaped by reward and punishment, just as S–R theory says. This fact is still widely used where we need to understand and to modify behaviour. For example: suppose you, as a child psychologist, are confronted by a 2-year-old child who is misbehaving wildly. The parents are at their wit's end. What to do? Often, in such situations, a trained observer will notice that in fact, the child's bad behaviour is 'attention seeking'. He or she desperately wants the parent's attention, but only gets it when misbehaving. Even the mother's criticism is more rewarding to the child than being ignored, so the child plays up more to get more attention, and the problem is made worse. The parent's behaviour (ignoring the child unless he or she is misbehaving) is creating the bad behaviour! The solution is straightforward; as Skinner puts it:

The remedy in such a case is simply for the mother to make sure that she responds with attention and affection to most if not all of the responses of the child which are ... acceptable and that she never (rewards) the annoying forms of behaviour.
(Skinner, 1961)

Behaviour modification, in other words the identification of the rewards and punishments that are controlling existing behaviour and altering these to create more satisfactory behaviours – just as described by Skinner – remains a powerful tool for psychologists dealing with problem behaviour today, particularly in dealing with children.

Social learning theory

Social learning theory (Bandura, 1973) provides one way of preserving the important insights of S–R theory as to how reward and punishment shape behaviour, while beginning to allow for the action of mental processes. Bandura studied aggressiveness in children, and found that children who watched a film where another person behaved aggressively toward a doll were more likely to behave aggressively when allowed to play with that doll themselves than was the case for children who had not watched anyone else being aggressive. This is hard to explain in purely S–R terms: where is the reward that is eliciting the aggressive behaviour in the child? Bandura suggested that the children are *learning by observation*. In effect, the observing child mentally identifies with the person he or she is watching, and so notices and is affected by any reward or punishment that person's behaviour attracts. If aggression is rewarded in the person the child watches, then aggressive behaviour is implicitly rewarded in the observing child too, and so becomes more likely.

Observational learning is an important factor in development. Children learn a great deal from watching others and then imitating them, both in their social behaviour and in the acquisition of skills. In fact, so important is observational learning and imitation in development that it now seems strange that psychology took so little notice of it until the 1960s! That social factors were ignored for so long is a tribute to the dominance of behaviourism in Western psychology. But in other cultures, such factors were recognized as important long before this.

Vygotsky and social interactions in development

The first to recognize the importance of social interactions in development was the Russian psychologist Lev Vygotsky. According to Vygotsky (1962), at any one time a child has a certain level of ability and is able to perform, alone and unaided, tasks up to that level of ability. Just beyond this level are new ideas and new skills that are too difficult for the child to manage alone, but that he or she can manage in collaboration with an adult or a more skilled older child. These new ideas and skills are the next thing to be mastered. Vygotsky called them the *zone of proximal development*. The support of a more skilled collaborator allows the child to enter and explore this zone, and so to learn, and to raise his or her mastery to a new level. This new level too will have a zone of proximal development, another step beyond – and so development proceeds.

For example, a baby learning to use a spoon to feed herself may be helped by an adult, who guides the spoon to the child's mouth more accurately than the child can manage alone, or who deals with the tricky problem of loading the spoon (and so on). The adult's help not only allows the child to achieve a performance beyond his or her own independent level of skill, but also provides the experience and practice to let skill develop.

For Vygotsky, such supportive social interactions are the key to human development. And in fact, the suggestion that practical skills and knowledge can be passed on in this way makes obvious sense. But Vygotsky's theory goes much further, suggesting that social interactions of this type not only foster the development of practical skills but also play a key role in creating mental processes.

For example, children's earliest efforts to communicate are supported by adults (or older siblings) in just the same way as their early efforts to feed themselves. The baby makes an effort to communicate (a noise of some sort), and the more skilled partner supports that effort by interpreting what the child means, saying the right words for the child, behaving as if there is a reciprocal conversation. In effect, the adult partner is 'shaping up' the child's language, just as his or her help shapes up the use of a spoon. At first the child's language depends on this help from the adult world: the child's language skills exist only in the social interaction between the child and skilled others. Gradually the child's independent skill as a speaker develops further, until the child can produce and structure language for him or herself. Now the child can begin to internalize language, to be able to reflect on it and with it, and thus become able to use it for private thought processes. Thus thought processes, according to Vygotsky, have their origins in social interactions.

Vygotsky's work does not provide a complete account of development. However, his insight into the role of social processes in fostering development has had a vast and continuing influence in developmental psychology. For example, followers of Vygotsky such as Luria (1976) extended his work to explore how the development of mental processes is structured by the surrounding culture as well as by individual social interactions, a powerful idea with increasing influence over developmental research.

Piaget and cognitive development

Piaget is, beyond any doubt, the most influential developmental psychologist of the 20th century. Only Darwin has had as great an impact as Piaget. Like Darwin, Piaget was originally a biologist. Like Darwin, his ideas have irrevocably changed how we think about human development.

Where ethologists, sociobiologists, learning theorists and behaviourists focused on the development of behaviour, and social learning theorists and Vygotsky focused on social processes in development, Piaget focused on the development of the mind. Specifically, he was puzzled by the development of knowledge, or *cognition*. The general assumption before Piaget was that babies are born without knowledge of the world, their minds empty, 'blank slates' waiting to be filled up through learning and experience. It was assumed that information from the world or from other people could provide this waiting mind with knowledge. Piaget realized that this cannot be right. Knowledge involves understanding and insight rather than blind rote learning. To achieve insight, there must already be structures in the mind able to capture and make sense of the information received. For if there are no structures capable of receiving it, the information will no more stick in the mind than a whispered word stays in an empty room. And if there are no structures capable of making sense of the information received, it will remain meaningless even if it can be recorded. (A tape-recorder, for instance, can record human speech. But it has no processes capable of interpreting the meaning of that speech, nor processes capable of learning how to interpret speech.) An infant, therefore, could learn nothing, could develop no knowledge or insight, unless the structures needed for doing those things were already there. This opens up entirely new problems for research: what structures does the infant mind contain, and where do they come from?

Piaget argued that the mental structures necessary for human knowledge and insight must be rooted within the organism, because they cannot (as we have just seen) be provided from outside. They must therefore develop from biological mechanisms. His theory was that the basic mechanisms of adaptation that serve evolution as a whole must be sufficient to explain the origins of intelligence, both in individuals and across evolutionary history.

For Piaget, human intelligence is continuous with that of all other living organisms. He argued that, through evolutionary history, intelligence arose through the development of the senses. With no senses at all, an organism cannot even detect that it has suffered damage, let alone keep out of harm's way. A first tiny step toward awareness and intelligence is the ability to detect the presence of other creatures or objects impinging on one's body, through the two proximate senses of touch and taste. Touch allows an organism to pull back at the first prick of a thorn rather than impaling itself, for instance. Taste gives an organism the basis for a choice between swallowing or spitting, a first small step toward anticipating consequences. The senses of smell, sight and hearing greatly extend the organism's ability to anticipate events: to smell food, a potential mate, a poison or a predator before you taste or touch it, to hear it coming or see it in the distance greatly increase the organism's scope for adaptive action. These three 'anticipatory' senses already imply some degree of ability to draw inferences and predict events (there is no advantage in being able to detect a lion in the distance unless this suggests danger and the wisdom of taking evasive action). The ability to reason and predict the future comes to fruition in the 'sixth sense': intelligence proper. With this sixth sense, an organism can not only draw inferences and make predictions on the basis of concrete present events ('I see a lion'), but can make predictions about the future, conceptualizing possibilities ('This looks like lion country, there *might* be a lion here').

Many species have begun to develop this sixth sense, this ability to anticipate (predict) events that have not yet happened (my dog, for example, predicts the viability of successful scrounging from strangers on a beach very well). Human beings have gone a step further, developing a powerful abstract intelligence capable of imagining hypothetical situations and possibilities way beyond concrete experience (only we worry about the danger of being abducted by alien spacecraft we have not yet detected, and so on).

Piaget's account of why intelligence evolved is intriguing and compelling. It is also extraordinarily universal: the adaptive value of senses, and the consequent steady progression toward abstract, predictive intelligence apply equally to a Martian, a human and a bird (or any other living thing), although species differ in terms of how far they progress through the process. His view of individual development is equally intriguing.

Human babies are born, according to Piaget, with nothing but a few reflexes (such as sucking, orienting to the breast and the like). They have no conception of the world or of themselves (nor any idea that there is a distinction between these things). Through very basic mechanisms of adaptation, each child must build on the simple reflexes to construct for him or herself all the mental structures necessary for the development of knowledge. This takes many years: it is completed at about 12 years of age. The process follows the same pattern and sequence of events in every child. This is not because it is 'pre-programmed' in any way. Rather, the universal sequence of events through development reflects the fact that knowledge itself has a certain structure, and the growing mind must reflect this. The sequence of cognitive development is therefore not specific to human beings – Martians would have to develop in the same way.

Piaget identified four stages in the process of cognitive development. Each stage is more powerful and sophisticated than the one that came before. Each produces a qualitatively different character of thinking. And each stage creates the conditions for the next stage to develop, until an adult form of reasoning has been reached. We shall study these stages in detail in later chapters. Briefly, they are:

■ *The sensori-motor stage*, which occurs between birth and about 18 months. This period is spent constructing the basic mental structures for memory and perception. Gradually, the baby becomes able to recognize that the world is separate from the self. He or she becomes aware that the world has its own properties, and becomes able to represent and remember those properties.

- *The pre-operational stage* occurs between 18 months and about 7 years of age. Initially, the child's thinking is very bound to specific physical actions in the world, so that thinking is tied to *doing.* The child becomes progressively more competent in *imagining* rather than actually doing as a basis for thinking. But his or her ability to connect one thing to another, or to bear two aspects of a situation in mind at the same time is still very limited. This means that the ability to draw inferences (for instance) is still very limited.

- *The concrete operational period*, which begins around 8 years of age, is a great breakthrough. The child becomes able to connect one thing with another, because it is now not only possible to do a thing in the imagination, it is possible to mentally *reverse* that action as well. For the first time, the child understands the logical connection between the situation before an event and afterwards, because he or she now knows what that relationship is. The difference this makes to reasoning is illustrated in **Box 1.2**.

- *The formal operational stage*, which begins from about 12 years of age, is adult reasoning. The concrete operational child can reason logically, but is very literal minded, very tied to concrete physical events. Gradually, the child's thinking is freed from concrete fact, and can handle the abstract and the hypothetical.

Piaget's theory has dominated psychology for half a century. The questions he asked and the data he collected pose a lasting challenge for developmental psychology. Perhaps most importantly, his idea that children must play an active part in constructing their own minds rather than being the passive products of biology or learning has revolutionized how we think about development.

Piaget's theory has difficulties (as we shall see in later chapters). Like behaviourism, for example, it underestimates the extent to which the newborn are innately primed to learn certain things. It underestimates the role of social processes in supporting development. Nor is logic as good a model of human reasoning as Piaget supposed. Nevertheless, it would be hard to overestimate the importance of Piaget's work.

Information processing and cognitive development

One legacy of Piaget's work is that developmental psychology is now very aware of the need to understand what knowledge a child may have at any given point, and what cognitive processes the child has for handling that knowledge. These issues have been explored in research that draws analogies between human minds and computers.

A computer is, basically, a device that performs *operations* on *information*. It can be programmed to behave like a calculator, performing simple logical or numerical operations. With more complex programming, it can solve much more complex problems. Just what problems a computer program can solve and how successfully it does that depends

Conservation of liquids: the effect of
being able to mentally 'undo' actions

Imagine you are asked to say, is there
the same amount of liquid in each
container in Figure (a)?

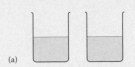

(a)

Now how about Figure (b)? Do these two
containers hold the same amount of
liquid?

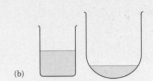

(b)

You probably answered 'Yes' to Figure (a), and 'Don't know, doesn't look like it' to
Figure (b). From these two 'still snapshots' there's no way of knowing. This is just
how Piaget says the world looks to the pre-operational child. But suppose you could
connect the two snapshots?

Suppose you could remember that
situation (b) was created by pouring
liquid from one of the two containers in
(a) into the new container, which is now
standing next to the other one from
situation (a) ...

and you were also able to mentally
reverse that act of pouring, and so 'see'
where the liquid in the new container
came from.

Now you would realize that the amount
of liquid must be the same in both
containers in (b), since it's the same
liquid as shown in the two containers in
(a). This is the position of the child with
reversible concrete operations.

on the exact information the program has and on the specific operations
it can perform on that information. So a program with a few very simple
rules might be very successful in solving easier problems in some area,
but produce poor answers or no answer at all to harder problems. Add
more information or more rules, and the program might 'develop' the
ability to solve more of the harder problems.

Various theorists have suggested that this may provide a good model of what is happening in childhood cognitive development. Like a computer, the human mind can be thought of as an information-processing device, one whose programming, and therefore performance, changes as it develops.

For example, Robert Siegler suggested that developmental changes in the solutions children offer when solving balance problems might reflect different states of knowledge, and therefore different rules children of different ages use in thinking about how things balance (Siegler, 1976). A 5-year-old uses a very simple rule, an 8-year-old a more complex one, and a 14-year-old uses a more complex rule still. Siegler showed that a computer program armed with the 5-year-old's rule produces the same answers across a set of problems as would a 5-year-old child, whereas a program armed with the 8-year-old's rule solves the problems in the same way as does a real 8-year-old, and so on. Furthermore, if you teach an 8-year-old the rule typical of a 14-year-old, the child's performance changes to be the same as a 14-year-old's, just as changing the computer's rule from the 8-year-old to the 14-year-old rule changes the program's performance.

Such *computer simulations* of the effects of different information or sets of rules for using that information, have helped to clarify what may be changing as children develop, across a range of different kinds of task. This approach has often been used to explore qualitative changes of the kind described by Piaget in the way children think (Klahr and Wallace, 1976): quite small changes in the rules a program uses can create a qualitative change in the factors it takes into account and the kind of solutions it produces, effects that can parallel the changes Piaget saw between one stage of cognitive development and another.

Other factors too can be explored through computer simulations of children's thinking. For instance, what would be the effect on reasoning if there were developmental changes in the sheer amount of information that the mind can use at one time? In other words, could it be that younger children's weaker reasoning reflects a smaller *memory capacity*, and that developmental change in reasoning occurs as this memory capacity increases? Advocates of this theory (Case, 1985; Pascual-Leone, 1970) argue that many of the changes we see in children's cognitive abilities through childhood can be predicted and simulated by assuming a developmental increase in the memory capacity available, as we shall discuss in Chapter 7.

Some researchers (Klahr, 1984) suggest that even the very process through which developmental change occurs can be explored through computer simulations, by creating programs that modify themselves. Various different ways of doing this have been tried: for example, by building an extra layer into programs using rules for solving problems: this extra layer of program ('a meta-program') monitors the problem-solving layer below, looking for patterns and modifying the lower program to reflect these patterns (cutting out redundant steps, for example, or chunking into one procedure elements that started out as separate steps but that turn out always to go together). Programs like this can be set up to modify themselves, turning themselves from a rule-set that behaves like a 5-year-old to one that behaves like an 8-year-old, for example. But the way they do this does not look very much like the way this process happens in children. For a start, the program achieves in minutes what children take years to learn. Obviously, the human process must be importantly different from what is happening in the computer.

Responding to this (and other) problems, some researchers have argued that human minds are not set up in the way a rule-following program is structured. Human brains create *neural networks* as they learn. That is to say, human learning involves the gradual creation of patterns of connection between many neurons, where many neurons within the pattern may be active at the same time, or may switch on and off in complex interaction with one another. Computer systems can be set up to simulate this sort of process (Plunkett, 2000). Such systems are called *connectionist systems*, and can indeed learn from experiences. But even this line of approach has yet to produce any system that convincingly mimics human development.

The possibility of simulating children's cognitive processes on computers opened up whole new ways of understanding cognitive development, and of testing theories about children's thinking (Klahr and MacWhinney, 1998). Of course, computer programs cannot fully simulate a child's mind: children are flesh and blood, and may have a dozen thoughts in their mind that have nothing to do with the problem-solving task itself ('I'm bored, is it lunch time, am I doing this task well enough or do I look stupid?' and so on) that the computer cannot share. Children develop in complex, multi-faceted environments, where computer programs exist in simple, abstract worlds. And children have insight and understanding, where computer programs don't. Nevertheless, simulations allow us to test the idea that developmental changes in specific states of knowledge or in the memory space available for using that knowledge might play a key role in qualitative changes in children's reasoning through childhood.

Sigmund Freud

Where Piaget and information processing approaches emphasize the universal aspects of the development of human thought and reasoning, other theorists have focused more on the development of individuality. The first and most famous of these was Sigmund Freud.

Freud's initial interest was in the peculiarities of the human mind. It would be easy, reading only the theories reviewed so far, to imagine the human mind as straightforwardly adapted to circumstances and rational. As Freud pointed out, this is not the case. We human beings can suffer great angst and confusion apparently over trivia, and like a character in Lewis Carroll's book *Alice's Adventures in Wonderland* we are perfectly capable of believing any number of impossible things. We harbour delusions, concoct fantasies, and sometimes these play a more important role in our lives than 'reality'.

Freud's explanation for all this was that human behaviour is as much a product of desires and motives as of learning or reasoning. According to Freud (e.g. 1933, 1940), the *ego*, which is the rational, conscious mind, is only one of three elements controlling our behaviour. Far more powerful in generating behaviour is the *id*, our unconscious mind, where our desires and motives bubble and boil. These are restrained by the ego, and by the *superego*, which is our moral conscience.

According to Freud, many of the desires of the unconscious mind (id) are unacceptable to the ego or the superego. These desires are rooted in our biology: in the core motivations of our sexuality, and in basic fears and needs. The ego and superego try to *repress* these unacceptable thoughts and feelings, but the drive of these desires is too great to simply turn off. This leads to the development of a number of *defence mechanisms* which work to disguise the unacceptable desires as something else, and so sneak them past the superego to influence behaviour.

The activity of our busy unconscious minds can best be seen in dreams, when unacceptable thoughts are symbolically transformed into more acceptable images (dreaming of a train going into a tunnel had an obvious sexual symbolism for Freud, for instance). They are also visible in the slips of the tongue we commonly make (such as saying 'Give me a hug' when we meant to say 'Give me a mug') which Freud argued were not innocent mistakes but reflect the real desires of the unconscious mind seeping through our ego defence mechanisms (hence this kind of mistake is called a 'Freudian slip'). The power and character of unacceptable unconscious thoughts is also evident in neurotic behaviour and fantasies.

By analysing the dreams, fears and fantasies of his neurotic patients through a process of *psychoanalysis*, Freud came up with a theory of the development of personality through childhood. Like Piaget, he believed that development passes through a number of stages; but Freud's stages are *psychosexual* rather than cognitive. That is to say, for Freud, the key to each stage of development is the biological drive that dominates the unconscious mind:

- *The oral stage* runs from birth to about the first birthday. The baby's chief desires relate to food, and to his or her mouth. Sucking is the greatest of pleasures. A child whose desire to suckle is fully satisfied during this stage may become, in later life, a sunny *oral optimist*, whereas one who is deprived may become a sour *oral pessimist*.

- *The anal stage* runs from the first birthday to about the third birthday, and coincides with the period of potty training. Now the child's pleasure centres on the anus, and the process of retaining or eliminating faeces. Freud suggested that children may become fixated at this stage, as a reflection of whether they are frustrated in their anal desires or not. He suggested that artistic activity, for example, is an extension of *anal expressiveness*: a symbolic revelling in the expression (smearing) of faeces, where miserliness is an extension of anal retentiveness, a symbolic hanging on to what is yours.

- *The phallic stage*, from 3 to 6 years of age, is when pleasure shifts from the anus to the genitals. The child fantasizes sexual pleasure with the opposite-sex parent, and suffers turbulent passions of lust (for that parent) and fear (of reprisals from the rival, the other parent). This is the period of the *Oedipus complex* in little boys, and the *Electra complex* in little girls.

- *The latency stage*, from 6 years to adolescence, reflects the resolution of all this turbulence. Defence mechanisms act to suppress and disguise the child's dangerous lust and so escape the fear of reprisal. The boy 'escapes' castration at the hands of his rival (father) by 'becoming' the father: adopting the father's ideals and values, and thus is formed the superego. According to Freud, little girls, with less to lose (no phallus), form weaker superegos than boys.

- *The genital stage*, which begins at adolescence, is the start of true, adult sexuality, bringing its own challenges for the superego.

Freud's theory has always been very controversial. The consensus of opinion is that many of Freud's specific claims either have not been supported by scientific work, or cannot even be scientifically tested. For instance, there is little evidence for the Oedipus complex. How could you test the claim that the superego develops through fear of castration? Psychoanalysis itself tends have a circular, rather than a scientific orientation to evidence. For example, if you refuse to believe a psychoanalyst's interpretation of your behaviour you may well be told that this is *proof* that it is correct – your defence system has obviously been alerted, you are clearly in denial! However, Freud's identification of the power of unconscious impulses, and of the role of motivations and desires in forming our minds and personalities, has had a lasting impact on psychology as a whole, as has the notion of defence mechanisms.

Freud's youngest daughter Anna Freud developed a more explicitly developmental application of Freud's psychoanalytic ideas, placing more emphasis on development in adolescence than Freud had done. Erik Erikson too applied and extended Freud's idea of development as shaped by the resolution of inner conflicts, though he viewed these conflicts as passing through a series of psychosocial stages rather than psychosexual ones, reflecting more general social processes rather than purely biological desires. We shall return to these ideas in a later chapter.

table **1.2**   Key theories in the history of developmental psychology

	Key idea	Samples of key works
CHARLES DARWIN (1809–1982)	Theory of evolution: all living creatures have been shaped by the biological process of natural selection	Charles Darwin: *The origin of species by means of natural selection* (1859) Charles Darwin: 'A biographical sketch of an infant' (1877)
BEHAVIOURISM (20th century)	That all behaviour is learned, either as an anticipatory response made to a stimulus associated with reward or punishment, or as an operant response aimed at achieving reward or ending punishment.	Ivan Pavlov: *Conditioned Reflexes* (1927) John Watson: *Psychological Care of Infant and Child* (1928) Burrhus Frederic Skinner: *About Behaviourism* (1974)
ETHOLOGY (mid 20th century)	That much animal behaviour reflects innate responses or tendencies, and that basic human behaviours may be explained in the same way	Niko Timbergen: *The Study of Instinct* (1951) Konrad Lorenz: *On Aggression* (1966) Irenaus Eibl-Eibesfeldt: *Love and Hate* (1971)
JOHN BOWLBY (1907–1990)	Influenced by ethological accounts, Bowlby suggested that human babies attach to their mothers through the operation of instinctive drives important to development and quite separate from the child's material needs	John Bowlby: *Child Care and the Growth of Love* (1953) John Bowlby: *Attachment and Loss* (1969)
SOCIOBIOLOGY	The idea that animal behaviour (including human behaviour) is shaped by the need to secure the survival of genes, rather than individuals. Thus we will sacrifice our individual interests to give our genes a better chance of survival.	Richard Dawkins: *The Selfish Gene* (1976) E. O. Wilson: *Sociobiology: The new synthesis* (1980)
LEV VYGOTSKY (1896–1934)	Skills and intelligence are developed through social interactions	Lev Vygotsky: *Thought and Language* (1962)
JEAN PIAGET (1896–1980)	Intelligence must be constructed from basic adaptive processes; the organism is an active contributor to this construction, building intelligence up through a series of stages each more sophisticated and powerful than the one before	Jean Piaget: *Genetic Epistemology* (1968)
INFORMATION PROCESSING	The human mind can be understood by analogy to a computer, wherein both the programming and the memory space may vary. Development may reflect increases in the 'programs' the child has available for processing information or in the memory space available to the program, or both.	Robert Case: *Intellectual Development: Birth to adulthood* (1985) Robert Siegler and Erik Jenkins: *How Children Discover New Strategies* (1989) Klahr and MacWhinney: 'Information processing' (1998) Kim Plunkett: 'Development in a connectionist framework: rethinking the nature-nurture debate' (2000)
PSYCHOANALYSIS	Our behaviour is controlled as much by unconscious, instinctive drives (especially sexual drives) as by our conscious minds. To understand childhood development we must understand the process whereby children gain control over raw instinctive drives to become civilized (and neurotic).	Sigmund Freud: *The Pathology of Everyday Life* (1904) Anna Freud: *Beyond the Best Interests of the Child* (1973)

The full details of each of these references are listed in the references at the back of this book.

Current research and the legacy of the 20th century

The influential theories of the 20th century (**Table 1.2**) can seem bafflingly diverse and contradictory. Sometimes they asked different questions. Sometimes they proposed radically different answers to the same questions. No consensus about development emerges across these different theories. Nevertheless, there are common themes in the history of developmental research, common questions that different theories tried to address in one way or another. These questions form the backdrop for the modern research we shall review in the remainder of this book:

- To what extent (and how) does our biological inheritance shape our human development and individuality? What are the roles of 'nature and nurture' in shaping who we are?

- What kinds of experience (reward and punishment, mental reflection, social interaction) shape development? How do these things interact with one another, and with biology?

- Is the child a passive passenger in this process, or an active influence on his or her own development?

- Where do individual differences come from?

- Is human development continuous (in the way the growth of an oak tree is continuous: its structure stays the same, it just gets bigger) or discontinuous (in the way spawn is different in structure from a tadpole, or from the frog it will become)? Could discontinuities in development reflect the action of a single developmental process, or do they imply that the process itself changes?

- What drives development? Why does it happen at all? Are there evolutionary constraints on how far development can go?

Studying development scientifically

In studying developmental psychology, you are studying a science, and learning to think and to do research scientifically. The core feature of science is that its theories depend on *empirical evidence*. Rather than simply speculating about things as philosophers and others do, scientists go out there and collect things, measure things, do experiments and record what happens. In many ways, this commitment to evidence is, and always has been, the defining characteristic of science. But our understanding of the status of empirical evidence ('facts'), and our understanding of theories has changed radically over the past 50 years. We have become much more sophisticated in our view of what it means to be a scientist.

table 1.3

Some differences between scientific
and unscientific thinking

Scientific thinking	Unscientific thinking
Is driven by the evidence: a theory must fit the evidence or be rejected.	Gives far less importance to evidence. A belief may be held without looking for evidence to support it, or despite the existence of evidence that refutes it.
Uses formal and systematic methods for collecting and testing evidentiary data.	Anecdotes, personal opinions, commonly held beliefs may be treated as self-evidently true, without any test.
Understands that all data are potentially biased, affected by the methods used to collect them. Different methods might produce different results.	Assumes that facts are facts.
Strives to create explicit, internally consistent and empirically testable theories to explain data.	Theories may be implicit, internally inconsistent and untestable.
Understands that we cannot 'prove' any theory to be the truth: theories are our best explanation in the light of what we know at the moment. Any theory may turn out to be wrong, or be replaced by a better one.	Believes certain things to be true beyond any question.
Is progressive, always open to new data and better theories.	May be rigidly committed to a particular theory.

The problem with 'facts' (and the nature of data)

In Darwin's day, the general view was that knowledge (theories, under-standing) derived from 'facts' – that is, from empirical observations and measurements. Collect enough facts and the truth would eventually emerge. (This theory of science is described by philosophers as 'inductivism'. It is still pretty much the layperson's view of science today.)

One problem with this view is that it assumes that human beings can perceive reality ('the facts') in some absolute, objective way. We now know that this is impossible. Every measurement we take is made with tools that have limitations which affect what we see. Every observation we make is made by a mind that is constrained by pre-existing theories which affect the 'facts' we find. Every measurement is made in a particular context.

For instance, imagine a new species of flying rodent. Does it communicate vocally? In 1877, a rigorous researcher makes a 2-year study and hears not a sound. For him, the 'fact' is that the rodents are not vocal. In 1977, a new researcher, armed with new equipment able to 'hear' signals way beyond the range of human hearing, discovers a plethora of communications in these rodents. For her, the 'fact' is that the rodents are vocal. In 2077, a researcher not yet born, armed with equipment we can no more now imagine than the researcher of 1877 could have anticipated the equipment of 1977, may make discoveries that will change our understanding of these rodents' communications again. The data we collect are always constrained by the tools we use to collect them. This is inevitable. At any moment, a new tool may come along and radically alter our view of 'the facts'. This has happened many times in developmental research, as we shall see through the course of this book.

Furthermore, however good our measurement tools and techniques, we can only make discoveries about the things we choose to look at, which are normally influenced by what we already know and expect to find. Suppose a researcher is studying the effect of particular elements in the diet on undesirable behaviour in children. Already, he is biased to expect a correlation between those behaviours and certain foods. So he will measure the correlation between behaviour and the specifics of the child's diet; he probably won't measure the correlation between (say) the child's behaviour and his or her popularity. Now, it may be that he finds a correlation of the type he is expecting: perhaps children who prefer junk foods show more undesirable behaviour? He is likely to see this as vindicating his theory that diets of that kind are damaging, and publish reports condemning the nutritional content of junk foods. But it is possible that there is nothing intrinsically wrong with eating junk food in itself (compared with the average diet, which is actually pretty much as deficient in fruit and vegetables and also includes too much salt, fat, sugar, etc.). It may be that quantity, not quality, is relevant here: junk food portions are simply larger and hence more fattening, and obese children are less popular. Unpopular children are less happy, and this is reflected in their behaviour. Our researcher will never see this: his preconceptions determined what he measured, and they shape how he interprets the results he gets. Another researcher with a different theory will make slightly different measurements – and come up with slightly different results.

Our theories always determine what we measure and how we measure it, and so our preconceptions bias the 'facts' we find. This too is inescapable: you cannot measure absolutely everything, you always have to be selective. Inevitably, your theories shape your choice of what to measure and what to ignore. As our theories grow to encompass more factors, our view of what is or is not relevant changes.

And however good our measurement tools, however good our initial theory may be, the results we observe can depend on who is doing the measuring and where that measurement takes place. For example, a doctor measuring your blood pressure in a clinic will get a higher reading than you would if you measured it yourself at home. This effect of context is so well known that doctors label it 'white coat syndrome' and make allowances for it in diagnosing high blood pressure. Any doctor's clinic causes white coat syndrome, but the effect is greater if the doctor happens to be sexually attractive (or repulsively ugly). Who does the measuring and where they collect these observations greatly affects the results in many contexts in developmental research.

So the truth is that there are no absolute, objective hard and fast 'facts'. There are only *data* measured in a certain place, using certain methods, by certain people who chose where and how and what to measure in the light of their pre-existing theories and expectations. This is why research papers have such detailed introduction and method sections. When two researchers come up with different results, we can look at precisely what they did and why, and try to work out what affected their data. We can form hypotheses that would explain the difference, and do new research to test those hypotheses. In the process, we may well make new discoveries that extend our understanding of both theories and methods.

The trouble with truth (and the nature of theory)

If there are no absolute, hard and fast facts, can we say that any theory is true? The answer is obviously, no. However well a theory may fit all the data we have today, new data may always come along that it cannot explain. This point is more important for science than may appear at a casual glance. The philosopher Karl Popper was the first to draw out the key implication: *no amount of data that fits a theory can ever prove that it is true, whereas one datum that contradicts the theory can prove it false.* Popper used the example of the very simple theory: 'all swans are white'. Now, millions of swans *are* white. For long periods of history, a researcher testing this theory in Europe would have made endless observations confirming it, but he would have been foolish to conclude that it was true. The discovery of one black swan in the southern hemisphere discredited it.

Popper argued that *falsification* is more pertinent to science than the search for truth, since we can never know that a theory is true (it's always possible that new data will falsify it). According to Popper, science progresses by proposing theories and testing the predictions these theories make against the data until a prediction proves wrong and the theory must be altered, or discarded in favour of another.

Every theory we have, then, is provisional: it is not the absolute truth, merely a useful way of explaining what we presently know. But that does not mean that any theory is as good as any other. A theory that doesn't fit the data we have now would obviously be less useful than one that does. And even where two theories both more or less fit the data, one may be better than the other because it predicts and explains a wider range of phenomena, or gives a simpler explanation. For instance, a theory that explains the development of both rational and irrational reasoning is better (more complete) than one that explains only rational reasoning, or only irrational reasoning. Equally, a theory that explains both rational and irrational reasoning as different facets of the same kind of process is better than one that explains these two things in terms of two entirely different processes: it is simpler, and simpler explanations tend to be more useful (the principle of always choosing the simpler of two equally good explanations of the same phenomena is called *Occam's razor*). In many ways, the ideal goal of science would be to find a complete theory that accurately explained all the phenomena of the universe in terms of a few simple principles: the elusive 'theory of everything'.

Data, theories and progress in science

Our theories do not arise out of 'objective facts' as inductivism supposed, and are not 'true', but merely useful (or otherwise) in predicting data. These insights suggest that the relationship between data and theory is far more complex than was supposed in Darwin's day.

Where do theories come from? What role does data play in the creation of a theory, or in its development? Popper gives only a partial answer. His principle of falsification is now generally accepted as an account of how science discards ideas. But it does not explain where new theories come from, nor why it is that some falsifications lead us to abandon a whole complex theory, and others don't.

The philosopher Thomas Kuhn (1970) has proposed that science develops in stages. In the first stage (which he called *pre-paradigmatic*) there are many different, often rather poorly specified theories about the phenomenon in question, theories that differ on very fundamental issues (whether behaviour is instinctive or learned, for example). Data is collected rather haphazardly (and in partisan ways) to bear on these controversies. The conflict over the nature of development between sociobiology, behaviourism and psychoanalysis is typical of pre-paradigmatic science.

Gradually, conflicting theories begin to find common ground: a set of assumptions that all can share evolves and comes to dominate research. (For example, in the last quarter of the 20th century it was widely agreed that all behaviour, whether biologically pre-programmed, learned or psychodynamically driven, reflects underlying information processing, and that theories should be expressed at this level.) Kuhn calls these shared assumptions a *paradigm*. Now research moves away from old controversies and focuses on applying these shared assumptions to more and more phenomena. According to Kuhn, this is *normal science*. At this stage, although individual hypotheses (that this particular behaviour reflects that particular set of information, for instance) are still falsified and rejected, the basic assumptions of the overall paradigm (that behaviour always reflects information processing of some sort, for example) are retained and defended.

'Normal science' continues until either there have been just too many failures and falsifications in the theories the underlying paradigm suggests, or someone comes up with an alternative, even more powerful new paradigm. In either case, scientists begin to challenge the old dominant paradigm and develop an alternative view. Kuhn calls this stage of competition between paradigms *revolutionary science*. It continues until one paradigm or another comes to dominate and 'normal science' resumes. Many think that developmental psychology is in the throes of a new period of revolutionary science, as we shall see through the course of this book.

Is developmental psychology a science like physics?

Even 30 years ago, it was common to hear it said that psychology was not a 'hard' science like physics. Physics was said to study phenomena where firm deterministic laws could be discovered, whereas psychology studied messier, more ephemeral phenomena where laws could only be probabilistic, where phenomena behaved in curious non-linear ways, data must be relative to some context and the very presence of an observer could unsettle the phenomenon to be observed and distort the data. Psychology was thus dismissed as an inferior branch of science, or even scarcely scientific at all.

For decades, the pressure seemed to be on psychology to find ways round this, to find a 'more scientific' (i.e. more strictly regular and deterministic) explanation of human development and behaviour: in other words, to be more like physics or to accept that psychological research is not 'real' science. As a consequence, psychology tended to shy away from tackling obviously 'messy' problems (such as intentions, consciousness and so on) and focused on the more tangible things (perception, overt behaviour and the like).

Ironically, the tables have turned in an unexpected way. It turns out that physics itself is not at all what we thought it was. In fact, it is much like psychology... For example, as Einstein's theory makes clear, measurements in physics are as relative to context as are measurements in psychology. (If you throw me a book in a train travelling at 100 miles an hour, on a rotating planet, how fast is the book travelling? There's no one absolute answer. The question is: relative to what?) Heisenberg has shown that, even in physics, the act of observing something (photons, say) changes the behaviour of what you are observing. And chaos theory shows that the relationship between cause and effect is not necessarily linear in the physical world either.

In sum, the physical universe is less deterministic and more probabilistic than old concepts of 'hard' science supposed, and psychology and physics are more similar than we thought. In fact, as we shall see in later chapters, the same principles that physicists use to describe the genesis of the infinite diversity of snowflakes or the origin of a star system can also be applied to explain developmental changes in human beings.

Methods for studying human development

Every science shares a number of methodological problems: for example, we want measuring instruments that are reliable and valid; we want our data and theories to have a degree of generality; and we want to be able to distinguish mere correlations from causal relationships. In addition, every branch of science studies a different set of phenomena, and each has its own particular problems in doing so, reflecting the nature of the phenomena studied.

Common methodological issues in science

Reliability and validity

Every science wants the tools it uses in collecting data to be reliable (in other words, to measure or record things accurately) and valid (in other words, to measure what we intend them to measure). Sometimes, establishing that our methods of collecting data are reliable and valid is fairly straightforward. For instance, I can compare what I weigh on my bathroom scales with the weight other scales produce on the same morning, and so see how reliable they are. Or I can check that my questionnaire is a valid measure of people's tendency to buy organic goods in the supermarket (rather than, say, their desire to impress a researcher with their 'green' credentials) by comparing the results it obtains against a film of what they actually bought.

But few measuring tools are perfectly reliable, and few are perfectly valid. Errors in reliability and validity are collectively known as *error variance*. Error variance is often regarded as no more than a nuisance, a weakness in our measurement tool. Sometimes this is true: some problems are purely technical (a bathroom scale that gives two different readings for the same naked person seconds apart, for example). But sometimes error variance is more interesting than this. It can point to the existence of 'real' factors that we have not yet understood (for instance, that a young child's popularity reflects his or her possessions – which we have not measured – as much as the personality traits that our test assesses). As we identify new variables that our original theory did not realize were relevant and begin to take these into account, we convert variance we did not understand (and so called 'error') into variance we do now understand – and so drive our theories forward.

Generality

There would be very little interest in the theories of science, if those theories applied only in the special circumstances of the laboratories in which the research took place. What use would a careful measure of the temperature at which water boils be, for instance, if it applied *only* in the particular laboratory where it was measured?

Generality is an issue for every science. As we all know, the boiling point of water varies with atmospheric pressure: it's different at sea level and up a mountain. The effect of a cancer drug may be very different in a mouse and a human being. A child's ability to solve logical problems may be different when the problem is couched in the concrete terms of a familiar situation and when it is posed abstractly, as we shall see later in this book. In sum, a great many phenomena in the physical, biological and psychological world are strongly affected by context. If things vary from one context to another, how can theories ever be general?

We can never *assume* that a theory will generalize. Some things do, some don't. The trick is to bear both possibilities in mind, and to test the issue directly. But it is also worth noticing that by understanding just how a given phenomenon varies from one context to another, we come to understand more about the processes at work across contexts. For example, by understanding *why* a given drug works in mice but not people (or understanding how logical reasoning relates to context), our overall understanding of how drugs work (or how reasoning develops) increases, taking in more and more contexts – and so becoming more general.

Correlations and cause and effect

Many things correlate; that is to say, changes in one factor are systematically related to (*co-vary* with) changes in another. For example, certain illnesses are correlated with high levels of anxiety. Such correlations are interesting, but they do not tell us much. Is the anxiety causing the illness? Or is the illness causing the anxiety? Or are both being caused by some third factor, so that there is no causal association between the illness and anxiety in either direction? Merely establishing that there is a correlation between factors cannot answer these questions.

Experiments provide science with a systematic way of exploring cause–effect relationships. The basic principle of an experiment is that, if there is a causal relationship such that factor A causes factor B, then intervening to change factor A should change factor B. So, for example, if anxiety is causing a given disease, then treating and reducing the anxiety should reduce the symptoms of the disease. If, on the other hand, anxiety is not causing the disease, treating the anxiety will have no effect on the disease. To test this causal connection, a sample of patients with the illness are divided into two groups. One group is the *experimental group*, and receives treatment ('an intervention') to reduce anxiety. The other is the *control group*, and receives no treatment for anxiety. This control group provides a check on the extent to which the disease would have abated in any case during the course of the experiment, rather than as a result of the experimental intervention. If, at the end of the experiment, the experimental group shows much better recovery than the control group, it can be inferred that the difference had been caused by the intervention, and hence that anxiety was playing a role in causing the illness. (Of course, the control procedures in a real experiment would be rather more elaborate than in this simple illustration!)

Special issues for research on human development

Studying change

Our primary aim is to understand the process of change through human development. But development takes a long time. At any one moment it is hard to detect much changing in an individual child. What we have is a snapshot of that child as he or she is now, a 'still' photo, when what we want to understand is the movie that runs from conception to adulthood. So our first problem is: how can we study developmental change or the processes that produce it? A number of research strategies (*research designs*) have been developed to help us study change through childhood. Each has strengths, and each has weaknesses.

The quickest and easiest of such strategies is the *cross-sectional* research design. Here, age-related changes in performance on some task or activity are explored by comparing groups of children of different ages. So, for example, a study might compare a group of 5-year-olds, a group of 8-year olds and a group of 12-year-olds. The vast majority of developmental research uses this strategy. It can produce rich data about different age groups.

This approach needs care: if the different age groups are not matched on all the factors besides age that might affect their behaviour in the task concerned (such as social background), then the results might reflect these other factors rather than age. Even if all the normally relevant factors are matched across the groups, it may still be possible that one age group has happened to have some extreme unusual experience that distorts the age effect. For example, 5-year-olds tested in October 2000 may be different in the kinds of anxiety they report from those tested in October 2001, reflecting the media coverage of the 9/11 attacks on the World Trade Center. This is known as a *cohort effect*. These two problems can be handled by alert awareness of the possibilities, and by careful choice of samples (in other words, the children studied) across both populations and time.

But the cross-sectional approach has another limitation that cannot be so readily handled: it creates a picture of each age group by averaging across children. There is no way to know what individual development between one age and another would look like. This problem of following individual development can be handled by a *longitudinal study*, in which the same children are followed for a period of time (weeks, months or years), and are repeatedly tested through that period on the measures of interest. Individual case studies and baby diaries fall into this category of research, though longitudinal studies generally follow a group of children rather than just one individual.

Longitudinal studies are rich sources of information both about age-related developmental change and about the pattern of change within individuals. They are rarer than cross-sectional studies because they are harder to do: the research inevitably takes a great deal longer, and over a period of months or years, a number of participants will drop out as families move away or children change schools (and so on). The drop-out rate can be a real problem: it may be that those who leave the study are systematically different from those who don't, making the results hard to interpret. For instance, what if the more entrepreneurial or imaginative families move more often? Then a longitudinal study of creativity might systematically lose those individuals most likely to have a background that fosters creativity. Furthermore, the repeated testing itself may distort the results, as children become sophisticated (or self-conscious, or bored) about testing.

Although longitudinal studies come closer than cross-sectional studies to tracking actual developmental change, it's still the case that they take snapshots, albeit in sequence, rather than directly observing change as it happens. This is inevitable: it takes time, often years, for a child to show clear developmental change. It would be impossible (and probably unethically intrusive) to record the child's behaviour in any detail over such a duration.

A comparatively recent solution to this problem is the *microgenetic study*. Here, a child's behaviour is recorded (often filmed) in very great detail for relatively short periods of time as the child engages in some activity that is likely to stimulate change in understanding or behaviour. For example, a child might be filmed for 20 minutes while trying to solve a building task that requires the discovery of counterbalance. Here, some participants will make new discoveries and adopt new strategies on camera (some won't). By very detailed frame by frame analysis of exactly what the child did and what feedback he or she received from the task, it is possible to develop hypotheses about the mechanisms of new discovery operating in childhood (see Chapter 7). Microgenetic studies are extremely labour-intensive and slow to do. They offer the best way we yet know of actually observing development as it happens. But how does what we observe relate to development as a whole, and to changes occurring over long periods of time?

Making mental processes visible

Much of what we want to understand in studying development is not visible: we cannot see a child's intentions, thoughts or feelings. All we have to go on is what we can see and hear: what the individual says and does, and what we can infer from this.

There are many ways of gaining insights into children's minds from what they say. Quite a few such insights have come from simply listening to *what children say spontaneously* to adults, to themselves or to one another, as they go about their everyday lives. For instance, it was only when I listened to my 3-year-old son's muttered dirge that I realized that he thought his chicken-pox was a life sentence, condemning him to a life of lonely itchiness forever. His concept of chickenpox was utterly different from my adult view. Maybe all 3-year-olds have the same confused ideas? On the basis of many such observations in casual conversation with her children, Susan Carey (1985) proposed a new theory of how children's conceptual understanding develops, as we shall see later in the book.

Open-ended interviews, where the researcher sets out to discuss a particular topic but lets the child lead the direction the conversation takes, give a slightly more formal way of collecting these useful data. Like a child's spontaneous remarks, such conversations tend to be idiosyncratic so that it can be difficult to gauge whether the insights they provide relate to all children of that age, or just to this individual. This issue can be more systematically explored in *structured interviews*, where the researcher asks a series of children exactly the same questions.

We can also gain insights about children's mental processes by asking them to 'think aloud' and explain their actions as they tackle a given task. Transcripts of such running commentaries are called *verbal protocols*. Of course, very young children cannot tell us what they are thinking. And in fact, even adults may have a surprisingly limited insight into their own mental processes (I do not always know, for example, exactly why I am irritable, or how I solved a particular crossword clue), and what they say is sometimes mistaken, and sometimes less than completely candid. For these reasons, what children *do* is often a more important source of data than what they *say*.

Like their speech, children's behaviour can be observed in a wide range of contexts. Their *spontaneous behaviour* in everyday life, out shopping, at school, playing alone or with others, interacting with their families, is a rich source of insight. Like spontaneous conversations, observations of individual children can be hard to compare: they may have been doing entirely different things, or have been influenced by different factors in the richly complex world which every child inhabits. It can be hard to know whether insight gained from spontaneous behaviour applies just to that individual child, or to children of that age at large. Again, this issue can be explored by observing children in more *controlled situations*, where the researcher puts a series of children in the same situation, or asks each of them to *complete a particular task*.

The level of detail that can be taken from observations of children's behaviour in such situations can vary enormously, from recording only whether the child *succeeds or fails* in a given task, right down to *recording every action* or even *every eye movement*. Either type of data can be used to test hypotheses about the child's mental processing. 'Pass/fail' data can provide a quick and easy way to test many types of well-formulated hypothesis. More detailed data are more useful for testing hypotheses about mechanisms of change, and for gaining new insights, and new hypotheses about mental processes (see **Table 1.4**).

table 1.4   Experiments, observations and data

	Natural contexts where the child's behaviour is free and spontaneous	Experimentally controlled tasks/ situations
Only specific responses, or pass/fail data are recorded	*Example:* Counting how many times children fight or cooperate in a nursery playground *Plusses:* Natural behaviour in a natural context *Minuses:* Lack of control of the situation may mean the relevant behaviours don't occur Narrow data focus may miss relevant factors/unexpected effects	*Example:* Recording children's success and failure in an experimental problem-solving task *Plusses:* Good for testing hypotheses *Minuses:* Narrow data focus may miss relevant factors/unexpected effects Experimental situation may distort child's responses
A full record is made of the child's behaviour	*Example:* Film of children playing together in a playground *Plusses:* Natural behaviour in a natural context Full record allows new factors and hypotheses to emerge *Minuses:* Labour-intensive analysis Lack of control of the situation may mean that little relevant behaviour occurs	Example: Microgenetic analysis of film of a child solving a problem *Plusses:* Good for testing hypotheses Detailed record allows behavioural change to be tracked, and new factors and hypotheses to be discovered *Minuses:* Labour-intensive analysis

No matter what data we collect, we still cannot see a child's mental processes, his or her thoughts or feelings. All we can do is draw inferences about those things from the data available to us. We can test those inferences by drawing new predictions from them, and testing those in new, more extensive data, or by constructing interventions and experiments designed to clarify what mental processes underlie a child's behaviour. But like every other theory in any science, our inferences about children's mental processes may be wrong. New data or new insight may change our understanding at any moment. So like any other theory, inferences about children's mental processes must be treated with care: they are our best understanding in the light of what we know now, not 'truth'.

Studying development ethically

Developmental psychology studies living creatures, the young of our own species, rather than inanimate matter or forces. This imposes an ethical responsibility on developmental researchers that exceeds that of other branches of science. There are things a physicist, say, may do to the material that he or she investigates (such as decomposing it into its constituent elements, or depriving a process of factors believed to be essential to its progress to check that theory) that we may not (and would not want to) do to a human child. How can we study development in an ethical way? Do ethical standards impose limitations on how far developmental research can progress?

Ethics has become an increasingly prominent part of research and practice in developmental psychology over the last century. Many studies done in the past would be regarded as inappropriate and unethical today (a prime example would be Watson's studies involving the induction of a conditioned fear in a baby). In the early days of research, ethical issues were left entirely to the individual researcher – not always with wholly edifying results. Today, there are strict, formal codes of ethics by which all psychologists are bound. Full statements of this ethical code are available from organizations such as the British Psychological Society, or the Society for Research in Child Development in the United States. In brief, as a developmental psychologist you must:

- Think about the consequences of your research or intervention for the participants and for those to whom the results may apply. You are responsible for those consequences.

- Do no harm. Don't expose participants in research to risks they would not have run ordinarily in the course of everyday life.

- If at all possible, explain the research and its potential consequences to the participants before you start, and get their informed consent for their participation.

- Where participants are too young or otherwise unable to give their consent, seek the consent of others who have some investment in the participant's best interests. This might include a child's parents, or a formal committee designed to uphold ethical standards (ethics committee).

- Give participants, however young, a real choice to refuse to participate.

- Don't deceive participants about research or interventions unless there is an overwhelming reason to do so that has also been endorsed by independent opinion (an ethics committee).

- Debrief participants after research or interventions: tell them what it was about and what you discovered in terms they can understand. Correct any false impression the participant may have gathered.

- Respect participants' privacy. All the information obtained about an individual must be absolutely confidential.

This code of ethics makes certain kinds of research impossible. For example, PET scans (positron emission tomography) can build up complex pictures of the structure and activity in a living brain, offering the possibility of new and more detailed information about developmental changes in the brain. But PET scans require the injection of a radioactive marker. This is too invasive to be ethical, if it is done solely for the purposes of developmental research. Equally, it would be shockingly unethical to deprive a child of nutrition, ordinary stimulation or love for the purposes of research, or to induce genetic or other physiological damage, however informative the results might be.

However, data are sometimes available because some situation has occurred completely independently of research, creating a *natural experiment*: the opportunity to study a phenomenon that it would have been unethical to arrange. Children are born with genetic damage; they suffer illnesses and accidents, and endure medical tests for diagnosis or treatment of these things. These natural events can provide us with information that would otherwise be outside all possibility of ethical research.

More extreme natural experiments occur in parts of the world where children are victims of famine, war, poverty, unchecked disease, often enduring brutalization and deprivation almost beyond our comprehension. The primary aim of research with such children is, of course, to find ways of mending the damage they have suffered. But in identifying what that damage has been, and what 'works' to put it right, we may gain information about the process of child development as a whole.

About this book

This chapter has introduced the basic questions that drive developmental research, and the basic methods that we use in trying to answer those questions. It has put this material in its historical context. This sets the scene for the remainder of the book, which surveys what we now know, and what we still don't know about development.

The nature of science means that in studying developmental psychology you aren't going to be discovering 'the truth' or learning lists of 'facts'. As we have seen, it is much more complicated than that. What you will be doing is developing an educated or 'critical' opinion about human development: that is to say, you will be learning how to evaluate theories and data about development in a rigorous and scientific way. How well does this theory explain the phenomena we are interested in? How valid and reliable are the data we have about this?

Each chapter of this book reviews research in a given area of developmental psychology. At the end of the chapter there is a synopsis of key material covered, for revision. The book can be read from cover to cover, but the chapters can also be used in any order you like. Where material in another chapter would provide useful background, a brief summary is included and cross-references in the text indicate where more detailed material can be found. Each chapter aims to cover its topic comprehensively. If you master the material in the text, you will have a sound grounding in developmental research. To take this knowledge to a deeper level, you can read the original work that this book reviews, following up on references in the text. There is also a short list of suggested reading to take you more deeply into key issues, at the end of each chapter.

At the end of each chapter you will find exercises designed to help you gain a critical grasp of the material that has been covered. Each has been chosen both to revise key themes from the chapter and to stretch your understanding of core issues. These exercises are intended to be completed first by you working as an individual. But having completed them, you might find it useful and illuminating to discuss your ideas with other people.

Exercises

1. In many ways, the cognitive developmental approach of Piaget and information-processing theories became a dominating paradigm in developmental psychology. What are the key features of this paradigm? In what ways does this cognitive approach differ from other approaches such as sociobiology, behaviourism, psychoanalysis? What assumptions does it share with these other approaches?

2. How would you design a study, and what kind of data would you collect, to test the hypothesis that 3-year-olds are less likely than 8-year-olds to remember what they had for lunch yesterday? Why would you use this approach, and what problems would you need to think about in setting up the study?

3. On a small island, children are suffering horribly from malnutrition. Many are dying. The island is rich in food, but the islanders' religion forbids them from eating most of the available things. Elders enforce the religious rules. You are hired as a psychologist to work on this problem. What practical and ethical issues should concern you?

Suggested further reading

For an overview of the history of developmental psychology read:

- R. B. Cairns (1998) The making of developmental psychology. In R. Lerner (ed.), *Handbook of Child Psychology, Vol 1: Theoretical models of human development*. New York: Wiley.

For discussions of how history has influenced the work of various key modern researchers, read:

- R. Parke, P. Ornstein, J. Reiser and C. Zahn-Waxler (eds) (1994) *A Century of Developmental Psychology*. Washington, DC: American Psychological Association.

For the key ideas of the major theorists in the 20th century, there is no substitute for reading their own words.

- Box 1.4 suggests specific readings for each theory. The full references for these readings are listed in the bibliography at the back of this book. Many of the older classics have been reprinted, and where this is the case, the details are for the reprint.

For an excellent and very readable introduction to the nature of science, read:

- A. F. Chalmers (1999) *What is This Thing Called Science?* 3rd edn. Buckingham: Open University Press.

For discussions of research methodologies in developmental psychology read:

- D. Teti (2004) *Handbook of Research Methods In Developmental Psychology*. Oxford: Blackwell.

- C. Robson (1993) *Real World Research: A resource for social scientists and practitioner-researchers*. Oxford: Blackwell.

For ethical issues read:

- M. Bulmer (ed.) (1982) *Social Research Ethics*. London: Macmillan.

- British Psychological Society (1991) *Code of Conduct, Ethical Principles and Guidelines*. Leicester: BPS.
- Society for Research in Child Development (2000) *Directory of Members SRCD*, pp. 283–4.

Revision summary

What is developmental psychology?

■ Developmental psychology is the scientific study of how individuals develop from conception through infancy, childhood, adolescence and into adult life.

■ From its beginning, developmental psychology has influenced childrearing practice and policy, influencing children's lives as well as contributing to a deeper understanding of human nature.

A short history of key ideas in developmental psychology

■ The beginning of developmental research was profoundly influenced by Darwin's theory of evolution through natural selection, and is still very much influenced by biological issues.

■ Ethologists and sociobiologists sought for innate or instinctive behaviours or tendencies in human development. There is little evidence for instincts, and explanations of behaviour in terms of survival advantage have been heavily criticized: they are plausible, but critics say they lack credible supporting evidence. Nevertheless, work exploring human behaviour in its evolutionary context has raised intriguing possibilities for important topics (such as attachment and altruism).

■ Learning theorists and behaviourists claimed that all behaviour develops through learning processes that parallel natural selection in the individual's life: rewarded behaviour survives, punished behaviour doesn't. Reward and punishment certainly do shape human behaviour. But such processes cannot explain the creative nature of human behaviour: this implies a vital role for mental processes. Nevertheless, this approach has given us useful tools for interpreting and modifying children's behaviour.

■ Vygotsky suggested that the development of children's skills, and even their mental processes, occurs in interactions with more skilled individuals, who support the child's efforts as he or she tackles the next area of challenge. Important aspects of human development may be carried by the culture, rather than constructed by the individual. These ideas have a powerful continuing influence on research.

■ Piaget argued that children must construct mental processes for themselves, starting from a few basic reflexes and using only very simple biological processes for adaptation. The nature of knowledge means that every child would go through the same stages during this process, each stage being qualitatively different in its thinking from the one before. Piaget's work was the greatest single influence on developmental research in the 20th century.

■ Information-processing theory drew an analogy between human minds and computers, arguing that computer programs can simulate the effects of

part

1

the
beginning
of life

Overview

The three chapters that make up Part I focus on one basic question: *where does it all start?* What are the first origins of human psychology, of our minds and our emotions, our personality, our sense of 'self'? How are these things possible?

Chapter 2 explores the biological history of our species, our roots in evolution, and how that evolutionary history is passed on to us through our genes. It follows the process of development from conception to birth. This chapter focuses on the development not only of the body, but of the functioning of the brain. When do our senses develop? What can we learn in the womb? How do babies gain physical control over their bodies through infancy?

Chapter 3 focuses on the mind, on the origin of intelligence, insight and understanding. What do these uniquely human abilities involve? How could they arise in an organic structure like the brain? What building blocks has evolution given us to spark the genesis of a reflecting, self-aware mind? What experience, what learning is needed to bring this potential to fruition?

Chapter 4 looks at social and emotional development, and at the origins of personality and a sense of self. How does a fertilized egg become a person with an individual character, able to form relationships with other people? How does the genetic legacy of our species, or the particular genetic legacy of our family, contribute to this process? What role does experience play?

The scope of these three chapters is at one and the same time unimaginably enormous and ridiculously tiny, covering the millions of years of the evolution of our species and the brief period between conception and 18 months of age. What holds the research reviewed here together is the puzzle of how psychological development emerges from its biological roots. As we shall see through these three chapters, a new type of theory ('dynamic systems theory') proposes a new way of understanding this process. It now seems possible that the very same mechanisms are responsible for development at both the evolutionary and the individual level.

chapter

2

bodies
and
brains

Human intelligence and personality are *embodied*. That is to say, these things (we) exist in a physical body that has an evolutionary history, is composed of biological processes and is constrained by the natural forces of the physical world. The fact that we are embodied in this way has important implications for who we are and how we develop.

What is the evolutionary history of our species? How does this *phylogenetic* (that is, evolutionary) history impact on our *ontogenetic* (in other words, individual) development? How do the properties of the bodies we now inhabit affect development? How, for that matter, do those bodies themselves develop? These are the questions addressed in this chapter.

Human evolution

Like every other living organism, our species, *Homo sapiens*, is the product of an evolutionary process that has systematically shaped us through the process of natural selection (Darwin, 1859, and see Chapter 1) to survive successfully in a particular environmental niche. That premise is 'axiomatic' in biology and psychology: that is to say, it is the core assumption of current research in these disciplines. But there is much more that we want to know about our evolutionary history.

Early ancestors

Three and a half million years ago, a shower of volcanic ash fell on the land around what is now called Laetoli, in Tanzania. Many animals and birds walked in this ash while it was still wet, leaving their footprints. As the ash dried, it became as hard as cement, preserving these marks in detail in its surface. Even the pinpricks made by raindrops are still clearly visible. Among all these fossilized indentations are the footprints of two hominids, walking upright (Leakey, 1979).

The hominids who walked across the Laetoli mudpans were *Australopithecenes* (specifically, *Australopithecus Afarensis*, which is normally written as *A. Afarensis*): members of a now extinct species that was transitional between apes and humans (**Figure 2.1**). They were very much like modern apes, in both their body shape and proportions, and the size of their brains (450–550 cc in size, about a third of the size of a modern adult human brain). But they were more like humans than apes in other ways: their teeth, for example, had smaller canines than an ape, and more dental enamel, just as human teeth do. And the footprints they left were remarkably like human footprints today, where an ape's foot leaves a print more in the shape of a hand.

The most complete skeleton we have of an Australopithecine is 'Lucy', found in Ethiopia in 1974. Lucy lived in roughly the same period as the pair who crossed the Laetoli mudflats. She was 3 ft 6 in (1.07 m) tall, though she was an adult. She was probably in her mid-20s when she died, though she already had signs of arthritis. She is the most ancient, as well as the best preserved, skeleton of any upright-walking human ancestor we have found so far (Johanson and Maitland, 1990). Who were the descendants of Lucy and her like? There is still so much we don't know, in answer to that question. But it seems certain that we humans are among the descendants of A. Afarensis.

Our uncertainty about our lineage comes from the fact that we must reconstruct our early history from fragments of information: usually the odd bone found here or there, the presence or absence of tools or other evidence of humanoid intelligence (fire, burials, artwork and the like). We are reconstructing our evolutionary history from the partial remains of potential ancestors, and the debris they happened to die with – which may or may not be representative of the items they lived with (imagine the different conclusions future archaeologists might draw about modern humans from a body killed on a camping trip as opposed to one found immured in their own home after a volcano).

Until recently, studies of human evolution relied heavily on comparisons between fossil bones, especially skulls and teeth, to establish connections between one find (species?) and another. And we relied on our knowledge (theories) about the age of the surrounding things (rocks, other animals, etc.) to date the fossil finds of potential ancestors. But as you will see so often through this book, on many topics, new and better methods are progressively changing our understanding and raising new questions. Among the new technologies relevant here are *carbon dating*, which gives a fairly precise age to organic remains, and *DNA analysis*, which allows us to establish the degree of relationship between one individual and another very

figure **2.1**

An illustration of hominid evolution by Victoria Edwards showing Australopithicus afarensis, Homo habilis, Homo erectus, Homo heidelbergensis, Homo neanderthalensis and Homo sapiens

© The Natural History Museum, London

accurately. These new methods have cast doubt on some old certainties.

What is clear is that we are *primates*, members of one of four primate groups. We are not descended from any other modern primate species: rather, about 5 million years ago we shared a common ancestor (long extinct) with the other great apes of the Old World, a group (labelled *Catarrhini*) which includes baboons, macaques, orangutan, chimpanzees, gorillas and gibbons. Modern species of apes, including humans, are all variants of this common ancestor which separated from other lines of development at some point in evolution, to produce the different species we see today. Australopithecenes seem to have diverged from other apes about 5 million years ago. Dental comparisons suggested that our closest living relatives (in other words, the species most recently divergent from us) are the orangutan. But DNA studies show that this is wrong: our closest relatives are first chimpanzees, and next gorillas.

As Figure 2.1 shows, A. Afarensis (the earliest of the Australopithecenes) was just the first ancestor of many bipedal sub-species. Some of these seem not to have progressed much beyond the great breakthrough of bipedalism. Others made new breakthroughs, becoming skilled tool users, learning to control fire, to think and to speak. Exactly which of these sub-species were our direct ancestors is controversial, though we are clearly the product of the 'Homo' sub-group. What is also clear is that gradually, all but one line of the descendants of A. Afarensis disappeared from the fossil record, leaving ourselves, Homo sapiens, as the sole survivor.

Just why Homo sapiens is the sole survivor of our branch of evolution is unclear. This is an issue with great implications for our understanding of human nature. Did we have some adaptive (survival) advantage over other hominoid species, so that natural selection inevitably favoured us above all our rivals? But it's far from clear what survival advantage early Homo sapiens might have had over contemporary rivals. For instance, Neanderthal man, like Homo sapiens, used tools, had ritualistic burials, had the capacity for speech. Neanderthals may have been at least as bright as us. In fact, their brains were larger. Neanderthals were clearly present in Europe 35,000 years ago, alongside our ancestors. But they are long extinct, while we flourish. Why?

Perhaps Homo sapiens had no survival advantage over Neanderthals, but interbred with that line, subsuming it into our human history? This would explain their 'disappearance'. But so far, DNA evidence refutes this theory. We have found no trace of Neanderthals in human genetic material.

Research on our nearest relative, the chimpanzee, suggests a third, more sinister explanation of why Homo sapiens is alone, the sole survivor of a rich evolutionary line. Chimpanzees turn out to be shockingly aggressive, vicious, capable of murder and even of systematic genocide (Goodall, 1986). So perhaps our ancestors made their own luck, wiping out their rivals. Looking around the world at the end of the 20th century, the start of the 21st, this hypothesis seems depressingly plausible.

One species

DNA research suggests that all modern human beings are descendants of the same small group of individuals, and that this original ancestral group lived in East Africa only about 200,000 years ago (we may all, in fact, be the descendants of one woman, the ancestral 'Eve'). The evidence that all human populations are so closely related lies in the fact that the genetic differences within any racial group are greater than the genetic differences between racial groups. In other words, for all their surface differences, people of Chinese, African or European (for example) origins are genetically more or less identical: the human blueprint is clearly the same across every racial type. All that differ between us are variations on the minor genetic differences that create individuality, variations that occur in some degree everywhere.

Like other hominids, our ancestral group originated in Africa. Like other hominids, Homo sapiens spread first across the African continent, and then out of Africa to populate the world. Exactly how long ago this exodus from Africa happened is not clear. But there is a great deal more individual genetic variation within African populations than anywhere else in the world, suggesting that Homo sapiens has a far longer history in Africa than elsewhere.

The evolution of the brain

Of particular interest to psychology is the puzzle of the evolution of the brain, for it is our brains that make human beings what we are. Surprisingly, the human brain has more or less the same structure as the brain of other apes. In fact, virtually all the structures of the human brain are also present in almost all other mammal species (Johnson, 1998). So whatever it is that makes our human brains special, it is not their basic structure.

Brain structure is complex. It can be thought of as falling into a number of main components. First, there is the *brainstem*, which is the most primitive area of the brain. It connects to and is continuous with the spinal cord. The brainstem regulates the vital functions of life: breathing, heart rate and the like. Next, there is the *cerebellum*, which nestles at the back of the brainstem, low down in the skull. The cerebellum contributes to balance, and to the control of movements of the muscles. The largest area of the brain is the *cerebrum*, which fills the rest of the skull. The innermost centre of the cerebrum is the *thalamus*, which is the centre through which sensory information passes en route to the cortex. The *cortex* is the outer layer of the cerebrum. It is divided into two halves or hemispheres, connected by the *corpus callosum*. The cortex is composed of many thin layers of cells that bunch up, folding over one another to create complex convoluted patterns of rucks and twists. It is the cortex that provides our distinctive human intelligence: this is the seat of all the higher brain functions – thought, feeling, action, language and so on. Different areas of the cortex specialize in different functions (**Figure 2.2**).

The key difference between a human brain and that of a chimpanzee (or most other mammals) lies in the sheer volume of our cerebral cortex. Not only do human babies develop more cortex before birth than do other species, but this area of the human brain continues to grow after birth and through childhood.

Australopithecus Afarensis had a brain size of about 450 cc. Through evolution, the size of hominid brains increased steadily, so that Homo habilis (Figure 2.1) had a brain of between 500 and 800 cc; Homo erectus's brain was 750–1225 cc; Neanderthal brains were 1400–1450 cc, larger than the modern human brain, which is 1400 cc.

We do not yet really understand just what it is about the human cortex that makes it function in so radically different a way from the cortex of other animals. In fact, we still know remarkably little about the way the cortex functions at all, either in our own or in other species. Unravelling this mystery calls for a collaboration between psychology and neuroscience which is only just beginning. However, it seems that as well as increasing in size, the way that the cortex functions has changed through our evolutionary history. For example, casts of brains from fossilized skulls suggest that less of the cortex is dedicated to vision in the modern human brain than was the case for our hominid ancestors, or is the case for modern chimpanzees (Holloway and Coste-Larey

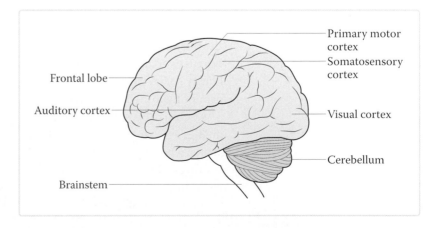

Primary motor cortex

Somatosensory cortex

Frontal lobe

Auditory cortex

Visual cortex

Cerebellum

Brainstem

figure 2.2

The structure of the brain

Mondie, 1982). Areas of cortex in the human brain have also become dedicated to peculiarly human functions such as speech (Wernicke's area, Broca's area), which again differentiates the human brain from that of other species.

What led to these evolutionary changes in the size of the human cortex and in the way it is organized? The answer is that we are not really sure. The general presumption has been that the brain evolved through natural selection just as, say, the beaks of birds evolved to fit their survival needs in a given environmental niche. Where a bird needs to suck food from long thin flowers, a longer thinner beak conveys survival advantages to the individual, giving it greater reproductive success, so that thin beakedness is 'selected for', and comes to be the common characteristic of the species over a number of generations. The presumption was that something in the environmental niche occupied by our early ancestors created a survival advantage for intelligence in just the same way, shaping our brains through the same process of selection.

No scientist would deny the importance of natural selection in the evolution of human brains (or bodies, or behaviour). However, the history of how the human brain developed seems to demand a new, more detailed understanding of the process of evolution and the way natural selection works. It poses puzzles for a simple theory of natural selection.

For instance, in its basic form, the theory of natural selection gives the greatest control over evolution to the environmental niche that the species occupies. It is the demands of the environment that determine survival, reproductive success and hence shape evolution. But what environmental niche could have *necessarily* called forth abstract human intelligence in the way fluted flowers call forth long thin beaks? The predators, the food sources, the climate our ancestors dealt with were similar for other African primate species. Yet our ape relatives managed very well with a concrete, pragmatic intelligence very different from ours.

Of course, the environment a species occupies is always partly created by its own behaviour (for example, if a bird were not trying to drink from long thin flowers, it would not need a beak shaped for that). It has been suggested that human intelligence might have evolved specifically to serve the complex *social* environment our species creates (the intrigues, the deceptions, the need to track each other's reputations for trustworthiness and so on). But in fact, many other primate species inhabit social worlds as complex as this without needing our particular form of hypothetical abstract intelligence.

Where is the survival value in a mind that goes beyond pragmatic intelligence, so that it can fantasize hypothetical threats (spirit world ghosts who can jinx the hunt unless appeased by ritual dances, wall paintings, the sacrifice of much needed foodstuffs or even close relatives) and treat these as if they were as real (if not more important) a problem as a visibly charging rhino? What environmental niche could possibly demand such an evolutionary response? No ape but the human ape thinks in this way. Piaget (1967) has proposed that human intelligence is a natural extension of the senses (see Chapter 1). He suggests that, after a certain point, intelligence would become *self-organizing*, becoming an end in itself rather than merely a tool serving basic survival needs – in other words, that the evolution of intelligence would eventually transcend the demands of adaptive survival. There is much in the content of human intelligence to suggest that he was right.

Another puzzle is that human intelligence seems to have evolved with inexplicable rapidity. Our ancestors apparently moved from using primitive tools no more sophisticated than those used by (say) otters, to the complex forms of reasoning unique to ourselves in less than 2 million years. Given the pace of evolution at large, this is a breakneck gallop. How was this possible? How could mere chance have provided the genetic permutations and mutations to allow so extraordinary a phenomenon as human intelligence to develop so rapidly?

In fact, there is evidence that the evolution of the human brain was not the result of random mutations, but rather the result of complex interactions between a great many different factors, each influencing the other. For example, bodies need management or control systems, and the structures of the brain must provide these, evolving to meet changing needs. A species that began to use tools more (say) would need finer control of hands and fingers, and brain structures would need to develop to manage this. If such 'direct demand' were the sole factor in brain evolution, we could predict that the relative size of different brain structures would reflect the importance (demands) of the activities those structures serve. But it is not so. In fact, the size of a given brain structure is predicted as much by its interaction with other brain structures during *neurogenesis* (that is, the growth of the individual's brain at the embryonic stage) as by its functional importance (Finlay, Darlington and Nicastro, 2001). In other words, it seems that the way one part of the brain grows in the uterus affects how other parts are able to develop.

The implication of this discovery is that the structure of the brain itself played a part in shaping its own evolution, rather than simply being passively shaped by the demands of adaptive behaviour by itself. Is it possible that the neurogenic processes for building a human brain in the fetus happened, through such interactions, to create excess capacity in some areas – and that Nature then found work for idle brain cells to do?

The notion that evolution might involve a degree of serendipity in this way is intriguingly plausible. There are a number of cases where what seems to have evolved for one reason may have created fortuitous knock-on effects that go beyond the original pressures driving natural selection. Standing upright is a good example. Standing gives the immediate survival advantage of seeing further, and many apes will stand briefly to look around. It happens also to raise the brain higher above the

African heat haze and so into cooler air. Cooling is an important constraint on the growth of the brain, so the mere fact of standing might have changed what was possible in the evolution of the brain.

Standing certainly had other fortuitous effects that affected our evolution. For example, standing alters the centre of gravity of the body, creating new structural pressures on the skeleton. Weight must be spread out laterally across the two legs in a way that is unnecessary in a four-legged creature. The effect was to elongate the human pelvis, changing the shape of the human pelvic girdle (through which the baby must pass at birth) from circular (as it still is in the chimpanzee) to oval. This in turn creates a challenge for the process of birth: the relatively large skull of a human baby barely fits through the pelvic girdle, and must turn sideways to pass through successfully. Babies who turn their heads to one side would therefore have a better chance of successful birth, and would be selected for. This almost certainly explains why modern human babies have a reflex that ensures this crucial turn in the last weeks of pregnancy: almost all are born facing sideways, and the vast majority turn the same way.

Now, this turning reflex is associated with the increased *lateralization* which characterizes human brain function: that is to say, it is connected with the specialization of one or other brain hemisphere for certain functions. It is associated with handedness, and may explain why most humans are right-handed (Butterworth and Hopkins, 1988). And turning the head also means that one ear is turned toward the outer wall of the uterus, and so is more exposed to sounds than the other, which may have played a role in the specialization of the left hemisphere in processing language (Previc, 1994).

It seems likely, then, that the evolution of the human brain and mind reflects the interaction of a great many factors. It's worth noticing that these factors include not only direct survival needs, but the laws of physics (temperature gradients, gravity, etc.), the properties of the body itself (the shape of the pelvic girdle, and so on), the structure of biological processes (the sequence of development in embryo neurogenesis, the turning reflexes and the like). You can imagine this evolutionary process as a complex sort of feedback loop, where one thing influenced another: a loop that took advantage of happy coincidences and so produced surprising effects in human evolution, effects very different from what could have emerged from any one factor acting alone. Of course, this approach in no way contradicts Darwin's theory of evolution: rather, it enriches and expands it.

Dynamic systems theory

The idea that radical qualitative change of the kind involved in the evolution of the human brain (and in fact, characteristic of many aspects of child development) is the product of an interaction between many different factors, and that serendipity plays a key role in shaping the outcome of such interactions, are at the heart of a new type of theory in developmental psychology as a whole: *dynamic systems theory*. This is not one single theory so much as a set of theories which share common assumptions.

Dynamic systems theory starts from the assumption that behaviour and development are *always* shaped by many factors interacting with one another. We are always embodied: that is to say, whatever we're doing, we do it in a body that has certain physiological characteristics (a certain genetic inheritance, a particular anatomy, neurological and other systems) and that generates certain psychological characteristics (mental and emotional processes, goals and so on). And our bodies always exist in a context: the physical context of a planet with certain characteristics (a gravity which constrains how far we can leap, what we can lift; temperature variations which we must respond to, objects with this property or that, diverse ecological niches which make food easier or harder to obtain or which expose us to greater or lesser dangers). Equally importantly, we live in a social context formed by culture and by our interpersonal relationships with others, the roles we play. According to dynamic systems theory, all of these factors interact to shape how we behave from moment to moment, and to shape how new patterns of behaviour develop.

Of course, no one would ever have denied that we are embodied and exist in a context, and that these facts influence how we behave and develop. There are long traditions of research through the 20th century exploring the effect on development of a wide variety of facets of our embodiment or our environment (see Chapter 1). What is new about dynamic systems theory is the claim that studying these factors separately, as 20th-century theories do, won't work. This is because these factors don't operate separately. Rather, they combine to form a complex *dynamic system*. Because of the properties of such systems, we can only understand human development, whether through evolutionary history or in the development of an individual child, by understanding the way the system functions as a whole.

Complex systems produce effects that reflect more than the sum of their constituent parts. The interaction between many different factors can yield results that no individual factor could have produced or can explain – results which can be quite surprising. Such results aren't programmed to happen: there's no guiding plan, nothing which pre-specifies what will develop. They simply emerge from the dynamics of the system, from the way one thing impinges on or constrains another, reflecting chance effects as well as more predictable ones. In this sense, a dynamic system is *self-organizing*: it shapes itself.

Thus the dramatic claim of dynamic systems theory is that the phenomena of evolution or development in effect 'just happen': they are *emergent functions* (that is, by-products or spin-offs) of the operation of a dynamic system. The theory that brain lateralization for language emerged from the consequences of the development of bipedalism is a good example of a self-organizing system in action: the dynamics of the system producing a surprising, unexpected outcome.

Self-organizing systems tend to become more complex over time. Each new emergent function sets the scene for others, progressively building up new and more sophisticated patterns of behaviour. Some innovations produce only slight modifications of the system, but some unleash a torrent of new possibilities, a cascade of change. Walking and talking are both examples of such potent innovations – both in evolutionary history and in individual child development.

Advocates of dynamic systems theory argue that all of the phenomena of evolution, and all of the striking qualitative changes we see as a child develops from conception to adulthood, are emergent functions of the operation of a complex dynamic system (Lewis, 2000; Spencer et al., 2006; Thelen and Ulrich, 1991). It's worth pausing a moment to note the importance of this claim. Qualitative changes, discontinuities in development have always puzzled us. How can something completely new, such as the evolution of human intelligence or the stage-changes in conceptual understanding in childhood described by Piaget, ever develop? Where do such things come from? What makes them happen? How is such change possible? Twentieth-century theories provided no satisfactory answers. The idea that qualitative developmental changes are emergent functions of self-organizing systems is a radical new idea, and an exciting one.

Dynamic systems theory draws parallels between biological/psychological systems and other systems in the physical world to further explore the way the dynamics of a system can produce sudden, discontinuous qualitative changes. Physics recognizes two kinds of dynamics. *Linear dynamics* were described by Newton to explain mechanical interactions (such as the movements of snooker balls) where one event produces a consistent and predictable quantitative effect on another (the harder one snooker ball hits another, the faster the other ball will move away). Linear dynamics produce changes that are smooth and continuous (**Figure 2.3**). *Non-linear dynamics*, by contrast, produce changes that are discontinuous and occur in sudden steps (Figure 2.3). Here, cumulative repetitions of the same simple interaction yield smooth quantitative changes *up to a point*, but at some point the system becomes unstable – 'wobbly' – and then it undergoes a sudden change (a *phase shift*) and settles into a new, qualitatively different way of behaving. For example, if you cool a glass of water, up to a point you just get colder and colder water. Then suddenly, the dynamics of the situation changes and there is a phase shift: now you get the radically different structure of ice. Many of the phenomena we see in child devel-

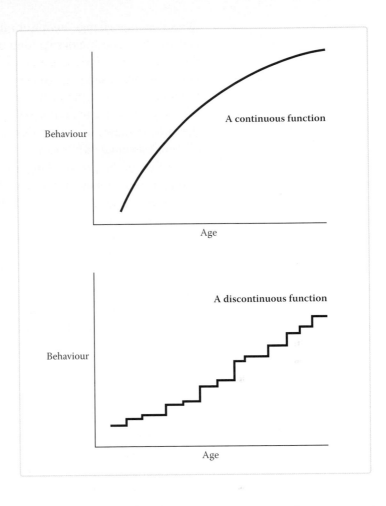

figure **2.3**

Continuous and discontinuous functions

opment and infer in human evolution seem to show the phase shifts of non-linear dynamics. Dynamic systems theory argues that non-linear dynamics offers us a new way of understanding how such qualitative step-changes can emerge from the apparently continuous functioning of a system.

By drawing on non-linear dynamics and the *chaos mathematics* which capture such effects, dynamic systems theory puts explanations of human development on a par with explanations of change in the physical world. The same non-linear dynamics can potentially be used to model the origins of any complex system, from the way the universe itself developed to how a snowflake forms, the patterns on a snail's shell – or the development of intelligence through evolution or in the individual child. For the first time, this approach gives psychology the possibility of explaining its subject matter in terms of principles that are common across the sciences as a whole (Lewis, 2000). This is exciting: is it a step toward the elusive 'grand theory of everything'?

Certainly, dynamic systems theory provides a unifying framework for research in developmental psychology. All behaviour and all developmental change stem from the dynamic functioning of a complex system. Both continuities (getting better at a given way of thinking) and discontinuities (developing a new way of thinking) are the product of the operation of the same dynamic system, reflecting the specific 'settings' of the system at a given moment. And since subtle differences in the setting of a dynamic system can produce subtly – or dramatically – different results, the same dynamic processes that yield development as a whole can also explain individual differences.

Because of the potential impact of subtle differences in the setting of a complex self-organizing system, dynamic systems theory predicts that there will be a great deal more individual variation between children in every aspect of development than has traditionally been supposed. There's little research testing this theory as yet, but what there is supports the prediction (Spencer et al., 2006).

The prediction of individual differences between children seems to raise a question: if individuals differ, how come there are so many *universal* features of development, so many common milestones and outcomes? How come the overall trajectory of development is more or less the same for all children? But the basic principles of dynamic systems theory predict this too. Common features of what it is to be human (the fact that we share the same planet, the same genetic blueprint to be human, the same basic anatomical plan, that we have the same basic survival needs) will tend to lead to common outcomes. In other words, the exact path individuals take in reaching a given milestone (such as learning to talk) may vary, but we all tend to reach the same basic milestones (even if details, such as which language we learn, differ) because we are all living in much the same bodies, much the same world and are solving much the same problems. To give a simple concrete analogy, imagine rolling a dozen balls down the sides of a cardboard valley which slopes down to a box. Start each ball in a slightly different place and no two balls will follow exactly the same path – but all of them will gravitate toward the floor of the valley and end up in the box at the bottom, because of the overall dynamics of the situation.[1]

Dynamic systems theory provides a powerful and intriguing new view of the process of development. It's a *dangerous idea*, just as Darwin's concept of natural selection was a dangerous idea (Dennett, 1996; Lewis, 2000). Darwin's theory changed our understanding of human nature and its origins in a very fundamental way. Many researchers believe that dynamic systems theory, which builds on Darwin's work, will have just as revolutionary an effect on how we understand ourselves and our relation to the world (Lewis, 2000).

---

[1] This way of thinking about the relationship between individual variation and universal milestones in development was originally explored by Waddington (1966), in connection with fetal development.

And just as Darwin's theory of natural selection had unsettling implications (were we really descended from apes, when we had thought we were created in the image of God?), so dynamic systems theory has implications which some will find unsettling. Let a dynamic system operate in only a subtly different way, and something quite different would emerge. The implications are both fascinating and disturbing. Was the development of human consciousness to some degree an accident of the specific settings of the dynamic system governing our evolution? Could tiny differences between our ancestors and other hominid species explain why we are as we are, and they are long gone? Were we just *luckier* than other hominid species? Physicists have worked out that we're actually far luckier than we realize. Tiny differences in the settings of the myriad of factors (parameters) that define the dynamic system (universe) in which we live could have made the evolution of intelligent consciousness impossible. The odds against all the settings being 'just right' for human consciousness to emerge are phenomenal. Some physicists have begun to wonder about this – Paul Davies (2006) calls it the 'Goldilocks enigma'. Did the universe just happen to have those settings by chance? Was there something that systematically *caused* the universe to be set up this particular way? Or are we living in the one universe where the development of human consciousness was possible, surrounded by countless barren alternative universes where it was not?

Dynamic systems theory is new. It began to emerge only at the very end of the 20th century. There's a long way to go, and many a problem to be resolved before the promise of this approach can be realized. But in every area of research there is growing interest in dynamic systems theory as a framework for understanding the process of development. We shall encounter this theory, and explore more of its implications, in many places through the rest of this book. Can this new approach provide a unified account of development as a whole? We shall return to that question in Chapter 13.

Genes

Human mothers have human babies. We pass on the fruits of our evolutionary history to our young, the basic recipe for becoming human, by passing on our genetic code. At the start of the 21st century we were able, for the first time, to create a map of the *human genome*: in other words, the full set of genetic instructions that make a human being. We are still many years away from fully understanding exactly how genes control development, but we already know far more about our genetic make-up than any previous generation did.

The structure of our genetic material

It turns out that we are far simpler than we thought: the total number of *genes* in our genome is only about 30,000, rather than 140,000 as we had speculated. Each gene consists of four chemical bases (adenine, guanine, cytosine and thymine, usually abbreviated to A, G, C and T) arranged in a complex sequence of pairings. Each gene contains many thousands of such pairings.

Genes themselves are arranged in chains along molecules of DNA (deoxyribonucleic acid) called *chromosomes*. The number of genes in each chromosome varies: the largest chromosome (chromosome 1) carries 2968 genes, while the smallest (chromosome Y) carries only 231. Chromosomes are arranged in pairs. Human beings have 46 chromosomes in all, arranged in 23 pairs. (Chimpanzees have 48 chromosomes in 24 pairs, while fruit flies have eight, forming four pairs.)

Our genes are the basis for the process of development from fertilized egg to birth, and on to our adult form, even contributing to our ageing and death. Some of our genetic code is very old, passed on from remote ancestors far back in evolutionary history and so shared with many other species. For example, the gene that carries the instructions to build legs is the same in human beings and centipedes (and most other species). That we grow two human legs rather than a hundred insect ones reflects the interaction between this 'leg-making' gene and other genes that moderate and specify the details of what kind of leg and how many (Pennisi and Roush, 1997). Most aspects of development are the product of interactions between many genes in this way.

A great deal of our genetic material is exactly the same in every human being. It constitutes a blueprint for making a human being, rather than for making an individual. If we were to reproduce asexually (in effect cloning ourselves), our offspring would contain exactly the same genetic information generation after generation, bar random mutations of genes. Many species do reproduce this way, apparently with great success. But such *asexual reproduction* has the disadvantage that, if the environment changes in ways that the organism finds hard to survive, adjustment is slow or even impossible: there is not enough diversity in the gene pool to allow natural selection to work effectively.

Sexual reproduction gets around this problem by combining genetic material from two individuals (each of whom will have slightly different versions of the basic human genetic code, reflecting both mutations of genes and previous mixings in earlier generations) to create a new individual with a unique version of the genetic code. Close relatives will have very similar genetic codes, and distant relatives will have much less similar codes. Over generations, as a population expands, genetic diversity will increase. This diversity gives great scope for natural selection to act quickly to reshape the species to new circumstances and demands. For instance, if individuals differ in their tendency toward fatness, there is scope for natural selection to quickly reshape the species toward greater or lesser fatness as changes in the environment (for example climate) demand.

Sexual reproduction requires special arrangements for the transfer and recombination of genetic material. Every cell in the body carries a complete version of the individual's entire genetic code (in other words, all 46 chromosomes) with the exception of the reproductive *germ cells* or *gametes*, the male sperm and the female ova. These gametes carry only half of the parent's genetic code: specifically, 23 chromosomes, one from each of the 23 pairs that parent carries. This halving of the genetic material in sperm and ova is essential for reproduction: otherwise, the fertilized egg would have double the normal amount of genetic material, and no cell could survive that. The reduction of the chromosomes in gametes is achieved by a process called *meiosis*. In girls, this process occurs while the baby herself is still in the womb: a girl is born with every egg she will ever have already formed and waiting in her ovaries. In boys, meiosis is still occurring in old age: men create new sperm continuously throughout their lives.

Which part of each chromosome is shed and which preserved during meiosis is random. It has been estimated, therefore, that a given man and woman could potentially produce many millions of different patterns of genes in their offspring, ensuring a unique genetic code for each individual.

There is much more variability between individuals in some parts of the genetic code than others. For instance, genes controlling the basic structure of the leg tend not to vary much from one individual to another, while genes controlling hair colour and other surface characteristics vary very much more.

Nature, nurture and genes

Every characteristic we have is affected by our genes. This includes not only the shape and functioning of our bodies, but also many aspects of our behaviour (as will be discussed in later chapters). For example, there is a strong genetic component to intelligence, to our basic temperament and to some gender-typical behaviours. Nonetheless, development is never fully determined by our genes.

The complete set of genetic codes we carry is called our *genotype*. Not all of these codes will be expressed in our development: for instance, I might carry the gene to form blue eyes, but I also carry the more dominant gene for brown eyes, and so I have brown eyes. The genetic codes that we actually exhibit are called our *phenotype*.

Which aspects of our genotype are expressed in our phenotype reflects two things: the interaction between one gene and another (as in the example of eye colour), and the interaction between the genotype and the environment. This latter interaction is complex and two-way. Environmental factors can affect what aspects of the genotype find expression. For example, an embryo genetically equipped for high intelligence might not realize this potential if the mother contracts a damaging disease like rubella; or different experiences may lead one of a pair of identical twins to suffer from a genetic disorder where the other does not, even though they share the identical genotype (having developed from a single egg, hence the term 'monozygotic' twin). The genotype can also affect the environment the infant experiences, creating situations that foster certain developmental paths rather than others. For example, a baby with a genetic disposition to be calm and peaceful will create a very different family dynamic (social environment) than one with a genetic disposition to be tetchy and easily upset, just as a beautiful woman lives in a rather different (and not necessarily more attractive) world from a plain one.

Genes play a greater role in development in the prenatal period than in later life: there is a powerful genetic 'programme' directing the sequence and process of construction of the organs of the body. But even in the womb the unfolding of the genetic code can be affected by the environment, as later sections of this chapter show. Furthermore, the fetus is not simply the passive construct of a genetic code and an environment, but is a dynamic contributor to a complex developmental system (for example, see **Box 2.1**). The way the fetus functions and behaves makes a vital contribution to how it forms, at many different levels.

box **2.1**

Genes, hormones, sex and intersex

The first question anyone asks when a baby is born is, *is it a boy or a girl?* Surprisingly, for one child in every 4500, the answer is – *it's hard to say.* In those babies, the external genitals on which we base our judgment are sufficiently ambiguous that we just can't tell. Such babies are diagnosed as 'intersex' babies. In a population of 60 million (Britain, for example), there are nearly 14,000 people who were born with this problem: neither obviously male nor obviously female.

The phenomena of intersex provide an interesting insight into the complexities of embryonic development: this development is not under genetic control in the absolute way we often imagine. The situation is very much more complex.

Intersex occurs when something goes wrong with the usual process of sexual differentiation in the embryo. We think of genes as the prime cause of gender, but this is only partly right. The main contribution to gender made by our genes is that the presence or absence of the Y chromosome determines whether the embryo will develop testes. Up to about 6 weeks, all embryos grow generic gonads. At about 6 weeks after conception, information on the Y chromosome instructs these gonads to become testes. If there is no Y chromosome, the gonads develop into ovaries. Once testes have developed, they begin to secrete male hormones or androgens (ovaries produce little or no hormones in the fetus). Androgen levels are many times higher in male fetuses than female ones, particularly between weeks 8 and 24 after conception. It is these androgens, rather than genes themselves, that control sexual differentiation. Any embryo with high androgen levels at the critical period for developing genitals will tend to develop male genitalia; any embryo that experiences low androgen levels at this time will tend to develop female genitalia. This is true whatever the genes. It's true, therefore, whether the fetus has XX or XY genes.

In most cases, sexual differentiation goes according to plan: XX babies develop ovaries, experience low levels of androgens and develop female genitals, while XY babies develop testes, experience high levels of androgens and develop male genitals. However, things sometimes don't work out this way.

Some XY fetuses develop testes and produce androgens – but don't develop the receptors to respond to these hormones. This is AIS, or *androgen insensitivity syndrome.* In its 'complete' form (CAIS), the baby develops apparently normal female genitalia despite the XY chromosomes, and the anomaly only comes to light at puberty, often because there is no menstruation. Partial forms of AIS (PAIS) result in ambiguous genitals, partly female, partly male.

A second major cause of anomalies in sexual differentiation is CAH or *congenital adrenal hyperplasia.* Here, inadequate levels of a key enzyme mean that the XX embryo has too little cortisol and so is exposed to excessive levels of androgens. This imbalance will need corrective treatment for life, to maintain health. The fetus may develop apparently normal male genitalia despite the XX chromosomes, or may show a very confused pattern of intersex, developing ovaries, womb and the upper part of a vagina – but also a penis.

Both AIS and CAH are problems originating in the fetus itself. But many environmental factors can affect the levels of androgen the embryo experiences, creating very similar results. For example, mothers who have been prescribed androgens during pregnancy may produce babies who have the same problems as those produced by CAH; or exposure to factors that reduce androgen levels can produce the same effects as AIS.

It isn't just physical genitals that are affected by hormone levels. For example, sexual orientation is affected too: genetically male XY individuals with CAIS develop female genitals and are sexually attracted to men rather than women (Hines, Ahmed and Hughes, 2003). This is a 'brain' effect rather than a genital effect. Much more than sexual orientation may be involved in gender-related brain differentiation. For instance, XX girls with entirely normal female genitalia who experienced high levels of androgens in the womb show male-typical behaviours and orientations, both in how they play as children (Hines et al., 2002) and how they behave, sexually and otherwise as adults (Udry, Morris and Kovenock, 1995). They are more interested in the mechanics of this or that, and are more likely to be bisexual or lesbian (Hines, 2004) than unaffected sisters.

Thus it seems that sexual differentiation is very far from the simple dichotomy implied by the question 'is it a boy or a girl?' Rather, it seems likely that there are a variety of degrees of being male or female, reflected not only in our genitals but in the development of our brains (we shall come back to the issues this raises in Part III). The phenomena of intersex challenge some of our fundamental views about human beings. These phenomena may be far more subtle, and more common than we suppose, and offer new insights into gender differentiation, homosexuality and the bases of gender identity and trans-sexuality.

Prenatal development

Conception

At the moment of conception, a sperm cell from the father penetrates the outer covering of the egg provided by the mother. Immediately, a chemical reaction begins that seals the outer membrane of the egg, preventing any other sperm cell from penetrating. The process of development has begun.

Already, nature has made sure that the new conception has the best chance of success. A man's ejaculation may place many millions of sperm cells in the vagina. These sperm cells are some of the smallest cells in the human body (the female egg is by far the largest single cell). Each sperm consists of a large head, containing all the genetic material to be contributed for conception, and a long tail. The tail propels the sperm cell on the journey from the vagina through the uterus and up the fallopian tubes, a journey of about 6 in (15 cm) that takes these tiny cells about 6 hours. Here, sperm may meet the egg, which is travelling down the fallopian tube toward the womb.

Few sperm make it all the way to the egg. Some are simply too weak or defective to make the journey. Others fail because they get their tails entangled with one another. Others go the wrong way, swimming up the wrong fallopian tube. (Normally, a woman's ovaries ripen and release just one egg each month, the two ovaries alternating as to which produces this egg, so that only one fallopian tube contains an egg. Occasionally, two eggs are released at the same time and both are fertilized, resulting in non-identical or 'dizygotic' twins.) In the end, fewer than 500 of the millions of sperm cells that set out get anywhere near the egg. These are likely to be among the fittest – and the luckiest – of those released in the ejaculation.

As the triumphant sperm cell smashes itself into the egg its head bursts open, releasing its 23 chromosomes to pair up with those in the egg to form a new complete set: a new individual with half its genetic material from the father, and half from the mother.

From conception to birth

Prenatal development (**Figure 2.4**) is divided up into three stages, each involving a very different process.

The zygotic stage

The first stage begins at conception, from the moment the egg is fertilized. The new conception is called a *zygote* at this stage. Within 12 hours of fertilization, the egg cell begins to divide, first into two cells, then into 4, 8, 16 and so on. This process of *cell division* is steady and rapid: the number of cells in the zygote doubles roughly twice a day (by birth, the original cell will have become many millions of cells). Each newly

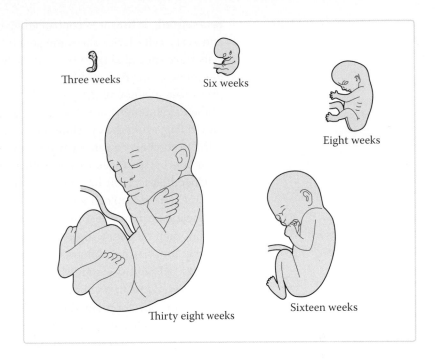

Prenatal development

formed cell contains a complete copy of all the genetic material present in the fertilized egg. Each is identical to all the others.

Roughly 4 days after conception, the cells in the zygote have arranged themselves into a hollow sphere called a *blastocyst*. Inside this is an inner mass of cells that will become the baby. The blastocyst travels down the fallopian tube towards the womb. A week after conception, it implants itself in the lining of the uterus. Two weeks after conception the blastocyst has embedded itself in this lining, burrowing in and becoming dependent on the mother for its nutrition.

The embryo stage

Once implanted, the second stage of development, the *embryo* stage, begins. Some cells in the blastocyst develop into the support system for the developing conception: the placenta, the amniotic sac and fluid, the umbilical cord and so on, while the inner mass, the embryo, begins to develop into a baby.

At first, all the cells in what will become the embryo are *stem cells*. Stem cells are all exactly alike, identical. They are entirely interchangeable: they have the potential to turn into any type of cell in the body (this is what makes them interesting for medical researchers seeking ways to regenerate damaged organs). But after a number of cell divisions, these stem cells start to specialize, differentiating into different types of cell and so beginning to build different parts of the body.

We don't yet fully understand how this process of *cell differentiation* gets started, or how it is controlled. Every cell in the zygote is the same, and every cell carries the same genetic code. So how and why do some cells start specializing to become nerve cells and others skin or bone? Hormones, enzymes and other chemicals secreted by the embryo itself play a role in shaping the physical structures of the body at a later stage in the development of the embryo (for example, hormones play a vital part in triggering the development of the genitalia, as you can see in Box 2.1). Do they play a role early on, too?

In the early stages of cell differentiation, stem cells go on being produced and go on having a degree of flexibility as to what they will become. For example, if you surgically move the region of a frog embryo that would normally become its eye to the area that will normally become its abdomen very early in the embryo stage, the area you have moved will develop into normal abdomen rather than eye. But if you do this later on, after the cells in the eye area have begun to differentiate, then the embryo will grow an eye in its abdomen (Wolpert, 1991). It seems that early in embryonic development the *location* of a stem cell within the overall structure of what is developing determines what it will develop into, whereas later in the embryonic process the cell is committed to a certain path in development, whatever its location in the body.

Interestingly, stem cells also migrate of their own accord before settling down to a given structure and function. For example, stem cells are created through cell divisions deep inside the cortex of the embryonic brain (the area that will one day support intelligent functioning). They then travel to the perimeter of the cortex as it now exists, and differentiate into the kinds of cells needed to expand it, so building the cortex layer by layer (Vaughn, 1996).

This whole process of differentiation into an embryo begins when the inner mass inside the blastocyst develops into three layers, each committed to a different developmental plan. The first of these will eventually form the outer surface of the skin, the nails, teeth, the ears and eyes, the nervous system. The middle layer will eventually become the inner layers of flesh and skin, the circulatory system, muscles, bones and other organs. The third layer eventually becomes the lungs, digestive and urinary systems and the glands.

Once these three layers have developed, a groove develops in the first, the sides growing toward one another until they fuse to create the neural tube, which will become the brain and spinal cord (**Figure 2.5**). Development progresses from the head downward: so head, face and brain start developing before the body; arms begin to develop before legs. Already, five weeks after conception, the embryo has a recognizable head, and the beginnings of eyes, arms, legs. Even fingers and toes are beginning to be visible.

One surprising feature of all this development is that it involves not only the *creation* of new cells, but also the systematic *death* of some

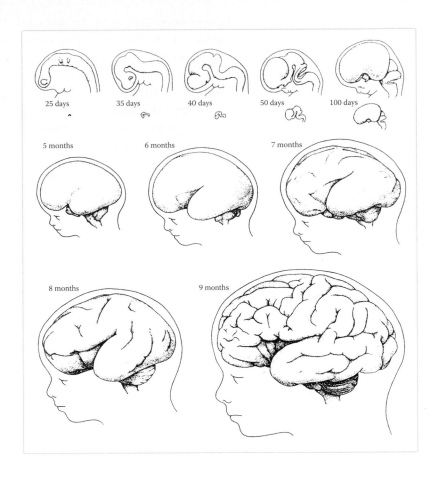

figure **2.5**

Prenatal development of the brain

Source: adapted from W. Cowan, 'The development
of the brain', *Scientific American*, vol. 241, 1979.
© Reproduced with permission from
Norman H. Prentiss

cells. For instance, the hand forms, at first, as a rounded blob or bud on
the end of the arm. Ridges develop in this blob, ridges that will later
become fingers. It is the systematic death of the cells between these
ridges that allows the fingers to separate (Wolpert, 1991). If these cells
did not die, or if too few died, the hand would be either fingerless or
webbed.

Eight weeks after conception (the time when most mothers first
realize that they are pregnant), the embryo stage is over. All the internal
organs of the body are there, skin, limbs and bones are visible, even the
fingernails are growing. The conception has become a fetus, and has
begun to move, and will respond to touch. He or she will turn the head,
for example, if touched on the side of the mouth.

The fetal stage

The third stage of prenatal development, the *fetal* stage, runs from the
end of the eighth week after conception until birth, which is typically
about 38 weeks (9 months) after conception. At the start of this stage,

the basic structures of the body are all already present. From now on, these will continue to develop more slowly, growing in size and detail. By 28 weeks after conception, the fetus is capable of surviving by itself if it should be born prematurely – and even at around 22 weeks, premature babies can survive with medical help. The last months of pregnancy allow the baby to gain in size and weight (more than doubling in weight in this period) and so becoming more robust in preparation for birth, and for life after birth.

Birth

In a normal, full-term baby, birth is triggered by the release of a hormone in the baby's brain. This hormone begins the contractions of labour which will deliver the child. How long this process takes varies: perhaps 12 to 14 hours or so is about average, though many deliveries last longer.

Most babies are born head first (only about 4 per cent present with some other part of the anatomy, which makes birth considerably harder and more dangerous). Almost immediately, the baby takes a lungful of air and lets out a cry. He or she is no longer dependent on the umbilical cord through which the mother has provided nourishment through pregnancy, which can now be cut.

A healthy baby scores from 7 to 10 on the Apgar test (**Table 2.1**), which is done 1 minute after birth and repeated 5 minutes later. A score between 4 and 6 is poor, while a score below 4 indicates a cause for concern.

Birth is a dramatic transition for baby and mother alike. Most women automatically cradle their new child to their breast, and many breastfeed within the first hour after birth. Human babies are extremely vulnerable and immature, much more so than the young of any other species. They need more support, and more care. These first moments of interaction between mother and baby are precious. Do they lay the groundwork for bonding (see Chapter 4)?

Methods for studying prenatal development in more detail

Until relatively recently, our knowledge of what a fetus even looks like at different stages of development came entirely from studying the dead: babies aborted by natural causes or human intervention. Such *post mortem studies* were informative. But the data they produced may also have been biased. Nature aborts when natural processes have gone wrong, and the deliberate termination of a pregnancy may cause injuries to the fetus that distort our impression of what is normal. Healthy development might look different from the remnants of abortion, however caused. And in any case, post mortem studies can never reveal how a fetus behaves, or what it can learn. Technological advances have opened table **2.1**   The Apgar scale

Score	0	1	2
Skin colour	Blue or pale	Body pink, extremities blue	Completely pink
Heart rate	Absent	Slow: less than 100	Over 100
Muscle tone	Flaccid	Some flexion of extremities	Active motion
Reflex irritability	No response	Grimace	Coughing, sneezing, crying
Respiratory effort	Absent	Slow, irregular	Good, crying

up a whole new world in studying living fetal development, which has greatly enriched our understanding of the beginnings of human life.

Fibre optics, ultrasound and heart rate

A variety of new technologies allow us to see the living fetus, watching its actions and reactions. One such tool is the *fibre-optic camera*. Miniscule cameras attached to flexible tubes have allowed us to enter and look inside all sorts of organs of the body: the heart, the bowel, the stomach and the womb. With such devices, we can see not only that a fetus has already developed a thumb, but that he or she is sucking that thumb. We can gently stroke or touch the fetus in the womb and observe its reactions.

But fibre-optic intrusion into the womb is just that: an intrusion. Like any other invasive procedure, it raises ethical issues. The risks to the individual fetus filmed may mean that such a technique is only appropriate where it also gives that individual some benefit: in other words, where the fetus itself has a direct medical need for such an invasive procedure.

Less invasive than fibre optics is scanning by *ultrasound*. Here, very high-frequency sound is bounced off structures within the body, reflecting back to equipment that interprets the echoes to create pictures, in much the same way that radar reveals coastlines, ships and so on in navigation. Ultrasound pictures allow us to see an astonishing amount of detail in the developing baby, from the grosser facts (such as the development of limbs, or sexual organs) to finer details (such as the adequacy of the structure of the heart). Ultrasound also allows us to see the fetus moving: kicking a leg, waving an arm, sucking a thumb, even grimacing. This kind of scanning carries little (if any) risk to the fetus. Most mothers in developed countries will have a number of routine ultrasound examinations during each pregnancy. (Stills taken from these films are the first pictures in many a baby album: there is something inexpressibly moving in a tiny arm, a curled back, a small, vulnerable face. Few parents fail to respond to the nascent humanity of their fetus.)

Another non-invasive way of measuring fetal responses is to measure *heart rate*. Monitors on the mother's belly can pick up and record the fetus's heartbeat from very early on in gestation. We can track the fetus's increasing ability to react to different stimuli by monitoring whether heart rate changes as these stimuli are presented or removed. Startling events make the heart beat faster, in a fetus as much as an older person. Concentrating, paying attention, make the heart beat slower and more steadily (Richards and Cronise, 2000; Kitajima, Kumoi and Koike, 1998).

Habituation designs

A key research method for studying the unborn child's sensory and mental capacities is the *habituation study*. Such studies start from the fact that living organisms tend to react to new stimuli. As they learn to recognize that a stimulus is familiar, they stop reacting to it (this is called *habituating*), although they will start to react again if a new stimulus comes along. This allows us to find out three basic things:

- what stimuli the fetus can detect: in other words, what stimuli the fetus reacts to

- whether (and perhaps how quickly or easily) the fetus can learn to recognize particular stimuli as familiar: in other words, whether (and how easily) the fetus habituates to a given stimulus

- how sensitively the fetus can discriminate between similar stimuli: in other words, how big a change in the stimulus will the fetus notice?

Virtually all research into fetal (and early infant) responsiveness and learning uses a habituation design of some sort, as we shall see later in this chapter, and in Chapters 3 and 4.

Behaviour and learning in the womb

Movement

Already, by the time a woman suspects that she may be pregnant, the 6-week-old embryo is beginning to move. The earliest of movements are generalized flexes of the whole embryonic body, which begin at about 5 or 6 weeks after conception. Gradually, as development progresses, the fetus begins to move arms, legs, fingers, toes, to move the head, to yawn, to suck fingers or thumbs and swallow the amniotic fluid in which it lives (De Vries, Visser and Prechtl, 1984). By 16 weeks the mother is able to feel the larger of these movements, and becomes aware of her baby kicking and squirming, 'jumping' when startled by a loud noise, and in many cases (for some reason no one understands) having attacks of the hiccups.

At first, the fetus moves more or less continuously. After a few weeks this activity starts to settle into patterns: periods of great activity alternating with short periods of inactivity. By the second half of the pregnancy, the fetus rests more and more, perhaps between 70 and 90 per cent of the time (DiPietro et al., 1998). Over the last weeks of the pregnancy, the fetus spends the majority of time asleep, sometimes showing the same patterns of rapid eye movements (REM) that are associated with dreaming in adults (James, Pillai and Smoleniec, 1995).

What makes the activity of the fetus slow down in this way? We don't really know the answer. However, we have some clues. In some (thankfully extremely rare) cases, the cortex of the brain doesn't develop: it's simply not there. The fetus often survives pregnancy and even birth. Such *anencephalic* (that is, without a brain) babies are obviously terribly disabled: they can't live long, and will never develop. Unlike a normal fetus, an anencephalic fetus stays very active throughout pregnancy. This has been taken to suggest that the development of the cortex is somehow related to the slowing down of activity in the normal fetus, and the establishment of 'sleep/wake' cycles (James et al., 1995). Perhaps the cortex takes over control of movement from more primitive, reflexive brain structures.

Why does the fetus move so much in the early stages of development? It seems that movements play a vital part in the proper development of the organs and muscles. Anyone who has ever had a wrist or an ankle immobilized in a cast after a fracture, or been confined to bed for a few weeks of illness, can tell you how much immobility wastes the muscles, tightens and shrinks the tendons and stiffens the joints, and how vital movement is in regaining strength and flexibility! And this is in an adult body, where these structures are already formed. The evidence is that movement is still more vital at the fetal stage, in that it plays an important role in ensuring that the limbs develop correctly in the first place.

For example, if a fetus is persistently prevented from moving in the womb for some reason (crowding in multiple births; anaesthesia associated with maternal alcohol abuse; malformation of the central nervous system in areas controlling movement, either through genetic or environmental effects, and so on), the infant is likely to be born with deformities of the joints (Chen, 2004). The hypothesis that these deformities are caused by the lack of movement has been tested by experimentally restricting leg movements in chicks before hatching, which indeed results in the deformity of leg joints (Forsyth et al., 1994). Even quite short periods of restriction are enough to prevent the normal development of these chick's joints.

Equally, sucking and swallowing help shape the development of the digestive system. Movements of the tongue as the fetus drinks amniotic fluid help shape the palate correctly, and processing the fluid through the digestive organs and excreting it back into the amniotic fluid helps these organs to mature and to be ready to function at birth. In a similar way, the fetus practises 'breathing', by inhaling small amounts of amniotic fluid into the lungs and exhaling it again (James et al., 1995).

The senses

The structures needed for the five senses (touch, taste, smell, sight and hearing) are present from the end of the embryonic stage of development. Some ingenious experiments have shown that these senses are functional well before the baby is born, allowing the baby to respond to events, and to learn in the womb:

Touch

Almost from the very start of the fetal period, babies respond to touch. Already at 8 weeks, the fetus will turn its head if lightly stroked near the mouth. As the mother moves and changes her posture, standing or sitting and so on, the fetus moves to accommodate to the change (mothers have to make similar adjustments to the fetus's activities too, especially in the later stages of pregnancy). Furthermore, as most mothers can tell you, the fetus has certain likes and dislikes, reflecting its developing sense of touch. My son, for instance, objected violently, thrashing about and kicking me furiously if I drove over a rough road surface (so much so that I gave up and changed my car for one with better suspension!). On the other hand, this same baby loved to be stroked, and would bunch himself up under my hand if I rubbed my belly, lying still until I stopped. The vast majority of mothers stroke their babies in just this way through the last few months of pregnancy, and know what sorts of touch their baby enjoys.

Taste

Equally, the fetus clearly has a sense of taste, and preferences for certain tastes over others. For example, if the amniotic fluid is made sweeter, the fetus will drink more of it than otherwise (Carlson, 1994). Physicians have tried to use this fact to practical effect: for example, where too much amniotic fluid has been produced, the fetus will help to solve the problem by drinking more and excreting more through the placenta, if the fluid is sweetened (Gandelman, 1992).

Smell

The amniotic fluid in which the baby floats can have quite a variety of flavours. These reflect what the mother has eaten, and the fact that the fetus is excreting into the fluid (overall, the smell of this fluid has been unattractively described as 'rancid' – Schaal, Orgeur and Rognon, 1995). Because the fetus is inhaling this fluid, the receptors for smell as well as taste are exposed to these flavours. Evidence that the fetus can discriminate between different smells, and learn preferences for familiar ones, comes from a study that showed that newborn babies whose mothers have eaten strongly flavoured foods such as anise during pregnancy clearly recognize and prefer the smell of those foods, whereas babies whose mothers did not eat such things do not. This is true right from birth, way before the newborn has had any opportunity to experience such smells outside the womb (Schaal, Marlier and Soussignan, 2000). As unattractive as the general smell of amniotic fluid sounds to an adult, it seems that the newborn baby finds this familiar smell more attractive and calming than any other smell, or than an odourless environment (Porter et al., 1998).

Sight

There's not a great deal to see inside the womb, perhaps particularly not in societies where there are not only the amniotic fluid and the mother's flesh but also clothing blocking off light most of the time. Nonetheless, sunlight or other bright lights can filter through, giving a slight degree of illumination. The fetus's eyes move at about 18 weeks (De Vries et al., 1984) and are clearly open at around 27 weeks after conception. There is some evidence that, at this stage, the fetus will react if a bright light is shone onto the mother's naked belly, suggesting that the eyes are already functional, even if there is not yet much to see (Kitzinger, 1989; Vaughn, 1996).

Hearing

Probably the most varied sensory experience a fetus has, and the best source for learning in the womb, comes from hearing. Hearing is also the sense we know most about, since it is easier to make noises and see how the fetus reacts than to manipulate odours or flavours in the womb.

We don't know just how early on the fetus can hear. Probably, the development of hearing (or any other sense) is not a sudden 'switching on' of the circuits (as you might switch on a light) so much as a gradual progression. The younger the fetus, the cruder and larger the noise must be before there is any sort of reaction (Joseph, 2000). But by late pregnancy, the fetus responds to a wide range of sounds, and is able to make some impressive discriminations. Thirty weeks after conception, the fetus is certainly able to learn to recognize sounds: he or she will stop reacting as a noise becomes familiar, and react again if the sound changes to something different (Joseph, 2000).

Babies in the womb learn to recognize their own mother's voice. The fetus's heart rate slows briefly when the mother begins to speak (Fifer and Moon, 1995). Immediately after birth, a baby can recognize, and prefers, his or her own mother's voice to that of another woman. But what has been learned from listening to the mother is very much more than simply the sound of her voice. For instance, newborn babies have learned to recognize their own mother tongue (in other words, the language their mother speaks). They will treat a different language as a new stimulus in habituation studies.

More impressive still, the newborn baby has already learned to identify 'happy talk' from other sorts of speech, so long as that happy talk is in their mother tongue! This involves far more than just recognizing the mother's voice: a newborn can identify 'happy talk' when a researcher, rather than the mother, is speaking, so long as it is in the mother tongue (Mastropieri and Turkewitz, 1999). Of course, the fetus is not learning the meanings of words: rather, he or she is learning to recognize patterns of speech. Given such impressive learning, it seems very likely that the fetus can also learn to recognize pieces of music or other familiar patterns of speech besides happy talk.

Genes, uterine environments and problems in development

Human prenatal development is a remarkably robust phenomenon: time after time, women deliver healthy babies even in the most unfavourable of circumstances. So if you happen to be pregnant as you read this section, don't forget: the problems we are about to review are rare! But for all its robustness, prenatal development is a complex and subtle process. There are many stages at which it can go wrong, and for some conceptions, things do go wrong at one stage or another.

Genetic problems

The first thing that can go wrong for a new conception relates to the genetic material it carries. Sometimes, bits of the genetic code from one parent or the other are missing, or extra material remains that should have been deleted as the process of meiosis forms the germ cells. Or it may be that the particular conjunction of the genetic material from the father and the mother creates a problem. In rarer cases, a single gene causes illness or deformity.

If too much genetic material is missing, or if there is too much extra material or a very dysfunctional conjunction of chromosomes, the conception dies. It may fail to begin cell division, or fail to form a blastocyst capable of implanting in the womb. Or if cells fail to differentiate into different structures as they should, the blastocyct or early embryo may be grossly deformed and so not viable. More than half of all conceptions fail at this very early stage. It is believed that the majority of conceptions lost in these early days of pregnancy are grossly defective in some way. This is difficult to test, of course: while the failed conceptions we do see are often defective, the majority of conceptions that fail are never even noticed by the mother. Many are lost in the important first 2 weeks, before a period is even missed.

Relatively small errors or problems in the genetic code the conception inherits are survivable. Some embryos with genetic anomalies develop comparatively normally, but others show characteristic patterns of developmental distortion. Much depends on the nature of the chromosomes and anomalies involved.

For example, if either the egg or the sperm cell fails to shed half the material on chromosome 21, the new conception will have three chromosomes instead of the normal two on the 21st chromosomal pairing. This is called 'trisomy 21', and produces the condition known as *Down's syndrome*. Babies affected this way have classic physical characteristics, including unusually flat faces, low bridge to the nose, high cheekbones and eyes that slant outward. They are typically poorly coordinated, and have learning difficulties that may be relatively mild or very severe. Typically, children with Down's syndrome also have lovely, gentle temperaments.

Equally, a conception may have too much or too little genetic information on the chromosomal pair that determines sex. A baby who inherits two X chromosomes, one from each parent, will be female; one who inherits an X chromosome from his mother and a Y chromosome from his father will be male. All conceptions need at least one X chromosome to survive: the X chromosome carries a great deal more genetic information fundamental to development than the Y, which is concerned primarily with creating maleness. A conception that inherits only one sex chromosome, an X, will therefore necessarily be a girl, but she will have *Turner's syndrome*: she is likely to be very short, and not to develop normally at puberty. She may also have learning difficulties, especially if the single X came from the mother. A child who has too many X chromosomes will have problems too: for example, a boy with two or more X chromosomes and a Y chromosome (*Klinefelter syndrome*) will have genital malformations and a feminized body shape, as well as learning difficulties and auto-immune problems (which are inhibited by male hormones and fostered by female ones). The more surplus X chromosomes the boy has, the more severe will be his developmental problems.

The differences between the amounts of information carried by the X and Y chromosomes explain why males are more vulnerable to a wide range of genetic problems than females. Many genetic defects are *recessive*. That is to say, the fetus must inherit two copies of the defective gene, one from each parent, to have the problem (examples are sickle cell anaemia and cystic fibrosis). If one normal copy of the gene is present, the defect can be corrected and the individual will be normal, though he or she will still carry the defective gene, and may be able to pass it on to their offspring. If a defective gene is carried on the X chromosome (as is the case, for example, in haemophilia), a girl is very likely to have a non-defective version on her other X and so not to experience any problem. A boy has no second X, no counter to the defective gene, and so will manifest the problem.

A small number of genetic problems are *dominant*. That is to say, inheriting one defective gene is sufficient to cause the associated developmental difficulties. Dominant genes rarely cause serious problems because seriously disrupted development reduces the individual's chances of reproducing, and so reduces the odds of the gene being passed on. Most dominant genetic problems are associated with difficulties later in life. The classic example is *Huntington's disease*, which causes early senile dementia, but not until mid-life, by which time the individual has probably already had children.

Over 1000 separate developmental problems caused by genes have been identified so far. We don't yet understand the mechanism by which the genes cause these problems. (For instance, why is it that the very same genetic error, such as trisomy 21, can produce very severe learning difficulties in one child, but only mild problems in another? Is this a difference in phenotype produced by the interaction of the developing child with environmental factors, or does it reflect a difference in genotype, perhaps the interaction between a whole pattern of genes? Or maybe a bit of both?) The rapid advances in genetic research are likely to answer these questions in the coming decades. It is even possible that through such research, we shall find ways of identifying conceptions with genetic problems and intervening to correct these at an early stage in embryonic development.

Environmental problems

Even though the fetus is safely embedded in amniotic fluid inside the mother's womb, protected by her immune system and liver, many things may still damage development. Substances that can cross the placenta and distort the development of the fetus are called *teratogens*. Teratogens can cause anything from a mild developmental problem to serious disruption and deformity or even death. The timing of the exposure to a teratogen is vital in determining its effect.

The organs of the body each have a critical period during their formation, when they are particularly susceptible to damage (**Figure 2.6**). So, for example, the developing nervous system is at its most vulnerable in the first 6 weeks after conception, while the genitalia are most susceptible to damage between weeks 7 and 12. Exposure to a teratogen that distorts the development of hand structures would have a major and serious effect if it occurred during the 5th week after conception, but relatively little effect at 8 weeks.

The impact of a teratogen is also related to the amount of exposure the fetus suffers. Alcohol, for instance, has a disastrous effect if the fetus is repeatedly or consistently exposed to high levels. The occasional very small amount does less harm, although there is no absolutely safe level. Many women 'go off' alcohol (and other things) during pregnancy even though they have enjoyed it beforehand, now finding that it makes them feel nauseous. The sickness often experienced in pregnancy (often called 'morning sickness', though it occurs all day) may actually have been selected through evolution to protect the fetus by steering mothers away from teratogens (Profet, 1992). It's a universal feature of pregnancy,

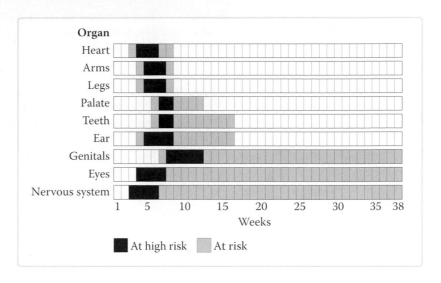

figure 2.6

Critical periods in fetal development

found all over the world. Women who have morning sickness are less likely to miscarry than those who don't. The damage done by a teratogen may also reflect the individual characteristics of the mother, or of the baby. One genotype, for example, may be very much more sensitive to substances like alcohol than another, or less efficient in clearing such substances from the system.

Many teratogens with different effects have been identified (see **Table 2.2** for some examples). These include alcohol; tobacco, recreational drugs such as heroin, marijuana and methodone, prescription drugs such as birth control pills, and many medicines. The classic example here is thalidomide, which was prescribed to counter the effects of morning sickness. Women who took this drug between weeks 4 and 7, the critical period for the developing limbs, gave birth to babies with severely deformed or largely absent legs or arms. Environmental pollutants such as lead, PCBs, mercury and radiation can also have teratogenic effects.

Maternal health and age can also affect the developing fetus. The babies of mothers over 15 and under 35 suffer fewer abnormalities and difficulties than those of older or younger women. Poor nutrition in the mother can affect the development of her fetus (Pollitt et al., 1996), resulting in a smaller brain and a less reactive baby (Lozoff, 1989). Nutrition tends to correlate with many things, including the socio-economic status of the mother. But the effects of poor diet in themselves are enough to adversely affect the fetus, independently of such factors (Stein et al., 1975).

The mother's stress levels can affect the developing fetus too, affecting the subtle dynamics of the process through which fundamental table **2.2**

Environmental hazards before and at birth

Hazard	Effect
Alcohol (over three units daily, but much lower levels can have measurable effects on the fetus)	Fetal alcohol syndrome (FAS): small head, characteristic facial abnormalities, growth problems, learning disabilities, poor concentration, poor social skills
Tobacco	In early pregnancy, malformations of the limbs and urinary tract; in late pregnancy, small birth weight and retarded growth; childhood respiratory problems; higher risk of sudden infant death syndrome (SIDS)
Marijuana	Some evidence suggests that heavy use might damage the fetal brain
Heroin, methadone	The fetus is born addicted and suffers pain/convulsions from withdrawal
Cocaine	Growth is retarded, premature birth, smaller head, possible learning difficulties
Solvents	Small head, eye abnormalities
Lead, mercury, PCBs, radiation	Neurological problems and learning difficulties, deformities
Hormones	Can affect sexual differentiation – see Box 2.1
Maternal malnutrition	In early pregnancy, severe physical defects; in late pregnancy, low birth weight babies with smaller heads
Maternal stress	Low birth weight; immunological and neurological problems; cognitive, emotional and behavioural problems in childhood
Various diseases, of which the most dangerous is rubella	In early pregnancy, devastating effects including severe malformations, deafness and blindness, mental retardation
Sexually transmitted diseases such as cytomegalovirus (CMV)	Damage to the central nervous system
Genital herpes	If the infant is exposed to active lesions during birth, blindness and even death can result
HIV	Can be passed to the infant in the womb or during birth or breastfeeding
Many prescription drugs (the most famous example of which is thalidomide)	Anything from minor to severe deformities or even death, depending on the drug and when the embryo is exposed to it

bodily systems are formed (Wadhwa, 2005). High maternal stress levels during pregnancy can damage the baby's immune and neurological systems (Ruiz and Avant, 2005), affecting health and physiological functioning (Di Pietro et al., 1996; Wadhwa, 2005) and causing low birth weight (Wadhwa, 1998). The effects continue after birth, with children exposed to high levels of stress hormones in the womb being more likely to have cognitive, behavioural and emotional difficulties (Foster, 2006; Huttunen and Niskanen, 1978; Van den Bergh et al., 2005; Wadhwa, 2005).

Most illnesses have little effect on the developing fetus, which is protected by the mother's immune system and the placenta. But some diseases do cross the placenta to affect embryonic development, or cause difficulties through infections at birth. For example, rubella is a mild disease in the mother, but can have catastrophic effects on the developing embryo if it occurs in the early months of pregnancy, resulting in deformity, deafness, blindness and severe learning difficulties. Many sexually transmitted diseases can adversely affect the fetus: cytomegalovirus can damage the central nervous system; genital herpes caught during birth can cause blindness or even death. HIV can be passed to the baby in the womb or during birth or breastfeeding (though many babies are not infected).

Physical development after birth

At the moment of birth, the baby already has all of the physiological systems he or she will need to develop into an adult man or woman. A truly astonishing transformation has taken place, converting a single, simple cell into a complex organism with millions of cells arranged in sophisticated structures. Nonetheless, the body is still vastly immature. There is a great deal of development yet to come.

Postnatal development of the brain

A newborn baby's brain is very different from an adult brain, in many ways (Johnson, 1998). In the first place, it is less than a quarter of the size of an adult brain. This size difference does not reflect differences in the structure of adult and newborn brains: all the main structures of the brain are present by the seventh month after conception. Nor does it reflect a difference in the number of neurons in adult and newborn brains: 18 weeks after conception, the fetus already has as many neurons he or she will ever have: about a million million (Rakic, 1995). Where adult and newborn brains differ is in the connections between these neurons.

In adult brains, each neuron may be connected to many thousands of other neurons, in complex patterns. It is these patterns that allow us to think, to understand the world, to feel, remember, even to operate our limbs effectively. Few such connections or patterns exist in the newborn brain. They must be built up through learning and experience as the child develops. This is the key to the development of the brain. The growth of the nerves and fibres connecting up the neurons (**Figure 2.7**) is what accounts for the dramatic growth in the size of the brain through childhood, and for the differences between human and other primate brains (Johnson, 1998).

Intriguingly, infant brains initially make many more connections between neurons than we find in adult brains (Huttenlocher, 1994; Johnson, 1998). A great deal of development then consists of editing or pruning this excessively complex pattern of connections until adult structures have been formed. At first, this overgrowth of connections seems wasteful. But in fact, the greater the variety of neural connections formed in the infant brain, the more different patterns the child can experiment with. The first pattern the baby constructs may not be very efficient, and is unlikely to be the best, just as the first thing you do when you try to solve a problem may not work too well. Trying different ways of doing things gives the greatest chance of finding the best way. So by creating many alternative neural patterns in connection with a given activity, the infant brain gives itself the best chance of finding an efficient and effective one. Less successful patterns can then be deleted (Johnson, 1998).

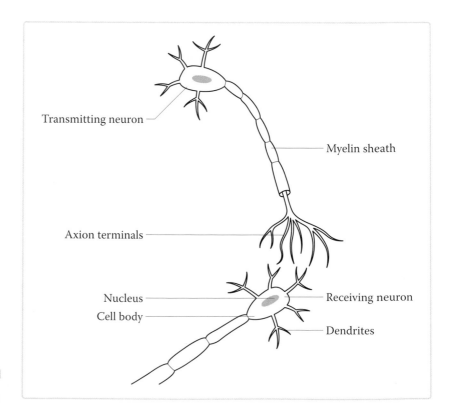

figure **2.7**

The structure of a neuron

80

The greatest increase in size in the postnatal brain occurs in the first 3 years of life. A 3-year-old brain is already 80 per cent of the size of an adult brain, though the rest of the body is proportionately much smaller. Growth continues, more slowly, through childhood – and, it has recently been discovered, in adolescence (Kuhn, 2006). Size is not the only change that occurs in the brain after birth. For example, the myelin sheath that surrounds and protects the nerves (Figure 2.7) is not fully developed in the newborn brain. This means that newborn brains are less efficient than adult ones in transmitting messages: information is transmitted more slowly and less reliably in the infant brain (Johnson, 1998). The myelin sheath takes many years to develop fully, and develops at a different pace in different areas of the brain. For instance, it develops first in areas that serve more basic functions, and later in areas of the cortex that serve higher mental functions. Some areas of the brain have not completed the process of myelination as the child enters the second decade of life.

At one time, it was thought that the immaturity of the myelin sheath limited the efficiency of the infant neural system in ways that restricted what could be learned. Under this hypothesis, the speed of mental development would be limited by maturational constraints in the brain. But this may not be the case. Even partly myelinated nerves pass information fairly efficiently. It may be that partial myelination supports the flexibility of the infant brain, making learning easier rather than more difficult (Johnson, 1998).

An immature neural system may be useful to the newborn in various ways. For example, the immaturity of the newborn visual system means that the baby can only focus on things that are nearby. The effect is to make salient those parts of the world the baby needs to understand first: the mother's face as she cradles the child, for instance. If newborn babies were able to focus on the broader world, as adults can, they would be swamped with so much information that it would be difficult to make sense of anything at all (Bjorklund and Pellegrini, 2000).

The way the brain develops is the result of complex interactions between the potential of the genotype and the experience of the individual. Even the way brain structures function may be shaped by this interaction (Johnson, 1998). For example, in a baby born blind, the areas of the cortex that would normally serve vision may develop to serve another function: processing sound, say. So even the 'hardware' of our brains can be reshaped by learning and experience.

For many years it has been believed that the flexibility of brain structures is greatest in the very young and declines with age, so that children under 10 years of age are more able to recover from brain injuries than adults. This thesis was associated with the belief that all the neurons we will ever have are formed early in fetal development (Rakic, 1995), so that damaged structures cannot regenerate. Recent research on the effects of alcohol on the brain suggest that this view may be wrong.

Alcohol abuse causes the death of neurons, and the shrinking of the brain. Studies in adult animals have found that abstinence from alcohol is associated with a regeneration of the brain: new neurons are produced to gradually replace the damaged ones. Studies with human adult alcoholics have shown the same effect: after as few as 7 days of abstinence, new neurons begin to be produced and brain structures repaired, though substantial regeneration takes many months or even years, and beyond a certain point, the damage is too great to reverse.

It now seems that *neurogenesis* (the production of new neurons) may continue throughout life. It may be that the reason that the absolute number of neurons is about the same in newborns and adults is that neurogenesis acts to replace damaged or dead neurons, rather than to increase the absolute number. Why, then, if adults also produce neurons, do children often seem to make a better recovery than adults after brain injuries? One suggestion is that this may reflect the different expectations of medical professionals treating older and younger patients, and the different treatment offered as a result of these expectations as much as anything else (Webb et al., 1996).

The growing body

Human bodies develop for a far greater proportion of life than is the case in other species. Mice, for instance, complete their physical growth after only 2 per cent of their lifespan. Human beings only complete physical growth after about 33 per cent of the lifespan: it is only at about 25 years of age that the ends of human bones cease to grow.

Growth is at its most rapid during the first 2 years of life, and again at adolescence. Increases in overall size are accompanied by changes in the proportions of different parts of the body: the head accounts for quarter of body height in the newborn, but only a sixth of the height of a teenager or adult.

For the first 10 to 11 years, boys and girls grow at roughly the same pace and are roughly the same size. Girls have their adolescent growth spurt earlier than boys, at around 12 years of age, and may grow taller than boys at this stage. Boys catch up and overtake girls when their adolescent spurt kicks in, at around 14 years. (Other physical changes associated with adolescence are discussed in Chapter 11.)

Many different things affect height. Genetics play an important role: tall parents will tend to have tall children, and short parents will tend to have short children. But this potential in the genome is affected by many environmental factors. Bad nutrition can stunt growth, as can illness in childhood, and such factors may be more influential than genotype in producing final height. A few hundred years ago Europeans were considerably shorter than we are now, so that suits of armour made for grown men would scarcely fit many modern 13-year-olds, reflecting the improvements in nutrition and healthcare in modern times. As conditions improve in a society at large, differences between socio-economic groups in height and physical growth decline: such differences were very marked in Europe during the early years of the 20th century, but are very slight now.

Until recently, the only factor developmental psychology had to worry about in relation to healthy nutrition was insufficient nourishment. In many parts of the world, this is still true: the World Health Organization estimates that over half the children in the world are still inadequately nourished a decade into the 21st century, as the result of wars, natural disasters and poverty. However, in affluent countries there is the new problem of child obesity produced by overeating. Like malnutrition, obesity affects the health, activities and social world of the child in ways that may cause substantial damage to development.

Motor development

The newborn gazelle stands up and runs after its mother within hours of birth, as do the young of many herbivorous species: it is essential to their survival. Even among mammals that are born relatively helpless (puppies, for instance), motor control over the body develops very rapidly, so that after a few weeks the young are vigorously mobile. Human motor development takes very much longer, as **Figure 2.8** shows. Even the basics of mobility and hand control take human babies about

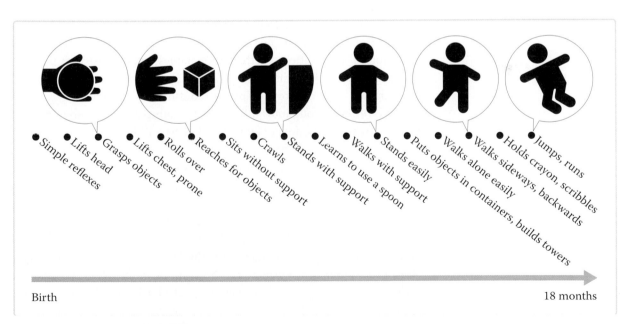

Birth

18 months

figure **2.8**

The pattern of human motor development

18 months to master, and both continue to develop in precision and coordination for many years after this.

At birth, the human baby has only a few innate reflexes, which include sucking, turning the head to find the breast if the cheek is stroked (*rooting*), *grasping* (a newborn will grasp anything placed in the hand with a grip strong enough to hold his or her whole bodyweight) and *stepping* (hold a newborn so that the feet touch a flat surface, and the baby will make stepping motions as if he or she were walking).

The role of these reflexes in development is unclear. Sucking and rooting are obviously immediately useful for the child's survival, but the function of other reflexes, such as stepping, is less obvious. For instance, the stepping reflex looks as though it were shaped by evolution to help a baby learn to walk. But the young baby is far too weak to manage anything like an upright posture or balance or carrying the weight of the body as walking requires. The stepping reflex typically disappears at around 2 months, long before the baby is anywhere near strong enough to walk. This makes it hard to see how this reflex could serve any useful function in the development of walking – so much so that it was believed that the reflex was no more than a dysfunctional remnant from evolutionary history which vanishes as the baby's neurological system matures. Ingenious research has recently shown that this conclusion is wrong (Thelen, Fisher and Ridley-Johnson, 1984).

Thelen and her associates noticed several things about the stepping reflex. Seven-month-olds in whom the reflex has disappeared many months previously will show it again if their weight is supported over the moving surface of a treadmill (Thelen, 1986). If it can be revived in this way, it's hard to see how the reflex could have disappeared as a result of neurological maturation. Furthermore, babies given consistent practice in stepping don't lose this reflex (Zelazo, Zelazo and Kolb, 1972). And even babies who do stop 'stepping' continue to show a very similar kicking reflex throughout infancy, alternating leg movements as if walking, when lying down (Thelen and Fisher, 1982).

Thelen speculated that the stepping reflex might not disappear so much as be suppressed by the increasing weight of the baby's legs. In the first months of life babies put on weight very quickly, much faster than they gain in strength. She speculated that the infant's legs might simply become too heavy to move, even if the reflex to step remains. If so, adding weights to the legs of a baby who still shows the reflex should stop it, while removing weight from the legs of a baby who no longer steps (for example, by suspending the child in water) should reveal the reflex intact. Both predictions were correct (Thelen et al., 1984). If this reflex is still available, as it seems to be, it may yet play a role in the development of walking at a point where the child's muscular strength is equal to the task of holding body weight.

Early work on motor development suggested that learning to reach, grasp, sit, crawl, stand and walk are all directly controlled by the unfolding (or maturation) of an innate biological programme (Gesell and Ames, 1940). This would explain why there is such a consistent sequence in the development of these skills, and why babies tend to achieve key milestones at fairly consistent ages. But this theory has long been discredited. Given more experience and opportunities to practise, motor development can be significantly speeded up (McGraw, 1945), which should not be possible if the process were purely one of maturing innate behaviours.

Recent research has looked at motor development more from a dynamic systems theory perspective. From this approach, the consistent sequence of motor development can be seen to reflect the dynamics of the situation. Control over the head comes first because the head is disproportionately heavy: if it cannot be balanced in a controlled way, nothing else is possible. Sitting is a more stable posture than standing, and learning to balance the upper body in this stable position is a prerequisite for learning to balance it on the more unstable platform of the legs. Being able to hold your weight on your legs is a prerequisite for taking steps bearing that weight – and so on. Each advance takes time: time to learn the skills, and to build up the necessary strength. Thus the consistent sequence we see in motor development reflects the properties of the body in interaction with the physical world, rather than maturation.

The dynamic systems approach has opened up a whole new way of understanding how motor skills develop in infancy. For example, it alters our understanding of what must be pre-programmed into the baby. Take the case of crawling. Babies seldom see others crawl – their elders walk, or at worst, toddle. Since they aren't copying anyone when they crawl, where does the 'idea' come from? Early research assumed that crawling must be pre-programmed, as part of the instinctive maturation of motor behaviour. Dynamic systems theory shows that this need not be the case. Crawling can emerge serendipitously as the surprising by-product (emergent property) of the way the body works in the world (Adolph, Vereijken and Denny, 1998).

For instance, the baby may reach out toward an attractive object. His or her only intention is to grab that object, nothing else. But the further the stretch, the more the centre of gravity shifts, until the baby's position is unstable and he or she topples forward onto the outstretched arm. Now the body is in a new posture, with the weight on that arm – and the baby has, quite without meaning to, and without any pre-programming to do so, taken a step toward crawling. Early crawling is as inefficient and disorganized as this implies, but nonetheless, once a set of events has happened, the infant can learn from the experience and build on it, so that crawling can now become progressively more focused and deliberate.

Thus a dynamic systems approach views motor development as the result of an interaction between neural mechanisms and infant reflexes, the shape and properties of muscles, bones and so on, the laws of physics, and the child's own activities, experiences and intentions. No one factor alone is enough to shape development. The same general theory can be applied in understanding other aspects of motor development throughout childhood and adolescence (Spencer et al., 2006; Thelen, 1995).

In conclusion

Human development is *embodied*. It takes place in a physical body, and in a physical world. It cannot exist outside these things. The details of its form and shape are the product of this embodiedness: of the interaction between the properties of the body, its structures, processes and behaviours, and the properties of the physical world. Development is a multi-factorial affair. The message of the research reviewed in this chapter is that this is equally true of the evolution of the species, of the development of the individual body, and of the development of motor behaviour. It may be true of every aspect of human development. A new theoretical approach, *dynamic systems theory*, offers a powerful way of exploring the nature of the interactive systems that influence development, and the way these systems create developmental change.

Exercises

1. How would you design a study to test at what age (on average) a fetus can tell the difference between classical music and jazz?

2. The mother of a newborn anencephalic baby is unsure what to do. Should she allow the child to die peacefully or fight for treatment to prolong its life? Should she allow the baby's organs to be used for transplants, though that would hasten its death? Taking the ethical code of psychology into account, what is the responsibility of a developmental psychologist whose advice the mother solicits on these issues?

3. What are the key features of dynamic systems theory?

Suggested further reading

For an account of human evolution read:

- D. Johanson and E. Maitland (1982) *Lucy: the beginnings of humankind.* London: Paladin.

For an approachable view of dynamic systems theory read:

- M. Lewis (2000) The promise of dynamic systems approaches for an integrated account of human development. *Child Development* 71, pp. 36–43.

For an introduction to genetics read:

- C. Dennis and R. Gallagher (eds) (2002) *The Human Genome.* London: Palgrave Macmillan.

For neurological development and learning before and around birth, and methods for research, read:

- M. Johnson (1998) The neural basis of cognitive development. In D. Kuhn and R. Siegler (eds), W. Damon (series ed.), *Handbook of Child Psychology*, vol. 2, *Cognition*. New York: Wiley.

For genetic and environmental contributions to mental retardation read:

- Chapter 9 in E. Mash and D. Wolfe (1999) *Abnormal Child Psychology*. New York: Wadsworth.

For motor development in infancy read:

- E. Thelen (1995) Motor development: a new synthesis. *American Psychologist* 50, pp. 79–95.

Revision summary

Human evolution

- Human beings are primates, sharing part of our evolutionary history with other primates. Our closest relatives are chimpanzees, and next, gorillas, although our last common ancestor was 5 million years ago.

- We are one species: despite the surface differences between races, all human beings share a common genotype. In fact, the genetic variation within a racial group is greater than the variation between racial groups. The core genes that define a human being don't vary much. Only the surface characteristics that create individuality vary.

- Our species emerged only 200,000 years ago, in Africa.

- We were not the only intelligent hominid species – but we are the only survivor of our line. We don't yet know why that is so, but studies of our closest relatives (chimpanzees) suggest that our capacity for violence and war may have played a role in this.

- Exactly how abstract human intelligence, or the brain to support it evolved is not yet clear. Many different factors may have played a part in this process – some directly driven by survival advantage, and some the fortuitous consequences of events: perhaps one thing led to another, in ways no specific environment, no specific biological process could have required or predicted.

Dynamic systems theory

- The idea that astonishing qualitative changes (from the emergence of human intelligence to many of the phenomena of child development) could emerge as the fortuitous consequence of the way one thing impinges on another is explored by a new theoretical approach: dynamic systems theory.

- This approach postulates that all biological change from human evolution to the development of the individual child takes place in the context of an interactive system comprising all that characterizes the organism, and all that characterizes the environment in which that organism lives. Only by understanding the dynamics of how this system operates as a whole can we understand how the dramatic and discontinuous qualitative changes of human evolution or child development occur.

- This approach further postulates that the occurrence of the discontinuous qualitative changes characteristic of the development of organic systems can be modelled by the same non-linear dynamics that physics uses to explain the origins of the universe, the shape of a snowflake or the pattern of a snail's shell. In other words, mathematical equations of the type sometimes known as *chaos maths* can explain how repetitions of a relatively simple quantitative process can suddenly produce surprising qualitative change.

- If the postulates of dynamic systems theory are correct, then this will provide a powerful new way of understanding human development: a new insight as radical as Darwin's theory of evolution, on which it builds. It will also, for the very first time, allow psychology to explain the phenomena it studies in terms of principles that are common across all the sciences.

- There is much work to do, before we can simply accept a dynamic systems theory approach to development. Nevertheless, dynamic systems theory represents the first major new theoretical framework for developmental psychology in the 21st century.

Genes: a blueprint for development

- Whatever else, it's clear that our evolutionary heritage is passed on to us through our genes.

- The 'human genome' project is opening up an understanding of genes that would have been unimaginable to previous generations.

- We are simpler than we thought: human development draws on less than a third of the genes we supposed it would need, and some of these genes are shared with vastly different life-forms (centipedes, for example).

- Genes are powerful contributors to every aspect of our development, throughout our lives. But they are not the sole contributor: events and experiences can intervene, so that our actual form is the result of a complex two-way interaction between genes and environment.

Prenatal development

- From conception to birth, genes play a vital role in shaping the formation of our bodies, although the uterine environment and the baby's own behaviour also play a part.

- New methodologies have opened up new ways of studying this process.

- We are now able to describe not only the physical changes in the new baby, as he or she progresses from conception to birth, but also the degree to which the fetus can respond to the world, or can learn.

- Well before birth, the fetus is learning from experience in a variety of ways: learning, for example, to recognize the properties of the 'mother language' he or she will learn in infancy.

Genes, uterine environments and problems in development

- Prenatal development is a subtle, complex and intricate business. Far fewer than half of the ova that are fertilized make it anywhere near birth. Most that fail are desperately damaged. But some of those that survive may have important difficulties.

- Genetic factors are a key contributor to developmental difficulties. Too many or too few genes, damaged genes or the wrong combination of genes can create developmental problems which affect body shape, intelligence, temperament, gender, health or even survival.

- Environmental factors too can radically influence development: poisons in the environment or diseases, stress, malnutrition in the mother can disrupt embryonic development. How bad the impact is depends on exactly when it occurs: each system of the body has a special or 'critical' period for development when it is most vulnerable to such factors.

Physical development after birth

- Human brains go on growing after birth. Much of this growth involves new connections between neurons (reflecting learning and experience) rather than the growth of neurons in themselves. But it now seems that neurons continue to grow through childhood and in adult life too.

- After birth, human bodies change dramatically in size, and in the relative proportions of different areas of the body

- The properties of the body play a crucial role in determining the sequence of mastery of motor skills, and in shaping what it is that is discovered. Motor development is the result of an interaction between the reflexes the infant brings to the situation, the laws of physics in our universe, and the primitive desires and intentions of the infant: precisely the kind of interaction dynamic systems theory describes best.

3

infant minds: perception, inference and understanding in the first 18 months

We take the existence of our minds for granted: we've got a brain, and it therefore seems natural that we have a mind. But in fact, if you reflect on it, this is probably the most puzzling of all phenomena. How can anything as astonishing as human intelligence derive from a lump of organic material like the brain? How can it develop in the individual brain?

Efforts to answer these questions have created controversy stretching back long before the start of developmental psychology, or even of science. Our early ancestors could not imagine how human awareness could possibly have an organic explanation, and argued that spirit or soul rather than bodily organs must be the basis of consciousness or sentience (Osmond, 2003). Later philosophers accepted that the brain is indeed the seat of mind and consciousness, but argued about the mechanics of how intelligence could arise in the newborn brain. Their argument is at the heart of the 'nature-nurture' debate (see Chapter 1).

Nativist philosophers (for example, Descartes, 1637, and later Kant, 1781) believed that certain very basic mental abilities (such as the ability to perceive depth or shape) must be innate: a part of the inherent structure of the brain and nervous system passed on to us as our evolutionary inheritance. By contrast, *empiricist* philosophers (for example, Locke, 1690) argued that ideas cannot be inherited in that way: rather, the newborn mind must be entirely empty, a blank slate (*tabula rasa*), since all concepts and understanding, including the basic ability to interpret information from the senses, must derive from learning and experience in the world.

How does intelligent understanding begin? Do we inherit some sort of ability to make sense of the world, or must we learn how to do that? These questions have been at the very heart of research into the development of intelligence in infancy for the past half-century (and more), and still shape modern research. These are the questions that structure this chapter.

Is the newborn mind a 'blank slate'?

What exactly would it mean to say that the newborn mind is entirely blank, or empty? Early advocates of this theory suggested that the infant is little more than a bundle of reflexes, unable to make sense of the world, and perceiving only 'a buzzing, blooming confusion' (James, 1890). Even the basic perceptual skills needed to see simple shapes such as triangles or squares are not present, but must be gradually learned through repeated experiences of their key components (Hebb, 1949).

According to Hebb, the newborn cannot detect where one shape starts and another ends, any more than an adult can tell, in an unknown language, where one word starts or ends. And just as the adult language student must learn to recognize discrete segments in the new language, to recognize units and interpret their meaning, so must the infant learn to recognize discrete shapes and dimensions, the cues for distance and depth in visual perception. The same is true for all sensory data, whether visual, auditory, tactile or kinaesthetic (that is, deriving from movement): the baby begins with no ability to make sense of this data, and must learn how to interpret it.

Accepting this profoundly blank state as the start of intelligence, Jean Piaget described the newborn baby's visual world as entirely devoid of meaning: 'a world of pictures, lacking in depth or constancy, permanence or identity which disappear or reappear capriciously' (Piaget, 1954). One way and another, this view dominated research in developmental psychology through the body of the 20th century. Piaget's theory was, and still is the single greatest influence on developmental psychology to date (see Chapter 1 for a short overview of the theory as a whole). The main drive of 20th century research on infant cognition has been the exploration of whether or not Piaget was right.

However naïve and lacking in understanding we believe the newborn infant to be, it's clear that the infant mind cannot be *completely* empty, or *completely* passive. If it were, learning and development would not be possible at all. How could a baby learn from experience, without some sort of equipment for learning, some sort of framework for making sense of experience?

The need for a starting point in learning is very well illustrated by a display in the Natural History Museum in London. This shows a 'talking head' of an alien, uttering strange speech sounds. No matter how long you listen to these, you will make no sense of them: they are completely new, like nothing you have ever heard before. But press a button, and you can see the same alien speaking the same 'words', but now no longer just a 'talking head': now you see gestures and expressions as well. Suddenly, you can make sense of the words: you can infer that *these* sounds tell you the alien's name and ask for yours, and *those* sounds offer you food. Your understanding of the gestures (social meanings) provides a framework within which it is suddenly easy to make sense of the alien speech. And note: your own efforts to make sense of things are just as important as this framework in allowing you to learn. If you didn't pay attention or weren't trying to understand, you wouldn't notice the implications of the gestures and so wouldn't unravel the meaning of the sounds.

At the very least, the newborn baby must have something to build on or there could be no learning, no development of the mind. It was Piaget who first really drew our attention to this fact (Piaget, 1968). And it was Piaget who offered the first account of what that 'something' could be, and how all the subtleties of human intelligence could arise in an infant born with no more than basic reflexes.

Piaget's theory of infant cognition

Babies are born with a number of simple reflexes: in other words, a number of automatic and involuntary responses to certain stimuli. Blinking if something flies toward your eye is such a reflex, as is the twitch of the knee when a doctor taps it with a special hammer. Babies share these (and other) reflexes with adults. They also have various reflexes peculiar to infancy: they will reflexively grasp anything put into the palm of their hands, gripping so tightly that their entire body weight can be lifted on their own grip; they make stepping motions as if walking, when held so that the soles of their feet touch the ground; they 'root', turning toward a soft stroke on the cheek, rooting for the nipple; they reflexively suck anything placed in their mouths; their eyes swivel to look at novel or startling stimuli; they startle at loud or unexpected sounds; curiously, the newborn also show reflexes against drowning, making swimming motions while the tract to the lungs automatically closes as they submerge.

Piaget argued that these reflexes give newborn babies a basic, minimal way of interacting with the world around them and responding to events. He argued that these simple reflexes also provide the fundamental building blocks for the whole of human intelligence.

Assimilation, accommodation and adaptation

Every living thing must *adapt* to its environment if it is to survive. That is to say, every organism has to modify or *accommodate* its behaviour to fit in with the environment, and also has to find a way of subduing or *assimilating* that environment to make it serve its needs. Accommodation and assimilation always occur together, creating the process of *adaptation*. A crude example is a rabbit eating a carrot. The rabbit assimilates the material of the carrot, incorporating this material to build its own bodily structures – but it necessarily also accommodates to the carrot, moderating its biting and chewing to reflect the fact that this is a carrot and not a jelly or a stick of rock, and moderating its digestive processes to reflect the nutrients on offer. In the same way, an infant sucking her fist accommodates her mouth to the shape of the fist, and assimilates information derived from her experience of sucking it. Piaget believed that adaptation of this bilateral kind is the basic tool not only of physical survival, but of the growth of intelligence, of the mind. It is through the processes of assimilation and accommodation that reflexes come under voluntary control and form the basis for intelligence.

Some reflexes are rigidly fixed, such as the knee jerk or blinking reflexes. Such reflexes don't change or develop, they remain always outside our voluntary control. But other infant reflexes are more flexible: for example, sucking, looking, listening, grasping. Piaget argued that reflexes like these are never passive, they are always affected by details of the situation. For instance, the breast is not always the same shape – it may be more full or less full of milk. The nipple is not always in the same place relative to the baby's mouth. Babies rooting for the breast must respond to these facts, modifying their search for the nipple and how hard they suck to get milk accordingly. Equally, a baby will suck not just the nipple but anything placed in the mouth. Each experience of sucking provides new information about the objects sucked for the baby to assimilate, and causes the baby to accommodate to events. Thus even when responding reflexively, the baby is not just reacting to events: he or she is also taking action. Through this adaptive interaction, each experience with the reflex teaches the child something new, and the reflex gradually becomes more flexible and less automatic, easier to generalize to new situations and more under intentional or voluntary control. As Piaget puts it, the reflex gradually evolves from a fairly rigid and limited response much like a knee jerk to a much more flexible or plastic *schema*.

According to Piaget, acting on the world in this way and reflecting on the consequences of actions is the key to all mental development. The gradual transformation of the simple, rigid reflexes present at birth into flexible schemas through repeated experience provides the baby with the basic building blocks for intelligence and awareness.

Sensori-motor intelligence

Piaget called the first stage of cognitive development the *sensori-motor* stage. Through this period the baby gradually constructs the ability to mentally or symbolically represent objects and events, to remember, to draw inferences and to plan through repeated cycles of accommodation and assimilation. Piaget identified six sub-stages in this process (see Table 3.1).

As you can see from Table 3.1, there is a gradual expansion of the infant's abilities from dominance by simple reflexes (stage i) which gradually, through assimilation and accommodation come under voluntary table **3.1**   Stages in Piaget's theory of infant sensori-motor cognition

Age	Bases of infant cognition	Understanding object permanence
(i) Birth to 6 weeks	Simple reflexes such as sucking are applied adaptively.	Babies don't search for a hidden object because they don't realize the object still exists if they can't see it.
(ii) 6 weeks to 4 months	Simple actions (such as sucking the thumb) become deliberate rather than reflexive, and are repeated over and over in *primary circular reactions*.	Babies can accommodate their actions to reflect the fact that objects have physical properties, but still don't understand that these properties exist outside their own interactions with the object, and don't search for hidden objects.
(iii) 4 to 8 months	The baby notices the effect of a simple action (that arm flailing makes a cot rattle move, for example), and repeats the action to recreate the effect. This is called a *secondary circular reaction*.	Babies explore objects and their properties through repetitive interactions. They recognize and can remember objects, but still show no awareness that the object exists independently of their own interaction with it, and still won't search for an object hidden out of sight.
(iv) 9 to 12 months	The baby can coordinate a sequence of actions (pulling a cloth retrieves an object resting on it, for instance) to achieve an effect, rather than dealing with only one action at a time. This is a *coordinated secondary circular reaction*.	The baby will search for a hidden object, showing a dawning awareness that the object still exists even though it is out of sight. But the search suggests that the child's insight is only partial: the baby will search where the object was last found (location A) even though he or she has seen it hidden at a new location (B). It is as if the baby believes the action of searching 'recreates' the object – hence the repetition of what worked last time. This is known as the *A-not-B error*.
(v) 12 to 18 months	The baby can deliberately vary a sequence of actions to explore what happens. This is called a *tertiary circular reaction*.	Babies can now find an object where they saw it hidden, but have difficulty finding objects when part of the hiding process is out of sight (an object placed in a box which is then tipped out behind a screen, for example) and must be imagined.
(vi) From 18 months	The baby can mentally or symbolically represent events and actions, and so can imitate things that happened in the past, or pretend that one thing is another. This is the stage of *symbolic representation*.	The baby can mentally represent or imagine the object and recall what has happened to it, and so at last understands that a hidden object still exists, and can infer where it must be from what has happened.

control as ends in themselves (stage ii). The infant then notices the consequences of certain actions and sets out to deliberately cause those effects (stage iii), eventually becoming able to coordinate different actions into a sequence to produce an effect (stage iv). This is the beginning of the ability to plan, and allows the baby to begin more extensive and planful experiments in exploring the world (stage v), eventually coming to an ability to mentally represent objects and events when they are not directly present (stage vi). This stage of *symbolic representation* marks the end of infancy and the sensori-motor stage, and the start of a new phase in the development of intelligence (see Chapter 6).

It's important to notice that it is the baby's own actions, and reflections on actions and their consequences, that build intelligence up in this way. The baby is, in effect, constructing intelligence for him or herself, from these experiences. Piaget is a *constructivist*, giving the infant the prime role in the creation of cognitive processes. In fact, Piaget argued that this must be the case: the individual can only make sense of what he or she already has the mental structures to understand. New mental structures must therefore always come from within. If the only mental structures available to the newborn are reflexes, then all intelligence must be built on these reflexes.

Infant egocentricity and understanding objects

Some interesting phenomena follow on from Piaget's assumptions about the newborn mind and the way it develops. For instance, Piaget argues that newborn infants are profoundly unaware. They have no sense of themselves as entities, and no sense of there being any distinction between the self and the physical world. Possessed only of simple reflexes, they lack the mental apparatus for understanding such a distinction. Instead, it is as if the infant mind 'believes' that the outside world is only an extension of itself, existing only to serve its needs, no more than the other half of its own basic reflexes. In this sense, the newborn baby is profoundly *egocentric*: not in the sense of being selfish or self-obsessed (since those things require a sense of self, which the newborn don't have). Rather, the baby is simply profoundly unconscious of anything but a basic set of needs and actions (hence the name 'sensori-motor' for this first stage of development: intelligence revolving around sensory impressions and motor actions).

One consequence of this egocentricity is that young babies don't realize that objects exist separately from themselves and their actions. To put this another way, so far as the baby is concerned, an object only exists while he or she is directly engaging it in some way. This naivety can be diagnosed from certain very strange behaviours typical of young infants (see Table 3.1). It is worth understanding this aspect of Piaget's theory in some detail, since in one way or another it has been the focus of the vast majority of research on infant cognition.

Up to the age of about 9 months, babies will not search for an object that disappears, even if they see you hide it, and even if the hiding place is very obvious (under a cloth on the table right beside the infant, say). According to Piaget, the object has ceased to exist so far as the baby is concerned, because it is invisible. At this stage, babies have no idea that an object has a permanent existence of its own, separate from their own perceptions and actions.

Step by step (Table 3.1), through the processes of assimilation and accommodation, babies become more familiar with the properties of objects, coming to recognize that objects have their own characteristics (such as being hard or soft), and that these characteristics exist whether you want them to or not: they are independent of the child's actions or wishes. Furthermore, the baby realizes that an object retains its identity whether it is this way or that way up, close or far away, even though these things can greatly alter how it looks. Eventually, at around 9 months, babies understand that the object exists separately from themselves in some way: that it continues to exist whether or not they can see it. Now, for the first time, the baby will search for a hidden object.

Despite the fact that the 9-month-old has made a giant mental leap toward understanding *object permanence* (that is, the separate existence of objects), he or she has not yet fully understood how objects and people interrelate. This is evident, according to Piaget, from mistakes babies typically make when searching for hidden objects. Between about 9 and 12 months of age, babies will search for an object they have seen hidden at location A, and will retrieve it successfully. But then, if they watch the same object hidden again at location B, *they still search for it at location A* (Table 3.1). This is known as the 'A-not-B error'. Piaget suggests that although the 9-month-old has realized that objects don't cease to exist just because they aren't visible, the baby has not yet understood that the object's existence is entirely independent of his or her own actions. It is as if the baby believes that the action of searching recreates the object, rather than discovering it. So to retrieve (recreate) the object the second time, the baby does what worked the first time – and searches at location A, expecting the object to reappear (be recreated) there, as before.

Completely disentangling the existence of objects from our own actions takes time. It depends on the ability to mentally represent objects and events separately from our own actions. This requires the ability to represent things symbolically, whether they are physically present or not, whether we are engaging them or not. It is through interactions with objects and trying to make sense of them that babies construct, by about 18 months of age, the mental structures to allow such symbolic representations and so finally understand object permanence.

Piaget was the first researcher ever to offer any sort of explanation of how the flexible, intentional intelligence characteristic of the human mind could actually begin to develop in a newborn baby possessed of no more than a few simple reflexes. His account of how this is possible is elegant and fascinating. But it assumes that there is a very profound qualitative difference between newborn and adult mental or even perceptual processes, that the newborn child must construct these adult processes through interacting with the world. Is this right? Does the newborn baby truly start out in life with no more than a few simple reflexes? Must even basic perceptual processes be constructed through experience?

Gibson's theory

A very different view of infant minds comes from the work of James Gibson. Gibson's theory is nowhere near as far-reaching as Piaget's: he was concerned with the development of the visual system, where Piaget tried to explain cognitive development as a whole. But Gibson's work challenges some of the basic assumptions from which Piaget and other 'blank slate' theories started.

Where Piaget was a constructivist emphasizing the importance of experience in development, Gibson was a nativist, emphasizing the importance of our biological inheritance. Gibson argued that there is no need for the baby to interact with the world to discover the fundamental nature of objects as Piaget supposed. Rather, babies are born with a visual system that is already innately 'wired up' to interpret sensory information from the world and to use this information to guide actions.

For instance, everything we see has a texture, and this texture changes as we move nearer or further away. Thus the flowers in a garden may be a single blur of colour from a distance, but become separate and distinct as we come closer. Gibson's (1979) theory was that the human brain is innately preset to use such textural information to perceive depth and distance, so that textures directly convey information about how distant an object is without any need for learning or for cognitive interpretation at all: depth perception is a *direct perception*. The capacity for such direct perception is present from birth (Gibson, 1979), and can support or structure the infant's actions. For example, guided by textural cues, babies will reach out toward nearby objects but not distant ones.

According to Gibson, texture is only one of many rich sources of information available from the visual environment that the human mind is innately programmed to use. We are also preset to respond in certain ways to information about the relative size of what we see. For example, if we see an object getting larger, we see it as looming toward us rather than as being stationary and just growing. If we see just one part of the visual field getting larger we see that thing as moving toward us; but if everything we can see is getting bigger, we feel ourselves to be moving forward. Infants and adults share these instinctive reactions. They are built into our visual systems, 'hard wired' and inescapable.

Gibson's classic demonstration of direct perception in infancy involves the 'visual cliff' (**Figure 3.1**). The apparatus consists of a sheet of thick glass laid over a chequered pattern. Along opposite sides the squares of the pattern are large. In the centre, the squares become small as they would if all the squares were the same size but the ones in the centre were further away – at the bottom of a drop, say. Manipulating the size of the squares in this way creates the visual illusion of a cliff edge, though there is no actual drop. Gibson placed the infant at one side of this 'cliff' and the mother at the other, and found that the babies would not crawl over the 'drop' to reach their mother, though they were happy to crawl on the 'cliff top' areas. He argued that this study demonstrated that infants directly perceive the visual cues from the chequered pattern as information about depth, and use this information to direct their actions. The 'cliff edge' does not look to the babies as if it *affords* safe crawling, and so the babies don't crawl across it.

figure **3.1**

The 'visual cliff'

Source: S. Thornton, *Growing Minds* (Palgrave Macmillan) © 2002. Reproduced with permission from Palgrave Macmillan.

The idea that visual information 'affords' action is at the very heart of Gibson's theory. Visual perception and action are intimately interconnected, so that certain visual configurations directly suggest the viability of (that is, afford) certain actions. For instance, a flattish, firm and solid surface affords sitting, standing or crawling where a flimsy or watery one does not. Such affordances are not universal: they reflect the characteristics of the individual or the species. A twig that affords perching to a small bird would not afford support to a child, and so would be perceived differently by bird and human. A branch that affords a safe seat to a small child might not offer support for an adult, and would be perceived differently by child and adult. Gibson believed that babies and birds are born with visual systems already attuned to perceive affordances in a very direct way, without needing the very rational understanding of the world that Piaget argued for. All that experience does, according to Gibson, is to fine-tune this innate system.

Two views of infant minds

Thus Piaget and Gibson presented two radically different views of what a newborn mind is like and what early mental development involves:

■ Where Piaget views the infant mind as blank, possessed only of reflexes and adaptive processes, unable to make sense of the world, Gibson sees the newborn mind as already furnished with sophisticated perceptual capacities, already able to interpret and use a wide variety of visual information.

- Where Piaget believed that perceptual understanding must be constructed from individual experience, Gibson believed it was innately specified as part of our biological inheritance, needing only fine-tuning from experience.

- Where Piaget saw perception as a very cognitive process involving explicit understanding and reasoning, Gibson proposed a very direct, more unthinking (almost reflexive) connection between perception and action.

How can we judge between these two starkly contrasting views of the newborn mind and of early development? How can we explore which, if either, is right? In other words, what methods can we use to test the different predictions made by different theories about infant minds, or to explore new avenues of research?

Studying infant minds

Methodological issues in infancy research

Understanding how someone else's mind works, how that mind sees or interprets the world, or what thoughts it holds, is always difficult. We can never see thoughts or feelings directly: these things are always hidden, and our understanding of them always rests on inferences drawn from what we can see and hear: from what the people we study say and do.

Finding ways of discovering more about mental processes is one of the major challenges for psychology as a whole (see Chapter 1). This challenge is particularly acute with babies: we can ask an adult, or even a child to tell us what they know or what they feel, but babies cannot use language. They can't understand or answer our questions (and in fact, even adults can't always articulate accurate answers to such questions). Newborn human babies are more helpless and less active than almost any other species, and take a long time to master their bodies (see Chapter 2). They can't do very much, so we have very limited behaviour to go on in drawing inferences about their minds.

The infant mind is, therefore, even more hidden and difficult to study than that of an adult or older child. Nevertheless, a number of powerful techniques for revealing the capacities of the young baby have been devised in the past few decades. Each has opened up a new level of detail, and provided us with new bases for drawing inferences about infant cognition. As is often the way with research, these new methods have been critical in increasing our understanding of the infant mind, resolving some old controversies, and opening up whole new areas of research.

Baby diaries

The oldest method of studying infants is the baby diary: a detailed record of a baby's behaviour from day to day, usually focusing on some specific aspect of development. The first person to use this method was Darwin (1877), who kept a diary of his son Doddy's facial expressions to explore whether emotional expression is innate or learned. This was a significant breakthrough in methods for studying infant development: Darwin's baby diary was the first systematic record of an infant's behaviour. Before that, theories were based on much more casual observations (or even on mere preconceptions).

Many psychologists since have kept diaries of one or another aspect of their own babies' development. Such records have been a rich source of data, both in shaping the development of new theories and in providing evidence in relation to those theories. The most influential baby diaries of all are those made by Piaget, studying his children Jaqueline and Laurent (for example, Piaget, 1954).

Piaget was an extraordinarily acute observer, as well as the most painstaking and profound theorist of 20th-century developmental research. As you can see from the short extracts shown in **Box 3.1**, the observations Piaget recorded in his baby diaries are detailed and intriguing, and bear very directly on the theoretical ideas he was working on. They use the child's reactions as a basis for inferences about quite subtle aspects of the baby's understanding. The extracts shown here clearly relate to the question of whether a baby understands that objects are permanent, for instance.

<table>
<tr>
<td>

box **3.1**

A short extract from Piaget's baby diary

Source: Piaget (1954).

</td>
<td>

Observing his son Laurent at the age of 5 months and 24 days, Piaget wrote:

Laurent's reaction to falling objects still seems to be non-existent: he does not follow with his eyes any of the objects which I drop in front of him.

Two days later, Piaget notes:

At 05.26 on the other hand, Laurent searches in front of him for a paper ball which I drop above his coverlet. He immediately looks to the coverlet after the third attempt but only in front of him, that is where he has just grasped the ball. When I drop the object outside the bassinet Laurent does not look for it (except around my empty hand while it remains in the air).

</td>
</tr>
</table>

As these extracts show, a baby diary can be an enormously powerful tool for research. In fact, Piaget's diary observations identified very universal phenomena that no one had ever noticed before: phenomena which reveal facets of infant minds that certainly need explaining.

Nonetheless, baby diaries have limitations. In their classic form, baby diaries follow a single baby over a long period of time. They are examples, therefore, of *longitudinal* studies of development (see Chapter 1). Such single case studies can be very valuable. But they also provide data that, at least potentially, confuse what is idiosyncratic (that is, particular to the baby observed) and what is general (true of all babies). The obvious way round this is of course to study many different babies in the same way (in a series of longitudinal single case studies), or to design experiments to test whether the developmental phenomena the diarist has noted are individual or general by comparing babies of different ages (in 'cross-sectional' research studies – see Chapter 1) .

Baby diaries also have the drawback that they can be rather selective and subjective: the observer is interested in a particular thing, and has certain views about it, and these biases influence what is observed and how it is interpreted. There is no-one to challenge the diarist's claims as to what has been seen or what it means since the fleeting moment has passed. To put this another way: the reliability and validity of the data reported in baby diaries is not always clear.

Again, the core strategy in handling the problem is to test the diarist's claims in new research, either by repeating a similar case study or series of case studies, or by devising new experimental tests of the reported phenomena. But modern technology has given us an extra tool here: unlike Darwin or the researchers through most of the 20th century, we can capture babies' behaviour on camera, creating a permanent record.

Recording behaviour for research

A recording of a baby's behaviour can be played over and over. It can be analysed by several researchers who all see the same events, allowing good estimates of the reliability or subjectivity of the data obtained. This is enough to make recording behaviour an important tool for research, but that is far from its most important contribution. The ability to record data allows us to examine new kinds of data: data reflecting much more subtle aspects of the child's cognitive processing.

Once you have a permanent record of a sequence of behaviour, it becomes possible to observe things in much more fine-grained detail than is possible while the event is actually happening. You can freeze the tape and examine it frame by frame so that very subtle aspects of behaviour can be seen. This makes it possible to measure all sorts of things that we could not readily measure otherwise: exactly where a child looks, and for exactly how many minutes, seconds or even nanoseconds, for example; or we can watch exactly how a child moves fingers and thumb in reaching for an object, and note whether he or she has anticipated the shape and size of the object – and so on.

Detail at this level provides rich information from which to draw inferences about the infant mind and its ability to perceive and under-stand the world. Fine-grained analyses of recordings of babies' behaviour have completely transformed research on cognitive develop-ment in infancy. This technology is used everywhere, from the baby diary to the experiment.

Drawing inferences from patterns of attention

We can use certain universal features of living organisms to devise experiments to explore how they perceive or understand the world. For instance, most living creatures orient to, and pay more attention to things that they find significant or attractive than to things they find unattractive or uninteresting. They will work to get more of what they find attractive. And in general, novelty is more attractive than 'the same old thing': however interesting something is when it is new, we eventually tire of it and would rather have something different. These three characteristics yield methods for studying infant minds that have been very fruitful in expanding our knowledge, though they need care in interpretation (Slater, 2004), since we are necessarily drawing inferences about what the child's reactions mean.

Visual preference

The visual preference task presents a baby with two things to look at: say, a human face and a jumbled pattern. By observing which the baby looks at more, we can deduce which he or she prefers (the answer in this particular case is the human face – Johnson et al., 1991). By varying the two stimuli on offer, we can explore not only what babies prefer to look at, but how subtle their powers of discrimination are, or what features of certain stimuli make them attractive or recognizably different from one another (for example, what cues does the very young baby use in recognizing the mother's face? We shall return to such questions in Chapter 4).

Habituation

When some new stimulus comes along, babies (like the rest of us) tend to pay attention to it: we look, or we listen. After a while it becomes familiar and we lose interest: we have become *habituated* to it, and we stop responding to it. An example of this comes from people who live near railway lines, who often simply don't hear the trains any more. They have habituated to the sound of the trains passing, though a weekend guest might be unable to sleep through the unfamiliar noise. This is a function of familiarity, not hearing of itself. Let some new noise come along (a car backfiring outside, say) and the host will wake up and pay attention as much as the guest.

This tendency to habituate provides us with a powerful way of testing what newborn babies can perceive. For example, can the baby tell the difference between a triangle and a square? One way to find out is to habituate the baby to squares, and then replace the square with a triangle and see what happens. Specifically, in such a study you might first project the image of a square on a display in front of the baby, and measure how long the baby looked at this stimulus before losing interest. You would then change that square for a different one (a bigger or smaller one, for example), and see how long the baby took to lose interest in the new square – and repeat this process with a succession of squares until the baby habituates to squares altogether (rather than to one specific square), becomes a little bored, and looks at the display less and less often despite the changing squares. At this point, you would display not another square, but a triangle. Now, if the baby can't tell the difference between a triangle and a square, he or she will go on being bored by the 'same old thing', and will not stare at the display. But if the baby responds differently to the triangle, looking at it for longer and showing a new interest in the display, we can infer that the baby has recognized something new, and so can perceive the difference between triangles and squares.

Habituation studies can be done even with newborn babies, within hours of birth. In fact they can be done before birth, allowing us to detect what stimuli the fetus can respond to, and what discriminations the fetus can make between one stimulus and another (see Chapter 2), although the range of stimuli you can present to the fetus is limited. After birth, of course, we can explore the child's ability to perceive and discriminate between a much wider range of phenomena.

Conditioning

Conditioning studies take advantage of the fact that even very young babies learn to associate one thing with another. They can learn that sucking on a teat keeps a tune playing, say. This allows us to extend habituation studies to babies' recognition and discrimination of sounds. Babies habituate to sounds just as they do to visual stimuli. Presented with a new sound, a baby will be interested, and will suck hard on a teat to keep the sound going. After a while the baby loses interest in that sound and stops sucking. Change the sound to something new, and the baby will be interested again and start sucking again. Studies of this sort can explore what sorts of sounds a baby can discriminate. Can the baby distinguish between one language and another, say, or between the mother's voice and the voice of another woman? How subtle a difference between one sound and another can the baby notice?

Measuring physiological responses

Studies that observe babies' behaviour either in their natural environment or in an experiment are enormously revealing about the mental processes of the very young. But such studies rely on the baby doing something, whether it is looking, sucking or reaching out for an object (and so on). Adults don't always react in such overt ways to events: for instance, I can tell the difference between a Porsche and a fire truck perfectly well, but this is not a difference that elicits any sort of response in me. The arrival of a Porsche after a sequence of pictures of fire trucks in a habituation study would not rekindle my interest in looking at the screen at all. Nonetheless, I might have a physiological reaction (probably palpitations at the fear that I might now be shown pictures of 30 more vehicles by the madman who bored me with the last 30 ...). The newest technologies of all in infancy research look directly at physiological reactions such as heart rate in asking what sorts of discriminations a baby can make between one stimulus and another.

Heart rate

Our heart rate changes in response to what is going on around us. When we are startled or alarmed, our hearts beat faster; concentrating and paying close attention to something makes the heart beat more slowly and steadily (Kitajima, Kumoi and Koike, 1998; Richards and Cronise, 2000). By measuring heart rate we can pick up much more subtle responses in the young baby, and can draw more soundly based inferences as to the nature of the baby's reactions.

Brain activity: PET, MRI and ERP

More exciting still is the possibility of using techniques that capture activity in the living brain to tease out infant mental capacities. Procedures originally developed for diagnosing damage and dysfunction in the brain, such as *positron emission tomography* (PET scan), *magnetic resonance imaging* (MRI) and *event related potentials* (ERP) offer three ways of doing this.

PET and MRI scans build up an image of the structures and activity in the conscious brain. In principle, we could use these techniques to look at how these things change through infancy and childhood. However, there are ethical objections to this. PET scans require the injection of a radioactive marker, which is an invasive procedure and carries a degree of risk for the child. We don't know how big that risk actually is, but it is hard to justify exposing a child to any risk purely for research purposes (see the ethical code for developmental psychology, Chapter 1). MRI exposes the child to vibration and noise, which many adults find unpleasant or frightening, and also to a strong magnetic field which may be damaging to the developing brain. Again, we don't know how large that risk is, but we cannot simply dismiss it. Ethical research, then, can only expose infants to PET or MRI when the individual exposed to these things gets some direct personal benefit from it. This means that the data we have from such scans comes from children who have some sort of damage or dysfunction in the brain, and so are not typical of normal development.

On the other hand, ERP involves nothing more than placing electrodes on the baby's head to pick up the patterns of tiny electrical currents in the various areas of the brain as the baby responds to a stimulus (hence the name 'event related potentials'). The electrodes can be fitted to a cap, so that the baby experiences nothing more sinister than wearing a rather funny-looking hat. There is no ethical objection to this!

ERP studies offer the possibility of answering questions of a kind we have never contemplated before. For instance, at what age do babies start controlling their eyes deliberately, or moving their eyes in a planful way? It would be very difficult to provide a clear answer to this question simply by recording and analysing eye movements themselves. Quite apart from the technical problems, there is the problem that they may have a plan before they can competently execute it (for example, someone might *plan* to write a brilliant essay or play a brilliant shot in tennis, but *actually* get in a muddle or miss the ball entirely). Planning and executing a plan are not the same thing, and what we see when we watch a baby's eye movements is what he or she is actually able to do, which may lag some way behind his or her plans. ERP studies offer a way around this type of problem.

In adults, planful eye movements are associated with electrical activity in certain areas of the brain, and this activity comes before the actual eye movement. Using ERP techniques we can explore the age at which infants start to show the same patterns of electrical activity before an eye movement, implying that they have begun to plan these movements (Csibra, Tucker and Johnson, 1998).

Many questions about mental processes can be explored using ERP techniques. For instance, when do babies show the same patterns of ERP as adults, in response to recognizing or anticipating events (Ackles and Cook, 1998; Nelson et al., 1998)? When do they start to respond differently to different aspects of language (Schafer et al., 1998)?

ERP studies are very new. Not all researchers as yet place much faith in them, because there are practical problems in getting accurate data from very young babies (Hood, 2001) which may distort the results. However, such problems will be solved. ERP studies offer a new and exciting way into exploring what the infant mind is like and how it changes with development.

Current research on infant minds

As in every field, research on infant cognition is very heavily influenced by its own history. This history was dominated by the very different views of infant abilities proposed by Piaget and Gibson. Thus the key issue has been to document exactly what the cognitive abilities of the newborn baby are, and how these abilities grow through infancy. Research driven by this question has led us to new ways of conceptualizing infant cognition and the processes involved in development, new controversies, and a new view of the issues involved in the 'nature–nurture' debate. And gradually, the focus of research is shifting from what babies can do to how they do it.

Perceiving shapes

Newborn babies have rather poor visual acuity: that is to say, they can't focus on things as well as an older child or adult can, and their best area of focus is closer up than that of an adult, so that their distance vision is poor. Nevertheless, they can perceive shapes very well. Studies using habituation techniques as described above have established that newborn babies can tell the difference between simple shapes such as circles, triangles, crosses and squares (Slater, 1997; Slater, Morison and Rose, 1983). They can also distinguish colours and sizes (Slater, 1997).

The ability to tell the difference between shapes is important. But it is not necessarily clear that this means that newborn babies perceive shapes in the same way that you or I do. For instance, you and I see a square as a whole: that is to say, we see the component parts of the square as integrated in a single unit, and not as a jumble of separate parts. But it would be possible to tell the difference between a square and a triangle without seeing either as a whole object, by just noticing differences in some individual feature of the two shapes. Do newborns see shapes as wholes, as adults do, or as collections of separate elements?

Answering this question is really rather difficult. An ingenious study by Slater and colleagues (1991) habituated newborn babies to two stimuli: a green diagonal bar and a red vertical one (see **Figure 3.2a**). Then they offered two test stimuli: one of the two original figures, to which the child was already habituated (the red vertical, say) and a novel stimulus which might be either a red diagonal or a green vertical bar (**Figure 3.2b**). If babies process stimuli in terms of their separate component parts rather than as wholes, then both the test stimuli should be equally boring: the baby has seen and habituated to all the components (red, green, vertical, horizontal) already. It's only the *combination* of these elements to make a new whole that is novel in one of the test stimuli. If babies see objects as wholes, they should recognize one of the test stimuli as new and look more at that than at the other, familiar one. In fact, newborn babies do look more at the novel test stimulus, showing that they do see objects as wholes rather than as jumbles of parts.

This, of course, does not necessarily mean that newborn babies process shapes in exactly the same way as older individuals do. In fact, there is some evidence that they don't (Westermann and Mareschal, 2004). There seems to be developmental change in the way younger and

Do babies perceive whole objects or just their components?

Source: after A. Slater, 'Visual organization in early infancy', in G. Bremner, A.Slater and G. Butterworth (eds) *Infant Development: Recent Advances*. © 1997. Reproduced with permission from Thomson Publishing on behalf of Taylor and Francis Books.

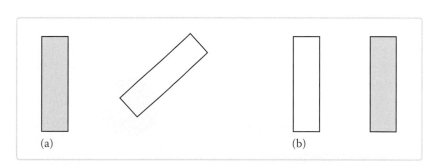

(a)   (b)

older infants process the relationships between elements of a whole, for example. Even very basic aspects of how we process shapes may develop through early infancy, despite the newborn's basic skill.

One aspect of shape perception that seems to develop through infancy is the perception of what is called 'subjective contour'. If you look at **Figure 3.3**, you will probably see a white triangle occluding three black discs (although of course, there is nothing there but three partial discs). This reflects a very general tendency of the visual system to fill in missing bits and to see what Gestalt psychologists call 'good' shapes (Koffa, 1935). Three-month-old babies perceive subjective contour (Ghim, 1990), though newborn babies seem not to.

Are newborn babies 'preset' in some way to perceive certain shapes, or are they merely born with innate perceptual biases that happen to allow shapes to be perceived? We don't yet know the answer, though recent research has raised new questions about this. For example, we've known for a long time (Johnson et al., 1991) that the human face is very attractive to the newborn baby, who prefers this to any other stimulus (this is discussed in more detail in Chapter 4). Some researchers suggest that this is evidence that newborn babies are innately programmed to recognize and process the specific features of the human face (Johnson and Morton, 1991). But other research suggests that newborns simply prefer any stimulus where the features are gathered more densely at the top ('top heavy' stimuli). Human faces may just be a very good example of such top heavy stimuli. Thus the newborn's apparent preference for the human face may be no more than an instance of this very general tendency to like top heavy configurations, rather than the reflection of

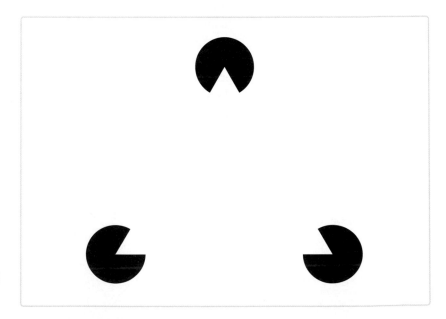

figure 3.3

Perception of subjective contour

any innate capacity to recognize or respond to faces per se (Cassia, Turati and Simion, 2004). This is discussed further in Chapter 4.

Shape and size constancy

Another crucial element in understanding objects is recognizing that the object is still the same – the same shape (hence the term 'shape constancy') and the same size ('size constancy') – even though it might look very different from different angles or distances.

Using habituation techniques, Slater and Morison (1985) have shown that even newborn babies perceive shapes as constant. They familiarized newborns with a given shape: a square, say, presented from many different angles, so that the baby was habituated to changes in the orientation of that shape. They then tested the baby by presenting a new shape (a trapezium) and at the same time presenting the familiar square in a new orientation that the baby had not seen before. Would babies still recognize the square as familiar, and the new shape as novel, as they should, if they have shape constancy? They did.

Similar studies reveal that newborn babies also have size constancy (Slater, Mattock and Brown, 1990). An object nearby makes a larger image on the retina than one further away. The key question is whether babies can disregard this fact, and recognize the relative size of an object regardless of its distance and the size of image it therefore makes on the retina. Slater and his colleagues habituated babies to changes in the retinal image size of a cube, by showing it at various distances from the baby. They then tested whether the babies would be able to differentiate that familiar cube from a novel one of a different size, regardless of the distance (in other words, regardless of the retinal image size) of the cubes, as an individual with size constancy should. And in fact, babies can do this.

Perceiving sounds

Just as it seems that babies are born with quite a sophisticated ability to recognize shapes, so they are born with the ability to discriminate a great many different sounds and patterns of sounds. Babies are particularly sensitive to the sounds associated with human language. Newborn babies are attracted to speech, and prefer it to other types of sound (Aslin, Pisoni and Jusczyk, 1983). Shortly after birth, they can distinguish between their own mother tongue and another language (Mehler et al., 1986). Obviously, some of these phenomena must reflect learning in the womb (recognition of the difference between the mother tongue and a strange language, for instance). But the ability to learn about sound, and particularly language, in the womb suggests that babies may have innately specified perceptual abilities and biases. This is discussed further in Chapter 5, in relation to the development of language.

Habituation display

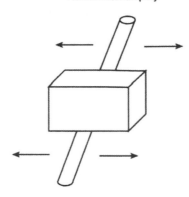

Test displays

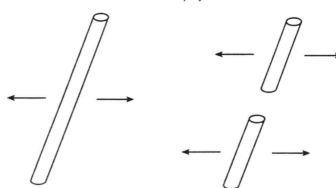

figure **3.5**

An 'occlusion' task

Source: A. Slater, 'Visual organization in early infancy', in G. Bremner, A.Slater and G. Butterworth (eds) *Infant Development: Recent Advances*. © 1997. Reproduced with permission from Thomson Publishing on behalf of Taylor and Francis Books.

rather than one long one, since the occluded part of the rod that adults infer is there wouldn't exist for the baby.

We can test which way babies see the display by habituating them to it, and then changing it for a test display showing either a single long rod (the bottom left of Figure 3.5) or one showing two short rods (the bottom right of Figure 3.5). Babies should be more surprised by (interested in) the two short rods if they saw the original display the way adults do, and more surprised by the single long rod if they didn't think that the invisible part of the rod existed.

Newborn babies in this task behave as if they do not understand that the occluded part of the rod exists: they are more surprised by, and look longer, at the long rod on the test display than at the two short rods (Slater et al., 1990; Slater et al., 1996). This is true even when the training display is altered so as to make it much more salient that the rod is behind the cube (Slater et al., 1994). These results are just what you would predict from Piaget's theory that newborn babies don't understand that objects exist when they can't directly see them.

However, studies of this sort suggest that babies realize that invisible things exist at a far younger age than Piaget's theory states (which would be at about 9 months of age). At 2 months, babies in this task behave as if they are unsure whether there were two short or one long rod in the original display (Johnson and Nanez, 1995). By 4 months of age, babies' responses show that they 'see' one long rod moving behind the cube in the training display, just as an adult would (Kellman, Spelke and Short, 1986). Other studies of responses to occluded objects show that babies of 3 months understand that things hidden behind something else still exist (Rosander and Von Holsten, 2004).

What can we conclude from these results? Clearly, the ability to represent invisible things is present in the baby at a far younger age than Piaget's theory states: 3 months, rather than 9 months. This conclusion is generally accepted in research. What is less clear is whether we can conclude that the ability to represent invisible things is not present in even younger babies. The problem is that, like Piaget's search task, this type of occlusion task involves other skills besides the ability to represent invisible objects. Specifically, it involves the ability to interpret visual displays such as the habituation display shown in Figure 3.5.

Look again this habituation display. Seeing this as a long rod moving behind a cube is an inference. That inference is based on our ability to interpret and integrate three clues: the fact that the two visible parts of the rod look very much alike; depth cues suggesting that the rod is behind the cube; the fact that the two visible pieces of rod move together. Now, even very young babies can interpret these cues correctly, but they are much less adept at putting them all together and drawing the right inferences than are adults (Slater, 1997). For example, babies are much more dominated and distracted by immediate visual cues, such as the fact that the rod is always seen as two pieces rather than as one. So it could be that the newborn baby's apparent expectation that there are two separate rods rather than one long one is a reflection of difficulties in interpreting the specific display, rather than an indication that he or she cannot represent the existence of invisible things. In sum, results from this type of task can't demonstrate that the newborn can't represent invisible objects. All we can say is that they don't, in this situation.

Inferences about the properties of invisible objects

Corroboration for the conclusion that babies can represent invisible objects at a much younger age than Piaget thought comes from a second type of task known as the *violation of expectation task*. Wynn's (1992a, 1995) task for studying babies' understanding of number is an example of such a task: the baby is habituated to a display representing a sequence of events, and then presented with test displays involving either possible or impossible variations on the test situation. If babies understand the situation, then they will react with more surprise and attention to the impossible event: it will violate their expectations.

For example, Baillargeon and her colleagues (1985) habituated babies to a situation where a hinged screen rotated from flat on a surface with its top toward the baby, up into the vertical position, and on over through 180 degrees until it lay flat with the top away from the baby. Then they put a block on the surface in the path of this movement such that it would be occluded (invisible) as the screen became vertical, and presented the baby with either a possible situation (where the rotation of the screen was stopped by encountering the block) or an impossible one (where the screen carries on moving as if the block were not there). Using this technique, Baillargeon and her colleagues have shown that by about 5 months, babies are surprised by the impossible situation: they know that the invisible block still exists, and should therefore impede the movement of the screen. Furthermore, Baillargeon's studies with this task show that 5-month-olds know quite a lot about the properties of different objects: for example, they know that the screen should travel further down if the obstacle is small than if it is large, and that the screen can compress soft objects but not solid ones.

In a second task, babies see a track which slopes down and then runs flat, disappearing briefly behind a screen. They are habituated to seeing a small truck travel down the track behind the screen and out the other side again. The screen is then lifted, and the baby sees a brick placed either behind the track or across it, and hidden again behind the screen. The baby then sees the truck run down the slope, behind the screen and out again as before. Babies of 6 months (Baillargeon, 1986) and 4 months (Baillargeon and DeVos, 1991) were more surprised, and looked longer, when this was impossible (they had seen the brick blocking the track) than when it was possible (they had seen the brick behind the track, where it did not block the track). Since the bricks are invisible behind a screen, this means that 4-month-olds not only understand that the invisible brick still exists (in other words, understand object permanence), but also understand something about the nature and solidity of objects. In a slight variation on this task, Spelke and colleagues (1992) have shown that the same is true of 2-month-old babies.

Almost always in research, it is possible to argue for more than one interpretation of the results we see in experiments. Some researchers have criticized Baillargeon's conclusion that very young babies can draw quite complex inferences from the properties of invisible objects, for example, arguing that their responses reflect some sort of rote learning during familiarization tasks, rather than inferences. Baillargeon has ruled out this possibility by repeating her tasks without the familiarization trials, so that the baby only sees the test trials (the track blocked by a brick, or the brick clear of the track). Here, mere rote learning can't be the cause of the baby's response: the baby could only be surprised by the impossible situation if he or she is capable of drawing inferences about the properties of invisible objects. The results are just the same as before. It is clear that very young babies can reason about the properties of hidden objects and infer likely outcomes (Wang, Baillargeon and Brueckner, 2004).

Despite their precocious understanding, Baillargeon's work suggests that there are important developmental changes in infant understanding in this area. For instance, there are developmental changes in what babies understand about occlusion. At 2 months, babies understand that an object can be either visible or occluded, but they make few finer distinctions. By 3 months, they understand more about how one object occludes another: that, for example, if the screen doesn't go all the way down to the surface, then the bottom of the occluded object should still be visible, and that the top of an object that is taller than the screen should still be visible over the screen (Baillargeon, 1999). At 4 months, babies will be surprised if they see a tall object disappear *behind* a short pot, but not if it disappears *into* the pot. But by 5 months, babies are just as surprised if the tall object disappears into the pot as if it disappears behind it (Hespos and Baillargeon, 2001).

Alternative explanations for search errors

The overwhelming evidence now is that, whatever it is that causes younger infants not to search for hidden objects and older ones to make the striking A-not-B error, it is not an inability to represent invisible objects as Piaget supposed. And yet infants persistently make those errors. Why?

Factors affecting search

Of course, many factors affect the ability to search effectively for something, besides realizing that it exists. You have to be able to remember the object long enough to think of looking for it, long enough to remember where it was hidden. You need the motor coordination to carry out the actions needed to retrieve it, and you need some sort of plan as to what those actions are. You need some notion of where it might be, if your memory isn't all that clear. Difficulties with any one of these factors might cause a problem.

Memory

Even very young babies are able to remember things. If that were not the case, they could hardly recognize things as familiar or learn anything. And in fact, there is evidence that babies' memories sometimes work very well: by 6 weeks of age: for example, babies can remember – and imitate – facial expressions they have seen as much as 24 hours earlier (Meltzoff and Moore, 1994).

Nonetheless, there are developmental improvements in memory through the first few months of life. The ability to recognize things across different contexts and over relatively longer periods of time increases with age, with babies of 6 to 12 months recalling less than babies of 18 to 24 months (Robinson and Pascalis, 2004). Short-term memory improves with age, too: babies below 5 months of age show poorer recall over a period of a few seconds than those over 5 months old (Reznick et al., 2004). And both short-term memory (Pelphrey et al., 2004), and longer-term memory (Learmouth, Lamberth and Rovee-Collier, 2004) show a steady improvement between 5 and 8 months of age.

The fact that memory, especially short-term memory, shows clear improvements between 5 and 8 months fits with the notion that memory is playing some sort of role in the young infant's search problems. But we can't just conclude that younger infant's failures to search are simply because they can't remember the object long enough to think of looking for it: babies of 6 months don't search for an object hidden under a cloth right in front of them only seconds earlier, yet younger babies (5-month-olds) can reason about objects that have disappeared from view 3 or 4 minutes earlier (Luo et al., 2003). The young infant's failure to search is not a simple problem with memory.

Memory also seems to play some role in the older baby's tendency to make the 'A-not-B' error, since the error is more likely to occur when the delay between the object being hidden and the baby being allowed to search is longer (Wellman, Cross and Bartsch, 1987), But again, the problem is not a simple problem with memory. Infants make the 'A-not-B' error, searching where the object used to be rather than where it is, *even when the object is in plain view in the new location* (Bremner and Knowles, 1984; Butterworth, 1977; Harris, 1974; Piaget, 1954), when there is no need to remember its location at all.

Thus the data we have suggest that remembering does play some sort of role in search errors. But straightforward estimates of the infant's general memory capabilities don't predict the search errors in either younger or older infants. Something else is involved.

Motor coordination

Young babies are not well coordinated. The ability to coordinate hand and eye, to reach out and lift or grasp things, shows quite striking developmental change through early infancy (Bruner, 1974; Gesell and Ames, 1940). Could difficulties in this area explain infants' problems in searching for a hidden object? The data suggest not.

For example: Bower and Wishart (1972) found that a young baby who watches an object in easy reach covered by a cup will not lift the cup to retrieve the object if the cup is opaque – but will do so if the cup is transparent. The two cups are identical in every respect except transparency. If the child has the coordination to lift one, failure to lift the other can hardly be the result of lack of coordination. The child's search problem really does seem to reflect something about invisibility in itself.

Planning

A further possibility is that infants' problems in searching for hidden objects may reflect limitations in the ability to make effective plans. Young babies are very poor at planning how to retrieve things, even when the object to be retrieved is in plain view. For example, if an attractive toy is placed on a cloth, and the cloth is within the baby's reach, babies over 7 months of age will deliberately pull on the cloth to retrieve the toy, but babies of 6 months or less don't (Willatts, 1997, 1999). This seems specifically to reflect a difficulty in working out the two-step plan (pull cloth, retrieve toy) needed. The data don't fit with the suggestions that younger babies are simply not interested in retrieving the toy (Baillargeon et al., 1990; Willatts, 1997), or that they haven't the motor coordination to do it (Willatts, 1984), or that the 6-month-old lacks the mental capacity to hold the simple means–ends analysis in mind (Bushnell, 1985).

The young baby's difficulty in planning is intriguing. It is not due to a general failure to realize that a two-step sequence of actions is needed: at 5 months, babies are surprised if, having seen a bear placed under a cover and then hidden by a screen, a hand goes behind the screen and retrieves the bear without first removing the cover (Baillargeon et al., 1990). In other words, these young babies understand *in principle* that retrieving a toy may require a two-step plan. They apparently just can't make one for themselves.

At first, it may seem absurd to say that a baby knows in principle what sort of plan is needed (remove cover, retrieve bear) but is unable to make that sequence of events happen him or herself. But in fact, that sort of thing happens to adults too. As Willatts points out (1997), you may know very well that a dishwasher can be repaired by taking the front off and replacing the faulty parts, but still have no idea how to take even the first step yourself – although you can easily tell whether the repairman has done it properly or not. Knowing what needs to be done is not the same as knowing how to do it.

Difficulties in planning aren't the whole explanation for infant search problems: Shinskey (2002) devised two versions of a task, each of which required the same level of planning, but where one version involved searching for a visible object and the other for an invisible object. Six-month-old babies were more likely to search for the visible object than the invisible one, again endorsing the conclusion that there really is something problematic about invisibility for these young infants.

Nonetheless, limitations in the ability to make effective plans do contribute to the 'A-not-B' error. The more complex the plan the infant needs to solve the search problem, the more likely he or she is to fail (Berger, 2004). So, for example, the likelihood of the 'A not B' error increases as the number of possible hiding places to be considered increases (Wellman et al., 1987), or as the possible hiding places become less distinctive from one another (Deidrich et al., 2001).

Understanding invisibility and searching for hidden objects

Just what the young baby's problem with invisible objects is, we are not yet sure. We know it isn't that the baby thinks the object has popped out of existence (Lecuyer, 2001). The developmental changes in babies' understanding of how one object can occlude or contain another described above (Baillargeon, 1999) may indicate that young babies are simply confused about what has happened when an object vanishes, where it has gone, making searching for it perhaps prohibitively difficult.

This suggestion fits with the interesting observation that exactly how an object vanishes affects search: even very young babies will reach out toward an object that disappears because the lights go out (Bower and Wishart, 1972; Hood and Willatts, 1986), although they don't search for objects that disappear in other ways. Bower suggests that the baby's visual system may be primed to interpret sudden darkness as the disappearance of light, rather than the disappearance of physical objects, and that this instinctive reaction means that, when objects disappear in this way, there is no mystery for the baby as to where they have gone, even though vanishing into or behind other objects may still be hard to fathom.

Equally, it may be that technical difficulties in figuring out exactly where an object has gone are responsible for confusing the older infant and yielding the 'A-not-B' error. After all, you and I know perfectly well that objects exist separately from our thoughts and actions, and that a missing object that we put down not long ago (the car key, say) is definitely still *somewhere*. The problem is – *but where?* Surely you and I are not alone in repetitively searching the spot where the key *ought* to be, as our understanding and experience predicts, even though we have (several times already) established that it isn't there? And then there is the gender divide in such matters: *when you scour the fridge for butter, should you look behind things and lift things up?* (Statistically, women do and men don't.) Theories of just how things may be hidden are a key component driving search.

A new theoretical understanding

Two things seem clear from the research reviewed above. First, a number of different factors are involved in searching for hidden objects; second, infants' problems with search tasks probably reflect a combination of these factors, rather than just one. What is required is a theoretical framework within which we can understand how these factors combine, and why they produce the developmental changes we see in infant's searching skills.

To produce such a theoretical framework we need to go beyond quantifying separate factors (how much a baby of a given age can remember, plan or understand) and look at the processes by which memory, planning and understanding work and interact. Two types of research, connectionism and dynamic systems theory, have contributed new insights in this area.

Connectionism and infant cognition

How do the basic processes of perception, memory, planning or reasoning work? All such processes are rooted in the physiological functions of the brain. Fundamentally, the brain is a network of interconnected neurons (a 'neural network'). Our every thought, perception and action creates a particular pattern of activity among these neurons, a particular pattern of 'firing' of interconnected neurons. The theoretical approach that seeks to understand cognitive development by exploring neural networks is called *connectionism*.

A new event (an action, a perception) creates a new pattern of connections within this neural network. At first, this new pattern is fragile, easily lost or overwhelmed by a stronger pattern: it leaves only a weak trace. But each time that action or perception is repeated, the specific pattern of neural connections that supports it is strengthened, creating a clearer, stronger trace. A good analogy would be to think of a garden lawn. A thousand people can walk across that lawn and leave no mark, if they all take slightly different routes, but if they all follow just the same route, a clear path is worn into the grass. Repeated actions or ideas are strengthened, isolated events are lost. Learning, then, is a matter of strengthening certain neural pathways, and perhaps weakening others (an idea rather similar to the ideas of the behaviourists – see Chapter 1).

From a connectionist perspective, the infant's problem in search and in the 'A-not-B' error reflects the fragility of the patterns of neural networks required for the task. The encoding (in other words, memory) of where the object has been hidden is fragile, easily lost among other encodings of where it was before. The neural patterns that connect actions and goals (in other words, plans) are also fragile, easily lost among other patterns associating the same goal with different actions, or the same actions with different goals. The neural patterns associating a given 'memory' with a given 'plan' are also fragile and easily lost.

All this neural fragility is not a function of the baby's age so much as a reflection of his or her lack of experience in searching for hidden objects. At any age, the neural patterns associated with new perceptions and actions, memories and plans can be fragile and easily lost. For example, almost everyone who studies psychology has a 'now I've got it – now I've lost it again' experience when first trying to understand and apply inferential statistics. We forget things and make mistakes in ways that can seem as absurd to a stats teacher as the baby's search problems seem to any adult. Our problem is the same as the baby's: the task is so new to us at first that we have no ready-made 'grooves' in the mind to slot it into. The neural patterns our early efforts create are therefore disconnected and exasperatingly easy to lose. Only repeated effort (strengthening the neural connections) will solve the problem.

The connectionist way of thinking about what is involved in memory and planning gives a new insight into those processes and how they interact and develop. It's worth noting that, from this perspective, terms like 'memory' and 'planning' are handy *labels* for certain aspects of what neural networks do, but they aren't, at least at first, actually special *operators* in the mind. To give a very simplistic analogy, if you press an earring into a lump of Plasticine, you end up with an earring-shaped mould, which is, in effect, both a 'memory' of what the earring is like and a 'plan' for casting another just like it. In this case, 'memory' and 'plan' are our labels for the emergent functions of the way the Plasticine happens to work. The Plasticine doesn't have an operator to store memories or an executive to make plans. These functions simply emerge from the nature of its substance.

From a connectionist point of view, memory and planning are our labels for the emergent functions of the impressions made on our neural systems by experience. And in the same way, 'insight' and 'understanding' are emergent functions of the development of stronger and more coherent patterns in our neural networks. This development allows us to behave consistently, coherently and effectively in relation to some problem – precisely the behaviours that we take as evidence of insight or 'joined up thinking'.

Connectionist theories offer new ways of thinking about how complex psychological phenomena could begin to emerge from the basic biology of our brains. It's worth noticing that the biological properties of neural networks are enough to ensure the emergence of the cognitive phenomena of memory, planning and insight without there needing to be any guiding rules or instructions in the system to shape these phenomena. Plasticine takes impressions, can be squished to a new shape and eventually dries out without 'rules' to tell it what to do, simply because of its physical properties. Connectionist theory makes the same claim for intelligence: it develops because of the physical properties of our 'wet ware', in other words, the physiology of neurons. The automatic 'impressions' created, strengthened or weakened by our actions and perceptions are enough to create, strengthen or weaken neural connections and so to generate behaviour and learning. And it's easy to see how innate structures (neural patterns preset through our genetic programming) and learning (neural patterns shaped through experience) could combine in such a system to produce our peculiarly human development.

The process shaping neural networks can be simulated on a computer, in what is called a connectionist program or C-net. Simulations of this kind have been created to explore all sorts of developmental phenomena in infant cognition, from the 'A-not-B' error (Munakata, 1998) to the perception of parts and wholes (Westermann and Mareschal, 2004) or the development of perceptual categories (Cohen, 2004). This line of research has very obvious promise – it has already made an important contribution to our understanding of the development of cognitive processes (Munakata and McClelland, 2003). But there is still relatively little work in this vein. Only tiny fragments of development have been modelled in C-nets. As yet, no computer simulations based on the theoretical principles of connectionism come anywhere near reflecting the facts or the complexity of human development, as even the supporters of this approach would admit (Munakata and Stedron, 2002). It isn't yet clear whether that is simply because the research task is enormous, perhaps still beyond our technical power and resources, or because there is some problem in the theory.

A dynamic systems approach to infant cognition

Many of the key assumptions of connectionist models are shared by dynamic systems theory (see Chapter 2 for an overview of this approach), although there are also important differences (Thelen and Bates, 2003). Like connectionism, dynamic systems theory emphasizes the idea that behaviour is *self-organizing*: that is to say, it emerges from the basic functioning of the system, without the need for any sort of controlling or conscious process directing it. The system of relevance to infant cognition includes every aspect of the child's environment, as well as every aspect of the child's own processing, each element interacting with and influencing all the others. Small changes in any one aspect of the system can create changes in behaviour, including developmental changes which may be sudden or slow, robust or fragile, or even apparently involve regressions (Gershkoff-Stowe and Thelen, 2004).

From a dynamic systems perspective, the 'A-not-B' error is the product of the normal processes that underlie searching and reaching for objects (Smith et al., 1999; Thelen et al., 2001). These processes involve an interaction between visual and attentional processes for perceiving where objects are, motor processes for planning and executing actions in relation to those objects, short-term memory processes that allow the baby to maintain relevant information from second to second when there are no clues to support recall, and longer-term memory for previous actions.

Specifically, Thelen and her colleagues suggest that, during the repeated trials where the baby sees the object hidden at location A, he or she constructs a strong longer-term memory for that location. When the object is then hidden at location B, the baby makes a new plan to go to B but this plan is weak (because it is new and has not had the opportunity to be strengthened) and so decays if there is any delay in being able to execute it. After a few seconds, the new plan has decayed to the point where it is weaker than the old plan in long-term memory of going to location A, and so the baby reaches to A, not B.

According to this view, the 'A-not-B' error becomes less probable in situations where there is less chance of 'plan B' decaying before it can be acted on, and where there are external supports (salient clues) to direct the search to B. This fits very well with Wellman and colleagues' (1987) review of the factors associated with the 'A-not-B' error in infants. It fits, too, with Diamond and Doar's (1989) observation that the shorter the delay between hiding an object at B and allowing the infant to search for it, the less likely the error. But it also makes new predictions. For instance, dynamic systems theory predicts that much older individuals will also make 'A-not-B' type errors, where the situation stretches their capacity to maintain a search plan effectively. This turns out to be the case (Spencer, Smith and Thelen, 2001): for instance, even 2-year-olds make the 'A-not-B' error when searching for an object hidden in a sandbox which provides no distinctive clues as to where the object is buried, and so imposes more difficulty on the task.

In conclusion

It is now quite clear that Piaget's view of the infant mind as empty bar a few simple reflexes is wrong. Even newborn babies already have impressive perceptual abilities and are able to make sense of the world to a far greater extent than Piaget supposed. By 2 or 3 months of age, babies' understanding has become quite sophisticated. They know a good deal about objects – certainly that objects still exist even if they aren't visible. They can represent and reason about invisible objects, drawing inferences based on the properties of objects. These inferences show that these young babies also have rudimentary concepts of causality, number, trajectory and so on.

Two-month-old babies are far too young and immature to have constructed all this cognitive sophistication through feedback from their own actions, as Piaget's theory proposed. The data suggest instead that Gibson may be more nearly right in suggesting that much of what a baby needs in order to understand the world is already pre-programmed at birth. Of course, babies do learn a great deal in the first months of life (Slater, 1997; Bremner, 1997). But the data suggest that this development is much more like the fine-tuning of an innate system through observation, as Gibson described, rather than the construction of the bases of cognition from experience as postulated by Piaget.

However, to conclude that Piaget was wrong and Gibson right would be a gross oversimplification of the situation. The young baby's perceptual system is very sophisticated, as Gibson suggested. But their ability to use the information it provides is quite limited. For instance, in studies involving occluded objects and violation of expectation tasks babies as young as 2 months clearly show that they understand hidden objects exist, and that they can reason and draw inferences about the properties of those objects. But they don't use this understanding in practical contexts: for example, in retrieving a toy or searching for a hidden object (Bremner, 1997; Willatts, 1997). Eight-month-old babies have moved on, and will readily retrieve or search for a hidden object. They are perfectly capable of remembering where an item has been hidden for more than a minute. But they will still make the 'A-not-B' error and search for the item where they found it last time rather than where they saw it hidden a few seconds earlier, if the hiding place is changed. Cognitive development through infancy is very much about the child's progressive development of the ability to use the rich information from the perceptual system to guide actions – and Gibson's theory offers no explanation of what is involved in this developmental change.

For perceptual information to be useful, it has to be integrated with the actions it serves (Bremner, 1997). For example, when you learn to drive a car, you have to integrate your perception of the changing direction of the road, corners and the like and your actions in turning the steering wheel or holding it straight. You can see the road perfectly well, but what you see does not instantly suggest what to do, so that the learner driver's steering is at first very wobbly even on relatively straight stretches, and tends to begin a turn a little too soon or too late for the corner. A key part of becoming a skilled driver is integrating what you see with what you do, until the whole operation is smooth and coordinated. Steering comes to seem automatic, with no need to work out when or how hard to turn the wheel as you did at first. Bremner's suggestion is that the young baby is very much in the same position as a learner driver: he or she has all the perceptual equipment needed for various activities, but like the learner driver, has not yet learned how to integrate perceptual information and action. Just as you cannot learn to drive a car without trying, a baby's perceptions cannot become integrated with actions unless the baby tries out those actions. It's only by becoming mobile, for instance, that a baby starts to need, and so to develop, perceptions about which surfaces 'afford' safe crawling and which don't (Bremner, 1997). So Piaget's emphasis on the importance of acting on the world as the basis for developing an intelligent, functional understanding seems right.

Understanding just how perception and action become integrated requires much more detailed theories of the processes underlying the behaviour than Piaget provides. His theory viewed development in this area very much in terms of the construction of mental processes, insight and understanding. New approaches such as connectionism and dynamic systems theory take a different approach, viewing the infant's developing skill as an emergent function of a complex dynamic system operating at a more basic level.

Approaches such as connectionism and dynamic systems theory offer a new way of conceptualizing not just development, but what mental processes as a whole are like, and where they have their origins. 'Nature–nurture' ceases to be a controversy focusing on which factor is crucial, and becomes a question of how these factors interact. From these perspectives, the processes supporting cognition and cognitive development are not qualitatively different from those supporting much more physiological functions. The distinction between 'cognition' and other functions is softened: the general assumptions of dynamic systems theory apply equally to intelligent search, the discovery of motor skills such as crawling and the formation of the embryo (see Chapter 2). In some senses, the question of how intelligence is possible in an organic system becomes less mysterious.

The emergence of theories such as dynamic systems theory is exciting. Dynamic systems theory has the potential to become a new paradigm in developmental psychology (see Chapter 1), shaping how we view all aspects of development (Lewis, 2000). But as always, the promise of a new approach carries with it new problems for research to solve. We have as yet no comprehensive account of development from this perspective. There are many empirical questions to be answered before such an account would be possible. So we don't yet have all the answers to the problem of how intelligence develops in infancy – though we do have a new way of exploring the question.

Exercises

1. How would you test the hypothesis that dogs can count up to 3? In what ways is this methodological problem similar, and in what ways is it different from the problem of finding methods to test the hypothesis that young babies can count to 3?

2. Why does it matter whether babies are born understanding that invisible objects still exist or not?

Suggested reading

For a taste of Piaget's theory and methods read:

- J. Piaget (1954) *The Construction of Reality in the Child*. New York: Basic Books.

For an account of Gibson's theory read:

- J. Gibson (1979) *The Ecological Approach to Visual Perception*. New York: Appleton Century Crofts.

For a discussion of the pluses and minuses of various methods used in studying infant cognition read:

- A. Slater (2004) Novelty, familiarity and infant reasoning. *Infant and Child Development* 13, pp. 353–5.

For reviews of research on infant cognition read:

- C. Rovee-Collier, L. Lipsitt and H. Haynes (eds) (2003) *Progress in Infancy Research*, vol. 1. Hillsdale. N.J.: Lawrence Erlbaum Associates.

For a dynamic systems account of infant cognition read:

- E. Thelen, G. Schoner, C. Scheir and L. Smith (2001) The dynamics of embodiment: a field theory of infant perseverative reaching. *Brain and Behavioural Sciences* 24, pp. 1–86.

- E. Thelen and E. Bates (2003) Connectionism and dynamic systems: are they really different? *Developmental Science* 6, 378–91.

Revision summary

Is the newborn mind a 'blank slate'?

- Research on infant minds was driven by the question: is the newborn baby's mind innately equipped to perceive the world, or is it a blank slate, so that everything from the simplest concepts on must be learned from experience?

- The debate is a very old one, stretching back to nativist philosophers such as Descartes (1637) and empiricist philosophers such as Locke (1690).

- Key protagonists of the 20th century were Jean Piaget and James Gibson.

Piaget's theory of infant cognition

- Piaget believed that babies are born with no more than a few reflexes and basic adaptive processes. They have no understanding of the world and cannot make sense of events. They don't understand that they are a separate entity, different from the objects around them, or that those objects exist independently of themselves.

■ According to Piaget, all knowledge must be constructed by the baby through experiencing active interactions with the world.

■ At first, these interactions are confined to fairly rigid reflexes. But even reflexes must adapt to the environment: for example, the sucking reflex must adapt to suck more strongly when the breast is empty, and the mouth must adapt to reflect the different shapes put into it (a nipple, a teat). Through progressive interactions, reflexes become more flexible, gradually coming under voluntary control. This allows the infant to explore the world ever more deliberately, and so to construct the mental structures needed to make sense of it.

■ In support of his theory, Piaget emphasized two strange phenomena of infancy. First, until about 8 months of age, babies don't search for a toy that disappears, even if they have seen it hidden under a cloth in front of them: *as if the baby believed the object ceased to exist when it went out of sight*, as his theory claims. Second, although 10-month-old babies will search for an object hidden that way, they will search for it in its usual hiding place rather than a new hiding place, even though they have seen it hidden in the new location seconds earlier, *as if they believed that it was their action in searching that recreates the object, so that redoing what they did before will 'find' it*, as Piaget claims.

Gibson's theory of infant perception

■ By contrast, Gibson argued that babies are born with a perceptual system that is already innately 'wired up' to interpret sensory information and use it to guide actions.

■ For instance, babies don't have to learn about distance and depth as Piaget supposed. Rather, their innate systems let them use cues such as texture to perceive these things. This perception is direct: there is no need for cognitive interpretation or insight. The reaction is instinctive and inescapable.

Studying infant minds

■ Resolving the controversy between these two views requires data about what newborn babies can understand about the world: data that can only be obtained by subtle methods.

■ Piaget's theory grew out of very detailed observations of his own children. Baby diaries of this sort can be a fertile source of new theoretical ideas, but have limitations.

■ Modern technology allows much more detailed observations of infant behaviour, through permanent audio or visual records.

■ Detailed studies of infants' patterns of interest and attention can reveal a lot about their minds: for example, which of two stimuli they prefer (visual preference tasks), or whether they can detect the difference between a familiar stimulus and a new one in habituation tasks.

■ Measures of heart rate change or of electrical activity in the brain may open up yet more ways of discovering what infants can respond to.

Current research

- Shows that Gibson's view of the infant's abilities was in many ways more accurate than Piaget's: newborn babies already have impressive perceptual skills. Babies as young as 2 months understand that invisible objects still exist, and can draw inferences from the properties of invisible objects. In fact, these very young babies already have some notion of number, trajectory, causality and so on.

- Nevertheless, Piaget's observations about infant's difficulties in search tasks are valid: the phenomena really exist, and need explanation. Babies seem to have difficulty using their knowledge about objects in search tasks – difficulties that Gibson's theory does not explain.

- A number of factors that might cause such errors have been explored, including difficulties in remembering, planning, motor coordination and understanding how things disappear.

- Connectionism and closely related dynamic systems theory offer new ways of conceptualizing the processes underlying the infant's difficulties in search tasks. These approaches offer a detailed account of how the basic processes of visual attention, planning, short and long-term memory involved in search tasks may cause the errors typical of infancy.

- Connectionism and dynamic systems theory, also new insight into the basic mechanisms underlying the development of cognitive processes as a whole.

4
growing emotions: social and personal development in the first 18 months

Just as philosophers have long been intrigued by the problem of how human intelligence could arise in a blob of flesh, the single cell of a fertilized egg, so we have puzzled over how all the rich emotions that characterize human experience could emerge from such a simple start.

We human beings are not dispassionate or disembodied observers of the world: we are creatures whose consciousness is as much emotional as it is rational. Our experience of ourselves is embedded in goals and actions that may (satisfyingly) succeed or (frustratingly) fail, in hopes and fears that may generate passionate yearning or paralyzing anxiety. Crucial to our experience is our ability to relate to others, to respond to them emotionally not just as 'yet another' part of the physical world but as persons: sentient beings who think and feel, who love and hate, hope and fear as we do, and with whom we can share ideas and empathy.

Where does the capacity for all this emotional reaction come from? How does it emerge in infancy? Why does one baby react differently from another? How does the infant come to understand that other people are persons like him or herself? For that matter, where does the sense of 'self', the awareness of our own unique identity come from? These are the questions that structure this chapter.

The beginnings of social responsiveness

Piaget (1968) argued that the newborn baby is profoundly unaware, utterly without any sense of 'self'. At the start of life, the child cannot even understand that there is a self that is separate from other things, let alone comprehend that some of those things are alive and sentient and others aren't. The newborn baby has none of the awareness that is necessary for personhood or for relating to other people as persons. This awareness must be gradually constructed through infancy and childhood, using the only tools at the baby's disposal: the basic mechanisms of biological adaptation (see Chapters 1 and 3).

According to Piaget there are no 'special' processes for social development. Rather, the infant's understanding of personal and interpersonal phenomena derives from the very same processes that allow the child to construct an understanding of the physical world. Development, in whatever area, reflects the progressive construction of mental structures that allow ever more powerful logical reasoning in making sense of experiences and events. In other words, for Piaget, the social and the physical worlds are not distinct. There are no innate or instinctive roots for understanding in either area, and there is no difference in the developmental process working to yield progress.

Piaget's theory dominated developmental psychology for many decades. As a result, the main focus of research in infancy was on the origin and development of very general cognitive structures for knowledge and understanding, without much regard to what was to be understood. Most of this focused on the baby's understanding of objects. There was relatively little research directly exploring social development in infancy. The situation began to change in the last decades of the 20th century, as evidence mounted up suggesting that Piaget's theory is importantly wrong in key assumptions (see Chapter 3). This evidence strongly suggests that we humans are born already primed with various perceptual biases, already pre-set to respond to (and learn about) physical objects in certain ways.

This discovery radically changed our approach to understanding infant development. It pushed the emphasis away from looking at the construction of very general processes in development of the kind described by Piaget, and toward looking for the innate foundations of knowledge, foundations that seem to be specific to particular areas. If evolution has given us specific perceptual biases on which to build an understanding of the physical world, it seems very likely that we are also endowed with similar tools for building an understanding of the very different phenomena of the social world. Current research focuses on identifying what these innate foundations might be, and how they contribute to the development of social understanding in early infancy.

Social responsiveness in the newborn

How can we possibly discover whether newborn babies are already primed to react to social stimuli in special ways? As ever in psychology, research methods are an important constraint on our theories. Piaget relied on careful observations of his own children's behaviour. Modern research has developed a number of more subtle and more objective techniques. These are reviewed in detail in Chapter 3, and summarized here in Table 4.1.

The evidence suggests that babies differentiate between human beings and other things right from birth (Legerstee, 1992; Poulin-Dubois, 1999; Rochat and Striano, 1999; Slater and Butterworth, 1997).

table **4.1**

Methods for studying infant development

Baby diaries	Detailed observations of individual babies recording their spontaneous behaviour and reactions over a fairly extended period of time
Filming	Detailed recording of a baby's behaviour over a short period of time, for example, while interacting with another person
Habituation studies	Babies get bored with the same old thing to look at or listen to. How much does the stimulus need to change before the baby's interest revives? In other words, what discriminations can babies make?
Conditioning studies	Babies can learn to do something (such as sucking a teat harder, turning their heads) to get to see or hear a stimulus (such as a human face or a cot mobile, mother's voice or music). What do they prefer to see/hear?
Visual preference	Given a choice of things to look at, what do babies prefer?
Physiological measures	Heart rate or electrical activity in the brain measured as event related potentials can clarify how a baby is reacting

For example: newborn babies look longer at human faces than at other stimuli, and make more effort to watch a face than to watch other sorts of thing (Fantz, 1961; Johnson et al., 1991). They imitate facial expressions (Field et al., 1982; Kugiumutzakis, 1999; Reissland, 1988; Vintner, 1986), and particularly movements of the lips and tongue (Kugiumutzakis, 1999; Meltzoff and Moore, 1977) as **Figure 4.1** shows, though they don't imitate inanimate objects even when these move in similar ways. Furthermore, newborn babies prefer human speech to other sounds (Mehler et al., 1986). They imitate very simple speech sounds (such as the vowel sound 'aa'), though they don't imitate other kinds of noise (Kugiumutzakis, 1999). And detailed analysis of recordings of newborn babies shows that their arm and finger movements are different when looking at a person from when looking at an object (Ronnqvist and von Hofsten, 1994).

Quite clearly human babies are, in some sense, 'primed' to be social from the very first. This conclusion, once controversial (Hayes and Watson, 1981), is now generally accepted. However, exactly what this means is still controversial.

Conflicting interpretations of early social responsiveness

What, exactly, does the newborn baby know or intend when he or she reacts to another person in a special way? Some researchers believe that babies are born with an innate understanding that other people are importantly similar to themselves, and with an innate urge to communi-

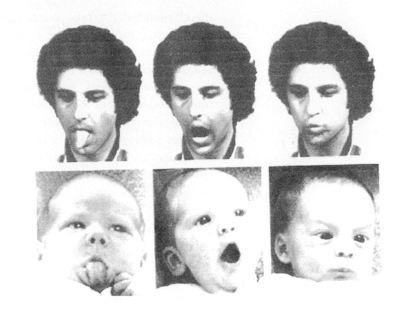

figure **4.1**

Imitating facial expressions

Source: A. Meltzoff and M. Moore (1977) 'Imitation of facial and manual gestures by human neonates', *Science* 198, pp. 75–78. Reproduced with permission from the American Association for the Advancement of Science.

cate with others (Trevarthen, 1993a, 2005; Trevarthen, Kokkinaki and Fiamenghi, 1999). Very detailed frame-by-frame analyses of young babies interacting with objects or with another person (Trevarthen, 1993a, 1993b) seem to support these claims. Babies match the facial expressions of an adult they are interacting with, their breathing takes on a pattern characteristic of the breathing pattern that will later allow language and turn taking, and the baby gives off every sign of pleasure. The interaction looks, for all the world, like a real social exchange – a 'proto-conversation' (Trevarthen, 1993a, 1993b). Things are very different when the baby interacts with inanimate objects: with a mobile or a cot gym, for instance. Babies seem to react socially to people, but not to objects (Legerstee, Anderson and Schaffer, 1998).

Watching Trevarthen's films of proto-conversations between adults and young babies, it's easy to believe that there is a real interpersonal interaction taking place. You get the same impression when you yourself interact with a young baby. The sensation of a responsive communication can be overwhelming. But critics of Trevarthen's conclusions have pointed out that this adult reaction may be misleading: after all, even animated triangles moving about a cartoon world can suggest all sorts of complex emotions and relationships to us. We can 'relate' to them, project motives and thoughts onto them, although no one would argue that these things really had intentions or feelings or knew we were there. Are we seeing what we expect or hope to see, when we interact with young babies, rather than what is actually there?

Critics of Trevarthen's theory argue that in fact, babies have no more than a few simple reflexes that lead them to imitate faces and simple speech sounds and to take pleasure in such imitation (much as they have reflexes for rooting for the breast and enjoying sweet fluids). Nevertheless, we adults are primed to interpret the babies' reflexive behaviour *as if* it were a real attempt to interact and communicate, and to respond accordingly. As the 'senior partner' in such interactions, we adults moderate our behaviour to fit in with and please the child, thereby creating the appearance of a responsive interaction even though the baby has no intention of either interacting or communicating, nor any understanding that these things are even possible (Poulin-Dubois, 1999; Rochat and Striano, 1999). In other words, the appearance of an interaction is created entirely by the adult's behaviour.

An alternative to Trevarthen's view (Neisser, 1991; Rochat, 1995) draws on Gibson's (1979) work on the visual perceptual system for an explanation of the infant's early social responsiveness (see Chapter 3). Gibson argued that the newborn perceptual system is already pre-wired to interpret and respond to visual information in certain ways. For example, newborns are biased to interpret an object expanding in the visual field as looming closer rather than getting bigger, though either may be possible. And Gibson argued that the visual system is pre-wired to interpret certain stimuli as *affording* (that is, supporting, eliciting, enabling) certain actions: a chair affords sitting where a teacup doesn't, for instance. Neisser and Rochat argue that the newborn perceptual system is also pre-wired to respond to social stimuli in certain ways, so that human faces or voices 'afford' social responsiveness without the need for any cognitive mediation (neither learning nor conceptual understanding). Social responsiveness would be 'directly' elicited by the perception of the human face. This 'Gibsonian' explanation of the newborn baby's social responsiveness would mean that babies need not construct social understanding from scratch, as Piaget argued: they can build on innate perceptual biases. But they would not necessarily understand the information or responses this perceptual system creates, or be able to use it intentionally, as Trevarthen suggests.

Unravelling this controversy poses difficult problems for research. What methods could we use to establish whether a baby's apparent social responsiveness was 'real' or merely the reflection of a reflex perceptual 'affordance'? The way forward lies not in more film of babies' interactions, but in more knowledge of babies' capacities in other contexts (just as we know that animated triangles have no intentions, not because of anything they do in cartoon interactions with one another, but because we know a lot about the characteristics and limitations of animations and triangles). So how do babies recognize human faces? How do they distinguish between living things and inanimate objects, understand emotions or experience 'self'? How do their relationships with others develop? Answering these questions throws light on just what it is that the newborn's social responsiveness actually means.

Recognizing people

When you or I look at a human face, we don't see a pattern of shapes and colours, contours and so on, we see a person. Eyes are not blobs of flesh to us, they are 'windows' into another entity, sentient like ourselves (and in fact it can be quite disturbing if this perception is fleetingly lost). Emotional expressions carry meanings denoting the mood of that other, and in reading these expressions we gain information about another person's feelings and intentions. Speech, even grunting, is not just an interesting pattern of sound to us but a communication. In other words, we adults have a rich and *meaningful* perception of other people. Newborn babies quite plainly orient to human faces and are attracted by them, imitate them. But do they intuitively 'see' faces as we do? Or are their responses just the result of perceptual reflexes, and devoid of awareness or understanding?

At a bare minimum, babies must be born with some kind of perceptual mechanism already pre-wired to draw their attention to the human face. Otherwise, how could they possibly be attracted to faces above other things within minutes of birth (Mehler et al., 1986), way before there has been time to learn anything about them? But there is no reason that this innate perceptual mechanism need necessarily be very sophisticated. For instance, human faces are more complex and mobile than other stimuli the baby sees. We know that babies' attention is drawn more readily to complex moving stimuli (whatever they may be) than to simple static ones. So it could be that it is only complexity and movement that draws the baby's attention to the human face, not the configuration of the face itself, or any insight into the meaning of a face. However, the evidence shows that this is not the case (Fantz, 1961; Johnson et al., 1991).

That babies are specifically primed to orient to human faces has been demonstrated in studies comparing their reactions to stimuli that vary in their resemblance to a face, such as those shown in **Figure 4.2**. The blank stimulus is substantially less complex or face-like than the other two. The scrambled stimulus has all the same features, and is as complex as the 'face', though it does not resemble the structure of a face. Johnson and colleagues (1991) showed babies these three stimuli, one at a time. Once the baby had begun to look at the stimulus it was moved in a shallow arc so that the baby had to rotate his or her head to go on looking at it. They found that while babies would turn their heads through about 20 degrees to follow the blank stimulus, they would turn about 40 degrees to follow the scrambled one, confirming their preference for complexity. However, babies would turn their head over 50 degrees to follow the face-like stimulus. There is more to the newborn's interest in faces than mere complexity.

Clearly, something about the specific pattern of the features of the human face attracts the baby's attention. But still this need not imply

figure **4.2**

Face-like stimuli

Source: M. Johnson, S. Dziurawiec, H. Ellis and J. Morton, 'Newborns preferential tracking of face-like stimuli and its subsequent decline', *Cognition* vol. 40, pp. 1–19. © 1991. Reproduced with permission from Elsivier Science.

Face   Scrambled   Blank

that there is anything more than a basic perceptual reflex at play, as opposed to an intuitive insight into faces as Trevarthen implies. After all, the face-like stimulus used by Johnson and colleagues is not really all that face-like. That babies treat it as something special implies that their responsiveness to the human face may be triggered by very simple perceptual cues. And in fact, there is evidence that the key factor that babies are primed to orient to is no more sophisticated than a crude pattern of blobs (**Figure 4.3**), two horizontally level and slightly apart, the third centred below them, and all contained in an oval or square frame (Johnson and Morton, 1991; Simion et al., 1998).

Thus there are grounds for supposing that the newborn's interest in faces reflects the action of a simple perceptual mechanism, a pre-wired neural reflex rather than any intuition about what a face actually is. Other species have innate reflexes orienting them to stimuli that are important for their survival. Certain fledglings, for example, freeze at the sight of specific silhouettes or shadows: the silhouettes and shadows

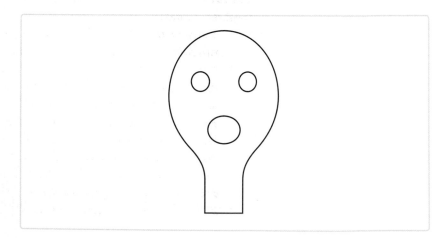

figure **4.3**

The 'face' a baby responds to

of predator hawks (Manning, 1972). For a human baby, other people hold the key to survival. A perceptual reflex orienting the baby to the human eyes and mouth makes sure that babies focus on the most important stimuli in their world. Such a reflex would not only make sure that the baby is looking in the right direction to learn important things about people, but also that he or she is more rewarding to a caregiver, and so more likely to elicit the arduous care that bringing up a baby requires. Who wouldn't prefer to cuddle a baby who gazes into your eyes (for whatever reason), rather than one that stares elsewhere, seemingly showing no interest?

Johnson and Morton (1991) suggested that babies have two distinct neural mechanisms orienting them to the human face. The first (which they called *conspec*) is a crude perceptual reflex which simply attracts the baby's attention to patterns suggestive of eyes and mouth. Conspec operates right from birth. The second more sophisticated system (which they called *conlern*) provides the mechanisms through which the baby can gradually learn to discriminate between different faces and to identify individuals.

The details of Johnson and Morton's theory are complex and controversial. Not all the data we have fit well with this theory. For example, it's clear that 2-day-old babies can reliably identify their mother's face (Bushnell, Sai and Mullin, 1989; Walton, Bower and Bower, 1992), which one would not expect from Johnson and Morton's account of how the conlern mechanism works. Even the claim that it is a pattern of eye/mouth blobs that newborn reflexes respond to has been questioned: for example, work by Cassia, Turati and Simion (2004) suggests that it is the 'top-heavy' nature of the face (with hair and eyes dominating the shape) that attracts attention, rather than internal features in themselves. But the general claim that neonatal face recognition rests on simple perceptual reflexes of some kind is widely accepted.

It's worth emphasizing that it would be a mistake to conclude that we fully understand what these perceptual mechanisms actually are. For example, there is the intriguing discovery that, right from birth, babies prefer to look at attractive faces rather than unattractive ones, just like the rest of us (Slater et al., 1998; Slater et al., 2000). It's not clear how this fits with the idea of a perceptual orientation to faces resting only on a crude detector of eye/mouth patterns or top-heavy structures: the same patterns are present in both attractive and unattractive faces.

Clearly, the newborn's preference for attractive faces must be innate: babies have not yet had time to learn the difference between attractiveness and unattractiveness. What makes a face attractive is its averageness. If you superimpose and average a number of human faces, however attractive or otherwise, you end up with a beautiful face. In other words, beauty reflects the archetypal configuration of the human face. Does the fact that babies respond to this archetype mean that they are innately provided with some sort of perceptual template of it? If so, how does this fit in with other perceptual mechanisms triggering an orientation to face-like stimuli? We don't yet know.

Learning about faces

We don't yet know just what a baby 'sees' when he or she looks at a human face. But the evidence suggests that the newborn orientation to faces is a reaction to a perceptual pattern rather than to the meaning of a face. This conclusion is supported, for instance, by studies of the way babies scan faces. Young babies seem not to know what features of a face are important. Studies of infant's eye movements show that 1-month-old babies scan the outer contour of the head, only glancing at the eyes, as if the significance of the internal features of the face was not yet apparent to them (**Figure 4.4**). Two-month-old babies focus on the inner features, especially fixating on the eyes and mouth, as if they now recognized these as more significant than other features (Maurer and Salapatek, 1976).

This same developmental change is evident in studies of babies recognizing their own mother's face. The newborn orient to gross characteristics such as the outline of the mother's face and her hairline rather than to her facial features, as a 2-month-old baby would. Thus even the newborn can tell the difference between their own mother and another woman with the same hair colour and hair length provided the two women have different hairlines. But put both women in the same wig, and they can't tell who is who (Bushnell et al., 1989), where an older child wouldn't be fooled.

Clearly, by the age of 2 months babies have discovered which parts of the face matter and which don't, but it's far from clear that they understand the meaning of eyes and mouths in any real way. For instance,

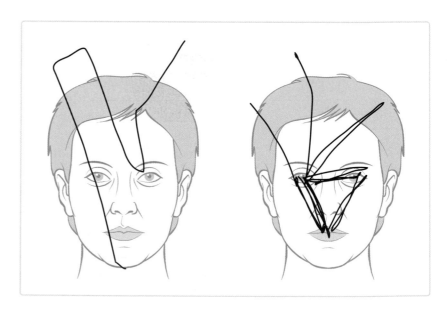

figure 4.4

How a baby scans a face, at age 1 month (left) and 2 months (right)

Source: after D. Maurer and P. Salapatek (1976).

even at 6 months, babies don't follow another person's gaze, don't look to see where the other is looking, as if they still haven't discovered the real significance of the eyes, or understood that the other person can see things (Bushnell et al., 1989).

Real insight into what a face means requires much more than the perceptual ability to distinguish between faces and other things, or the ability to recognize individual faces. It requires insight into what lies behind the face and its expressions. Evidence from other lines of research suggests that these things only begin to develop in the second half of the first year of life.

Distinguishing between living and inanimate things

Somewhere between 7 and 9 months of age, there is a 'revolution' in the baby's understanding of faces and people (Poulin-Dubois, 1999; Tomasello, 1999). For the first time, babies begin to follow someone else's gaze, looking to see what the other person is looking at. For the 7-month-old, the tendency to do this is inconsistent, affected by a variety of factors such as the emotional expression on the other person's face (Flom and Pick, 2005), or where the object the mother is looking at lies, relative to the child (Butterworth and Jarrett, 1991). But by 9 months babies are able to use this *joint attention* more confidently. And at 9 months, babies begin to direct others to look where they themselves are looking, pointing at things for the first time and looking at the other person's eyes to check that they are looking in the right direction.

This new ability to share a focus of attention with someone else, and to coordinate eye contact, vocalization and gestures such as pointing is the first step toward real, intentional communication (Camaioni, 1992; Poulin-Dubois, 1999). It seems to reflect a breakthrough in the infants' understanding of living things, and a consequent recognition that a human being is alive. How is this insight possible?

There is some evidence that babies are innately pre-wired to notice the difference between the way living things and inanimate objects move, even though the data suggest that at 3 months of age, they don't *understand* this difference (Bertenthal, 1993). The data come from studies of babies' reactions to the 'point light' displays shown in Figure 4.5. In each of the four panels shown, the black dots represent lights against a dark background. The lights in panels A and B are lights placed on the head, neck, hip, elbows, knees and feet of a human being, whereas the lights in panel C and D are in random positions.

So long as these point light displays are static (A and C), adults see both patterns as random. But when the lights move as the arrows show (reflecting the movements of a person walking in panel B, and equivalently large but random movements in panel D), adults still see D as random, but see a human form in B, and can identify its action (running, walking, dancing and so on).

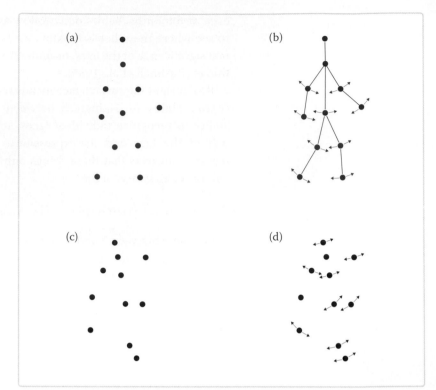

figure **4.5**

Point-light displays

Source: after A. Slater, 'Visual organization in early infancy', in G. Bremner, A.Slater and G. Butterworth (eds) *Infant Development: Recent Advances*. © 1997. Reproduced with permission from Thomson Publishing on behalf of Taylor and Francis Books.

Habituation studies show that 3-month-old babies prefer the pattern suggesting a person in motion to the static patterns or the pattern reflecting random movements, though they respond as if using a perceptual reflex, rather than comprehension of the display (Bertenthal, 1993; Slater, 1997). But by 5 months of age, babies respond to point light displays very much more as an adult would, suggesting that they now beginning to understand the meaning of what they are seeing (Slater, 1997). They have moved from a reflexive interest in certain kinds of movement to a recognition that that pattern of movement indicates a human being.

A reflexive interest in movement, especially the movement of living things, is a very useful thing. It orients the baby to attend to the way things move, and so sets the scene for a crucial discovery. Some things (the supreme instance being people) are self-propelling: that is, they can move themselves. Other things are not self-propelling, and will only move if something else propels them. Associated with this insight is another, still more important one: you have to touch some objects to get them to do things, but people can be controlled and induced to do things without touching them, by making noises, pointing and the like (Poulin-Dubois, 1999; Premack, 1990). It is these insights, which develop between 7 and 9 months of age, that kick off the baby's efforts to share attention and command other people through pointing and vocal gestures.

The change in the baby's behaviour at this point is dramatic. At 9 months, babies now clearly have the *intention* of sharing attention with someone else, and are *deliberately* interacting with another person in a communicative way. This is a giant step forward. But it still need not imply that the baby has much awareness or insight into other people (Moore and Corkum, 1994).

As adults, when we communicate with one another, we understand that we are interacting with a creature that has a mental interior: ideas, goals, beliefs, desires, fears and other emotions. We understand that the 'self propelling' nature of other people, and our ability (sometimes!) to affect how they behave, are mediated by this mental interior. And we understand that, in communicating, we are sharing ideas and feelings with another mind, perhaps influencing the interior state of that mind. But the evidence is that, even at 10 months or more, babies don't understand that communicating involves sharing feelings or ideas with another mind. In fact, the evidence suggests that they still don't understand that mental or emotional states exist at all, either in themselves or anyone else (Poulin-Dubois, 1999). We shall revisit this issue in Chapter 9.

Understanding emotions

Emotional expressiveness

Right from birth, babies use the same facial expressions in response to events as adults do (Darwin, 1877). For instance, they smile a little when offered a sweet liquid, and grimace when offered a bitter one (Ganchrow, Steiner and Daher, 1983). It seems that we don't need to learn to cry when distressed, or to smile when satisfied: these things are innately specified, a conclusion reinforced by the fact that people all around the world, across very different cultures, use the same emotional expressions and can 'read' one another's emotions from facial expressions (Eibl-Eibesfeldt, 1971).

Most mothers believe that they can detect a wide range of primary emotions such as happiness, sadness, interest, surprise, fear, anger or pain on their babies' faces within a few months of birth (Campos et al., 1983). But this conviction may reflect the mother's skill in interpreting the baby's state from the context, rather than the clarity of the baby's expression itself. Independent observers find it easy to tell whether a young baby is basically in a positive or a negative mood simply from his or her facial expression (Izard et al., 1980). But they have difficulty making more subtle distinctions, particularly between negative emotions (Oster, Hegley and Nagel, 1992).

This difficulty in making subtle distinctions between a baby's emotional expressions does not necessarily mean that babies' emotional expressions are less clear than an older child or adults. After all, it can be quite hard to make subtle distinctions between emotions in adult faces, too. Furthermore, emotional experience is seldom pure: that is to say, we are seldom *just* angry or *just* sad (for example). These emotions tend to co-occur, either simultaneously or one swiftly replacing the other, which can make identifying a mood from a facial expression hard. Even babies experience sequences of emotion that shade into one another: a single episode of crying might begin with an angry face that slides into deep distress before subsiding into sadness, for instance (Saarni, Mumme and Campos, 1998).

Nonetheless, very detailed observations of infants suggest that there is some increase in the clarity of emotional expression through the early months of life (Case, 1991; Darwin, 1877). And certainly, there is a clear developmental change in the range of emotions babies express: younger babies express all the primary emotions (happy, sad, angry, afraid and so on), but not the secondary ones (shame, pride, guilt, jealousy and the like).

Feelings and emotions

The developmental change from expressing only primary emotions to expressing secondary ones is revealing. *Primary emotions* such as pain, anger, pleasure, fear and the like reflect very direct reactions to events, and are probably innate. By contrast, *secondary emotions* reflect a more subtle understanding of the world (Barrett and Campos, 1987), and almost certainly develop as the child's social understanding and insight develops. To feel guilt or shame, for example, you have to be able to recognize that your behaviour has betrayed some standard, and this requires a degree of self-awareness, and the ability to reflect on events and compare one situation with another. To feel embarrassed, you have to realize that other people are aware of your shortcomings and are disapproving, which requires an ability to imagine other people's thoughts and feelings. There is very little evidence that infants in the first year of life have the understanding of either themselves or other people that these secondary emotions require (Perner, 1991; Saarni et al., 1998).

The idea that we can't feel certain emotions unless we are capable of certain degrees of conceptual understanding may at first seem strange. We tend to assume that an emotion is a feeling, not a thought. But in fact, the situation may be much more complicated than that, even in the case of primary emotions such as fear or pleasure.

From the early days of research, psychologists have doubted whether feeling is the primary element in any emotion. For example, one of the founding fathers of the discipline, William James (1890), argued that our feelings are always an interpretation of events and actions. Famously, he suggested that we feel afraid because we run away from a predator, rather than that we run away because we are afraid. Another seminal study (Schachter, 1965) reinforced the view that our feelings reflect our interpretations of events, rather than being integral to a given emotional state. In this study, Schachter injected a number of participants with adrenaline, which creates a state of arousal, and asked them to sit in a waiting room for a while 'before taking part in an experiment'. In fact, the waiting was the experiment. Each participant shared the waiting room with a stooge, who behaved either as though waiting was an infuriating imposition or as if it were a pleasurable opportunity to mess about. Participants in the first condition interpreted their high arousal as anger, where those in the second condition interpreted it as pleasure, even though the underlying physiological condition was the same: it had been created by the same dose of adrenaline.

There are a great many criticisms of Schachter's study, but it serves to illustrate an important point: a particular physiological state of the kind associated with emotion can be given different interpretations, and it can be these interpretations that generate the 'feeling', rather than the underlying physiological state itself.

The idea that feeling might arise from interpretation rather than being the fundamental element in an emotional reaction raises some interesting questions. For instance, newborn babies lack the conceptual ability to interpret events. Does this mean that they do not feel emotions as we do? A number of researchers have argued exactly that, claiming that newborns do not *feel* happy when they smile, nor angry when they yell (Lewis and Michalson, 1983; Sroufe, 1979). According to such theorists, emotional feelings only become possible when the baby has started to make sense of the world, and in particular, to become aware of him or herself as a definite entity, at around 9 months of age. It is this increasing conceptual understanding that allows the baby to reflect on events, to begin to differentiate and interpret interactions with the world and so to subjectively experience (feel) his or her own emotional states.

But this view of the young baby as unable to feel emotions raises a new problem: even the newborn can *express* emotions – only too clearly! If these emotional expressions don't reflect feeling, what are they and how do they occur?

Some theorists in this area suggest that the physiological responses that express our emotions (from the clamminess of our skin, the rate of our heartbeat, the levels of our hormones to the contraction or relaxation of certain muscles in the body and face) are reflexively tied to the neurological systems that manage our goals and motivations. When our goals are met, our physiology automatically responds in one way. When our goals are frustrated, the physiological reflex responds differently (Saarni et al., 1998). Through such a reflex mechanism, emotional *expression* need not necessarily be associated with emotional *feeling*. A newborn baby could, through such a mechanism, express primary emotions just as adults do even if he or she cannot interpret or reflect on events, and even if, without such interpretation, the baby cannot feel the emotion being expressed as an adult would. Even newborn babies have simple goals (comfort versus discomfort, for example).

However, the view that young babies don't feel emotions is controversial. It rests on a very simplistic view of how emotions 'work', in any of us. For instance, shape your face into a smile. Sit like that a while. You'll probably notice that just the act of smiling makes you feel a tad happier. There's an old adage that says 'the mood of your day follows the corners of your mouth', and there's a degree of truth in that. In other words, the evidence is that the *feeling* associated with an emotion is generated by the physical expression of that emotion, without rhyme or reason, let alone insight or interpretation of the situation. Saarni and colleagues (1998) argue that there is no reason to suppose that newborn babies cannot feel emotions in this way, given that they have innate neurological mechanisms that produce facial expressions and other physiological responses.

But the view that even newborn babies can feel primary emotions does not mean that there is no developmental change in the subjective experience or expression of these emotions through infancy. Many aspects of emotional experience, expressivity, reactivity, and later, even the way emotions are categorized and named, are affected by the beliefs and practices of the society or culture in which a baby is raised (Parke and Buriel, 1998; Saarni et al., 1998). As the examples in **Box 4.1** show, our experience of emotions is 'socially constructed': that is to say, guided and directed through interactions with other people, rather than being a simple reflection of individual or innate inner states.

Understanding and sharing emotions

One striking thing about very young babies is that they imitate other people's emotional expressions (Kugiumutzakis, 1999; Meltzoff and Moore, 1977). This phenomenon is universal. It occurs in newborn babies in cultures all round the world, and is generally accepted as reflecting an innate predisposition to imitate.

This innate imitation is very curious. It occurs before babies have seen their own face, before they can have learned the connection between certain movements of their muscles (tongue and lip movements) and the visual effect (protruding tongue). The implication is that we are somehow pre-wired to make these connections between perception and action in relation to facial expressions (Gibson, 1979; Neisser, 1991; Rochat, 1995), again supporting the view that there is a complex innate neurological system at work here. And in fact, very recent research (Dapretto et al., 2006; Stefan et al., 2005) has identified a specific neural system, the *mirror neuron system*, which may well be the innate mechanism through which the imitation of emotional expressions occurs. (We shall explore this in detail in Chapter 9.)

Whatever the origin of this imitation, it provides babies with a primitive means of 'sharing' someone else's emotions. As we saw earlier, making a face (a happy face, say) is enough to induce the emotional feeling associated with that facial expression. So by imitating your facial

Many aspects of emotional expression and experience are universal: for example, facial expressions are the same across all human societies. But cultural practices and mores also affect emotional development in various ways.

For example, cultures differ in whether they swaddle infants or not, whether adults share a bed with the infant, and in how vigorously the baby is handled. These cultural differences have different effects on the infant's emotional development.

Swaddling babies so that their movements are restricted encourages calm and passivity, where allowing a baby to move freely fosters more activity and emotional volatility. Co-sleeping with babies encourages closer emotional ties to the parent, where sleeping alone in a crib fosters more independence. Babies who experience light tossing and vigorous handling in the first few months of life are less fearful than those handled more delicately.

Equally, cultures differ in the forms of interaction they encourage or discourage. For instance, Western cultures enjoy eye contact, and mothers hold their babies where eye contact is easiest, fostering warm and lively exchanges. Certain African societies actively disapprove of eye contact, holding babies so that eye contact is impossible, and thereby fostering a cool, subdued emotional tone in their infants.

Furthermore, cultures differ in the overall emotional climate they support. Some cultures are loud, expressive, readily moved to laughter, tears, hugs or bellows of rage. Other cultures foster a controlled 'stiff upper lip'. Some cultures present a generally gentle, approving emotional atmosphere, where others project more hostility and criticism. The emotional climate babies live in affects what they take to be normal, what model of emotionality they internalize. Babies in expressive cultures tend to be expressive, whereas those in restrained cultures tend to be controlled. The prevailing atmosphere sets the tone for the child's dominant moods, so that babies in tense, hostile social contexts become anxious and insecure.

expression, a baby can at the very least experience the emotion you are expressing in parallel with you. This process is called *emotional resonancing* or *emotional contagion.*

It's worth noting that emotional contagion is not enough to provide real empathy with the person being copied. A baby imitating a sad face and feeling sad as a consequence is feeling his or her own emotion, not the other person's. This effect can happen even if the baby has no awareness of the significance of the other person's emotional expression, no insight into what the other person may be feeling, no understanding even that the other person can feel at all. The research suggests that this profound lack of insight is exactly the situation for the newborn.

The data strongly suggest that babies don't understand the significance of facial expressions. Within a few days of birth, they can tell the difference between one primary emotional expression (happy, sad) and another (Field et al., 1982). By 7 months of age, they are adept at making such discriminations (Soken and Pick, 1999). But the evidence suggests that even 7-month-olds are making these distinctions on the basis of crude perceptual clues rather than recognizing the emotional meaning of expressions. For example, at 4 months of age, babies can easily tell the difference between a face with visible teeth and one without. This is often enough to allow the baby to distinguish between primary emotional expressions: we tend to expose our teeth when smiling and cover them when sad. But teeth can be misleading! Babies can't tell the difference between a happy and a sad expression if the smile doesn't expose the teeth (Oster, 1981). Such subtleties are learned with time. Even at 9 months, babies can't differentiate between a toothy smile and teeth bared in anger (Caron, Caron and Myers, 1982).

The view that young babies don't understand facial expressions is supported by data that show that, at 4 months of age, they find frowning faces as attractive as smiling ones (Nelson, 1987; Walker-Andrews, 1997), as if the meaning of the expression had no importance or relevance to them. Only from about 7 months of age do babies begin to behave as if other people's emotional expressions mattered in any way, beginning to prefer to look at a smiling face rather than a frowning one (Soken and Pick, 1999).

It seems, then, that babies have to learn the significance of facial expressions. At first this seems surprising: couldn't even a young baby work out what an expression means, given the direct information available from emotional resonancing? But recognizing a facial expression as denoting an emotion is a complex thing. The significance of a facial expression lies in the fact that it indicates an interior emotional state. To understand this, babies must understand that other people have interior emotional states. The evidence is that this insight only begins to emerge around the second birthday (Perner, 1991; see Chapter 9). Thus it seems that babies up to the age of 18 months can't really understand other people's emotions, and can't really empathize with them as older children and adults can.

Signalling and communicating with emotions

Babies are utterly dependent on adult carers for their survival. They have no means of communicating their needs to those carers except through emotional expressions such as crying or smiling. There need be no *intention* of communicating on the baby's part: a reflexive cry in the face of cold or hunger would bring help from the carer, and smiling and reflexively imitating bring pleasurable social interactions and cuddles, whatever the baby did or didn't intend.

Like any other living creature, babies learn the association between one thing and another very rapidly. If reflexive crying brings food or warmth, the reflex will gradually become an 'operant'[1] tool to fetch those

---

[1] See the section on Skinner and learning theory in Chapter 1.

things, and so gradually become a deliberate signal. Note that babies can learn to use emotional expressions as signals in this way purely by associating an action with a result, without having any insight into the fact that they are communicating with another living being. (It's interesting to speculate on how this kind of process helps the child to discover the different effects of yelling at people and inanimate objects discussed earlier, and so eventually helps the discovery of the possibility of communication.)

Late in the first year of life babies also begin to use other people's emotional expressions as signals, a process known as *social referencing* (Feinman, 1982). For example, Sorce and colleagues (1985) showed that babies looked at their mother's faces for 'advice' as to whether it would be safe to crawl across a glass surface over an apparent drop in Gibson's 'visual cliff' task (described in Chapter 3, Figure 3.1). Twelve-month-old babies would not cross the glass if the mother's face expressed anger or anxiety, but would cross it if the mother looked interested or happy.

Social referencing is a common phenomenon of infancy, becoming particularly clear and important as the baby begins to become mobile, crawling off to explore the world independently. From this stage and right through early childhood, babies will typically look back and check on their mothers or care takers from time to time as they explore, reacting to their expression and using it as a guide to their actions. And as babies become more mobile, mothers use their emotional expressions more deliberately to convey information to the child, exaggerating a frown or look of anxiety, for example, to stop an infant in mid-(undesirable) action.

We don't yet entirely understand what the infant's ability to use other people's emotional expressions in this way implies, or how it develops. For instance, does emotional contagion play a role in the ability to use social referencing, so that the baby is put off crawling over the glass in Sorce and colleagues' study by his or her own feelings of anxiety, acquired by sharing (imitating) the mother's facial expression? Do babies progressively learn to associate their mother's facial expressions with good or bad outcomes, and so gradually coming to give a significance to her emotional expression? Do both processes work together? Given their lack of insight into other minds, it seems unlikely that babies of 12 months realize that the mother is feeling anxious. But do the phenomena of social referencing and learning to associate a look with an outcome contribute to the child's future discovery that the mother has feelings?

Insight into other minds requires complex knowledge of many kinds: knowledge that goes on developing for a lifetime, as the frequent misunderstandings about motives and meanings that undermine even adult relationships demonstrate! Understanding other minds is a long, hard journey, to which we shall return in Chapter 9. One crucial first step in understanding other people is the ability to recognize them as beings like ourselves. To do this, we must obviously have at least some conception of 'self'.

Developing a concept of self

Our sense of self is the defining centre of social, emotional and personal development. It is our awareness of self that creates 'personhood' and allows us to organize our subjective experience and our understanding of and relationships to others (Bretherton, 1991; Cassidy, 1990).

What is the 'self'?

At one level, we all know what we mean by 'self'. But things are more complex than we suppose. For example, William James (1890, 1892) pointed out that our sense of self has two major and quite distinct components. There is the *I-self*, the self that is characterized by my subjective experience and by my sense of having a continuous identity across situations and through time. This is the self that directly engages the world, acting in pursuit of goals and reacting to events. Then there is the *me-self*, the self I can reflect on and whose characteristics I can discover and describe – that I am female, for example, quite tall, Lillian's friend, mostly quite kind. James suggested that the me-self is multifaceted, comprising the *material self* defined by my appearance, possessions, job and so on; the *social self*, or rather our many social selves, each brought into being by the self created in social interaction with particular others: the responsible citizen reflected in my neighbour's eyes, the reassuring companion reflected in my child's eyes, the half-wit I am in the eyes of most car mechanics, and so on; and there is the *spiritual self*, which James considered to be the heart of self, comprising the attitudes and values that provide continuity and meaning to our interactions with the world. James's analysis of the nature of the self has become increasingly influential over the past 30 years, particularly in research on the origins of the self in early infancy (Lewis, 1994; Lewis and Brooks-Gunn, 1979).

Studying the origins of 'self' in infancy

How can we study the origins of self-awareness in infancy? How, for that matter, can we study consciousness (*self*-consciousness) at any age? It's very difficult to devise methodologies that will allow us to measure or probe the secret world of individual subjectivity: hardest of all when our subjects are babies, unable to answer questions or share our assumptions about what the relevant questions are, or what the answers 'ought' to look like[2] (Harter, 1998). All our evidence is indirect: a matter of drawing inferences from data, of putting two and two together across different research studies, studies with different aims.

There is a great deal of theory about the development of the self concept in infancy. Little of this is supported by *direct* empirical

---

[2] See Chapter 10 for a discussion of how our social expectations affect the answer to such questions.

evidence, although all of it has roots in research. In evaluating it for yourself, you're going to need a new critical skill. You must move beyond looking for an authoritative experiment that will justify this claim or that. You must move to the higher ground of asking, does the story this theory tells make sense? Is it internally consistent, does it fit with the information we have in other areas? Does it offer an adequate explanation of the phenomena in question? For the pure empiricist, the absence of direct experimental tests is unnerving. But the truth is that many (if not most) of the *interesting* questions for science cannot be resolved by a quick experimental test. The ability to evaluate speculative theories in a rigorous way, to cross-reference claims in one area with research in another, is vital to mature science, and to critical reasoning. It's vital to understanding the origins of the self-concept in infancy.

Explaining the origins of 'self' in infancy

You will often read statements such as 'Children first become self-aware at about 18 months.' The evidence suggests that this is a gross over-simplification, ignoring a fascinating process that brings together many of the phenomena of social, emotional and personal development. There are three elements to this process which begin at different times through infancy, but all of which go on developing throughout infancy and childhood, and indeed, to some extent through our whole lives (Thompson, 1998; and see Chapter 10).

Discovering a consistent self (from birth onwards)

The most basic sense of self is an awareness of my direct and immediate experiences: for example, of being *cold and wet, hungry and tired.* Even the youngest baby has this primal experience of self.

Older children and adults have a subjective sense of self that includes but transcends this primal response to this one moment. We can integrate this subjective state with others, fitting it into a broader pattern that gives perspective to our present reaction. We know what is likely to come next, and how our present experience of self will change as a consequence. Our sense of self is thus integrated across different situations, reflecting familiar patterns rather than one-off events, and providing a sense of a consistent identity in different contexts. None of this is true for the newborn baby.

Newborn babies are notoriously unpredictable and inconsistent. There is no timetable to their lives, no regularity in when they sleep, eat, defecate and so on. The first 6 weeks of a baby's life are in fact disorganized enough to challenge any nearby adult's sense of having a coherent existence! Certainly, there is not enough pattern or consistency to provide the baby with a consistent sense of self. For the very young baby, therefore, subjective experience is limited to the immediate: to what is happening *now*. There is no sense of self that transcends the moment (Harter, 1998).

Gradually through the first 6 weeks of life babies become more regular and predictable in their habits. This regularity creates patterns of experience: just what is needed for the infant to begin developing a sense of self that transcends any one moment, a sense of self as a coherent, consistent entity (Harter, 1998). This allows the beginning of a recognition of the integrity of the 'I-self'.

Notice that the regularities and rhythms of life that create the baby's sense of a consistent self at this stage are not controlled by the baby. Mothers (or other primary carers) provide the structure and pattern of the baby's life, even if they adapt their own rhythms somewhat to match the baby's. The regularities of the baby's subjective experience are created in the social interaction between mother and child, so that the child's I-self is deeply embedded in the symbiotic relationship with the mother. In other words, what babies experience of themselves is inextricably intertwined with what they experience of the mother.

The notion that our core concept of ourselves grows out of our symbiotic interactions with others is at the centre of many powerful theories of the development of self-awareness (Baldwin, 1895, 1906; Cooley, 1925; Mead, 1934). Most researchers believe that, from the very beginning, our concept of our self is *socially constructed*.

This basic sense of self as consistent and coherent, as a predictable entity with certain characteristics, continues to grow throughout infancy. In a profound way, the first step to experiencing self depends on understanding the self as a 'permanent' being, persistent across contexts. This understanding of 'person permanence' (of the self, of others) is initially shaky, just as the baby's ability to respond to objects as 'permanent' is shaky (Chapter 3). An understanding of person and object permanence develop together through the first year of life, fostering the emerging sense of 'self'.

Discovering 'self as agent' (from 4 months on)

At first, babies are more or less completely helpless: they are utterly dependent on other people to move, to eat, to be comfortable or uncomfortable, to survive or die. Their sense of self is utterly defined by the patterns other people create in serving or failing these needs. But between 4 and 9 months of age, babies begin to make a marvellous discovery: they are not completely powerless! In fact, they can influence events (Bertenthal and Fischer, 1978; Lewis and Brooks-Gunn, 1979; Stern, 1985). This discovery gives the baby a sense of personal efficacy that is highly gratifying (Case, 1991), and that creates a new sense of *self-as-agent* (Bandura, 1990).

In part, of course, this discovery depends on the baby's growing conceptual ability to recognize cause and effect: to recognize that *this* action caused *that* effect, and that by doing the same thing again 'I' can produce the same result. But it is also importantly encouraged by social interactions with the child's family or caretakers. Games such as 'peek-a-boo', or the one where the baby chucks everything out the pram and you pick it up again (over and over) foster this potent sense of agency, as does the parent's encouragement when the baby tries to help out with everyday activities, clutching the spoon or the food, holding an arm helpfully for dressing, and so on.

Experience of the self-as-agent grows alongside, merges with, builds on and contributes to the self-as-consistent. As these attributes of the 'I-self' develop, babies become more assertive, more demanding and more picky, increasingly frustrated when their efforts to control events fail. This phenomenon reaches its peak as the toddler approaches 18 months, and the start of the 'terrible 2s'.

Discovering the me-self (as the child approaches 18 months)

Self as consistent and as agent are very direct subjective experiences: states of being characteristic of the I-self. The me-self is a later development, involving a more self-conscious and reflective process, a reflection less on our subjective state and more on our attributes (for example, what we look like, whether we're lovable). This me-self is only just beginning to emerge as the child reaches 18 months.

The classic test of a child's me-awareness is the *rouge test* (Berten-thal and Fischer, 1978; Lewis and Brooks-Gunn, 1979). The baby sits in front of a mirror for a short period. Then, under pretext of wiping the child's face, the experimenter puts a dab of rouge on the child's nose, and puts the child back by the mirror. In Lewis and Brooks-Gunn's study, the majority of 2-year-olds immediately put their hands up to their nose when they spot the rouge, but no babies under the age of 12 months did so. Fewer than 20 per cent of 15-month-olds touched their noses, and only 25 per cent of 18-month-olds did so. It seems that awareness of what we look like is only just beginning to emerge at 18 months.

Some of the things that define the me-self (such as what I look like) are discovered directly through the child's own observations. Others (such as whether I am good and lovable or not) develop from interactions with other people. As we've seen earlier, the young baby's experience of even the I-self is at first deeply embedded in a symbiotic relationship with the mother. The young infant experiences what Emde (1988) calls a 'we-self', reflecting the properties of the relationship rather than the individuals involved (for example, 'Mummy always cuddles me when I'm sad'). Gradually this symbiotic perspective is teased apart, so that the child can reflect on properties of the two individuals involved ('mummy is kind/I am lovable') and thus begin to understand the social me-self. This differentiation may occur implicitly, before the child can describe it in words (Bretherton, 1991; Cassidy, 1990). The me-self disentangled from such relationships is the basis for our self-esteem, our evaluation of who we are and how important we are in the world, whether we matter or are insignificant.

Thus key elements of who we believe ourselves to be are 'socially constructed' (Cooley, 1925). That is to say, the social me-self is a reflection of 'me' in someone else's eyes rather than a property of the individual in themselves. It's as much a product of that other person as of me. A relationship with someone who values and respects the child will produce a social me-self that confidently believes in its own worth. A relationship in which a child is criticized and devalued will produce a social me-self with a negative self-image. The spiritual me-self, too, has its roots in the relationships the child experiences in infancy (Kochanska, 1993). The symbiotic relationship between parent and child, in which the parent provides the structure and the child connects through emotional contagion and social referencing, gives rise to shared views of what is good or bad, fun or frightening and so on. Here are the roots of values, and the origins of conscience. Thus early social relationships are of immense importance in personal and emotional development.

Social relationships in infancy: attachment and development

Typically, the most important and influential relationship for any child is with his or her mother. Sigmund Freud believed that the mother–child relationship is 'unique, without parallel, established unalterably for a whole lifetime as the first and strongest love-object and as the prototype of all later love relationships' (Freud, 1940). Coming from a very different theoretical background (see Chapter 1), John Bowlby (1953) agreed.

Bowlby's theory of attachment

Bowlby was a psychiatrist much concerned with the highly disturbed children coming through orphanages after the Second World War. These children showed severe emotional damage, damage very like that produced in other young primates deprived of their mothers (Harlow and Zimmerman, 1959). Work by ethologists such as Konrad Lorenz had shown that young goslings (for instance) were innately primed to bond with the mother during a critical period shortly after birth (Chapter 1). Bowlby suggested that human babies, too, have a biological drive to bond with one significant other (the mother), and that the existence of such an attachment, particularly between the ages of 6 months and 3 years, is essential to healthy emotional and personal development (Bowlby, 1953, 1969). According to Bowlby, deprivation of this bond (*maternal deprivation*), whether through the complete absence of such a bond or even through the separations involved in daycare or hospitalizations for childhood illness, would cause irreparable long-term damage to the child's emotional health.

Bowlby argued that infant attachments develop through four phases:

- Phase 1: *pre-attachment* (0 to 2 months). During this initial phase, the baby responds socially to anyone, without showing any preference for one person over another.

- Phase 2: *early attachment* (2 to 7 months). Gradually through this period the baby begins to discriminate between different people, and begins to form preferences for one person over another. By the end of the period, babies smile more readily at the preferred person (mother), and are more easily comforted by them.

- Phase 3: *attachment* (7 months to 2 or 3 years). By 7 to 9 months, babies show a clear preferences for their care givers (mothers), protesting if separated from them (*separation anxiety*). They become wary of strangers, shy of interacting with them (*stranger anxiety*). These two forms of anxiety are the behaviours that mark the existence of a real attachment.

- Phase 4: *partnership* (from 2 or 3 years). Whereas younger children use their attachment partners very much as a resource, by 2 or 3 years of age, a relationship of greater reciprocity is developing, with the child accommodating to the other's needs too.

Bowlby's theory has received a great deal of criticism. First, its roots in ethology turn out to be far less secure than Bowlby supposed. The kind of bonding observed in goslings doesn't occur in primates, whether human or not (**Box 4.2**). Furthermore, the emotional damage caused by maternal deprivation in Harlow's studies is not irreversible (Novak, 1979): other attachments later in life can, in the right circumstances, undo this damage. These discoveries were taken to undermine Bowlby's claims for an innate biological basis for bonding, and for a special relationship with the mother.

This kind of criticism may cause us to look more closely at the biological bases of attachment, but it doesn't really damage the core of Bowlby's theory. The data we have today overwhelmingly suggest that human babies are indeed innately primed to orient to and interact with other people: strong evidence for a biological drive to be social, even if the achievement of attachment also reflects conceptual development (such as person permanence, the development of the distinction between self and other).

Far more open to criticism is Bowlby's emphasis on the importance of the mother in a child's life. At one level, this thesis has had powerful practical effects, to the benefit of babies and children. For example, the practice of separating babies from mothers at birth or when the child is hospitalized for an illness has changed so that mothers are now allowed to stay with the child, undoubtedly relieving many a sick child of a great deal of distress. But the implication that mothers are somehow special and should stay home with their children rather than using daycare has been far more controversial. It wasn't what feminist women wanted to hear, and the evidence doesn't really support Bowlby's view, either (**Box 4.3**).

box 4.2

Bonding

Studies of certain animal species suggested that there is a 'critical period' shortly after birth during which infants become instinctively bonded to their mothers and vice versa, creating a relationship vital to the physical and emotional survival of the infant. At one time it was believed that this *early bonding* also occurs in human beings. Beliefs of this sort led to the practice of keeping mother and baby together in the first hours after birth, to facilitate the formation of such bonds.

However, recent research has cast considerable doubt on this theory. Although human babies can recognize their mother's voice at birth, and quickly learn to recognize her face, there is no evidence that they are particularly attached to the mother in the early months of life. In fact, babies don't form particular preferences for one person over another until around 7 months of age. Up until then, they are happy to be handled by almost anyone. The evidence suggests that 'early bonding' does not occur in human babies, or in the young of other primate species.

Klaus and Kennell (1976) suggested that even if babies do not bond to their mothers, mothers bond to their babies. Their study showed that mothers with access to their babies immediately after birth formed deeper and more effective attachments to their babies than mothers whose infants were separated from them (as had been the norm in many maternity hospitals). The benefits of this early bonding were claimed to be visible up to a year later. However, Klaus and Kennell's study involved only a small number of women, and had methodological flaws. Efforts to replicate their results in better studies have generally failed to find any effect at all, or have found only small or transient effects (Myers, 1984).

Thus despite its continuing hold on the popular imagination, early bonding between human mothers and babies now seems more myth than reality.

The idea that there is something special about the relationship between a child and his or her mother that cannot be replaced by anyone else turns out to be both right and wrong. There is nothing special about the mother herself, when it comes to forming attachments. Babies can and do form primary attachments to other people besides the mother, such as fathers, siblings, grandparents, foster or adoptive parents, carers, and these attachments can serve the child's emotional development just as well as attachment to the mother. The fact that in most cultures, the primary caregiver and attachment partner turns out to be the mother reflects economics, politics, social norms and practicalities as much as biology. Nevertheless, there is something special about early attachments. How successfully a child forms such an attachment does indeed play a crucial role in shaping the child's emotional development (Ainsworth, 1973), creating effects that can last a lifetime. It's the fact that these attachments *happen*, usually, to be to the mother that makes mothers special.

Bowlby's emphasis on the importance of one primary attachment has also been widely criticized. Many researchers believe that social and emotional development actually occurs in the context of a number of different relationships rather than just one. These various relationships form a *social network* in which the child experiences attachments of

box **4.3**

Daycare, development and the growth
of love

Bowlby's claim that babies need their mothers to be home with them for the first 3 years of life has caused a great deal of heart searching. Almost all women want the very best for their baby. But economic circumstances, personal aspirations and the like mean that not all women can stay home for those 3 years without a major sacrifice. Who pays the bigger price? Does a baby in daycare necessarily suffer, as Bowlby suggested?

The data in Table 4.2 seem to support Bowlby's position: American babies in daycare seem to be less securely attached – with all that that implies – than babies reared at home with their mothers. But these data hide a multitude of complexities. And there is more to development than attachment.

A major study by the National Institute of Child Health and Development in the United States has found that security of attachment to the mother is not affected by daycare unless the child spends many hours of the week in poor-quality daycare, and the mother is also relatively insensitive to the infant's needs. It's maternal sensitivity that predicts the growth of love, rather than daycare of itself.

Some researchers have argued that daycare may actually have benefits for the infant: for example, in promoting better cognitive and social development through providing a more stimulating environment than a mother at home can sustain (Lamb, 1998). Such benefits do occur, where the quality of daycare is high, and the socio-economic status and education of the mother is low. Overall, it's the quality of care that matters, not who provides it.

different intensities and forms with different people (Lamb, 2005; Lewis, 2005). Many researchers would agree that a focus on the social network rather than on a primary attachment provides a broader understanding of social development, particularly after the age of 18 months (see Chapters 10 and 11).

For all the criticisms levelled against it, Bowlby's concept of attachment still dominates research on social development in infancy, and still provides us with powerful insights (Lamb, 2005; Thompson, 1998; Waters, Corcoran and Anafarta, 2005). The notion that early attachments are vital for emotional development fits very well with more recent research on the ways in which concepts of reality, self and other are socially constructed in the interactions between parent and child. The four phases of the development of attachment Bowlby described occur across a wide range of cultures and social contexts (Ainsworth, 1973), suggesting that the process of attachment formation is the universal human mechanism through which these social constructions of self and other arise. At the same time, analysis of the different effects of different degrees of success in forming such attachments offers valuable insights into how a universal developmental process (attachment) can yield a diversity of emotional and personal development across individuals.

Measuring the quality of attachment

The principal procedure for measuring attachment is the 'strange situation' (Ainsworth et al., 1978), which provides the opportunity for observing whether infants display the key markers of attachment: namely separation anxiety and stranger anxiety, together with evidences of trust.

In this procedure, a mother and baby spend a few minutes alone together in an experimental room full of toys. A stranger enters, sits to one side for a few moments, then tries to engage the child in play. The mother then leaves, and the stranger continues to try to play with the infant for a while, then stops. The mother returns, and the stranger sneaks out. The mother then leaves too, so that the child is alone. The stranger returns and tries to settle the child, then sits quietly for a few minutes. The mother then returns, the stranger leaves, and the mother sits with her baby for a few minutes. The whole procedure takes about 20 minutes.

Using this procedure, Ainsworth found three patterns of attachment: types A, B and C. A fourth has subsequently been identified, type D (Main and Soloman, 1990). These are:

- *Insecure avoidant (type A)*: the child is subtly avoidant of the mother, often turning away from her or ignoring her while she is in the room. These children are not particularly distressed when the mother leaves, and greet her only casually or not at all when she returns. Greetings are mingled with avoidance: turning away, moving away.

- *Secure attachment (type B)*: the baby uses the mother as a base from which to explore the toys in the room, returning to her or glancing at her from time to time. The child is usually (but not always) distressed when the mother leaves the room. But when the mother returns, these children greet her and are clearly pleased to see her. If they were upset during her absence, they go to her for comfort and are easily calmed, often quickly resuming their exploration again.

- *Insecure resistant (type C)*: The child is clingy throughout the session, hanging onto the mother rather than exploring the room. These infants are very distressed when the mother leaves, and cling to her firmly when she returns – but resist the mother's efforts to comfort them. For example, they may demand to get on the mother's knee, but having got there, squirm to get down. Their orientation to the mother is highly ambivalent.

- *Disorganized (type D)*: these children don't fit into any of Ainsworth's categories. They seem to be simply disoriented by the strange situation, unable to cope, sometimes freezing or giving up on an action part-way through. Their behaviour is often contradictory: for example, they might approach the mother while smiling fearfully and looking away from her. They may even approach the mother backwards. It's as if the child simultaneously wants to approach and avoid the mother, both needing her and fearing her.

These four types of attachment appear to be universal: babies from cultures all round the world can be categorized in the same way (see

Table 4.2). In most cultures, secure attachments predominate, and disorganized attachments are rare. However, as the figures in Table 4.2 show, the proportion of each type of attachment varies between one culture or social situation and another.

It's particularly interesting to note the results for Germany and Japan in this figure, by comparison with Britain, the United States and each other. Germany produces the highest number of insecure-avoidant attachments. Japan produces an unusually high number of insecure-resistant attachments. The implications of these cross-cultural differences are unclear. Do they reflect cultural differences which affect the accuracy of the strange situation as an assessment of attachment (Levine and Miller, 1990)? Or do they reflect cultural differences in parenting strategy that produce different patterns of attachment (Grossmann et al., 1985)? The issue is hard to resolve.

For example, German mothers actively encourage their babies to become more separate and independent at 12 months of age, which might produce more insecurity as these young children struggle with the challenge, or might mean that the German infants were simply more self-sufficient in the strange research situation and so appeared more avoidant. Similarly, the extreme clinginess and distress of so many Japanese babies might arise because Japanese babies are seldom or never

table 4.2 Distribution of attachment styles across cultures

Source: modified from R. Thompson, Early sociopersonality development. In N. Eisenberg (ed.), W. Damon (series ed.), *Handbook of Child Psychology*, vol. 3: *Social, Emotional and Personal Development*, 5th edn. © 1998. Reproduced with permission from John Wiley & Sons.

Country	Type A %	Type B %	Type C %	Type D/ unclassifiable %	N
Great Britain	22	75	3	0	72
Germany	49	32	12	7	49
Netherlands	34	66	0	0	41
USA (middle class)	16	69	14	0	43
USA (low income, high risk)	22	55	23	0	212
USA (early daycare)	23	57	21	0	58
USA (home reared)	12	76	12	0	91
USA (Chinese Americans)	25	50	25	0	36
USA (low income Hispanics)	30	50	20	0	50
USA (low income recent immigrants)	32	32	37	24	93
Japan	0	68	32	0	60
Chile	23	50	22	0	40

parted from their mothers, and so basically panic in the unnervingly unfamiliar context of the strange situation; or it could be that the constant proximity of the child as the mother goes about her daily work means that her attention to the child is intermittent, producing an insecure-resistant attachment.

Questions such as these underline the fact that any way of measuring a phenomenon may have limitations or drawbacks. For this sort of reason, other ways of measuring attachment have been developed. The chief of these is the *Q sort* (Vaughn and Waters, 1990). Here, an observer records descriptions of an infant's behaviour across different situations, which could be both in the home and in other locations. These descriptions are then compared with descriptions typical of the various types of attachment, to arrive at a conclusion about the child's attachment. This procedure endorses the existence of the four basic types of attachment. It produces scores that correlate with those produced in the strange situation, although the correlation is not perfect.

What causes secure or insecure attachments?

The principal influence on the quality of a child's attachment appears to be the sensitivity of the adult partner to the child's needs. Mothers who interpret their baby's behaviour accurately and respond swiftly and effectively tend to have securely attached children. Mothers who are less sensitive to their children's needs produce insecure, or in extreme cases disorganized, attachments.

A study by Van den Boom and Hoeksma (1994) assessed the way mothers interacted with their infants at home. Mothers who typically ignored crying for long periods and seldom approached or cuddled the baby when soothing tended to produce babies who were insecure-avoidant at age 12 months. Mothers whose response was very inconsistent, so that sometimes they would respond swiftly and effectively to the baby's cries and sometimes either ignore crying or respond ineffectively (often upsetting the child further) tended to produce babies who were insecure-resistant at 12 months.

It's easy to see how an unresponsive mother could foster avoidance in her child, creating a distant relationship in which the child does not rely on her. It's equally easy to see how an inconsistent mother could create ambivalence in her child, a basic doubt whether the mother will be supportive or not. That the maternal behaviour, rather than anything else, is responsible for the child's insecure attachment is demonstrated by the fact that retraining these mothers to intervene more reliably and effectively improved the situation, moving babies into secure type B attachments (Van den Boom, 1994).

Disorganized (type D) attachments also arise from the mother's insensitivity toward her baby. In this case, the insensitivity is extreme: it may involve actual abuse or neglect, or derive from serious mental illness in the mother. Recent research has identified a link between disorganized attachments and 'borderline personality disorder' (Hobson et al., 2005). The features of this disorder are shown in **Box 4.4**. Mothers who exhibit these characteristics present an extreme form of inconsistency. Such a person exhibits wild and unpredictable mood swings and changes in behaviour, a ready paranoid interpretation of events. This is the kind of person of whom adults say, 'You never know where you are, or what to expect.' Intuitively, it makes sense that such a mother would produce a baby who is both fearful of her and drawn to her, whose attachment is utterly confused. It is also sadly not surprising that infants with disorganized attachment often themselves exhibit borderline personality disorder later in life (Holmes, 2005).

box **4.4**

Characteristics of 'borderline personality disorder'

Source: *Quick reference to the diagnostic criteria from DSM-IV* © 2000. Reproduced with permission from the APA.

A pervasive pattern of instability of interpersonal relationships, self-image and affects, and marked impulsivity beginning by early adulthood and present in a variety of contexts, as indicated by five (or more) of the following:

- frantic efforts to avoid real or imagined abandonment
- a pattern of unstable and intense personal relationships characterized by alternating between extremes of idealization and devaluation
- identity disturbance: markedly persistent unstable self-image or sense of self
- impulsivity in at least two areas that are potentially self-damaging (e.g. spending, sex, substance abuse, reckless driving, binge eating)
- recurrent suicidal behaviour, gestures, threats or self-mutilating behaviour
- affective instability due to marked reactivity of mood (e.g. intense episodic dysphoria, irritability or anxiety usually lasting a few hours and rarely more than a few days)
- chronic feelings of emptiness
- inappropriate intense anger or difficulty controlling anger (e.g. frequent displays of temper, constant anger, recurrent physical fights)
- transient stress-related paranoid ideation or severe dissociative symptoms.

Attachment and development

Attachment relationships provide the context in which child and adult partners develop a shared world of activities and meanings, through which the child's view of reality, of the self and of others is gradually constructed. The earliest conceptions of the me-self develop through the child's perception of his or her role in the relationship. The child's model of what other people are like, and what relationships are like, derives from the separation of the dyadic entity into self and other. It is therefore no surprise that the quality of an infant's attachments has profound effects on social and emotional development, which often persist through childhood and adult life.

Infants who enjoy secure attachments learn that they are loved and worthy of being loved. They learn that other people are reliable and can be trusted. They approach life confidently and positively as a consequence, and are constructive and cooperative (Kochanska, Aksan and Carlson, 2005). Furthermore, securely attached children are relatively robust in handling negative emotions, perhaps because they have been allowed to express these emotions in the security of the infant relationship and have learned to manage these strong feelings in this context (Cassidy, 1994).

Children with insecure attachments learn a very different lesson. They experience low self-esteem, seeing themselves as unworthy of love. They are generally insecure, less positive and less cooperative. They expect others to reject them or to be unreliable. They lack confidence. These children have difficulty in handling negative events and emotions, perhaps because expressing negativity was problematic in the insecure infant attachment relationship (not allowed, or punished by the mother's withdrawal or criticism) so that the child has learned that such emotions are dangerous without learning how to handle them (Cassidy, 1994).

Children with disorganized attachments are still more insecure, negative and lacking in confidence. They are also disproportionately likely to show emotional disorders of one kind or another, including eating disorders (Pearlman, 2005) and borderline personality disorder (Holmes, 2005).

Thus infant attachment experiences affect a wide range of characteristics that we think of as providing individual personality. These effects tend to be long-lasting: secure attachment in infancy is associated with better adjustment throughout school, both in forming friendships (Schneider, Atkinson and Tardif, 2001) and in scholastic success (Jacobsen and Hofmann, 1997).

Some researchers have challenged the assumption that the better subsequent adjustment of the securely attached infant is a carry-over from infancy, as Bowlby claimed: after all, parents who were sensitive to an infant might be equally good at parenting through the whole of development (Lamb et al., 1985).

Certainly, changes in the home such as arise from conflict or divorce or other stressors can affect the security of a child's attachment and consequent adjustment (Frosch, Mangelsdorf and McHale, 2000; Lewis, Feiring and Rosenthal, 2000). New relationships formed either with new people (Rushton and Mayes, 2005) or after a parent has been trained to respond more sensitively (Van den Boom, 1994) can rescue children from insecure attachments and create security. The child's current attachment style predicts his or her adjustment better than a historic one (Thompson, 1998).

Nevertheless, quality of attachment in infancy does seem to be associated with some lasting effects: it is associated with more secure romantic attachments in adult life, for example (Lamb, 2005; Roisman et al., 2005), and with parenting styles: children who had secure or insecure attachments in infancy (**Box 4.5**) tend to grow up to produce children who have the same style of attachment as themselves (Fonagy, Steele and Steele 1991; Levine et al., 1991). Both of these things suggest that Freud was, to some extent, right in saying that infant attachment forms the prototype for subsequent relationships.

box **4.5**

Infant attachment and adult parenting

Assessments of the quality of an adult's attachment to his or her caretaker can be made by exploring the adult's recollections of their relationship with the parent in early life. Four different attachment styles emerge (Hesse, 1999), the first reflecting secure, the others insecure attachments:

- *Autonomous* (securely attached) adults produce coherent, consistent accounts of their parenting, recalling both positive and negative aspects of their relationship with the parent. They view their relationship with their parent as important and influential.
- *Dismissing* adults often say that they can't remember much about their childhood relationship with their parents, and deny the importance of this relationship. Their stories may be inconsistent: idealizing the parent, but also reporting rejecting experiences.
- *Preoccupied* adults are intensely focused on their childhood relationship to the parent, and provide accounts that are often hostile and confused.
- *Unresolved* adults may provide accounts that are irrational and disturbed, reflecting abuse or loss.

Some researchers believe that these four responses directly reflect the adult's infant experience of attachment (Hamilton, 2000). Others dispute this, suggesting that these responses are more a reflection of the adult's current theories about relationships and level of personal development (Thompson, 1998).

Whatever their origin, these four attachment styles correlate with both the adult's sensitivity to his or her own child, and the quality of their child's attachment to them. Autonomous parents tend to have securely attached infants; dismissive parents tend to have insecure/avoidant infants; preoccupied parents are more likely to have insecure/resistant infants; unresolved parents are most likely to have disorganized infants (Van IJzendoorn, 1995).

Temperament

So far, the research reviewed in this chapter has emphasized the role of social interactions in laying the groundwork for a great deal of what we think of as the self, or as individual personality. But babies are not passive players in these processes. The way a child develops is also affected by his or her temperamental constitution.

Personality is a complex thing, reflecting an individual's skills, habits, values, the way he or she thinks about the world, the self, other people, relationships (Rothbart and Bates, 1998). Much of what we call personality develops through experience (as we shall see in Chapter 10). But underlying all of this is the baby's individual temperament.

Temperament is, by definition, the inborn constitutional component of personality (Rothbart and Bates, 1998). That is to say, it is composed of the stable, unchanging dispositions with which we are born, and which persist through life. It derives from the 'setting' of our individual neurological system (Bates and Wach, 1994). All living organisms must be *reactive* to events, or they could not survive, still less learn. And all living organisms must be able to *regulate* their reactions, or they will be overwhelmed by them. But species and individuals vary in the extent to which they are reactive or self-regulating. For example, one infant's neurological system may be 'set' to be more sensitively reactive than another's, so that small stimuli produce a reaction in one but not the other. One infant may be constitutionally biased toward damping down reactions, where another allows them free rein. Such differences are the basis for differences in temperament.

Temperamental differences very similar to those we see in human beings also occur in many other species, including dogs and cats, fish, birds and so on, as well as other primates (Kagan, 1998). The implication is that temperamental variables (in other words, different settings of reactivity and self-regulation) have been bred into us for many millions of years. They are part of our evolutionary heritage (Gunnar, 1994; Strelau, 1983).

But for all its genetic base, the temperament we are born with may also reflect events in the womb. As the fetus takes shape it responds from moment to moment to the nutrients available to it, the hormones circulating in the mother's blood and so on. Some of these responses require 'decisions' that divert resources from one task to another, or alter the settings of the neural system. Once these decisions are taken they can't be undone, so that the effect is locked in forever. Temperamental variables may be affected in the womb in this way. For example, high levels of maternal stress seem to affect the physiology of the monkey fetus, generating a more nervous disposition (DiPietro, 1995; Schneider, 1992). Similar effects occur in human development (Di Pietro et al., 1996; Wadhwa, 1998; 2005).

Measuring temperament in babies

There are numerous difficulties in measuring temperament in babies. In many ways, the person best placed to assess a baby's temperament is his or her mother, since she (typically) has the greatest experience of the child. Early efforts to measure temperament (Thomas and Chess, 1977) used mothers' ratings in devising their scales. But this approach has problems. As we have seen, a baby's behaviour is very much structured by the mother, who in effect creates the world the child exists in. A mother who is slow to react to her baby's cries will have a baby who cries more, whatever the child's underlying temperamental disposition. The mother's perception that this baby is irritable may not be a pure reflection of the baby's temperament so much as a reflection of the relationship between mother and child. Furthermore, mother's assessments of their babies may be biased by love, or by inaccurate oversimplifications. Nonetheless, for all the problems and the need to treat the results with care, mothers' assessments of their baby's temperament can provide useful information which is hard to get in other ways (Rothbart and Bates, 1998). For example, assessing temperament by observing a baby's reaction to a particular event (such as the removal of a pacifier) may provide a more objective measure. But this approach provides a far narrower view of the range of a baby's behaviour than a maternal assessment can, and may not tell us what is consistent or what is variable across different situations.

Second, there is the problem of how we are to characterize the dimensions along which temperament varies. Thomas and Chess (1977) identified nine dimensions of temperament in their analysis of the ways mothers describe their babies (**Box 4.6**). Within this, they identified two basic temperamental patterns: *difficult* babies (negative, unadaptable, irregular) and *easy* babies (positive, adaptable, regular). Both the nine dimensions and the two patterns make an intuitive sense to us. But they don't hold up to experimental test, and nor do the dimensions of temperament measured by revised versions of the scales (for example, those of Carey and McDevitt, 1978, and Windle and Lerner, 1986). Using complex statistical techniques for identifying the relationship between one thing and another (a technique called 'factor analysis'), it emerges that the nine dimensions are not independent of one another: they overlap and intertwine (Sanson et al., 1987).

box **4.6**

Thomas and Chess's (1977) nine dimensions of infant temperament

- Activity level
- Rhythmicity or regularity of bodily functions such as sleep, hunger, elimination
- Initial reaction to unfamiliarity: approach or withdrawal
- Ease of adaptation to novel situations
- Responsiveness to subtle stimuli
- Amount of energy
- Predominant mood (happy, irritable)
- Distractability
- Attention span and persistence

40 per cent of babies are 'easy' babies: regular; positive approach to novelty.
15 per cent of babies are 'inhibited': slow to warm up, withdraw from novelty and are mildly distressed by it.
10 per cent of babies are more 'difficult': little regularity; irritability; withdrawal from novelty, poor adaptation.

Starting from a factor analysis of questions intended to measure 11 possible dimensions of temperament, Rothbart (1981) identified only six separate dimensions: smiling, fear, distress, orienting, activity and soothability. These six dimensions may themselves hide subtleties we do not yet understand (for example, is distress in the face of novelty the same dimension of temperament as distress in the face of losing a pacifier? – Kagan, 1998). But they are all subordinate to the two over-arching dimensions of temperament (Rothbart, 1989a): *reactivity* (how easily motor, emotional, hormonal or other physiological responses are aroused) and *self-regulation* (the disposition to modulate reactivity through processes such as approach, withdrawal, self-soothing, inhibition, switching attention).

Cultural differences in temperament

Although analyses of temperament show that individuals vary across the same dimensions in all cultures, the average temperament is different between cultures. For example, Asian-American babies are calmer and more placid than European-American babies, and more easily consoled (Freedman and Freedman 1969); Chinese-American babies are less active, less vocal, less likely to smile and more inhibited than European-Americans (Kagan, Kearsley and Zelazo, 1978). Such effects could easily reflect differences in the genetic pool of Americans from different backgrounds: systematic differences in temperament between groups can be created within a few generations through selective breeding in quail (Jones, Slatterlee and Ryder, 1994) or dogs (Scott and Fuller, 1965), so why not human beings? But it is also possible that these cultural differences reflect social or developmental factors, for example, the way parents respond to their babies, or whether they use practices that encourage calm (such as swaddling) or not (Saarni et al., 1998). In this case, cultural practices might not affect the underlying temperament so much as the way it develops.

Temperament and development

At first, the suggestion that temperament can change developmentally or through the action of social factors seems a contradiction in terms. After all, temperament is *defined* as the stable constitutional disposition that underlies all our behaviour, the disposition set for us at birth. So how could it change?

It's worth pausing to note that our surprise at this suggestion stems from the assumption that there is some necessary relationship between what is innate and what is unchanging over time. But this is not so. My first language is consistently English, for example, but that is a happenstance of my nationality rather than a genetic disposition. On the other hand, my adult sexual capacity is clearly part of my genetic inheritance – but was not present in childhood. And even the most genetically based of tendencies (such as the tendency to develop hands) can be modified by events (such as the drug thalidomide). In fact, the clear message of research is that our genetic dispositions never completely determine any aspect of our behaviour. Genetic disposition always interacts with other factors to produce the individual we see at any moment (see Chapter 2).

The way we express our temperamental disposition is modified by developmental factors, even if the disposition itself remains constant. For example, a highly distress-prone baby signals his or her distress in unrestrained crying or screaming. By 7 years of age, increasing self-control and social censure mean that the highly distress-prone child responds with withdrawal, comfort seeking, nervous activities and the like rather than crying. By the age of 22, the highly distress-prone individual may seek solace in a chocolate cake or a violent game of squash, a phone-fest with friends or a bottle of vodka. Such developmental changes in the way temperamental dispositions manifest in behaviour make it difficult to track just how stable these dispositions are over time. Obviously, we can't define any temperamental disposition in terms of specific behaviours. Rather, we need an abstract concept of what a given temperamental disposition implies, so that age-appropriate measures can be identified. Research that takes this approach has found that many neonatal dispositions, and particularly proneness to distress, emerge as very stable through the lifespan (Rothbart and Bates, 1998).

But notice also how, in this example of distress-proneness, the expression of a stable underlying disposition is affected by social factors. We tend to do what our community expects of us. Gender and cultural expectations as well as age affect the ways we express and manage distress, and also the contexts in which we are 'allowed' to feel distress. Footballers aside, in our society 'big boys still don't cry'.

A child's social experiences can affect not only how he or she learns to express a given temperamental trait, but also what aspects of an overall temperamental constitution dominate behaviour. As we've seen (Box 4.1), certain cultural practices can foster a greater or a lesser emotional volatility. The child's social circumstances can have similar effects, working to either exaggerate a given temperament or counteract it. Imagine, for example, a highly distress-prone baby born into either a calm, stable household or one in turmoil. In either case, the child is constitutionally distress-prone. In the calm household, there are relatively few threats, there is instant reassurance, and the child's tendency toward distress will be damped down. In turmoil, threat is constant, reassurance rare, and the tendency toward distress will be magnified.

But babies are not the passive products of circumstances. A baby's temperament can itself act to exaggerate a given disposition. For example, a baby more disposed to distress will, at 7 months, be more distressed by strangers than will another child who is less prone to distress. The greater distress of the first child will make strangers seem very noxious, reinforcing the child's anxiety and tendency to withdraw. By contrast, the less distressed child may be able to discover pleasure in interacting with the stranger, so that his or her distress is reduced, and confidence in life is enhanced (Rothbart and Bates, 1998). Equally, a positive child elicits a better response from care givers, thus creating a more positive environment and enhancing a disposition to be positive, where a negative child elicits negativity from the parent, so creating a negative environment and enhancing a negative disposition (Scarr and McCartney, 1983). Thus each child's basic temperamental disposition pushes the child toward reactions that entrench a constitutional tendency.

Through processes such as those described, temperament may show marked development of one sort or another (Rothbart and Bates, 1998). Further change occurs because not all aspects of temperament are expressed at birth: they develop as the baby's repertoire of behaviours expands (Rothbart, 1989b). For example, babies learn to inhibit their reactions as their general ability to regulate themselves increases. Only when this has happened can temperamental differences in self-regulation fully emerge.

Temperament and attachment

Does the baby's innate temperament play a role in shaping the quality of his or her early attachment to the mother? In other words, is the mother's reaction to her baby a reflection of the child's temperament? You would expect that it would be, at least to a degree: 'easy-going' babies are so much more rewarding than 'difficult' ones. But the evidence on this subject is ambiguous, and the issue is controversial.

If we assess parent–child attachment in Ainsworth's 'strange situation', the data suggest that there is no consistent relationship between the child's innate temperament and the quality of the attachment relationship (Seifer et al., 1996; Shaw and Vondra, 1995). By contrast, if you assess the security of a child's attachment by 'Q sort', a clear relationship between security and temperament emerges. Distress proneness and negativity are associated with insecure attachments (Seifer et al., 1996; Vaughn et al., 1992). But which came first: the negativity or the poor relationship?

Studies by Van den Boom and Hoeksma (1994) tried to answer this question by making direct assessments of how irritable and negative babies were at 10 and 15 days of age, and relating this to the quality of attachment at age 12 months. Babies assessed as irritable in the second week of life were more likely to be assessed as having an insecure-avoidant attachment, even though their mothers had not initially been assessed by researchers as insensitive. These mothers rated their babies as 'difficult'. Objectively, the babies showed few positive responses and many negative ones.

These results seem to suggest that babies may play quite an important role in creating their own attachment destinies, rather than simply being the passive products of a process imposed on them by the mother. However, there are reasons for being rather cautious about accepting this conclusion. Van den Boom and Hoeksma's own data demonstrate that mother and child are not equal partners in shaping their attachment relationship. When the mothers of negative babies were trained in more sensitive parenting skills, they were able to establish much better-quality attachments with their child. In other words, parenting skills are clearly more important than innate temperament in establishing the quality of the parent–child attachment, and can overcome the impact of a baby's negative temperament (Van den Boom and Hoeksma, 1994).

The conclusion that parenting skill rather than innate temperament plays the key role in determining the quality of parent–child relationships is supported in other studies of this relationship (Goldsmith and Alansky, 1987). Very recent studies of the relationship between innate temperament and the quality of parent-child attachment have concluded that the effect of the baby's temperament is negligible (Roisman and Fraley, 2006).

In conclusion

It's quite clear, from the research reviewed in this chapter, that newborn babies are not entirely devoid of social skills, or as devoid of the ability to differentiate between people and objects, as Piaget supposed. In fact, human babies are born already equipped with a range of innate mechanisms to support social interactions. Newborn, we are already able to orient to others, to imitate them, and to take pleasure in their interaction with us.

The evidence suggests that the newborn baby's social skills reflect the action of innate perceptual systems, perhaps systems in which perception and action are linked, paralleling the systems Gibson proposed for visual perception of the physical world (see Chapter 3). Devoid of conceptual insight, these perceptual systems provide the baby with the behaviours that attract a carer and that focus attention where it needs to be: on learning about other people.

Long before babies have any awareness of the existence of other minds (or even of their own minds) or any understanding of human interaction, these instinctive reactions ensure that they are already integrated into a rich, dynamic social system. Adults behave as though the baby were sentient and aware, supporting and shaping his or her behaviour, crafting responses and patterns of interaction with which the baby can engage. Whatever the infant initially understands of such interactions, participating in them provides the ideal experience for the development of insight. Through such interactions a world of consistency and meaning is created, which the child gradually becomes able to represent and interpret.

Processes individual to the child play an important role in the discovery of the social world: temperamental processes that determine a child's first response to events, conceptual discoveries that people are 'permanent', that little red fire trucks (for example) can't move themselves or be commanded where dad can, that 'I' can make this teddy fly out the cot, and so on. Nevertheless, it is social processes that construct crucial realities for the child. Social information guides the baby's activities and perceptions first through emotional contagion and social referencing, and later through attachment relationships in which the child's descriptive account of the self, others, relationships and reality is constructed. At 18 months, a baby's grasp on self and other, the notion that others have minds and feelings, is still slight. But the scene is set for the development of real insight in these areas. And already, infants are locked into the relationships which may well, unless something radical intervenes, set the tone for self-perception and self-esteem, for confidence or distrust, for love, for many years to come, if not for a lifetime.

The picture we have of development in these areas today is strikingly different from views in the mid-20th century. Then, the growth of social and emotional skills and awareness, the origins of individuality and the sense of self were attributed to this factor or that: to genetic dispositions, or to learning from specific experiences, or to the process of socialization. Different theories argued for the importance of different factors. Now, the consensus among researchers is that no one factor can account for development in this area: it is the combination of different factors interacting together to form a complex system that yields both social insight and individual personhood (Sroufe and Sampson, 2000). Understanding development therefore calls for a new kind of theory: a theory about how complex systems function. And at the very end of the 20th century, 'dynamic systems theory' began to address this issue (see Chapters 2 and 3 for an introduction to this approach).

From a dynamic systems perspective, all the phenomena of social and personal development *emerge* from the dynamics of the interactions between many different factors. There is no guiding plan for this development, no blueprint for the path development will follow. It just so happens that, given a genetic bias to react *this* way, a physiology with *those* features, a social context with *these* characteristics, one thing leads to another. Social awareness and personhood are *assembled* bit by bit by the dynamic interaction between these various factors as the baby engages with the world. No one factor necessarily dominates this process, though some factors may be more influential than others at a given time – for example, the mother plays a leading part in shaping an infant's world at certain moments. Even chance events can affect the way the system works and so can influence the course of development. It is the system as a whole that matters. And systems are more than the sum of their parts: complex systems can produce surprising outcomes, radical qualitative changes (Chapter 2).

Various aspects of social development have been explored from a dynamic systems perspective – for example, the emergence of emotional expressiveness from the interaction between innate reflexes, physiological reactions, the child's goals and social experience (Messenger, Fogel and Dickson, 1997; Fogel and Thelen, 1987); the emergence of attachment relationships from the dynamics of the interaction between baby and parent (Coleman and Watson, 2000; Lewis, 1999; Lewis, Lamey and Douglas, 1999). These analyses have begun to provide new insights into the detail of developmental processes.

One key insight highlighted by dynamic systems analyses is that emerging patterns in infant social (and all other) behaviour are necessarily fragile and easily changeable. Behaviour is assembled in the moment by the dynamics of the situation. Inevitably, the precise details of the situation change from moment to moment – if only because the emerging behaviours change things. And as the details of the situation change, new behaviours emerge. Dynamic systems theorists describe emerging behaviour as a *soft assembly* to underline this fragile dependence on circumstances. Only as the system settles to consistently function in the same way over time do particular patterns of behaviour become entrenched.

Soft assembly has many advantages for the developing child. Subtle (or not so subtle) variations in behaviour allow the child to react flexibly to a variable world, to explore the consequences of different reactions and so to increase the probability of settling into effective patterns of behaviour. In many areas (such as learning to walk or to understand the concept of balance), physical properties of the world play a leading part in shaping what behavioural patterns become established. For social development it is our interaction with others that plays this leading part. Parents in particular shape the dynamics of a child's social world. The fluidity of emerging social behaviours in infancy underlines the fact that we adults are more responsible for children's personal development than we like to think.

Through concepts such as soft assembly, dynamic systems theory predicts that there will be marked differences between children, not only in the characteristics that we identify as individual personality and which we expect to vary, but also in the detail of how basic social skills and insights develop. We are only just beginning to explore this prediction, so we don't yet know just how much variability between children there actually is. But the probability of variability in this area raises an important question.

If, as dynamic systems theory asserts, there is no guiding plan for social development, no blueprint determining the path development in this area will follow, and if what emerges from the dynamics of social development is a fragile soft assembly, then how is it that there is a common trajectory for the emergence of social skills and insight? How come there are characteristic patterns of development across children as a whole, for example in responding to facial expressions, forming attachments and the like? How can such a fragile, variable system produce such consistent results?

The dynamic systems answer points to the fact that the behaviours assembled through dynamic interactions are *functional*: that is to say, they are shaped by the tasks we engage in, the problems we try to solve (Thelen, Kelso and Fogel, 1987). The fundamental tasks and problems facing the infant in the social domain are the same the world over: we all face broadly similar problems in learning to understand and relate to others. Furthermore, core features of what we bring to these tasks are common to us all: a human body for example; dependence on a care giver. Addressing broadly the same tasks with broadly the same resources, the overall trajectory of social development will be broadly similar for us all, even if there turns out to be considerable variation in how individual children reach a given milestone.

Could dynamic systems theory provide a single overarching framework within which we can explain all the remarkable gains of infancy, from motor development to conceptual, emotional, social and personal development? Work in this vein is still new. But many researchers believe that the dynamic systems approach will be increasingly important in coming years.

Exercises

1. It's clear from the evidence that parenting styles affect a child's security, and that security has an impact on the child's later adjustment. Parenting styles are themselves affected by culture, socio-economic status, and by the parent's own childhood experience. What implications might this have, in a society where there is a marked diversity of culture, affluence and childhood experience? What practical and ethical issues would be involved in securing a more equal start for all babies?

2. A new study reports that infant temperament varies between affluent, well-educated families and those of low education and poor economic status. How would you interpret this result? How reliable is it? What artefacts might contribute to the result?

Suggested reading

For an overview of social development in infancy read:

- P. Rochat and T. Striano (eds) (1999) *Early Social Cognition: Understanding others in the first months of life.* New Jersey: Lawrence Erlbaum.

For a comprehensive and detailed review of emotional development read:

- C. Saarni, D. Mumme and J. Campos (1998) Emotional development: action, communication and understanding. In N. Eisenberg (ed.), W. Damon (series ed.), *Handbook of Child Psychology*, vol. 3: *Social, Emotional and Personal Development*. New York: Wiley.

For a discussion of the developing self read:

- S. Harter (1998) The development of self representations. In N. Eisenberg (ed.), W. Damon (series ed.), *Handbook of Child Psychology*, vol. 3: *Social, Emotional and Personal Development*. New York: Wiley.

For a discussion of attachment in infancy read:

- S. Gerhardt (2005) *Why Love Matters: How affection shapes a baby's brain.* Philadelphia: Routledge.

For a discussion of temperament in infancy read:

- M. Rothbart and J. Bates (1998) Temperament. In N. Eisenberg (ed.), W. Damon (series ed.), *Handbook of Child Psychology*, vol. 3: *Social, Emotional and Personal Development*. New York: Wiley.

Revision summary

Are newborn babies socially aware?

- Newborn babies treat people very differently from other objects, orienting to the human face and voice and preferring them to other sights and noises, imitating facial expressions and simple vowel sounds. The data overwhelmingly suggest that this responsiveness reflects innate predispositions and skills.

- Key research questions focus on what these innate skills mean. Do babies realize that, in interacting with others, they are interacting with a person, a creature like themselves, or is their sociability the result of innate reflexes devoid of insight? Do they deliberately intend to interact at all, or is that an illusion created by the adult partner?

Emotional understanding

- Babies display primary emotions (sadness, happiness, pain, fear, surprise, interest) from birth. Some researchers suggested that they do not experience (feel) these emotions as adults do, because they lack the conceptual skills to interpret and make sense of events. More recent research suggests that this is wrong: there is a physiological component to emotion, and there is no reason to suppose that babies are any less able to 'feel' primary emotions than anyone else, even if these feelings are less conceptually differentiated in infancy.

- Babies can tell the difference between one emotional expression and another from birth, but only begin to react as if they had any insight into the meaning of the expressions after 7 months. Even at 15 months there is little evidence that they understand that an emotional expression means that the other person is feeling the implied emotion, or even that other people feel emotions at all.

- Babies' imitation of emotional expressions reflects innate reflexes rather than social understanding. Nevertheless, through imitating a happy face a baby will be stimulated to feel happy, and so can co-experience another person's emotions through emotional contagion. This is a first, primitive, step toward empathy.

- Despite lacking insight, babies can use emotions as signals very effectively. Their own direct expression of their feelings signals their needs to others. By 12 months, they use other's emotional expressions as signals to guide their behaviour, a phenomenon known as 'social referencing'.

- Real insight into other people's emotions requires understanding that others have feelings and desires like your own, an insight only beginning to emerge at 18 months.

Developing a self-concept

- 'Self' is a complex construct. As William James pointed out, there is the 'I-self' that experiences life directly and is our subjective experience of ourselves; and there is the 'me-self', composed of the descriptions I have of myself: my material being and possessions; my social relationships and roles; my spiritual values.

- The 'I-self' develops first, rooted in feedback from the body (comfort, discomfort and so on). As the newborn baby's sleeping, eating and eliminating develop a routine, the patterns of this routine feed the sense of continuity and consistency at the root of the 'I-self'. Further advance comes between 4 and 9 months, as babies become aware of themselves as agents able to make things happen.

- The 'me-self' begins to develop as babies learn about their bodies and material circumstances, starting to be able to recognize themselves in mirrors or photographs at around 15 to 18 months. The social and spiritual 'me-self' is constructed in symbiotic interaction with the carer who structures the baby's world, creating a shared definition of reality, self and others.

■ The symbiotic relationship between carer and infant at first creates a 'we' self in which both parties are inextricably intertwined. Gradually this is separated into a conception of self and other as distinct entities with different characteristics.

Attachment

■ The psychiatrist John Bowlby claimed that secure infant–mother relationships in infancy are crucial for emotional development. 'Maternal deprivation' would produce irreversible emotional damage for life. Subsequent research shows that his theory was wrong in certain respects. Mothers are important because they're usually the one caring for the baby, not because of any biological bonding between mother and baby. Any carer can potentially provide the secure attachment the baby needs. The damage done by poor attachment in infancy can be reversed later, if the child makes a new and effective attachment, or the parents cope better, or through therapy in later life. But Bowlby was right in emphasizing the importance of infant attachments.

■ Attachments develop through the first two years of life, beginning at around 7 months. Ainsworth measured the security of an infant's attachment in the 'strange situation'. While many infants show secure attachments (trusting and enjoying the mother), others are either 'insecure-avoidant' (cool and not reliant on the mother) or 'insecure-resistant' (clingy and ambivalent about the mother, demanding her nurturing and rejecting it at the same time). A few show 'disorganized' attachments (profoundly ambivalent toward the mother, fearing and needing her, readily disorientated and panicked).

■ Quality of attachment reflects parenting style. Sensitive parenting yields secure attachment. Slowness/coolness in attending to a baby's needs leads to insecure-avoidant attachment; and inconsistent parenting (sometimes good, sometimes bad) leads to insecure-resistant attachment. Disorganized attachment reflects serious maternal problems such as 'borderline personality disorder'.

■ Secure attachment in infancy is correlated with better social and academic achievement. It also seems to provide the template for future romantic relationships, and for the infants' own subsequent parenting style.

Temperament

■ Temperament is the innate component of our constitutions, the basic way we react to life. Mary Rothbart identifies two core traits: reactivity (how easily aroused we are, either positively or negatively) and self-regulation (how effectively we manage this arousal). These two basic components give rise to a number of more specific traits such as proneness to distress, activity and smiling.

■ Underlying temperament is constant, but the way it is expressed and the degree to which a given trait dominates are affected by social and developmental factors.

■ Although we might expect a baby's temperament to affect the quality of parent–child attachment, research suggests that parenting skills are the dominant factor.

Dynamic systems and social development

■ Dynamic systems theory offers new insights into how social and personal development emerge from the complex interaction of many different factors.

cognitive development from infancy to adulthood

Overview

The four chapters that make up Part II focus on the question: how does human intelligence grow through childhood, adolescence and on into adult life? What is it that changes as our minds develop, and how does this change come about?

Chapter 5 explores the development of language. No other species uses language as we do. Language provides us with an extraordinarily rich and flexible means of communicating, describing the world, reasoning. In many ways, it's the hallmark and foundation of human intelligence. This chapter describes the emergence of language through infancy, from the reflexive reactions of the newborn to the articulate verbal fluency of the child, and explores the complex processes that allow this development to occur.

Chapter 6 focuses on conceptual development: on our ability to interpret and make sense of the world around us, to draw inferences and to reason. Conceptual understanding continues to grow throughout our lives – you are developing new concepts and new ways of reasoning right now, as you study psychology. This chapter explores the processes that underlie the growth of knowledge and the power of inference, and how these things change as we develop from infancy to adult life.

Where Chapter 6 explores the structure of the human mind, **Chapter 7** examines the mind in action. What exactly happens, as we try to create plans or solve problems? What happens as we recognize or recall things from memory? How do we learn new things or make new discoveries? Can understanding problem-solving processes help us to understand the mechanisms of cognitive development as a whole?

Every normal child learns to speak, to understand the world, to reason, to plan, solve problems and recall past events. Nonetheless, some individuals are very much better than others at all of these things. Chapter 8 explores the origins of individual differences in cognitive development. Is there a general factor (IQ) that explains this variation between individuals, or must we look elsewhere for an explanation? What goes wrong, when a child fails to develop normal intelligence? And what is involved in creativity or genius?

5
language

Think back over your day. From start to finish, you have been bathed in language: in words you have spoken to yourself or to other people, words you have heard or read. Can you imagine life without language?

Language is a vital, central component of our human intelligence. It's a multi-purpose tool. We use it for all sorts of things: communicating with and controlling one another, passing on ideas, reasoning and problem solving, reflecting and remembering, coaching and directing ourselves, creating our histories and personal narratives – the story of who we are as a culture or an individual. The ability to talk is fundamental to what it means to be human.

The speed with which human infants master language is truly astonishing. Newborn babies have none of our rich linguistic ability, and yet by 3 or 4 years of age the average child is fairly fluent, well able to hold his or her own with the complexities of language. It's easy to underestimate just how impressive this speed of progress really is. Most adults have enormous difficulty in learning a new language: unoscapolofornitodiunbuonpatrimonio???[1] Even working out where one word ends and another begins is hard. As for producing sentences in the new language ourselves, unless we are one of the gifted few, even after years of effort our accents are quaint, our grasp on grammar negligible, even the intonation of our speech is quite wrong. And this, despite the fact that we adults already know what language is, already know that things have names, that grammar has rules, and can already understand enough about the world to guess what might be meant from gestures and context. Yet infants, with none of these advantages, are somehow far better linguists than we are! What underlies this remarkable talent? How does the baby do it? These questions structure research on language development, and are the focus of this chapter.

---

[1] This is in Italian with the words run together, and part of a very famous sentence: 'e verita universalmente ammessa che *uno scapolo fornito di un buon patrimonio* debba sentire il bisogno di ammogliarsi' – in the original, English, 'It is a truth universally acknowledged that a single man in possession of a good fortune must be in want of a wife', the opening line of Jane Austen's *Pride and Prejudice*.

What is language?

Like us, other species communicate in all sorts of ways. They use facial expressions (**Figure 5.1**), body postures, even vocal signals to indicate threat, say, or sexual attraction, or the imperious 'feed me!' of the young. Garden robins, for example (like every other bird), have elaborate rituals, territorial songs, threat displays. Bees can dance a complex geographical message, directing their companions to rich pickings. The haunting songs of whales express a variety of emotions. Recently, we have discovered that even lowly caterpillars sing songs to soothe and seduce ants, and that ants themselves create war music, one anthem for the determined advance into battle, another for the triumphant return with the spoils.[2]

But for all that the communicative systems in other species are vital and useful, binding communities or mates together, mediating interactions, protecting from danger and the like, they are actually extremely limited. They rest on very stereotyped patterns of display or

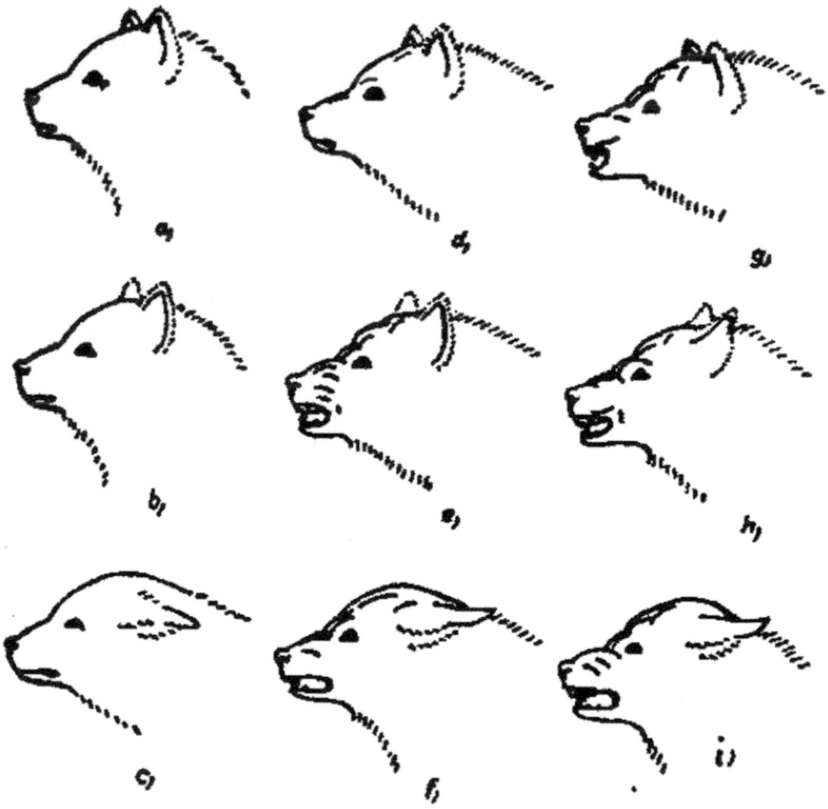

figure 5.1

Canine facial expressions

Source: K. Lorenz (1952) 'Die Entwicklung der vergleichenden verhaltensforschung in den letzen 12 jahren', in: *Verhandlungen der Deutschen Zoologischen Gesellschaft in Freiberg*, pp. 36–56.

[2] The extent of insect communication through sound is a recent discovery, much of it first recorded for a television documentary *Life in the Undergrowth* presented by David Attenborough, BBC 2005.

vocalization. A warning cry is always and only a warning cry, even if it can be modulated to indicate whether the danger is on the ground or in the air (Seyfarth and Cheney, 1993). The seductive gestures of courtship are always and only that. Each communicative signal has a particular practical function, acting as an immediate cue to other individuals. The information conveyed is direct: as direct as the information in a human scream of agony. Other species do not take bits of one signal and combine it with bits of another to create new messages as we humans do. This crucial difference is what we point to when we say that no species but human beings uses *language.*

Where other species communicate simple messages through a limited repertoire of separate and stereotyped *signals,* human language is an infinitely flexible system capable of endlessly combining *symbols* in new ways to create new meanings. We think of language as being vocal, resting in sound. But in fact, it can take many different forms: from spoken words to signs expressed through the hands, from written text to patterns of flags, Morse and other codes, shorthand and so on. The defining feature of human language is not sound, but rather the grammatical rules that govern how symbols (words) are combined, organized and ordered to convey particular meanings.

Could other species learn to use human language?

Other species can certainly master some facets of human speech. Parrots, for example, can imitate the human voice very accurately, reproducing both the sounds (*phonemes*) and the rhythms and intonations (*prosody*) of whole sentences, even if they have no grasp on the meaning (*semantics*) of what they 'say'. Dogs (and many other species) can learn the meaning of a range of individual words ('sit, stay, walkies, biscuit, no!' and so on) even if they can't reproduce these sounds. And they understand enough about how language is used in context (*pragmatics*) to know when they (rather than someone else) are being addressed, and whether the tone or volume of a voice spells trouble or a treat. Where other species differ from us most clearly is in the ability to master the grammar (*syntax*) that defines language.

If any other species were capable of mastering the intricacies of syntax, it would surely be our nearest relatives, chimpanzees or gorillas. Both chimpanzees and gorillas can certainly learn the meaning of quite a number of words or even phrases (Gardner and Gardner, 1969; Hayes and Hayes, 1951; Patterson and Linden, 1981). But they don't have vocal tracts adapted to speech as we humans do, and cannot pronounce recognizable words any more than a dog can. To get round this, researchers have tried to teach chimpanzees sign languages devised for the deaf (Gardner and Gardner, 1969; Patterson and Linden, 1981), or taught them to pick out symbols on a specially designed keyboard (Savage-Rumbaugh, 1986).

Studies of non-human primates learning language have had very mixed results. Washoe (a standard or 'pan troglodyte' chimpanzee) and Koko (a gorilla) both learned to sign the names of objects and people, and even to put two signs together, producing, for instance, 'more fruit' (Gardner and Gardner, 1969; Patterson and Linden, 1981). But their communications showed no evidence of the sort of complex grammatical structure that defines language (Wallman, 1992).

More recent studies have focused on bonobos (pan paniscus or 'pygmy' chimpanzees). Bonobos are brighter than pan troglodytes and have a more complex system of social communication. One bonobo in particular – Kanzi – showed great promise. He learned to use Savage-Rumbaugh's keyboard by watching his mother being taught: he himself had no direct tuition from humans. Kanzi learned to understand about 60 symbols, and could use about 50. He also learned to combine two or three symbols to convey messages. More interesting still, Kanzi was adept at understanding the meanings of spoken speech, and was clearly able to use word order in speech to interpret meaning. For example, he could correctly interpret and act on the implications of the different word order in the instructions 'pour the lemonade in the coke' and 'pour the coke in the lemonade' (Savage-Rumbaugh et al., 1993).

In fact, Kanzi was better at interpreting the implications of word order than a human child tested alongside him (Alia, the daughter of one of the researchers) until the child was about 2 years old. At around 2 years of age, human infants really begin to get a grip on the syntactical properties of language. It is at this stage that the human child begins to master *morphology* – in other words, the rules governing how nouns are modified as they become plural (hat/hats), or how verbs are modified to reflect tense (push/pushed). This grasp on morphology is what really sets the scene for proper syntactical processing (Bates, 1993): in other words, for the development of real language. There is no evidence that Kanzi ever began to develop such morphological knowledge. Whereas after her second birthday Alia's speech became progressively more structured, combining more and more symbols, Kanzi's communicative efforts did not develop in this way. He was quickly left far behind. The general consensus is that even bonobos are not capable of mastering the syntactical structure of language as every normal human infant does (Tomasello, 1994). Only human beings are capable of language.

Patterns in language development

Mastering language is a complex, multi-faceted process. There are common, universal patterns in this process. Girls and boys don't differ much, though boys are slightly more likely to have difficulties in some areas of language development (Kovas et al., 2005). But there is a great deal of individual variation, in both the speed and the detail of how language develops.

Early days

Even before we are born, we human beings are already biologically prepared to learn language as other species are not. In the womb we develop the core vocal tract anatomy needed to produce all the subtleties and complexities of speech, although this tract only matures sufficiently to produce coherent sounds 6 to 8 weeks after birth. And in the womb, we develop structures in the brain dedicated to processing language.

In the vast majority of people the left hemisphere of the cerebral cortex is specialized for speech. This left hemisphere specialization is associated with handedness: it occurs in all of us who are right-handed, although it is less marked in the left-handed or the ambidextrous (see Chapter 2). Damage to the left hemisphere of the cerebral cortex can produce problems with the comprehension and production of language. Exactly where the damage lies determines what aspect of language is affected, because there are specific areas within the left hemisphere that specialize in different things. For example, damage to Broca's area (**Figure 5.2**) causes problems in finding the words to express an idea, whereas damage to Wernicke's area is associated with the fluent production of meaningless speech (Goodglass, 1993).

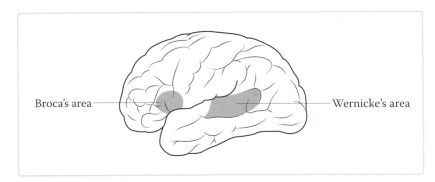

figure 5.2

Areas of the brain specializing in language processing

This specialization of the left hemisphere for speech seems to be set very early in life, probably before birth. Evidence for this comes from studies measuring electrical activity in the brain (EEG studies). Like adults, young infants show more activity in the left hemisphere than the right when listening to speech (Molfese and Betz, 1988), though the bias increases with age (Mills, Coffey-Carina and Neville, 1997).

These physiological preparations for language are associated with a variety of innate predispositions and skills for language (see Chapter 4). Newborn babies already orient to human speech, preferring it to other sounds (Aslin, Pisoni and Jusczyk, 1983). They imitate simple vowel sounds (Kugiumutzakis, 1999). Most remarkably of all, the newborn is more adept at differentiating speech sounds than an adult!

Habituation studies (described in Chapter 3) show that young babies are capable of distinguishing all the speech sounds (*phonemes*) that their parents can distinguish – the difference between 'B' (buh) and 'P' (puh), for instance (Aslin et al., 1998; Eimas et al., 1971). Very young babies can also make distinctions that adults can't hear at all: adults distinguish between only those phonemes relevant to their own language, whereas young babies can also distinguish between speech sounds that are differentiated in other languages but not in their own mother tongue (Jusczyk, 1997). For example, young Japanese babies can hear the difference between 'L' (luh) and 'R' (ruh), a distinction important in English and obvious to an English speaker but irrelevant in Japanese and notoriously difficult for adult Japanese speakers to hear or produce. It seems as if babies are born capable of making all the distinctions between speech sounds found in every human language in the world (Jusczyk, 1997). This ability must be innate: since many of these sounds don't occur in any given language, the baby cannot be learning them all from experience.

Newborn babies can already tell the difference between their mother tongue, which they have heard in the womb, and an unfamiliar foreign language (Mehler et al., 1986). At this early stage, babies cannot differentiate individual words, still less understand meanings, so that their ability to detect the difference between languages must reflect an inborn ability to recognize the characteristic *prosody* of language. Prosody, the typical rhythms and intonations of speech, is an important aspect of language. It varies enormously between one language and another: for example, American English is flat by comparison to British English, which is far more melodic. And British English itself subdivides: the markedly 'sing-song' intonation of the Welsh English speaker is very different from the more drawling speech of the West Country, or the staccato patterns of London English. A French or a German native speaking accented English still sounds French or German because they speak with the prosody (and phonemes) of their native tongue, even though they are using English vocabulary and grammar.

The first months of life

Despite their impressive abilities to perceive key features of speech, newborn babies cannot yet segment speech into separate units, still less understand the meaning of words. Their ability to make speech-like sounds is extremely limited: they will imitate the simplest of vowel sounds ('a'), but their vocal tract is not yet mature enough to achieve more.

The ability to make the variety of vowel and consonant sounds typical of human language reflects the low position of the human tongue relative to other structures in the vocal tract, such as the pharynx. The higher position of the tongue in chimpanzees and other non-human primates is what prevents them from forming these phonemes. In newborn infants, the vocal tract is like that of a chimpanzee in crucial respects, limiting the phonemes that can be produced (Liebermann, 1992). The vocal tract matures through the first year of life, becoming progressively like the adult human tract.

For the first 6 to 8 weeks of life, babies cry or grunt (for example, as they fill a nappy), but make few if any speech-like sounds. But by 2 months of age, the vocal tract has matured enough to allow the baby to begin making simple vowel sounds such as 'aaaaaaaa' or 'oooooh'. At around 6 months of age, babies begin to put vowels and consonants together to form syllables: for example: 'ma' or 'ba'. This is the beginning of *babbling*. By 8 months of age, babies are repeating these syllables over and over, for example: 'mamamamama'. Soon after this babbling progresses to combining different syllables: for instance 'ma-me' or ba-da' (Oller, 1980).

Babies babble enthusiastically to themselves in their cots as well as sociably with other people, playing with sounds as well as copying what they hear. It used to be thought that this babbling included all the phonemes the young baby can distinguish, whether or not these are used in the language to which the child is exposed. But more recent research shows that although babies do produce some sounds not found in the language they hear around them (for example, French babies say 'ha', though French does not include the phoneme 'h' – Vihman, 1992), such 'foreign' sounds are relatively rare (Aslin, Saffran and Newport, 1998; Boysson-Bardies, 1999). Babbling tends to focus on a relatively limited range of speech sounds, most of them represented in the language the child hears, repeated in different combinations.

The noises of the young baby and the babbling of the 6-month-old are ways of exploring and experimenting with the elements from which speech is constructed. The tendency to play with noises in this way seems to be biologically primed: babies with profoundly limited hearing start out making the same sorts of noises as the hearing. But their babbling (like other aspects of language development: see **Box 5.1**) progresses much more slowly than that of a hearing child, suggesting that auditory feedback is also important in the way babbling develops. For instance, where hearing babies are exploring syllables before the age of 10 months, deaf babies are not (Oller and Eilers, 1988).

Gradually, babies refine their babbling to reflect the characteristics of the language they hear around them. They drop any speech sounds that don't occur in their mother tongue from their babbling, so that by 8 months or so they are using exclusively the phonemes of the mother tongue (Aslin et al., 1998). By 12 months of age they will also have lost the ability to hear distinctions that don't occur in their own language (Mehler and Dupoux, 1994; Werker and Tees, 1984), although we don't yet understand why (Aslin et al., 1998).

Babbling progressively takes on the prosody of the mother tongue: long before they make any word-like sounds, babies babble with the characteristic intonations and rhythms of the language around them. So marked is this effect that adults hearing this babbling can tell the difference between a baby 'babbling in French' and one 'babbling in Arabic', although neither produces any actual words (Boysson-Bardies, Sagart and Durant, 1984).

box **5.1**

Language and sensory impairment

Hearing and sight play a vital role in the development of language, so it is no surprise that children with impairments in one or both of these senses are at risk of significant delay in developing language, and may not master language fully at all.

That deaf children should have difficulty learning language is easy to understand. Such babies begin by making noises just as hearing babies do, producing simple vowel sounds and other noises such as grunts and coos. But without feedback from their own noises, without the ability to hear speech sounds, they quickly fall behind: whereas hearing babies spontaneously move on to babbling with consonants and with strings of syllables, deaf babies don't. Where hearing babies begin to identify, comprehend and produce spoken words, deaf babies don't.

Teaching deaf children to speak presents some serious problems. In some cases, it's possible to give the child a degree of hearing through a cochlear implant, and the earlier this is done, the less damage to language development. Such implants allow the child some scope for developing language in the normal way. For other children, verbal communication will always be problematic if not impossible, and for these children, only non-verbal language is a real option.

Sign languages for the deaf provide an alternative to spoken language. It's intriguing that deaf children growing up with people who don't use a sign language develop communicative signs for themselves. This, and the fact that these children spontaneously progress from communicating with single signs to putting two or three signs together, has been taken as evidence that the urge to communicate is a strong instinctive drive, and that the tendency to develop grammar is also inbuilt. The first of these conclusions is hard to dispute, but the second is controversial. As with apes, the mere fact of stringing signs together does not necessarily indicate any grammatical knowledge or usage: and in fact, not even all formal sign systems are grammatical in any real sense.

This last point is illustrated by Signed English. This system is often the one preferred by those rearing deaf children in English-speaking communities, on the grounds that learning to sign in English seems to be the best basis for easing the child toward literacy in English – an important step, in that the ability to write and read opens up a far wider scope for participating in society than is possible with sign languages used only by the minority. However, Signed English is not grammatical: it omits crucial syntactic features, so that people sign 'he is walk' rather than 'he is walking', for instance. Some critics argue that it is not, therefore, really a language at all.

Studies looking at the effects of teaching deaf children Signed English show that not all signing systems are beneficial: children taught only Signed English make very poor progress in mastering written English, even at college level.

By contrast, sign systems that do possess a real grammatical structure, such as ASL or BSL (American and British Sign Language respectively), are far more effective in developing the deaf child's capacity for language. ASL is not English. It's as different as any other foreign language, and has its own grammatical structure, which is very different from that of English. Children taught both ASL and written English are, in effect 'bilingual'. But these children do far better than those taught only Signed English, becoming far more literate in written English. It seems that exposure to grammatical structures is critical for language development, providing the key for learning other languages (such as English).

The problems of the blind child in learning language are less obvious, but equally severe. A blind child can hear sounds, and so can imitate them, but cannot see what these sounds refer to, cannot learn the names of objects by having them pointed at or by looking to see what others are talking about. Blind children often show echolalia – parroting words or phrases without understanding their meaning. Furthermore, where the deaf child cannot imitate sounds because he or she cannot hear them, the blind child has difficulty in imitating speech sounds accurately because he or she cannot see other people's mouth and lip movements, and so cannot imitate these. Moreover, blind children know less about the world than do the sighted: they can make sense only of events in which they participate in a meaningful way, where the sighted child can observe events involving others. Overcoming these handicaps requires both direct phonological tuition helping the child to imitate sounds, and a very tactile approach to naming things and explaining events.

Children who are both deaf and blind face the greatest difficulty in developing language, and until comparatively recently few ever did so. The plight of such children is hard to exaggerate. Intelligence is unaffected, so that a bright mind may be trapped for life in very considerable sensory deprivation and isolation. This double handicap is not rare: as we reduce one common cause (rubella in pregnancy), another increases: deaf-blindness is caused by the sexually transmitted CMV.

Helen Keller is perhaps the most famous instance of a child born deaf-blind who, thanks to the painstaking efforts by her care givers, learned to communicate fluently. The methods used for Helen Keller are still the basis for language teaching for these children: simple signs made touching one another's hands, and a very tactile approach to exploring the world and naming things.

The fact that children with severe sensory impairments are significantly handicapped when it comes to learning language underlines the fact that experience of the world plays an essential part in linguistic development. That these children learn to communicate at all, and that they contribute to the creation of communicative systems, is testimony to the powerful biological basis of language.

Discovering words

By 8 months of age, babies are producing speech sounds that, although meaningless, have many of the characteristics of the language they hear around them. But they don't yet show signs of understanding the meaning of words, still less producing words themselves.

Recognizing words as units in speech

One challenge for anyone learning a language is to identify units within a stream of speech: to identify where one word starts and another one ends. Picking out individual words is hard enough for adults faced with a foreign language, even though we know that we're looking for meaningful units. For a baby who has not yet discovered the existence of words, the task seems impossibly daunting. And yet, babies are adept at segmenting speech in this way.

Eight-month-old infants, for example, can identify units in speech ('words') simply by learning to recognize patterns of sound (for example, the syllables of a word) that regularly occur together, even when there is no pause between one word and another (Aslin et al., 1998; Saffran, Aslin and Newport, 1996). Saffran and colleagues presented infants with a 2-minute tape in which nonsense words were repeated in different orders, with no pauses at all between one word and another, for example:

gobalutupirobidakupadotitupiropadotegobalubidakubidakugobalu

and so on. Later tests showed that the infants had learned to recognize frequently occurring patterns in this stream of sound (the 'words' gobalu, tupiro, bidaku, padoti), differentiating them from 'non-words' (such as balupad, pirobid, lutup and so on), even though the syllables of the non-words had been juxtaposed at least once in the tape.

Tiny pauses between words make the baby's task of identifying the basic units of speech easier (Myers et al., 1996). The exaggerated pauses characteristic of what used to be called 'motherese' – the simplified speech adults adopt when talking to babies which is now called 'infant-directed speech' – may play an important role in helping babies to segment speech into words (Thiessen, Hill and Saffran, 2005).

Comprehending the meaning of words

Identifying words as separate units in speech is a major advance, but how do babies move on from there to discover that words have meanings? How do they come to realize that a particular segment of speech has a particular meaning? This problem is harder than it looks. For example, suppose I say 'blargle' to you. Am I referring to an object, an action, a person? Unless you have some understanding of what I am up to, you will have no idea what I might mean by this word.

Macnamara (1972) and Bruner (1975a) argue that it is precisely by understanding other people's behaviour and intentions that babies begin to associate words with objects or events, and so begin to give words meaning. It's quite clear that babies can make sense of the world around them long before they show any sign of understanding the meaning of words or producing words themselves. They become familiar with everyday routines, so that they can anticipate what comes next. For example, at 3 months, babies are very familiar with routines such as mealtimes and being fed. They open their mouths in anticipation of the spoon. Regular phrases said during such routines ('Open wide!') become part of the activity, so that the baby begins opening his mouth when he hears that phrase, or even waits for the phrase before opening his mouth.

One of the first words babies come to recognize is their own name. Most babies orient to their name by 4 months of age (Mandel, Jusczyk and Pisoni, 1995). By 6 months of age, they understand the referent of words such as 'mummy' or 'daddy', and look toward the relevant parent when they hear each word (Tincoff and Jusczyk, 1999).

The great breakthrough in learning the meaning of words comes when, at about 9 months of age, babies begin to point at things, and to look to see where other people are pointing (Poulin-Dubois, 1999; Tomasello, 1999; see Chapter 4). Pointing is unique to human beings. No other species points or understands the significance of pointing: animals just stare at your finger if you point, rather than looking to see what you're pointing at. Human babies below 8 or 9 months of age do exactly the same. Coming to understand pointing as a reference to something 'over there' creates the powerful possibility of *joint attention*. For the first time, the baby is able to *explicitly* share a point of reference with another person. Now, if mother and child are both attending to a dog (say) and the mother says 'Bargle', it's a good bet that she's referring to the dog.

Mothers tend, almost as if it were a reflex, to name the things their babies point at (Masur, 1982). Babies attend longer to new things that have been pointed out to them than to things than haven't been pointed at, and they pay even more attention if the object pointed at is also named (Baldwin and Markman, 1989). Both pointing and naming are ways of referring to things, in other words, ways of bringing them to other people's attention. The child's discovery of pointing is pivotal in the discovery that things have names (Harris, Barlow-Brown and Chasin, 1995), and pivotal in discovering what the names of particular objects may be. Shortly after this great breakthrough, babies produce their first words.

As useful as pointing is in the discovery that things have names, it still leaves the child with a dilemma. Let's take the example above in more detail: 10-month-old Jack points to a dog gambolling on the lawn. He glances at his mother's eyes to check that she is looking where he is pointing. She looks, and says 'doggie'. Mother and child are looking at the same thing – but what has she named? The object or the activity? And if the object, what aspect of it has she labelled? Is she labelling the category of animal (dog) or naming that individual (Jingle-the-family-pet), or referring to some specific feature of this dog – its colour, for example?

The problem of disentangling what is being referred to by pointing or labelling should be much harder than it actually is for the young infant. As it turns out, the labels we typically offer babies are nouns referring to the whole object and at a general level of description. For example, mothers are most likely to respond by saying 'doggie' when their infant points at a dog, even if the dog in question is their own pooch Jingle, and even if its activity is unusually interesting. And babies typically take words to refer to whole objects rather than to actions or individual features of objects (Woodward and Markman, 1998), and take labels to be generalizations rather than specific names. (They often call any man 'daddy', for example, as if they had interpreted the word to mean man in general rather than this specific man in particular.)

The adult tendency to offer generic nouns as labels, and the child's tendency to assume that whole objects are the referent of pointing and labelling, are obviously very useful in the process of learning word meanings. These biases also explain why, for the great majority of children, the first words comprehended and produced are nouns (Nelson, 1973). But where do these biases come from? Neither mothers nor babies need to be taught to offer or interpret labels in these helpful ways. Some researchers have suggested that these biases must therefore be innate, part of a specialized biological pre-specification for learning (or teaching) language. But this need not be the case. Human beings have a very general perceptual bias toward seeing things as wholes, rather than as collections of parts (Koffa, 1935; Slater, 1997). While this general perceptual bias may well be innate, it is not specific to language. It may be that in seeking to simplify language for the novice, mothers instinctively label the simplest perceptual unit (the whole object), which is what babies are also most likely to be attending to.

Building a vocabulary

Infants begin to comprehend the meaning of words long before they first produce a word of their own. Typically, a baby produces his or her first word somewhere between the ages of 10 and 15 months. These first words are often not conventional words: they may be idiosyncratic, peculiar to the child, or simplified and shortened versions of a word and so easier to pronounce (Gerken, 1994). Typically, the part of the word the infant produces is the part where emphasis falls. For example, my son's first word was 'awa', which he used to mean a variety of plants, but particularly those in bloom. This was probably his best effort to say 'flower', the emphasized part of which is very like 'awa'.

It's not always easy to tell when a baby has produced his or her first word. Various sequences common in babbling (mama, dada) sound awfully like words to an adult ear – words we can't wait to hear! There's a tendency to treat such sequences as words, even though they are not. It's interesting to speculate that this parental enthusiasm may be responsible for shaping the types of words most languages use to label mother and father. And by treating these baby sounds *as if* they were referential words, parents may also lead the baby toward using sounds in that way. But we can only be sure that a baby is really producing a word when he or she consistently uses a particular sound to refer to the same thing.

The first words most babies we've studied produce are nouns (Nelson, 1973; Gentner, 1982), which is what you would expect if the meanings of words are first discovered through reference in joint attention. At first, the baby's progress in word learning is slow: only ten or so words are learned over several months. Gradually the speed of learning picks up, so that by 18 months the average infant has a vocabulary of about 50 words. Verbs and other parts of speech begin to be added to the vocabulary, as children try to describe events, people, feelings, actions as well as things.

Between 18 and 24 months there is a sudden explosion of progress in word learning (Goldfield and Reznick, 1990) so that by 24 months of age most children have a vocabulary of several hundred words. This explosion of word learning may reflect the infant's discovery that you can learn new words by deliberately asking what an object's name is, rather than waiting to hear the name used and working it out for yourself (Vygotsky, 1962). It also reflects the child's growing ability to draw inferences about word meanings on the basis of his or her developing understanding or the world. And it is directly encouraged by social interactions. For example, as toddlers begin to learn words, adults start playing naming games with them ('Where's your nose? Touch your toes!' and so on). Nouns and verbs are learned in this way, and through the action rhymes and songs of infancy.

By 18 to 24 months of age, children can also use insight into other people's intentions to infer word meanings: for example, if an adult says he or she is 'looking for the gazler', picks up an object and looks disappointed and then picks up another and looks pleased, most 18-month-olds conclude that the second object is the searched-for gazler, although the adult never says so (Tomasello, Strosberg and Akhtar, 1996). If an adult peeks into a container and says 'There's a modi in here', the child infers that the item that later emerges from that container is a modi (Baldwin, 1895, 1906). In both of these examples the infant is using the pragmatics of language as a basis for inferring the meaning of the words. These preschool children can also use the grammatical structure of language to infer word meanings, as we shall see later in this chapter.

From 18 months until school starts, vocabulary expands at breakneck speed, with children learning between five and ten new words every day (Anglin, 1993). Vocabulary continues to grow, albeit at a slower pace, throughout childhood and adolescence until the individual knows many thousands of words. Even in adult life we go on learning new words as we take up new studies, careers or sports, or as new ideas enter our culture (I have just discovered the meaning of 'blogging', for example).

Vocabulary, culture and experience

The account of the way vocabulary grows given above is supported by study after study, revealing general patterns in development. But it would be premature to conclude that word learning always develops through these same characteristic phases.

It's hard to document developmental change in a child's vocabulary. It can be done by keeping detailed records of individual children's comprehension and production of words over a period of months or years, for example in 'baby diaries', but to do this rigorously the observer must be skilled, committed, and able to spend considerable time with the individual child. Few people can meet these criteria. As a result, the children studied in such diaries tend to be from better educated middle-class homes, and indeed are often the children or grandchildren of the researchers themselves. Furthermore, analysing such data is arduous and time-consuming, so that few studies of word development involve more than about 20 children. Thus our basic picture of word learning (and, for that matter, language development at large) reflects the way a small number of middle-class children in the United States or Europe – most of them from English-speaking homes – learn words.

Even within this group of children there is considerable variability between individuals in the speed of development, as **Figure 5.3** shows (Brown 1973). For example, whereas some children show a steady incremental progress once they have produced their first word, others seem to stick with only a few words for a long time, then suddenly, well after their peers, produce a string of words (Boysson-Bardies, 1999). Furthermore, there are differences between children in the basic pattern of word acquisition. The first words some children produce are not nouns, as is the case for most, but verbs or pronouns or other pro-social words such as 'please' (Nelson, 1973). The subsequent pattern of word learning may be different for children whose first words are referential (nouns) and those whose first words are more interpersonally oriented or expressive (Bates, O'Connell and Shore, 1987; Nelson, 1981). For example, a child whose early words are referential tends to focus on mastering the phonemic structure and meaning of individual words (getting the right label and saying it right), whereas a child whose early words are expressive focuses more on the conversational aspect of speech, stringing together sounds correctly inflected with the prosody of questions or comments without much regard for the production of recognizable words (Boysson-Bardies, 1999).

We have already identified more variation between individuals in word learning (and language development as a whole) than in most other aspects of development through infancy (Brown, 1973). The scale

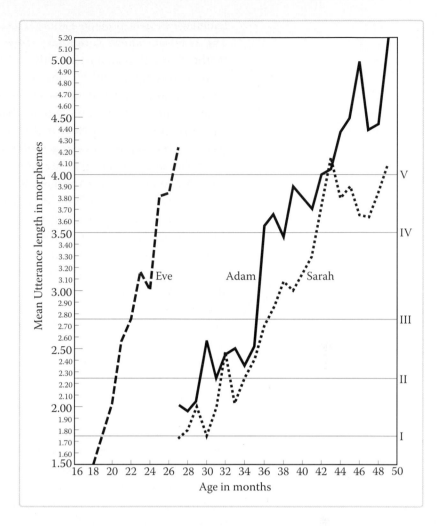

figure **5.3**

Individual differences in the
development of lengthier utterances

Source: R. Brown, *A First Language: The early
stages*. © 1973. Reproduced with permission from
Harvard University Press.

of this variation may be far greater across different social and cultural groups than we yet know. Understanding this diversity is an essential task, if we are to develop a better understanding of what is universal in language development, and of the underlying process by which children learn to talk.

Recently, both large-scale studies using new methods to track language development (for example, the Bristol Language Project: Ellis and Wells, 1980), and also cross-cultural studies have begun to clarify the range of variation in children's word learning, and to deepen our understanding of how children learn words.

For example, we have known for some time that the more a mother talks to her child, the faster the child's vocabulary develops (Huttenlocher et al., 1991). We know also that the better educated the mother, the more she talks to her infant, and the larger the infant's vocabulary as a result (Huttenlocher et al., 1991). Data from the Bristol

Language Project provide a more subtle analysis of this kind of effect. The children whose vocabulary grew the fastest were those whose mothers' speech was most directly and sensitively focused on the child's current ongoing activities: commenting on what was going on, asking questions and giving instructions (Ellis and Wells, 1980).

Cross-cultural studies show that a baby's first words are very directly influenced by the words their mothers tend to use in speaking to them (Hart, 1991). English-speaking mothers tend to use more nouns than verbs, and this is reflected in the infant's tendency to learn nouns before verbs. By contrast, Korean and Mandarin-speaking mothers tend to use more verbs, and their infants' early words are as likely to be verbs as nouns (Gopnik and Choi, 1995; Tardif, 1996). English-speaking mothers tend to focus on objects and activities, giving their babies directions and asking them questions, whereas Japanese mothers focus more on the child's feelings and emotions (Fernald and Morikawa, 1993; Todo, Fogel and Kawai, 1990) – differences that are reflected in their infant's early word learning.

Mothers (and others) from different cultures not only use language in different ways in speaking to their children, they also use words to identify different concepts. For example, the German word *Schadenfreude* has no equivalent in English. Do the words we learn influence how we think? In other words, does language influence our conceptual understanding, as well as growing out of it (**Box 5.2**)?

There is much that we don't yet know about how children learn the meanings of words (Bloom, 2005). But it is increasingly clear that patterns of development typical of children from educated, middle-class English-speaking families may not be representative of all children. Experience, social interactions and cultural practices affect word learning, contributing both to individual variations between children within a society and to cross-cultural differences in the speed and style of word learning.

Grammar

The key defining characteristic of language, as we have seen, is not the ability to comprehend the meaning of words or even the ability to use words oneself: it is mastery of the grammatical or syntactical rules for combining and modifying words to convey precise meanings.

Responding to grammar

Even before they begin to produce their first words, babies are already sensitive to some grammatical constraints. The evidence for this comes from *preferential looking tasks* devised by Hirsh-Pasek and Golinkoff (1996). Here, the child sits on mother's lap, between two television screens. Both screens show pictures incorporating all the same elements, but in different configurations (see **Figure 5.4**). A voice-over describes a

box **5.2**

Language and thought

What is the relationship between language and thought? Can we think without language? Can we entertain a concept for which we have no word? Do the words we use shape and constrain how we see and construe the world?

For behaviourists such as Skinner (1957), there is no thought without language, since – by his definition – thought is no more than internalized language, no more than 'sub-vocal verbal behaviour'. Although Skinner's work is long superseded by other theories, the basic notion that thought is intimately connected to language is not.

Vygotsky too saw a close connection between thought and language. According to Vygotsky, children first learn language through social interactions, their early efforts at speech 'scaffolded' by adult partners. Gradually the child becomes more competent, until he or she can produce speech independently. Now this speech can be internalized and used as a private medium for thought. Although the child is now free to think his or her own thoughts, the medium (language) he or she will use has been profoundly shaped by the social practices for which it was evolved. Socially constructed language will continue to constrain and influence the way the child thinks about the world.

The notion that the particular words we know mould our thoughts has a long history in philosophy and psychology. The seminal claim of this kind was made by Sapir (1929) and his student Whorf (1956). For these theorists, language evolves to reflect the social and physical realities of the society that speaks it. Thus (for example) the Inuit have many words for snow that English speakers do not need. Because they use these words, the Inuit can make conceptual distinctions between grades of snow that the English cannot see. In its strongest form, the Sapir-Whorf hypothesis views language as the medium through which we construe social and physical reality, shaping what we see and how we think about it. And because the social and physical realities carried by different languages are different, translation between one language and another is problematic, if not sometimes impossible.

The 'strong' version of the Sapir-Whorf hypothesis has long been discredited: quite obviously, we can conceptualize things that as yet have no words in our language. Language evolves all the time to accommodate this fact: new words are being invented for new ideas, new social realities ('blogging' being an example, or 'boomerang generation'). Even very young children invent words for new concepts. Translation may not be an exact science, but cross-cultural communication of even subtle ideas is not impossible. Nonetheless, it is also quite clear that the words we use do affect how we think about things, how we perceive them: were this not so, the drive for 'politically correct' non-racist, non-sexist language would be meaningless. Language influences how we think and how we perceive things, even if it is not the only factor determining our thoughts.

scene, for example, 'Big Bird is hugging Cookie Monster.' (Big Bird and Cookie Monster were familiar characters from a popular television programme, *The Muppets*.) On one screen, this is true. On the other, it's the other way round: Cookie Monster is hugging Big Bird. A child who looked longer at the screen that matches the voice-over would be assumed to have understood the implications of word order for meaning.

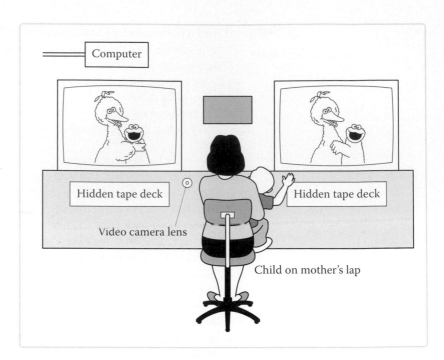

figure **5.4**

Hirsh-Pasek and Golinkoff's
preferential looking task

Source: K. Hirsh-Pasek and R. Golinkoff, *The Origins
of Grammar: Evidence from early language
comprehension.* © 1996. Reproduced with
permission from MIT Press.

Using this method, Hirsh-Pasek and Golinkoff showed that infants
understand word order at 18 months, but don't understand more subtle
aspects of morphology (such as the way word endings change tense or
meanings) until around 2 years of age. In other words, the real use of
syntax to provide meaning begins at the end of the second year of life.

Producing grammatical utterances

Babies' earliest utterances involve only one word: ball, say, or cat, or
mummy. At first these words may be used in a very restricted context.
For example, one small boy initially used the word 'mummy' only in the
context of handing a toy to his mother (Harris et al., 1988). But words
are quickly generalized and used in broader contexts. In fact, infants
typically overextend the meaning of words: for example the word 'ball'
might be used to refer to balls, balloons, marbles, apples, eggs and a
spherical water tank (Rescorla, 1980).

Furthermore, early one-word utterances may carry the meaning of a
whole sentence, so that 'nana!' may mean 'I want a banana', and pointing
at the dog basket and saying 'doggie' may mean 'There's the dog's bed'.
Meaning in these one-word sentences is often carried as much by
contextual cues and the pragmatics of how language is used in context
as by the words themselves.

Somewhere between 18 and 30 months of age (Brown, 1973), children begin to put words together, forming two-word sentences such as
'Where daddy?' or 'Jack shoe!' These simple sentences are called *telegraphic speech* because all the non-essentials (morphemes indicating

tense, plurality and so on; auxiliary verbs such as was and is; function words like in, on, a, the) are left out. Children all round the world, learning very different languages, produce telegraphic speech (Boysson-Bardies, 1999), indicating that this is an important stage in development.

For all its simplicity, telegraphic speech is grammatical. That is to say, it already reflects the syntactical structures of the language the child is learning (Slobin, 1979). For example, two-word utterances follow the grammatical rules of word order of the language the child is learning, and juxtapose parts of speech in a grammatically correct way. A child might say 'little dog', which is grammatically correct but not 'little it', which is not.

Gradually the sentences that children produce become longer and more complex. They begin to include words omitted from telegraphic speech, and begin to reflect rules for modifying words to convey precise meanings (for example, 'pat dog' becomes 'patting dog' and then 'I am patting the dog'). Progressively the child moves on to ever more complex speech structures, producing sentences with more than one clause ('I want *that* bowl because it's got more cherries'). From here the child moves on to master other syntactic rules: for example, mastering the word order for interrogatives ('Why I don't have a cake?' becomes 'Why don't I have a cake?'), and expressing negatives through syntax rather than by bolt-on 'no's' ('No want cake' becomes 'I don't want a cake'). The speed and timing of these developments varies enormously between individual children, even children in the same family. But on average, children begin expanding telegraphese at about 24 months, and start mastering the more complex forms of speech from about 30 months onward.

Using grammar to reveal meaning

As we have already seen, babies are sensitive to syntax well before they produce grammatical sentences of any complexity themselves. They can use this sensitivity to discover the meaning of words. For instance, Gleitman (1990) pointed out that word meanings cannot always be deduced from understanding the events to which they refer. Many scenes can be described in different ways, using different verbs: for example, 'The goose chased the hen' is one way to describe a scene that could also be described by saying, 'The hen fled from the goose'. It would be impossible to work out individual word meanings in either sentence just by observing the event. But by using syntactic clues, one can work out word meanings. For instance, word order and the preposition 'from' which modifies the verb in the second sentence reveal the meaning of both verb and nouns. Using the whole structure of a sentence to infer the meaning of the words in this way is called *syntactic bootstrapping* (Fisher, 2000; Gleitman, 1990).

Two-year-olds can use the syntax of sentences to bootstrap their understanding of word meanings in this way. For example, Naigles (1990) showed 2-year-olds a video of a duck pushing a rabbit over, while both creatures waved their arms about in circles. Some children were told, 'The rabbit and the duck are kradding', and others were told, 'The duck is kradding the rabbit'. On a later test, the children who had heard the first description thought 'kradding' meant waving your arms about in circles, while those who had heard the second description thought 'kradding' meant pushing. In other words, the children inferred the meaning of the verb from the grammatical structure of the sentence in which it occurs.

Working on the rules of syntax

Children are surprisingly interested in grammatical forms and in getting morphology right, as the conversation between a 3-year-old and a 6-year-old shown in **Box 5.3** shows. This conversation also illustrates a classic phenomenon of young children's language: the tendency to over-generalize regular rules for morphological changes (tall/taller/tallest), applying them to irregular words (bad/worse/worst) and so creating incorrect forms (worsest, badder, baddest). Such mistakes are called *over-regularizations*. Common examples of such mistakes applied to verbs and nouns would be 'I goed' or 'I wented' instead of 'I went'; and 'two foots', 'some mouses', 'my tooths' instead of 'two feet', 'some mice', 'my teeth' (Berko, 1958; Xu and Pinker, 1995).

box 5.3

Grammatical concern in the young

Source: Bee (1989).

> 6-year-old: *It's worse to forget to feed them.*
> 3-year-old: *No, it's badder to feed them too much.*
> 6-year-old: *You don't say badder, you say worser.*
> 3-year-old: *But it's baddest to give them too much food.*
> 6-year-old: *No it's not. It's worsest to forget to feed them.*

Over-regularizations of this kind are rare in very young children's speech: few if any children under 2 years of age produce such errors (Fenson et al., 1994), whereas 25 per cent of 2½-year-olds make mistakes of this kind. Often, the child has successfully used the correct irregular form of the word before beginning to produce the over-regularized error. In a curious way, getting word endings wrong in this way is the clearest evidence that young children learn rules about morphology.

Reflecting on language

For all that they learn and apply morphological rules for word endings and syntactical rules for word orders and the like, young children find it very hard to reflect explicitly on language. For example, 4-year-olds are fairly fluent speakers but they are still confused about what is or isn't a word (Karmiloff-Smith, 1992). At this age, children will readily agree that nouns such as 'table' are words, but assert that function words such as 'the' are not. Young children also have difficulty understanding that names (such as 'table') are arbitrary symbols rather than being in some way determined by the object to which they refer. Even 6-year-olds can be confused about this: they're stumped by questions like 'What sounds would cats make if they were *called* dogs?' (Osherson and Markman, 1975), as if the name and the properties of the animal were somehow intertwined.

Karmiloff-Smith (1992) argues that young children are concerned to achieve what she calls 'behavioural success' in speech (in other words, getting the words and the word endings right), but that children under the age of about 6 years don't reflect on language as an object in itself, and don't explicitly reflect on the rules of language. Explicit reflection on language and grammar begins at around 6, and continues through childhood and beyond. Six-year-olds are already explicitly correcting their own utterances (and other people's, as Box 5.3 shows) in the light of strictly linguistic considerations, although they cannot explain why. By 10 years of age, the child can articulate the principle involved.

This developmental change is illustrated in a task where the experimenter hides a child's watch and asks the child to describe what she did (Karmiloff-Smith, 1992). Six-year-olds may say things like: 'You hid my wat ... the watch'. Ten year olds say 'the watch' from the outset, and can explain why that's better:

Well ... 'my watch' because it belongs to me, but I said 'you hid the watch' because there are no other watches there. If you'd put yours out I would have had to say 'you hid my watch' because it could have been confusing, but this way it's better for me to say 'you hid the watch' so someone doesn't think yours was there too.
(Karmiloff-Smith, 1992)

Both the self-correction of the 6-year-old in this task and the comment of the 10-year-old reflect a degree of awareness of the way specifically linguistic considerations convey meaning. This metalinguistic awareness is hard to detect in younger children, and is not yet explicit or articulate in the 6-year-old as it is at 10 years of age. *Metalinguistic awareness* goes on developing well beyond the age of 10, fostered not only by the child's own efforts but also by explicit lessons in grammar in school. Nonetheless, metalinguistic knowledge can be sketchy even in adults: you and I use the subjunctive easily in talking. Can you (or I) define what a subjunctive actually is?

Theories of language development

The phenomena of learning to talk described above are rich and multi-layered. What shapes and drives this development? There is still a great deal of controversy on this issue. Different theories propose entirely different explanations of the processes underlying the development of language. No one theory has yet convincingly explained all of the phenomena.

Biology and language

It is quite clear that our human capacity for language has a strong biological base. All but the most damaged of human beings develop language, where no other species do. We alone possess certain brain structures dedicated to language. Newborn human beings have an impressive ability to differentiate the phonemes, patterns and rhythms of speech, and an inbuilt fascination with these things. Furthermore, human infants seem to have a strong drive to learn to talk, doing so without much prompting: as Flavell (1985) put it: 'Draconian measures would be needed to prevent most children from learning to talk'! The power of this drive is revealed by studies of children born deaf to parents who don't learn sign language: though not exposed to language, these infants develop their own hand signal systems, systems that spontaneously show some of the characteristics common to all natural human languages (Goldin-Meadow and Feldman, 1979). All these things indicate that language is quite clearly part of our evolutionary heritage.

The conclusion that we are born biologically prepared to learn language is no longer controversial: every researcher in the area would agree. But exactly what this biological endowment involves is a matter of continuing controversy. The controversy centres around how we develop grammar. As we have seen, it is grammar that defines language. And as we have seen, species that don't share our capacity for grammar can (to some extent) learn word meanings and can learn about the phonetics, prosody and pragmatics of language, suggesting that these things may develop from very general cognitive capacities rather than from language-specific mechanisms. Only grammar is unique to humans. Why? Is it innately programmed into us? If not, how do we master this complex phenomenon?

Chomsky and innate mechanisms for language

A number of theorists have argued that grammatical structures are just so very complicated that there is no way a baby could master these things without the help of very specific innate mechanisms (Pinker, 1984). This idea goes back to nativist philosophers such as Kant (1781). Its most influential modern exponent has been Noam Chomsky (1957, 1980), who proposed a detailed and complex theory of the innate mechanisms that may underlie the development of grammatical language.

According to Chomsky, since grammar is too complex to be learned, it must somehow be pre-wired into the infant brain. But this poses a problem: different languages have very different grammatical structures (for example, rules for word order are importantly different in English and French; sentences without nouns or pronouns are allowable in some languages, where this would not be grammatical in others; some languages allow verbs to stand alone where others do not – the single word 'nevica' is grammatical in Italian, for example, where in English we'd have to say 'it's snowing' to convey the same meaning grammatically). Obviously, whatever is wired into the human brain, it cannot be the specific grammatical structures of any one human language.

Chomsky argued that in fact, underneath all the 'surface' variations between one language and another there is a single, common grammar: the *Universal Grammar*. Every human language is a variant of this Universal Grammar. The analogy of a drinks vending machine may be useful in understanding this idea: there is a single machine whose overall structure is pre-set and unchanging. Set its buttons one way, and you get back coffee, set them another and you get a milky tea, or soup. By analogy, the Universal Grammar is the pre-set and unchanging 'machine' for producing grammatical speech. Set its 'buttons' one way and you get the grammatical forms of English; set them in other ways and you get the grammatical forms of Arabic or Urdu, and so on.

According to Chomsky, then, we inherit a fixed 'machine' for mastering grammar. This machine (the Universal Grammar) is a special *module* (Fodor, 1983) in the mind, dedicated only to the acquisition of grammatical speech and separate from other mental functions (just as the vending machine is specialized to produce beverages, and has no connection with machines for cooking food, say). Because the Universal Grammar already contains all the grammatical possibilities of human language, babies have no need to learn these things. All they need do is to 'set the buttons' to produce the particular version of grammar needed for the particular language they are learning. According to Chomsky (1979), exposure to a given language is enough to 'set the buttons' appropriately.

To put this complicated idea another way, Chomsky (1979) argues that we do not learn grammar at all: we are born with a powerful grammatical device all ready and set to go. All we need do is to 'prime' this device for the particular language that will be our mother tongue. This priming involves 'setting' a relatively small number of the key parameters that differentiate the grammatical rules of one language from another (word order rules, for example). A relatively small experience of the mother tongue is enough to allow the innate grammar machine to automatically 'set' itself.

Chomsky's innate grammar machine has been called the *language acquisition device* or *LAD* (McNeill, 1970). According to Chomsky, the LAD is controlled by an innate biological programme that takes time to mature, which explains why, despite possessing this powerful device, babies don't begin to acquire grammar until the second year of life. The idea that the timing of language development is biologically controlled is associated with the idea that there is a special time or critical period in development at which language is 'supposed' to be mastered, and that the acquisition of language will be considerably harder if this critical period is missed.

This account of how children master grammar is very intriguing. It would certainly explain how individual children acquire grammar, although, of course, it doesn't offer any sort of explanation of how our species acquired the LAD in the first place. But the theory is very controversial. The data we have do not provide clear support for it, and key assumptions are open to serious challenge.

Evidence for the LAD

The key evidence used to support Chomsky's theory was the observation that young children tend to over-apply grammatical rules, producing the errors of 'over-regularization' noted above ('I goed', 'tooths', 'mouses' and so on). Such mistakes are surprising: obviously, they are not copied from other people, since adults and older children tend not to make such errors, so whatever generates the over-generalization of grammatical rules is *inside* the child. Furthermore, over-regularizations seem quite different from the errors children make in other areas: for example, children begin by over-extending the meaning of words (using 'ball' to refer to anything round, for instance) and progressively refine their usage until it matches other people's. But children produce over-regularization errors *after* they have previously produced the correct irregular forms, the forms that other people use. Again, this looks like evidence for the action of an internal grammar machine rather than learning.

This conclusion seemed to be powerfully endorsed by the discovery that deaf children who are not exposed spoken language or to official sign languages invent their own, creating systems that have been claimed to have grammatical structure: structure that could not have been learned from experience, and must therefore have come from within (Goldin-Meadow and Feldman, 1979).

All of this evidence has been challenged. First: over-regularizations are rare (Marcus et al., 1992). The data suggest that 75 per cent of children may never make such errors at all (Fenson et al., 1994). Even the children who do make such mistakes also use the correct irregular forms, making the error only occasionally. These data do not fit with the idea that there is a powerful LAD controlling the acquisition of language and driving the child to apply grammatical rules. A very different explanation fits the data better: namely, that young children learn irregular forms (go/went, tooth/teeth and so on) by heart, and produce these whenever they can remember them. Over-regularization errors occur not out of any drive or desire to be grammatical, but simply on occasions where the child has forgotten the correct irregular version of the word and applies the rule by default, as an intelligent guess (Marcus, 1996). This still implies that children know something about grammatical rules for word endings. But this knowledge could be learned, rather than the product of an innate Universal Grammar.

Nor do the communicative systems invented by deaf children with no experience of language provide support for the claim that there are powerful internal mechanisms for grammar. In fact, it is easily possible for a sign system of the kind these children invent to show patterns without having grammatical structure. For example, Signed English is a widely used sign system that is not grammatical (see Box 5.1). Many researchers argue that the systems invented by deaf children are not grammatical either, and so provide no evidence for the existence of innate grammatical devices.

Maturation and development

The notion that there is a biological programme that sets the speed and direction of development in relation to the acquisition of grammar has been profoundly challenged both by evidence and by new theories.

As we have seen earlier in this chapter, there is a great deal of variation in the speed with which children progress from one-word utterances to complex grammatical sentences, and in the steps they take in the process (Brown, 1973). Some researchers argue that there is simply too much variation between individuals for the development of grammatical speech to be governed by a pre-set biological programme (Maratsos, 1983). Certainly, experience seems to play a role in shaping how development occurs, a role that goes beyond merely priming the release of innate skills (Ellis and Wells, 1980). Both the speed and shape of language development are affected by social and cultural experience (Gopnik and Choi, 1995).

Evidence that there is a critical period during which language learning is made especially easy by the support of a maturing biological programme has also been questioned. It's true that children who miss out on learning language in infancy for some reason (such as deafness or social isolation) do often struggle to catch up, but their struggle could be explained in many other ways besides missing a biologically programmed 'critical period' (**Box 5.4**). It's also true that young children are better at learning a second language than are older children or adults (Box 5.4). But again, this does not necessarily point to a biologically programmed critical period for language learning: the young are better at learning a great many complex tasks than their elders, from the old craze for Rubik's Cube to the intricacies of computer games – but no one would suggest that evolution could have primed us specifically to learn these things at a certain age! An alternative explanation is that the very simplicity of the child's mind allows a focus on specific, concrete patterns in learning language (or Rubik's Cube, or computer games), the very level of analysis optimal for learning. It may be that adults learn more slowly because we over-complicate things (Box 5.4).

box 5.4

Critical periods and second-language
learning

One implication of the notion that there is an innate program driving the development of language is that there may be a 'critical period' during which language learning is easiest, and after which, the capacity to learn a language declines.

Early tests of this hypothesis looked at so-called 'feral' children: individuals who had, for one reason or another, been deprived of contact with language in early childhood. For example, one child had been abandoned by his family, and had somehow survived by living among animals. Another had been kept tied to a chair in isolation throughout her childhood. Such children, when rescued, tend to make relatively little progress in mastering language. Certainly, they do not make a full recovery to become fluent speakers.

At first, the evidence from feral children seems to support the idea that there is a critical period for language learning, and that these unfortunate children had missed it. But this conclusion is unsafe. Such children have suffered far more deprivation and damage than the absence of language. This greater damage may be responsible for their failure to recover or to learn to speak. They may also have had some sort of handicap in the first place, and have been abandoned or hidden away for that reason.

More recent research has looked at second-language learning. If it's true that there is a critical period for language learning in early childhood, then we should expect young children to learn a second language more easily than do their elders. This seems to be the case.

For example, individuals who had emigrated from Korea to the United States before the age of 7 years were, in adult life, as fluent in English as individuals who had been born and raised in the United States (Johnson and Newport, 1989). Those who emigrated between the ages of 8 and 10 years had become fairly fluent in adult life, but were not as fluent as indigenous Americans. The older the age of emigration (and the start of learning English), the less fluency the individual would achieve.

More interesting still is the discovery that adults who learned a second language before the age of 3 years show a completely different pattern of brain activity on grammar tests in the second language from those who had learned that language after the age of 3 (Neville and Bavelier, 1999). Those who became bilingual before 3 years of age showed a bias toward greater activity in the left hemisphere than the right, as would be normal for first-language processing. The later the second language had been learned, the more both hemispheres were involved in processing.

Data such as these certainly support the conclusion that it is easier to learn a language in childhood than later on. But they do not necessarily support the idea that this is because there is a maturational 'programme' with a biologically specified critical period for language learning. Other interpretations are possible. For example, Newport (1991) suggests that young children are better language learners because they have a cognitive rather than a biological advantage: the younger the child, the more limited his or her memory and conceptual complexity. As a result, the younger the child, the smaller and simpler the block of language that will be identified and learned. Small, simple blocks are inherently easier to learn than large or more complex ones – hence the younger child's greater success.

Furthermore, the theoretical models of development produced by dynamic systems theory (Chapter 2) are beginning to show that even very complex phenomena (such as language) can develop without there being any innate pre-specification of what is to be developed or how it is to develop (Gershkoff-Stowe and Thelen, 2004; Thelen and Smith, 1994). Just as crawling can develop as almost a 'happy accident' of the way the dynamic system that is the child's physical world works (Chapter 2), so language can develop through the complex interactions of the factors that comprise the child's social world, without any biological programme to guide it. We shall return to this later in this chapter.

Identifying grammatical universals

Chomsky's theory depends on the idea that there is a Universal Grammar which captures all the features of every human language. But it has turned out to be very difficult (if not impossible) to specify what this Universal Grammar looks like, or to identify the features and parameters on which languages vary, or to specify any set of rules that could relate the variation across individual human languages to this one hypothetical root (Maratsos, 1998; Slobin, 1985).

If the diversity of grammars across different human language systems can't be reduced to a single set of universal underlying principles, then it is hard to see how babies could be innately provided with a general syntax allowing them to learn whatever human language they might encounter as their mother tongue, as Chomsky suggests.

Modifications to Chomsky's theory

In response to these kinds of criticism Chomsky's followers have abandoned some aspects of his theory but endorsed the core idea that the acquisition of grammar reflects the action of innate modules in the mind specifically geared to the development of language (Fodor, 1983; Gleitman, 1990; Pinker, 1984).

For example, Pinker proposes that, while there may be no complete Universal Grammar, babies' minds are innately pre-wired to expect to discover things like nouns and verbs and rule-governed relationships between them (Pinker, 1984, 1987). The child does not need, therefore, to learn that these grammatical structures exist. All he or she need learn is how these elements of speech are handled in a particular language (Grimshaw, 1981). According to Pinker, such learning comes about through a process that he has called *semantic bootstrapping*. The child understands the meaning (semantics) of events: who did what to whom. The structure of this semantic understanding maps onto the grammatical word classes (noun, verb) and categories (subject, object, transitive/intransitive verb and so on) that the child is innately primed to expect. Having made this mapping, the child is now well placed to notice the details of how these grammatical elements operate in the language being learned.

The idea that children could use their understanding of the meaning of events to discover the structure of grammar is appealing. It offers an elegantly simple solution to the problem of how a child could ever start mastering the complexities of grammar. But Pinker's theory has also been criticized.

First, even if children do use their understanding of the meaning of events to discover the structure of grammar in the speech that describes those events, there is no reason why this process need necessarily involve any innate pre-specification of grammatical categories or structures (Maratsos, 1998). Such discoveries might just as easily reflect the child's general cognitive capacity for learning to identify patterns and categories, without any innate pre-specification of what those categories would be (Bates and MacWhinney, 1989; Braine, 1994; Bruner, 1975b, 1975c).

Furthermore, whether there are innate mechanisms at work or not, semantic bootstrapping can't entirely explain how children master grammar. The theory has to assume that the structure of meanings maps neatly onto the structure of innate grammatical categories (that action words are always verbs, for example), otherwise the bootstrapping could not explain learning. But action words are not always verbs. For example: 'bath' is not a verb, but it is an action word ('I bath daily'). 'Bath' behaves like a noun rather than a verb. Up to 15 per cent of the action words that a young child learning English hears violate the 'verb expectation' in this way (Pinker, 1984). If children can only learn about verbs by extrapolating from action words, these violations ought to disrupt development – but they don't. Young children are efficient in learning about the grammatical properties of verbs, and they also learn to understand and to use non-verb action words like 'bath' without difficulty. They use non-verbs such as 'up' or 'away' in specifying actions even in two-word 'sentences' (for instance 'car away' – Nelson, 1996). Semantic bootstrapping does not explain how this is possible.

Grammar from cognitive and social processes

A number of theorists reject Chomsky's claim that there is an innate grammar acquisition device, or a biological programme pre-set to yield grammatical speech (Bates and MacWhinney, 1989; Bloom and Tinker, 2001; Bruner, 1983; Lieven, Pine and Baldwin, 1997; Snow, 1999; Tomasello, 1992, 1998). It's worth noting that these theorists agree that there is some sort of biological basis for language: that the baby is genetically equipped with predispositions and perceptual capacities that are useful for learning about language. What they reject is specifically the claim that there is some special 'grammar module' in the mind of the kind described by Chomsky and his followers. These theorists argue instead that children learn grammar as they learn everything else, through applying very general cognitive and perceptual skills to the problem.

Grammar and the structure of social meanings

An influential theorist in this area was Jerome Bruner, who claimed that, in fact, the structure of social interactions and meanings is sufficient to allow the child to master grammar, without the need for any innate representation of what is to be mastered. Just like Pinker, Bruner (1975a, 1975b) argued that by understanding the meaning of events (who did what to whom or what) children can identify grammatical structures in language (subject, verb, object and so on) and so can learn about grammar.

Bruner argues that the structure of social interactions is rich enough to allow the child to discover *all* the subtleties and nuances of grammar. It is this last claim that nativists like Pinker reject, arguing that there are complexities of grammar that are not evident in the structure of social interactions, and which can only be discovered by specifically grammatical processes (Pinker, 1984). This conclusion is now widely accepted: there are things about grammar that you can't discover simply by understanding the structure and meaning of social interactions and events. But there are many alternatives to Pinker's suggestion that grammatical development would therefore be impossible without special innate mechanisms to generate it.

Scaffolding, infant-directed speech and language

So far, the theories we've looked at have emphasized the role of the individual child trying to figure out or acquire language and grammar from the speech he or she hears. An individual trying to deduce the grammatical structure of a language from first principles in this way faces a difficult task, perhaps an impossibly difficult one, as Pinker suggests. But in reality, children do not learn language as isolated individuals by the power of their own efforts alone. The *point* of language is social communication. The child's efforts to master language are embedded in social communications with others. Some theorists believe that these interactions play a crucial role in shaping up the child's progressive linguistic skills, with the adult partner effectively teaching the child language.

Adults certainly encourage babies to communicate in a variety of ways. By the time a baby is 2 months old, parents are engaging in 'proto-conversations' with the child (Trevarthen, 1993b), each partner watching the other's face intently and alternately making noises or facial expressions that the other then copies. Trevarthen believes that these proto-conversations are genuine interactions in which the baby is trying to communicate (Reddy et al., 1997; Trevarthen, 1993a). Other researchers believe that it is only the adult who is really taking turns or intending to communicate, interpreting the child's reflexive reactions *as if* they were communications and matching their own behaviour accordingly (see Chapter 4). At one level, it doesn't much matter who is right:

treating babies as if they were trying to communicate provides exactly the right input to encourage the baby to *develop* the intention of communicating, just as creating a pattern of turn-taking provides exactly the right context for babies to develop this skill.

Treating children 'as if' they possess skills beyond their actual abilities and supporting their fragile efforts in this way provides a very powerful tool through which many aspects of language could be shaped up in the child. This type of interaction between adult and child has been called *scaffolding* (Vygotsky, 1978; Wertsch, 1979) and is not peculiar to language development: social interactions of this type support development in many areas (see Chapter 1).

In addition, adults tend to speak to young children in very distinctive ways – ways that make the business of learning language easier. The distinctive speech addressed to infants used to be called 'motherese' (Newport, Gleitman and Gleitman, 1977), but is more properly called *infant-directed speech* since it is not just mothers who produce it (even children do this when speaking to younger infants – Sachs and Devin, 1976). The two clearest features of infant-directed speech are that it is generally warmer and more affectionate in tone than adult-directed speech, and that the characteristics of speech are exaggerated: the voice is pitched higher, pauses between words are longer, patterns of intonation are emphasized more than usual. Furthermore, the pattern of conversations between adults and young children tends to be distinctive. When a baby points at something, adults almost always react by labelling the thing pointed at (Masur, 1982) – which would be a strange response if they were speaking to another adult. And adults tend to repeat back what the very young say, expanding and correcting the utterance to be longer and more grammatical (for example correcting 'Daddy coat' to 'That's daddy's coat': Nelson et al., 1984).

It's easy to see how these modifications make infant-directed speech more attractive to babies (Cooper and Aslin, 1994). It's also easy to see how the exaggerated features of infant-directed speech make the baby's task of learning language easier – and infants do in fact learn more words from infant-directed speech than from adult-directed speech (Golinkoff, Alioto and Hirsh-Pasek, 1996). Even the exaggerated intonation patterns may help the child to extract meaning from vocalizations. All round the world, adults 'bark' negatives (for example 'no', said sharply, with an aggressive tone) and 'croon' positives (yeees, drawn out and sing-song). At 8 months, babies take meaning from the intonational pattern rather than the words said. As Fernald (1989) puts it, 'the melody is the message'.

Many people have observed that it's almost impossible to resist the urge to use infant-directed speech when speaking to a small child. In fact, it almost feels as if this tendency is an instinctive response in adults. But this seems not to be the case. It's true that adults in many cultures around the world use infant-directed speech (Boysson-Bardies, 1999). But infant-directed speech is not universal, as an instinctive response should be. In some cultures adults don't speak to babies at all, believing it to be pointless (Le, 2000; Watson-Gegeo and Gegeo, 1986). And whilst adults from many cultures hold proto-conversations with very young babies, some don't. For example, some cultures believe it is dangerous to make eye contact, and avoid face-to-face interactions with babies and young children altogether. The tendency to hold proto-conversations and to use infant-directed speech seem to be culturally learned, rather than instinctive.

Just how big a role does infant-directed speech, or direct tuition by adults, play in the development of language? The answer to this question is not yet clear. Infant-directed speech certainly makes it easier for the baby to take the first steps in language development. But babies in cultures where infant-directed speech is not used take those first steps too, albeit more slowly (Lieven, 1994). The implication is that infant-directed speech is useful but not essential in the early stages of language development.

Most puzzling of all is the role of adult input to the development of grammatical speech. Adults provide potentially useful input for the child's mastery of grammar in two ways. Their own speech provides a model of grammatically correct speech (although adult speech itself is ungrammatical more often than we suppose). And adults correct and expand children's utterances, providing correct models of the child's own efforts ('I goed fridge': 'You went to the fridge?'). Obviously, models of grammatically correct utterances must play *some* role in the development of language, otherwise, the child could not master the peculiarities of the mother tongue at all. But the influence of such modelling is not as powerful as you might expect.

For example, children whose mothers speak with greater grammatical correctness and complexity do not master these things faster or more effectively than those whose mothers' speech is less grammatical and less complex (Gleitman, Newport and Gleitman, 1984), suggesting that this kind of modelling has little direct influence over development. And in fact, it seems that parents very seldom make deliberate efforts to teach children grammar, and children profit very little when they do. Parents tend to focus more on the content of the communication than on correct grammatical forms, so that the child's part of a conversation may go uncorrected even though it includes gross grammatical errors (Maratsos, 1998). This is probably just as well. Trying to correct a child's grammar is largely wasted effort, as the examples in **Boxes 5.5** and 5.3 show.

Data like these make it hard to see how social interactions, scaffolding or tuition could explain how infants learn grammatical structures. The child certainly uses input from the interactions and conversations he or

box 5.5

Grammatical indifference in the young

Source: McNeill (1970).

Child: *Nobody don't like me.*
Mother: *No, say 'Nobody likes me'.*
Child: *Nobody don't like me.*
Mother: *No, now listen carefully, say 'Nobody likes me'.*
Child: *Oh! Nobody don't likes me.*

she hears and participates in. But grammatical speech seems to develop stubbornly at its own pace. Chomsky and his followers still argue that this supports their theory that children are not learning grammar from the environment at all, but rather priming an innate programme for pursuing grammatical speech which produces errors as part of its normal maturation. Recently, new research has proposed a radical alternative explanation.

Building blocks for conversations

Neither the innate mechanisms described by Chomsky and his followers nor the accounts of language learning through general conceptual understanding or social interaction have explained how or why children learn grammar. But what if children *aren't* learning grammar at all? What if language production is *not* driven and directed by grammatical rules, as has always been supposed? What if grammar is entirely in the eye of the beholder, and not in the head of the speaker at all?

This suggestion is not as bizarre as it may at first sound. The fact that we can *describe* language in terms of grammatical word categories and syntactical structures does not necessarily mean that these things are part of the *process* generating language. A process is not identical with its product. For example, fire produces ash, but the process of combustion is not at all like the residue it leaves. Snowflakes grow into complex and beautiful structures that can be *described* by mathematical equations, but there is no question of these equations being present in any way in the snowflake. It is possible that, like the snowflake, children produce complex patterns of behaviour (grammatical speech) without in any way knowing that they do that, and without directly using grammatical rules in the process. Many facets of human cognition show complex structures, although they develop organically rather than through the application of rules (Plunkett, 2000), as we shall see in later chapters. Why not language?

Some theorists (Lieven et al., 1997; Tomasello, 1998) suggest that children learn to speak very specifically as a tool for conversation and communication. Initially, they learn very concrete words or phrases off by heart ('Where daddy?' for example, or 'Mummy eating cake'), and use these in very specific situations. The child has no innate expectation of grammar and develops no representation of parts of speech or grammatical rules at all: no notion of nouns and verbs, no notion of the subject–verb–object structure of a sentence. All the child has is a collection of useful concrete speech units. These form the basic building blocks for language.

Learning by rote, the child gradually accumulates a number of speech units with common features (for example: 'Where daddy?' 'Where doggie?', 'Where sock?' and so on). Generalizing across these parallel units, the child abstracts a *template* reflecting their commonalities: 'Where … ?'. This process of abstraction has nothing to do with grammatical processes or insights. It's a straightforward product of the child's very general conceptual skill in detecting patterns and regularities. Nevertheless, the creation of this template provides the child with a *frame* into which new words can be slotted ('Where coat?', 'Where Jack?' and so on). By slotting new words into this frame, the child can generate new utterances that have not been learned by rote (Lieven et al., 1997; Tomasello, 1998).

Detailed recordings of children's early speech fit with this view of how language develops. Early speech is constructed around verb forms, which are initially learned by rote in concrete contexts and then gradually abstracted as the centre of a template with several slots that can be filled (Tomasello, 1992). For example, 'eating' may form the centre of a template with the form ' … eating … ', allowing the child to construct a variety of utterances such as 'Mummy eating cake', 'Dog eating hat', and so on. Whole phrases, or even other template phrases, can be put into these slots: for example, 'hungry dog' 'eating' 'all the cake', or 'where daddy' 'eating' 'the cake'?

In this way the child can gradually develop the ability to construct longer and more complex utterances. From an objective point of view it is possible to identify sophisticated grammatical structures in these utterances (subclauses, say), but there is no sense in which these structures are represented in the child's mind, nor any need for grammatical principles to be involved in generating the utterance. For example, sentences containing subclauses can be constructed simply by slotting whole phrases into the primary template.

According to this approach, specifically grammatical structures are only recognized long after the child has already learned to speak in grammatical ways – if at all. Even adult language may be constructed from basic building blocks rather than drawing on a process involving any sort of representation of grammatical rules and structures (Lieven et al., 1997; Tomasello, 1992, 1998), although once an individual is speaking grammatically, 'grammar' is there to be discovered as an emergent property of speech. Karmiloff-Smith's work (1992) suggests that children do eventually make some discoveries about grammar, though these have nothing to do with achieving behavioural success in speech. But these discoveries need not be very articulate. It may be that only trained linguists have real representations of grammatical structures.

Of course, young children obviously do extract rules for speech: rules for word endings, for example, that are evident in their errors of over-regularization. But these rules need not be grammatical rules as such: that is to say, they may reflect a very general cognitive tendency to generalize across a collection of concrete examples (Bruner and Kenney, 1965), rather than any concern with specifically linguistic rules about nouns or verbs as such. The fact that children make relatively few errors of over-regularization, and make such errors patchily rather than consistently, having previously got the correct irregular form right, fits better with the idea that the error arises when the child forgets the word ending and must fill the gap by generalizing (Marcus, 1996) than with the theory that the child is driven by zeal for a grammatical rule.

This account of how language develops has yet to be fully elaborated and tested, so it's not yet clear just how far the process Tomasello and Lieven and colleagues propose could account for the development of grammatical speech. However, the approach has many strengths. It fits with most of our observations of the phenomena of language development. It integrates the development of language very directly with general conceptual processes, and with the social and communicative functions that language serves. It suggests an elegant account of how simple, general cognitive processes could generate all the complex structures of speech, without the need for innate mechanisms or language-specific developmental processes.

Connectionism and dynamic systems approaches

Tomasello and Lieven's thesis that language can develop without the need for innate representations of grammatical structures, and without special innate mechanisms for learning language, is strongly supported by both connectionist and dynamic systems theories (see Chapters 2 and 3 for an introduction to these approaches).

Connectionist systems are computer-based neural networks which simulate the way patterns of neurons become interconnected in the human brain as we learn. The more often a particular pattern of neural activity occurs, the more that pattern is strengthened, and the easier it is to find and reuse it. Sub-patterns which regularly co-occur become ever more firmly linked into a larger overall pattern, building up ever more complex patterns of neural connections, supporting ever more complex behaviours. Learning occurs in this way in every area, no matter what the activity, because this is the way neural networks learn.

Many different aspects of language development have been explored through connectionist systems, from learning to interpret meaning (Sugita and Tani, 2005) to the acquisition of syntax (Chang, Dell and Bock, 2006). Connectionist systems show an impressive ability to mimic certain aspects of language acquisition in children. For example, given only a minimum of pre-programming and no language-specific learning mechanisms at all, a neural network devised by Rumelhart and McClelland (1986) learned the past tense of English verbs through exposure to a large number of sentences of the kind young children hear, containing regular and irregular verbs. In the process, it showed patterns of behaviour very similar to those observed in young children, including errors of over-regularization, even though it had no representation of grammatical rules whatever. Rumelhart and McClelland claim that the success of programs like theirs demonstrates that all the information needed to acquire language is inherent in language itself and is extractable by general-purpose learning processes, so that there is no need for innate mechanisms or special language development devices.

But as impressive as such demonstrations are, it would be premature to conclude that connectionist models can resolve the mysteries of human language development. Each connectionist model concentrates on a tiny fragment of language development – no system comes anywhere near simulating the complexity of even the young child's mastery of language. Furthermore, the specific pre-programming built into any one connectionist system (the details of exactly how connections are made, strengthened or discarded, activated and so on), and the particular experiences the programmers allow it (exactly what examples or activities it encounters) determine its performance – and neither the pre-programming nor the system's experiences necessarily correspond to those of a human child. The fact that connectionist systems typically learn very quickly what children take years to master suggests that there are important differences between the way such programs address language learning, and the way human infants do it.

The starting assumptions of a connectionist model (its pre-programming, the kinds of experience the researcher assumes that it needs to develop) play a vital role in determining just how successful this approach can be in simulating the development of language in infancy. Many of the basic ideas about learning inherent in connectionist models are shared by dynamic systems theory, which offers new ways of exploring what those starting assumptions should be.

Like connectionist models, a dynamic systems approach assumes that language develops without the need for language-specific mechanisms of the kind postulated by Chomsky or his followers. Rather, language emerges from the same general process as all other behaviour, through the dynamic functioning of the human system. This human system includes all the physiological and neurological characteristics of the child, all the innate predispositions and reflexes the child brings into the world, the people with whom the child interacts, the characteristics of these interactions, the child's goals and activities, the details of the language to be mastered. These things interact, combining to create a complex dynamic system. Language develops as an emergent function (see Chapter 2) of the dynamic action of this system, without there needing to be any innate recipe for the path this development will take.

From a dynamic systems perspective, language develops through the interaction between an infant who is 'configured' for learning to communicate through language, and an environment which provides special support for this. The infant is primed with physiological structures, innate perceptual biases and dispositions, and with social and emotional needs and reactions which combine to produce a powerful orientation toward language learning. The social environment bathes the child in language, and includes the child in the language game from the start: most parents speak to their newborn baby, welcoming this precious newcomer as we would welcome any arrival, and carrying on 'conversations' as they cuddle, play with or nurture the child thereafter. Adults, and particularly the parents, provide all kinds of specific support for language learning, from a rewarding enthusiasm for the child's earliest efforts to communicate, to infant-directed speech, naming strategies which make word meanings particularly easy to learn, offering corrected versions of the child's utterances, word games and so on.

Thus a dynamic systems approach argues that to understand the development of language we have to understand the details of how the characteristics of the language-configured child and those of the language-supportive environment interact and combine to shape the emergence of language. What differences in one or other of these account for the individual variations we see in the development of language? What essential features of either account for the fact that all normal children eventually master the structures and meanings of language and become fluent? This way of thinking about language development is new. There is still comparatively little work exploring these issues (Gershkoff-Stowe and Thelen, 2004). But dynamic systems theory holds out considerable promise for a strong account of the development of language (Lewis, 2000).

In conclusion

Language is one of the defining features of the human mind, a uniquely subtle and flexible symbol system with a complex and intricate structure. The task of learning language looks daunting – and yet virtually every human baby succeeds. We do not yet wholly understand how this is possible.

Many aspects of language, from the meaning of words to the phonetic and prosodic sounds of speech, and the pragmatics of how we use speech in different contexts, are learned. Since other species who do not share our linguistic abilities can, to some extent, master these things, it seems likely that development in this area reflects general processes for learning, rather than language-specific ones, even if human babies are born with perceptual biases and reflexes that particularly dispose us to orient to and learn about speech. Like every other human characteristic, language has a strong genetic base.

But just how far has evolution gone in preparing us to develop language? Human beings are unique in mastering grammar. For 30 years, research in this area has been dominated by controversy over whether or not the grammatical structure of language is innately 'hard-wired' into babies' brains. Would it be possible to learn grammar if it weren't? Claims that there is nothing in the child's experience, nothing in social interactions that can explain how children master all the subtleties and complexities of grammar unless there is an innate grammar device have been countered by claims that the evidence just doesn't support the existence of such a grammar machine.

As is often the case with such controversies, the resolution may lie not in proving one or other 'side' right, but in a complete reconceptualization of what language is and how it develops. This reconceptualization suggests that in fact, we neither inherit grammar acquisition devices nor learn to speak grammatically by learning grammatical principles: in fact, the *process* of generating language is not grammatical at all, even if an observer can identify the patterns that we call grammar in what is produced. This new view of language suggests that we learn the building blocks of speech by rote, learning to generalize from one to another and to combine and recombine these building blocks in ever more complex ways. Grammar as such is in the eye of the beholder, rather than in the processes producing speech.

This radical new view of the development of language fits well with the new theoretical understanding of learning provided by connec-tionist computer models that mimic the way neural systems work in the brain. It fits well, too, with the view of development proposed by dynamic systems theory, which explores how complex phenomena (such as language) can emerge through the action of a complex dynamic system (such as the human baby in his or her social context), without there being any need for an innate programme to ensure that develop-ment takes a given path, or any representation in the child to specify what is developing. Will these new theoretical ideas be able to resolve the puzzles of language development?

Exercises

1. What are the core differences between Chomsky's theory and the account of language development given by Tomasello and Lieven? Is there compelling evidence that one of these theories is better than the other?

2. How could we devise a methodology to test the hypothesis that girls learn to speak earlier than boys? What factors would you have to control for, to test such a theory? How would you do it?

Suggested further reading

For a discussion of non-human primate language learning read:

- M. Tomasello (1994) Can an ape understand a sentence? A review of *Language Comprehension In Ape and Child* by E. Savage-Rumbaugh et al. *Language and Communication* 14, pp. 377–90.

For an overview of language development read:

- K. Karmiloff and A. Karmiloff-Smith (2001) *Pathways to Language: From fetus to adolescent*, Developing Child Series. Cambridge, Mass: Harvard University Press.

For cross-cultural comparisons of language development read:

- B. Schieffelin and E. Ochs (eds) (1986) *Language Socialization across Cultures*. Studies in the Social and Cultural Foundations of Language no. 3. New York: Cambridge University Press.

For a discussion of the origins of individual (and gender) differences in language development read:

- Y. Kovas, M. Hayiou-Thomas, B. Oliver and D. Bishop (2005) Genetic influences in different aspects of language development: the etiology of language skills in 4.5-year-old twins. *Child Development* 76, pp. 632–51.

For detailed discussions of ongoing issues in language development read:

- L. Bloom (1998) Language acquisition in its developmental context, pp. 309–70 in D. Kuhn and R. Siegler (eds), W. Damon (series ed.), *Handbook of Child Psychology*, vol. 2: *Cognition, Perception and Language*. New York: Wiley.
- M. Maratsos (1998) The acquisition of grammar. In D. Kuhn and R. Siegler (eds), W. Damon (series ed.), *Handbook of Child Psychology*, vol. 2: *Cognition, Perception and Language*. New York: Wiley.

Revision summary

The nature of language

- The ability to communicate with language is central to human intelligence and experience. Other species also communicate with one another in various ways, from vocalizations to body postures and behavioural displays. But their communication systems do not provide rich and flexible symbol systems as human language does. Only human language has grammatical structure, and it is grammar that creates the flexibility and sensitivity of language.

- Chimpanzees and gorillas can master some aspects of human language, and can even use simple grammatical structures such as word order to infer meaning, but a 2-year-old human's grasp on grammar far outstrips that of the most linguistically sophisticated non-human primate, no matter how intensely trained.

The development of language

- Human babies are born already equipped to learn language.

- Our young are born with brain structures specifically dedicated to language. And we are born with a vocal tract that has the potential for speech, although this tract must mature through the first weeks of life, before speech sounds are possible.

- Human babies are also born predisposed to find language interesting and to attend to it, and with an impressive ability to hear the sounds (phonemes) and rhythms (prosody) of speech. These innate skills are already in play in the womb, so that at birth babies can differentiate their own mother tongue from a foreign language.

- Through the first months of life babies practise speech sounds, cooing and babbling to others, copying the sounds other people make, and experimenting with noises alone in their cots. Even deaf babies play with sounds in this way, suggesting an innate predisposition is at work, though they soon fall behind the hearing.

- Babbling begins with very simple vowel sounds (aaa). Gradually consonants are added (ma, pa, ha) and then strung together (mamama). Early babbling includes sounds not found in the adult language the baby hears, but progressively focuses on the phonemes of that language, taking on its prosody, so that French babies babble with the rhythms and intonations of French and English babies babble with the rhythms and intonations of English.

- Babies show an astonishing ability to pick out words from a stream of speech, apparently simply by recognizing often-repeated sequences of sound. They first recognize the meaning of certain words, such as their own names and the words 'mummy' and 'daddy', at around 4 to 6 months. At 9 months, they discover the possibility of sharing a joint attention with someone else by looking where the other is looking, or pointing to attract the other's attention. This shared attention provides a vital route into working out the meaning of words.

- Word meanings are comprehended long before the baby produces words of his or her own. The first word is typically produced between the ages of 10 and 15 months. At first, vocabulary develops fairly slowly: a baby may take months to learn ten words. But at around 18 months vocabulary begins to expand at an vast rate – possibly reflecting the child's ability now to ask what words mean – so that by the time they enter school children know many hundreds or even thousands of words. We go on learning new words, albeit at a much slower rate, right through our lives.

- Most children's early words are nouns. But this is not always the case: in some cultures and social situations, children's early words are as likely to be verbs or

6
reasoning and conceptual understanding

As impressive as our human capacity for language is, it would be of very little use without our even more extraordinary ability to reason, to draw inferences and to reach conclusions that 'go beyond the information given' as Jerome Bruner (1975c) puts it. This ability to analyse the implications of what we know, to extrapolate and to draw conclusions from a few facts and so to discover new ideas, is the foundation of all our human knowledge, from the complexities of science and technology to the speculations of philosophy and religion. And even from early childhood, it's at the root of our everyday understanding of the world, our everyday intelligence, as the examples in **Box 6.1** show.

box **6.1**

Two examples of toddler inferences

Sources: DeLoache, Miller and Pierroutsakos (1998) and Thornton (1995).

1. Laura (aged 3 years, removing can of soda from refrigerator, to mother): 'Whose is this? It's not yours, cause it doesn't have lipstick.'

2. James (aged 2 years, very aggrieved): 'Jack broke my car!'
   Mother: 'I'm sure he didn't ...'
   James: 'He did! He did! Harry didn't go there [the playroom]. Jack broke my car!'

It's worth pausing a moment to think about the examples given in Box 6.1 These toddlers have drawn quite sophisticated inferences from the facts available to them. If you spend some time today just noticing the occasions on which you and other people round you draw inferences in this way, 'leaping' from a few facts to some new conclusion or insight, you'll be impressed. We deploy our extraordinary powers of reasoning almost without noticing.

How are we able to reason as we do? What processes of the mind allow us to make inferences, to interpret the world around us and make sense of it all? Where do these processes come from, and how do they develop through childhood, adolescence and on into adult life? And why does our reasoning sometimes go so horribly wrong? How can a species as gloriously intelligent as we so frequently add 2 and 2 and make 5? These are the issues explored in this chapter and the next.

Logic, reasoning and development

Ask the average person in the street what reasoning involves, and as like as not you'll be told 'logic'. Reasoning that is careful and painstaking, that comes to a conclusion that can be justified and defended (the 'right' conclusion) tends to be labelled 'logical', whereas reasoning that doesn't take the facts into consideration, doesn't work through the implications carefully or comes to the wrong conclusion is labelled 'illogical'. Children's thinking, by this account, is illogical and quaint, even fantastical (**Box 6.2**); development involves the growing ability to think more logically.

This apparently commonsense approach to the development of reasoning is anything but that. In fact, it reflects the theories of two great thinkers, Aristotle and Piaget. And although this view captures certain important insights, it rests on a great many assumptions that now seem quite dubious. Worst of all, the average person in the street generally has an entirely mistaken understanding of what 'logic' actually is!

The nature of logic

Suppose I say to you, 'If dogs aren't taught to swim, then they drown in ponds. My dog Luddy hasn't been taught to swim, therefore he will drown in that pond he's fallen into'. Am I right? Is my conclusion correct? Am I being logical?

From a practical point of view I am probably wrong: Luddy may not be able to swim, but he's chubby enough to float rather than drowning. More likely his normal response of trying to run away from danger will lead him to discover doggie-paddle for himself, even though no one is there to teach him. (And if not, I might even rescue him myself, of course.) But from a purely logical point of view, my conclusion is correct: it is *logically valid*. It's worth understanding this point properly.

My *argument* about dogs and drowning could be formally stated this way:

If the dog hasn't been taught to swim, then he will drown.
He hasn't been taught to swim.
Therefore he will drown.

To put this argument in abstract terms:

If X is true, then Y will occur.
X is true.
Therefore Y will occur.

From a factual point of view, my *premises* are wrong (dogs don't in

box **6.2**

Do children engage in more 'magical' thinking than adults do?

It's commonly believed that young children are much more inclined to engage in fantastical or magical thinking than adults, more inclined to hold irrational beliefs about the way the world is, and less able to distinguish between fantasy and reality. After all, young children believe in Father Christmas, don't they, and in the Tooth Fairy, and the possibility that wishes can come true? But in fact, a major review of research in this area (Woolley, 1997) suggests that children and adults may not be so very different.

What makes an idea 'fantastical' or 'magical' is that it violates our normal understanding of the way the world really works (Broad, 1953), and is not supported by empirical evidence. In other words, it doesn't fit with what we know to be demonstrably true. Lots of things that adults believe fit this description: for example, belief in paranormal powers such as telepathy or telekinesis, belief in 'alternative' medicine, or that UFOs full of aliens have visited the earth and so on. Many adults also believe in superstitions such as the idea that black cats are lucky, and walking under ladders is not. Many of us cross fingers or 'touch wood' for luck. In fact, adults may be just as prone to magical thinking as children, even if exactly what we believe in this way is different from what the young child believes (Woolley, 1997).

Nor is there much evidence that the way adults and children understand the basic reality/fantasy distinction is different. Even 3-year-olds know that there is a difference between a thought in their head and external reality (that they have *imagined* a monster rather than seen it, for example). Some researchers have suggested that young children believe that imagining something (a monster under the bed, say) is enough to make it real, 'a mistake that adults don't make'. But the evidence here suggests something more complicated. Adults too sometimes behave as if what we imagine might now be real. Watch a creepy film and it's easy to find yourself anxiously glancing around for madmen lurking in the shadows (or even under the bed) as you go home. It's not that we think that our imagination has created these monsters – it's that *having had the thought* raises the possibility that they're there. The young child may be in exactly the same position. As Woolley points out, children don't generally behave as if they thought they could create reality simply by imagining it: a toddler who wants a cookie asks for one rather than trying to create it through an act of imagination.

Magical (fantastical, superstitious) reasoning involves the adoption of a conclusion that violates our normal understanding of the world (whether or not that conclusion turns out to be true: it's the form of reasoning that is magical, rather than necessarily the conclusion). In adults, this kind of thinking tends to occur in certain contexts. For example, it occurs where we accept the word of authority figures for things that don't fit our naïve theories about the way things work (that flying to holidays is destroying the planet, for example). It's common when we are helpless and afraid and desperately wish that things were different (sales of books advocating fantastical and superstitious beliefs go up in times of trouble, and many seriously ill people believe in the power of the mind, or in untested 'alternative' remedies as a means of cure). And magical thinking is found when we simply don't have much real knowledge and so invent speculations to fill in the gaps (Woolley, 1997).

Woolley suggests that the circumstances in which adults tend to think magically offer an explanation of the apparent differences between adults and children in this area. Young children live in a world where they are routinely required to take what authority figures say on trust, and so to believe things for which they themselves have no evidence and can mount no reality-based argument. These authority figures actively encourage magical and fantastical beliefs in children (in Father Christmas, the Tooth Fairy, the possibility that Uncle Albert can really conjure coins out of thin air behind your ear, that rubbing the 'wishbone' on a chicken can make your wishes come true, and so on). The younger the child, the less knowledge of the world he or she has, and the less confident he or she can be in assessing or dismissing the reality of such claims (or dismissing the faint possibility of a monster under the bed). And the less knowledge of the world, the more common the situations in which the child can only invent fantastical speculations if pressed for explanations. Children are also less in control of their lives, more helpless than adults, and so more often in situations where wish-fulfilment fantasies are emotionally attractive.

In sum, Woolley (1997) argues that age-related changes in fantastical thinking may reflect age-related changes in social circumstances and knowledge, rather than any fundamental difference in how children and adults think.

reality need to be taught to swim to avoid drowning), and so my conclusion is *factually wrong*. But though factually wrong, the conclusion is *logically valid*: looking only at the abstract form of the argument, it's clear that the conclusion (Y will occur) *necessarily* follows, *given those premises*. Logic is concerned only with the form of an inference, the abstract relationship between premises and conclusions, and not with the factual accuracy of the premises (however vital that may be in real situations).

The same *logical principles* for drawing inferences apply, no matter what the content of the information to which they are applied. This makes logic a very powerful, very general tool for reasoning: master the principles of logic, and you can reason logically about anything.

If human reasoning is logical, the development of reasoning involves the development of very abstract, general (logical) tools for drawing inferences. Specific factual knowledge in any area would be an entirely separate matter, developing separately from the capacity to reason. These conclusions were taken to be true, until comparatively recently. But is human reasoning logical? Are factual knowledge and the processes of reasoning independent of one another, things that develop separately? These questions have been at the heart of research into the development of reasoning for the past 30 years. To understand this research, we must begin with Piaget.

Piaget and the development of reasoning

Piaget's theory dominated research on the development of reasoning for many decades, and still has a powerful influence over research today.

Piaget assumed that human reasoning rests on logical structures in the mind. He was the first to wonder how such structures could develop in a biological organism such as a human baby, and the first to offer a serious answer to this puzzle. A basic outline of Piaget's overall theory of the development of intelligence is given in Chapter 1. His account of the origins of the mind in infancy is discussed in detail in Chapter 3. Here, the focus is on his account of what it is that changes as the child moves from infancy to adult reasoning, and what it is that drives this development forward.

Piaget believed that human babies are born without any innate mental structures for reasoning, without any insight or understanding: in other words, with absolutely no capacity for logical reasoning. All of this must be constructed by the individual child, using only primitive reflexes and basic adaptive mechanisms (Inhelder and Piaget, 1958, 1964), as is described in Chapter 1. According to Piaget, the construction of logical reasoning passes through four stages, each building on what has gone before, and each producing a qualitatively different form of reasoning.

Sensori-motor intelligence: birth to 18 months

The earliest stage of this development has been discussed in detail in Chapter 3. The first 18 months of life are spent building the basic framework for intelligence: perception and memory. Gradually, the baby comes to see the world as separate from the self, with properties of its own, and to be able to represent and remember things that are no longer visible. But even at the end of this stage the baby is not capable of logical inference or reasoning.

Pre-operational reasoning: 18 months to 7 years

At the start of the pre-operational period, the baby's understanding is still very concretely rooted in physical doing. He or she can mentally represent or remember specific actions, such as the action of *hiding* an object or the action of *finding* it, but cannot yet connect these two different mental pictures. The result is a very fragmented consciousness, where the relationship between one action and another is not understood. As a consequence, the child is still dominated by the way things *look*: logical connections between one state of affairs and another cannot be understood.

This very complex idea is best explained by an example: for an adult mind, *hiding* and *finding* again are connected. They are necessarily two aspects of one single reversible operation: what we did in hiding an object can be mentally (if not physically) undone, to recreate in imagination (or reality) the original situation. Because the possibility of mentally undoing or reversing an action is an integral part of our understanding of that action, we can link the present situation (object hidden) with the previous or future situation (object revealed), and understand the relationship (in other words, the causal connection) between one situation and another. We can therefore draw logical inferences about what must necessarily be true. For the pre-operational child who does not represent the connection between separate actions such as hiding and finding, these actions are not reversible: they cannot be mentally undone to discover the logical relationship between the way things look now and the way they looked before. Thus the pre-operational child cannot understand cause and effect, and cannot draw inferences about what logically must be true. Piaget supported his thesis in a number of tasks which show that young children do indeed make bizarre mistakes in reasoning of exactly the kind his theory predicts.

Perhaps the most famous task Piaget used to demonstrate pre-operational reasoning is the *conservation* task (Inhelder and Piaget, 1964), which is illustrated in Chapter 1, in Box 1.2. For example, the child is shown two identical glasses, each containing an identical amount of water, and asked to confirm that the amount of liquid in each glass is the same. The child then watches as the contents of one glass are poured into another glass of a different shape: a taller and thinner glass, say. The child is then asked to say whether the amount of water in this new glass is the same as that in the remaining original glass. Below the age of 6 or 7 years, children will say that the amount of water in the new glass is not the same.

According to Piaget, this is evidence that they do not have 'reversible mental operations', thus cannot mentally undo the act of pouring the water from one glass to another, and so cannot understand the causal connection between the present situation and the original one. They therefore cannot understand that the amount of water *must necessarily* (logically) still be the same in the two glasses, because it has only been poured from one place to another *and could easily be poured back*. Unable to understand the links between how things were before and how they are now, the pre-operational child relies on perceptual appearances to make judgments. Do the amounts of water look the same?

Another classic task used by Piaget to demonstrate this same developmental limitation of preoperational intelligence is the *transitivity* task (Inhelder and Piaget, 1958). Here, the child is shown two sticks, a green one and a yellow one. The green one is longer than the yellow. Then the green stick is removed, and the child is shown the yellow stick and a red one, the yellow stick being longer than the red one (**Figure 6.1**). The child is then asked to say which is longer, the red stick or the green one. Up to about 6 or 7 years of age, children will say that they can't tell: they have never seen the green and the red stick compared. Their problem, according to Piaget, is again the inability to mentally undo actions and so connect one situation with another: the pre-operational child cannot represent the relationship between the green and yellow sticks *at the* *same time* as the relationship between the yellow and red sticks, and so cannot understand the logically necessary connection between the green and red ones. With no direct perceptual comparison to hand, the pre-operational child cannot answer the question.

This inability to mentally reverse actions and understand connections is perhaps most clearly illustrated by Piaget's *class inclusion* task (Inhelder and Piaget, 1964). The child is shown a set of items such as those in **Figure 6.2**. Seven-year-old children know very well that dogs are animals, and can count up very well how many dogs there are in such a display, and how many animals. But if you ask them, 'Are there more dogs or more animals? children of 6 or 7 will tell you that there are more dogs! Piaget's explanation is that this is because these children can only make one grouping at a time. Once they have assigned the dogs to the class 'dog', they cannot mentally undo that and include the dogs in the larger class 'animals'. Without reversible mental operations, the classes of animal and dog cannot exist simultaneously in the child's mind, and so the relationship between them cannot be understood.

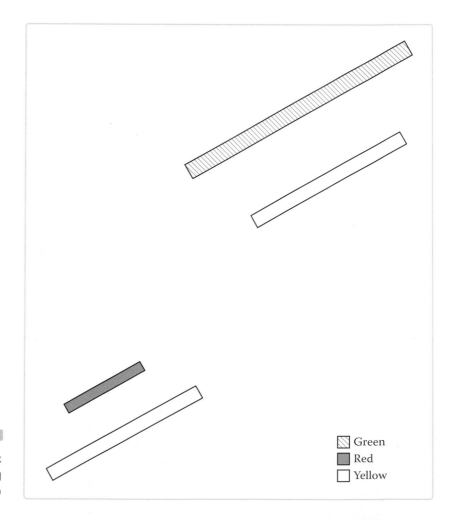

figure **6.1**

The transitivity task

First comparison (top) and second comparison (bottom)

☒ Green
■ Red
☐ Yellow

figure **6.2**

The class inclusion task
Are there more dogs or more animals?

Concrete operations: 7 to 11 years

According to Piaget, children develop reversible mental operations at around 8 years of age. From this age they start to solve the conservation task, the transitivity task and the class inclusion task successfully, and most significantly, they can explain *why* their answers *must* be right. For the first time, understanding how events came about and being able to mentally undo that process allows the child to deduce necessary logical relationships between things, rather than relying on perceptual appearances. It is important to Piaget's theory that all these tasks come within the child's talents at about the same time. According to Piaget, reversible operations reflect the emergence of a very general logical structure in the mind, one that can be applied across all sorts of tasks.

Nonetheless, the 7 to 11-year-olds' reasoning is still very limited in many ways. Reversible operations are tied to specific, concrete things. That is to say, the child can understand logical relationships in relation to specific situations where particular actions or events can be mentally reversed. But he or she cannot detach reasoning or logic from these concrete situations. It's only specific, concrete actions which can be mentally reversed, not hypothetical ones. To put this difficult idea another way, the child's ability to understand causal connections is tightly tied to concrete reality – to what is now, or recently was, or shortly could be. He or she cannot yet take the extra step and understand that this concrete reality itself could – hypothetically, in principle – be different (undone, reversed), even if that isn't possible in the physical world. Reversibility is concrete and practical, not an abstract principle. As a consequence, the concrete operational child can't reason in the abstract about hypothetical situations or events, and can't understand the abstract *idea* of logic or the *principle* of logical necessity. At this stage, the child is very literal-minded. Having made one concrete connection or created one concrete situation, other hypothetical possibilities will not be explored.

Formal operations: from 12 years on

Some children never progress beyond the stage of concrete operations. For those that do, from about the age of 11 or 12 years reasoning gradually becomes independent of concrete events, until the child is able to reason in the abstract and to think about hypothetical things. This is the stage of *formal operations*, the crowning achievement of adult intelligence.

According to Piaget, the impact of formal operational reasoning is enormous. Where the concrete operational child can see only one concrete reality, the formal operational adolescent can see that concrete reality as only one of a number of potential alternatives, and so can imagine different hypothetical universes, different ways of solving a problem, different perspectives on truth or morality. The formal operational thinker can reason systematically about a problem, reviewing all the different possibilities, testing all the possible hypotheses, opening up the possibility of real logical and scientific thinking (**Box 6.3**). As with the development of concrete operations, the structures that underlie the development of formal operational reasoning are, according to Piaget, very general. Once the child has begun to reason at this level, he or she can apply formal operational thinking to any topic area. The idea of logic and logical necessity can now be understood in abstract terms.

Critiques of Piaget's theory

Piaget's account of the origins of reasoning is impressive. It seems to provide a coherent theory of developmental change from birth to adulthood, explaining a number of striking peculiarities (such as the 6-year-olds' problems with class inclusion and conservation tasks, and the 10-year-olds' literal-minded inability to consider hypothetical alternatives). However, Piaget's theory has been criticized at many different levels.

Alternative interpretations of failure in Piaget's tasks

Piaget's experimental tasks provide really rather startling demonstrations of just how different the conclusions young children reach can be from those reached by older children or adults. These demonstrations are very robust: if you do just what Piaget did, you will get the same extraordinary results. These data certainly need to be explained. But do they mean what Piaget said they meant?

As we saw in Chapter 3, critics of Piaget's work on infant cognition argued that his tasks seriously under-estimated the baby's cognitive

box 6.3

Concrete and formal operational reasoning

Look at the apparatus below. If you attach any one of the weighted strings to the hook here and give it a push, it will swing like a pendulum. What determines how long it takes for the pendulum to swing through a complete arc? How would you find out?

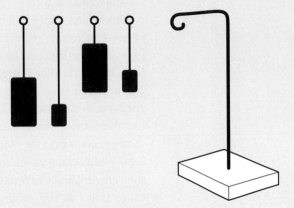

Both children and adolescents start out believing that the speed of the swing reflects the heaviness of the weight, but they test this theory in very different ways.

'Concrete operational' children test out different lengths of string and different weights, but not in a systematic way. For example, they might compare the speed of a light weight on a short string dropped from quite low with that of a heavy weight on a long string dropped from much higher. They do not control for the effect of different factors, and so cannot disentangle one from another or gain new insights.

By contrast, 'formal operational' adolescents approach the task more systematically, exploring how each of these three variables affects the speed of the pendulum: for example by comparing the effect of different weights on the same-length string released from the same position, or by comparing the same weights on different lengths of string, or the same weight and string length released from different heights. This systematic approach allows them to discover that neither the weight nor the dropping position is relevant: the swing of the pendulum reflects only the length of the string.

abilities and so provided a misleading picture of what is developing and how. The same accusations have been made about the tasks he used in studying childhood cognition. The most powerful attack on Piaget's results came from Margaret Donaldson (1978). Donaldson argued that Piaget's tasks don't make 'social sense': where is the sense in asking if pouring water from one jar to another changes its volume, if we all know that it doesn't? Where is the sense in asking if there are more dogs or more animals, if we all know that dogs are animals? To answer such questions correctly you have to divorce them from the normal social expectation that adults won't ask daft questions, and treat these questions as purely abstract intellectual challenges. Older children are wise to the ways of adults, and have learned to handle questions in the abstract in this way, and so can deploy their logical skills effectively. But younger children are simply confused by the social peculiarities of the task, and their ability to reason logically is derailed as a consequence (Donaldson, 1978).

Donaldson argued that in everyday contexts that make sense to them, even very young children are capable of drawing quite sophisticated logical inferences (as the examples in Box 6.1 show). She demonstrated that, if you modify Piaget's tasks so that they make 'social sense', even 3-year-olds can succeed, although they continue to fail in the original versions. For example, if you use a collection of plastic cows in the class inclusion task, some standing, some lying down, and ask, 'Are there more cows or more sleeping cows?' (a perfectly sensible question), 3-year-olds can answer correctly, even though this task presents exactly the same logical challenge (and need to hold two classes in mind at the same time) as the original class inclusion task in which children fail (Donaldson, 1978).

There are a great many demonstrations that if Piaget's tasks are made less abstract, less difficult and more familiar, young children are very much more successful than they are in the original versions (Bryant, 1974; Bryant and Trabasso, 1971; Donaldson, 1978; Light, Buckingham and Robins, 1979; McGarrigle and Donaldson, 1975; McGarrigle, Grieve and Hughes 1978). Such data suggest that young children can reason logically at a far earlier age than Piaget thought, and therefore that his account of what is involved in the development of reasoning through most of childhood is wrong.

Defenders of Piaget's theory objected to this conclusion. They argued that in making the tasks easier and more familiar, Piaget's critics had changed the nature of the task so that it no longer needed logical inferences at all, but could be solved in a simpler way: for example, by using perceptual, linguistic or social cues rather than logic (Moore and Frye, 1986; Tollefsrud-Anderson et al., 1992). In other words, Piaget's defenders claimed that his critics had demonstrated young children's ability to succeed in certain tasks, but not their ability to draw logical inferences.

This debate went on for about a decade. The contenders could not agree on a 'pure' test of a child's logical competence, and went round in circles each trying to prove that their version of the tasks was the purer measure, and their results therefore the more accurate. Nevertheless, this controversy played an important role in driving research forward.

The need to study mental processes more directly

The crucial breakthrough in the apparently deadlocked controversy over interpreting Piaget's data was the eventual acceptance that success or failure (that is, *performance*) in any version of a task can never definitively establish the existence or absence of any given skill or ability (that is, *competence*). You can always succeed or fail in any task in lots of different ways. And in fact, factors that affect your performance right now (being tired, hungry, hungover, misunderstanding the instructions, not feeling cooperative, not realizing that a given idea or skill is relevant here, not knowing how to generalize skill from one situation to another and so on) can be as important to the outcome as your underlying competence (Sophian, 1997).

If we want to understand how children's reasoning develops, we must therefore look directly at the processes through which children come to their conclusions, whether successful or not (Sophian, 1997; Thornton, 1982). In doing so, we must pay as much attention to the processes affecting performance as to those reflecting competence (Gelman and Meck, 1992; Gelman and Brenneman, 1994; Greeno, Riley and Gelman, 1984). This conclusion had dramatic consequences for research on the development of reasoning.

Challenging the importance of logical structures

Both Piaget's defenders and his critics assumed that human reasoning depends on logical processes in the mind, even if they couldn't agree as to the age at which such processes develop. But the shift from a focus on whether or not children of a given age succeed or fail in various tasks to a focus on how and why they succeed or fail ended up fundamentally challenging this basic assumption.

To examine how any behaviour is generated you need a way of thinking about active mental processes. The best analogy we have for this is the computer program, which can represent the information available to the thinker and the operations that can be performed on that information to generate inferences or actions. Piagetian tasks were explored from this *information-processing* perspective (Chapter 1), often resulting in theoretical models expressed as computer simulations (Klahr and Wallace, 1976; Simon and Klahr, 1995; Trabasso et al., 1978).

Information-processing models of this kind suggested that all the phenomena described by Piaget could be explained by developmental changes in the information available to the child and in the ways this information is handled, rather than involving logical processes (Klahr and Wallace, 1976; Simon and Klahr, 1995; Trabasso et al., 1978). For example, Trabasso and colleagues' (1978) model of processing in the class inclusion task showed that developmental changes in how key information is encoded and in the exact procedures used in quantifying (counting) the class and sub-class could account for developmental change in success between younger and older children.

At first, the idea that logical inferences might not derive from logical processes seems strange. But there is actually no reason that the process that produces a thing should have the same sort of structure as the thing that is produced. For example, the flames of a fire are not at all like the ash they produce. Could it be that Piaget was wrong to assume that the development of reasoning has anything to do with the development of logical structures in the mind? If so, his whole account of what drives cognitive development through childhood would be wrong. There is strong evidence in support of this conclusion.

Mental models and logical reasoning

In the main, we draw inferences in order to make practical decisions and to understand the world around us. Factual accuracy is therefore important: it's more important to get your facts right than to draw an elegant inference that has no basis in reality (Johnson-Laird, 1993; Legrenzi, Girotto and Johnson-Laird, 1993). Strictly logical processes take no account of factual accuracy, as we saw earlier in this chapter. If you were designing an intelligent creature from first principles, it's likely, therefore, that you would root reasoning processes in information and meanings rather than around the abstract rules of logic. A priori, it seems likely that evolution would take the same course.

Johnson-Laird and his colleagues have produced a great deal of evidence which suggests that human reasoning is in fact based on the construction of *mental models* that reflect our factual understanding of the world (Johnson-Laird, 1993; Legrenzi et al., 1993). That is to say, when we want to draw an inference or make a decision, we use the relevant information available to us to build up a 'picture' of what the situation is, and then use that mental model to draw inferences and conclusions about the relationships between one thing and another. Using mental models in this way allows us to draw both logical and non-logical inferences. Johnson-Laird argues that there are no structures in the mind that reflect the structure of logic as such: all reasoning draws on mental models, even when the results of this psychological process can, from an observer's point of view, be described as 'logical' reasoning.

Transitive inferences from mental models

Take the case of transitive inferences. Adults can solve such problems fairly well. But the evidence is that they do not use logical inference processes in doing so (Potts, 1974), as Piaget thought. Potts gave participants in his study (college students) information about adjacent pairs of items in six-term series such as the one depicted in **Figure 6.3** (Jane has longer hair than Mary, Mary has longer hair than Sue, and so on). He then asked them to make transitive inferences, just as in Piaget's task, comparing pairs they had not seen together (for example, who has longer hair, Jane or Sue?).

With a six-term series, the closer together the pair to be compared are, the fewer the inferences needed to reach a conclusion. Comparing Jane and Sue needs only one transitive inference, to establish that since Jane has longer hair than Mary, and Mary has longer hair than Sue, Jane

figure 6.3

A six-term series: Jane, Mary, Sue, Kate, Betty and Louise

must have longer hair than Sue. But comparing Jane and Betty, who are separated by three intervening girls, would need three transitive inferences: one to establish that Jane has longer hair than Sue, one to establish that Sue has longer hair than Betty, and finally one to infer that therefore Jane must have longer hair than Betty.

Assuming that it takes time to make a transitive inference, we should expect it to take longer to compare faces far apart in the series (where more inferences are needed) than those close in the series, if the process of solving such puzzles relies on logical inferences. But Potts found that comparisons far apart in the series are made faster than comparisons close in the series! This result suggests that even adults cannot be using logical inferences in solving transitivity tasks.

Potts' data suggest that adults actually solve transitivity problems by making a mental 'picture' or model of the series as they learn it, and then by reading off the answer from this imaginary 'picture', rather than by using any process resembling logical deduction as such. For example, the fastest comparison of all is where the two ends of the series are to be compared. This is the exact opposite of what one would predict, if logical inference were involved (it should be the slowest), but it's just what we should predict if people were answering by 'looking' at a mental 'picture': the ends of the series are easiest to find and therefore easiest to compare, when you are looking at a picture.

The most impressive result in Potts' data is that adults can actually make comparisons between items at the extreme ends of a series (which they have never seen directly compared) faster than they can answer questions about adjacent pairs in the middle of the series, even though they have been directly shown those pairs. This is exactly what we would expect if someone were reading answers off a 'picture', but quite incompatible with the idea that the problem is being solved by logical inference.

Logic, mental models and the development of reasoning

There is overwhelming evidence now that Piaget was wrong about the nature of mental processes. Even adult reasoning does not derive from logical structures in the mind as he thought. The development of reasoning through childhood cannot, therefore, involve the gradual construction of logical structures as described by his theory. Nevertheless, the phenomena described by Piaget (the erratic inferences of young children and the failure of 10-year-olds to think systematically) still need to be explained. We also need to understand why it is that young children seem to be able to draw logical inferences in some circumstances but can't do so in others.

Reasoning and knowledge

Young children can build mental models and draw inferences from them perfectly well (Johnson-Laird, Oakhill and Bull, 1986). In fact, babies as young as 5 months of age have been shown to be able to mentally represent objects and events and to draw simple inferences from these mental models (Baillargeon, 1986; Baillargeon, Spelke and Wasserman, 1985, and see Chapter 3). Thus it seems that the basic processes on which adult reasoning is based are present even in the very young.

However, the young often have less knowledge than their elders in any given context, and typically have knowledge in a narrower range of areas. Age-related changes in knowledge mean age-related changes in the mental models from which inferences are drawn. This may go a long way toward explaining both the different conclusions younger and older individuals reach in reasoning, and the greater variability of success in younger children's reasoning across different contexts (Halford and Andrews, 2004).

There is now a great deal of evidence that, in situations where they have good relevant knowledge, even pre-school children are adept in constructing logical arguments and drawing logical conclusions (Halford, 1993; Halford and Andrews, 2004; Hawkins et al., 1984; Johnson-Laird et al., 1986; Komatsu and Galotti, 1986; Miller, Seier and Nassau, 1995; Moshman, 1990). In fact, in some contexts, even toddlers can draw inferences as effectively as adolescents (Klaczynski, Schuneman and Daniel, 2004; Nakimichi, 2004). It's where younger and older children have different knowledge that developmental differences in reasoning are most striking.

Logical necessity

The ability to draw logical inferences is one thing. Insight into the nature of logical arguments is another. Piaget claimed that young children don't understand logical necessity or consistency at any level, and that even pre-adolescents don't explicitly understand the principles of logical necessity and can't use such principles in a rigorous, abstract way. According to Piaget, this explicit insight and formal logical ability develops in adolescence (the stage of 'formal operations'). Part of this description of developmental change in children's reasoning seems to be accurate, even if the age at which these effects occur is not as Piaget said and the underlying processes are not what he thought.

For example, Ruffman (1999) presented children with two 'stories', telling them that one would make sense and the other wouldn't. One story might be that Bill is wearing a hat, but also not wearing a scarf (sensible story); the other might be that Bill is wearing a hat but also not wearing a hat (logically inconsistent story). All the 6-year-olds were easily able to detect the logically inconsistent story as nonsensical, showing that they understand logical necessity and consistency. Only 10 per cent of 3-year-olds and 29 per cent of 5-year-olds could do this. Although some of the younger children's difficulties seemed to relate to their lack of relevant knowledge, Ruffman demonstrated that children under 5 years of age do lack insight into logical necessity.

What is involved in understanding logical necessity? How does this understanding develop? It seems likely that insight emerges gradually rather than in one fell swoop. For example, the fact that 6-year-olds understand that some things are logically inconsistent does not mean that they can tell the difference between conclusions that are logically valid and those that aren't (DeLoache, Miller and Pierroutsakos, 1998). Told 'if you're noisy, you won't get a treat', children are adept at inferring the logically valid conclusion that, having been noisy, their treat is now off the agenda. But having been quiet, they tend to infer that they will get the treat – and this conclusion is *not* logically valid. If you think about it, no such promise is made by the literal form of the statement. The fact that children don't distinguish between the logically valid and the logically invalid conclusions suggests that they are not reflecting on or sensitive to the *logical form* of the argument as such.

But if Piaget was right to point to the young child's lack of insight about logical necessity, he was wrong to assume that this deficit disappears through the course of development. Most adolescents and adults have as much difficulty as children do in distinguishing between conclusions that are logically valid and those that are merely probable or factually accurate but don't necessarily follow logically from the premises (Balacheff, 1988; Chazan, 1993; Lee and Wheeler, 1989; Martin and Harel, 1989). And even highly educated and intelligent adults fail to apply their understanding of logical necessity in many situations, even if they can apply it in some (Evans, 1989; Johnson-Laird and Byrne, 1991; Kahneman, Slovic and Tversky, 1982). Like young children, adults are more swayed by factual knowledge than by considerations of logical validity (Evans and Pollard, 1990; Evans, Barstow and Pollard, 1983; Evans, Newstead and Byrne, 1993; Oakhill and Johnson-Laird, 1985; Oakhill, Johnson-Laird and Garnham, 1989; Morris and Sloutsky, 1998). It seems that it is very hard for the human mind to acquire or to deliberately apply insight into logical necessity. Most of us never achieve these things at all, and even the highly intelligent and educated are not consistently logical.

Literacy, mathematics and formal reasoning

As rare and difficult as logical insight is, it's obvious that some individuals do achieve it, at least to some degree. The general consensus of research is that this is the product of cultural tools and specific training, rather than being the natural result of the way our minds develop, as Piaget thought.

The idea that logical insight and systematic formal reasoning are cultural artefacts originally came from studies of traditional, non-industrialized rural communities where there is no formal schooling. Early studies found no evidence for any sort of abstract logical reasoning of the kind Piaget labelled 'formal operations' in such societies (Cole and Scribner, 1974; Luria, 1976; Scribner and Cole, 1981). Subsequent researchers objected that this was because the experimental measures used were not appropriate for use in such cultures (Hutchins, 1983). But even the most arduous and culturally sensitive search for evidence of abstract logical reasoning in pre-industrial societies finds it only in very circumscribed contexts, such as the skills needed to navigate a boat over hundreds of miles out of sight of land from one island to another (Hutchins, 1983). The evidence that such skills involve logical inference is stronger than the evidence that they involve logical insight.[1] But in any case, marine navigation is hardly a 'natural' facet of cognitive development. It is itself a cultural tool, socially shared and formally taught from one generation to another. If anything, the contexts in which we have found logical reasoning in non-industrialized cultures confirm the view that this skill is a cultural tool rather than a natural part of development.

---

[1] As a sailor myself, I am anxiously aware that crew can often apply the procedures for navigation with great success, but with very little insight into the principles involved.

There is a natural affinity between human language (itself culturally shaped) and logic in that logical inference involves learning to take the meaning of certain words (if, and, or, unless, then and so on) seriously. Learning to use these words in everyday speech is generally believed to help the child to begin drawing logical inferences in practical contexts. But this is not enough to foster an explicit understanding of logical necessity. A closer look at how we understand language suggests *why* this is so. Everyday language is fairly imprecise. Even adult speech often means something rather different from the literal force of the words. For example, if I say to you, 'Could you lend me your coat?' you would probably assume that I actually meant, 'Please give me your coat for a while,' and act accordingly. But if you took what I said strictly literally, my question asked only whether you were *able* to lend me your coat, not whether you were *willing* to do so. In everyday conversation we rely heavily on our understanding of the social context in interpreting messages. Taking the words used absolutely literally would often be inappropriate and annoying. Thus inferences in everyday situations are embedded in the situation which language describes, rather than in the literal force of the words.

Spoken language doesn't encourage us to take the meaning of words literally, but literacy does. Writing stands alone, rather than being embedded in a social interaction. In learning to read, the child must learn to treat language as an abstract entity, paying careful attention to the literal words on the page rather than using extraneous social cues to infer meaning. The reader must consider the possibility of alternative interpretations of text, using language alone to resolve ambiguities. In sum, becoming literate lays the foundations for an abstract, analytic, reflective and literal use of language, which is exactly what is needed for logical insight. Logic requires us to interpret key words in a strictly literal way. Once we can do that, we can reason logically regardless of the specifics of what we are reasoning about. And once we can reflect on the strict literal meaning of words, we are ready for an abstract understanding of logical necessity (Cole and Scribner, 1974; Donaldson, 1978; Scribner and Cole, 1981).

However, although learning to read (**Box 6.4**) may lay a crucial foundation for logical insight, it isn't enough to ensure that such insight will develop. In fact, the evidence suggests that only teenagers who have received very direct tuition in abstract ways of reasoning show any real understanding of logical necessity (Morris and Sloutsky, 1998). Learning mathematics (**Box 6.5**), and specifically developing a conceptual understanding of the abstract principles of algebra, plays an important role here. It's easy to see why this should be so: mathematics, and particularly algebra, is a strict logical system that uses abstract symbols, and so forms a perfect context in which to develop insight into these things. Sadly, few of us ever gain much conceptual understanding of algebra. Few of us are able to profit from its potential in providing insight into logical necessity.

box 6.4

Learning to read

Like most cultural tools, the scripts used for writing things down vary from one society to another. For example, English and other European languages use an alphabetic system, defined as a script in which each symbol (letter) represents a *phoneme*, the smallest unit of sound within a word. Chinese, by contrast, uses a non-alphabetical system in which each symbol represents a *morpheme*, that is, a whole unit of meaning. But whatever the details of the script, writing offers the same potential for magnifying the power of human intelligence and altering the way we think.

Learning to read involves mastering a number of separate skills. These may vary depending on the precise nature of the script involved. Most of our research has focused on alphabetic scripts in European languages, and that is the focus here.

Children, particularly those from middle-class homes where parents read to them often learn a lot about reading before they even start trying to decode writing for themselves. For example, they learn that books tell stories, that books have a right way up and a wrong way up, that you turn the page to get more of the story, even that writing goes from left to right and that at the end of one line you jump back to the start of the next. Very young children may play at 'reading', demonstrating much of this knowledge and pretending to decipher a story.

Many children (again particularly from middle-class homes) have learned to say the letters of the alphabet before they start learning to read. Such children tend to be more successful in learning to read than those who haven't learned the alphabet (Vellutino and Scanlon, 1987), but this seems to be because learning the alphabet is associated with a much more general interest in reading: teaching children the alphabet by itself doesn't make learning to read easier (Adams, 1990).

What really makes the crucial difference in the early stages of learning to read is *phonemic awareness*, namely the realization that words can be broken down into separate sounds (Juel, 1988; Thompson and Nicholson, 1999). If you can't break words down into their constituent sounds, it's very difficult to learn connections between sounds and written letters (Bryant, 1993). Children have enormous difficulty with this (Bruce, 1964; Ferreiro and Teberosky, 1983). Children aged from 4 to 6 years tend naturally to break words down into syllables rather than phonemes (Liberman et al., 1974). Phonemic awareness is often not taught explicitly, although teaching children to break words down into constituent sounds in this way provides enormous and long-lasting help in the process of learning to read (Bradley and Bryant, 1983).

It seems that the normal way that children become aware of phonemes may be through nursery games that focus on rhymes. Words rhyme when the sounds at the end of words match and the sound at the start doesn't (rocks/locks; picks/sticks; ham/jam and so on). Nursery rhymes often present rhyming words where only the first phoneme changes, providing the opportunity to discover this phoneme. The greater a 3-year-old's knowledge of nursery rhymes, the greater his or her phonemic awareness (Maclean, Bryant and Bradley, 1987). There is direct evidence that children use rhymes in learning to read (Goswami, 1986), and that learning to read itself also increases phonemic awareness (Cardoso-Martins, 1991).

The key task in learning to read fluently is learning to decode script into meaning. This can be done 'bottom up' (that is to say, by spelling out each phoneme and building up the word) or 'top down' (that is, by remembering the overall visual appearance of a word as a whole and identifying its meaning from that, without spelling it out letter by letter). The evidence is that children use both of these strategies, adaptively choosing the one appropriate to the circumstances (Siegler, 1986). Familiar, easy words are read through visual recognition whilst new or difficult words are spelled out phonetically.

Most children who go through our school system learn to read to a basic level. That is to say, they learn to identify and read written words. But it is possible to do this without having much comprehension of what is read. Indeed, children vary enormously in the extent to which they can extract meaning from text. Millions of adults in Britain are functionally illiterate. Surveys for the United Nations suggest that as much as 25 per cent of the population of every Western industrialized society is functionally illiterate to the point of being unable to understand the instructions on a medicine bottle or fill out a tax form. The average adult is reckoned to have a reading age of about 11 or 12 years. Like most things, comprehension skills improve with practice: the more you read, the better your comprehension skills become. But when text is hard to understand, there's little pleasure in reading and little incentive to try.

Understanding the meaning of what we read calls for most of the processes involved in the intelligent construction of a mental model, one that is updated continuously as new text is decoded. The more generally intelligent the child, the more easily he or she will be able to construct such models fluidly and so comprehend the meaning of the text. Comprehension is helped by good decoding skills: the less you have to focus on deciphering individual words, the more resources you have to devote to understanding meanings. Comprehension also fosters decoding: the more you comprehend the meaning of a text, the more easily you can guess at the meaning (and sound) of unfamiliar letter sequences. Children who are good comprehenders sometimes get the gist of material rather than reading literally every word. Again, good readers use different strategies in different contexts, skimming when a summary will do and slowing down when the exact meaning is important – although this skill doesn't begin to develop until around 14 years of age (Kobasigawa, Ransom and Holland, 1980).

Cultural tools and cognitive development

It's worth pausing a moment to underline the fact that cultural tools such as literacy and mathematics play an enormous role in the development of human intelligence, both in society as a whole and in the individual. These formal systems contribute much more than the basis for logical reasoning. For example, the ability to write things down creates a shared memory, so that knowledge can be accumulated across a far wider range of people than is possible if communication is limited to the spoken word. Sharing knowledge in this way allows many individuals to contribute to its development. Writing things down rather than having to remember them or work things out in our head also greatly expands the sheer amount and complexity of information

box **6.5**

Number and mathematics

There has been considerable controversy (see Chapter 3) over whether or not basic number skills such as counting, adding and subtracting are part of the innate equipment of our minds. Some research finds evidence for basic number skills in very young babies (Wynn, 1992a, 1995), though other researchers have failed to replicate this result (Wakely, Rivera and Langer, 2000). This controversy is presently unresolved. Recent research suggests that number skills very like those of the young human baby are also found in other species (Feigenson, Dehaene and Spelke, 2004; Lipton and Spelke, 2004), which may imply that there is indeed an innate basis for these skills. But whether that turns out to be true or not, it's also clear that mathematics is very importantly a learned skill.

Like writing, number systems and mathematics are cultural tools and vary from one society to another. The ways we represent numbers differ from one society to another (for example, Roman numerals I, II, III, IV, V, VI encapsulate numerosity more directly than the more arbitrary Arabic numerals 1, 2, 3, 4, 5, 6). The procedures we use for making calculations vary culturally too (for example, the procedures for calculations on a Chinese abacus are very different from those in Western mathematics). The way numbers are represented and the procedures for making calculations can greatly affect how easy it is to master number and mathematics. For example, children growing up in European and American societies find it harder to count from 1 to 20 than do their counterparts in Asian cultures (Stigler and Perry, 1990), probably because in the latter societies, the numbers from 11 to 20 are named as 'tenty-one, tenty-two' and so on, whereas in European languages we use more arbitrary words (eleven, twelve and so on).

Learning to count involves far more than learning the sequence of number names, or even the convention connecting number words to their mathematical symbols (six = 6, for example). The crucial factor is the connection between these names and numerosity: that is, realizing that 'six' refers to a given number of objects, and that if there are six objects here and six objects there, there are the same number of objects in each place.

Gelman, Meck and Merkin (1986) suggest that there are three crucial components in learning maths. These are the acquisition of procedures for performing operations such as addition, subtraction, division or multiplication; the ability to understand the principle underlying the procedure: in other words, to understand what it does, rather than simply being able to execute it by rote; and understanding when to apply a given procedure.

Donlan (1998) has documented the development of children's knowledge of the procedures used in mathematics. Often, children know of more than one procedure for achieving the same result. For example, it's possible to do a long division on paper, or the answer may be learned off by heart or worked out in your head. Which strategy is used varies with the context, and with the difficulty of the sum. Siegler and Jenkins (1989) have demonstrated that even very young children can use alternative procedures for adding, as will be discussed further in Chapter 7.

It's quite easy to learn mathematical procedures by rote without really understanding them. For example, 6- to 9-year-olds become progressively more adept at adding and subtracting numbers, but don't always realize that the operations of adding a number and then subtracting the very same number (2 buns plus 7 buns minus 7 buns equals 2 buns) cancel out, so that there is no need to go through the procedure of addition and subtraction for these digits (Bisanz and Lefevre, 1990). In other words, they have mastered the procedure but not the principle.

Knowing when to use a mathematical procedure is as important as knowing how to use it. Often, children who can use a given procedure very well in one context fail to use it in another. The classic demonstration of this looked at the multiplication strategies used by Brazilian street vendors aged 9 to 15 years (Nunes, Schliemann and Carraher, 1993). In the street, these children were typically very effective in calculating the price of their wares (how much for four coconuts at 35 each?). Confronted with exactly the same problem (4 x 35) in the abstract in a classroom, they failed to apply the effective procedure they had used in the street, probably because they lacked enough conceptual understanding of that procedure (or of the different procedures taught in school) to realize the relevance of transferring the street procedure to the classroom problem. The teaching that is most effective in producing children who can apply their maths procedures effectively across different situations focuses on fostering conceptual understanding of mathematical principles rather than on procedural success in itself (Stigler and Hiebert, 1999).

The need to foster conceptual understanding is particularly acute when children encounter more sophisticated forms of mathematics such as algebra. Many children treat algebra as a completely arbitrary and meaningless set of rules, and never comprehend that it is actually a very general and principled system for solving mathematical problems. Only when the principles of algebra are understood can this form of mathematics open the way to insight into logical necessity. It's only when the teaching of algebra includes direct tuition fostering conceptual understanding that studying algebra is associated with the growth of logical awareness (Morris and Sloutsky, 1998).

we can handle. These cultural tools thus greatly magnify the power and potential of human reasoning. They change what we can reason about and how we reason in all sorts of ways, even if they seldom fulfil their potential to make us abstract logical thinkers.

Cognitive development in adolescence

The consensus of research today is that adolescents do not develop the abstract logical mental structures Piaget described as 'formal operations' (Kuhn, 2006). However, there is good evidence for developmental changes in performance in reasoning tasks between childhood and adolescence which are very like the effects described by Piaget, and these still need explaining.

Even very young children can reason scientifically in some circumstances, considering alternatives and using data to reject or refine hypotheses (Ruffman et al., 1993; Sodian, Zaitchik and Carey, 1991). But children are more likely to be disorganized in their approach than adolescents, just as Piaget claimed. Children are more likely than adolescents to try to investigate all the potentially relevant factors simultaneously and in no particular order, to foreclose on a conclusion on the basis of only partial data, to ignore information that could falsify their hypothesis and focus instead on information that endorses it (Ford, 2005; Klahr, 2000; Kuhn and Dean, 2005; Schauble, 1996). The young are also more reluctant than adolescents to take implausible-seeming hypotheses seriously, tending to reject them out of hand without testing them (DeLoache et al., 1998). By ignoring hypotheses that don't fit their pre-existing theories in this way young children explore a narrower range of possibilities than adolescents do, and so are more likely to miss out on new discoveries.

If these changes in reasoning in adolescence are not due to the development of the logical and abstract processes of Piaget's 'formal operations', what does cause them? Recent reviews suggest that one key factor is *executive control* over mental processes (Keating, 2004). The evidence suggests that adolescent reasoning is as focused on the factual aspects of the task as is the child's, and is as little driven by explicitly logical considerations or awareness as the child's. But adults and adolescents are markedly better at monitoring and managing their own mental processes than children are, and this allows them to approach tasks in a more controlled and systematic (scientific) way, to organize a coherent and efficient plan, to suspend disbelief in the implausible and to explore alternative possibilities more rigorously.

The development of greater executive control over mental processes is correlated with developmental changes in the brain, which goes through a growth spurt in early adolescence. There is a marked overproduction of neural connections followed by a reduction through the pruning of discarded neural patterns, and there is an enhancement of the myelination of nerves (Chapter 2), which allows for the more efficient transmission of neural messages (Giedd et al., 1999). The result is that by mid to late adolescence, there are fewer, more selective and stronger neural connections than there were in childhood.

It's possible that these changes in the adolescent brain allow more efficient processing, and hence allow the development of better monitoring and executive control. On the other hand, we know that the way we use our brains stimulates growth, so that learning new skills and thinking in new ways can stimulate neurological expansion (see Chapter 2). It's possible that the physiological changes in the adolescent brain are the result, rather than the cause, of changes in monitoring and control of mental processes (Kuhn, 2006).

Executive control over reasoning requires knowledge. It requires knowledge about the task in hand, about what is and isn't relevant or possible, about the strategies that might be used in this situation: which ones work in specific circumstances and which ones don't (Kuhn, 2001). Only when we are armed with this kind of awareness can we make systematic choices and plans. The older the individual, the more time

and opportunities he or she has had to gather such knowledge in relation to any task, or in relation to problem solving as a whole.

Furthermore, the older the child, the greater the social demand that he
or she behave in responsible and reflective ways – in other words, that
behaviour of all kinds should come under executive control. We expect
adolescents to be rigorous and autonomous where we allow children to be
disorganized and dependent. Social expectations have powerful effects in
shaping the emergence of many patterns of behaviour (Rogoff, Gauvain
and Ellis, 1984). Could social expectations be a factor in the development
of executive control over reasoning in adolescence?

Heuristic reasoning

Piaget's theory, with its emphasis on logic, dominated research on the
development of cognition for 30 years. A very different approach to
reasoning looks at the ways in which we can derive inferences from the very
basic perceptual process that we share with many other species. Even the
processes of recognizing similarities and recalling previous experiences
and events can provide some remarkably powerful tools for intelligence.

For example, recognizing that one situation has generally been associated with food in the past, and that another has been associated with
something bad happening allows even birds to learn to anticipate events
and to take the correct action, securing the food or avoiding the disaster.
Learning of this type gives even mice a primitive response to the balance
of probability: a situation that is *always* associated with disaster is
avoided absolutely, where one that is *sometimes* associated with disaster
and *sometimes* with food is treated quite differently. Recognizing that
there are similarities between one situation and another allows an
animal to *generalize* behaviours to the new context (itself a form of inference), rather than having to learn afresh in each situation. We human
beings take these simple perceptual and memory functions a step
further, to provide surprisingly powerful general tools for reasoning and
decision making.

Heuristic reasoning, perception and memory

Which kills more people: asthma or plane crashes? Statistically, the
answer is asthma, but most people believe that plane crashes cause more
fatalities. This is an example of a *systematic bias* (a systematic error) in
human reasoning. Human reasoning shows many such biases: as we've
seen, it often fails to correspond to the principles of probabilistic or
logical analysis (Evans, 1989; Johnson-Laird and Byrne, 1991; Johnson-
Laird, 1993; Johnson-Laird and Shafir, 1993; Kahneman et al., 1982;
Kahneman and Tversky, 1973; Tversky and Kahneman, 1973).
Understanding how these systematic biases come about reveals the way
we ordinarily draw everyday inferences.

The 'availability' heuristic

For example, the tendency to over-estimate the frequency of plane crashes comes from the way we use our memory as a basis for inference. Other things being equal, it is easier to remember things that are common or frequent than to remember things that are rare or unusual (you can probably recall the school you went to more easily than you can recall a school you visited once for a sports match). This bias in memory toward easier recall of the common or familiar is so powerful that studies of how memory works have to take care to control for the familiarity of the items to be recalled, to avoid biased results (Baddeley, 1976).

We use this memory bias in drawing inferences: since frequently experienced things are easier to recall, we infer that things that come easily to mind must be more frequent than things which are harder to remember. Kahneman and his associates called this the *availability heuristic* (Kahneman et al., 1982). Normally it works quite well, and provides us with a useful rule of thumb in estimating how common or likely something is. But memory is affected by other things besides how frequent or familiar things are. For example, something shocking or very vivid is very easy to bring to mind. These other influences on memorability can mislead us into believing that rare but vivid events (such as plane crashes) are far more common than they really are.

The 'representativeness' heuristic

Another example of a heuristic inference process uses the way we perceive similarities as a basis for drawing inferences. In formal systems such as logic, categories are supposed to be defined by specific principles or criteria. That is to say, membership of a category such as 'dog' should be defined by possession of certain critical features, such as having fur, four legs and a tail and barking. But our perceptual systems do not ordinarily recognize category membership in that way: a bald three-legged dog who has lost his tail and never barks is still recognizably a dog, albeit an unhappy one!

In fact, Rosch (1978) has shown that we normally recognize the members of a category by comparing them to our prototype or stereotype of what members of that category should be like. For example, for most people, a labrador or a collie better fits the stereotype of a dog than, say, a dachshund or a chihuahua. In deciding whether some new individual is a dog, we compare it to that stereotype. The more the new individual resembles the stereotype, the more sure we are that it really is a dog. So in a way, even recognizing things involves a sort of inference: *if it looks like a typical elephant, it is an elephant.* Extending this simple perceptual process only slightly provides what Kahneman and his colleagues call the 'representativeness' heuristic: if it looks like a member of the category X, assume that that is what it is.

As with the availability heuristic, the representativeness heuristic is normally a very useful and accurate basis for inference. But as with the availability heuristic, it can lead to biased reasoning in certain circumstances. Take the case of the room containing 70 doctors and 30 musicians. If one individual leaves the room, the objective statistical probability is that it is a doctor, since there are so many more of them than musicians. If adults are told nothing whatever about that individual, they will use statistical probabilities to judge the profession of the one who leaves. But if they are told anything at all about that individual (that he has long hair, say, or is wearing a psychedelic waistcoat) people ignore the statistical probabilities and use the representativeness heuristic, and since the information given here is more like our stereotype of a musician than of a doctor, most people would guess that the leaver was a musician.

Interestingly, adults will ignore the statistical probabilities and try to use the representativeness heuristic even where the information given about the individual in question is irrelevant to either stereotype (such as that he has blue eyes, or is 6 ft (1.8 m) tall). The representativeness heuristic doesn't cue either profession here, so people infer that the individual is equally likely to be a doctor or a musician, despite the clear statistical probability that he is a doctor (Kahneman et al., 1982).

Is heuristic reasoning rational?

Kahneman and his colleagues have identified quite a number of inference heuristics deriving from basic psychological processes in the same way as do the availability and the representativeness heuristics. Even highly educated adults, including those trained in formal logical or probabilistic reasoning use heuristics such as availability and representativeness to draw inferences, and this is true even where more formal mathematical or logical procedures could or should be used (Block and Harper, 1991; Kahneman et al., 1982; MacLeod, Williams and Berkian, 1991; Scheiderman and Kaplan, 1992). Heuristic reasoning extrapolating from memory and perception is characteristic of adult intelligence.

Is heuristic reasoning rational? Certainly, it can lead us into a variety of errors, and very probably contributes to some of the less attractive prejudices and biases to which our species is prone. But it is important not to over-estimate the extent to which such reasoning causes mistakes, or to assume that logical reasoning would result in fewer errors of judgment.

Heuristic and logical reasoning work in very different ways. Logic provides rules which guarantee answers that are *necessarily* valid: that is to say, answers that *must* be valid, if the rules of logic have been correctly followed. But these rules are only concerned with the logical form or the inference, and not with factual accuracy. Logic provides no means of testing the factual accuracy of a conclusion. If your premises are factually wrong, then your logical conclusion may be perfectly valid but it may be factually wrong, and so lead to errors of judgment. ('There are no poisonous spiders in London. I am in London. Therefore that giant spider in the kitchen is not poisonous.' Faultless logic, but ...)

By contrast, heuristic reasoning gives no guarantee of a necessarily correct answer: it provides more of an informed guess. But it has the advantage of being rooted in our experience and understanding, our mental models of the world, and therefore is directly based in what we believe to be factually accurate. This is a good enough basis for rational inference in most contexts. For the purposes of everyday life, rooting reasoning in factual knowledge is often more rational than applying the rules of logic. ('That looks awfully like a tarantula ...')

The development of heuristic reasoning

Knowledge and understanding change dramatically as an infant passes through childhood. A 3-year-old has not had the time or experience to build up stereotypes of doctors and musicians, and will have different vivid memories from an older child or adult. So even if very young children make judgments through heuristics such as availability or representativeness, they will probably come to different conclusions, and show different biases than their elders. But do they in fact make heuristic judgments in this way at all?

Kahneman and his associates argued that heuristic inferences are innate, automatic and involuntary, so natural a part of the way our memory and perceptual systems work that they are hard to inhibit in favour of more sophisticated strategies. On this basis, we should find that even very young children use heuristics such as representativeness and availability, and indeed, we would predict that they will do so to an even greater extent than adults do, since adults have the choice of more formal alternatives such as logical or probabilistic strategies (Fischbein, 1975; Ross, 1981). But this is not the case. Six-year-olds are very much less likely than older children to use either the representativeness heuristic (Jacobs and Potenza, 1991), the availability heuristic (Thornton, 1996), or other everyday inferential heuristics identified by Kahneman (Krouse, 1986).This is a surprising result, and worth considering further. Given how simple and natural these heuristics seem, what restricts the child's use of them?

If you ask college students, 'Are there more mice or more ducks in cartoons?' and then ask them to recall as many as possible of each category, you find that those who say there are more mice subsequently recall more mice, and vice versa. This is the availability heuristic at work. Eight-year-olds behave in much the same way as adults, but younger children don't: they are very good at remembering ducks and mice from cartoons, but the judgments they make before doing so are not biased toward over-estimating the more easily recalled category (Thornton, 1996).

This is not a unique finding. If you read out a number of names, listing an equal number of male and female names but using very familiar names for one gender (Nelson Mandela, Martin Luther for example) and unfamiliar ones for the other (Jane Black, Susan Jones and so on), and ask adults whether there were more male or more female names on the list, they will systematically over-estimate the number of the gender represented by the familiar (and therefore more memorable) names (Kahneman et al., 1982). With children, of course, you cannot use politicians and celebrities' names in this task, since these may or may not be familiar to young children. You can substitute the names of the child's school classmates for the familiar names. Again, 8-year-olds spontaneously show a bias toward over-estimating the gender represented by familiar names, indicating the action of the availability heuristic, but younger children do not (Thornton, 1996).

Obviously, then, heuristic reasoning drawing on the properties of perception and memory is not automatic, as was initially supposed. But do these data mean that young children *cannot* draw inferences in this way? Or do the data mean that we have to learn how to invoke our basic psychological processes to draw inferences?

The youngest children tested for their ability to use heuristic inference processes so far are 5- and 6-year-olds (Thornton, 1996), so we do not yet know whether very young children can reason on this basis or not. But the evidence is that 5- to 6-year-old children *can* use heuristics such as availability, if something in the situation cues them to recall the things to be compared before making their judgments, or if they have a special reason to pay attention to the task in hand.

For example, 6-year-olds show no availability bias in judging which gender is more numerous on a list of names including their schoolmates as the familiar names, if asked to make the gender judgment *as an end in itself*. But 90 per cent of these children show a strong availability effect if they have a personal interest in the list of names: if the list tells which children will get a treat, for example (Thornton, 1996)!

The implication of this result is that, to understand the development of reasoning, we must focus on how skills are brought into play as much as on what skills the child has, even when the skills in question are apparently very simple, and very tightly tied to the child's basic perceptual and memory processes. It seems that young children do not automatically mobilize their memories or other mental processes in the service of reasoning as older children and adults do. This result endorses the conclusion that a crucial aspect of what develops through childhood and adolescence is executive control over mental processes.

The development of knowledge

It's clear from the research reviewed so far that the child's developing knowledge, his or her conceptual understanding of the world, plays a vital role in reasoning, forming the basis for inferences from mental models and perceptual heuristics. But how does knowledge itself develop? Are there more things to discover about how what we know affects how we think?

Concept formation

Take a look at **Figure 6.4**. What is the object silhouetted on the left? What would you do with it? Probably your reaction is, 'How should I know? I can't tell what it is! I've never seen it before.' But that isn't really the problem. The thing on the right is just as new to you, you've never seen that before either, and yet you do know what to do with it. For all its novelty, it is obviously some kind of mug. You know a lot about it, simply because you can 'see' it as a mug. Your problem with the object on the left is that you don't have any conception of what it is: in other words, you can't slip it into any familiar category, so you can't draw on any past experience to help figure out how to react to it.

This demonstration reveals the fundamental importance of our ability to recognize one thing as similar to another, to group objects in categories. Without this basic conceptual ability, every mug and every blade of grass would seem unique and unfamiliar. You would have to learn about every individual object you encountered right from scratch – an impossible mental burden. Dividing the world into concepts (such as 'mug') greatly simplifies things: now you can build up knowledge about categories of things rather than individual objects or experiences, and can generalize from past experience. The ability to form concepts, to generalize from one thing to another, is the root of all learning, the basis of all knowledge.

Babies are able to form concepts right from (and even before) birth. This is obvious from the habituation studies described in Chapter 3: a baby could hardly become bored with 'yet another square' unless he or she was able to form the concept of 'square', recognizing objects of different sizes and shapes as examples of this concept (Slater and Morison, 1985).

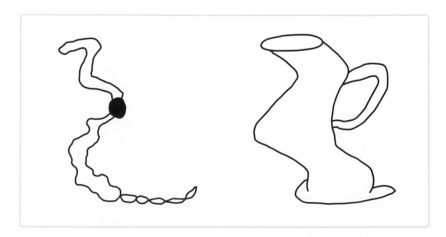

figure 6.4

What are these?

Children undoubtedly create their own concepts on the basis of their personal experience and efforts to make sense of the world: this is clear from the idiosyncratic ways they lump things together under a label, as they first learn to speak (Dromi, 1987; Mervis, 1987), for example, using the word 'ball' to refer to almost anything that rolls. But quickly, better mastery of language brings their concepts in line with those of the culture around them (Banigan and Mervis, 1988). All our knowledge is, in an important sense, socially constructed (see **Box 6.6**).

6.6

Knowledge as a social construction

It is easy to assume that when a child learns about the physical world he or she is learning objective facts from a fixed universe. But this is not so: you and I, for example, 'know' that the world is sort of spherical, whereas our remote ancestors believed it to be flat. But our 'knowledge' is as much hearsay as that of our ancestors: *someone told us*. Few of us have checked it out for ourselves, or would have the slightest idea how to do so. A very great deal of what we understand about the world is socially constructed and transmitted to us by our culture.

Quite young children in our society come to understand things which it took the greatest minds of our species many hundreds of years to discover (Carey, 1985). They do this either through being directly taught these ideas or through being deliberately exposed to the kinds of experience likely to make a given discovery salient. You can see this effect for yourself, in studying the research into child development reviewed in this book. Ideas that seem obvious to us now (such as the notion that we can solve logical problems without necessarily using mental processes that have a logical structure) took decades of research to discover. Every individual's apparently objective knowledge rests on discoveries made by others, and is shaped by the way a given culture views the world.

Even at a very mundane level, the 'facts' we know about the world are influenced by social conventions. Take, for example, Piaget's famous 'conservation' task in which a child is shown two identical glasses, A and B, containing identical amounts of water. The water from glass A is then poured into a third, different shaped glass: a taller, thinner one, say. The child is asked to say whether the amount of water in the tall thin glass is the same as that in glass B. In this task, children are scored as answering correctly if they answer (as those over about 8 years do) that the amount of water is the same. But objectively, this is the wrong answer! In fact, the emptied glass will still be damp inside, because some of the water has adhered to the glass instead of pouring into the new, thin glass. So if the amounts of water in the two original glasses were absolutely identical, there will now be less water in the thin glass, because some remains in glass A. But this is a difference which is socially agreed to be too small to matter (Light and Perret-Cleremont, 1989). To a far greater extent than we realize, learning to think like an adult is a matter of learning to share the way our own particular culture looks at things, the meanings and assumptions that define our shared understanding of the world and determine what is or is not a good solution to a problem.

The power of cultural expectations over the way we think and reason is illustrated by two studies from cross-cultural research. In the first, shortly after the Second World War, soldiers joining the Gurkha regiments in Nepal were asked to complete IQ tests, 'as fast as possible'. They did so, and scored extremely badly: they had entirely sacrificed accuracy for speed. Asked to try again, and get as many right as possible this time, they laboured extremely slowly and painstakingly over the test, failing to complete it in a time that allowed for a meaningful interpretation of the results: they had now entirely sacrificed speed for accuracy. Their culture simply did not prepare them for the notion of a balanced trade between speed and accuracy, although this is so fundamental a concept in our own culture as to seem too obvious to need explanation.

In the second study (Cole and Scribner, 1974), researchers were comparing the categorizing skills of tribesmen from a remote African area with those of American college students. Asked to group the things that go together, the American students made taxonomic groupings (all the tools in one category, all the vegetables in another, and so on). But the Africans made completely different groupings, for example putting a mattock with the root vegetables, and so on. To the researchers, the Africans' behaviour seemed bizarre and immature: surely adults ought to understand the greater sense in sorting like with like? They asked the Africans why they had sorted as they did, and were told that it was because this was how a 'wise man' would arrange things: the things you need for planting a field all in the same place, for example. Asked to sort the things as a 'foolish man' would do, they produced taxonomic categories just as the Americans had done! Cultural norms and expectations had dictated the perception of what is or is not a mature way of reasoning, for both the African tribesmen and the American researchers.

Conceptual organization

Our concepts are hierarchically organized (see **Figure 6.5**). That is to say, they form interconnected patterns, with higher-order concepts such as 'animals' subsuming progressively lower-order ones ('dog' , 'spaniel') and themselves being subsumed into progressively higher-order groupings ('living things' versus 'inanimate objects').

It is easier to discover concepts at some levels within this hierarchy than at others. For example, it's easier to notice commonalities at an intermediate level in the hierarchy (such as 'dog') than at either super-ordinate ('animal') or subordinate ('spaniel') levels. On the one hand, the members of the intermediate-level category are more recognizably similar to one another than those at the superordinate level (members of the category 'dog' look more alike than members of the category 'animal', which includes dolphins, mice, bats and giraffes, which don't look much alike at all). On the other hand, two intermediate-level categories ('dog' and 'mouse') are easier to tell apart than are subordinate categories (different breeds of dog or mouse can be hard to tell apart). Rosch (1978) calls these easiest to identify intermediary categories *basic-level categories.*

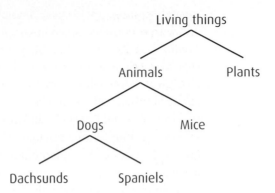

figure **6.5**

The hierarchical organization of concepts

Because they are the easiest to pick out, the first concepts children discover are basic-level categories, and these are also the concepts adults first encourage babies to learn. We tend to provide basic-level category names when first teaching children words, or when naming things they or we have pointed out (Nelson, 1973, and see Chapter 5). Basic-level categories form the reference point from which the rest of the hierarchy of concepts can be learned. We tell toddlers, 'Dogs and cats and foxes are all kinds of animal', or 'A spaniel is a sort of dog' (Callanan, 1985; Taylor and Gelman, 1989). Through such remarks we teach children not only individual concepts at different levels of abstraction, but also how concepts fit together to create a coherent, integrated structure of knowledge.

Core concepts

Some concepts are more important than others, and some provide a more useful way of structuring the world than others. For instance, the distinctions between inanimate and living things, between plants and animals, and between our own species and other animals, are helpful to our survival in a way that the distinctions between (say) white things and things that aren't white, big white things and little white things, and little white things in trees and little white things on the ground, are not, although the structure of the two category systems is the same. Equally, concepts of time, place, causality and number are more important than most others in interacting effectively with a world full of events, opportunities and threats.

It's no surprise, then, to discover that human beings around the world structure their knowledge around the distinctions between animate and inanimate things, plants and animals, human beings and other creatures, and that concepts of space, time, causality and number are also universal. Knowledge is already structured in this way in very young children (Wellman and Gelman, 1998).

Some researchers argue that these core concepts are so vital to our evolutionary survival that they are programmed into us: that we are innately equipped with basic knowledge in each of these vital domains, and with specialized mechanisms for learning in each area (Atran, 1998; Medin and Atran, 2004). They suggest, for example, that we have a special 'module' in the mind dedicated to directing the development of biological knowledge, and another specialized module for learning about number, and so on. This theory is very controversial. Virtually all researchers would agree that knowledge in the core domains (that is, knowledge about human beings, biology, physics, time, space, causality, number) is indeed fundamental to human intelligence. But is that because we are innately primed with knowledge in these areas, or because intelligence naturally focuses on what is most relevant for its needs, without requiring any such priming? And even if there is some sort of innate basis for knowledge in these core areas, does it necessarily involve separate modules for each domain rather than deriving from general mechanisms?

There is nothing intrinsically absurd in the notion that human beings may have some sort of innate predisposition to attend to certain things and to learn in core areas. Other species certainly come pre-equipped with knowledge relevant to their survival. For example, birds may have to learn their own species' love songs, but they 'know' what a song is, know what to pick out of the auditory environment to learn (Marler, 1991).

If core knowledge in key domains is innately specified, then we would expect to find that very young babies show this knowledge (this prediction fuelled much of the research on infant skills reviewed in Chapters 3 and 4). The evidence suggests that we are indeed innately primed to perceive and react to the world in certain ways. For example, newborn babies can perceive shape, colour and size (Slater, 1997), and very young babies have some degree of understanding of the physics of objects, the way objects exist, move, can't hover in space unsupported and so on (Spelke, 1994; Spelke et al., 1992). From birth, too, babies are strikingly fascinated by people, by the human face (Johnson et al., 1991) and voice (Mehler et al., 1986), and are precociously competent at recognizing individual faces (Bushnell, Sai and Mullin 1989; Walton, Bower and Bower, 1992). From surprisingly early they can tell the difference between the way animate and inanimate objects move (Slater, 1997), are able to recall time sequences (Haith, Wentworth and Canfield, 1993) and draw simple causal inferences (Oakes and Cohen, 1995). Young babies may even be able to handle addition and subtraction with small numbers of objects (Wynn, 1995).

Most researchers now agree that the precocious abilities of very young babies do imply the existence of innate mechanisms of some sort. But do they necessarily imply the existence of special modules for each core area of knowledge? Do innate modules continue to direct the way knowledge develops in core domains? Many researchers doubt this. The baby's precocious talents could just as easily be explained in terms of simple reflexes on which general, rather than 'modular' developmental processes build.

The theory that there are innate modules in the mind that direct the way knowledge in core domains develops predicts that key aspects of conceptual understanding should develop in the same way all round the world, even though children in different cultures have different experiences and opportunities to learn. There are some data that seem to support this prediction. For example, the idea that eggs laid by a duck will hatch into ducklings even if incubated by a hen is understood by very young children from working-class and middle-class American families, urban and rural Native Americans, middle-class Brazilians, children from a fishing village in Madagascar, and unschooled Yukatek Maya children from Mexico (Astuti, Solomon and Carey, 2004; Atran et al., 2001; Johnson and Solomon, 1997; Medin and Atran, 2004; Sousa, Atran and Medin, 2002). This has been claimed as impressive evidence that the idea that creatures pass on their 'essence' to their young must be biologically primed, because it emerges in the same way across cultures that offer children very different opportunities to learn it, either through their own observations of eggs hatching or through parental or formal tuition (Atran, 1998).

However, this conclusion has been strongly criticized. The very same studies that identify common themes in biological understanding across different cultures also show that there are important differences in how children and adults from different cultures naturally understand biological phenomena and structure their knowledge (for example, Medin and Atran, 2004). The supporters of innate modules of knowledge overestimate the commonalities across cultures, and therefore the extent to which biological knowledge could be innately specified (Ingold, 2004). Furthermore, such commonalities as are found need not necessarily imply innately pre-specified knowledge: they could simply reflect the facts of nature. As it happens, duck eggs *do* produce ducklings the world over, for example. Even if children in some cultures are not directly exposed to this fact, they are exposed to a great deal of information from which it could be inferred (Gelman et al., 1998).

The present consensus of research is that we are born with reflexes that predispose us to orient to certain aspects of the world, but not with specialized modules that direct the development of knowledge in core domains. Knowledge in all domains develops through the same general mechanisms, rather than through special modular processes dedicated to a given topic (Astuti et al., 2004; Carey, 1985, 1999; Gelman, 2003; Springer, 1999). Knowledge grows through the child's own efforts to put two and two together to make sense of things (Astuti et al., 2004; Carey, 1985), sometimes resulting in rather idiosyncratic ideas, as in the case of a 3-year-old quoted as asking, 'Why doesn't my blood come out when I open my mouth?' (DeLoache et al., 1998). But the major influence on the way knowledge develops in any area is social. Adults shape children's basic concepts as they teach them words, and influence the overall structure of their knowledge through both social practice and direct tuition (Bruner, 1986; Keller and Keller, 1996; Lave and Wenger, 1991; Rogoff and Lave, 1984; Vygotsky, 1978). Most of what we know is socially constructed (Box 6.6), shaped by the shared knowledge of our culture so that adult understanding varies between societies (Ingold, 2004) and within a society over time (Carey, 1985).

Conceptual understanding, causality and reasoning

Differences in social and individual experience, and in the idiosyncratic theories the individual child creates for him or herself, mean that there is no neat pattern in exactly what children of a given age know. Even within a given culture, there will be differences between children of the same age in what information they have gathered and what they have made of it. Between cultures, the range of variation is likely to be far greater. For example, 10-year-olds in London undoubtedly understand far more about the internet than do their counterparts in a rural Nigerian village, whereas the African village children understand far more about the way the seasons affect animals than do the Londoners. The speed, pattern and content of knowledge development, even in core areas, may vary very widely from one culture to another (Astuti et al., 2004; Luria, 1977; Medin and Atran, 2004; Rogoff and Lave, 1984; Vygotsky, 1978).

There are some patterns and regularities, of course, in the way knowledge develops, reflecting systematic influences on the child such as the shared school curriculum within a culture, or the fact that the physical world has the same properties (for instance, gravity, or the way plants grow) the world over. Identifying patterns in the development of children's conceptual understanding in various core areas such as time (**Box 6.7**), space (**Box 6.8**), number (Box 6.5), basic physics (Chapter 3), other people's minds (Chapter 9), is an important dimension of research into cognitive development. But for the rest of this chapter we shall focus on understanding how the structure of knowledge in any area develops, and how the changing structure of knowledge affects the way we reason.

<table><tr><td>box **6.7**

Understanding time</td><td>The essence of a sense of time is the experience of things happening in a given sequence: that is to say, knowing that such and such a thing happened first, and then that happened, and now this is happening, and in a while something else will happen.

This basic experience of time is vital to the way we make sense of the world, as was entertainingly explored in a novel by Rob Grant (1996) about a world in which time runs backwards. For example, our understanding of the sequence of events determines how we see causality. In our world, St Francis of Assisi picked</td></tr></table>

up injured birds, then he healed them and then he released them from his hand – a saintly action. In Grant's backwards world the time sequence is reversed: healthy birds fly to Francis' hands, then they are injured and then he puts them down – a sequence of events that is more sadistic than saintly. If we saw no sequence in the events, we could make no causal connections between one thing and another at all.

Given how vital the order of events is for understanding the world, it's no surprise that even very young babies are able to detect and anticipate sequences of events. They are certainly able to do this by 3 months of age (Haith, Wentworth and Canfield, 1993), at least in relation to ongoing events. Since most living creatures can recognize and anticipate such sequences, it seems probable that there is some innate neurological basis for this skill.

Children can become confused about the order of events over long periods of time. For example, asked in mid-February whether Christmas or Valentine's day was the more recent, most 4-year-olds know the answer (Friedman, 1991). But asked which was more recent, their birthday or Christmas, few children under the age of 9 years can answer correctly if both events were more than 2 months earlier (Friedman, Gardner and Zubin, 1995). This age effect probably has little to do with the basic ability to understand time sequences. Even adults often have difficulty in remembering the relative order of events that happened some time ago (for example, I have difficulty in remembering whether the serious flooding in Cornwall was before or after the even more dramatic floods of New Orleans). If the events in question are causally connected (for example, one led to the other), we may be able to use our understanding of the causal connections to reconstruct which must have come first. The older the child, the more relevant understanding he or she will have, and the more able he or she will be to make such reconstructions. When events aren't causally connected, we may be able to work out which came first by referring to the conventions we use for measuring time (hours of the day, days of the week, months of the year, years of the century). The older the child, the more likely it is that he or she has learned these time conventions and can use them as a framework for working out the sequence of long-past events.

Learning to use time conventions is a more complex business than most of us remember. It involves the rote learning of the names of days of the week and months of the year, and the order these come in. It involves mastering the skills of reading clocks and calendars and keeping track of time. But none of this is of much use unless the child has the conceptual insight that these things are devices for measuring and labelling time.

The notion that time comes in different-sized units seems to develop fairly young. By 5 years of age, children are also fairly adept at judging short periods of time: the difference between 10 seconds and 30 seconds, say (Fraisse, 1982). But their understanding of the measurement of time is shaky. Young children who count to measure time periods often don't realize that this only works if you count at an even rate (Levin, 1989). Nor do they always focus on time itself in such measurements. For example, if two toy trains travel along parallel tracks for the same amount of time, but one ends up farther along than the other (because it went faster), 5-year-olds think that the train that went further also travelled for longer (Acredolo and Schmidt, 1981). Their problem seems to be one of disentangling the different factors that combine in the concept of speed.

box **6.8**

Understanding space

Fundamental to our ability to function intelligently in the world is the ability to locate ourselves relative to objects and places, and to understand the way one thing or place is located relative to another. There is some evidence that we are born innately prepared to perceive the relative distance of objects (Chapter 3), and to construe their location relative to ourselves. Young babies reach for the nearer of two objects (von Hofsten and Spelke, 1985), and orient in the direction of noises in the dark, for example (Clifton et al., 1993).

Evidence that babies initially construe the location of objects relative to themselves rather than relative to the environment at large comes from the observation that, having seen an object on the left, they look to the left to find it again even if they themselves have been turned around so that it's now on the right (Acredolo, 1978).

Understanding the location of objects relative to the environment rather than the self develops through infancy. Becoming mobile seems to play an important part in this: babies who have had the experience of moving themselves either by crawling or propelling themselves in a 'walking frame' tend to have a better representation of the location of one object relative to others than those without such experience (Bertenthal, Campos and Kermoian, 1994). You have probably experienced a similar phenomenon yourself: we all learn far more about an environment when we walk around it navigating for ourselves than we do when driven around in a bus or car.

The ability to make mental maps of the environment, to locate objects relative to one another and to use these in navigation, continues to develop through infancy and childhood, and even through adult life (Bremner, Knowles and Andreasen, 1994; Gallistel, 1990; Overman et al., 1996). There is even some evidence in support of the popular stereotype that men are generally better at such skills than women (Pease and Pease, 2000). This may reflect biological differences, but may as easily reflect social differences: boys are often allowed more freedom to explore the environment, and men are still more likely to be the driver than a passenger, so that males get more practice with spatial skills. Cross-cultural research shows that the degree of practice in spatial skills, and the social importance of ability in this area, have a clear effect on development (Kearins, 1981).

Making causal connections

As we have seen earlier (Figure 6.5), conceptual knowledge is arranged in a hierarchical structure, each concept connected to other, related concepts. This interconnectedness of concepts provides a powerful basis for inference. For example, knowing that a mouse is an animal allows me to conclude that mice have certain characteristics (such as eating or defecating) even though I have never seen a mouse before and know nothing about the species.

But *why* is a mouse an animal? To the adult mind, the answer is easy: it is obvious, from our rich understanding of how biological systems work. But what if we didn't have that biological knowledge? Often, when we begin to learn in a new area, new concepts are simply juxtaposed. We connect them only because we've been told there is a connection, or because they happen to turn up together, or because they look rather similar somehow. We don't really understand much about *why* they are connected, and may misunderstand or misinterpret the connections as a result. A great deal of conceptual development involves coming to understand the real basis of connections between things: gathering enough *causal information* about how things work to understand just why one concept relates to another.

Causal understanding increases dramatically through childhood and even on into adult life. It's not that the very young cannot understand causal connections in principle (as Piaget suggested). Even babies have the general idea that one thing can cause another (Oakes and Cohen, 1995): for instance, that one object knocking into another can cause the second object to move. The problem for the young child is that causal understanding involves knowledge that they have not yet had time to gather. For example, you need to know how hooks work before you can realize that a hooked tool is better for retrieving things than a straight one, a piece of information that toddlers lack at 18 months but have generally discovered by 24 months (Chen and Siegler, 2000). We come to understand causality by discovering very specific information in a specific area. Understanding about hooks doesn't help you understand why one thing melts in the sun and another doesn't! Causal understanding comes from the acquisition of very specific information, topic by topic.

Children work hard on understanding how things work (endlessly asking 'Why … ?' for example). But they must gather a great deal of information, before the structure of their knowledge can be shaped by causal connections. This takes time. The project is an important one: changes in the degree of causal understanding in an area affect not only the connections we see between concepts, but also the ways we understand those concepts, and the tools we can use in reasoning about them. The classic demonstration of how increasing causal understanding can create qualitative change in how children reason about a particular topic is Carey's (1985) study of how children understand the biological concept 'alive'.

Understanding what is alive: a case study

As we have seen in Chapter 3, even young babies distinguish between living creatures and inanimate objects on the basis of the way these things move: animate objects can move themselves and are goal-directed, whereas inanimate ones cannot propel themselves and have no goals (Slater, 1997). It seems that our perceptual systems may be pre-set to be alert to this distinction (Slater, 1997).

By the age of 3 years, many of the child's judgments about whether something is alive or not are very like the judgments made by an adult.

They know, for example, that dogs are alive and dolls are not. But this apparent competence hides some radical differences in the way younger and older children conceptualize the notion of 'being alive', and how they reason about it. The differences emerge if you ask younger and older children whether trees are alive, for example, or whether lizards eat. The young child will probably say that trees are not alive, and be very unsure whether lizards eat or not, whereas the older child has no difficulty with such questions.

Despite their inborn predisposition to orient to animate entities, children below about 7 years of age generally have little or no real biological knowledge. They have no real idea what a biological organism actually is, or what is inside it, or how it works. They do not understand biological processes such as reproduction or death. They know that they must eat and defecate, but do not understand the purpose of digestion or the nature or function of the digestive organs. They know that wounds bleed, but do not understand the purpose of blood or the role of the heart: at this age hearts are for loving, not pumping oxygen and other vital substances around the body (Carey, 1985).

Since these young children don't understand what a biological organism really is, they have no conception of any characteristics that might be common across all organisms. Thus they have no basis for inferring whether or not something is a living organism, or will do the things a living organism does, other than its similarity to the things they already know are alive. In other words, they have no basis for reasoning except Kahneman's representativeness heuristic: the more something looks and behaves like the prototypical animate creature (which for us is a human being), the more likely it is to judged to be alive (Carey, 1985). Monkeys and even dogs look and behave somewhat like people, and therefore young children confidently judge them to be alive, and to do the things that people do, such as having babies. But daffodils and shrubs do not look or behave like people, and will be judged to be inanimate, and not to reproduce. Lizards don't look much like people either, though more so than a daffodil, creating uncertainty in the young child's mind.

By the age of 10 years or so children[2] have typically learned quite a lot about biology, and how biological systems work. They know, for example, that respiration supplies the blood with oxygen, which must then be pumped around the body by the heart to feed the tissues, and which subsequently removes waste products. They understand the purpose of digestion, the relationship between functions such as eating and defecating, and so on. Crucially, they understand that all living organisms must feed, eliminate, breathe, reproduce and die, because that is what *defines* life.

---

[2] This is true in our culture, as result of schooling. The same may not be true in cultures where formal biology is not taught, as indeed it wasn't in our culture 300 years ago.

Conceptual change from causal understanding

The 10-year-olds' new knowledge about how biological systems work radically changes both the way concepts in this area are structured and the way the child can draw inferences.

For example, understanding the process of reproduction means that the 10-year-old now defines a baby as the newborn young of a species, whereas for the younger child, the defining feature of a baby is smallness, because that's what babies look like, relative to adults. As a consequence of this change, 10-year-olds have no trouble in understanding that an elderly miniature dachshund is older than a month-old Great Dane, whereas younger children may insist that this cannot be true: the smaller dog must be younger (Thornton, 2002)! Greater causal understanding has restructured the child's concept of 'baby': features that seemed to be at the core of this concept when it was based on perceptual appearances (such as size) shift to peripheral importance, and are replaced by other criteria as the child comes to understand biological processes better. This kind of conceptual restructuring happens in every area of knowledge, as the child shifts from concepts based on perceptual similarities to concepts based on causal understanding.

Redefining concepts in the light of causal understanding in this way has radical effects on reasoning. For the child without causal understanding, reasoning is rooted in generalizing from concrete perceptual similarities, just as Piaget described. As we've noted, the child has no basis for drawing inferences except the representativeness heuristic (if it looks like a human being, assume it has the characteristics of a human being; if it doesn't look like a human being, assume that it hasn't got those properties). By contrast, causal understanding provides a more abstract and principled basis for defining categories and for drawing inferences: it no longer matters what a thing looks like, it only matters whether or not it has the properties that define membership of the category in question. Confronted by a new entity, the 10-year-old can decide whether or not it is alive by asking whether it has the defining properties of 'aliveness', no matter what it looks like, so that plants and insects can be recognized as alive despite looking entirely different from people. Conversely, knowing that a cactus is alive, the 10-year-old can infer that it must reproduce, even if the means of reproduction is not understood.

It's worth underlining just how fundamental a change in reasoning the acquisition of causal understanding provides. A child reasoning on the basis of similarities is very much limited to generalizing from his or her concrete experience of the world, unable to imagine things other than the way they are (an alien would have to look pretty much like a human being to be recognized as an intelligent being, for example). But a child reasoning on the basis of principled category definitions is not concretely tied down in this way. Such a child can draw more formal, analytical inferences, and can entertain abstract hypothetical ideas (that there may be alien intelligences that are pure air, or made of stone and so on, even if there's nothing like that around here). Thus an increase in causal understanding of the kind Carey is describing explains the same shift from reasoning embedded in concrete (perceptual) experience to more abstract formal reasoning that Piaget sought to explain, but in a very different way. Carey's work shows how the important developmental change in reasoning that Piaget observed can derive from changes in factual understanding, rather than arising from the construction of abstract logical structures of the mind as Piaget thought.

Developmental stages versus domain-specific knowledge

Piaget's theory described reasoning as developing through four distinct stages, each one characterized by a particular level of the development of logical structures for reasoning. According to this view, all of a child's reasoning, in whatever area, would have the quality of the stage he or she has reached, since logical structures are abstract and independent of the content of the information to which they are applied.

The picture of the development of reasoning arising from Carey's work is very different. According to this new view, the quality of a child's reasoning in any area is directly related to his or her level of causal understanding in that specific area or domain, and it is this *domain-specific knowledge* that creates the tools the child uses in reasoning. The sophistication of a child's knowledge can vary very greatly from one topic to another, and so the quality of reasoning will vary across topics as a consequence, being perceptually based where there is little knowledge and principled where knowledge is richer. Thus according to Carey, reasoning does not develop through general stages as described by Piaget, but more patchily, topic by topic. The evidence supports Carey's theory.

Piaget is right to point out that reasoning is typically rooted in concrete, perceptual processes in the very young, and more likely to be based on more abstract principled reasoning in older individuals. But this is not invariably true, as a 'stage' theory such as Piaget's must predict. Even very young babies draw principled inferences from category membershp rather than perceptual similarities in some areas (Smith, 1989). Three-year-olds can disregard striking perceptual similarities and reason on the basis of category membership, given the right information (Gelman and Markman, 1986, 1987). Conversely, even college students resort to similarity-based reasoning in areas (such as physics) where they lack causal understanding (Chi, Feltovich and Glaser, 1981). The switch from similarity-based reasoning to category-based reasoning is not related to age or stage, but to the level of causal understanding the individual has about the topic in question. It just happens that, the younger the child, the less likely he or she is to have gathered much causal understanding in any area.

Novices and experts

Research on adult novices and experts supports the view that it is domain-specific knowledge, rather than general reasoning tools that creates skilled performances in reasoning. We have a naïve tendency to assume that expertise reflects 'super-intelligence', so that we expect that a brilliant scientist or chess player will be brilliant at everything else, too. There is a grain of truth in this idea (as will be discussed in Chapters 7 and 8.) But the fact is that brilliance in one area is not necessarily associated with brilliance in another: being an expert scientist does not make someone more adept than the average person at managing the family budget, say, or repairing the family car, still less at forging fulfilling relationships (as our stereotype of the 'mad professor' suggests). Conversely, being useless at chess does not necessarily mean that someone will be bad at their job, or at handling the intricacies of playing the stock market or running an international business. Expertise reflects not so much general mental power as specific knowledge in the particular domain of that expertise. People can be (and usually are) an expert in some areas and a comparative novice in many others.

Experts and novices conceptualize problems and their solutions in an entirely different way (Chi et al., 1981; Chi, Glaser and Rees, 1982; Larkin, 1983). The difference is very much the same as the difference Carey (1985) noted in children's biological knowledge: like young children, adult novices lack understanding of how one thing relates to another and so conceptualize things in terms of perceptual similarities, where the expert organizes knowledge around principles guided by causal understanding. As a consequence, novices and experts construe problems differently and draw inferences in a different way, paralleling the developmental change reflecting changing causal knowledge that we see between younger and older children.

The rich conceptual structures of expertise actually make problem solving easier in many ways. The expert has a vast store of past experience to draw on, a detailed understanding of what is involved in problem solving in this area. This allows a more planfully aware and organized approach to reasoning, a more informed choice between strategies: in other words, a greater executive control over reasoning. Lacking such knowledge the novice may thrash about in more or less random trial and error. Experts can also often recognize a problem as familiar, and can simply recall and reapply what worked last time, where a novice meeting that same problem for the first time must reason out the solution from scratch.

For example, chess experts can understand what they must attend to, and can marshal plans in ways that novices can't. They can recognize patterns in the play that novices don't see (De Groot, 1965), and can decide what to do by recalling how different responses to those patterns worked out in the past, where the novice must try to calculate what will happen next. Such expertise, even in chess, depends on knowledge and not age (Chi, 1978): experienced child chess players behave more expertly than adult novices to the game.

Developing from novice to expert?

Thus, in many lines of research the evidence is mounting that the sophistication of the reasoning we bring to a task reflects the relevant domain-specific knowledge that we have. Where adults lack relevant knowledge, we behave very much as children do, trying things out by trial and error, making incoherent plans and using primitive concepts and processes in default of other options (Brown and DeLoache, 1978, and see Chapter 7). Where children possess more relevant knowledge, they can reason in more sophisticated ways than adults. Expertise (or naivety) in reasoning is a function of what you know.

Should we conceptualize the development of reasoning as the development of expertise? In a profound sense, the young baby is a 'universal novice': a novice at everything. Through childhood, adolescence and on into adult life we gradually acquire more and more information, developing a progressive degree of expertise in a wider and wider range of areas (Brown and DeLoache, 1978; Carey, 1985; Chi and Ceci, 1987; Wellman and Gelman, 1998). It's this general progress towards expertise across more and more areas that gradually creates a developmental change from perceptual to principled reasoning across the board, and a more general ability to exert executive control over our mental processes and strategies.

Can change in domain-specific knowledge and the expertise it creates explain all the phenomena of developmental change in the quality of reasoning through childhood and adolescence? A number of researchers have argued that it can (Carey, 1985; Chi and Ceci, 1987; Wiser and Carey, 1983). Certainly, it is generally accepted now that the acquisition of domain-specific knowledge is a critical factor in the development of intellect (Kuhn, 2000).

In conclusion

Our human capacity to draw inferences, to understand and make sense of the world, is extraordinary. Some of our skills we share with other creatures: the ability to remember, to notice similarities, to generalize and draw inferences from these things. But it's beyond dispute that we far surpass other species in our ability to reason. What, exactly, is the basis for our special human capacity in this area?

For decades the answer to this question was dominated by the work of Piaget, emphasizing the development of reasoning through progressive stages of construction of logical structures of the mind. The specific knowledge the child might have was thought to be relatively unimportant, from this perspective: logical structures function without regard to the content of the information on which they operate.

Modern research has turned this around. It seems that even when we draw logical inferences we don't use logical structures. Rather, the inferences we draw, whether corresponding to the rules of logic or not, are produced by extrapolating from mental models of the information we have, the facts that we know. Where our knowledge is slight we are reduced to generalizing on the basis of perceptual appearances. Where we have a richer causal understanding we can reason in a more principled, categoric and abstract way. Reasoning develops topic by topic as our knowledge grows, therefore, rather than in overarching stages as Piaget argued.

This change in the way we understand what is involved in the development of reasoning has put a new emphasis on the need to explore conceptual development. What knowledge do children of different ages typically have? How do they acquire this knowledge? To what extent has evolution primed us to acquire certain kinds of knowledge, certain ways of thinking about things? Cultural and individual variations in experience mean that there can be no rigid schedule for the development of any specific piece of knowledge. To create a theory of the development of reasoning we need to understand the principles of conceptual development and their effect on inferences, issues explored in this chapter. To understand how particular children solve (or fail to solve) particular problems, we must investigate what they specifically know about the domain of the problem in hand, and how this knowledge is deployed and managed. These issues are explored in more detail in Chapter 7.

Exercises

1. How would you set up a study of developmental change in children's understanding of the concept of death across different cultures? What methodological and ethical problems would there be, and how could you circumvent them?

2. Why does it matter whether reasoning develops through coherent global stages as Piaget claimed, or patchily through the acquisition of relevant knowledge, as Carey suggests?

Suggested further reading

For an excellent and approachable account of Piaget's theory read:

- M. Donaldson (1978) The appendix to *Children's Minds*. London: Collins/Fontana.

For a collection of essays on reasoning, logic and mental models read:

- P. Johnson-Laird and E. Shafir (1993) *Reasoning and Decision Making*. Amsterdam: Elsevier Science.

For a flavour of modern experimental research on children's understanding of logical necessity read:

- T. Ruffman (1999) Children's understanding of logical inconsistency. *Child Development* 70, pp. 872–86.

For essays on human heuristic reasoning read:

- D. Kahneman, P. Slovic and A. Tversky (eds) (1982) *Judgment under Uncertainty: Heuristics and biases.* Cambridge: Cambridge University Press.

For a flavour of classic experimental analyses of children's knowledge read:

- S. Carey (1985) *Conceptual Change in Childhood*. Cambridge, Mass. and London: MIT Press.

For essays on the role of knowledge in cognitive development read:

- S. Carey and R. Gelman (eds) (1991) *The Epigenesis of Mind: Essays on biology and cognition.* Hillsdale, N.J.: Erlbaum

Revision summary

Logic and reasoning

- For thousands of years, people have believed that human reasoning is logical. The most influential theory of cognitive development of the 20th century – that of Jean Piaget – accepted this premise, and provided an elaborate account of how logical operations might develop in the individual human mind from infancy through childhood and adolescence.

- Piaget's work raised questions and identified phenomena that every other theorist must address. But it has been profoundly challenged by more recent research. Piaget's data are open to other interpretations besides the theory that developmental change in children's performance reflects the growth of logical structures in the mind.

- In fact, recent research shows that human reasoning does not use logical *processes* of themselves, even when drawing logical inferences: rather, we draw inferences from mental models of relevant information.

- Nor is the ability to reflect explicitly on logical propositions the normal outcome of human development as Piaget thought: it is the product of literacy and education, a cultural artefact rather than an inherent aspect of human intelligence. It is rare and inconsistent even in educated adults.

- It is now generally accepted that cognitive change between childhood and adolescence does not reflect the development of abstract logical reasoning processes ('formal operations') in the way Piaget claimed. Instead, the increasingly systematic scientific reasoning of adolescents seems to reflect a marked increase in executive control over problem solving and reasoning.

Heuristic reasoning

- Much everyday reasoning involves heuristic processes: rules of thumb for extrapolating from basic perceptual and memory functions which provide useful rather than necessarily valid conclusions.

- For example, we infer that memorable things are more common than unmemorable ones, and we infer that things are what they look like. Generally, these rules of thumb work well. But they also produce systematic biases in reasoning. Not all memorable things are common (plane crashes, for example); we over-estimate the probability of rare but memorable events. Not everyone who dresses like our stereotype of an artist is an artist: but we apply stereotypes rather than probabilities in making judgments, even though we have the information to calculate the probabilities.

- Even these very simple heuristic inferential techniques are not automatically used by children below the age of 8 years, although younger children can draw inferences in this way when highly motivated or cued to do so. Again, the data point to increasing executive control over mental processes as a crucial factor in cognitive development.

Knowledge and reasoning

- What a child knows affects how he or she uses heuristics and mental models in drawing inferences. Studying the development of knowledge is now a prime focus for research on the development of reasoning.

- Concept formation begins at (or even before) birth, and escalates as the child acquires language. 'Basic'-level concepts, those intermediate in a conceptual hierarchy, such as 'dog', are learned before either superordinate concepts (animal) or subordinate ones (spaniel), and form the reference point from which concepts at other hierarchic levels can be learned. This reflects both processes in the child (basic-level concepts are the simplest to pick out) and social processes (adults use basic-level labels in teaching children to speak, and refer to these categories in extending the child's understanding).

- Some concepts are of particular importance to our evolutionary survival: the distinction between living and inanimate things, the distinction between plants and animals, and between animals and our own species; and concepts of time, space, causality and number. Researchers such as Atran (1998) suggest that there may be innate modules in the mind to ensure the development of these core concepts.

- It's true that even young babies show primitive understanding of core concepts, suggesting an innate predisposition to orient to these areas. However, the data suggest that this reflects basic reflexes and that knowledge grows through the action of general cognitive processes, rather than through the action of specialized modules in the mind. Even core knowledge is vitally affected by learning and by social and cultural factors.

- As knowledge increases, children begin to make causal connections between things, and this radically changes both what they view as important for category membership, and the bases on which they can draw inferences. Without causal understanding of the relationship between members of a category, a child has no basis for drawing inferences except perceptual similarity. A 4-year-old may say that a cactus is not alive because it doesn't resemble his or her stereotype of a living thing (a human being). By contrast, a 10-year-old, having discovered that all living things reproduce and die, and that this applies to cacti as much as to people, is confident that the cactus (or any item that reproduces and dies) is alive. The 10-year-old can thus use principled, category-based reasoning to draw inferences rather than relying on similarities.

- Conceptual change of this kind produces a shift from 'concrete' perceptual reasoning to more abstract, principled formal reasoning of the kind described by Piaget, but through a very different mechanism from that proposed by Piaget.

Novices and experts

- Both in adult and child, the quality or expertise of reasoning depends on the richness of causal understanding in the area addressed, rather than on age or stage of development.

- The amount of knowledge an individual has varies from one topic to another, and the sophistication of the individual's reasoning varies with it. The younger the child, the less knowledge he or she is likely to have in any area, which is why the young tend to reason in a less sophisticated way than their elders in many situations. Where children know more about a task than adults, their inferences are more sophisticated.

- Expertise involves rich knowledge of the task, and of the different strategies that may be used in addressing particular problems: what works and what doesn't. This is precisely the kind of knowledge needed for planful executive control over reasoning.

7

memory, problem solving and mechanisms of cognitive development

The previous chapter looked at the way our minds are structured: the way our conceptual understanding develops from infancy and through to adult life, and the way this changing knowledge allows us to develop new tools for reasoning and making sense of the world. This chapter looks in more detail at the processes involved in using knowledge and tools for reasoning. How do we remember the experiences, the knowledge that we have? How do we use knowledge in solving problems? What are the processes through which our conceptual understanding and strategies for reasoning grow?

The development of memory

Fundamental to all intelligence is the ability to learn: to take in information, store it and retrieve it – in other words to *remember* it. Memory plays a key role in everything we do, from the deliberate learning we put in before an exam to the casual recall of things that happen to us in our daily lives. Without memory, no learning or knowledge would be possible. Everything we encounter would seem new and unique, and unconnected with anything else. Nothing could even become familiar: we could know nothing about the world, nor even about ourselves. It's not surprising, then, that the ability to remember is part of the innate equipment of the mind, and that it's an ability we share with every other living creature.

Recognition and recall

Even before birth babies are able to recognize that some situation or event is familiar, in other words that they have experienced it before (Schneider and Bjorklund, 1998). The clearest demonstration of this comes from the 'habituation' studies used to test how babies perceive the world (described in Chapters 2, 3 and 4): an unborn baby could hardly become accustomed to certain sounds and cease to respond to them if he or she could not recognize them as familiar (Joseph, 2000).

Nor could a newborn baby become bored by 'yet another square' if he or she could not recognize that each successive square was like the ones before (Slater, 1997).

Does the ability to recognize things change in childhood?

Recognition is the most basic function of memory. Is it fully formed at birth, or does even the basic ability to lay down a memory and to recognize the familiar develop through infancy and childhood? This question is harder to answer than it looks. Some researchers argue that babies get better at recognizing things as they get older, because whereas a newborn baby may need quite a few trials to habituate to a given stimulus such as a square, an infant of 5 months or so may habituate after only one or two exposures to the stimulus (Fagan, 1984). But this difference in habituation need not necessarily reflect a difference in the power of the basic processes that allow us to learn to recognize something as familiar in itself. It could equally well be, for example, that the older baby has had so much more time to experience the world than the newborn that the stimuli used in habituation tasks (including squares) are generally less novel, and so less interesting to the older infant, thus yielding a lower threshold of habituation or boredom.

Controversies like this can be difficult to resolve, and we don't yet know the answer. New research methods offer the possibility of exploring the question in a different way. For example, using 'ERP' techniques[1] (see Chapter 3) we can detect patterns of electrical activity in the brain: which areas of the brain are active, the latency (speed) with which the brain reacts to some stimulus, the characteristics of the brain waves generated by that reaction, and so on. With such techniques we can begin to explore how the patterns of electrical activity in the brain differ when we see familiar and unfamiliar things, how one pattern changes into the other as new items become familiar, and whether these things change through infancy, childhood and adolescence (Brown and Chiu, 2006; Wiebe et al., 2006). Research in this area is only just beginning, and has yet to produce clear answers.

Overall, it seems likely that there may be at least some developmental changes in the ability to recognize things, although it isn't clear why this is. For example, while some research suggests that children's ability to recognize that they have seen some item before is as good as an adults by 4 years of age (Brown and Campione, 1972; Brown and Scott, 1971), other studies suggest that this is only true where the items to be recognized have a fairly simple structure. Young children recognize fewer items when the stimuli are complex (Nelson and Kosslyn, 1976;

---

[1] *Event Related Potentials* are the changing patterns of electrical activity that are triggered by some event, such as seeing a particular object. They can be measured by electrodes embedded in a special hat.

Newcombe, Rogoff and Kagan, 1977). Is this developmental effect to do with the process of recognition in itself, or something to do with more general developmental changes in encoding complex material? In either case, the young child's powers of recognition are impressive: 4-year-olds may recognize over 100 items as having been present in a given test situation.

Developmental change in recall

Far harder than recognizing familiar things, even for an adult, is recalling things (Shepard, 1967). It's not hard to see why this is so. Recognition involves considering whether something presented to you is familiar or not. By contrast, recall involves bringing to mind items or events that are not present – a far more open-ended and difficult task.

Even very young babies can recall absent objects (Baillargeon, 1986). By 2 or 3 months of age, they can recall how to make a mobile move when confronted with it afresh (Rovee-Collier, 1984, 1987). Few 2-year-olds have much trouble remembering promises made to them, or in deliberately remembering to remind mother to buy them sweets (Somerville, Wellman and Cultice, 1983). Three-year-old children can recall events that happened nearly 2 years before (Perris, Myers and Clifton, 1990).

Nevertheless, younger children consistently recall much less in experimental memory tasks than do their elders (Kuhn, 2000). For example, if you show children a tray with, say 12 objects on it, cover it up and ask for recall ('Kim's game'), a 4-year-old might remember one or two items, where an 8-year-old might remember eight or nine (Brown, 1975). The ability to recall things improves steadily between 3 and 12 years of age. Most of the research on the development of memory has focused on why this is.

Conceptual understanding and developmental change in recall

What we know about the world has a major effect on what we can recall, or how easy it is to remember a given thing. This is just as true of adults as it is of the very young. But the younger the child, the less he or she typically knows in any and every area. This developmental change in knowledge produces developmental change in memory in a number of different ways.

Item familiarity

Look at the two lists of items to be remembered shown in **Box 7.1**. Which is easier to memorize? Even adults do better when the items to be memorized are familiar (Baddeley, 1976; Ebbinghaus, 1913). The reason is not hard to understand: with familiar items, you don't need to learn the words themselves, only to remember that they were on the list. But with unfamiliar items you must learn the words as well: two tasks, rather than one.

This type of item familiarity effect contributes to age-related change in recall. For example, a 3-year-old who is only just in the process of learning animal names will face a far harder task in memorizing a list of such names than will a 10-year-old, to whom the names on the list have been familiar for years. Many items are less familiar to the younger child than to his or her elders.

box **7.1**

Materials for recall: familiarity and unfamiliarity

List A	List B
ELEPHANT	TORVIGON
TIGER	MRINGO
RACOON	SCIGLE
SNAKE	TRINF
GAZELLE	FIMONOL

Causal understanding and recall

Knowledge is not about learning lists. As we gather more information about a given topic we develop a rich, integrated *causal* understanding in that area. This gives our knowledge a new structure and creates powerful new tools for reasoning (Chapter 6). It also has a major effect on how we store and retrieve information from memory (Carey, 1999; Chi and Ceci, 1987).

For example, if you understand how and why one thing is connected to another, you can see patterns that are simply invisible to someone without such insight, and you can use these patterns to memorize and recall the material (Chi, 1978; Chi, Feltovich and Glaser, 1981; De Groot, 1965). The result is a dramatic improvement in memory. The classic example of this comes from the studies of people memorizing the positions of pieces on a chessboard. Individuals who know nothing about the game of chess memorize the position of each piece separately, and typically recall the exact location of only about seven pieces, give or take a few (Miller, 1956). If the pieces have been randomly placed on the board, expert chess players behave the same way and do no better. But if the pieces are set up in a way that makes sense within a real game of chess, the experts see meaningful patterns in the way pieces are placed, and they encode (that is, memorize) those patterns rather than memorizing (encoding) the position of pieces individually. The probability is that the expert will recall the position of all of the pieces (De Groot, 1965). It doesn't matter how old the novice or the expert are: child experts recall more than adult novices, so long as the pieces are positioned in patterns they can recognize as meaningful (Chi, 1978).

We remember best what we understand best, as any student revising for an exam knows. What makes sense can be learned almost effortlessly, as part and parcel of the very process of understanding it. But what we can't understand must be bludgeoned into the mind by rote, and is far harder to reproduce at all, let alone in a useful way. In a profound sense, then, memory is not a separate function of the mind, not a separate 'box' in which we stow things but rather, it is an integral part of the process by which we encode information and store knowledge (Kuhn, 2000).

The data suggest that where causal understanding is relatively sophisticated, information is encoded more efficiently and recalled better, whatever your age. But in general, the younger the child, the less causal understanding he or she has in any given area. On this basis alone we should expect recall to improve as children get older (and understand more).

Reconstruction and recall

Causal understanding affects what patterns and connections we can see, determining how we encode material (that is, store it), as we have seen. But it also affects the processes through which we retrieve information from storage.

Retrieval is not simply a matter of collecting a memory from a store, the way you might collect a book from a library. Rather, it involves actively *reconstructing* that material. This was first demonstrated by Bartlett (1932), who showed that our recall for a story evolves over time, drifting in the direction that makes the most sense to us. Bartlett read the story of the war of the ghosts (**Box 7.2**) to British students. This story is a North American Indian legend. It's rather bizarre to a British mind: it includes all sorts of cultural assumptions and references that we don't understand. Rather than recalling the material verbatim, the British students recalled the gist of the story. Asked to recall it repeatedly over a period of weeks and even years, their recall changed. Gradually the alien and incomprehensible elements of the story were dropped out or reinterpreted, transformed into something that made more sense to a British mind.

Both adults and children reconstruct memories in this way: inevitably, since this is how recall works. We seldom remember things verbatim. We drop bits out, and we add bits in. This can create uncertainties in recall. For example, if a character in a story does something that implies using a tool, we assume that the tool must have been there, and we're very bad at telling whether the tool was actually mentioned in the story or not (Kuhn, 2000).

The reconstructive nature of memory has some intriguing implications for developmental changes in what a child remembers. For example, a child's recall of a sequence of different-length rods may be far better a few months after he or she first saw the sequence than it was a few moments after seeing it! This surprising phenomenon was first noted by Piaget and Inhelder (1973), and has been replicated many

box 7.2
box 7.2

The 'war of the ghosts' story

Source: Bartlett (1932).

One night two young men from Egulac went down to the river to hunt seals, and while they were there it became foggy and calm. Then they heard war-cries, and they thought, 'Maybe this is a war-party.' They escaped to the shore, and hid behind a log. Now canoes came up, and they heard the noise of paddles, and saw one canoe coming up to them. There were five men in the canoe, and they said, 'What do you think? We wish to take you along. We are going up the river to make war on the people.' One of the young men said, 'I have no arrows.' 'Arrows are in the canoe,' they said. 'I will not go along. I might be killed. My relatives do not know where I have gone. But you,' he said, turning to the other, 'may go with them.' So one of the young men went, but the other returned home. And the warriors went on up the river to a town on the other side of Kalama. The people came down to the water and they began to fight, and many were killed. But presently the young man heard one of the warriors say, 'Quick, let us go home: that Indian has been hit.' Now he thought, 'Oh, they are ghosts.' He did not feel sick, but they said he had been shot. So the canoes went back to Egulac and the young man went ashore to his house and made a fire. And he told everybody and said, 'Behold, I accompanied the ghosts, and we went to fight. Many of our fellows were killed, and many of those who attacked us were killed. They said I was hit, and I did not feel sick.' He told it all, and then he became quiet. When the sun rose he fell down. Something black came out of his mouth. His face became contorted. The people jumped up and cried. He was dead.

times (Liben, 1977). The explanation is simple: the rods in the original display were arranged in an ordered series, ranked by length from left to right. When they first saw this display, the children had no conceptual understanding of a rank-ordered series of this kind, so in recalling the display, they had no concept to guide them in reconstructing a ranked series, and so drew different-length rods in no particular order. A few months later the children had understood the concept of a rank-ordered series; now, they were able to use that concept in reconstructing their recall of the display, and so were able to recall it more accurately.

Everyday recall

In everyday activities, learning or memorizing is very seldom an end in itself. For example, in baking a cake the aim is to create the cake, not to memorize the list of ingredients. Nevertheless, the next time you want to bake that cake you will probably find that you can recall the recipe anyway.

As we have seen earlier, memory is not a separate store, but an integral part of ongoing processing. In everyday contexts memories are almost incidentally embedded in a meaningful, functional pattern of activities and goals which not only serve to structure our learning in a useful way, but also provide a rich constellation of cues for recall. Even very young children can memorize things very well in such contexts, far better than when they are asked to memorize something outside the context of a goal or activity they can understand and share (Ceci and Liker, 1986; Saxe, 1988).

For example, young children recall many more items on a list when told that it is a shopping list than when given no context or rationale for remembering the items (Istomina, 1975). Five-year-olds mobilize their memories far more effectively when addressing a question with personal importance (such as who gets a treat) than when completing experimental tasks in which they have no personal investment (Thornton, 1996). Toddlers are more likely to do things deliberately to help themselves remember, such as staring at the hiding place to be remembered, when the task matters to them, for example when the hidden object is chocolate they can win by finding it, rather than when asked to remember things of less obvious importance, such as where the experimenter hid her pencil (Bjorklund and Zeman, 1982).

Is the young child's everyday recall as good as an adult's, when it is embedded in personal goals and meaningful activities? As ever, there are difficulties in answering this question: other factors (such as differences in conceptual understanding between younger and older children and adults) cloud the issue, making straightforward comparisons of the simple ability to recall things difficult. Many things affect how we recall our own experiences.

Children's eyewitness testimony

Take, for example, the question of eyewitness recall. Here, a child is asked to recall events that he or she has experienced. Often these events are of immense personal significance to the child, involving interactions in the family or among playground friends, or events made significant by their dramatic or traumatic nature. In general, the younger the child, the less reliable the eyewitness testimony provided. Young children more often give distorted accounts of what happened than do their elders (Ceci, Leichman and White, 1999), and their accounts may even include fantastic elements. At first this seems to suggest that the younger child's memory for everyday events is just shakier than that of an older child or adult, but there are a number of other possibilities.

What we get when we ask children for eyewitness testimony is not a pure measure of the ability to create or recall a memory, it's a measure of *what is recalled in the particular circumstances of the case*. In other words, the young child's unreliable eyewitness testimony may reflect factors affecting recall in the special circumstances of a legal enquiry, rather than the process of everyday remembering as such.

As we've seen, recall is always a matter of reconstruction, drifting in ways that make the memory fit better to our understanding of the world (Bartlett, 1932). Developmental changes in how children understand the world will inevitably influence how they recall what they've seen: a rape, for example, may seem as bizarrely incomprehensible to a 3-year-old mind as the 'war of the ghosts' did to Bartlett's students, and recall may drift in ways that make sense to the child's mind, but which seem 'unreliable' to an adult.

Recall is also importantly affected by our emotions (van Vreeswijk and de Wilde, 2004). When we're happy, we tend to recall positive things. When we're depressed, we tend to recall negative things. Even the very same event can be remembered quite differently in different moods (self-confident, I recall how well I answered that tricky question after Tuesday's lecture; in moments of lower self-esteem I recall only how stupid I must have looked not having anticipated it). Recently we have discovered that people who are depressed or stressed tend to have vaguer, more generalized memories than normal (Kuyken, 2006). Whereas people who are not stressed or depressed remember specific episodes with vivid imagery (the patch of the sunlight on your lover's face, the smell of the sea, what you said and did, the grittiness of the sand under your toes), such detail tends to get lost when the depressed or stressed person remembers events, to be replaced by a more abstract memory (we walked on the beach). Giving testimony to a court is stressful for us all. The younger the child, the fewer the resources he or she has for managing that stress. It may be that stress itself robs the younger child of the very detail the courts want to hear. And when we are pressed to recall what we can't bring to mind, we confabulate, telling the best story we can.

Sometimes witnesses of any age lie deliberately, to protect themselves or other people, or out of embarrassment. Such 'faking good' takes insight to do well: you have to know what lies to tell to best achieve your goals, which requires a degree of understanding of other minds that small children don't have (see Chapter 9). Sometimes we just try to please, saying what we think others want to hear. The younger the child, the less understanding he or she will have of the consequences of false witness, and the less internal restraint there is on such fudging. Either intentionally or unintentionally, then, witnesses edit their reports to suit the circumstances. Younger children may be more prone to such effects than their elders, through ignorance and innocence.

There is considerable research on suggestibility: on how easy it is for an adult 'interrogator' to lead a child into 'remembering' what the questioner wants the child to recall (Ceci and Bruck, 1993). Anyone can be browbeaten into 'remembering' what is required by an interrogator prepared to push hard enough, as the many false confessions obtained by the police demonstrate. Children are easily led to remember things that didn't happen, even very bizarre things, especially if they are asked the same questions over and over, or if the questioner suggests things they might 'remember' (Ceci et al., 1999). The young may be more vulnerable to such pressure than their elders: they have fewer resources to resist it.

But questioned less aggressively and without leading questions, even the very young can recall things quite well, and do not usually invent or embroider stories (Howe and Courage, 1997). Suggestibility may be less a product of memory processes as such, and more a reflection of social pressure and personal factors. And suggestibility is a feature of personality: even at 3 years of age, some children are more vulnerable to suggestibility than others (Scullin and Warren, 1999).

Developmental change in the reliability of children's eyewitness testimony is an important issue in its own right. We need to understand what affects recall in such contexts, if we are to respect the rights and protect the welfare of both children and adults. But the factors that affect developmental change in eyewitness testimony are also revealing for our broader understanding of the way recall works, and what affects it.

Scripts and autobiographical memory

Eyewitness testimony is a special case of 'autobiographical' memory: that is to say, memory for the specific events and experiences that make up our own personal stories. Autobiographical memory provides another arena in which we can explore whether the basic processes of everyday memory change developmentally, or are the same from infancy to adult life. And here, there is a very striking developmental effect: the curious phenomenon of early childhood amnesia (Pillemer and White, 1989).

What's your earliest memory? What can you remember from the first three years of your life? For most of us, the answer is: more or less nothing (Perlmutter, 1986). The great divide is at about 3 years of age. For example, Sheingold and Tenney (1982) asked adult students to recall the events on the day that a younger sibling was born. Students who had been 3 years old or more when the sibling was born could recall quite a lot about that day, but those who had been less than 3 years old at that time recalled almost nothing. This complete forgetting of early infancy is intriguing. It is not simply a matter of the passage of time: people of 20 cannot recall the birth of a sibling 18 years earlier, whereas people in their 60s normally have very clear recall for important events such as the birth of a child 40 years earlier. To understand the phenomenon of early childhood amnesia we must understand how everyday and autobiographical memory works.

Our experiences and our memories of those experiences are organized into 'events' at various levels of abstraction (Conway and Pleydell-Pearce, 2000): 'being at university', for example, or 'going to a lecture', or 'the lecture last Tuesday on primate evolution'. The middle level in this hierarchy is a sort of generalized scheme for going to lectures: it has been called a *script* (Schank and Abelson, 1977). Scripts shape how we expect events to unfold, providing a recipe for the event: who will be there, what will happen and so on. Scripts are built up by generalizing across repeated experiences of the same kind, picking out the consistent features. The more experience we have of events of a given type, the clearer our script for such events will be.

The scripts we have shape what we expect and how we behave in the situations to which they apply. They also provide the framework for our memories of our own experiences: specific experiences of particular lectures (for example) are slotted into the general script 'going to a lecture'. When we try to recall a specific event we refer back to the general script and try to reconstruct the specific details of the event from there (Schacter, 1996). This is often very useful: for example, knowing that the 'lecture script' has a slot for being given a handout prompts us to search for memories of the specific handout for that lecture (just as 'being at university' is a higher-level script which includes the slot 'going to lectures' and so can structure our search for autobiographical memories of that period of our lives). But scripts can also contribute to faulty memories: we may 'remember' that there was a handout at last Tuesday's lecture because there usually is (it's part of our script), even though on that occasion there wasn't.

The younger the child, the fewer scripts he or she has yet had the opportunity to elaborate, which will have implications for the ease with which autobiographical events and experiences can be encoded, stored and retrieved. But far more important than this is the fact that scripts are organized around words. It's the label 'lecture' that triggers the script. Scripts are structured and organized by language (Nelson, 1996). Before 3 years of age the child simply has too little language to encode scripts linguistically, and so stores memories of experiences in some non-verbal, sensori-motor way. As the ability to construct language-based scripts develops, the early 'un-scripted' memories become very much harder to retrieve, and so are effectively lost (Sheingold and Tenney, 1982; Spear, 1984). This research explains the phenomenon of early childhood amnesia. It suggests, too, that even the ability to remember everyday events develops: first, through the revolutionary switch from sensori-motor encodings to the use of linguistic scripts, and second, through the progressive elaboration of scripts, creating an ever richer framework for experience and remembering.

Deliberate memorizing

There are developmental processes that affect children's ability to recall events even in everyday life, as we've seen. Nevertheless, even young children have an impressive degree of recall for things that are embedded in their own goals and activities. It's when it comes to learning or remembering as an end in itself that developmental differences become very clear. In experimental tasks or school contexts where material must be learned solely for the purpose of recalling it later, the younger the child, the poorer the recall (Flavell and Wellman, 1977).

Understanding the point of the activity

One factor in developmental differences in deliberate memorizing is that young children do not understand the point of tasks where memory or reasoning must be used not to serve a meaningful goal, but as ends in themselves (Donaldson, 1978). For example, my son (then 3 years of age) took part in a memory experiment run by one of my students. She showed him a tray with 12 things on it, covered the tray with a cloth, and asked him what was on the tray ('Kim's game'). To my intense embarrassment, he failed to recall even the normal few items one would expect of a 3-year-old. He just stared at her and at the covered tray, flummoxed. I took him later that day to buy some shoes. In the car on the way, he said, 'Mummy, why did that lady want to know about the things on the tray?' Ever the psychologist, I asked: 'What things?' whereupon he recalled nine of the 12 items! When I asked him why he had not answered her question at the time, he told me that it was because *she already knew the answer, as she had seen the tray for herself, and could lift up the cloth if she really wanted to know.* And quite right, too! Memory tasks may seem perfectly sensible to the adult mind, but may appear so pointless or absurd to the young child that he or she does not really participate.

Strategies for remembering

However, a key factor limiting the younger child's recall in formal tests of memory (that is, memorizing as an end in itself) is that, even when they understand and accept the aim of the task, younger children are far less likely than their elders to use effective strategies for memorizing and recalling the material.

There are a great many strategies that we can use to improve our chances of recalling things, from very simple ruses (such as staring at where something was hidden) to more elaborate mnemonics. For example, suppose I asked you to memorize the list of items shown in **Box 7.3**. What would you do? You might read the list passively, and hope for the best. Far more likely, you would work through the list from top to bottom, *rehearsing* the items as you go (for example kettle, fridge, potatoes! kettle, fridge, potatoes *spoon*! Kettle, fridge, potatoes, spoon, *apple*, and so on). Or you might notice that the list can be simplified by *restructuring it into meaningful groups of items* (a group of vegetables, a group of utensils and so on) and then separately memorizing each sub-group. Or you might try to *make a single picture* incorporating all the elements into one meaningful pattern, for example, visualizing a kitchen and placing all the items in it. All of these are effective strategies which would greatly improve your recall of lists such as this.

Occasionally, in situations where remembering really matters to them personally, toddlers will use very simple strategies, such as staring at where the chocolate is hidden (Bjorklund and Zeman, 1982). But even 4-year-olds seldom spontaneously use even the simplest strategy when

box 7.3

Materials for recall: an organizable list

KETTLE	FRIDGE	POTATO	SPOON
APPLE	CARROT	DISHWASHER	BANANA
FREEZER	SAUCEPAN	FORK	CABBAGE
BOWL	KNIFE	ORANGE	SINK

memorizing lists of items in experiments (Baker-Ward, Ornstein and Holden 1984). Only 10 per cent of 5-year-olds spontaneously rehearse items to be remembered, whereas the majority of 7-year-olds and nearly all 10-year-olds do so (Flavell, 1985). And even where the majority of 5-year-olds do spontaneously rehearse material to be recalled, their rehearsal attempts are less structured and less efficient than those of 12-year-olds (Kunzinger, 1985; Ornstein, Naus and Liberty, 1975). The use of more sophisticated memory strategies shows an even greater developmental effect.

What explains this developmental change in the tendency to use deliberate strategies in remembering? One possibility is that there is a *mediational deficiency* in early childhood: in other words, that the younger child lacks the mental capacity to use mnemonic strategies and so simply cannot use them (Flavell, 1985). There is some evidence to support this view: for example, Ornstein, Medlin, Stone and Naus (1985) found that 7-year-olds could be taught to use the strategy of grouping items for recall, but only if all the items to be recalled were visible all at once, which reduces the effort needed in learning (we shall return to the issue of memory capacity shortly). However, the bulk of research suggests that even very young children can be taught to use strategies such as rehearsal effectively, and even to benefit from more complex strategies such as organizing a list into groups (Brown et al., 1983; Kail, 1990). The implication is that these mnemonic strategies are within the child's capacity.

Nevertheless, even when children have been taught to use a mnemonic strategy and have been using it to good effect to improve recall, a child below about 8 years of age will stop using the strategy if the experimenter stops encouraging that approach – and recall drops down again (Flavell and Wellman, 1977). The implication is that there is some sort of developmental deficit affecting the child's tendency to produce a mnemonic strategy (often referred to as a *production deficit*). Researchers such as Flavell and Wellman (1977) suggested that this reflects the fact that young children have too little knowledge about how their own memories work or what the limitations on their memories are to recognize the power and usefulness of mnemonic strategies, or to understand when and where to use them.

Meta-cognitive awareness

The suggestion that children's poorer performance in formal memory tests reflects a lack of understanding of the limitations of memory or of the power of mnemonic strategies was a seminal insight. It drew attention to the fact that the proper exercise of human intelligence depends not simply on *possessing* certain mental tools, but on *knowing enough about those tools* to be able to control and deploy them effectively and deliberately. In sum, it depends not merely on *cognitive* processes such as memory, but on the *meta-cognitive* processes which create *executive control* over them. To put this another way, becoming more expert in memorizing (or any other cognitive function, such as planning or drawing inferences) requires the child to acquire and manage knowledge not just about the specific material to be recalled, but about memory processes (or other cognitive functions) themselves (Brown et al., 1983; Schneider and Pressley, 1989).

Meta-cognitive awareness of memory processes develops gradually. There is evidence that even very young children know that we must do something to help recall. For example, DeLoache, Cassidy and Brown (1985) found that 2-year-olds know that pointing to, or repeatedly glancing at, the hiding place of an object they will have to find later helps recall (these are both forms of rehearsal). Four-year-olds know that long lists are harder to recall than short ones (Wellman, Collins and Glieberman, 1981). Nonetheless, even 7-year-olds still over-estimate their performance in memory tasks, and under-estimate the effort needed to memorize things (Kreutzer, Leonard and Flavell, 1975). And 7-year-olds rely more on external strategies to support memory, such as writing things down, rather than on cognitive strategies such as mentally grouping like things together (Fabricius and Wellman, 1983).

One source of children's growing meta-cognitive awareness is likely to lie in their own experience. Increasing experience with memory tasks, for example, would clarify how hard such tasks are, and provide the child with a better understanding of the powers and limits of memory. Likewise, experience of particular mnemonic strategies is a source of information about the effect and utility of such things, and the contexts in which they are most relevant. However, it is also likely that the acquisition of meta-cognitive awareness has an important social dimension. Children are explicitly encouraged by others to recall things, and to learn to do so deliberately (Rogoff, 1998; Schneider and Pressley, 1989). Schooling in particular requires children to learn how to memorize things effectively, as an end in itself. It seems highly likely that this social demand is associated with more or less direct support for the development of meta-cognitive awareness of strategies for learning and for executive control over mental processes. We shall return to this issue later in this chapter.

Does the physical capacity of memory change in childhood?

Despite the role of changing knowledge, scripts, strategies and meta-cognitive awareness in creating developmental change in recall, it is still possible that there may also be other, more neurological bases for developmental change in children's memories. The physiology of the brain, and particularly its efficiency in transmitting information, continues to mature through infancy and early childhood, (see Chapter 2), and in fact goes through another growth spurt in adolescence (see Chapter 6). Might this not affect the child's ability to store and recall information? Specifically, might such neurological effects mean that there is a physiological change in the size or capacity of the child's memory through development (Rabinowicz, 1980; Thatcher, 1992)?

To explore this idea, we need to consider the structure of memory processes. There are in fact very many different theories about how memory works, each one dividing memory processes up in various ways to reflect the different functions of remembering. For example, there are some things that we recall for a very long time, such as our teenage adventures, or a poem, or the meaning of words or other symbols. Then again, there are things that we 'hold in mind' for a short while, and rapidly forget. Do these *long-term* and *short-term memories* reflect different processes, or different aspects of a single process (Craik and Lockhart, 1972)? And among the memories that last a long time, are the processes that underlie conceptual understanding the same as the processes that underlie autobiographical recall, or are there separate *semantic* and *episodic* memory processes for these different things? These issues are complex, and beyond the scope of this book.

But whatever position theorists take on the detail of such questions, there is general agreement that, somewhere along the line, there is a *working memory* which is pivotal in all our efforts to encode and process information: a *central processing unit* that can only handle a certain amount of information at any one time. The size of this unit (in other words, the amount of information it can hold) determines the complexity of the cognitive tasks we can complete. If the demands a task places on this working memory (the *M-demand* of the task) exceed the capacity of the working memory (*M-space*), we will not be able to hold enough information in mind at one time to complete the task. Some theorists believe that M-space grows larger through childhood, contributing to age-related increases in how much information children can encode into or retrieve from memory (Pascual-Leone, 1970; Case, 1985).

Pascual-Leone and Case argue that an individual's M-space can be calculated by assessing 'digit span': the number of digits an individual can accurately remember and repeat back in a memory task (Case, 1985; Dempster, 1985), or by a 'counting span' task, which requires the child to use working memory more dynamically, for example, by counting the number of spots on a card and recalling that number while counting the spots on the next card, and so on (Case, 1985). The results from either method suggest that there is a marked developmental increase in M-space through childhood. For adults M-space is about seven items (Miller, 1956). A young child may have an M-space of only three items.

Digit span measures suggest that there is a steady increase in M-space between the ages of 3 and 10 years (Case, 1985; Dempster, 1985).[2]

Some studies suggest that we can predict the patterns of children's success and failure in problem-solving and memory tasks at different ages by comparing the M-demand of various tasks with the M-space characteristically available to the child at each age (Case, 1985; Pascual-Leone, 1970). According to this view, developmental changes in M-space could explain why some memory strategies seem to be beyond the younger child, and why younger children have more difficulties with (for example) Piaget's tasks. However, this approach to explaining the development of memory and problem solving is very controversial. It involves a lot of assumptions which don't stand up to critical analysis very well, and it doesn't explain as much as it seems to.

What, exactly, is involved in the development of M-space? Is there literally a change in the physical size of working memory, perhaps some sort of physiological change that alters its capacity to hold information? Some researchers believe that there is (Cowan et al., 1999). But many believe that the evidence is better interpreted in other ways (Dempster, 1985).

The idea that there is a fixed capacity of M-space at each age and that this capacity increases through childhood is hard to square with the evidence. If that were so, surely adults (with the largest M-space) should outperform children in every context? And yet we know that where the material to be memorized is familiar to children and unfamiliar to adults, the children remember more (Chi, 1978; Lindberg, 1980).

In fact, as we've seen earlier in this chapter, the amount of information an individual can process (at any age) reflects his or her experience and expertise with that particular type of information rather than anything else (Chi, 1978). It varies across different tasks, reflecting relative expertise between one task and another (Chi and Ceci, 1987). Rich knowledge allows us to structure information differently, organizing it into patterns and remembering more: remembering seven whole patterns rather than seven individual items. It's hard to square this with the idea of a physiologically limited working memory space with a fixed capacity. What kind of bucket could have a total capacity of either seven[3] separate drops of water, or seven cupfuls? What kind of box could hold a maximum of seven individual shoes, or seven matched pairs? Fixed capacities ought to constrain the absolute volume of material to be held, and not be affected by the nature of the packages in which it arrives.

---

[2] Is this a pure measure of memory capacity? Might item familiarity effects or relative inexperience with counting contribute to the younger child's poorer performance?

[3] Seven is a 'magical' number in memory research: reliably, people can recall seven things 'plus or minus 2' (Miller, 1956), although it doesn't seem to matter whether the 'things' are individual items or whole patterns.

Case (1985) has tried to deal with these criticisms by arguing that greater knowledge and expertise make certain aspects of a task *automatic*, so that they require less attention, or less effort (M-space) to do. For example, when you learned to write, forming each letter took effort and concentration, and involved a number of separate elements to remember (/, then \, then – to make A, for instance). But nowadays, not only do you form each letter as a single unit but you are unlikely to be aware of forming the individual letters that make up words and sentences at all. The task of writing has become automatic, and takes up less processing effort (imposes less M-demand) than it did when you first learned to write, so there is more mental capacity (M-space) left over for other things.

Case's defence of the 'M-space' hypothesis is interesting, in that it points out that expertise affects how efficiently we can process information, which affects our success and failure in a wide range of memory and problem-solving tasks. Few researchers would disagree with that. The controversy is about how best to understand what is involved here. Do we need a theory of 'M-space' to explain this phenomenon? Case's own thesis here seems to suggest not. If expertise, the way knowledge is structured or compiled is the crucial factor determining how much information can be processed, then surely the concept of M-space is redundant? What is there left for it to explain? Where is the evidence that developmental changes in M-space as such even exist, let alone play any role in age-related changes in performance in memory and problem solving?

The development of problem-solving

From the earliest moments of life we human beings address our minds to solving problems: we investigate the world around us with restless curiosity, actively trying to work out what things are, what it all means, how to make things happen as we want them to. The baby working on how to make that crib toy rattle, the toddler experimenting with Lego, the 10-year-old struggling with the difficulties of building a satisfactory spaceship in the garden, the adolescent (or octogenarian) puzzling over the vexing conundrums of human relationships, the engineer with his ship design or the politician trying to find a balance of social justice – all are engaged in the dynamic exercise of problem solving.

A striking thing about problem solving is that we human beings really *enjoy* it. For all the difficulties and frustrations problems present, we're never happier than when solving a problem of one sort or another. A great deal of childhood play revolves around problem solving. Adults deprived of the challenge of problems to solve can become bored or depressed (the frequent plaint of the retired). And at the end of a long day at work, we come home and find even more problems to amuse ourselves with (sudoko, golf, bridge, gardening, computer games, crosswords ...).

What is it that so drives us to engage in the often arduous and brain-taxing process of problem solving? The answer may lie in the nature of the activity itself. Problem solving is a multi-faceted process. It involves identifying goals, planning, finding an effective strategy, making new discoveries, coming to new insights. It's the archetype not only of intelligence but of creativity, of our human inventive genius. It's what the human mind *does*. Problem solving is cognition in action.

From this point of view, research on problem solving is not a matter of studying a special activity or aspect of human cognition. Every human activity can be construed as 'problem solving', because all involve the same basic cognitive processes at one level or another. What research labelled 'problem solving' does is to look in detail at the dynamic processes involved in learning, using knowledge, drawing inferences and the like, rather than looking more broadly at the way knowledge is structured or the basic character of reasoning, as the research reviewed in Chapter 6 does. The two approaches address the same issues in different ways, complementing one another and fleshing out our understanding of the nature of cognition and development.

New insights from studying knowledge in action

In general, as we saw in Chapter 6, the more knowledge we have in relation to a problem, the better able we are to reason effectively and so to reach the right solution. But detailed studies of knowledge in action reveal that the effects of knowledge are more subtle and complex than this, which explains several phenomena that at one time posed puzzles for our understanding of cognitive development.

Knowledge and rules for reasoning

How is knowledge brought into action in solving problems? Siegler (1976, 1981) explored the idea that we can conceptualize what children know about a given type of problem as creating the 'rule' they use in reasoning about such problems. Different levels of knowledge would produce different rules, and hence different patterns of success and failure.

Children in Siegler's study were shown a scale where each arm has a number of pegs on which weights may be placed in varying positions (see **Figure 7.1**). The arms are supported by blocks, and the child is asked to say whether different configurations of weights will balance or not when the blocks are removed.

Three-year-olds know next to nothing about what makes scales balance, and so have no rule. They simply answer at random. Five-year-olds know that balance is about weight, but don't know that the position of a weight relative to the fulcrum affects balance. Their rule is simply to compare the weights on each side of the scale.

Eight-year-olds know that the distance of a weight from the fulcrum

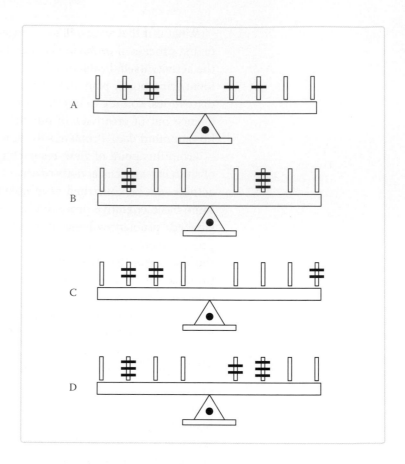

figure 7.1

Siegler's balance scale

Source: after R. Siegler, 'Three aspects of cognitive development', *Cognitive Psychology* vol. 8, pp. 481–520. © 1976. Reproduced with permission from Elsivier Science.

is also relevant to balance, but they don't understand how the two factors interact, and still give more importance to the amount of weight than to its position. These children use a slightly more complex rule: compare the weight on each side of the scale (as the 5-year-old does). If it is the same, look at the position of the weights relative to the fulcrum. But if the weight is uneven, disregard its position and judge solely in terms of weight.

Fourteen-year-olds are no wiser than 8-year-olds over how to take both weight and position into account, but they have realized that they can't simply ignore position when weight is uneven, as 8-year-olds do. They use a rule that always looks at both weight and position, and that produces good answers where these two factors can be handled separately. But when both weight and distance from the fulcrum vary and must be coordinated, they have no rule and so cannot calculate an answer. Few adults in Siegler's studies progress beyond this point to the most sophisticated rule, which is based on an understanding of how to take the cross-product of weight and distance from the fulcrum into account (Siegler, 1981).

Applying these different rules to the various types of problem depicted in Figure 7.1 produces clear predictions about which problems children of a given age will solve successfully and which not. These predictions are borne out in children's actual behaviour (Siegler, 1976, 1981; van der Maas and Jansen, 2003). The detailed patterns of success and failure that follow from different knowledge rules provided several new insights into cognitive development.

First, more knowledge doesn't always mean greater success. In fact, whether or not a given level of knowledge and the rule it generates will result in success or failure depends crucially on how the rule interacts with the detail of the task – which goes some way toward explaining why children are successful in some versions of a task and not in others. For example, consider problem B in Figure 7.1. Here, the amount of weight on each arm is the same, so a rule focusing solely on this will (wrongly) predict that the scale will balance – and 5-year-olds make just this mistake. A rule that takes the position of weights into account when this is not confounded with the amount of weight involved will get the right answer – and both 8-year-olds and 14-year-olds solve this problem successfully. This is a classic example of more knowledge producing better problem solving. But now consider problem C in Figure 7.1. A rule that pays attention only to weight (or one that pays attention only to weight when weight is uneven) will predict that the scale will not balance – and as it happens, this is correct. Five-year-olds (and 8-year-olds) solve this problem successfully. By contrast, a rule that requires that the position of the weights must always be taken into account, but which has no formula for coordinating the effects of different amounts of weight in different positions, provides no basis for judgment. There is no option but to guess, which will produce the correct answer at chance rates (half the time). Fourteen-year-olds solve this type of problem only at chance rates, and so are *less* successful than younger children.

Siegler's study solved a problem that had puzzled researchers for years. Developmental 'regressions', where children become less successful in problem solving than they were at a younger age before later going on to become more successful again, occur in many tasks. This phenomenon was known as the 'U-shaped curve' (Siegler, 2004). It was hard to understand why it should occur, if development involves a progressive increase in conceptual understanding (as it seems to do) and if better conceptual understanding is associated with better reasoning (as it generally is). All sorts of explanations for regression were offered. Siegler's detailed analysis of knowledge in action revealed that older children might become less successful than younger children in solving certain problems, not *despite* having better conceptual understanding (as had been assumed), but *because* of that better understanding. Better (but not yet perfect) conceptual understanding can result in *knowing that you don't know*, and hence in guessing, where a discarded simpler rule based on less knowledge would have been successful. Knowing that you don't know how to solve a problem may make you less successful in solving some problems than you were before, but this is not really a regression in development. In fact, it's an important step toward further progress: recognizing that you need to learn more about certain factors directs the attention in ways that make such learning more likely.

Siegler's analysis of knowledge in action also clarified the problem of why it is that, faced with the same feedback from the task, younger children often learn less than older children do. For example, both 5-year-olds and 8-year-olds get the wrong answer to problems of type D in Figure 7.1, because both use a rule which results in paying attention *only* to the uneven amount of weight. Eight-year-olds can learn from this mistake, whereas 5-year-olds don't. The difference is due to the fact that the knowledge rule used by the 5-year-old pays attention only to weight, so that the child doesn't notice anything about the position of the weights and is simply baffled. By contrast, the 8-year-old knows that position may be relevant, and so is much more likely to pay attention to it in trying to work out why the prediction was wrong. Siegler demonstrated that this analysis is correct by showing that, if taught to pay attention to the position of weights as 8-year-olds do, 5-year-olds can learn just as much as 8-year-olds do from their experiences with the task (Siegler, 1976).

Information processing, performance and knowledge

Siegler's study is an example of an 'information-processing' analysis of the way knowledge acts to shape performance in problem solving. Similar analyses have been made of a variety of other tasks, with similar results (Klahr, 1984; Klahr and MacWhinney, 1998; Klahr and Wallace, 1976; Johnson and Morton, 1991; Munakata, 1998; Siegler, 1996; Siegler and Chen, 1998; Siegler and Jenkins, 1989; Siegler and Shrager, 1984). Many of these studies involved the construction of computer simulations of the effects of rules associated with different levels of knowledge on problem solving (Klahr and MacWhinney, 1998; Klahr and Wallace, 1976; Siegler and Jenkins, 1989). Such simulations often provide very accurate models of the patterns of success and failure observed as real children of different ages tackle the task in hand.

This line of research has produced impressive demonstrations of the sheer power of knowledge in shaping problem solving and learning. In doing so, it has underlined the point that knowledge has its effect through the specific rules or procedures for reasoning that it generates. Are there other factors besides knowledge that affect which procedures we use in addressing particular problems?

The process of planning

Every problem needs a plan. That is to say, problem solving begins with an evaluation of our current situation, comparison of that situation to the goal state we would like to achieve, and the identification of a sequence of actions that will move us from the former to the latter. In almost every situation, the younger the child, the poorer the planning he or she produces (Brown and DeLoache, 1978; Fabricius, 1988; Klahr and Robinson, 1981; Willatts, 1997).

Strategies in planning

Researchers studying adults have identified a number of different strategies for planning. The simplest of these is *trial and error*. Suppose you want to find a way to fasten something securely to the roof of your car, but have no proper equipment. You might search the house, trying out different items you found there (a very long belt perhaps, or a piece of rope, or something stretchy) until you found something that worked.

A more sophisticated, more conceptually driven way to plan is to *analyse sub-goals*: to work out a series of steps which will provide the means of achieving your ends or eventual goal. Want to fish that hat out of the pond, without getting wet? Then you need to find some kind of pole, and some means of getting a hook near the hat: two specific sub-goals to fulfil.

The development of trial and error

Even very young babies use trial and error to solve problems, for example, swiping wildly in the general direction of cot toys to make a rattle spin. In fact, so simple is trial and error as a plan that it is hard to imagine any goal-directed organism that could not 'plan' in this way. Trial and error is what any creature must do, to achieve a goal for which it hasn't got a more conceptual basis for planning: without insight, it's the only option. Even adults fall back on trial and error in looking for the solution to a problem when they have no relevant knowledge. The best known example is Edison, who tried out hundreds of possible substances while looking for a filament for his invention, the light bulb, before finding an effective substance.

Although it's a strategy that remains in our repertoire for life, the character of trial and error tends to change as we develop. Up to the age of 2 or 3 years, toddlers try things pretty randomly. They experiment with solutions that (to an adult eye) could not possibly work, trying to post big square pegs into small round holes, for instance. And they try things in no particular order, repeating some options and overlooking others. As the child grows older, he or she becomes more *focused* in the options investigated, both selecting more plausible things to try than the younger child and considering a broader range of possibilities. Trial and error also becomes more *systematic* with age, so that the options are explored in a more orderly, programmatic fashion. By 12 years of age, trial and error can be a structured and scientific process, much as it was for Edison, who worked systematically through a coherent set of possibilities to narrow down on an effective solution. It's easy to see why even trial and error tends to work better for older children than for younger ones.

What is it that changes between the ages of 2 and 12, to generate the older child's more systematic approach to trial and error? Piaget believed that this developmental effect derived from the gradual construction of logical structures in the mind, specifically 'formal operations' (see Chapter 6). More recent research suggests that the tendency to be systematic in trial and error is less a matter of any general characteristic of the mind and more a matter of what we know, both about this particular task and about our own mental processes. The more you know about a situation, the more focused and plausible the things you try out will be. The more you know about the process of planning itself (the benefits of keeping track of what you've already tried, for example), the more systematic you will tend to be even in situations where you have little knowledge relevant to the task in hand. Both kinds of knowledge tend to increase with age as experience broadens.

The development of means–ends analysis

Piaget (1953) argued that trial and error is the only planning strategy that infants can use. Certainly, the evidence suggests that babies under 6 months of age don't engage in means–ends analysis (Willatts, 1997, 1999). For example, if an attractive toy is placed on a cloth so that the baby can reach the cloth but not the toy, the 6-month-old will not pull on the cloth to retrieve it. The problem is not that these young babies don't want the toy (Baillargeon et al., 1990; Willatts, 1997), or that they lack the motor coordination to pull on the cloth (Willatts, 1984), or that they lack the mental capacity to hold this simple means–ends analysis in mind (Bushnell, 1985). The problem is, as Piaget predicted, that the 6-month-old can't make the means–ends analysis of the situation necessary to work out how to retrieve the toy.

Exactly why young babies don't make means–ends plans has been a matter of controversy. Piaget claimed that it reflects the absence of certain mental structures that do not develop until around 18 months to 2 years of age. But as we've seen (Chapters 3 and 6), Piaget's theory does not fit the evidence. Research over the past 20 years has shown that the ability to use means–ends analysis emerges far earlier that Piaget thought. And just as the development of trial and error reflects the development of knowledge, so means–ends analysis reflects the growth of conceptual understanding rather than the emergence of general logical structures of the mind (Willatts, 1984, 1997).

Babies show the first evidence of means–ends analysis in Willatt's toy-retrieval task at about 7 months of age. Babies below 6 months either ignore the cloth on which the toy is lying, or they give up on reaching the toy and begin playing with the cloth instead. By contrast,

7-month-old babies treat the cloth as a tool, tugging it in a way designed to retrieve the toy.

Clever studies by Baillargeon and colleagues (1990) show that even the younger babies understand *in principle* that a sequence of actions (that is, a plan) may be needed to achieve a goal such as retrieving a toy (see Chapter 3). But the data suggest that they have not yet understood exactly *what* sequence of actions may be needed. They haven't understood that pulling on the cloth will bring the toy nearer, for example, so the idea of using this means to achieve their ends does not occur to them. The knowledge the baby needs in this task comes from experience: as the 5-month-old plays with the cloth, he or she *accidentally* brings the toy closer, and so the vital insight needed for future means–ends analyses in tasks like this can be discovered.

The ability to make even the simplest of means–ends analyses proceeds task by task (Willatts, 1997). Each new situation requires new knowledge about the effects of different kinds of actions: what actions will work in this situation and what won't. Knowing that pulling on a cloth brings everything on the cloth closer does not help you to understand that hooked rods work better than straight poles in trying to fish a toy closer, for example. Learning the consequences of different actions and the properties of different tools takes time. The younger the child, the less knowledge of this kind he or she will have, and the more limited the potential for means–ends planning. Even in adult life we are still making new discoveries of this kind, and extending our ability to make effective means–ends analyses to new areas.

Willatts' toy-retrieval task poses a very simple problem: although objectively there is a sub-goal (pull the cloth), the solution can be enacted as a single unit: there is no need to explicitly represent the sub-goal as a separate step, and 7-month-olds probably don't (Willatts, 1997). Only at 9 months is there clear evidence that babies can represent sub-goals as such (Willatts and Rosie, 1989). Even so, there is a marked developmental change in the number of sub-goals that can be handled, and in the ability to plan a sequence of sub-goals in the right order.

For instance, in a more complex version of Willatts' task, the toy is placed on the far end of a cloth as before, but a transparent screen is then placed over the cloth between the baby and the toy (**Figure 7.2**). To solve this problem, the baby needs a two-step plan, and the steps have to be in the right order: pull on the cloth before removing the screen and the toy will be dislodged by the screen and left out of reach, so the screen must be moved aside first. Up to about 12 months of age babies find this planning task impossibly difficult. Even at 18 months, the majority of infants are still flummoxed. Only one in three of this age group removes the screen first with any consistency, and even these few do so only half the time. It's not until somewhere between 2 and 3 years of age that toddlers can solve this simple problem consistently (Willatts, 1989).

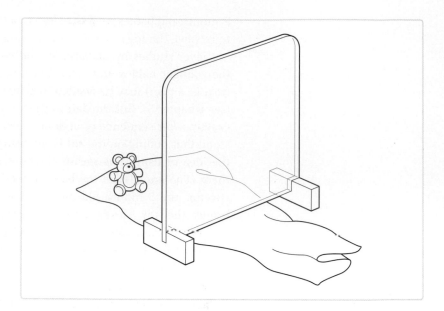

figure 7.2

A two-step plan: move the screen then pull the cloth

Source: after P. Willatts (1999).

The ability to plan a sequence of sub-goals in more complex tasks continues to develop throughout childhood. For example, 4-year-olds are far less efficient than 5-year-olds in planning a route to collect various baby animals and return them to their mothers: where 4-year-olds zigzag back and forth inefficiently crossing their own tracks, 5-year-olds plan more direct and economical routes (Fabricius, 1988). The younger children realize that a direct route would be better: they often go back and amend inefficiencies in their plans. The problem seems to be directly one of planning the sequence of steps or sub-goals.

Not all of the developmental change we see in planning tasks can necessarily be attributed to a developmental change in the ability to manage sequences of sub-goals as such. As ever in developmental psychology, there are methodological issues that we need to be wary of in interpreting the data in this area. A classic demonstration of this comes from Klahr and Robinson's (1981) study of developmental change in planning in the 'Tower of Hanoi' problem. In the traditional version of this task, three disks must be move from pole A to pole C (see **Figure 7.3**), subject to the rules that only one disk can move at a time and it must come to rest on a pole at the end of each move, and that no disc can rest on a disk smaller than itself. (If you are not familiar with this problem, try it for yourself, for example using three marks on paper to represent the poles, and three coins of different sizes for the disks.)

Even 6-year-old children normally do very badly in this task, which has traditionally been taken as a measure of their poor means–ends planning. But is their difficulty purely one of planning, or are there other factors at work here? For example, does the need to remember the rather arcane rules of the task limit the younger child's efforts? Klahr and Robinson

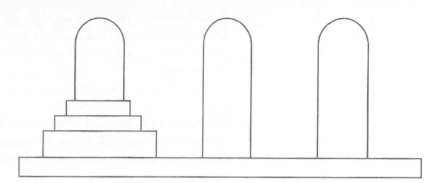

figure **7.3**

The 'Tower of Hanoi' problem

explored this question by devising a version of the task (**Figure 7.4**) in which there was no need for the child to remember the rules. They replaced the discs with 'monkey cans': a big 'daddy' can, a medium sized 'mummy' can and a small 'baby' can. These cans had to be balanced on the poles, and were so devised that it was only possible to put a larger can over a smaller one (of course, this reverses the usual rule of only having smaller discs on larger ones, but the structure of the task is unaffected). The child needn't remember the rule (only larger cans on top) because the cans would only balance the 'right' way. And so that the child need not remember where the monkey family are heading, Klahr and Robinson provided a physical model of the goal state to be achieved which was left in view all the time: the child had only to say how the cans should be moved to match it. Six-year-olds were much more successful in this task than in the classic version of the game, suggesting that, indeed, experimental tasks requiring children to remember arcane rules and goals may underestimate their ability to plan.

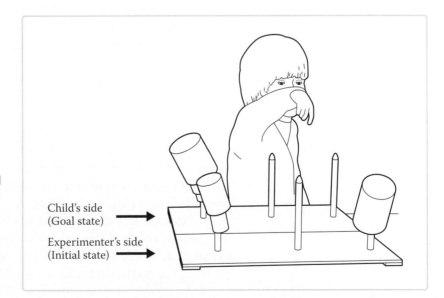

figure **7.4**

The 'monkey cans' version of the 'Tower of Hanoi' problem

Source: D. Klahr and M. Robinson, 'Formal assessment of problem solving and planning processes in preschool children', *Cognitive Psychology* 13, pp. 113–48. © 1981. Reproduced with permission from Elsivier Science.

Child's side
(Goal state)

Experimenter's side
(Initial state)

Nevertheless, there is a residual age effect in Klahr and Robinson's task which suggests that there is a real developmental change in the ability to plan a sequence of moves. The greater the number of steps to be planned, the more likely it was that older children would be more successful in this task than younger ones: 60 to 70 per cent of 3- and 4-year-olds could successfully make two-step plans in Klahr and Robinson's task, as could all the older children. Sixty-five per cent of 5-year-olds and nearly all 6-year-olds could make effective four-step plans, though very few 4-year-olds could do this. More than half of the 6-year-olds in the study made perfect plans even when six moves were required.

Task-specific knowledge and means–ends planning

It may seem tempting to speculate that this developmental change in the number of steps a child can plan reflects developmental change in the amount of information children can keep in mind at one time. But as we've seen earlier in this chapter, a physical limitation on working memory or M-space of the kind this speculation implies is not really a plausible explanation. In fact, the evidence suggests that the extent to which we can generate a sequence of sub-goals has more to do with the knowledge we bring to a task than with any sort of physical limitation in processing capacity (Brown and DeLoache, 1978).

For example, a professional researcher can plan the complexities of an elaborate experiment or a convoluted statistical analysis quickly, efficiently and almost without noticing, where a student struggles with what may well feel like an overload of factors to coordinate, too many balls to keep in the air at the same time. The researcher has no more M-space than the student. The difference in their planning comes from the fact that the researcher has expert knowledge to draw on where the student does not. As we saw in Chapter 6, expert knowledge allows the researcher to see the factors relevant to the problem in a more organized, coherent and principled way than a novice can, which greatly reduces the difficulty of identifying possible paths to solutions. The researcher knows more strategies that may work in this context, and more about their strengths and limitations, and so has less work to do to work out an effective plan. And in fact, the researcher may be able to simply reach into memory and pull out a plan that worked last time in this sort of context, where the student has to work it all out from first principles. Without rich knowledge of a task, planning is very much harder, and likely to be less sophisticated and less successful.

The younger the child, the less likely he or she is to have coherent, principled expert knowledge of the task to draw on. Some researchers suggest that the lack of such rich knowledge is the major factor limiting the younger child's ability to plan a sequence of sub-goals. It has been shown that, where they have the relevant knowledge, even the very young can plan effectively (Brown and DeLoache, 1978).

Is it really possible that the younger child's difficulties in planning a sequence of sub-goals is because of a lack of knowledge and experience in the task? Surely simple tasks like the Tower of Hanoi problem don't really require much knowledge, and so are measuring some other factor limiting the young child's ability to plan? But in fact, even planning in the Tower of Hanoi problem is more insight-driven than might appear. For example, which imposes the greater challenge to planning: a version of this task where three disks must be moved from A to C, or one where four, seven, 19 disks must be moved? The more disks, the more individual movements of each disk, and the more sub-goals will have to be identified and achieved. For the novice, the more disks, the harder the problem and the lower the probability of success. Even with only three disks, complete novices may solve the problem only half the time, which is no better than chance. But with experience in the task you will come to realize that there are a number of simple rules that make planning very much easier. First, you discover a rule that specifies whether the top disc should be shifted to B or C on the first move of the solution for a given number of disks. Then you discover that this rule changes with the number of disks to be moved. Later on, you discover that these rules are systematic: with an odd number of disks you start one way, with an even number, the other. This insight means that planning how to solve the task with any number of disks (30, say) is easier for the expert than planning how to solve the three-disk problem is for the novice!

Becoming an expert problem solver

It's worth noting that experience with tasks like the Tower of Hanoi puzzle (or any other problem) doesn't just teach us strategies specific to solving that particular puzzle. For example, the discovery that there is a simple rule that allows you to solve the Tower of Hanoi with any number of discs alerts us to the higher-order strategy of looking for simple rules of this kind in other tasks, too (there is one for 'noughts and crosses', for example).

As children gain experience with different tasks, they gain more higher-order insights of this kind. This creates a new and powerful tool for planning and problem solving: it allows the child to import knowledge about problem solving itself into a new situation. Such meta-cognitive knowledge allows a more organized and systematic approach even in novel situations where task-specific expertise is not available. This is an important step toward developing executive control over reasoning, and toward developing more generally applicable skill as a problem solver.

Generalizing problem-solving skills through analogy

Faced with an entirely new problem, we have two options. One is to treat it as unique, and to search for a brand new solution. The other is to try to find a similar sort of problem that is more familiar to us, and to search for ways to generalize our insight and expertise from the familiar to the novel situation: in other words, to draw an *analogy* between the current problem and one we know how to solve. The ability to reason by analogy in this way greatly enhances the power and generality of problem-solving skills.

Can young children draw analogies?

Children are notoriously bad at drawing analogies. Even 10-year-olds often fail to draw analogies which seem perfectly obvious to an adult mind (Inhelder and Piaget, 1958). This fact is the bane of many a teacher's life: it can produce a classroom of children who are adept at solving some mathematical problem in a given format, but who utterly fail to recognize the very same problem or to generalize their skills if the format changes even slightly (Bruner and Kenney, 1965; Werthheimer, 1945). The consequence is that children's success in problem solving is much more tied to specific tasks than is the case for adolescents, who more easily draw analogies and generalize their skills. How do we draw analogies, and why is the young child not so good at this as an adolescent?

Piaget claimed that in order to draw an analogy you have to be able to disregard the concrete specifics of the present problem and the analogous one, and focus on the abstract, logical parallels between the two. The ability to reason in this abstract logical way was claimed to develop only in adolescence (Inhelder and Piaget, 1958; Piaget, 1968). According to Piaget, then, young children can't reason by analogy.

More recent research suggests that Piaget's view of the process involved in drawing analogies, and his view of the young child's abilities in this area, were wrong. To recognize a useful analogy between a familiar and an unfamiliar situation we have to be able to map the structure of one situation onto the other (Gentner, 1983). That is to say, we have to be able to recognize that there is something useful in common between the two situations. Sometimes recognizing commonalities between two situations is a matter of recognizing that the concrete *elements* of the problem look very similar: both involve dealing with a mother infuriated by a broken item, say. Sometimes the elements of the problem may look entirely different, and the commonality between situations lies in the *structure of the relationships* between these elements: pedals and engines both involve mechanisms for propelling vehicles, for example. In either case, your ability to draw the analogy depends on having enough knowledge of both situations to recognize the commonalities between them.

The tasks that Piaget used in measuring children's ability to draw analogies (and in which they failed) involved rather obscure commonalities. For example, 'A bicycle is to handlebars as a ship is to ...?' Few

10-year-olds answer this correctly. But then, the elements of the problem don't look similar, and the structural relationship between then is rather esoteric (and apparently hard for even adults to grasp: the correct answer is generally taken to be 'rudder' but is in fact steering wheel or tiller). Few 10-year-olds know enough about boats to draw this analogy. When asked to solve analogies where the elements and the structural relationship between them are more familiar (for example: 'Chocolate is to melted chocolate as snow is to …?') even 3-year-olds can readily draw the analogy (Goswami and Brown, 1989).

Overall, the evidence we now have strongly suggests that the young child's ability to draw analogies is limited only by how much knowledge he or she has of the situations compared. When they have enough knowledge of the two situations to recognize commonalities, even very young children can solve analogies (Brown and DeLoache, 1978; Goswami and Brown, 1989; Johnson-Laird, 1983, 1993).

This conclusion is confirmed by studies of the detailed processes involved in drawing analogies. Sternberg (1977a, 1977b) identified five separate steps in this process: *encoding* the elements of the situation; *inferring* the relations between them; *mapping* links between the elements of the two situations; *applying* the relationship inferred in the given situation to the new one; and *justifying* the resulting analogy. Goswami (1992) has shown that 3-year-old children can be taught and can use all these elements of analogical reasoning. There is some evidence that the basic ability to draw analogies is present from birth (Goswami, 1995).

Using analogies in problem solving

As we have seen earlier in this chapter, being able to use a given cognitive process in principle does not necessarily mean that the young child will *actually* use it. But the evidence suggests that very young children do spontaneously draw analogies in solving problems (Gholson et al., 1989; Holyoak, Junn and Billman, 1984). For example, Holyoak and colleagues asked 4-year-olds to solve a problem which involved moving gumballs from a bowl in easy reach to another which was out of reach, without getting out of the chair. A walking stick, a big sheet of card and various other things were available to solve the problem. Before tackling this task, the child was told a story which involved someone solving an analogous type of problem: for example, a genie who moved jewels from one bottle to another either by using his magic staff to move the far away bottle closer, or by rolling his magic carpet into a tube and pouring the jewels down it to the other bottle (**Table 7.1**). Four-year-old children spontaneously used the analogies in the stories to solve their problems, even when the elements of the specific story they heard were less obviously similar to the analogous problem (Miss Piggy, a character from *The Muppet Show*, a popular television programme of the time, transferring jewels to a safe, for example). In still simpler tasks, even children as

table 7.1 Analogical reasoning

	Story analogues	Ball problem
Initial state		
Goal	Genie wishes to transfer jewels from one bottle to another.	Child wishes to transfer balls from one bowl to another.
Resources	Magic staff/magic carpet.	Walking cane/sheet of paper.
Constraint	Must not drop or lose jewels.	Must not drop or lose any balls.
Solution plan 1	Genie (a) uses magic staff to pull goal bottle closer to initial bottle; (b) drops jewels into goal bottle.	Child (a) uses cane to pull goal bowl closer to initial bowl; (b) drops balls into goal bowl.
Solution plan 2	Genie (a) rolls magic carpet to form a long hollow tube; (b) places tube so it extends from initial bottle to goal bottle; (c) rolls jewels through tube to goal bottle.	Child (a) rolls sheet of paper to form long hollow tube; (b) places tube so it extends from initial bowl to goal bowl: (c) rolls balls through tube to goal bottle.
Outcome	Jewels are transferred safely.	Balls are transferred safely.

Source: K. Holyoak, E. Junn and D. Billman, 'Development of analogical problem solving skill', *Child Development* 55, pp. 332–40. (c) 1984. Reproduced with permission from Blackwells Publishing.

young as 2 years spontaneously solved problems by analogy (Crisafi and Brown, 1986).

Even though young children are able to draw analogies and spontaneously do so in problem solving, it is not surprising that older children use this tool more extensively and more effectively. The older the child, the more knowledge he or she will have across a broader range of areas. Older children will therefore often be able to detect analogies still invisible to the less well-informed younger child, and so will be able to generalize skills through analogy to a far greater extent than younger children can. The impact of this progressive capacity for analogy on the power of the older child's reasoning is explosive. Analogy is a key vehicle through which skills begin to become general and abstract, rather than specifically tied to the content of the domain in which they were constructed.

Mechanisms of cognitive change

So far, we have looked at *what* it is that changes as children's cognitive abilities develop. But ultimately, the real question for research is *how* do these things develop? By what process or mechanism does the way we reason change? How do we discover new strategies and ideas? Research that looks at children's problem solving in detail lends itself to exploring these issues directly. How does the child's own individual processing in problem solving contribute to developmental change and new discovery? Can we understand development itself as a problem-solving process? How are these things influenced by social interactions and tuition?

Microgenetic methods for studying the process of change

Often, in exploring the general character of intellectual development, we collect data about a number of children and look for the patterns across children that characterize a given age group. We look for how many digits 5-year-olds or 8-year-olds can typically hold in mind, or what an average 8-year-old knows about biology, or whether children of a given age can create three-step plans or draw complex analogies. The answers to such questions give us a global picture of what it is that changes during development, and how progress proceeds through childhood. But it is only by studying the specific problem-solving processes used by an individual child in a given context that we can see how skills and knowledge come together to produce an actual strategy, or to yield new learning and new conceptual insight in a task.

Studying the detailed processing of an individual problem solver poses some challenges. The mental processes involved are invisible, so how can we study them? Early research asked problem solvers to introspect on what they were doing: to solve some problem, and to comment on how they were thinking as they went along (Ericsson and Simon, 1993). But this method (called taking a *verbal protocol*) has very serious drawbacks. First, there is good evidence that what people say they are doing when solving a problem and what they are actually doing are not necessarily the same thing at all. Much of the processing we do in problem solving is unconscious, hard to notice in ourselves. For example, I have no real advance awareness of exactly what words I will write next as I complete this sentence, still less any awareness of how I choose them. If you ask me to explain it to you, I would produce a plausible-sounding rationalization of what I probably did, rather than reporting the actual psychological processes, to which I have no access. The classic example of the point comes from Piaget's report of a number of philosophers: asked to crawl across the floor, all were able to do it, but none could accurately describe the sequence of movement of their arms and legs.

There is clear evidence that children introduce a new strategy into their problem solving before they can describe it (Siegler and Stern, 1998), as we would expect if its emergence, and the processes associated with that emergence, were not conscious. And indeed, the youngest children have great difficulty in telling us anything about their thinking at all: 3- to 5-year-olds seem not to have much ability to reflect on their own thought processes, or even to really understand what such processes are (Flavell, Green and Flavell, 1995), as will be discussed further in Chapter 9.

Rather than asking children to tell us about their problem-solving processes, then, researchers have developed *microgenetic* techniques for more direct scrutiny of precisely what a child (or an adult, for that matter) does while engaging a task. Such analyses focus on the detail of the child's actions in addressing the problem. In microgenetic studies, children are not asked to describe or reflect on their behaviour, although what they say spontaneously is recorded and analysed.

A microgenetic study has several key characteristics (Siegler and Crowley, 1991). First, the emphasis is on studying the behaviour of each individual child as he or she addresses a problem. The main interest is not in whether the child can complete a given task successfully, but on the *processes* by which their performance, successful or otherwise, is produced. Experimental sessions are recorded, and these recordings are then analysed in great detail to try to infer what specific goals and representations of the problem directed the child's behaviour at any one time, the processes through which these were brought to bear on the task, and how changes in strategy emerge. The aim is to study problem solving through a period of change or new discovery. The child is observed addressing the same kind of problem over many trials or attempts in a session, for example, or over repeated sessions, to allow time and opportunity for developments to take place. Microgenetic analyses have provided rich new insights into how reasoning operates and develops, changing our traditional views (Kuhn, 1995; Siegler, 2000; Siegler and Crowley, 1991).

Strategy selection and cognitive change: a new view of development

Perhaps surprisingly, one of the first discoveries made through microgenetic analysis of relatively short periods of problem solving has radically challenged our view of the process through which cognitive skills develop through childhood as a whole (Siegler, 2000).

Traditional views of how cognition develops were very much influenced by Piaget's theory (Inhelder and Piaget, 1958, 1964; Piaget, 1954). According to Piaget, cognitive development is a matter of progressive evolution: the baby begins with no mental skills beyond very basic reflexes and the biological mechanisms of adaptation (see Chapters 1, 3 and 6), and from these gradually constructs the mental structures that allow problem solving and reasoning. Through this process new and more sophisticated strategies develop out of the old less adequate ones, each old strategy being overwritten and replaced by its successor as the more powerful approach develops. The model of developmental change that this implies is schematically represented in **Figure 7.5**. According to this view, development follows a coherent path, always progressing in the direction of more adequate and more sophisticated strategies.

Studies using traditional methods (that is, comparing the performance of groups of children of different ages and inferring developmental change in skill from the patterns of success and failure in problem solving observed) supported this view: overall, there is a consistent movement through childhood from less to more adequate and sophisticated strategies. However, microgenetic studies of the problem solving

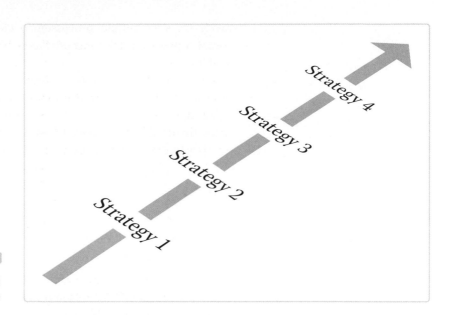

figure 7.5

Piaget's model of developmental
change

of individuals suggest that the process underlying this developmental
change is very different from what was traditionally thought (Kuhn,
1995; Schauble, 1996; Siegler, 2000; Siegler and Chen, 1998; Siegler and
Jenkins, 1989; Siegler and Shipley, 1995).

Microgenetic studies have revealed that, at any one time, children
(and for that matter, adults) normally have a range of different strategies
for solving any particular problem. Simpler, less adequate strategies
coexist alongside more sophisticated ones, and continue to be used long
after the more sophisticated strategy has come into the child's repertoire. Children (or adults) may use a variety of different strategies during
the course of even quite short period of problem solving, moving back
and forth between more and less sophisticated strategies (Siegler, 1996;
Siegler and Jenkins, 1989). In sum, there is no relatively clean transition
from less to more sophisticated strategies, as the traditional model of
development supposes. Furthermore, new and more powerful strategies
do not necessarily grow out of older and less sophisticated ones: rather,
they may develop entirely separately from the older strategy, and operate
on a quite different and unconnected principle (Siegler and Jenkins,
1989). There is no orderly connection between less and more
sophisticated strategies, as the traditional model assumes.

Siegler's 'overlapping waves' theory

In the light of these findings, Siegler has proposed a new theory of the
way cognitive development as a whole progresses. According to this
theory, the process of developmental change as a whole may be as much
a matter of change in how strategies are selected as of the generation of
new strategies. As a consequence, cognitive development may rely as

much on very simple processes for learning from feedback as on complex processes for conceptual construction of the kind described by Piaget.

This theory is best explained through a concrete example. Take the traditional 'post box' game for infants: the baby has a number of shapes, which must be posted into a box via a series of correspondingly shaped holes in the lid of the box. From a very young age, the infant has a number of different strategies for solving this problem:

- *brute force*, which relies on bashing a shape into the chosen hole harder and harder, if a first try doesn't work

- *twisting* the shape above the hole, to more deliberately search for an orientation which will fit

- *trying another hole* until one is found where the shape matches.

All of these strategies may appear in the baby's problem solving in a single session. It is hard to see one strategy as a primitive version of a better one, here: each strategy draws on a quite different approach, and looks more like a separate and different kind of strategy, even if an observer might want to rank order them for sophistication. The same variety of seemingly unconnected strategies can be identified in individual's problem solving in all tasks so far studied (Siegler, 1996), both in children and in adults.

How does the child choose which strategy to select at any one moment? Each of the strategies in the child's repertoire (such as the three for the post box game noted above) will have a 'history', in the child's experience. That is to say, each will have been used in the past, in analogous situations, with greater or lesser success. Siegler and Jenkins (1989) suggest that the child selects whichever strategy currently has the greatest historic association with success and the least association with failure. So, for example, a child who has had great success with brute force in similar situations in the past, but relatively little success with either twisting the shapes or trying other holes, will select a brute-force strategy first in the post box game. But each experience with the task provides more feedback. If the brute-force strategy doesn't work very well this time, its association with success may decline until one of the other strategies has a better 'track record', and the child will then swap to this second strategy. These associative processes controlling strategy selection need not be conscious (Siegler and Chen, 1998).

Siegler's theory explains why the young child's choice of strategies may appear very inconsistent, and why a new and powerful strategy may be in the child's repertoire for a long time before it becomes the dominant, most often used approach. In the early stages of experience with a task there may be no clear difference, from the child's point of view, in the efficacy of strategies which are, from an objective observer's perspective, quite different in their potential power. For example, brute force may work quite often in the 'post box' task if the materials are cheap and flimsy. Twisting shapes about to find a fit may not improve success much in practice, since the majority of holes simply won't accommodate a given shape, no matter how it is rotated. Even the objectively best strategy of trying different holes until one works may not produce much success for an inexperienced infant who does not search through the holes systematically, or who aligns shapes poorly and so misses potential matches. Where no strategy has a clear history of greater success than any other, the reasons for preferring one over another are slight. The child may select between strategies more or less at random, and so produce a performance that is very inconsistent, now using weak strategies, now more powerful ones.

Practice with a task gives the child considerably more feedback about the efficacy and properties of each strategy, until one or more strategies emerge as clearly more successful than the others. Now these more successful strategies will be systematically selected in preference to other, less successful ones, so that the child's performance will become more consistent, and more rooted in sophisticated approaches. This developmental process can take a surprising amount of time: older, weaker strategies may be used for a long time after newer and more powerful ones are available (Kuhn, 1995: Schauble, 1996; Siegler, 1994), particularly where the older strategy is already fairly successful, or where the newer one is much harder to use (Bjorklund et al., 1997). But where the advantages of a new strategy are obvious, it may become the child's normal approach fairly quickly (Alibali, 1999).

This theory suggests that cognitive development should not be represented as a linear progression as in the traditional model (Figure 7.5), but more as a succession of 'overlapping waves' (Siegler, 2000), as different strategies dominate the child's problem solving in some task (**Figure 7.6**).

Siegler's theory suggests that the processes that create cognitive development are not special to childhood or to development, but are ubiquitous. They are the basis for the evolution of all problem-solving skills throughout life. The very same processes that account for developmental change in children's strategies also account for problem solving and cognitive change in adults (Shrager and Siegler, 1998; Siegler and Shipley, 1995).

In fact, according to this theory, the progress of cognitive development is importantly the product of some extremely general mechanisms for learning: feedback mechanisms of the kind described by 'S–R' or learning theorists nearly 100 years ago (see Chapter 1). Feedback-driven learning processes of this type have received comparatively little attention in developmental psychology for a number of decades, despite their power and ubiquity (for example, similar reward–punishment processes of learning occur in all animals, and play a critical role in shaping the

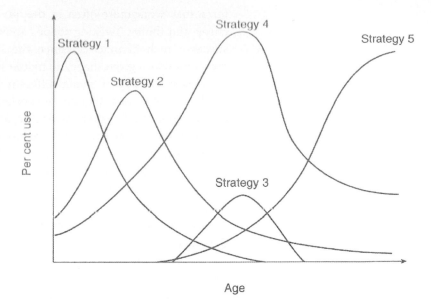

figure 7.6

Siegler's 'overlapping waves' model of developmental change

Source: R. Siegler, 'The rebirth of children's learning', *Child Development* 71, pp. 26–36. © 2000. Reproduced with permission from Blackwell Publishing.

rich patterns of adaptive behaviour across the species). This neglect stemmed from the fact that early research into conceptual development assumed that 'simple' associative learning of this kind could make little contribution to the development of the complex subtleties of human intelligent behaviour. It is only in the last decade or so that we have begun to see that learning processes are in fact an integral tool of development, with a critical role to play not only in shaping how and when we use the strategies in our repertoire (Lemaire and Siegler, 1995), but also in the construction of new strategies and understanding (Kuhn, 1995; Siegler, 2000).

Discovering new strategies

Even if the progress of development as a whole reflects processes for selecting strategies from alternatives in our repertoires, we must still explain how those alternative strategies were generated in the first place. In some senses, it has been clear for a long time that new strategies can be shaped through the feedback we get from a task. Every time we try to solve a problem to which we do not know the solution, we in effect expose ourselves to such feedback, and though a more or less trial and error process, allow it to shape our behaviour toward a successful strategy. Such 'data-driven' processes play a powerful role in new discovery: for example, in the infant's discovery that pulling on a cloth can bring a toy nearer, in Willatts' studies of infant problem solving (Willatts, 1997).

But what, exactly, is the role of feedback in creating new strategies? How does it interact with existing mental structures? This issue has been controversial for decades. There is a great deal of evidence to suggest that Piaget was right to emphasize that what we can learn from feedback is constrained by what we already know (Moore, 1996). For example, as we saw earlier, 5-year-old children learn very little by comparison with 8-year-olds from feedback in a balance scale task, because their conceptual understanding doesn't lead them to pay attention to the right things. Some theorists (for example, Piaget) have argued that all new discovery is ultimately driven, dependent on and limited by existing conceptual structures and strategies, so that feedback has a limited influence. Others argue that the simple feedback from success and failure is enough to generate entirely new strategies that have no root in existing behaviour or understanding (Siegler and Stern, 1998; Thornton, 1999), and indeed that if this were not so, it is hard to see how any genuinely novel discovery could ever be possible (Sophian, 1997; Thornton, 1999).

New strategies from existing procedures

Even those theorists who most strongly urge that real developmental change must come from within the child's own conceptual structures concede the point that behaviour, at least, can be shaped by learning processes in some task. Thus Piaget believed that all real developmental change in understanding comes from reflection on the effects of our actions in the world. But action must precede thought, and action can be structured by feedback from the world (Piaget, 1967, 1968). Many theorists agree with Piaget's thesis that development derives importantly from processes that come to explicitly represent structures which are implicit in patterns of behaviour, patterns which have themselves been shaped by 'data-driven' processes – in other words, by feedback from interaction with some task (Bremner, 1997; Gelman, 1982; Karmiloff-Smith, 1992; Wynn, 1992b).

Processes that explicitly represent what is already implicit in a child's behaviour undoubtedly make a powerful contribution to development in a number of ways. Such processes can bring new elements of a task into clearer focus, so that the child can recognize their relevance and use these factors in guiding new problem solving (Karmiloff-Smith, 1992). And they can allow the identification of recurring patterns in behaviour, so that these patterns can be 'chunked' into coherent units and so deployed more economically and effectively (Klahr and Wallace, 1976; Klahr and MacWhinney, 1998). Or they may allow the child to eliminate redundant elements of an old procedure and so discover a new and more efficient strategy (Siegler and Jenkins, 1989).

For example, Karmiloff-Smith's (1979) classic study asked children to make notes on the route to be followed by a toy ambulance. The ambulance travelled down a 'road' drawn on a roll of paper, passing a variety of bifurcating turns (see **Figure 7.7**). Some turnings had useful landmarks (such as trees) and others did not. Children saw the route a bit at a time,

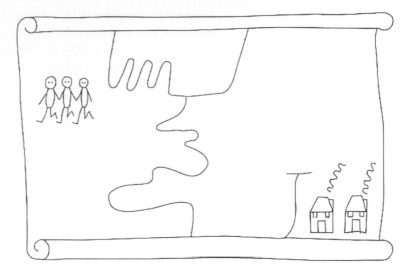

figure **7.7**

The route to be followed by a toy ambulance in Karmiloff-Smith's study

Source: A. Karmiloff-Smith, 'Macro and micro developmental changes in language acquisition and problem solving', *Cognitive Science* 3, pp. 81–118. © 1979. Reproduced with permission from Elsivier Science.

and so had to find a way of noting which turning to take at each junction. Children used a variety of strategies in this task, from redrawing the whole route to noting landmarks to simply recording 'turn left/turn right', and so on. Sometimes the strategy a child began with could not cope with all of the turns, and children reacted by modifying the strategy to cope better. But children also modified strategies (such as recording left or right turnings) which could successfully cope with all of the turnings.

For example, **Figure 7.8** shows an initial version of a child recording whether to turn left or right (A), and a subsequently modified version (B), in which the child has added redundant information. This change in strategy has no obvious objective utility, and is not driven by any aspect of the task in itself, or by a pursuit of success (since the original strategy is perfectly adequate). Karmiloff-Smith (1992) argues that such modifications occur as a result of the child's reflections on his or her strategy: the child observes and notes the properties of the successful strategy, and then makes these more explicit, perhaps becoming explicitly aware of why a strategy works, and what elements it draws on for the first time through such reflections.

A further example comes from studies of how children learn to add (Siegler and Jenkins, 1989). Four-year-old children typically add two numbers together in a rather laborious way. Asked to add five and three, for example, they first count out the five on one hand, then separately count out three on the other hand (**Figure 7.9**) before then counting all of the fingers together to make eight. Implicit in this strategy is that one can directly count on from the first sum: for example, counting out the first five on one hand, and then carrying on 'six, seven, eight' on the other, without counting the three extra fingers separately (Figure 7.9). This intermediary strategy then paves the way for a further refinement:

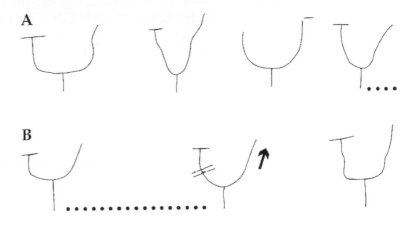

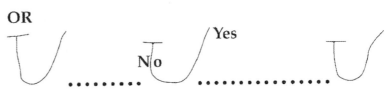

figure 7.8

Map drawings in the toy ambulance task

Source: A. Karmiloff-Smith, *Beyond Modularity: A developmental perspective on cognitive science* (Cambridge, Mass.: MIT Press). © 1992. Reproduced with permission from MIT Press.

not counting out the first five either, but starting 'five … six, seven, eight' (Figure 7.9). Thus a sequence of small steps, each making explicit something that was implicit in the previous strategy, has created a new and more streamlined strategy for adding (Siegler and Jenkins, 1989).

Similar analyses have shown how new strategies grow out of old ones across a variety of different tasks (Klahr and MacWhinney, 1998; Siegler, 1996). In fact, there have been a number of computer simulations of how one strategy can evolve from another through the action of processes which monitor ongoing problem solving looking for patterns (Klahr and MacWhinney, 1998; Shrager and Siegler, 1998; Siegler and Shipley, 1995).

But powerful as such self-reflective processes are in the construction of new strategies, they cannot really account for all the rich phenomena we see in childhood development, or even for the process of new, creative discovery in adult problem solving. The difficulty is this: the only thing that we can discover from this kind of self-reflective process is, by definition, *something that is already implicit in our existing strategy or understanding.* This means that all new strategies and discoveries constructed in this way must inevitably build on and resemble existing strategies, and share a conceptual structure with existing knowledge. We cannot discover a new, qualitatively different way of understanding the world or solving a problem simply by reflecting on the properties of our existing understanding or performance (Sophian, 1997; Thornton, 1999), because that, by definition, does not contain the new idea: it is not there to be discovered by reflection.

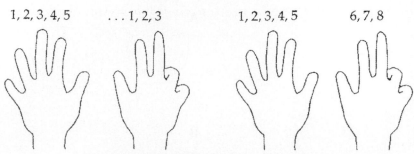

First strategy: counting everything out.

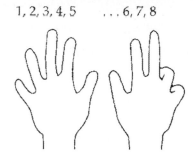

Intermediate strategy: counting out the first number and then counting on.

Final strategy: counting on from the first number.

figure 7.9

Children's strategies for counting

Source: S. Thornton, *Children Solving Problems*.
© 1995. Reproduced with permission from
Harvard University Press.

And yet the key feature of development, and of human intelligence as a whole, is that we *do* discover new strategies that are entirely different from and unconnected with our old strategies. And we do discover new ways of understanding the world which are qualitatively different from our previous ideas, even revolutionarily different (Brown, 1990; Gelman and Brenneman, 1994; Kuhn, 1970; Siegler, 1997). The obvious implication is that somehow, our interactions with the world and the learning processes involved in shaping our behaviour as we solve problems must import the seeds of these new ideas and strategies (Sophian, 1997). How could this be, if learning from feedback is itself constrained by our existing conceptual understanding?

Creative discovery from problem-solving processes

As Piaget pointed out, it is very hard to see how the mind could come to discover something for which it has no pre-existing structure or representation. How can we discover what we lack the mental apparatus to understand? But this problem may look harder than it is: for the structure of our conceptual understanding is not the only source of structure that influences our behaviour (Lewis, 2000; Sophian, 1997; Thelen and Smith, 1994; Thornton, 1999). There is also structure in the world, in the mechanics of our bodies and in the physical and social worlds with which we interact. These multiple sources of structure come together, acting as a 'dynamic system' (see Chapter 2) to shape problem-solving behaviour in unexpected ways, ways that need have no initial representation in our minds at all. This new behaviour is then available for review by self-reflective processes, which now have something new to discover.

One key characteristic of problem solving is that it is *goal-directed*. As we have seen earlier in this chapter, solving a problem involves finding a means of changing an initial state of affairs into a new one. This eventual goal may not be reachable in one step: it may be necessary to work through a series of sub-goals along the way. The exact nature of these sub-goals may be influenced by many factors, from our understanding of the social dynamics of the problem to be solved, to the physical characteristics of the problem or the world, or the limitations on the tools available to deal with it. The complex patterns of sub-goals we adopt during problem solving may change and redirect our problem solving in unexpected directions, and so lead us to novel strategies (Sophian, 1997).

An example of such processes at work comes from a microgenetic study of children's efforts to build a bridge between two towers either side of a 'river', using wooden blocks (Thornton, 1999). None of the blocks provided is long enough to span the river, so the child must construct a counterbalanced bridge to solve the problem as shown, for example, in **Figure 7.10**. Few children solve this problem immediately, even at 9 years of age, but the majority of 7- and 9-year-olds do solve it eventually, building bridges where counterbalance is either implicit or explicit. But 5-year-olds have enormous difficulty with this task. They do not know enough about balance to understand how to construct any sort of counterbalance. Only one 5-year-old in Thornton's study discovered how to build a counterbalanced bridge and so solved this problem, and it is clear from her problem solving that she did so entirely thorough the dynamics of her interaction with the task.

Table 7.2 summarizes how this child went about exploring this problem. This analysis shows how the child's goals gradually evolved through the course of problem solving as a result of feedback from the task. At first her goal is simple: find a block long enough to span the river (A). When none can be found, she adopts the sub-goal of making a block

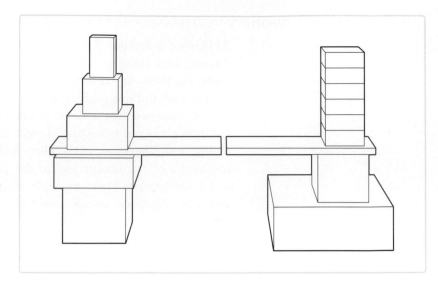

figure **7.10**

Building a counterbalanced bridge
across a river

Source: S. Thornton, *Growing Minds*. © 2002.
Reproduced with permission from
Palgrave Macmillan.

table **7.2**   Microgenetic analysis of a child's problem solving

Sequence of construction	Goal	Feedback available	Comment
A: Measures single blocks against the gaps between towers	Find long enough span	There isn't one	Always chose one of the four longest blocks, two or three repetitions with each
B: Measures two span blocks against the river	Make long enough span	Two blocks will reach	Still aiming at a support bridge
C: Juxtaposes two span blocks, varying the point of contact (end on/overlapping at centre – left over right, right over left): and varying the means of securing the join (squeezing join together very hard/ inserting another small block at centre join between spans – apparently as a 'fastener' – before release; holding in place by hand)	Fasten two blocks together	The point of join makes no difference: squeezing does not create a join; inserting a block does not create a join (this assembly is less stable, centre of bridge dips more strongly, ends of bridge lift away from towers more strongly); hands can enforce join; hand pressure maintains spans on towers	Focus is plainly on fastening things together to allow a support bridge to be built: no balance-related procedures; insertion of a 'fastener' block at central join confirms no recognition of need to bring bridge pieces into balance; proprioceptive feedback could cue the new goal of fastening bridge end to the towers; and also the idea that pressure (e.g. of hands) can fasten the spans to the tower
D: Moves small 'fastener' block from central join; after maintaining assembly by hand pressure, replaces one hand with small block at tower end of span; repeats with numerous different small blocks, using one block at a time	Use blocks to substitute for hand pressure in fastening span to tower	Blocks fail as fasteners	Still no recognition of weight as relevant here: successive blocks tried as 'fasteners' are all small and light (e.g. a semi-circle; triangle; small square; small pillar); only one is ever used at a time, so successive tries do not add weight – and often reduce it

table **7.2** continued

Sequence of construction	Goal	Feedback available	Comment
E: Returns to seeking one span long enough to cross the river in a simple support bridge	Reversion to original goal	This is still unachievable	This reversion confirms that the child did not recognize how promising her previous strategy was, and could not interpret the reason for its failure (i.e. inadequate weight on rear of span)
F: Alternates between Phases D and E, as above	Alternating between D and E as above	As for D and E above	The child faces two sets of negative feedback, but has prior experience of successful support bridges; the only positive feedback so far is that pressure (hands) can support the spans
G: As phase D, but widens the range of blocks tried as 'fasteners' – including some larger (heavier) ones	Use blocks to substitute for hand pressure in fastening span to tower	Larger blocks work better	This grew gradually from previous alternating strategies – during which search slowly widened both when looking for a single span and when looking for an effective 'fastener'
H: As phase D, but focusing on finding larger blocks to place on the towers, and now using more than one block to secure each span	Press spans into place with larger/heavier blocks	Larger/heavier blocks are more successful but often overbalance on unstable towers	The child's actions are now creating a counterbalanced bridge, though it is unclear that the role of weight in itself is explicitly recognized; the feedback from her actions is capable of revealing the role of weight and balance
I: Adjusts towers creating broader and more stable structures able to support more blocks; adds spans and fixes in place with stable piles of large blocks; successfully completes a counterbalanced bridge	Create stable towers to support more blocks; fasten spans in place with big/heavy blocks	Problem solved !	The child's actions now swiftly create an effective counter-balanced bridge; it remains unclear to what extent the role of weight or balance is explicitly recognized

Source: S. Thornton, 'Creating the conditions for cognitive change: the interaction between task structures and specific strategies.' *Child Development* 70, pp. 588–603. © 1999. Reproduced with permission from Blackwells Publishing.

long enough to do the job, by using two blocks to create a long enough span (B). This in turn leads to a new problem: the two blocks will not stay in place, they fall into the river. She adopts a new sub-goal of fastening them together to solve this problem (C). This sub-goal is doomed, since no means of actually fastening the blocks together has been provided. Nonetheless, this sub-goal is highly instructive, as Table 7.2 shows.

Like many 5-year-olds observed by Piaget, this child has a rather poor understanding of how we might fasten one block to another. She tries to do it by squeezing hard on the point where the blocks meet mid-river, as might work, if the blocks were structured like 'Lego' bricks, for example: but they are not, and this fails. She tries to fasten the spans together by putting something (another very small block) between them, as might work if the small block had been glue (Piaget has reported many children trying to use inappropriate things as 'magic' glue in this way). This makes everything worse. The only means she has of fastening any block to anything else is her hands: she can hold the join between the two spans mid-river, or she can hold each span to the tower on which it rests. But holding the assembly together by hand does not meet the social demands of the situation.

The child adopts the new goal of finding something to replace her hands in fastening the spans in place: blocks are the only available materials (D). This goal is far from immediately successful, and the child proceeds through trial and error, showing no sign of conceptual understanding of the solution she is now working towards. Indeed, her early efforts are so unsuccessful that she several times abandons this goal and goes back to looking for one block long enough to span the river (E, F). Eventually, feedback from the physics of the task shapes her toward discovering that bigger blocks make better substitutes for her hand pressure than smaller ones (though she may not yet realize that it is their weight that is relevant), until she has constructed a counterbalanced bridge.

Step by step, then, this child's goal-driven behaviour gradually exposed her to new feedback from the physics of the task in hand, which then gradually restructured her behaviour until an entirely new and qualitatively different strategy has been formed. This new strategy was not inherent in the child's initial understanding or behaviour, but is now available to be reviewed and reflected on, and in time, explicitly understood. Note that it is not just the child's actions that have changed: her attention has also been directed to the relevance of the size of blocks best used as substitute hands. She ends the task far better placed to attend to, and so learn about, factors relevant to counterbalance. And this qualitative change has been achieved without the need for the child to have any anticipation of the eventual outcome of her problem solving. Each small change in her goals on the way to forming this new strategy made sense to the child, from the perspective she had at the time (see Table 7.2). The crucial factor in the construction of this new strategy was the structure of the physics inherent in the task itself, which constrains both the goals and the actions the child adopts, without the child needing to understand what those physical forces are. Gravity will cause her simple two-span bridges to fall in at step C, whether the child understands gravity or not. And the principles of balance and counterbalance will apply at steps G, H and I , whether the child understands them or not.

The process described by Thornton (1999) is not new: at some level we have always known that the characteristics of tasks shape our problem solving. What has been under-estimated is the power of such apparently simple learning processes in creating the conditions for qualitative changes in the structure of our behaviour and in the factors we attend to in problem solving, and so their power in opening the gateway to qualitative conceptual development.

If simple learning processes have such power in shaping new ideas, why did only one 5-year-old in Thornton's study discover how to build a counterbalanced bridge? Of course, the answer must in part lie in the children themselves: the successful 5-year-old was very persistent in trying to meet each of her sub-goals, but did not persevere endlessly with any one effort. Other 5-year-olds either gave up on fruitful strategies too quickly without exploring them much, or persisted with unfruitful strategies to the exclusion of trying anything else. Getting the right balance between trying new things out and sticking with a strategy is a crucial factor in the development of new strategies (Siegler, 2000).

But analysis of the other 5-year-olds' problem solving in this task shows that very fine-grained details of a child's strategy can greatly alter the feedback the child gets from the task, and so determine the likelihood of making a new discovery. For example, two other 5-year-olds tried to hold spans in place atop their towers, as the child in Table 7.2 did, and so could have received the same useful feedback from the task as she received. But in both cases, the towers these children had built were so unstable that they collapsed. Thus these children received very different feedback, which discouraged them from exploring the avenue so fruitful to the successful child. In both this task and other types of problem solving, some strategies will be more effective in leading to new discoveries than others (Thornton, 1999), and some versions of a task will be richer in feedback likely to trigger strategy change than others.

Social processes in the development of problem solving

Individual problem-solving processes have a rich potential for new discovery which can drive development forward, as we've seen. But these are not the only processes contributing to cognitive development. Much human knowledge and skill is *socially constructed*: that is to say, it is shaped by social and cultural processes rather than being the product of the individual mind working alone.

Observation and imitation

Young children are keen observers of other people and wonderful mimics. Even newborn babies imitate others, suggesting that there is a strong genetic basis for this tendency (Chapters 3, 4 and 9).

Children spontaneously imitate adult activities and skills, apparently for the sheer pleasure of it. The strength of this enthusiasm is obvious from a short trip round a toy store. A high percentage of toys are props to support the imitation of adults: dolls, prams, bottles to imitate child care; 'doctor's bags' with plastic stethoscopes and hypodermics; 'work benches' with hammers, saws and so on. We also teach children how to do things by deliberately encouraging imitation ('Now, watch what I do and then you have a go ....').

It would be hard to over-estimate the importance of what we learn in this way: a great many aspects of the way we think about and approach problem solving are the product of observing and imitating other people.

Collaborating with other children

Children also learn a great deal through interacting with one another, playing together or working together in school. Intriguingly, it seems that even when two children are both fairly inexpert at some task they can sometimes achieve more working on it together than either would working alone (Doise and Mugny, 1984). There has been a great deal of research into exactly how such interactions foster new discoveries, and why some collaborations are fruitful in producing new insight and others aren't.

The traditional view was that a *conflict of ideas* where each child's perception of the way to do things challenges the other's (and particularly where one child's approach was more sophisticated) was the vital stimulus to new discovery (Doise and Hanselmann, 1991; Piaget, 1967). But this turns out not to be the case. The mere existence of different approaches between two children is not enough to ensure that either will learn anything (Glachan and Light, 1982). What matters more is the way the children interact.

The crucial benefit from interacting with another child comes from genuine collaboration and shared decision making. Such collaboration is not always possible: sometimes the children's ideas will simply be too far apart to allow any real meeting of minds. Sometimes the personalities of the children prevent collaboration, with a dominant child simply taking over, or an immature one being unable to provide sufficient concentration. If two children working or playing together can't find a way to share the decision making, neither is likely to gain much from collaborating. The dominant child will take over and do everything his or her way, and so learn exactly what he or she would have learned working alone. The passive child may feel too excluded to really pay much attention, and so may learn nothing at all.

Of the two, the passive child in such a lopsided interaction may actually be the better off, particularly where the dominant child understands more about the task. The passive child can still learn from observation, so long as he or she is able to follow what is happening and understand the dominant child's approach (Doise, 1978). If the dominant child also explains what he or she is doing, the passive child can learn even more. But in some situations the dominant child solves the problem so fast, and explains so little, that the watching child has no opportunity to learn (Doise, 1978). If your experience is anything like mine, you will have suffered just such a situation when someone tries to explain some computer function to you: the expert's fingers fly so fast, and the explanations are so paltry, that you are normally left at least as confused as before, if not more so.

How do children learn from sharing decisions when they do manage to establish a genuine collaboration? Each joint decision is necessarily influenced by both children's starting assumptions and their approaches to the problem. If these views differ, the children are likely to come to compromises which neither would have thought of alone. These compromises in effect disrupt *both* children's approaches, and so expose them to feedback from the task which they would not have encountered alone, and hence provide the opportunity to make discoveries that they would not have made working separately. So enriching is the effect of such new feedback that even two children starting out with very poor strategies can discover a much better one through their collaboration (Glachan and Light, 1982). A great deal of learning and discovery in childhood must derive from collaborative play through this sort of process. It seems likely that a great deal of new discovery in the adult world, including in science, derives from much the same process (D'Andrade, 1995).

Learning from apprenticeship

If children make important discoveries through interacting with their peers, they make still more fundamental developmental progress through interacting with adults or older children more expert than themselves, who often set out, more or less deliberately, to teach the child something or to support the child's own efforts in some way (Rogoff, 1990).

Vygotsky (1978) argued that in fact, joining in and sharing some activity with a more experienced partner is one of the main ways in which children learn to understand the world and to acquire skills, including intellectual and problem-solving skills. It is not simply that the child can learn by watching the more experienced person: sharing the activity actually extends what the child is able to do. For example, a 3-year-old can be very successful in baking cakes, say, when his or her mother is there sharing the activity, even though the child would be very much less successful if left to do it alone. In effect the mother provides a structure for the child's activities: prompting the next step, guiding and supporting the child's effort so that there is no need for the child to have a complete plan or to remember all the activities involved in baking cakes. By providing what Bruner and Wood have called a *scaffold* for the child's behaviour, the parent stretches the child's skills, giving the child the opportunity to make new discoveries and learn new things, until he or she is eventually able to complete the activity alone.

The classic description of this type of *symbiotic* interaction between parent and child is Wertsch's (1979) description of how young children learn to solve jigsaw puzzles by interacting with an adult. Very young children cannot complete even the simplest of puzzles, and may not automatically view such tasks as fun. At first, the adult has to suggest doing a jigsaw, and to foster the idea that this is a pleasurable activity to share. Typically, with a very young child the adult then does most of the work of completing the puzzle: searching for pieces that fit, commenting on progress and what needs to be done next, placing the pieces in position, and encouraging the child to do very specific things such as putting *this* piece right *there*. Gradually the child will understand more and more about solving jigsaw puzzles, and as his or her understanding grows, the adult reduces his or her input, allowing the child to take over more responsibility for solving the problem. As the child begins to evolve plans and to decide what pieces to search for and where to place them, the adult's comments become less directive. For example, the adult might say, 'Is that the right piece?' or 'Try twisting it round' rather than the more didactic 'Here's the next piece' or 'Turn it up the other way'. Eventually the adult offers still more global advice ('Why don't you leave the sky till later?'), as the child begins to move toward jigsaw expertise.

It's worth commenting that a child in such a symbiotic interaction is learning much more than how to solve a jigsaw, or that such activities are fun. By commenting on how well the task is going or on what needs doing next, the adult is also teaching the child higher-order skills and strategies for problem solving at large: how to plan and organize a coherent strategy; how to use analogies in looking for a solution; when to persist and when to give up and try something else; how to be reflective about actions and their effects in the course of problem solving. These are the things the child needs to learn in order to develop a meta-cognitive awareness of reasoning processes and to become able to apply and regulate problem solving effectively across different situations (Vygotsky, 1978). In other words, the adult is scaffolding not just skills specific to the task in hand, but the skills needed to establish executive control over cognitive processes and to establish a general expertise in problem solving.

Adults don't need to learn to scaffold their children's performance in the way described by Vygotsky and Wertsch: it comes naturally. So, for example, McNaughton and Leyland (1990) found that mothers sharing an activity with a 3-year-old spontaneously modify how much support they give to their child to reflect how much difficulty the child is having with the task. The greater the child's difficulty, the more the mother intervenes to help out.

The power of scaffolding to foster development is at its greatest when the adult lures the child into what Vygotsky (1978) calls the *zone of proximal development.* This is the area just beyond, but not too far beyond, the child's present abilities: in other words, the step the child is ready to master next. It's obvious why stretching a child to enter precisely this zone yields the most development. Too small a stretch, and there is too little to learn; too big a stretch, and there is too much to manage. Again, adults seem to instinctively recognize this, and to spontaneously alter the scaffolds they provide to lead the child into the zone of proximal development (McNaughton and Leyland, 1990).

The degree to which a child can learn through scaffolding depends on the adult partner's sensitivity to the child's needs. Some adults are far more sensitive than others (Pratt et al., 1988; Wood, Wood and Middleton, 1978), and so far more effective as teachers. Parents differ not only in their success in gauging the child's zone of proximal development, but also in the style of support they offer. Children learn the most when the adult partner strikes the right balance between nurturing the child's efforts and demanding good progress with the task (Pratt et al., 1988). Parents who clearly describe and demonstrate what needs doing teach their children more than those who do not (Wood et al., 1978). But the crucial factor in the child's success in learning from such interactions is that the adult is able to actually share decision making with the child, rather than simply being didactic or dictatorial, providing what has been called *guided participation* (Radziszewska and Rogoff, 1991).

Even quite young children can create scaffolds for others, and can modify their explanations of things and their behaviour to accommodate the needs of a younger or less skilled child, to some degree. But children are not as adept at this as are adults. For example, Radziszewska and Rogoff (1991) tested how much 9-year-old children would learn about how to plan effective routes between stores on a map either from interacting with an adult or from interacting with another 9-year-old who had already been trained to complete the task efficiently. Children learned more from interacting with the adult, because the adults were far better at explaining their decisions and actions than were the 9-year-old mentors, and far better at sharing the decision making with the pupil. Thus the ability to scaffold a child's learning must itself develop, perhaps out of our increasing ability to understand the child's needs and limitations, however natural the tendency to accommodate to a novice in this way may be.

In conclusion

The processes involved in remembering, in reasoning, solving problems and discovering new ideas are all far more subtle and complex than we imagined 30 years ago. The way we think about these things, the way we try to explain them, have changed dramatically over the last three decades.

Our ability to remember is a reflection of our knowledge and conceptual understanding, the way we use information in reasoning; and it is affected by our goals and emotions, and by factors specific to the situations in which learning or recall occur. It seems from this that memory is not a separate function of the mind as once thought, but rather that remembering is embedded in and emerges from intelligence in action, so that the development of memory is inexorably intertwined with the development of reasoning and conceptual understanding. From this point of view, old analyses of memory in terms of a series of 'stores', and old debates as to the number and kinds of memory store there might be (episodic, semantic, long-term, short-term and so on) and how much information a given store might hold at different ages seem progressively misguided. One prominent researcher has suggested that that approach is now on the 'endangered topics' list (Kuhn, 2000). We need new metaphors, new ways of conceptualizing how remembering works and how it develops.

Microgenetic analyses of individual children's behaviour have changed our view of the way cognitive development progresses: new, more sophisticated strategies emerge more gradually than we thought, existing alongside and competing with older strategies rather than growing out of and superseding those older strategies as was believed. Furthermore, both social processes and feedback from the task in hand play a larger role in supporting and shaping the development of new strategies and new insights than the dominant theory of the 20th century (Piaget's theory) allowed.

Most fundamentally of all, it is now clear that the qualitative changes that characterize cognitive development cannot be explained purely in terms of the action of meta-cognitive processes monitoring and reflecting on ongoing reasoning and abstracting new structures from it, as Piaget and his followers assumed. Rather, the strategies we select in the moment as we address a problem and the discoveries we make as a result of those strategies are the product of a complex interaction between all that we bring to the task (our past experience and knowledge, our general strategies for problem solving, our meta-cognitive processes, our motivations and so on) and the structure of the task itself (the constraints imposed by the physical and social properties of the situation, the feedback these constraints provide). Cognitive development as a whole is the product of the dynamic interactions between the child, the physical and social world across a myriad of problem-solving moments (Lewis, 2000; Sophian, 1997; Thelen and Smith, 1994; Thornton, 1999).

In many ways the research reviewed in this chapter seems to fit very well within the general framework offered by dynamic systems theory, and some researchers are beginning to explicitly apply the assumptions of that approach in exploring the development of cognition (Costa and Izquierdo-Torres, 2006; Thelen and Smith, 1994). Others, however, are more cautious (Bertenthal and Boker, 2004; Wallis, 2003). Dynamic systems theory asserts that behaviour is not only embedded in a social and physical context, but also embodied in our physiological and neurological systems as a whole. Now, at one level, this is obviously true: everything we do depends on bodily systems in some way. But there is debate as to the nature of this interrelationship, in the case of cognition.

Leading advocates of dynamic systems theory argue that cognitive processes are always inextricably interwoven with sensory and motor processes – in other words, that mental activity is always intricately connected to perception and action – in infants and adults alike (Thelen, 2000; Thelen and Smith, 1994). To understand cognition, then, we must always view it in its bodily context, rooted in the physiological processes supporting perception and action. This works well in studies of infant cognition: for example, Thelen presents a convincing case for the idea that the bizarre 'A-not-B' search error typical of 9-month-old babies (see Chapter 3) doesn't reflect a purely conceptual problem as Piaget suggested: the infant's problems in managing looking and reaching play an important role in generating this peculiar behaviour (Thelen et al., 2001). But is cognition always intertwined with perceptual and motor processes in this way, even in adults? Is this a useful way of understanding how ideas are represented in the mind? Will construing cognition as embodied in perception and action help us to understand how a child comes to understand abstract ideas such as 'democracy', say, or to master the procedures of arithmetic? We don't yet know. Researchers sceptical of the dynamic systems approach are not convinced. This debate is likely to continue for many years to come.

Exercises

1. What are the practical implications (for example, for education) of the differences between the linear model of cognitive development (Figure 7.5) and the 'overlapping waves' model (Figure 7.6)?

2. Ask someone unfamiliar with the 'Tower of Hanoi' problem to complete the task, first with three disks, then four, then five. Make a microgenetic analysis of their behaviour. How would you characterize their problem solving? What problems are there in making such an analysis?

3. What ethical issues do you think had to be addressed in running a microgenetic study such as Thornton's (1999) analysis of children's strategies in trying to build a counterbalance bridge?

Suggested further reading

For a review of research on the development of memory in childhood read:

- W. Schneider and D. Bjorklund (1998) Memory. In D. Kuhn and R. Siegler (eds), W. Damon (series ed.), *Handbook of Child Psychology*, vol. 2, *Cognition, Language and Perception*. New York: Wiley.

For a review of research on the development of problem solving including planning and analogy read:

- J. DeLoache, K. Miller and S. Pierroutsakos (1998) Reasoning and problem-solving. In D. Kuhn and R. Siegler (eds), W. Damon (series ed.), *Handbook of Child Psychology,* vol. 2, *Cognition, Language and Perception*. New York: Wiley.

For a discussion of Siegler's theory of cognitive development read:

- R. Siegler (1996) *Emerging Minds: The process of change in children's thinking*. New York: Oxford University Press.

For an analysis of why children's performance in some task must be a key source of conceptual development read:

- C. Sophian (1997) Beyond competence: the significance of performance for conceptual development. *Cognitive Development* 12, pp. 281–303.

For a discussion of social processes in the development of problem solving read:

- B. Rogoff (1998) Cognition as a collaborative process. In D. Kuhn and R. Siegler (eds), W. Damon (series ed.), *Handbook of Child Psychology,* vol. 2, *Cognition, Language and Perception*. New York: Wiley.

Revision summary

The development of memory

- Like every other animal, human babies are born already able to remember.

- Nonetheless, the ability to recall things shows a marked developmental change. In general, the younger the child, the poorer his or her recall. This can't be explained by the theory that the younger child has a weaker or 'smaller' memory.

- In fact, how much we can encode into memory or retrieve in recall is directly affected by our knowledge. The richer our conceptual understanding, the better we can make sense of and structure information and the more easily we can learn it and recall it. This is true for all age groups: it's the way memory works. Where children know more, they recall better than adults. The development of memory reflects the development of conceptual understanding.

- Even in everyday contexts the young child's conceptual structures are less well prepared for recall than those of older children or adults. Autobiographical memories depend on 'scripts' which provide the framework within which we encode events and which we use to cue recall (we have a script for what is involved in going to the dentist, for example). The younger the child, the fewer the scripts that have yet been elaborated, so the less support there is for reminiscence and recall of events. Furthermore, scripts are encoded in language. Events that occur before the child has learned to speak are not encoded in this way, and so are very much harder to recall. This accounts for the curious phenomenon of 'early childhood amnesia' – the universal inability to recall things that happened before about 3 years of age, when we learn to speak.

- Impoverished scripts and poor conceptual understanding may contribute to the unreliability of child eyewitness statements: recall is not a matter of simply pulling a memory out of store, it always involves an active process of reconstruction. Our reconstructions tend to drift in the direction that makes best sense to us. A young child's reconstruction of a rape is not informed by the same understanding as that of an adult, and will drift in a different way.

- But recall is also affected by many other factors, including the social mores, constraints and pressures of the situation (what others expect, allow, want you to recall). The younger the child, the more susceptible he or she is to such influences.

- In addition, children recall best what is of personal interest to them, what makes sense. The very young may sometimes perform poorly in memory tasks because they simply can't see the point of the task, and so never really get involved.

- There are very marked developmental changes in the child's tendency to deliberately use mnemonic strategies (such as rehearsing, grouping like with like) to assist recall, particularly in experimental situations. Even 7-year-olds often fail to use mnemonic strategies that are quite within their scope, and which have produced improved recall when imposed by a teacher or researcher.

- The developmental change in the tendency to use mnemonic strategies reflects developmental change in the child's insight into how memory works, and into the limitations of memory. The young child overestimates his or her ability to remember and shows little sign of understanding what strategies will help or where it is best to use such strategies. Awareness of, and a progressive ability to deliberately deploy, strategies to assist performance (meta-cognitive awareness) develops through later childhood.

The development of problem solving

- What we know affects the rules or procedures we use in problem solving. Studies of this knowledge in action reveal that success or failure in a task is always the result of the interaction between the detail of these procedures and the detail of the task, explaining one way in which a given level of knowledge can yield success in some versions of a task and failure in other versions. Furthermore, better understanding doesn't always mean more success: it depends on the task details. This explains the puzzling phenomenon of apparent regressions in skill found in many tasks.

- The ability to plan in problem solving also depends fundamentally on knowledge of the tasks in hand. In situations where we have no relevant knowledge or experience, even adults must rely on trial and error in searching for the solution to a problem, rather than more sophisticated 'means–ends' analyses. This situation befalls younger children more often than older children or adults, since the younger child has less experience in most situations.

- The success of means–ends analysis also depends on the extent of the individual's knowledge: more experience with a task can greatly reduce the difficulty of planning, either by allowing the retrieval of the plan that worked last time rather than needing a new analysis, or by structuring the problem in ways that readily suggest solutions. The novice lacks these fruits of knowledge and so must construct a plan from scratch, a very much more demanding task. The younger the child, the more likely he or she is to be a novice in any planning task.

- Through experience children develop not only knowledge of how to solve particular problems, but of how to go about problem solving in general. There is thus a developmental increase in the degree to which problem solving can be controlled and managed, and to which skills can be generalized across situations.

- A very powerful tool for generalizing skills comes from the ability to draw analogies. Again, this ability depends on possession of sufficient knowledge to be able to make relevant connections across different situations. Even the very young can draw analogies where they have the relevant knowledge. As knowledge grows through childhood, the range and power of analogy develops.

The process of development

- Microgenetic analyses of problem solving have given us a new perspective on the process of problem solving: how new discoveries are made, and how children's strategies evolve toward more adult and sophisticated forms.

- Cognitive development is not a smooth process. Naïve strategies are not necessarily the progenitors of more sophisticated ones, and are not necessarily abandoned when a better strategy is discovered. Development involves the generation of new strategies, and the gradual shaping of strategy selection toward a consistent use of the best strategy. Feedback from the task itself plays a vital role in both processes: providing the vector through which new information can alter a child's actions and so create the basis for new conceptual insight, and providing information on which of several strategies works best.

- New discovery and learning also come through social processes. Children learn through observing and imitating others. They also learn from one another: two children collaborating well can discover things neither would discover alone. But cognitive development is also deliberately 'scaffolded': supported and directed through shared activities between adult and child which teach not only specific skills, but also the meta-cognitive skills needed in controlling the mind effectively.

- The evidence suggests that cognitive development emerges from complex interactions between the child and the physical and social world he or she engages. Will dynamic systems theory provide new insights into this process?

8
individual differences in cognition

Every normal child recalls past events, develops a rich conceptual understanding of the world, learns to speak, to reason, to plan and to solve problems. But within this universal framework there are very marked differences in the way individual minds function. Faced with the same information two minds may come up with very different interpretations. Given the same problem to solve, two minds may make very different plans for solving it and may find very different strategies.

To a large extent the way individuals of a given age or of different ages reason reflects their experience and knowledge of the world, of the task in question and of mental processes themselves (as we've seen through Chapters 6 and 7). These factors affect individual differences too, as will be discussed in more detail later in this chapter. But beyond these 'knowledge' effects there are other differences between individuals, for example in their persistence and flexibility of mind (Thornton, 1999; see Chapter 7), and in the apparent sheer power of reasoning that one person or another brings to a task: some of us just seem to be quicker on the uptake than others. Do such differences reflect a difference in general intelligence? What determines how intelligently a given mind will function? What goes wrong when a child fails to develop normal intelligence? And what is involved in creativity or genius? These are the questions addressed in this chapter.

Individual differences and IQ

What's the first thought that comes to your mind, when you see someone present a brilliant essay at a seminar or solve a tricky problem adeptly, or conversely, watch another individual stumble ineptly through these activities? Almost as a reflex we attribute a high level of intelligence to the first person and a lower IQ to the second. This way of conceptualizing the differences between the individuals seems natural, obvious. But it's important to realize that this is a relatively modern perception. The whole concept of IQ would have been novel and surprising less than a century and a half ago.

The theory that individual human minds can be characterized as having a given level of general intelligence is just that – a *theory*, not a fact. It's a theory we need to examine closely: a theory that is controversial, and which has been accused of causing confusion and damage, of being more trouble than it's worth. It's one of the few theories in psychology that has actually caused riots! As scientists, we need a clear understanding of exactly what this theory is and how useful it is, both in explaining the phenomena to which it relates and in its power of predicting individual potential and development.

The concept of IQ

Historical origins

Just before the start of the 20th century, Francis Galton (1892) observed that abilities seemed to run in families: thus one family might produce talented writers, thinkers or musicians in successive generations where another family consistently produced individuals with little apparent ability in any area. Such observations led him to the hypothesis that there is a general capability for learning and reasoning, inherited from our parents, which varies between individuals and which characterizes each individual's overall level of mental ability through life. This hypothetical innate capacity is 'intelligence'.

Galton's observations led to the new science of *psychometrics*, which aimed to construct tests that would measure the level of intelligence possessed by a given individual. The intention behind this was benign: by measuring the innate potential of a child's mind these tests were supposed to allow us to identify, and so to rescue, able children performing badly through lack of opportunity to learn, or to make special provision for those without the innate ability to learn. Psychometrics could separate the potential high flier from the plodder, and so allow us to provide the optimal education or career for each. Through psychometric testing we could, in other words, fit round pegs to round holes and square pegs to square ones, and thereby save a lot of wasted effort, frustration and human misery.[1]

A psychometric definition of intelligence

Whereas research into cognitive development began from questions about what the processes that underlie intelligent behaviour might be and how these might change through childhood (Chapters 6 and 7), psychometrics focused on searching for ways of measuring the relative intelligence of one individual compared with another. Psychometric researchers paid more or less no attention to the invisible mental processes that underlie intelligent behaviour, and provided no definition

---

[1] The potential for such well-meaning ideas to spawn the less benign ideas behind Nazi eugenics, racism or the *Brave New World* Huxley's novel warns of is the root of much of the hostility to the IQ concept.

of intelligence in terms of those processes. For psychometric research, 'intelligence' was defined solely as 'what intelligence tests measure'.

Intelligence tests were constructed in a very pragmatic way, by collecting together items that people who are socially judged to be highly intelligent would answer differently from those who are socially judged to be of lower intelligence. These might include tests of memory, of verbal comprehension, spatial skills, pattern detection, general knowledge and the like. The whole focus was on creating a tool (an *intelligence test*) that would allow us to rank-order individual minds in terms of their innate power.

IQ scores

An IQ score is not simply the number of items you got right (your 'raw score') on an intelligence test. Rather, it's an interpretation of an individual's score in the light of the scores obtained in the comparable population as a whole. So, for example, in the case of children, IQ is the child's score in relation to other children of the same age. To understand how this works we have to understand something about the statistical concepts of a normal distribution and a standard deviation (SD).

Many human characteristics (including scores on IQ tests) are *normally distributed* through the population: that is to say, if we plot the distribution of scores on those characteristics we get a graph like the one depicted in **Figure 8.1**. Notice that the scores fall symmetrically around the mean, and that there are fewer and fewer scores the further we go away from the mean. In fact (by definition), 68 per cent of scores in a normal distribution are one standard deviation away from the mean, half of them being above the mean and half below it. A further 27 per cent of scores are two standard deviations from the mean, again, half above and half below it. Just over 4 per cent of scores are three standard deviations from the mean and a tiny fraction are four standard deviations away. These statistical properties are the basis of the interpretation of the scores on an IQ test.

In the early days of psychometric testing it was decided that the *average* IQ would be scored as 100. Thus, any individual who scored exactly the mean score (for his or her age) on a test would be assigned an IQ of 100. It's important to remember that this score is not an absolute measure of ability: it's a score that places the individual relative to a population. It turns out that the mean raw score on IQ tests goes up in successive generations, a phenomenon known as the Flynn effect (Herrnstein and Murray, 1994 – see **Box 8.1**). IQ test manuals are regularly updated to register this fact: the scoring is changed so that an IQ of 100 is always assigned to whatever the mean raw score currently may be. Thus an IQ of 100 always means that the individual is exactly in the middle of the range of intelligence, with 50 per cent of the population scoring higher and 50 per cent scoring lower.

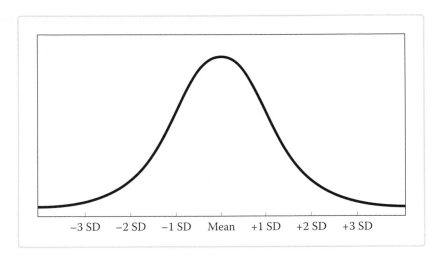

figure **8.1**

The normal distribution curve

box **8.1**

The Flynn effect: systematic changes in average IQs

The Flynn effect, named by Herrnstein and Murray (1994) after the New Zealand political scientist who first noticed it, is the year-on-year rise in scores on intelligence tests. The effect has been observed all round the world, although to varying degrees, often being higher in previously disadvantaged societies. On average there has been a 3-point rise in scores every decade, so that mean intelligence scores have improved a whole standard deviation since 1945 – a fact now taken into account in scoring IQs. This effect may have ended in some societies (Teasdale and Owen, 2005) including Britain, and may even be going into reverse, with mean scores dropping over time.

Various explanations for the Flynn effect have been proposed, including the idea that it reflects better nutrition or schooling, or the radically more stimulating environment provided by the progressive explosion in information technology from radio to television to internet over the past 50 years. No explanation that clearly fits the data has yet been found (for example, the effect occurs in societies where nutritional standards haven't changed as well as those where they have changed). Reasons for the reverse in the Flynn effect are even more obscure, although Teasdale and Owen suggest that this might reflect changes in the rates of entry into certain types of educational programme.

Whatever the specific factors involved, the Flynn effect and reversals in this effect are generally believed to reflect environmental factors rather than any change in the human genetic pool: the effect has simply been too swift to be genetic.

The standard deviation of most IQ tests is 15 points. That is to say, 68 per cent of the population will produce scores within 15 points of the mean, 34 per cent scoring up to 15 points above the mean and 34 per cent scoring up to 15 points below the mean. Equally, a further 27 per cent will score between 15 and 30 points of the mean, 13.5 per cent scoring between 15 and 30 points above and 13.5 per cent below the mean, and so on. Thus a child who scored 45 points below the mean score would be assigned an IQ of 55 (100 −45 = 55), and would score lower than 98 per cent of the population, just as a child who scored 45 points above the mean would have an IQ of 145 (100 + 45 = 145) and would be in the top 2 per cent of the population. An individual whose IQ is 115 has scored 15 points more than the mean, higher than 84 per cent of the population.

Does general intelligence exist?

Galton and his followers believed that intelligence is a very general feature of the mind: that an individual's relative power and quality of reasoning is the same across any situation, reflecting the same IQ, the operation of the same general intelligence (known as 'g') in every situation. The data are not entirely compatible with this view.

The level of ability an individual shows in one task does tend to correlate with the level he or she shows in another, as the theory of general intelligence predicts that it should (Anderson, 1992). But the correlation is not very strong: not as strong as you would expect if intelligence were a general function responsible for the calibre of our performance across tasks. The pattern of an individual's abilities can be very patchy. For example, you may be very good at solving verbal puzzles, but fairly poor at solving spatial ones. Or you may be good at science subjects but terrible at learning languages, and so on. This uneven pattern of abilities is actually the norm (Gardner, 1983). It suggests that there are a number of different factors at work in determining the calibre of our performance across different types of task, rather than simply a single unified general intelligence or 'g'.

One possible explanation for the patchiness of an individual's performance across different kinds of task is that 'g' itself has more than one dimension: a verbal fluency component, perhaps, and a spatial reasoning component (Spearman, 1927; Thurstone, 1938). Some theorists argued that 'g' has a great many components: for example, Guildford (1967, 1988) suggested that intelligence has 180 separate components, and that an individual's mental abilities reflect his or her profile across all of these. Other researchers have argued that, rather than reflecting an individual's profile across sub-components of 'g', variable performance across different types of task reflects the existence of a range of quite separate intelligences, each such 'module' being specifically evolved to deal with a particular area (Gardner, 1983; Howe, 1989). For example, Gardner suggests that we may have seven quite separate innate modules for linguistic, spatial, logico-mathematical, musical, social, self-regulating and physical skills.

The suggestion that we may have a number of separate biologically programmed intelligences has also been investigated by researchers studying the processes underlying cognitive development, who point to the newborn baby's precocious skill in (for example) social responsiveness, language, number, planning or inference as possible evidence for such modules (Chapters 3, 4, 5, 6). But whereas cognitive developmental research explored the possibility of modules as the universal foundations of conceptual development (that is, as the mechanism that kick-starts development in all children), psychometric research focuses on modular intelligences as the origins of individual differences in one skill or another, and as the explanation for the unevenness of skills within the individual: suggesting that we can inherit a strong language module but a weak mathematical module (for instance), or that the strength of your maths module and mine may be different even if our language module is the same.

The notion that the mind is modular in this way is very controversial in both lines of research. It's far from clear, for example, exactly what this would mean, or exactly what evidence would support or refute the hypothesis. Nor is it entirely clear that we need to postulate the existence of different kinds of intelligence to explain patchiness in performance across tasks. We already know that the competence and sophistication of an individual's reasoning reflects his or her knowledge in relation to the particular task in hand, and that knowledge does not develop evenly across all areas (Chapters 6 and 7). Some researchers believe that this is enough to explain why an individual's performance varies from one type of task to another. Others argue that, even allowing for this 'knowledge effect', some individuals seem to have a far greater natural aptitude for learning in a given area than others do: that not every child given Mozart's upbringing would have been capable of his musical genius, that a Mozart can only be explained by the existence of some special degree of innate musical intelligence.

Whether or not there are multiple separate intelligences as Gardner and Howe suggest, the fact remains that performance across very different types of task does show a clear degree of correlation, and this must be explained. Is there some underlying general intelligence that accounts for this correlation, even if other factors (whether knowledge and experience alone or modular intelligences) also affect performance in different areas?

Teasing out factors in intelligence

Many of the items on early IQ tests required knowledge in specific areas to complete successfully (for example, knowledge of word meanings, or the practical knowledge needed to draw analogies, or the procedural knowledge needed to solve mathematical or logical puzzles, or even 'test sophistication': the knowledge that the apparent absurdity of a test question should be ignored, an acceptance of the legitimacy of 'trick' questions). In a real sense, such items do not test the child's inherent capability in any particular area, still less any general capability. Rather, what they measure is the child's past experience and opportunities to learn. This is problematic at both a theoretical and a pragmatic level: the more the items in a test 'load'[2] on prior knowledge, the more likely it is that patchiness in a child's experience will throw up unevenness in performance across different types of item, obscuring the action and existence of any general factor in intelligence ('g'). And the more performance on an IQ test depends on prior experience, opportunities to learn and knowledge, the less it provides a fair test of the relative abilities of individuals from different backgrounds or different cultures. In sum, knowledge-dependent tests are not *culture-fair*: that is to say, not an equal test for children from different social backgrounds, still less for children from different cultures.

Recognizing this fact, Cattell (1963) proposed that intelligence should be conceptualized as having two major components or factors: *crystallized* intelligence, which reflects the knowledge and skill the individual has acquired and is therefore very much influenced by cultural advantages and experiences; and *fluid* intelligence, reflecting the pure intellectual capacity of the individual. Cattell argued that these two factors can be measured by different kinds of item. By careful control, fluid intelligence can be measured in a way uncontaminated by cultural advantages or experiences – in other words, by a 'culture-fair' IQ test.

It's not clear just how possible it is, in fact, to produce a genuinely culture-fair IQ test. For instance, typical measures of fluid intelligence use a series of puzzles like the one shown in **Figure 8.2**, which test the ability to detect visual patterns. Tests of this sort seem to require an absolute minimum of knowledge or experience, and so to present a 'pure' measure of the inherent power of the individual's mental processing ('g'). But even a test item like this is not entirely free of the effects of experience and specific knowledge. For example, IQ tests like Raven's Progressive Matrices require you to solve as many such puzzles as possible as quickly as you can, which involves knowing how to trade off speed and accuracy in an appropriate way. Ten-year-olds from middle-class Western backgrounds have a 'script' for being tested and know how to make this trade-off. Ten-year-olds or even adults from other cultures may know far less about the 'rules of the testing game', and may produce poorer performances simply through not knowing how to make this trade-off. And in any case, what is it that a test of fluid intelligence should be aiming to measure? Traditional psychometrics provides no definition. An answer to this question would make it a great deal easier to establish how best to measure this factor more accurately.

---

[2] 'Load' in this context means depend on, correlate with. The term 'loading' of an item on factors such as prior knowledge derives from the statistical process of 'factor analysis', which establishes correlations between sub-items in a test.

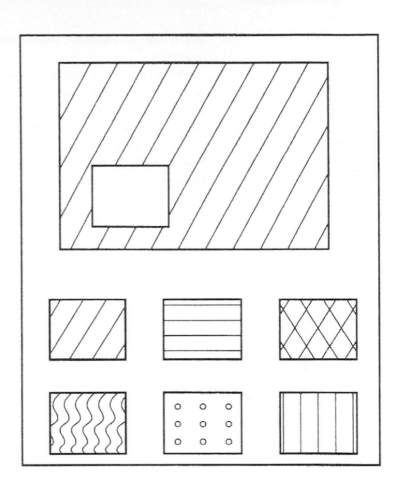

figure **8.2**

A visual puzzle of the kind used in
Raven's Progressive Matrices

A new theory of intelligence

Anderson (1992) argues that there is a basic processing mechanism underlying intelligence, the efficacy of which differs between individuals. Just as individuals inherit different physiological characteristics which affect our height, metabolism and so on, so we inherit neuro-physiological characteristics which determine the speed and efficiency with which connections are made in the brain. According to Anderson, these inherited neuro-physiological differences are the source of variation in general intelligence, since the speed and efficiency of this basic processor (which is, in effect, very similar to the concept of working memory discussed in Chapter 7) affects all cognitive activity. Inherited differences mean that some individuals can process information faster than others, and can process more information before their working memory becomes overloaded. The faster you process information and the more information you can process, the more complex the processing you can do, the more you can learn, and the better you can reason. The basic speed and efficiency of the individual's processing system would affect his or her performance across almost all tasks, thus yielding a fairly generalized basis for intelligence.

Theories such as Anderson's would explain why there is a degree of correlation between an individual's success in one area of cognitive skills and another: an element of 'g' reflected in our performances across different situations. However, Anderson argues that not all mental activity involves the basic processor, and that the efficiency of the basic processor is not sufficient to explain all the individual differences we observe in the ease of mastering particular skills.

In some cases, we see far less variation between individuals than we would expect, if all mental performances drew on this basic 'working memory' processor. For example, even children with severe cognitive disabilities are adept at interpreting visual depth cues, even though we might assume that this is quite a complex process: it involves translating two-dimensional images on the retina into three-dimensional objects. Anderson suggests that the lack of individual differences in seeing depth comes from the fact that this basic perceptual process is handled by a special pre-set module in the brain which needs no intelligent processing to function, and so does not draw on the power of basic working memory. And in fact, there is strong evidence that infants are born with quite a range of pre-set perceptual skills of this kind, as has been discussed in Chapter 3 (Slater, 1997).

In other cases, pure measures of the power of the basic processor cannot predict individual differences because the skills concerned draw on specific processes for reasoning in that particular domain. Anderson argues that there are specific processors for abilities such as verbal reasoning or spatial processing, mathematics, music and the like. Each individual has these specialized processors, but the speed and efficiency of each specific processor varies between one individual and another. Anderson argues that these specialized processors do not act alone. They are not truly separate modules of the mind, therefore. They draw on the central basic processor. Thus any given ability – in mathematics, say – will reflect the combined strengths or weaknesses of *both* the basic processor *and* the specialist processor, to yield the rich patterns of variation in ability we see between individuals.

Anderson's model of intelligence is innovative and in many ways coherent. It reflects a move away from research that simply tries to measure a hypothetical intelligence, and towards an approach more rooted in understanding the processes by which individuals actually process information. However, it is still within the historic tradition begun by Galton, in that it still assumes that the central element determining the intelligence of an individual's behaviour can be defined in terms of innate, stable properties of the power of his or her mental system in itself. For Anderson, the best test of general intelligence is a pure measure of processing speed.

Measuring processing speed

There are a number of ways of testing processing speed across individuals: for example, by using reaction-time (RT) tasks in which the speed of response to some stimulus can be measured in milliseconds. Historically such tasks asked the participant to make a motor response to the stimulus: pressing a button for instance, or calling out. More recent methods use 'evoked potentials' to measure reaction time: here, electrodes attached to the head monitor electrical activity in the brain (creating an EEG or electro-encephalogram trace), and the reaction time measured is the time between the presentation of a stimulus (flashing a light in the eyes, say, or sounding a buzzer) and evocation of the electrical spike in brain activity in response to the stimulus.

Individuals do vary in reaction speeds. However, it is still a matter of debate whether processing speed really is the best measure of general intelligence: for example, some studies find only a low correlation between evoked potential latencies (that is, speeds) and scores on tests of even fluid intelligence (Widaman et al., 1993). There is as yet no evidence that differences between individuals in the capacity to function intelligently in any task (still less a school career) can be predicted on the basis of processing speed alone.

Individual variation in intelligence and genetics

Is an individual's capacity to function intelligently genetically specified? This is an emotive question because it has become entangled with questions about racial differences, and with muddled thinking about what the implications of a correlation between intelligence and race might mean.

Leaving political issues to one side, the evidence is clear: cognitive abilities *can* be selectively bred for, implying that there is indeed a genetic component in intelligence. For example, Tryon (1940) tested rats for their ability to find their way through mazes. He identified two groups of rats, 'maze bright' and 'maze dull', and bred the bright with the bright, and the dull with the dull. Over a few generations the offspring of the bright rats systematically outperformed the offspring of the dull rats in running mazes. This was so even where the offspring were swapped round so that the bright babies were fostered by the dull parents and vice versa, so the effect was genetic, rather than to do with parenting.

Every aspect of a human being must have a genetic basis of some sort. We grow into baby human beings rather than kittens or ducklings through the unfolding of our genetic blueprint. Quite a lot of the variation between one human body and another is plainly inherited, so that tall dark-haired parents are more likely to produce tall dark-haired children rather than short blond ones. However, it cannot be the case that any cognitive ability is *entirely* inherited.

Even physical properties such as our height are affected by the environment in which we grow up and by our experiences. Poor nutrition can stunt the growth, and good nutrition can enhance it. Childhood illnesses and infections can also reduce growth and affect our adult height. The steady increases in the height of European and American populations over the centuries reflect the rise in living standards and reduction of disease rather than a genetic change in the population. The current generation of teenagers is the tallest ever, reflecting the vast explosion of preventive medicine and access to foodstuffs of the past 20 years: far too short a period to reflect genetic change. In the same way, intelligence is quite plainly affected by experience and environment. For example, children who have been severely malnourished show a marked decrease in intelligence. Those deprived of appropriate stimulation show clear decreases in the basic ability to learn. Thus the issue for research is not whether intelligence is inherited as opposed to being formed by our experience and environment: both *must* be involved. But even the question of how much nature and nurture contribute to intelligence is harder to answer than you might think (Petrill et al., 1998).

Identical twins develop from a single genetic code (since they develop from the same egg) and have much more similar levels of intelligence than do less genetically similar individuals, as we would expect if there were a clear element of heritability in intelligence. Likewise, adopted children's intelligence correlates more highly with that of the biological parents than with that of their adoptive parents, pointing to a clear hereditary element in intelligence. But even in identical twins, the correlation in intelligence is far from perfect, showing that intelligence is not entirely inherited, but is affected by other things.

Can we calculate what proportion of intelligence is inherited, and what proportion is due to the environment or experience? No: or at least, not in any generally meaningful way. This is because the relative importance of each factor will vary, reflecting the situation. Imagine a science fiction world where every child somehow has exactly the same experiences. In such a world, the relative lack of variation in the environment means that differences between individuals will almost entirely reflect genetic factors, and intelligence will appear to be very highly heritable. Or imagine a world in which a set of cloned children are each reared in vastly different environments. Here, the lack of genetic variation will mean that differences between the individual children will entirely reflect environmental factors, and intelligence will appear to be due to environmental factors. Of course, neither of the extreme worlds imagined here actually exists (yet). But the problem this 'thought experiment' reveals applies to measures of the heritability of intelligence. How much individual variation in intelligence seems to reflect genes depends on how much variation there is in the environment and in the gene pool in which the measure is taken. No absolute measure is possible.

Estimates of the heritability of intelligence are thus always relative to a given situation, reflecting both the degree of variation in the environment and the degree of genetic variation in the population studied in that environment. This may explain why estimates of heritability vary between 40 per cent and 80 per cent (Herrnstein and Murray, 1994). But many researchers argue that it scarcely matters what the heritability of intelligence may be in any case: even if it was 100 per cent heritable, the intelligence of individuals would still be modifiable by experience and education, just as any other inherited characteristic can be modified by events or experience (Anastasi and Urbina, 1997). And since the malleability of intelligence is not constrained by its heritability, heritability has no practical implications (Wahlsten, 1997).

Does intelligence develop through childhood?

In one sense intelligence obviously develops through childhood, as we have seen in previous chapters. A 5-year-old child is capable of a range of intelligent behaviour far beyond the powers of a 2-year-old, but far less than that of the average 12-year-old. Those components of intelligent action that reflect learning and experience change powerfully as the child grows older. However, Anderson (1992) argues that the power of an individual's basic processing mechanism (its relative speed and efficiency) does not change through childhood. In effect, his thesis is that an individual's basic mental ability is a constant.

Testing Anderson's thesis is quite difficult, in that it is hard to find tests of mental ability that are directly comparable across younger and older individuals. Usually, intelligence in infancy is measured by comparing the individual child's progress on various developmental milestones with that of the average child. For example, the Bayley Scales of Infant Development (Bayley, 1969, 1993) look at the child's motor skills (such as grasping and throwing objects), mental skills (such as searching for a hidden object, following instructions) and behaviours (such as goal directedness, social responsivity). Each child is given a development quotient (DQ), with a DQ of 100 representing average progress, DQ scores above 100 reflecting accelerated development, and those below 100 reflecting developmental delay behind the average. However, DQ scores do not correlate with the scores the child will later achieve on IQ tests (Honzik, 1983). Since what DQ tests measure is very different from the abstract reasoning power measured by IQ tests, or from the pure processing power proposed as the root of intelligence by Anderson, this is perhaps not surprising. More recent research has tried to make more direct estimates of basic processing power in infants, for example by measuring how fast 6-month-old babies habituate to a novel stimulus, and how much they prefer novel stimuli over familiar ones (Thompson, Fagan and Fulker, 1991). Such measures show a better correlation (0.46, on average) with IQ in childhood.

Do studies of older children's scores of intelligence tests support the idea that levels of intelligence remain fairly constant through life? For example, Honzik, Macfarlane and Allen (1948) followed 250 children from the ages of 4 to 18 years, testing their intelligence at regular intervals. The shorter the interval between testing, the greater the similarity in the IQ score achieved: so, for example, scores achieved at age 4 show a correlation of only 0.42 with scores achieved at age 18, whereas scores achieved at age 8 show a correlation of 0.88 with those achieved at age 10. But the low correlation between scores at ages 4 and 18 years is hard to interpret, since IQ tests are far less reliable for very young children than they are for older ones. And indeed, there is an impressive correlation (0.61) between IQ scores obtained at age 6 and those at age 18, suggesting a powerful stability in IQ through childhood.

However, Honzik and colleagues' data present the average relationship between IQ scores across a group of children. Other studies have looked at what happens to IQ scores for an individual child, and these data paint a rather different picture. For example, McCall, Applebaum and Hogarty (1973) found that, between the ages of 2½ and 17, more than half of the children studied showed changes in IQ, with the average change being over 28 IQ points. Twenty children out of 140 showed changes in IQ score of over 40 points in this study! These data suggest that IQ may be quite stable for some children, but fluctuate strongly for others.

Of course, the finding that IQ fluctuates within an individual child over time need not necessarily challenge Anderson's view that the speed and efficiency of the basic processor remains constant through childhood. The IQ tests used by Honzik and colleagues, and by McCall and colleagues, were traditional IQ tests, and not pure measures of processing speed as such. Scores on traditional IQ tests reflect many factors besides processing speed or efficiency, including motivation, confidence and learning (Cattell's 'crystallized knowledge'). The fluctuations in IQ reported by McCall and colleagues may reflect more changes in the individual's *performance* than in his or her basic ability to learn. This conclusion is reinforced by Honzik and colleagues' finding that the children in their study who showed the least stable IQ scores were from unstable home environments, whose life experiences would be less consistent than their peers, and who might well have experienced more fluctuations in factors likely to affect their cognitive performance (such as motivation or self-confidence) than their contemporaries from more stable environments.

Predicting future performance from measures of IQ

Originally, the concept of intelligence gained its popularity because it led to the construction of tests which could allow educationalists to identify children who were going to struggle with normal school work

(Binet and Simon, 1916). Certainly, those who scored very poorly on intelligence tests seemed to have very general problems, not just in education, but in many aspects of everyday life (Ross et al., 1985). At the other end of the spectrum, extremely able individuals who scored very highly on intelligence tests were found to achieve high levels of success across a wide range of measures (Terman, 1954). For example, Terman found that individuals scoring over 140 on IQ tests (gifted individuals) were systematically healthier, happier, better paid and more successful in their careers than those with average IQs.

These data seem to suggest that intelligence tests can be useful in predicting how well individuals will perform on various tasks, and through life. But this conclusion is more controversial than you might think. First, the two groups noted above are at the very extremes of the intelligence scale. It is scarcely surprising that individuals who are classed as 'learning disabled' should generally show consistent and markedly lower performance across more or less every task than those identified as 'normal' or 'gifted'. But in fact, even this apparently obvious conclusion must be handled with caution.

For example, Ross and colleagues (1985) followed up men who had been classified as retarded on the basis of IQ scores averaging 67, and who had been placed in special education for the retarded. Although in mid-life these individuals had lower incomes, poorer housing and poorer social relationships than their non-retarded peers or siblings, the differences were not as great as you might have predicted. For example, 29 per cent of the 'retarded' men held jobs in the retail trade or were skilled workers, compared with 32 per cent of their non-retarded siblings. Only 18 per cent of 'retarded' individuals were in fairly unskilled jobs, compared with 13 per cent of their non-retarded siblings. The major effect of this mild level of retardation was to create a bias away from professional or managerial jobs, towards semi-skilled or clerical ones relative to non-retarded peers. This is scarcely surprising, considering that the 'retarded' group had been given special education premised on low expectations of their achievements, and so in effect had been denied the educational opportunities offered to their siblings.

Ross and colleagues' results suggest that relatively low IQ need not be a bar to normal life, and that individuals with low IQs may blend with the normal population more easily than we expect. These data can, of course, be criticized: for example, as we have seen, IQ scores can fluctuate through childhood, and may reflect a child's performance on a given day, or his or her general life experiences rather than any consistent underlying ability. Some of those sent to special education may have been wrongly assigned low IQs. But the key point to note is that an IQ score is not sufficient to predict an individual's future achievement.

This point is also underlined by Terman's study of gifted children. All the children enrolled in his study had comparable and very high IQs, averaging around 150. One group of these children went on to show consistently high IQ, and to be successful in most aspects of life. Another group showed a marked decline in their IQ scores, their academic achievements and their later success in life. Those who were consistently successful came from stable homes with more intellectual stimulation and support than those who showed a decline. Twice as many of the latter group came from homes where there had been a divorce or other family disruption, and they were twice as likely to be divorced themselves.

Thus neither very high, nor very low scores on IQ tests are *sufficient* to predict how successful or happy an individual's life will be. The same is true in the average range of IQs: there is only a very modest correlation (about 0.3) between occupational success and IQ in the general population (Kline, 1991).

There is some correlation between an individual's present IQ score and his or her success in school. On average, the correlation is around 0.50 (Minton and Schneider, 1980). IQ scores are also fairly good at predicting future performance in school (Crano, Kenny and Campbell, 1972). However, it's important to remember that these correlations reflect the *average* over a group of children. An individual child's achievements might be very different from what you would expect from his or her IQ, as Terman's study of gifted children and Ross and colleagues' study of low-IQ children show. Thus an IQ score alone should never be used to predict or shape an individual's future.

Intelligence as an explanation of individual differences

If IQ can't predict the performance of individual children, can it explain why individual differences in cognitive abilities exist? To answer this question, we must pause and think a little about what we mean by an explanation.

Let's take a simple example. My son and I each have a propelling pencil. Mine is an entirely functional thing, made by a mass manufacturer and bought for a few pounds. His (as befits a stylish young man) is a thing of beauty, made by a specialist company, and probably cost enough to run a small house for a fortnight. If I tell you that his pencil works wonderfully, that the lead feeds down obediently to a twist of the cap and never jams or breaks, but that I spend hours wrestling with mine, unable to extrude a new lead or finding it stuck or broken, I'm sure you will not be in the least surprised. You'll probably think, you get what you pay for! Things with big price tags normally work better than things with small ones. And of course, this is a direct analogy with IQ scores: people with 'big ones' normally work better than people with 'small ones'. But is the price tag (or IQ score) a useful explanation of why the pencils (or brains) work differently?

Certainly, there is a *correlation* between what you pay for a propelling pencil and how well it works. But the correlation is not perfect: some expensive pencils are duds, and some cheap ones work just fine. It is not the *price in itself* that causes the pencil to work well or badly. So the price may be a *marker* letting us predict (more or less) how well the pencil will work, but it does not *explain* why one pencil works better than the other. To understand that, you have to take the two pencils to pieces and examine how they work. The expensive one has been made more carefully, and each mechanism inside it fits very well with every other, and works efficiently as a result. The cheap pencil has been mass produced, and the mechanisms inside it don't quite fit together tightly enough, and so it often doesn't work very well. To explain how something works, you have to understand the process or mechanism that makes it work.

IQ scores, whether they are from traditional tests or from tests of basic processing efficiency of the kind Anderson describes, are like price tags on propelling pencils. They provide markers which allow us to predict (but less well than you might suppose, as we have seen) individual differences in cognitive abilities. But the psychometric concept of intelligence is not enough to explain why such differences exist. Even if IQ were a perfect measure of an individual's *potential* ability (which it clearly is not), an individual's *actual* achievements will depend very strongly on a wide range of factors. However fast your basic processor, you still need to learn the rules before you can play chess, for example. However good your innate specific processor for musical skills, you cannot develop such skills without exposure to music and the opportunity to learn and discover in that area. And if your early efforts are met with praise and success, you are likely to persist with a task and learn more than if someone criticizes or tells you you're bad at it. Motivation and application can be as important as opportunity to learn or basic processing efficiency in determining individual differences in achievement. Indeed, motivation, experience and opportunity may yield greater explanatory power than processing speed in both predicting and accounting for achievement. As we all know intuitively, a potentially gifted child who does little or no work on a given topic will not outshine an industrious plodder.

Thus to *explain* individual differences in cognitive abilities, we need to look very directly as the detail of the processes by which individuals learn, make discoveries and approach reasoning or problem solving. Traditional IQ tests and concepts of intelligence do not do this. Some researchers (Howe, 1989) believe that the whole notion of IQ has distracted research from where it ought to be focused, namely directly on the processes yielding individual differences in particular levels of achievement. The psychometric concept of intelligence alone cannot possibly explain the rich variety of differences we see across individuals. Howe argues that psychology took a wrong turning: instead of inventing the idea of intelligence as a general property of the individual mind, we should all along have focused on understanding how intelligent behaviour is produced through the interaction of a diverse range of processes.

Modern psychometric measures of individual differences

No student of cognitive development can afford to be ignorant of psychometric research on intelligence, but the concept is one that needs to be treated with some caution. It may be much less useful than is commonly supposed. Indeed, recent efforts to measure individual differences in cognitive abilities have moved a long way from the search for some inherited, stable capacity in the individual.

For example, Sternberg (1988) argues that knowing how fast an individual can succeed in mastering some arbitrary task is not a useful measure of intelligence at all. Success can reflect the individual's past experience so that, in a task familiar to one child and novel for the other, the child who succeeds most easily may be using far less intelligence (because he or she is repeating a well-learned solution) than the child who struggles (who may be working for the first time through unknown territory). Equally, being able to master an arbitrary, abstract problem is not necessarily a good marker of how 'street smart' an individual is. Behaviour is not intelligent in the abstract, but *in context*. For example, we tend to admire the individual who can produce a complex analysis of a problem more than one who cannot. That is all very well. But if the problem to be solved is, say, putting a fire out, an individual who fetches the extinguisher and douses the flames is behaving more adaptively and so more intelligently than one who stands by and gives a lecture on the nature of combustion, however erudite.

Furthermore, traditional IQ tests may miss the point in asking only whether an individual can successfully solve a given problem, or how fast. Some ways of solving problems are better than others, as we have seen in Chapters 6 and 7. Some strategies are more richly informed, more sophisticated and will be more generally useful than others. These are the more intelligent strategies, even if they are slower, or even sometimes less successful (Siegler, 1976; see Chapter 7). Sternberg argues that a proper estimate of an individual's ability ought to look at what kind of strategies he or she uses to solve problems, as well as taking his or her past experience and ability to react appropriately to the context into account.

Sternberg's approach to measuring individual differences in cognitive abilities fits very much more closely with modern accounts of the processes which underlie skilled cognitive performance than was the case for earlier psychometric measures. Nonetheless, we should be cautious in assuming that even tests as sophisticated as Sternberg proposes provide a *definitive* measure of the child's abilities, or a basis for predicting that individual's future.

Of course, even within the psychometric tradition IQ is not the only factor believed to lead to differences in reasoning and problem solving between one individual and another. Ability is also importantly a function of a variety of other processes, which determine the style or flavour of the way the individual approaches cognitive activities.

Scores on IQ tests have a limited power to predict which individuals will make outstanding novel discoveries or be innovators (Guildford, 1967). Few individuals with very low IQs are creative. But for those with IQs over about 125, IQ does not predict who will or will not be successfully creative. Guildford (1967) identified two main styles of reasoning which he argued account for the difference between individuals who are creative and those who are not. There are 'convergent' thinkers, who think in very conventional ways and are unlikely to come up with new or unusual ideas, and there are 'divergent' thinkers, whose thought patterns are less conventional and who are more creative as a consequence.

Psychometric measures of divergent thinking tend to rely on measuring how imaginative an individual is in inventing different uses for common objects such as a brick (Guildford, 1967). The more uses the individual produces, the more divergent (that is, creative) he or she is said to be. However, this approach is subject to a number of serious criticisms. First, there is very little evidence to suggest that useful innovations are actually achieved through thinking of more alternatives, rather than better ones. For example, Darwin's seminal work on evolution was indisputably creative, but he can scarcely be imagined to have reached his conclusions by making a list of all the possible ways species might have arisen! Only where we solve a problem by guessing in a trial-and-error way would the ability to generate more possible solutions be likely to be relevant. And even then, it is only if we are able to recognize which solutions are better or are moving in the right direction that a useful new discovery is likely. Recognizing such things involves very different mental processes from merely listing more alternatives.

As with the concept of IQ, the psychometric concept of creativity in itself does not offer an explanation of the process by which innovative ideas actually arise. Nor is there convincing evidence that scoring high on tests of creativity is associated with useful innovation. We shall look at creativity again, from a different perspective, later in this chapter.

Process accounts of individual differences in cognition

Researchers who study the mental processes that underlie cognitive performance tend to focus on universal features of these processes, rather than on individual differences. As a result, there is an astonishing lack of research directly focused on how the mental processes of individuals who learn quickly differ from those of individuals who learn slowly, and filling in this gap may become an important issue for developmental research in the next few decades.

Every factor that contributes to the general nature of human mental processes as a whole can also contribute to the occurrence of individual differences in processing between one individual and another. Thus every influence on development noted in earlier chapters of this book, from biological factors to social and individual ones, may be a source of variation between one child and another.

Genes

Sexual reproduction involves a mixing of the detail of the genes defining the human blueprint as it passes from one generation to another. Subtle differences in this blueprint play a key role in creating diversity in a great many human characteristics, undoubtedly including characteristics that influence cognitive development. But the more we discover about genes, the more likely it seems that there is no simple or straightforward relationship between our genetic inheritance and individual differences. For example, the genetic pattern known as trisomy 21 (see Chapter 2) produces a variety of physical and mental characteristics known as 'Down's syndrome'. But children with this syndrome vary enormously in their intellectual achievements. Some are utterly dependent all their lives, while others manage well, holding down jobs and living fairly independently. Equally, the genetic endowment that allowed young children in Terman's (1954) study to show high intellectual ability was not enough to ensure that they would continue to be gifted in later life: some showed a marked decline in ability, as we have seen earlier in this chapter.

In part, the impact of genes on development is mediated by environmental factors. The child's circumstances may act to exaggerate or counteract the genetic disposition. The cognitive abilities that emerge in the individual are always the product of the complex dynamic interaction of many factors, as we shall see later in this section. But it also seems that genes interact with one another in very complex ways: the overall genetic pattern is as important as any single gene or set of genes the individual may possess, in determining how a genotype is expressed in the individual child. And it may be a mistake to suppose that cognitive development is affected only, or even primarily, by genes regulating mental ability as such: other genetically influenced characteristics that affect how the child interacts with the world (such as temperament, or manual dexterity) may be just as important.

Social processes and individual differences

Human knowledge and reasoning are, in a very important way, social constructions rather than simply the product of individual minds (see Chapter 7). We don't discover the world or develop abilities in isolation. We learn how to do things from watching and interacting with others, our strategies and skills shaped and scaffolded by more experienced people (Luria, 1976; Radziszewska and Rogoff, 1991; Rogoff, Gauvain and Ellis, 1984; Vygotsky, 1978; Wertsch, 1979). Even the way we approach thinking or problem solving is influenced by the mores of the various social groups (family, peers, education, society at large) we grow up in: some social groups reward intellectual activity, erudition, reason, reading where others don't. Some reward persistence, rigorousness or creative originality, others don't.

Cultural tools such as literacy, computer literacy, mathematics and the like radically affect the way our minds develop: literacy and mathematics play a vital role, for example, in paving the way for abstract logical thinking, leading the mind to operate in a quite different way than it would otherwise (Johnson-Laird, 1993; Kahneman, Slovic and Tversky, 1982; Morris and Sloutsky, 1998; Scribner and Cole, 1981). Computer literacy and other aspects of the IT revolution may be inducing new changes in the way the human mind functions, changes we as yet barely anticipate (Greenfield, 2003). Different societies, even different schools or families, offer different opportunities to acquire these cultural tools.

Culture sets the pace for development, too (Rogoff, 1998; Rogoff et al., 1984). In some societies children are regarded as 'delayed' if they have not mastered the rudiments of reading by the age of 6 years. In other societies, a child of 6 is regarded as too young to even begin mastering such a skill. In our urban industrialized societies we scarcely trust an 8-year-old to wash up the dishes unsupervised, where in many traditional African societies, 8-year-olds are entrusted with sole care of the family's main asset, being left to tend the cattle on which the whole family depends. Children tend to live up to what we expect of them, becoming intellectually adept or responsible when that is expected, remaining inept and childishly irresponsible when it is not.

It follows from all this that differences in the way children are parented and taught (Pratt et al., 1988; Radziszewska and Rogoff, 1991), differences in the way they are educated (Scribner and Cole, 1981), differences in the beliefs and practices of the culture to which they are exposed (Cole and Scribner, 1974; Luria, 1977; Scribner and Cole, 1981), differences in what the culture around the individual *demands and expects* (Rogoff, 1998), will create differences in cognitive functioning between one individual and another.

Individual characteristics and cognitive development

Temperamental dispositions of the individual child or adult, from basic motivations to the care or impulsiveness with which they approach problem solving, their persistence in worrying at an idea or trying to apply a given strategy, even the level of stress they find optimal, all contribute to the way reasoning and problem solving develop in and differ between one person and another. These factors produce effects over and above the more obviously cognitive features of individual minds, such as what particular knowledge they have of a given problem or what expertise in that area, what strategies they know for solving it or how efficient their basic mental processes may be, important as these factors are as sources of individual difference in reasoning (Carey, 1985; Chi and Ceci, 1987).

There is no advantage, for instance, in knowing exactly how to solve a problem if we lack the interest or motivation to apply that knowledge. Equally, persisting too long or not long enough in trying to solve a problem in a given way can mean failure where a more appropriate judgment of when to try something new will lead to new discovery and success (Siegler, 1996; Thornton, 1999).

Temperamental or stylistic differences in how individual children approach problem solving can have a surprisingly large impact on the speed with which a child learns, or the character of what is learned. For example, Siegler and Jenkins (1989) have shown that children differ in how sensitive they are to feedback from the environment. As we saw in Chapter 7, children typically have more than one strategy that they might use in any situation (Siegler and Jenkins, 1989). Which strategy they choose to use at any one time is a matter of the experience they have had with that strategy in the past: the more successful it has been, the more likely they are to use it. But until the difference in the relative success of two strategies passes some critical threshold, the child will continue to use both strategies more or less interchangeably. It is only once one strategy has become markedly more successful than another that the child will begin to systematically use that strategy and reject the other. However, exactly where the critical threshold for difference between two strategies lies varies from one child to another.

For example, Siegler and Jenkins have shown that, where one child will not begin to trust a new strategy until it has proven itself to be, say, twice as effective as older and more familiar strategies, another child might start to prefer the new strategy when it is only 25 per cent more likely to succeed. In effect, the first of these children is far more cautious and conservative in learning and making new discoveries than the second, and will change his or her approach to problem solving or reasoning more slowly. Often this will mean that the more cautious child develops more slowly. But occasionally, such a child will have an advantage, because he or she will avoid leaping prematurely to the conclusion that a strategy that happens to be good in particular circumstances is necessarily generally better when it is not. However, even this advantage may be rare: the more readily adaptive child will soon detect such errors and correct them. Overall, the more rapidly a child differentiates between one approach and another, the more he or she will learn about a task.

Stylistic differences in the child's approach to cognitive tasks may have some basis in inherited characteristics of the child's temperament (Kochanska et al., 1998). For example, babies differ from birth in how irritable or how readily soothed by cuddling they are, how upset by loud noises, and so on (Chapter 4). There may be innate differences in infant's tendency to seek out new stimuli, with one infant needing more stimulation to avoid a noxious boredom than another, or one infant unpleasantly stressed by a level of stimulation which merely excites another.

However, stylistic differences in problem solving between one child and another can also be reinforced or exaggerated by experience: success, however achieved, breeds success, and failure breeds failure. A child who *happens* to use a strategy that generates fruitful feedback, and who is therefore successful in making discoveries in that task, is not just learning about the task itself. Such a child is learning that he or she is *good* at solving that kind of problem, good at solving problems as a whole. There is clear evidence that this kind of experience makes us more confident and more successful problem solvers, where the opposite experience, namely failing in a task, can teach us that we are bad at solving those problems and can make our future efforts more inadequate and still less successful (Hartley, 1986; Seligman, 1975).

Equally, children who solve a problem through trying out many different strategies will learn to vary their approach more readily, where children who are successful through persistence will learn to persist with a single strategy, and so on. The experience of solving problems teaches the child not just how to solve that particular type of problem, but how to go about structuring the process of problem solving as a whole, and so can influence the development of a particular cognitive style.

The process of creativity

Psychometric research saw creativity as a distinct factor from intelligence, requiring a certain level of intelligence but operating separately (Guildford, 1967). Process-oriented accounts of creativity take a very different view. From this perspective, the same basic processes are responsible for all problem solving, for the new discovery that characterizes childhood cognitive development and for the outstanding acts of innovation in science or the arts that we call 'creative genius' (Boden, 1990).

Intellectual development through childhood involves an almost continuous process of new learning, new understanding and new discovery, creating revolutions in conceptual understanding in the child (Kuhn, Amsel and O'Loughlin, 1988). Every normal child shows an astonishing capacity of this kind, as the ordinary basis of developmental growth. The differences between children in the speed and range of new discoveries made reflect a variety of factors, from the specific detail of the strategy used to the child's willingness to try something new (both themselves the product of a variety of social, ecological and personal factors) rather than the operation of some special 'creative' function. Creativity is the characteristic of ordinary intelligent processing, as we saw in Chapter 7 (Boden, 1990; Siegler, 1996; Sophian, 1997; Thornton, 1999).

Why, then, do we recognize some individuals as possessing creative genius and others not? It's important to notice that this recognition is a social attribution, a social decision rather than an objective fact. There's no objective definition that specifies what an act of genius actually is. Creative genius is very much in the eye of the beholder: a million new ideas come up every day. Few stick, and fewer still are regarded as the product of genius. A brilliant idea is an idea whose time has come: in other words, an idea that society is ready to welcome and accept (not all of which turn out to be good ideas).

We pick certain ideas out as evidence of genius when they resonate with us in some way, even though no one has thought of them before, as if they were ideas waiting to happen. And in fact, that may be a very useful way of conceptualizing outstanding acts of innovation in the arts or science. For example, Darwin's explanation of the origin of the species through evolution had never occurred to anyone in past generations, although the same evidence was there all along, but it occurred to another man, Wallace, working alone in Australia at more or less the same time as Darwin. (Indeed, the news that Wallace was about to publish was a spur to Darwin to present his dangerous ideas – Dennett, 1996.) Likewise, the camera was invented more or less simultaneously by two men working entirely independently in England and in France. Movements in painting and music show the same character, with apparently startling innovations being discovered separately, *but at the same time* by different artists.

The implication of such parallel discoveries is that the keys to creative breakthrough lie not in the mind of the individual, but in the collective understanding of a culture. Gradual changes in the way a given culture reasons, and in the information it has, may lay the foundations for such revolutionary change in how we view the world. What appear as individual acts of genius may really be very collective and social things. Perhaps Darwin and Wallace were merely the right kind of men (of sufficient ability in reasoning and problem solving, open to information and ideas from their shared culture, well placed to make the observations which might explore the implications of those ideas) to mediate the transition to a radical new idea whose foundations were already culturally laid. Thus a process-oriented account of creative genius suggests that, not only does it not involve processes special and separate from those characteristic of ordinary problem solving, it need not involve exceptional prowess in those problem-solving skills either.

Developing differently

So far we have been concerned with normal development: with the patterns and regularities that characterize all children as they grow up and develop an adult mind. Within this normal process of development there is a vast scope for variety and difference between one child and another, with *this* child being musical, for example, and *that* child being tone-deaf but very good at science. But there are also patterns of development that are quite outside this normal range: children whose development is very delayed, or that takes a path very different from the norm.

Abnormalities of development come in all shapes and sizes. As we have seen, the normal process of development depends on a vast range of factors: genetic, physiological, social, environmental and individual. We are all the product of such a fantastically complex process that it is surprising that development does not 'go wrong' more often than it does. A failure in any factor can potentially derail development.

Diagnosing developmental abnormalities

As we have seen in this chapter, there is a great deal of variety between individuals in the speed with which they learn and develop, in the patterns of ability they display, and the levels of achievement they finally attain. All this variety is perfectly normal: we accept a fairly broad degree of variation in how normal individuals learn, think and reason. Abnormal development, then, is identified as a very *marked* deviation from the normal range of developmental progress, a marked failure of the child to behave as expected.

Exactly where the border between a 'normal' pattern of development and an 'abnormal' one lies is a little hazy. Some children are so very severely different from the average that there is no question but that their development is abnormal. But for milder problems, it can be rather unclear where the line should be drawn between a normal but very slow developer, say, and a child with a real difficulty that is worth diagnosing and treating.

Nor is it the case that all developmental abnormalities reflect abnormalities in the child as such. For example, imagine that you are a teacher. In your class of 5-year-olds, there is a very disruptive little boy. He can't be quiet or sit still, he can't make friends or get along with the other children, he's fairly destructive and aggressive. His command of language is very much behind that of his peers, and his progress on schoolwork is more or less non-existent. What is the matter with him? What is the solution? A pattern such as this might have very many causes. Perhaps there is something wrong with the child, some underlying failure in the developmental process. But it is entirely possible that the child himself is normal, but has come from a home that is very unsupportive or even abusive, and which has set him on a damaged developmental trajectory from birth. Poor parenting sets such a child off on a disastrous school career, in which his poor behaviour is likely to be interpreted as low ability whatever his actual potential might have been. His disruptive behaviour may be diagnosed as a conduct disorder, or a disorder of attention and impulse control. Once this reputation has been acquired the child will be treated differently, very often in ways that will lock him into his 'abnormality'. This is particularly sad in that developmental problems stemming from such social causes as poor parenting and poor tuition are the easiest to remedy, with the right input.

Diagnosing developmental abnormalities, particularly in milder cases, can be fraught with difficulty as the example in the last paragraph shows. Not least of the difficulties is that putting a label on a child carries a cost. Sometimes, identifying a specific sort of deficit (in learning to read, say) is very helpful to the child: it directs teachers to provide that child with the extra support he or she needs to master the skill in question. Having such a specific difficulty acknowledged and supported can be a great relief to the child, taking away a sense of hopelessness and failure. But labels can also be damaging. Social reputations ('Paul can't learn maths') can become self-fulfilling prophesies (Hartley, 1986), trapping a child in under-achievement or poor behaviour.

Delayed cognitive development

Some children progress toward the milestones of development much more slowly than the average: they learn to talk later than average, or struggle to keep up with their peers in motor skills, in maths, reading or analytical thinking. Marked delays of this kind are likely to be diagnosed as reflecting a *learning disability* or *learning disorder* (the two terms are generally used interchangeably).

Developmental delays can be a source of great consternation to parents and professionals. Sometimes this concern is well founded: development that is very markedly different from the average may be a sign of some serious physiological disorder, predicting a qualitative aberration in the path the child's development will take, as will be discussed later in this chapter. But often developmental delay is no more than that: a lag in the speed with which the child progresses down the normal path. Such developmental delay can be caused by many factors.

General factors in developmental delay

Where the child lags behind peers in most areas, the probability is that some general factor is responsible. In many cases, the child's difficulties may reflect a generally low level of ability, perhaps reflecting low inherent potential or intelligence. But low intelligence is far from the only factor that may be at work in producing generally lower performance.

The child's circumstances may reduce the rate of development. Poor nutrition, poor parental support, a deleterious home life, illness, depression, insecurity, low self-esteem or alienation can slow the child's overall cognitive development, as we have seen earlier in this chapter, slowing progress across the board. Even undiagnosed problems in hearing or sight can disrupt a child's general progress, whatever the underlying level of intelligence may be.

But even when there is a normal level of intelligence and a good family background, development may be affected by characteristics of the child that are not primarily a reflection of cognitive capacity in itself. The most familiar example is ADHD or *attention deficit/hyperactivity disorder*. Children with ADHD show an extraordinary level of energy and destructiveness, and an extraordinary inability to sit still or pay attention to anything. Box 1.1 (Chapter 1) gave a case study description of one such child.

ADHD is exhausting and depressing to deal with as a parent or teacher. It interferes with the child's ability to learn and to make friends: the child can't concentrate, and is too noxious to be attractive to interact with. The result is fairly widespread damage to the child's cognitive (and social) development. The causes of ADHD are not known. There seems to be no genetic or organic cause. Quite possibly, the problem is metabolic. The ADHD child may have an atypical level of arousal, either too high, so that the child reacts to ordinary life as if he or she were high on caffeine (say) all the time, or too low, so that the child becomes hyperactive to escape a noxious under-arousal. Drugs that affect the metabolism and alter the child's levels of arousal may have some effect in addressing this problem, although the issue is very controversial. The ADHD child is a very extreme case of the limited powers of concentration and the huge and poorly controlled energy of the normal infant. All children become more able to concentrate as they grow older, and more able to control their energy, and the same is true for ADHD children, many of whom gradually calm into a more normal pattern of development as they reach middle and late childhood.

Specific developmental disabilities

Where there are delays in specific skills (such as reading, say, or maths) in a child who is otherwise developing normally, it's tempting to speculate that there may be some specific learning disability reflecting a particular form of underlying neurological problem. Such interpretations are very controversial: do these specific disabilities really reflect neurological problems, however mild, or are they simply a reflection of the variety we generally see in human characteristics?

Take the example of *dyslexia*, the most commonly identified form of specific learning disability, diagnosed when a child has considerably more difficulty in learning to read and write than one would expect from his or her general abilities. Brain-imaging techniques show that the areas of the cortex activated by reading are different in dyslexic and normal children (Frith and Frith, 1996). There is also some evidence that dyslexia is associated with poor lateralization of the brain, so that the dyslexic child has general problems with spatial orientation, is generally ill-coordinated and does not develop a clear left- or right-handedness (Wolff et al., 1990). Some researchers point to such data as evidence that dyslexia reflects a particular minor neurological defect. Others challenge this interpretation, arguing that the different patterns of activity seen in brain-imaging studies may be the result, rather than the cause, of the different ways dyslexic and normal readers are processing information, and pointing out that the majority of children who are labelled as dyslexic show no evidence of any sort of neurological difference from good readers in any case (Scarborough, 1990). These critics of the concept of dyslexia argue that there is no neurological basis to the lag in reading at all. The debate has become murky: defenders of dyslexia countered with the idea that 'dyslexics' showing no evidence for different neurological functioning had been wrongly diagnosed; critics replied that, since the reading problems of the 'real' dyslexics and the supposedly 'wrongly diagnosed' ones were apparently indistinguishable, there was not even evidence of a correlation between poor reading and neurological deficits, let alone evidence of a causal link.

Direct analysis of the problems children labelled dyslexic have in learning to read suggests that the errors they make and the difficulties they have in learning to read are typical of the normal child, except that these difficulties persist much longer in the 'dyslexic' child. In other words, there is no evidence that 'dyslexic' children are developmentally abnormal in any *qualitative* sense at all: the process of development is apparently the same, it is only the speed of progress which is different (McGuiness, 1987).

McGuiness argued that in fact, learning disabilities such as dyslexia are more a reflection of the adult world's poor understanding of 'average development' than they are of any deficit in the child. Virtually every human characteristic is normally distributed (see Figure 8.1). This means that fully half the population will *always* be 'below the average' on any given measure. A sizeable percentage (about 13 per cent) will be appreciably below the mean. We tolerate this in relation to many characteristics: we don't worry, for example, that one boy reaches puberty at 10 and another not until 17 (both far from the mean age), or that some children find it very difficult to learn to carry a tune as well as the average person does, or that some will never be even averagely graceful skaters. But when it comes to school subjects, subjects that society has decided are vital, we forget about normal distributions and mistake the average for the baseline of achievement. We start expecting all children to achieve the average standard of reading for their age, and get upset when (inevitably) about half of them don't.

From this perspective, dyslexia as a 'syndrome' doesn't exist: variation in the speed with which children learn to read, even appreciable variation, is normal and just what we should expect. If we want those falling below the average to 'catch up', the solution is to provide special input, more support than the more adept reader would need. The concept of dyslexia may have made the provision of such special help more likely, but there is no need for such a concept and the attendant perils of labelling children abnormal, since helping those having difficulty is surely what we should have been doing in the first place, neurological deficit or not.

So long as the *pattern* of development is normal, even quite severe developmental delays may have no implications for the child's final achievements. This is particularly true for developmental delays in mastering skills that are cultural artefacts rather than basic to our human nature, such as reading, writing, maths and logic. For example, had they been at school today, Winston Churchill, Albert Einstein and Woodrow Wilson would very likely have been labelled as learning disabled: all had much less than successful school careers. There is a great deal of scope for variation in the speed with which skills are mastered, within the range of normal development.

Atypical cognitive development

For some children development does go very badly wrong, leading to persistent, pervasive and qualitatively different progress in cognitive development by comparison with normal children. Such atypical development can have many different causes, but generally has some sort of physiological basis.

Many serious developmental problems have a genetic basis. In some cases, defective genes or patterns of genes are passed from parent to child: for example, in 'fragile X' syndrome there is an inherited flaw on a particular gene on the X chromosome which results in very general cognitive deficits, accompanied by a distinctive physical appearance and social and emotional deficits. In other cases, chromosome damage seems to arise spontaneously, perhaps as a result of the decay of the older mother's ova, as in Down's syndrome. Down's syndrome produces widespread cognitive deficits together with distinctive facial peculiarities and often, a sunny disposition. Spontaneous damage may occur to other chromosomes too, for example, to chromosome 15, which produces 'Prader-Willi' syndrome which involves mental retardation and strange, obsessive eating.

Other serious cognitive deficits are associated with toxins, disease or injury (see Chapter 2). Many substances derail the development of the fetal brain to a greater or lesser extent. The most common such poison is alcohol. Babies born to mothers who drank too much during pregnancy typically have marked cognitive problems and again, distinctive faces. Viruses such as rubella, or even mumps and measles, can affect the development of the fetus in ways that damage the brain and distort development. Serious brain damage can also occur at birth, either very immediately through oxygen deprivation or injury, or through the invidious action of infections caught in the passage through the birth canal. Although most of the factors causing serious damage to normal brain development operate before or at the time of birth, serious injuries, poisons and illnesses such as meningitis can, of course, derail the functioning of the brain at any point through childhood, adolescence and adult life.

Over 1000 separate physiological causes of serious damage to the developing brain have been identified. Often, the result is a severe abnormality not only in the speed but in the pattern of development: normal milestones aren't reached, and the child's progress is strikingly different from the normal path. The exact degree or character of this developmental difference is not always easy to predict from the damage alone: for example, not all children with Down's syndrome are equally disabled, as we noted earlier in this chapter, even though all have the same chromosomal abnormality.

In fact, there's a great deal that we don't yet understand about why certain genetic or chromosomal flaws have the effects they do (Simonoff, Bolton and Rutter, 1996). We do not know exactly what it is that is disrupted, in the brains of these children, to limit their development in these ways. Nor do we wholly understand how poisons, illnesses or physical injuries damage the brain, or the power of the brain to recover from such insults. Even the basic nature of many syndromes that cause serious obstacles to normal development (such as autism, which is discussed Chapter 9) are still unclear. Cures are even further from our reach.

In conclusion

For all that there are clear universal patterns in cognitive development, there are also enormous differences between individuals in the conceptual understanding, cognitive style and skills that develop. Early efforts to explain this generated the concept of 'intelligence' – the notion that individuals differ in the general power of their mental processes as a result of their particular genetic inheritance from their family. But psychometric attempts to measure intelligence have had a rather chequered history. Mental ability turns out to be more multi-faceted, more uneven across different types of task than the original theory supposed. Scores on many IQ tests reflect the individual's experience rather than providing a pure measure of potential. IQ scores are less stable across time, and even when stable, are less effective in predicting future performance than the theory of general intelligence implies. The theory that our mental capacity is set at birth by our genetic inheritance is too simple to account for the rich phenomena of individual differences in cognition.

More recent research has focused less on measuring differences between individuals and more on analysing the processes by which an individual child's cognition develops along a particular path. This research suggests that the way the mind develops is the product of a complex interaction between biological factors (genetic temperament and neurological characteristics) and social factors (determining the ways of conceptualizing the world, the skills and expertise, the style of response or attitude to problem solving that is transmitted to the child from his or her family and surrounding culture). The implication is that individual development may be very malleable: the surprising product of a myriad of happenstances in the particular time and place the child grows up in, rather than predetermined by an underlying genetic programme.

As yet, there is no theory of individual development integrating all the factors that contribute to this process into a single coherent explanation. Only the dynamic systems approach (Thelen and Smith, 1994) seems to have the potential to provide the framework for such a theory (see Chapter 2), and this may become an important avenue for research in the next few decades. It's interesting to notice that when we take a dynamic systems approach to cognitive development, the distinction between universal and individual features blurs: both must be the product of the same dynamic system.

Normal developmental processes may account for both the gifted and acts of genius: there is no evidence that either exceptionally high ability or exceptional achievement involve anything beyond the same basic processes that yield all problem solving, reasoning and discovery of new ideas through development. Delays in development, either right across the board or in relation to specific skills, may also, in general, reflect only the action of these normal processes.

Some children are born with brains damaged by faulty genes, toxins, infections or injuries. Here development may take a very different course from the normal in both qualitative and quantitative ways, as may also be the case for individuals who suffer certain illnesses or injuries later in development. But does this different course imply a different process, or merely a distortion of the normal dynamic system through which cognition as a whole, and individual differences in particular develop? The answer has important implications, both for our theoretical understanding of the development of the mind and for practical strategies for intervening to support the development of the severely disadvantaged child.

Exercises

1. How would you test the hypothesis that the Flynn effect reflects the advent of more stimulating, information-rich environments? How would you extend that research to explore why, when information technology continues to expand, the Flynn effect seems to be reversing?

2. What are the key differences between a psychometric and a process-oriented approach to individual differences? Which is more useful in determining what support a given child needs to fulfil his or her potential? Why?

Suggested reading

For a taste of just how complex it can be to try to disentangle environmental and genetic influences on intelligence read:

- S. Petrill, K. Saudino, S. Cherny, R. Emde, D. Fulker, J. Hewit and R. Plomin (1998) Exploring the genetic and environmental etiology of high general cognitive ability in fourteen to thirty-six-month-old twins. *Child Development* 69, pp. 8–74.

For an introduction to Sternberg's work on measuring individual differences in cognitive functioning read:

- R. Sternberg (1988) Intellectual development: psychometric and information processing approaches. In M. Bornstein and M. Lamb, *Developmental Psychology: An advanced textbook*. Hillsdale, NJ: Erlbaum

For a discussion of the mental processes underlying creativity :

- M. Boden (1990) *The Creative Mind: Myths and mechanisms*. London: Weidenfeld and Nicholson.

For a review of abnormal development read:

- E. Mash and D. Wolfe (1999) *Abnormal Child Psychology.* Belmont: Wadsworth.

Revision summary

The concept of intelligence

- Early efforts to explain why high or low ability is consistent across generations within a family generated the concept of general intelligence: the notion that an individual's mental ability is set by his or her genetic inheritance.

- Efforts to measure intelligence generated the science of psychometrics. The initial focus was entirely on a test that would distinguish between individuals with different levels of ability. There was no interest in the cognitive processes underlying intelligence, and no definition of intelligence in those terms. Tests were devised pragmatically (what worked). Intelligence was simply defined as 'what an IQ test measures'.

- This agenda ran into a number of problems. First, intelligence is not so general as had been supposed: an individual might be quick on the uptake in one area but not in another. Then, the scores achieved on IQ tests reflect the individual's prior knowledge and opportunities to learn rather than his or her inherent potential, even where the relevance of prior knowledge is minimized.

Furthermore, IQ scores are less stable across time within an individual, and less accurate in predicting an individual's future achievements than the theory of intelligence implies. And although there is some correlation between genes and ability (identical twins are more similar than other siblings, for example, even when reared separately), the correlation is not high, and is affected by the relative contribution from the environment. The whole question 'how much of intelligence is inherited' is conceptually muddled.

■ Modern theories of intelligence are far more elaborate and sophisticated than early efforts.

■ Anderson (1992) suggests a multi-dimensional concept of intelligence, at the core of which is a 'basic processor'. The relative speed of this processor (in interaction with processors for specific skills) is inherited. It is this that determines the calibre of an individual's intelligence. Processing speed can be measured by evoked potentials, and does vary between individuals. However, there is no evidence that processing speed alone can predict general ability, let alone school achievement.

■ Taking a different view, Sternberg (1988) argues that intelligence cannot meaningfully be conceptualized in terms of the speed or power of a mental processor: intelligence is inherently a matter of using available knowledge to engage the environment in an appropriate way. A fast response is not always the most intelligent one; nor is the most intellectually complex response (analysing the nature of combustion, say) necessarily smarter than a simple practical action (putting out the fire). Sternberg argues that intelligence can only be usefully assessed by exploring the individual's response in context. But even Sternberg's sophisticated tests of intelligence are of limited value in predicting future achievement.

A process-oriented approach to individual differences in cognition

■ A completely different approach to understanding individual differences looks directly at the processes involved in cognitive development.

■ Biological processes contribute to cognitive development in different ways. Individual genetic inheritance plays a role, not merely through influencing the child's basic neurological characteristics (such as processing speed) but through shaping temperamental factors and physical dexterity, which affect the ways the child interacts with the environment and learns.

■ Social factors play an enormous role in cognitive development. An individual child's conceptual understanding, skills and even attitude to or style in approaching problem solving will profoundly reflect the beliefs and practices of the culture and the family he or she grows up in.

■ In fact, the very same complex and interacting processes that shape the universal patterns we see in cognitive development as a whole also shape individual differences in cognitive development. As yet we have no theoretical framework capable of integrating all these processes into a single coherent explanatory model. Dynamic systems theory would provide such a framework. Research in that vein may become increasingly important over the next decades.

Developing differently

- As with any human characteristic that is normally distributed, while the majority of children follow pretty much the same sort of developmental path, a few are very different: either gifted 'geniuses' or developmentally disadvantaged to some degree.

- Although psychometric theorists suggested that creativity (the root of genius) involved a special ability separate from ordinary intelligence, process-oriented accounts have demonstrated that this is not the case. There is no evidence that either the exceptionally high ability of the gifted or exceptional achievement of the creative genius involve anything beyond the basic processes that yield all problem solving, reasoning and discovery of new ideas through development.

- Likewise, a great many 'developmental delays' may reflect no more than the normal distribution of ability through the population. The evidence does not support the view that children with specific learning disabilities (such as dyslexia) have underlying neurological damage: their problems are merely an exaggeration of the normal process. And indeed, many children with specific learning difficulties grow up perfectly normally.

- However, a percentage of children are either born with brains damaged by faulty genes, illnesses or injuries, or suffer trauma at or after birth. The degree to which development is affected is variable. But in some cases, cognitive development is negligible or very seriously different from typical patterns. We don't yet understand exactly how genetic flaws or injuries create these severe developmental difficulties, still less how to provide support to help the affected child back toward a more normal developmental path.

social and emotional development from infancy to childhood

Our cognitive skills and understanding of the world are a crucial aspect of what it is to be human. But it's our sense of identity, our experience of ourselves and others as persons, our relationships and our emotional lives that define what it is to be an individual, what it is to be me. The four chapters that make up Part III explore how these things develop.

Chapter 9 explores the development of our understanding of human minds: the realization that people have intentions, desires, feelings, thoughts, beliefs. How do children make this momentous discovery? How does it affect our ability to relate to other people, to feel empathy and sympathy? Why is it that individuals differ in the ability to sympathize with others? How do the marked failure of 'mind reading' associated with autism, or the extreme failure of sympathy associated with psychopathic behaviour, arise?

Chapter 10 looks at the way personality and our sense of self, of personal identity, arise from the interactions between our individual characteristics and temperaments and the social world. How consistent is personality? What affects our conceptions of 'self'? Is adolescence marked by a period of 'identity crisis' as some theorists claim? Are there cultural influences in the development of identity?

Chapter 11 looks in more detail at social relationships and the way they affect us. How do the dynamics of family life, parenting styles, relationships with siblings affect our development? What is the effect of divorce? How does the ability to form friendships with peers develop, and how do such friendships affect us through childhood and adolescence? Why are some individuals popular, and others socially rejected, and what are the consequences of these different experiences?

Chapter 12 looks at the development of prosocial and antisocial behaviour. What leads us to develop in prosocial or antisocial ways? What role does our ability (or inability) to empathize or sympathize with others play in this development? How do we acquire moral values and beliefs, and what role do these play in motivating us to behave well or badly? How does conscience develop? How does one individual get to be a saint – and another a criminal?

9 chapter

understanding other people

We human beings are a profoundly social species. We depend on others to survive the long period of helpless infancy that is the price of our high intelligence. And as we have seen in Part II, the knowledge, skills, strategies and style that make up that intelligence are, to an important extent, socially constructed through shared ideas and activities, observation, tuition and collaboration.

But social interaction is not just a useful prop for survival and intelligence. In fact, for most of us, relationships with other people are what give life its meaning and purpose. Without people to care for and to care for us, with no one to discuss ideas or plans with, no one to mull over reminiscences or share a joke with, no one to console us in the face of setbacks or to rejoice with us over triumphs, life would be a wretched thing. Such loneliness kills.

We take the power and importance of human relationships for granted. But why do they matter so very much to us? What is it that gives other people their special importance in our lives? Imagine, for a moment, that you alone had been transported to a world where clever aliens had created robots programmed to look and behave in every respect like a human companion. Would you find a relationship with such machines emotionally satisfying? There's a long debate, both in science fiction and 'science factual', on this issue, most of which is entirely irrelevant to our purposes here. But I suggest that, if you believed that these robots were actually capable of *feeling, experiencing and reflecting on life* as you do, that they shared your motivations and concerns as a fragile mortal, that they could therefore *empathically share and sympathize* with your feelings and experiences (and you with theirs), then you could relate to them meaningfully. But if you saw their behaviour as merely an automated response, a sort of mechanical knee-jerk, then you would find them meaningless and empty as companions.

It is our awareness that other people are sentient beings like ourselves, comprised of the same hopes and fears, the same kinds of thoughts and feelings as we have that makes empathy and sympathy possible, and makes human relationships meaningful and valuable. But we are not born with this awareness, still less with the ability to 'read other minds' to know what particular thoughts and feelings another person may have in a given context. How does this precious insight and ability develop? In searching for an answer to this question, researchers have had to face some of the most challenging puzzles of recent decades. In the past few years, new discoveries in neuroscience have begun to radically change the way we understand this area of development – discoveries that have as yet only partly been digested. This is the research summarized in this chapter.

Becoming a folk psychologist

Through the bulk of our lives, understanding other people is a matter of working out what their situation is and how they are reacting to it. The older we get, the more practice and experience we have had and the better we are at this (although in truth, none of us is actually very good at it – sadly, not even those professionally trained in psychology). But for the newborn baby the challenge is more serious still. It is to discover that people are sentient: in other words, to discover that people are capable of having thoughts and feelings. The baby must discover the basic principles of human psychology, before he or she can start to become an adept psychologist.

Naïve psychology (that is to say, the everyday or 'folk' psychology lay people use in understanding one another) construes people in terms of three core constructs: intentions, feelings and beliefs. These constructs are seen as interconnected in complex ways, one thing causing another. For example, what we believe (about the thickness of ice on a pond, say), and our desires (to show off to a new lover, perhaps) influence our intention (to skate on it); conversely, the success or otherwise of the resulting plan affects our emotions (elation if the ice holds, distress if it doesn't), and so on. Infants discover these psychological constructs gradually, and only gradually make interconnections between them.

Discovering intentions

The first psychological construct that infants discover is that people have goals and intentions. Now, it is not entirely clear exactly how they do this. There is some evidence that babies are born with some sort of reflex that allows them to tell the difference between human movement and other forms of movement, even though they show no signs of conceptual understanding of the difference (Bertenthal, 1993, and see Chapter 4 for a discussion of this work). This reflex also makes human movement attractive, so that babies pay attention to it. Gradually, babies discover something very interesting about the way human beings (and other living things) move: they're *self-propelling.* That is to say, whereas you have to push or pull inanimate objects to get them to move, people and other living things move themselves. Most babies make this discovery during the first 6 or 7 months of life. By 7 to 9 months of age, they have drawn the inference that self-propelled things are goal-directed: in other words, that their movements are governed by goals and intentions (Flom and Pick, 2005).

Apparently uncaused movement is a very good clue in the discovery that living things are goal-directed, but it can lead to confusions, not only in babies, but in older children too, as **Box 9.1** shows. Children have a continuing tendency to assume that anything that appears to move of its own accord (such as the sun) is alive and has intentions.

By 9 months of age babies are able to draw simple inferences about other people's intentions: for example, they infer that an adult's word is

box 9.1

Childhood animism

Although even babies can differentiate between living and inanimate things to some degree, children don't make quite the same the distinctions that adults would make. For example, the 8-year-olds' lesser knowledge of biology creates uncertainties about whether certain things (such as cacti) are alive or not (Chapter 6). But in addition to this, children seem to project psychological characteristics onto inanimate things. For example, Piaget describes this conversation with a young child:

> Piaget: *What does the sun do when there are clouds and it rains?*
> Child: *It goes away because it is bad weather.*
> Piaget: *Why?*
> Child: *Because it doesn't want to be rained on.*

(Piaget, 1929)

Here, the child is attributing feelings and intentions – in other words, sentience – to the sun. Piaget suggested that children tend to attribute life to anything that shows spontaneous movement: that is movement that has no obvious mechanical cause and so appears to be evidence of a self-propelling entity.

Children also tend to over-extend psychological concepts from human beings to other living things, as this example (Linkletter, 1957) of a 6-year-old child explaining how to be a successful fisherman shows:

> When you throw in your line, the main thing is don't look hungry because if the fish sees you up there making faces and licking your lips, they'll know you want to eat them. But if you just pretend that you're not even interested in what's going on, they think you just like them and want them to eat what you've thrown in, and they bite it.

These over-extensions and errors are very probably reflections of the young child's imperfect conceptual understanding of both the physical and the psychological world. But it's also worth noting that such 'category errors' are not unique to children: many an adult attributes human psychology to their pet cat, dog, mouse or hamster. Nor is it unknown for adults to attribute psychological characteristics to inanimate objects (saying that a particular tool or machine is 'contrary', for example), even if we do this in a joking way. Children, too, play with the idea that inanimate objects are alive: they feed dolls, for example, and attribute emotions and desires to them, although it is clear from their behaviour that they are also fully aware that a doll is not alive in the way that a person is alive (Carey, 1985).

intended to label the object he or she is gazing or pointing at (Baldwin and Markman, 1989; Harris, Barlow-Brown and Chasin, 1995; and see Chapter 5). By 18 months of age, toddlers can draw quite sophisticated inferences about what another person intended, even where the intention is thwarted: for example, after watching an adult tug to no effect on the ends of a dumbbell, 18-month-olds imitate what the experimenter apparently meant to do (pull the ends off) rather than what he or she actually did (Meltzoff, 1995).[1]

The discovery of the existence of intentions is the first building block for a conceptual understanding of other minds. Nevertheless, it's worth noting that this early concept of intention is not like an adult understanding. In the first 12 to 18 months of life, babies may understand intentions very narrowly in terms of the specific actions they promote. If you are apparently pulling the end off a dumbbell, your intention is simply to pull the end off a dumbbell – no more. There is as yet no connection between intentions and other psychological constructs, so that intentions are not put in the context of any larger plan or emotional need. Construed in this simple way, intentions can't fail: what happens must be what was intended – by definition.

Discovering the 'psychology of desire'

We don't know exactly when babies first become aware that other people have emotions (see Chapter 4). The discovery probably arises through the phenomenon of 'emotional resonancing' in some way. Babies are born with a reflex to imitate other people's facial expressions. Assuming a facial expression tends to make us feel the emotion associated with that expression (smile and you'll feel happy, cry and you'll feel sad). So by imitating other people's expressions, babies are co-experiencing the other's emotion, whether they realize this or not. 'Resonating' with someone else's emotion in this way provides a situation in which the child might begin to consider the possibility that other people have feelings too, perhaps by gradually coming to impute what he or she is feeling to the other (Harris, 1992).

It's hard to say just what a young baby understands about another person's emotions, or just when he or she has realized that others have feelings too. But by 18 months of age, it's very clear that toddlers are aware of and responding to other people's feelings: they will comfort another child who seems distressed (Flavell and Miller, 1998) and will do things apparently deliberately aimed at annoying other people (Dunn and Munn, 1985). By the time they begin to produce two-word utter-

---

[1] Interestingly, these children did not infer that a mechanical device performing the same unsuccessful action as the human being had any intentions, and didn't pull the ends off the dumbbell after watching the machine. Clearly they already know that only living things have intentions.

ances, it's clear that toddlers have understood quite a lot about primary emotions (happy, sad, angry, afraid and so on).

Very detailed analysis of infant's spontaneous conversations shows that children begin to relate feelings to intentions by 18 months (Bartsch and Wellman, 1995), and are certainly doing this before their second birthday (Astington, 1993; Wellman, 1993). This allows the concept of intention to take on a new dimension: it relates not simply to an action (he picked up the banana because he intended to pick up the banana) but to a desire (he picked up the banana because he *wanted* a banana). Two-year-olds use 'sentences' like 'Want nana!' in ways that clearly show that they understand *wanting* to be a psychological state that is different from current reality.

In some ways, the 2-year-olds' understanding of psychology is now fairly sophisticated. At this age, children already know that what one person desires may be different from what another wants (Bartsch and Wellman, 1995), and that desires drive actions. For example, 2-year-olds can predict that a character in a story will act out his or her own intentions (for example, choosing to play with a truck), even when the child's personal goals (preferring to play with a doll) are very different (Astington, 1993, Gopnik and Slaughter, 1991). The 2-year-old also understands that people are pleased or happy when they get what they want, and sad or angry when they don't (Hadwin and Perner, 1991; Yuill, 1984). In other words, they understand not only that emotions (desires) generate goals and actions, but that the fulfilment or otherwise of those goals in turn generates emotion.

But for all its sophistication, the 2-year-olds' understanding of other minds is also quite limited, in two ways. First, the range of emotions and desires that 2-year-olds understand is initially small, and the kinds of evidence they use in inferring these states are naïve (Gnepp and Hess, 1986). Many desires that are straightforwardly familiar to the older child or adult (desires for status or sexuality or to avoid shame, for example) involve complexities beyond the 2-year-old mind, and will only be mastered gradually, as social sophistication grows through childhood and adolescence. Nor does the 2-year-old yet suspect the human capacity for dissimulation, dishonesty or duplicity: neither subtlety nor cynicism have yet set in (**Box 9.2**). For instance, even a 4-year-old does not know that disappointed people may hide their disappointment by smiling. Such understanding is still weak at 6 years, and increases up to the age of 10 years.

More fundamentally, the 2-year-old's comprehension of human motivation is two-dimensional. Although he or she has realized that intentions reflect desires, the toddler does not yet understand that intentions also involve action plans based on beliefs. For the toddler, there is a very immediate connection between an intended action and a desire: what you intend to do simply reflects what you want. And what

box 9.2

Dissimulation, deceit and cynicism

Although there is a natural tendency to smile when we are happy and to look miserable when we are sad, we human beings have a remarkable ability to control and disguise our emotional expressions. Partly this reflects social pressures: most cultures frown on the unrestrained expression of emotion, requiring us to restrain our tempers, inhibit certain desires and to feign gratitude for gifts and favours (no matter how unattractive): in other words, to pretend that we are happy (or at least content and calm) when we are not.

Children begin to learn to dissimulate – in other words, to control their emotional expressions – very young. As we saw in research on early attachment (Chapter 4), some families provide environments in which strong emotions are accepted and channelled constructively; others react to such emotion with withdrawal or even punishment. Either way the toddler learns to control how emotions are expressed, doing what is rewarded, avoiding what is punished. Such self-control is hard, and develops gradually. Toddlers understand little of what is required of them, though by 6 years of age children are aware of the need to be gracious in receiving gifts and the need to feign sympathetic intentions whatever they may feel. Sensitivity and self-mastery of this kind continues to grow through childhood and adolescence.

We can learn to dissimulate, to control the expression of emotion solely to gain reward or avoid punishment, without much awareness of other minds. Deceit is a different matter. To deliberately deceive another person we need at least some understanding that they have thoughts and feelings, at least some understanding that these things can be manipulated and misled. Even very young children tell lies: that is to say, they give accounts of events that are discrepant from the facts. However, it's not clear whether the motivation behind the lies of the very young is to deceive someone else – or to simply deny an unwelcome reality, to pretend all is well in the hope of making it so. Even we adults can 'do denial' in that way, as Freud pointed out! Evidence from experimental studies suggests that the ability to deliberately deceive someone else for gain is only achieved at about 4 years of age, as the child becomes proficient in working out what information another person has and how this may affect their expectations and behaviour (Russell et al., 1991). Our capacity to deceive grows as our insight into other people and social life develops.

Dissimulating one's own emotions to meet social mores, using insight into human minds to deceive others is one thing. Realizing that other people behave in the same ways is something else. The evidence suggests that this cynical insight develops later: the 4-year-old who masks his or her own emotional expressions and can manipulate to deceive does not yet realize that other people may smile to hide disappointment or tell lies for personal gain. Until recently it was believed that children are devoid of cynicism about other people's behaviour until quite late in childhood: perhaps as late as 9 or 10 years of age. Recent research confirms that 6-year-olds are more naïve in this respect than 8- or 10-year-olds, tending to assume that what people claim is the truth (Mills and Keil, 2005). But when told that the claims of a character in a story were false, even 6-year-olds show a degree of cynicism, identifying the claims as deliberate lies when they were in the character's self-interest but as mistakes when they went against the character's interests. And in fact, 6-year-olds in this study were, in a sense, even more cynical than 8- or 10-year-olds, in that they always interpreted self-serving claims as deceitful lies, whereas older children, like adults, understand that sometimes such claims may reflect unintentional wish fulfilment or other biases.

you intend is what happens: like the younger child, the 2-year-old still doesn't understand that actions may have unintended consequences (Astington, 1993). The implications of this are more profound than may at first appear.

For example, suppose you see John step onto a frozen pond and fall through. How to interpret this? As an adult, you understand that his intentions reflect not only his desire, but his belief. Given the general unattractiveness of plunging into freezing water, you would probably infer that John had believed that the ice was thick enough to support him, and that he had wanted to walk or skate on it. But a 2-year-old doesn't understand that intentions involve beliefs, or that actions can have unintended consequences. Seeing John crash into the water, the toddler may well infer that, since that was the consequence of his action, it must have been the intention of his action. And since his intention was apparently to fall in the icy water, that must be what he *wanted* to do. The whole notion of a failed plan based on a faulty belief is simply beyond the 2-year-old. If it becomes obvious that John *didn't* want to fall in the water, the toddler has no explanation except that he therefore can't have intended the disastrous action: if there's no desire for the outcome, then to the toddler's mind, there can't have been an intention.

Discovering beliefs

A belief is a mental representation (state of knowledge) of the world which reflects the information available to you. This is often very different from the way the world actually is. (Yesterday, for example, I firmly believed that my keys were in my coat pocket as I slammed my front door shut. Alas! They were still indoors.) To understand that people have beliefs, then, a child has to realize not only that others 'know' things, but that what they know reflects what information they have rather than the objective state of reality.

At about 9 months of age, babies begin to look to see where someone else is looking, and begin to point at things themselves, drawing things to other people's attention (Butterworth, 1991). At 18 months, infants will point something out to a given individual just once rather than repeatedly (Flavell and Miller, 1998), and will pull away hands covering another person's eyes if they want to show that person something (Lempers, Flavell and Flavell, 1977). These behaviours seem to suggest that between 8 and 18 months, babies realize that people only know about the things they have seen, and that I may see something you haven't seen. Does this amount to a primitive realization that people have mental representations of the world reflecting the information they have, representations that can be different from person to person? The question is hard to answer.

At 18 months, infants begin to enjoy pretend play, for example pretending that the arm of a chair is a horse or that a cup is a boat.

According to some theorists (Leslie, 1987), this is evidence for quite a sophisticated awareness of the existence of mental representations (I'm pretending this is a boat) as opposed to states of the world (it's really a cup). Other researchers object that, while pretend play certainly shows that 18-month-olds can hold two versions of events in mind at the same time, it doesn't necessarily indicate that children of this age understand that one of these versions is a mental representation or state of mind: both versions might seem like alternate states of the world (it is a cup and it is a boat) to the child (Harris, 1991; Perner, 1991; Perner, Leekam and Wimmer, 1987). Controversies of this kind are hard to disentangle. What evidence would Leslie need, to demonstrate that 18-month-olds *do* know that the pretence is a state of mind? What evidence would his critics need to prove that they don't?

Children first begin to comment spontaneously on what people believe at about 3 years of age (Bartsch and Wellman, 1995). However, it's unclear just what 3-year-olds understand about beliefs. They have difficulty in working out what other people may believe, and don't refer to beliefs in explaining intentions, for example (Shultz, 1980). Only at 4 years of age is there clear evidence that the child understands that beliefs are mental representations reflecting the information available to the individual, and can be wrong. Only at 4 is there clear evidence that the child understands that intentions involve beliefs as well as desires, and that the actions people plan can lead to unexpected and undesired outcomes if the beliefs on which the plan was based were wrong. Only at 4 years of age does the child become adept at manipulating other people's beliefs to manipulate their behaviour, deliberately misleading another child about where an object is to win a game, for example (Russell et al., 1991).

The 'false belief' task

The strongest evidence that there is a marked change at about 4 years of age in children's ability to disentangle states of mind and states of the world, and to understand the role of beliefs in intentions and behaviour, comes from studies using the *false belief* task (Wimmer and Perner, 1983). In this task, a child watches the experimenter hide some chocolate. A boy called Maxi also watches this, and then he leaves the room. In his absence, the experimenter retrieves the chocolate and hides it somewhere else, and the child watches this. The child is then asked where the chocolate really is, and where Maxi will think it is when he comes back.

To answer this question correctly the child must understand the difference between the real state of the world (where the chocolate is now) and Maxi's mental state/belief (where Maxi saw it hidden originally). The child must also realize that Maxi's mental state, rather than reality, will determine where Maxi will search for the chocolate. Typically, 3-year-old children fail in tasks like this whereas 4-year-olds succeed

(Perner et al., 1987; Wimmer and Perner, 1983). Similar results are obtained from many studies (Mitchell, 1997) and across different cultures (Avis and Harris, 1991): for example, Pygmy children growing up in isolated African communities show exactly the same developmental change between 3 and 5 years of age as do children growing up in the urban United States or in Britain, suggesting that there is some universal developmental change in the ability to reason about other people's mental representations at about 4 years of age.

'Appearance/reality' tasks

The same conclusion comes from studies using *appearance/reality tasks* (Flavell, Flavell and Green, 1983). The classic study of this kind asked children between the ages of 3 and 5 years to handle objects that looked just like rocks but were in fact sponges. The child was then asked what the object *really* was, what it *looked like* (that is, what you'd *think* it was if you saw it), and what someone else who hadn't been able to touch it would think it was. To answer all these questions correctly, the child would have to understand that there is a difference between objective reality (it's a sponge) and mental states/beliefs (you'd think it was a rock). In other words, they'd have to understand that mental states/beliefs exist, and that these are not direct reflections of reality.

Results from studies such as this show a clear parallel with results from false belief tasks: children below 4 years of age show no sign of understanding about mental representations, whereas those over 4 do. In Flavell and colleagues' study, for example, both 3-year-olds and 5-year-olds knew what the object really was: a sponge. But whereas 5-year-olds said that they would think it was a rock if they'd only seen it and not touched it, and that someone who hadn't touched it would think it was a rock, 3-year-olds said they'd think it was a sponge, and so would anyone else who saw it, even if they hadn't touched it.

Do 4-year-olds develop a 'theory of mind'?

Some theorists have suggested that the 4-year-olds' integrated understanding of the core constructs of naïve psychology provides them for the first time with a coherent *theory of mind*, and that it is this which accounts for the clear change in the ability to succeed in tasks such as the false belief and appearance/reality tasks at this age (Gopnik, 1993; Perner, 1991). They draw a parallel between this theory of mind and theories in the natural sciences such as Darwin's theory of evolution and Einstein's theory of relativity: some theories revolutionize how we think, so that, once we have grasped them, suddenly nothing ever looks the same again. These researchers believe that the 4-year-olds' development of a theory of mind creates a similar revolutionary change in thinking about minds (Gopnik, 1993; Perner, 1991; Wellman and Gelman, 1998), a qualitative step-change in how children understand other minds.

In some senses children are, of course, developing a conceptual understanding of the mind and of human motivation that could be described as a theory. This conceptual development begins early in infancy and will continue right through childhood and adult life (Frye and Moore, 1991; Thompson, 1998; Wellman and Gelman, 1998). And it's also true that development as a whole is characterized by qualitative changes in how we conceptualize things: new knowledge can restructure our ideas so that we understand and draw inferences very differently. For example, the child's developing biological knowledge turns his or her understanding of processes such as reproduction or elimination upside-down, allowing a whole new way of reasoning about living things (Carey, 1985; see Chapter 6). It seems likely that the child's progressive insight into mental states such as feelings, beliefs and intentions creates similar qualitative conceptual changes in how children understand human beings.

But is the radical change in children's performance in false belief tasks and the like at 4 years of age due to a sudden theory-like breakthrough in insight into other minds? Some researchers doubt this. In the first place, the change in 4-year-old behaviour is not as stable as we would expect, if it were due to the advent of a whole new conceptual structure for understanding minds: a given 4-year-old may succeed in one version of a false belief task but fail in another (Gopnik and Astington, 1988), or may solve a given task correctly one week but wrongly the next (Mayes et al., 1996). This suggests a model of development more like Siegler's (1996) 'overlapping waves' theory of development, where better knowledge and strategies gradually replace weaker ones, rather than a step-like change from one 'stage' of reasoning to another (see Chapter 7).

Furthermore, it's far from clear that the 3-year-old's problems in false belief and appearance/reality tasks are entirely because of a lack of insight into beliefs. These tasks pose problems over and beyond the application of naïve psychology in itself. Could such tasks underestimate the younger child's grasp on mental representations (beliefs)? If so, then the sudden change in success in such tasks at 4 years of age might reflect other factors, rather than the advent of a revolution in the child's grasp of theory of mind as such.

For example, both the false belief task and appearance/reality tasks depend on the child's interpretation of a question. There's quite an improvement in the child's grasp on language, between the ages of 3 and 4. Might 3-year-olds simply fail to display their understanding of other minds because they misunderstand the key question? Young children tend, generally, to answer the question that makes sense to them rather than the literal question asked (Donaldson, 1978). Might they misinterpret the key false-belief question ('Where will Maxi look?') to mean 'Where *should* Maxi look?' (Siegal and Peterson, 1994). If so, then their wrong answer (its real hiding place) is the right answer to the wrong question! And in fact, 3-year-olds are more able to succeed in false belief tasks when the question is reworded to be less ambiguous (for example, 'Where should Maxi look *first of all*?' – Siegal and Beattie, 1991).

But difficulties in understanding the question may not be the only factor that limits the 3-year-old's ability to use what he or she understands about minds in false belief and appearance/reality tasks. The basic form of the false belief task may pose a challenge to memory and reasoning that is simply too hard for the 3-year-old (Flavell and Miller, 1998). This possibility is underlined by a study comparing children's performance in the false belief task with their performance in a 'false photograph' task (Leslie and Thaiss, 1992).

In both tasks (see **Table 9.1**), the child is shown a scene (a doll sitting on a box, say). In the false belief task, another child (Maxi) sees this too, whereas in the false photo task the child takes a picture of the scene with an instant camera. In the false belief task, Maxi leaves the room. In both tasks, the doll is now moved (to a mat, say). The child is asked either 'Where will Maxi think the doll is?' (false belief) or 'Where will the doll be, in the developing photo?' (false photo). Four-year-olds answer correctly in both tasks. Three-year-olds answer wrongly in both tasks. Now, the form of these two tasks is identical: they pose the same challenge of remembering and inference. The fact that the 3-year-old fails when there is no other mind to be understood – only a photograph – strongly suggests that 3-year-olds' problems with the false belief task reflect problems quite unconnected with whether or not they understand mental representations as such. Again, this undermines the idea that the sudden change in success in false belief tasks at 4 years of age reflects the acquisition of a revolutionary new theory of mind. It could just as well reflect changes in general processing power that allow the 4-year-old to *apply* his or her insight into other minds, where the 3-year-old cannot.

A great deal of research has been done exploring different versions of the false belief task, trying to establish a 'definitive' measure of whether or not children under the age of 4 can recognize false beliefs (Mitchell and Lacohee, 1991; Saltmarsh, Mitchell and Robinson, 1995; Wimmer

table **9.1**   False belief and false photo tasks

	False belief task	False photo task
Scene one	The child sees a doll placed in one position: sitting on a box, say. A second child ('Maxi') is present and sees this too. This second child then leaves the room.	The child sees a doll placed in one position: sitting on a box, say. He or she is given an instant camera and asked to take a photo of this.
Scene two	The doll is moved to a new position: sitting on a mat, say.	The doll is moved to a second position: sitting on a mat, say.
Key question	'Where will Maxi think the doll is?'	'Where will the doll be, in the photo?'

and Hartl, 1991). This research has very much the same flavour as the debate about whether young children could think logically or not discussed in Chapter 6, and is probably just as misguided. What matters is not whether or not a child succeeds or fails in a task, but the process that underlies that success or failure. What we have come to understand is that tasks that require us to differentiate mental states and states of the world always impose other demands on processing as well – demands that can disrupt even adult performance.

For example, even though they understand the principles of naïve psychology very well, adults can have as much difficulty as 3-year-olds in some appearance/reality tasks. Fischoff (1975) described two (real) opposing armies to adults participating in a decision-making study. One army was better equipped and better organized; the other had more local knowledge, more men and a reputation for ferocious tenacity in battle. The participant's task was to decide which of these armies was, *on appearances*, more likely to win the battle. But before they made this judgment, Fischoff told them who had *actually* won the battle. Adults were not able to set aside their knowledge of the real outcome in judging which army would *appear* more likely to win (much as the 3-year-olds couldn't ignore their knowledge of the sponge in assessing what it *looked like* in Flavell and colleagues' 1983 study). Moreover, the adults in Fischoff's study couldn't ignore knowledge of the outcome of the battle in judging what people who had not been told this would think of each army's chances (just as 3-year-olds' views on how other children would perceive the sponge were biased by their own knowledge).

Solving both false belief and appearance/reality problems involves much more complicated psychological processing than simply having a good theory of mind – and this could prevent younger children from applying their knowledge of the mind, obscuring the depth of the 3-year-old's insight. Insight into the nature and function of beliefs may develop more gradually than the sudden change in performance in false belief and appearance/reality tasks at age 4 seems to imply.

Factors affecting the discovery of the mind

Three different factors have been identified as contributing to the child's progressive discovery of mental states and minds. These are social interactions (Perner, Ruffman and Leekam, 1994; Siegal, 1991), cognitive processing power (Frye et al., 1996), and biological preparedness (Fodor, 1992; Leslie, 1994). Of course, these three factors are not alternative explanations. All contribute and interact, as the child learns about the mind.

Social interactions and the growth of psychological insight

One important source of insight into mental states comes from the infant's interactions with other people (Perner et al., 1994). This is clear from the fact that toddlers with older siblings do better on false belief tasks than toddlers who don't have older siblings (Jenkins and Astington, 1996; Ruffman et al., 1998), and the fact that children who have a high level of interaction with adults show more advanced development in understanding other minds than those with less contact with adults (Lewis et al., 1996).

Detailed explorations of how social interactions contribute to the child's developing understanding of other people show that toddlers gain insight specifically from experiencing conversations about mental states. For example, children whose parents often talk to them about feelings at age 33 months, whose parents provide a rich commentary on the actions, motives, feelings and intentions of the people (or dolls) involved in an interaction, do far better than those whose parents don't discuss such things much, when tested on false belief tasks and other measures of their understanding of mental states at the age of 40 months (Dunn et al., 1991). The importance of verbal commentaries on social interactions is not limited to early childhood: 3-year-olds who take part in many discussions of feelings do far better than those who don't on tasks measuring their ability to infer someone else's feelings when they reach 6 years of age (Dunn et al., 1991). And even in adult life, we go on learning more about other people's feelings and beliefs by talking to and about them. Children (like the rest of us, gossip being one of the delights of human experience) are deeply interested in such commentaries. Their own 'pretend' play is rich in explicit discussion of such things, as the example in **Box 9.3** shows, providing an arena for exploring how others think and feel.

It seems likely that social interactions play a role not only in helping the young child to discover that other people have feelings, beliefs and intentions, but also in the developing sophistication of insight into just what another person's mental states may be. The older the individual, the greater the range and variety of social interactions he or she will have engaged in, each one offering further opportunities for elaborating psychological understanding. The character of social interactions changes as we grow up, producing a qualitative change in the range of emotions and motivations to which we are exposed and can therefore discover. The social world expects different behaviour of a 5-year-old, a 10-year-old and a 15-year-old, and in learning to comply with these expectations, children have another opportunity to identify new aspects of human psychology.

For example, society allows a 5-year-old to cry in frustration, but expects an older individual to mask his or her rage and woe. We aren't surprised or put out if a 2-year-old shows no pleasure when given a gift he or she doesn't find attractive, but would disapprove of an older child for failing to behave graciously as social convention requires. These changing expectations provide a framework within which the older

box 9.3
Pretend play

Children first begin to play games of 'let's pretend' at about 18 months of age. At first such games tend to involve pretending that an object is something else – that a shoe is a car, say, or that a biscuit is a bird or a plane. But progressively, such pretences take on a social focus. The majority of 3- to 4-year-olds have imaginary companions (Taylor, 1999) whose hands they hold on walks, for whom they set out a place at meals, who take part in all their activities and even get the blame for accidents and misdemeanours. Dolls and teddy bears are also treated like real people, given tea parties and the like. Children show great interest in the emotional states and reactions of these 'pretend' companions, attributing all sorts of thoughts and intentions to them.

Most deliciously of all, from the preschool years until almost the end of childhood children delight in elaborate games of 'make-believe' in which they themselves or their dolls and toys act out various scenes, as in this example (Jack, a child of just under 4 playing with a 6-year-old sibling, Mary).

Mary: (moving Teddy and a cardboard tube/tree appropriately across an elaborate terrain of 'roads', 'houses', 'shops', 'forest' and so on, constructed from toys, books, cushions, bits of clothing: 'Pretend teddy goes to the forest to get some wood and he chops a tree down and he carries it home.'
Jack: '... and he comes in the house and wants to play a game.'
Mary: 'No, he's all tired, he comes in the house and he wants a rest, but his rocking chair's all broken so he gets very cross.'

Make-believe games of this sort allow children to explore social roles and activities, and may be a valuable resource to the child as he or she tries to make sense of the adult world. But as this brief example shows, such games are a wonderful arena in which the child can impute mental states – feelings, intentions and beliefs – to dolls or to other players, discussing the different possible responses the various characters might have to one event or another, exploring the consequences of different beliefs and reactions. This is a rich arena indeed for discovering the way other minds work. The more such play a child experiences, the more advanced is his or her understanding of other minds, particularly where other players are older and more sophisticated.

child can discover that the relationship between an emotion and an emotional expression may be far less direct than the younger child suspects (Box 9.2).

Cognitive processing power and representations of others

Perner (1991) suggests that very young children have too little processing power to represent more than one version of reality at a time. As a consequence, a very young child can only represent the current situation. As processing power increases, the child comes to be able to represent two versions of reality: the present and the immediate past, for example. According to Perner, it is this increase in processing power that allows the 18-month-old to begin to be able to represent two alternative versions of the present: to imagine that the arm of a chair is simultaneously a chair arm *and also* a horse to ride on. The ability to represent two alternative realities in this way is, of course, the prerequisite for representing different people's versions of the same reality: *you* may think this is a chair, but *I* know that it is my horse.

What is it that limits the younger child's processing power? Some theorists suggest that there are physical limits on how much information a child can handle, limits that change with age (Case, 1985). But the evidence for an absolute capacity limit of this sort is poor (see Chapter 7). How much information we can handle seems to reflect how that information is structured (understood) and processed, rather than anything else (Dempster, 1985). But whatever the cause of the limits on children's processing power, there is strong evidence that difficulties in understanding different points of view do reflect the complexity of processing required to do this, and so could be a factor in the young child's failure in false belief and false photo tasks.

For example, long after they can successfully represent different realities in the false belief task, children still have great difficulty in understanding other people's points of view in other tasks, such as Piaget's *three mountains* task. Piaget invented this task to explore his theory that children are 'egocentric': unable to imagine another person's perspective, or even, in early childhood, that the other person has a different perspective (Piaget and Inhelder, 1956). The child sits on one side of a model of three mountains of different heights (see **Figure 9.1**). A doll is placed in a different position relative to the model. The child is asked to say what the doll could 'see'. Children aged from 4 to 6 years generally say that the doll sees just what they themselves see, as if they understood nothing at all about mental representations. Children aged from 6 to 8 years clearly indicate that they know the doll has a different perspective from their own, but can't work out what it is. Only at about 9 years of age do children begin to be able to solve this problem correctly.

Data from the false belief task make it clear that the younger children's difficulty in Piaget's three mountains task is not the result of any intrinsic inability to understand someone else's perspective: even 4-year-olds can do this in principle. What they don't yet have is the cognitive power to handle the complex information processing needed to work out what things would look like from a perspective they can't themselves directly see or apprehend.

In sum, the younger the child, the greater the difficulty he or she has in working out what another person can see or know, even when he or she is aware that the other has a different perspective. This is not surprising: working out what someone else knows involves a great deal of cognitive effort. The ability to handle complex processing grows throughout childhood and adolescence (Chapters 6 and 7), contributing to the progressive development of sophistication in understanding exactly what another person's mental state may be in a given situation (Frye and Moore, 1991; Frye et al., 1996).

'What can the doll see?'

figure **9.1**

Piaget's three mountains task

Biological bases for discovering the mind

It's a striking fact that a naïve psychology centring on the three constructs of feeling, belief and intention develops in all human cultures, and in children growing up in a wide range of different circumstances, and that generally it seems to become effective at about 4 years of age. This observation led some researchers (Fodor, 1992; Leslie, 1994) to suggest that the development of our theories about minds is controlled by a special module built into the human brain through the course of evolution, which matures at around 4 years of age. This hypothetical module was said to be pre-set to ensure that we will see minds in certain ways, directing the discovery of the core constructs of naïve psychology. This module was called the *theory of mind module* or *ToMM*. The idea is controversial at a great many levels.

It seems very likely that evolution has indeed 'primed' us in some way to develop insight into other minds. The sheer importance of such insight makes it likely that there is some inherent biological basis for it. And although some researchers claim that this phenomenon is uniquely human (Povinelli, 1995), there is evidence that clearly suggests that other primates also show this kind of insight. For example, chimpanzees spontaneously do things that seem to be aimed at deliberately deceiving other chimps, such as pretending there is no food when there is, or pretending to leave but sneakily hiding and watching another animal (Byrne and Whiten, 1988, 1991). Some researchers dismiss this sort of thing as merely 'learned behaviour' (Povinelli and Eddy, 1996), arguing that chimps can't have a theory of mind because they fail in false belief tasks.

But as the comparisons of false belief and false photo tasks show (Leslie and Thais, 1992), such tasks demand much more than a theory of mind. Such tasks may underestimate the chimp's understanding. And in fact, the chimp's deceptive behaviours actually seem to imply a fairly sophisticated theory of mind: the deceiver would have to understand that deceived and deceiver could have different beliefs, that the other animal's actions are going to be affected by its beliefs, and how to deliberately manipulate and mislead the other's belief – a level of sophistication that human children only achieve at about 4 or 5 years of age (Russell et al., 1991). The implication is that the biological bases of insight into other minds are part of our ancient evolutionary heritage.

What exactly is the biological basis for our discovery of the mind? What is it that has been built into our brains through evolution? Is there a ToMM containing processes already preset to help us discover a specific way of conceptualizing minds (in terms of the three core constructs that define naïve psychology)? Are we pre-programmed to come up with that solution? Although at one time some researchers did suggest that certain aspects of conceptual development may be directly shaped by pre-programming of some sort, the idea has been strongly challenged by others.

Researchers applying dynamic systems theory (Lewis, 2000; see Chapter 2) argue that complex conceptual development of the kind we see in the development of naïve psychology can arise systematically in every normal child without the need for any sort of pre-programming, through the interactions between simple biological characteristics as primitive as reflexes, the properties of the physical world and the structure of social relationships. If human beings the world over come up with a naïve psychology centred around the same three core constructs, dynamic systems theory argues that this is not because we are pre-programmed to develop that particular conceptual framework: rather, it is because, around the world human beings are in fact goal-driven information-processing creatures capable of powerful emotions and desires, engaged in social interaction with other people. It is this fact that determines what we discover as we formulate a naïve psychology.

Human beings are born with a number of innate reflexes and perceptual biases that orient us toward other people and to social interaction (Chapter 4), creating the ideal situation for learning about other people and other minds. Extraordinary new research suggests that we also have reflexes that more directly allow us to intuitively 'read' other minds. This discovery was made quite by accident: researchers studying neural patterns associated with the hand movements involved in picking things up in monkeys noticed one day that, when one of the experimenters picked something up, the neurons associated with hand movements fired in a monkey who had been watching – *even though the monkey had not moved its own hand at all!* Careful checks of the equipment showed that it wasn't faulty, so the researchers explored the phenomenon and discovered what are now called *mirror neurons* (Gallese et al., 1996): neurons that fire not only when a monkey performs an action itself, but also when it observes someone else perform that action. Mirror neurons also operate in the same way in the human brain (Dapretto et al., 2006; Stefan et al., 2005).

We do not yet entirely understand how the mirror neuron system functions. Watching someone else perform an action creates the neural pattern necessary to perform this action in the observer's brain, so that we can actually learn how to perform that action just by watching someone else do it (Stefan et al., 2005). This may well be the basis of newborn babies' reflexive imitation of other people, and of their imitation of facial expressions in particular (Rizzolatti and Craighero, 2004). Furthermore, there is evidence that the neurons involved in mirroring actions are integrated with other neural systems: watching someone else's action may fire not just action neurons but those associated with the *intention* behind that action as well (Bower, 2005). The neural bases of emotional feeling may also be activated by observing or imitating the physical movements of the relevant facial expression, through the activity of the mirror neuron system. Certainly, the mirror neuron system seems to allow us to co-experience other people's emotional responses in various ways. For example, when we watch someone else experience a painful event (such as being pricked with a pin) the neurons that would fire were it our own hand that had been pricked fire too, mirroring the reaction in the real victim (Avenanti et al., 2005).

It seems that, through the action of the mirror neuron system, our own mental states may 'resonate' with another person's, so that we in effect instinctively *simulate* in our own minds what someone else is doing and feeling, even though we may have no conceptual understanding of this. Some researchers (Harris, 1991) have long argued that simulating another person's mental states is an important means of discovering other minds: that we develop the notion that other people have mental states by coming to impute to them the feelings we experience in ourselves, and that we work out what someone else may be feeling in a given situation by imagining ourselves in their place. At first, the baby simply co-experiences other people's feelings through emotional resonancing, experiencing those feelings as if they were his or her own and not realizing that they 'belong' to someone else. As the baby becomes more aware of the distinction between self and other (see Chapter 4), the simulations generated by the mirror neuron system support a dawning awareness that the other has intentions and feelings and beliefs.

The notion that babies could come to conceptualize other minds through such simulations was originally rejected by other researchers on the grounds that the cognitive processing involved in reflecting on our own mental states and then conceptually projecting these onto someone else was far too difficult for the young child, let alone a baby (Gopnik, 1993). But the baby's earliest simulations of other minds may not involve cognitive or conceptual processing as this criticism assumes: The mirror neuron system provides an innate neurological basis for an instinctive, intuitive imputation of mental states to others (Gallese and Goldman, 1998), a reflexive foundation on which more conscious reflections and conceptual insight can subsequently be built.

Autism and the failure of mind reading

Research on the origins of autism provides strong support for the idea that our ability to discover and to 'read' other minds depends on a functional mirror neuron system and on the social reflexes which this provides, and for the idea that normal development in this area is the result of complex interactions between many factors.

The clinical syndrome of autism

Autism was first identified by Kanner (1943). The defining feature of this disorder (**Box 9.4**) is a marked lack of the sociability and social responsiveness that is characteristic of normal babies and children (Mash and Wolfe, 1999). Babies with autism aren't attracted by human faces as normal babies are, don't make eye contact, don't imitate, don't smile or use other emotionally expressive gestures. They don't point things out to other people, don't follow other people's gaze to share attention with them. They don't take part in the interactions typical of early infancy ('proto-conversations', peek-a-boo and the like). Infants with autism don't develop attachments to other individuals (such as the mother) as normal children do (Chapter 4).

At one time it was thought that children with autism simply couldn't recognize or distinguish individual people at all, could not form attachments of any kind. More recent research (Mash and Wolfe, 1999) shows that, although they have more difficulty in recognizing faces than normal children do, children with autism do respond differentially to their own parents, suggesting at least some level of recognition of individual people. And children with autism use the parent for security, which suggests that they do feel some sort of attachment, even though they don't show the emotional reactions normally associated with attachment. For example, where a normal child might become upset when left by the mother in a strange situation (Chapter 4), showing a variety of emotional expressions, the child with autism is likely to react in a dead-pan way, even if he or she searches for the mother.

The lack of sociability in individuals with autism is associated with very marked delay in the development of both language and non-verbal communication – or even a complete failure of development in these areas. And whereas symbolic, imaginative 'pretend play' exploring social

box **9.4**

Diagnostic criteria for autism

Source: *The Quick Reference to the Diagnostic Criteria*, from DSM-IV © 2000. Reproduced with permission from the APA.

A. A total of six (or more) items from (1), (2), and (3), with at least two from (1), and one each from (2) and (3).

(1) qualitative impairment in social interaction, as manifested by at least two of the following:

- marked impairment in the use of multiple nonverbal behaviours such as eye-to-eye gaze, facial expression, body postures, gestures to regulate social interaction
- failure to develop peer relationships appropriate to developmental level
- a lack of spontaneous seeking to share enjoyment, interests, or achievements with other people (e.g. by a lack of showing, bringing or pointing out objects of interest)
- lack of social or emotional reciprocity.

(2) qualitative impairments in communication as manifested by at least one of the following:

- delay in, or total lack of, the development of spoken language (not accompanied by an attempt to compensate through alternative modes of communication such as gesture or mime)
- in individuals with adequate speech, marked impairment in the ability to initiate or sustain a conversation with others
- stereotyped and repetitive use of language or idiosyncratic language
- lack of varied, spontaneous make-believe or social imitative play appropriate to developmental level.

(3) restricted repetitive and stereotyped patterns of behaviour, interests, and activities, as manifested by at least one of the following:

- encompassing preoccupation with one or more stereotyped and restricted patterns of interest that are abnormal either in intensity or focus
- apparently inflexible adherence to specific, malfunctional routines or rituals
- stereotyped and repetitive motor mannerisms (e.g. hand or finger flapping or twisting, or complex whole-body movements)
- persistent preoccupation with parts of objects.

B. Delays or abnormal functioning in at least one of the following areas, with onset prior to age 3 years:

(1) social interaction
(2) language as used in social communication
(3) symbolic or imaginative play.

C. The disturbance is not better accounted for by Rett's disorder or childhood disintegrative disorder.

roles and human motivations is characteristic of the normal toddler and child (Box 9.3), children with autism show no interest in this kind of activity and won't engage in it. Rather than orienting to people, individuals with autism orient to objects, and typically develop unusual and obsessive interests and rituals. In infancy these may involve (for example) twiddling a toy in a compulsive way or rocking back and forth repetitively, or repeating words or phrases they've heard over and over in a meaningless way (this phenomenon is called *echolalia*). In later childhood obsessions may relate to given activities or areas of interest: an obsession with types of car, for example, or lists of footballer's names, or working out the day of the week of any date in the past or future.

Autism is the syndrome associated with the 'savant': the apparently very abnormal individual who shows an extraordinary talent in one area. For example, **Figure 9.2** shows a drawing made by Nadia, aged 3 years: it's quite different, startlingly better than the drawings a normal 3-year-old (or most adults, for that matter) could make. Up to 10 per cent of those with autism may show this kind of savant talent (Happé, 1994).

Of course, autism is not the only syndrome associated with abnormal social development and delay in the development of language and other forms of communication. Anything that disrupts the child's ability to join in and learn from social interactions or from watching and listening to other people, will delay development in these areas, so that, for example, children born with severe sensory deficits (blindness, deafness) are often affected. Very low IQ can have a similar effect, disrupting the child's ability to make sense of social interactions or to master language, though this is by no means always the case. Children with Down's syndrome, for example, generally have very low IQ but are typically very sociable and often socially skilled.

Children with autism typically have very low IQ: over half score below 50 on IQ tests. But this is not what disrupts their social and

figure 9.2

A 'savant' drawing, by Nadia, aged 3, who has autism

Source: L. Selfe, *Normal and Anomalous Representational Abilities in Children.* © 1977. Reproduced with permission from Academic Press/Elsevier.

communicative development. Twenty per cent of individuals with autism have normal intelligence and are able to pass through the normal school system, even though they show the deficits in sociability and social insight characteristic of autism (such individuals are often labelled as suffering from Asperger's syndrome rather than autism, to reflect their lesser degree of handicap within the range of 'autistic spectrum disorders'). There are even instances of people with autism who have been academically successful enough to become university researchers or professors (most famously, Dr Temple Grandin, see **Box 9.5**), and who manage very well so long as no one expects them to have subtle interactions or relationships with other people. What is special about autism spectrum disorders is that the child's lack of social responsiveness appears to be the primary problem, rather than being the result of some other deficit.

box **9.5**

Dr Temple Grandin, autistic extraordinaire

Temple Grandin didn't talk until she was 3 years old. She was asocial, difficult and demanding, and was diagnosed as autistic. Her parents were told that her condition was hopeless, and advised to put her away in an institution. Luckily they took no notice of this. Temple was intelligent and able: with the support of her family she was able to learn to speak, able to pass (albeit unhappily and asocially) through the normal educational system to the extent of taking a PhD and becoming a professor at an American university. She is the most articulate of autistics, and in 1986 published a book on the experience of being autistic which has thrown new light on what this syndrome means for its sufferers (Grandin and Scariano, 1986, *Emergence: Labelled autistic*).

Temple Grandin's academic expertise is in designing equipment for handling cattle, particularly in designing the facilities of slaughterhouses to minimize the distress of the cattle. She says of herself that she is able to 'think like a cow', noticing the tiny details of shape, light and darkness that startle or sooth cattle and using this to redesign equipment to make it less stressful for them. Paradoxically, cattle have also given her an insight into how to handle the high levels of anxiety that her autistic difficulties in understanding other people generate: cattle coming for vaccination or other treatment are securely held in a 'squeeze box' that hugs and restricts them. As a teenager Temple Grandin noticed that this had a calming effect on the cattle and tried it for herself. She still uses her squeeze box to reduce anxiety, and similar equipment is now used with autistics in many treatment centres.

Dr Grandin is not a 'savant': she has outstanding insight into cattle, but has many other talents too. She is a prominent speaker and writer on autism, having published now a number of books on the subject. In doing this she displays a clear insight into her own psychological processes and those of other people, although she describes herself as still being without the intuitive empathy that would allow her to read other people's emotional expressions or gestures, and utterly uninterested in the human relationships that consume most of the rest of us. Her insights have implications that may radically change how we think of autism, and how we go about responding to it.

What causes autism?

In the 1940s psychiatrists drew parallels between autistic behaviour and the similar social withdrawal found in survivors of Nazi concentration camps, and hypothesized that autism was the result of severely dysfunctional and rejecting parenting. The idea seemed to be supported by studies of the attachment behaviours of children with severely disturbed mothers, who show somewhat similar dysfunctional social behaviour (Chapter 4). However, the evidence overwhelmingly refutes this theory of the cause of autism: the social dysfunction of autism is more profound and persistent than that deriving from poor attachment, and in any case, many of those with autism come from very normal, loving families. Nor is there a shred of credible evidence in favour of the theory that autism is caused by the MMR vaccination, hyped as that idea was in the popular media. In fact, it is now generally accepted that autism has a strong genetic component.

Evidence for a genetic basis for autism comes from the observation that the siblings of children with autism are 100 times more likely to have autism than are children in the general population. Furthermore, boys are four times as likely to have autism as girls, a sex bias commonly found in genetic disorders, reflecting differences in the way X and Y chromosomes function (Chapter 2). Despite these strong indications, the genetic contribution to autism has been harder to identify than was the case in other diseases with a similar genetic basis.

By the very nature of their problems, individuals with autism are not interested in social relationships. They seldom marry or have children, so that we don't find the family clusters following a line of descent that characterize diseases such as Huntington's chorea or certain breast cancers. And given the low incidence of autism in the general population, even the hundred-fold increase in risk for the siblings of a child with autism is hard to spot: the absolute risk of having a second child with autism is still only between 3 and 8 per cent, so that it is statistically likely that many paediatricians will pass an entire career without ever seeing two cases in one family. Nonetheless, some behavioural geneticists believe that 90 per cent of the characteristic disability of autism is a direct reflection of genetic factors.

The obvious hypothesis about the nature of the genetic defect in autism is that there is some damage to the neurological mechanisms which underlie normal social development and the ability to discover other minds. There has been some debate as to exactly what these mechanisms might be.

One hypothesis was that autism reflects the absence or serious dysfunction of the ToMM (theory of mind module), so that the child with autism lacks the normal pre-programming to discover the theory of mind (Baron-Cohen, Leslie and Frith, 1985; Baron-Cohen, Tager-Flusberg and Cohen, 1993). Studies using the false belief task produced a great deal of data which seemed to support this conclusion. Whereas normal children can succeed in false belief tasks by 4 years of age, even adolescents with autism typically fail in such tasks (Baron-Cohen et al., 1985). This isn't a reflection of the low IQ associated with autism: Baron-Cohen and colleagues compared children with autism and children with Down's syndrome with very similar IQs, and found that the children with Down's syndrome succeeded in the false belief task whereas those with autism did not.

Further evidence that the child with autism's problem is specifically connected to a failure to understand other minds comes from a comparison of the false belief and false photograph tasks. The mental demand of the two tasks is exactly the same. The only difference is that to pass the false belief task you must understand about other minds, whereas to pass the false photograph task you must understand about photographs but need know nothing about minds. Normal 3-year-olds fail both false belief and false photograph tasks: the mental demand of the task is too much for them. Normal 4-year-olds succeed in both tasks. By contrast, even adolescents with autism typically pass the false photograph task and fail the false belief task (Leslie and Thais, 1992).

However, as we have seen, many researchers reject the hypothesis that there are structures in normal brains (such as the ToMM) pre-set to ensure that our understanding will develop in certain ways or at a given age in a given domain (Lewis, 2000). Even researchers who support the general idea that development may draw on pre-programmed modules in some areas doubt that a faulty ToMM can be the explanation of autism, since autism can be detected in children under 3 years of age, and the ToMM is hypothesized not to be functional in normal children at this age (Smith and Tsimpli, 1996). The social difficulties of autism must therefore have some other origin. And indeed, there are data that raise doubts about whether the primary deficit in autism really is *specifically* an inability to master the conceptual principles that underlie a theory of mind, as an explanation in terms of a damaged ToMM assumes.

It's true that the majority of individuals with autism do seem to fail to develop a theory of mind. But this may not reflect a specific inability to master the conceptual insights necessary for a theory of mind so much as a very generalized difficulty for the autistic mind in abstracting conceptual insights of any kind. Normally, the human mind has an overwhelming tendency to notice patterns, to extract an overview of things, to orient to the whole rather than to the parts (Chapter 3). We take 'the big picture' rather than noticing every little detail. This tendency (which is hard to inhibit) is what allows us to move beyond a merely perceptual response and to abstract the conceptual insight which is the hallmark of normal intelligence. There is evidence that children with autism lack this organizing tendency: that they tend not to detect patterns as normal minds do, but to remain absorbed with individual elements, focusing on the parts rather than the whole (Frith, 1989). In other words, those with autism have greater difficulty than normal individuals in 'seeing the wood from the trees'. It's easy to see how this general cognitive bias in the autistic mind would make conceptual understanding more difficult in any and every area of knowledge, including conceptual understanding of other people.

Intriguingly, this characteristic of focusing on the parts rather than the whole may turn out to be the source of the prodigious 'savant' behaviours shown by some people with autism. Many savant behaviours involve extraordinary spatial or numerical abilities, where attention to the parts might well be an advantage over attention to the whole. This capacity has been identified as reflecting characteristic activity in part of the left temporal lobe of the brain in those with autism. By placing a pulsating magnet over this area of the brain in normal people (and so disrupting its normal function), Snyder and colleagues (2006) were able to induce prodigious savant-like counting skills in people without autism. Their hypothesis is that the magnetic pulse disrupted the mind's general tendency to orient to patterns, allowing 'raw' numeric skill to emerge.

Some highly intelligent people with autism actually do manage to develop a degree of insight into other people. Detailed examination of the nature of this insight raises more doubts whether the problem in autism is specifically an inability to develop a conceptual theory of mind. For example, Dr Temple Grandin (one of the most articulate of people with autism) describes herself as able to work out other people's feelings (that a colleague was jealous of her, for instance) by drawing principled inferences from their behaviour (that he sabotaged her work), although she was unable to 'read' people's emotions or motivations from their facial expressions or non-verbal behaviour as you or I might do. In effect, this individual seems to have and to use a conceptual theory of mind in drawing inferences about other people's minds, but to have no intuitive empathy with other people, no resonance with other minds, and no attraction to relating to others. Studies of other high-functioning people with autism find that they are much the same. The implication is that autism may involve a failure of intuitive mind-reading rather than an inherent inability to develop a conceptual theory of mind as such, although the absence of intuitive empathy may well make the development of a theory of mind much harder.

This conclusion led researchers to wonder whether the genetic deficit in autism might relate specifically to the mirror neuron system, which, as we have seen, seems to provide the basis for an intuitive empathy or resonancing with other minds in normal development. And in fact, there is now clear evidence that the mirror neuron system does not function in the autistic brain as it does in normal brains (Dapretto et al., 2006; Williams et al., 2001).

The development of autism

The absence of a functional mirror neuron system would deprive the baby with autism of the reflexes of social responsiveness, of imitation, and of the reflexive resonancing with other minds available to the normal baby. This could lead to what Williams and colleagues (2001) describe as a 'cascade of developmental impairments', a series of knock-on effects creating an escalating problem.

We can hypothesize that, without the basic social and 'empathic' reflexes of the normal baby, the baby with autism has no reason to find other people especially attractive as the normal baby does, and no neurological support in learning from or about other people. In normal babies these reflexes create orderly patterns of social interaction and experience – for example, as baby and parent take turns to imitate one another's facial expressions (Chapter 4). Patterns are what babies need, to begin to make sense of human behaviour (or anything else). Once a pattern exists, it can be observed, examined, explored, and what begins as a reflex response can begin to come under deliberate control, can begin to be conceptually understood. Without the reflexes that create and organize patterns in social interactions, the baby with autism is faced with an overwhelming jumble of experience. Not only is this much harder if not impossible to learn from, but it may also be frightening: the chaotic over-stimulation provided by this senseless jumble may make other people actively noxious to those with autism. There is evidence that those with autism do find other people dangerously unpredictable, a source of anxiety (Baron-Cohen et al., 1993): another reason to withdraw from contact with others.

Unresponsive to and uninterested in others, maybe even actively avoidant of people, the baby with autism doesn't experience the social interactions typical of early infancy: the interactions through which normal babies come to discover self and other (see Chapters 4 and 10). The problem escalates through infancy and childhood. Disengaged from other people, unwilling to interact or to engage in social or imaginative play, the child with autism misses out more and more on the activities and experiences which are important for the normal child's developing insight into other minds, developing social skills and developing language. The more social development and communicative skill deviates from the norm, the more socially isolated the child with autism becomes, and the more deprived of the very experiences that could foster healthy development, until he or she is locked in social isolation. Social withdrawal on this scale could be sufficient to seriously derail the autistic child's conceptual understanding (theory) of minds (Hobson, 1993), even without the additional handicap of dysfunction in reflexive resonancing with other minds which supports the normal baby's development.

The idea that autism reflects a 'cascade of developmental impairments' of this kind fits well with the 'dynamic systems' approach to explaining development (Lewis, 2000; Shanker, 2004; Thelen, 1995; Thelen and Bates, 2003; see Chapter 2). From this perspective, autism (and normal social development) are the product of a complex interaction between many different factors, each having knock-on effects, rather than reflecting the failure (or, in the case of normal development, success) of any overall developmental programme or module pre-specifying how interpersonal insight will progress. Some researchers believe that only dynamic systems theory offers an adequate framework for understanding either the difficulties of the autistic or the process of normal social development (Mundy and Markus, 1997). Models in this vein seem likely to become more important over the next few years.

Empathy and sympathy

Conceptual understanding, a theory of mind, is one important element in our ability to relate to other people. But understanding other people is not simply a matter of rational, analytical conceptual understanding. There is also the emotional dimension: the responses of empathy (feeling *with* others), and sympathy (feeling *for* others). These emotional reactions connect us to one another in ways that mere conceptual understanding can't. They are fundamental to the intersubjectivity that characterizes normal human relationships, the feeling of being in contact with another sentient being. They underlie the mutual caring that binds us together (Eisenberg and Fabes, 1992; Eisenberg and Miller, 1987; Saarni, Mumme and Campos, 1998).

The origins of empathy

The roots of empathy lie in the baby's early social reflexes (Saarni et al., 1998; Thompson, 1990; 1998), which, as we have seen in the previous section, may reflect the activity of the mirror neural system. As they imitate facial expressions, babies experience something of the emotion associated with that expression, and so co-experience (that is, experience in parallel) the feelings of the person whose expression they are copying. The young baby doesn't yet have any conceptual understanding that other people have emotions, doesn't yet make any clear distinction between him or herself and other people (Chapter 4), so that this co-experienced emotion doesn't yet involve any awareness of empathy with another person. Only as the infant begins to differentiate between self and other, and to understand that the other has feelings, does he or she become aware of sharing another person's emotions and hence able to experience a real empathy.

Strayer (1989) distinguishes between two different types of empathy: *participatory empathy*, where the child responds directly to another person's emotional distress without knowing what has caused that reaction, and *event-focused empathy*, where the child's empathic response is derived from an interpretation of a sequence of events (one child being shoved off a ride by another, for example) and an inference of the emotional reactions this will cause. Participatory empathy is obviously the more primitive of the two, and develops first, growing out of the reflexive co-experiencing of emotions, the resonancing with others that is probably provided by the mirror neuron system. Event-focused empathy is fundamentally dependent on conceptual understanding of human motivations and reactions, and begins to emerge in late infancy or early childhood. At first, the range of situations in which event-focused empathy is possible is small, reflecting the child's limited knowledge of human experience and reactions. Such knowledge grows through childhood and adolescence, and indeed, through adult life. The progressive expansion of the situations in which event-focused empathy is possible which this growing knowledge produces is a key facet of the development of empathy after infancy.

Empathy, sympathy and personal distress

Empathy is the root of sympathy. If we can't *feel with* another person, whether by directly experiencing a participatory empathy or by seeing or hearing of events that elicit an event-focused empathy, we can't sympathetically *feel for* them or be motivated to relieve their distress.

The ability to offer sympathy develops very early. For example, by 14 months of age, toddlers show sympathetic concern to others, trying to comfort another child by offering cuddles or a favourite toy (Zahn-Waxler, Robinson and Emde, 1992). In other words, by 14 months of age toddlers can not only empathize with another person's distress but have sufficient understanding to know how to offer a degree of help, and may be motivated to do so.

However, the relationship between empathy and sympathy is complex. For some individuals, empathically sharing another person's distress seems to be sufficient to elicit sympathy and help, but for others, it isn't. In some individuals, experiencing another person's pain generates only *personal distress*. That is to say, rather than experiencing a compassionate identification with the other and a sympathetic desire to help, they experience only a pain that is noxious to themselves. These individuals are motivated to protect themselves rather than to offer sympathetic help to others.

Sympathy and personal distress are very different reactions, although both arise out of empathic insight. Where sympathy is other-oriented, personal distress is a more self-centred response. Where sympathy motivates pro-social behaviours, personal distress motivates withdrawal, escape from the situation and the source of the pain – a response that can be far from pro-social. Even the physical response associated with the two reactions is different: where sympathy induces a compassionate facial expression and a slower heart rate, personal distress induces a fearful or horrified expression and a raised heart rate (Eisenberg et al., 1988).

The development of sympathy versus personal distress

The differential reactions of sympathy and personal distress are not age-related: that is to say, some individuals of any age from infancy to old age can and do show a sympathetic response to empathic insight, and others throughout the age span show only personal distress. How and why do these two different responses develop?

One factor disposing an individual towards either sympathy or personal distress seems to be underlying temperament (Chapter 4). Each of us has a level of arousal that is comfortable to us: too little and we are noxiously bored, too much and we are noxiously over-aroused.[2] Individuals who easily become emotionally over-aroused tend to find other people's distress too stressful, and to experience personal distress and withdrawal rather than sympathy (Eisenberg et al., 1988).

Temperament is largely genetic (Chapter 4). However, the tendency to respond with sympathy rather than personal distress seems also to be influenced by the quality of the child's attachment to the care giver in infancy (Zahn-Waxler, 1991). The dynamics of this early and all-consuming relationship create a world of shared meanings, defining the appropriate link between our own emotions and those of the other, providing a framework that, for good or ill, is then generalized beyond the parent-child relationship (Chapter 4). Children who receive consistent, sensitive parenting learn that other people are safe and predictable, and are secure in their ability to relate to, sympathize with and help others. By contrast, children who receive inconsistent or insensitive parenting learn that others can be unpredictable and unpleasant. Such children are less likely to feel safe in the face of strong emotions in others, and less secure in getting involved (such things may be dangerous), so that they are disposed toward personal distress rather than sympathy.

Although the characteristics of the child's relationship to the parent in early infancy can have lasting effects (Chapter 4), the tendency to respond either with sympathy or with personal distress is also shaped by the child's experiences throughout childhood and adolescence. Children in families or communities that encourage emotional expressiveness and sympathy tend to react in those ways, whereas children in families or communities that discourage these things tend to react with personal distress (Eisenberg et al., 1991). Those who grow up in social environments where positive emotions dominate tend to show sympathy, where

---

[2] This relationship between arousal and comfort can be plotted as a graph, yielding an inverted U-shaped curve. The principle relating arousal to comfort along this curve is known as the 'Yerkes-Dodson' law, after its discoverers. It applies to all living creatures.

those who grow up in environments where negative emotions dominate show personal distress (Eisenberg et al., 1992). Even in adolescence (Eisenberg and McNally, 1993) and mid-life (Koestner, Franz and Weinberg, 1990), individuals who received warm, accepting and positive parenting through childhood and adolescence are more likely to show high levels of sympathy and low levels of personal distress. Those with more negative family experience tend to show the reverse pattern, with high levels of personal distress and lower sympathy.

Right feeling, right behaviour

Children realize early on that personal distress and withdrawal are less socially acceptable than sympathy and helping out. Even children who respond with personal distress and so do not spontaneously offer help will often help if directly asked to (Eisenberg et al., 1992), although their reluctance to get involved communicates: their help is less willingly received than that offered spontaneously. Furthermore, most children claim that they would help someone in trouble, again, reflecting a general awareness that this is the 'right' answer, the socially acceptable intention. But self-report of an intention to provide sympathetic help is a poor predictor of who will actually offer help. A far better prediction can be made on the basis of facial expression and heart rate: those experiencing personal distress rather than sympathy as judged by these measures are much less likely to offer help, whatever they may say.

Gender differences in insight, empathy and sympathy

Cultural stereotypes suggest that women are more interested in and insightful about other people than men, and that women are more likely to respond with empathic sympathy. Certainly, an alien life-form who spent 10 minutes in any high street newsagent looking at the magazines on sale would come away with this conclusion. But in fact, it's quite difficult to say what these gender differences really reflect.

There is as yet no evidence that points to biological differences between male and female in the capacity to be empathic or in the inclination to be sympathetic. Both the basic discovery that other people have feelings, beliefs and intentions, and the basic ability to respond empathically to other people's emotions, seem to develop in just the same way in infancy, in girls and boys. Only in childhood are there observable differences between the genders, and these may reflect differences in behaviour rather than differences in empathy as such: for example, although girls are more likely to express sympathy and to offer help than boys, measures such as heart rate suggest that there is no gender difference in the underlying empathic response (Eisenberg and Fabes, 1998). Differences in behaviour may reflect social expectations and the way girls and boys are reared, rather than differences in underlying potential for sympathy (Saarni et al., 1998).

We expect girls to be nurturant, and accept boys who aren't. It's possible that these expectations reflect inherent biases in the male and female brain, as many popular books suggest (for example, Pease and Pease, 2000), but expectations also *create* behavioural biases (Rogoff, Gauvain and Ellis, 1984). Certainly, girls and boys are socialized to meet these gender expectations from the moment of birth. Given the direct tuition that this implies and the differential patterns of reward and punishment (for being 'a good girl'/a tomboy; a 'real boy'/a sissy and so on), it would not be surprising if girls were to allocate more effort to developing insight into other minds and a wider empathy than boys do.

Equally, in a culture which has long been suspicious (and, for all our progress, continues to be so) of close relationships between men but which regards intimate friendships as the sign of healthy femininity, it is hard to disentangle the degree to which the genders are biologically different in their need for intimate relationships rather than culturally disposed to differ in their behaviour. The social permission given to girls to have confidantes and to endlessly discuss other people's motivations provides them with a far greater opportunity to develop a broader insight and empathy than is typically allowed to boys. Thus, whether or not there are biological differences in underlying interest in other people, socialization practices in our culture can be expected to produce more women than men who are insightful and empathic in relation to others, and a greater average insight in women than in men.

Gender differences in the expression of sympathy tend to vary from one context to another. For example, girls and women tend to be more sympathetic than boys and men in the context of family and friendships. However, boys and men are more likely than girls and women to show sympathy to strangers (Zahn-Waxler, Cole and Barrett, 1991). Phenomena such as this suggest that there may be no fundamental difference in the predisposition to be sympathetic between the two genders, though there are social pressures and anxieties that mediate when and where sympathy occurs (Saarni et al., 1998).

Psychopathy and the failure of sympathy

It's probably the case that all human beings are, on occasion, capable of using insight into another person to deliberately cause hurt. In rows with parents, siblings, friends and lovers we say what we know will wound, even if we will regret it later. This is a 'game' that begins early in life, certainly by 18 months of age (Dunn and Munn, 1985). Furthermore, all of us are capable of a depressing degree of insensitivity. Of course, it's impossible to ever fully understand all the emotions and thoughts of another mind. But where that mind is very different from our own (a different generation, a different gender, a different social class, race or culture), the differences between us can make it very hard to have empathic insight, or to understand what the appropriate sympathetic response should be. These are the *normal* failures of empathy and sympathy.

However, there are also individuals whose failures of empathy and sympathy are *not* normal: not a reflection of a temporary loss of temper, nor the result of lack of empathic understanding. These individuals understand other minds very well. But they use this understanding only to exploit and to manipulate, and may even derive a sadistic pleasure from the infliction of pain (Hare, 1993; Strayer, 1987). Such individuals are popularly labelled *psychopaths*. More correctly, they are said to suffer from *antisocial personality disorder* or APD.

The clinical syndrome of antisocial personality disorder (APD)

Characteristically, individuals diagnosed as showing APD have very good conceptual insight into other minds, and are very good at using this insight to predict and influence other people's beliefs and feelings. They are often able to be socially charming, even likeable as a result (and even forensic psychologists and psychiatrists are regularly taken in by this). But typically, the individual with APD uses his insight into others to manipulate, deceive, bully or brutalize. He is utterly devoid of compassion or concern for his victim, and experiences no guilt and no remorse, not even social embarrassment (Hare, 1993), as the chilling example in **Box 9.6** shows. There is no conscience: no awareness of evil. It is as though the individual with APD has excellent event-focused or conceptual, theory-driven empathy – but the more emotional dimension of participatory empathy is awry. Something important is missing in such individuals.

Individuals with APD are substantially more likely than the average to engage in aggressive, delinquent, antisocial behaviours. Such behaviours in early childhood are known as *conduct disorders*. Some 25 to 40 per cent of children diagnosed with conduct disorder go on to develop APD in adult life (Hinshaw, 1994). A percentage of these individuals will go on to commit crimes of atrocious callousness – many serial murderers have APD. But the majority live within the law or commit only minor transgressions, 'white-collar' crimes and the like, working successfully as business-

box 9.6

Jason, a boy with no conscience

Source: E. Mash. and D. Wolfe, *Abnormal Child Psychology.* © 1999. Reproduced with permission from Wadsworth.

Thirteen-year-old Jason had been involved is serious crime – including breaking and entering, thefts, and assaults on younger children – by age 6. Listening to Jason talk was frightening. Asked why he committed crimes, this product of a stable, professional family replied, 'I like it. My f****** parents really freak out when I get in trouble, but I don't give a sh** as long as I'm having a good time. Yeah, I've always been wild.' About other people, including his victims, he had this to say: 'You want the truth? They'd screw me if they could, only I get my shots in first.' He liked to rob homeless people, especially 'faggots', 'bag ladies' and street kids, because 'They're used to it. They don't whine to the police ... one guy I got into a fight with pulled a knife and I took it and rammed it in his eye. He ran around screaming like a baby. What a jerk!'

people, surgeons or even psychiatrists. Indeed, the callous indifference of APD may be a positive advantage in many professions, allowing the individual to pursue courses of action from which more sympathy-prone individuals would flinch. Such 'functional psychopaths' have been described as wearing 'the mask of sanity' (Cleckley, 2003), although close inspection of the detail of their lives often reveals a pattern of poor relationships, bullying, and asocial or antisocial behaviour of one kind or another. Individuals of this kind are sometimes called *sociopaths*, reserving the term 'psychopath' for the minority of individuals with APD – perhaps 20 per cent – who are extremely dangerous.

Some researchers suggest that APD can be diagnosed in children as young as 3 years of age (Kochanska and DeVet, 1994). The first evidence for such a diagnosis is the failure to develop a conscience, the failure to show signs of guilt or remorse where normally developing 3-year-olds would do so (Chapter 12). Scored on the screening device for psychopathy (**Box 9.7**), a sub-group of school age children with conduct disorder show a callous, unemotional personal style: no guilt, no embarrassment, no empathy. Typically, this sub-group are more intelligent than others with conduct disorder (Christian et al., 1997), and more likely to go on to show APD in adult life. These are the children who, for example, torture the family pet without remorse.

box **9.7**

Screening device for psychopathy

Source: P. Frick and R. Hare, *The Psychopathy Screening Device* © 1997. Reproduced with permission from Multi-Health Systems, Toronto

Blames others
Engages in illegal activities
Is unconcerned about school
Acts without regard for consequences
Is shallow and ingenuine
Lies with skill and ease
Breaks promises
Brags excessively
Is easily bored
Uses or cons others
Teases or makes fun of others
Displays no feelings of remorse
Engages in risky and dangerous activities
Is charming but ingenuine
Reacts to correction with anger
Believes him/herself better than others
Fails to plan
Is unconcerned about others
Doesn't show feelings
Has unstable friendships

What causes APD?

It has long been known that brutal environments rear brutal children. Children learn what is 'normal', learn what to expect from others and how to behave toward them from the role models they see around them. We don't have to look far around the world or far back in our own history to see that previously quite normal people will do atrocious things in certain circumstances, even torturing others and ignoring their screams. Few of us are immune (Milgram, 1974).

But APD does not seem to be caused by the child's social environment in this way. It's true that many children who grow up to display serious APD come from dysfunctional families, or from families where antisocial behaviour is commonplace (Christian et al., 1997; Frick et al., 1994), and that growing up in such environments disposes any child toward antisocial behaviour and low levels of empathy or sympathy. But the psychopath seems to be qualitatively different from the average anti-social delinquent with poor empathy/sympathy. The average delinquent can (to an extent) be reformed by being led to a greater degree of empathic insight into the effects of his or her delinquency on others (this is the basis of all successful interventions in juvenile delinquency). By contrast, the psychopath is utterly unaffected by such interventions: he or she is totally indifferent to the rights or suffering of other people. Such callous individuals don't only occur in dysfunctional families: as is clear from the example in Box 9.6, a perfectly normal family may produce a psychopath (Hare, 1993).

Research suggests that in fact, there is a strong genetic basis for APD, which might contribute to the occurrence of family clusters of psychopaths (Hare, 1993). It's estimated that about 5 per cent of the population has APD. Of these, the vast majority are male: there are five times as many male as female psychopaths. This sex bias is consistent with a genetic disorder, reflecting the different functioning of the X and Y chromosomes (Chapter 2). Some research suggests that this disorder might be 70 per cent heritable.

As with autism, it has been suggested that psychopaths may have some kind of genetic dysfunction in the mirror-neuron system (Hare, 1999). As with autism, what the psychopath seems specifically to lack is the intuitive empathy with another person that the mirror neuron system might provide: the basis for caring and compassion. It's as if the psychopath doesn't feel with or identify with others' pain: it is simply meaningless to him. Without this instinctive empathy, aggression is not switched off by signs of fear, submission or appeasement in the other, as is the case for normal people, and indeed for most animals (Blair, 1995). This frees the psychopath to abuse others violently or even sadistically. What begins as a defect in empathy ends as a form of moral blindness (Chapter 12).

If both autism and APD are caused by genetic flaws in the mirror neuron system, why are the clinical syndromes so very different? Why can psychopaths easily master a conceptual theory of mind where individuals with autism typically cannot? Why do psychopaths exploit, manipulate and harm where those with autism don't? We don't yet know the answers to these questions. Perhaps the nature of the neurological defect is qualitatively different in the two disorders? Perhaps it is a matter of degree of damage to the same system? But what is clear is that, in understanding the neurological bases and development of these two disorders, we shall discover a great deal about the normal processes through which our ability to understand and to relate to other people develop.

In conclusion

Our ability to understand others is at the heart of what it means to be human. It's central to our ability to relate to one another, not just as objects that must be negotiated or manipulated, but as sentient beings like ourselves with whom we can share subjectivity. Ultimately, our understanding of other people becomes an articulate, conscious, cognitive process. As we gain experience of life we become progressively more insightful about the subtleties of how people might think and feel in relation to different events, and how their facial expressions might relate to their thoughts and feelings.

Early research into the way this insight into other people develops assumed that, because the final insight is so rooted in cognition, the origins of interpersonal empathy must also be cognitive. Studies focused on measuring conceptual understanding at different ages, charting the child's progress toward the realization that other people have intentions, feelings and beliefs. Debate centred around the age at which children could be said to have a 'theory of mind', and whether the emergence of this theory was biologically pre-programmed, the product of a special 'theory-of-mind module' in the brain.

Recent discoveries in neuroscience and new theoretical ideas about development have begun to transform our understanding of the development of insight into other minds. The roots of empathy may lie in the mirror neuron system, a system hard-wired into our brains through evolution that allows us to imitate others and so to effectively simulate their emotional states in ourselves, and through such simulations, to discover their intentions and feelings. Mirror neurons may provide the crucial starting point for the development of empathy, but they do not predetermine how development will proceed. It seems likely that there is no programme guiding us to discover a theory of mind of a particular kind: rather, the instinctive empathic reactions arising through the mirror neuron system interact with our experiences and our general cognitive tendency to reflect on and try to make sense of these reactions and events, so gradually constructing the articulate insights and empathy of the adult.

This theoretical interpretation fits well with the ideas of dynamic systems theory (Chapter 2), which argues that development is always the product of complex interactions between a great many different elements, interactions that produce effects that are unexpected and fortuitous, rather than pre-programmed into us. Dynamic systems theory offers a framework within which the interactions between physiological factors (such as the mirror neuron system) and experiential factors can be understood in new ways.

The extraordinary and very different deviations from normal development present in autism and APD may both reflect genetic defects of some kind in the mirror neuron system. Understanding exactly what these defects are, and how these neural defects interact with other things to generate the clinical syndromes of autism or APD will clarify the process of normal development, and may even suggest better interventions to reduce the impact of neurological damage in this area.

Exercises

1. How would you test the hypothesis that there are innate gender differences in empathy or sympathy?

2. What are the key differences between the hypothesis that autism is caused by the absence of an effective theory-of-mind module and the hypothesis that it is the result of damage to the mirror neuron system?

Suggested reading

For a taste of seminal research on theory of mind:

- J. Perner (1991) *Understanding the Representational Mind.* Cambridge, Mass., MIT Press.

For a review of the development of empathy, sympathy and insight into other minds:

- C. Saarni, D. Mumme and J. Campos (1998) Emotional development: action, communication and understanding. In N. Eisenberg (ed.), W. Damon (series ed.), *Handbook of Child Psychology*, vol. 3: *Social, Emotional and Personality Development* (New York: Wiley).

For research on the mirror neuron system and naïve psychology:

- V. Gallese and A. Goldman (1998) Mirror neurons and the simulation theory of mind reading. *Trends in the Cognitive Sciences* 2, pp. 493–501.

For an excellent description of the clinical syndromes of autism and APD from a developmental perspective:

- E. Mash and D. Wolfe (1999) *Abnormal Child Psychology*. New York: Wadsworth.

For an account of antisocial personality disorder:

- R. Hare (1999) *Without Conscience: The disturbing world of the psychopaths among us.* New York: Pocket Books.

Revision summary

Naïve psychology

- Fundamental to our ability to relate to one another is our ability to understand that other people are sentient beings like ourselves.

- The key insight is that other people have intentions, feelings and beliefs, and that these psychological constructs are causally interconnected.

- Children discover the constructs of naïve psychology gradually. By the end of the first year of life they have already understood that living things are goal-directed: that is, that they have intentions. By 2 years of age they understand that these intentions reflect desires. By 4 years of age, they understand that intentions also reflect beliefs.

Developing a theory of mind at 4?

- Seminal research using false belief and appearance/reality tasks suggest that there is a marked change at about 4 years of age in the child's ability to infer what someone else knows, and to predict how they will act, on this basis.

- It has been suggested that this reflects the development of a 'theory of mind': a radical new conception of other minds that induces a qualitative step-change in how children approach such tasks at about 4 years of age.

- Children certainly do develop conceptual understanding (theories) about minds, and all areas of conceptual development involve conceptual restructurings that qualitatively change the way the child thinks.

- But the data suggest that conceptual insight into the mind develops gradually, rather than through a sudden revolutionary insight. Four-year-olds are not as consistent in showing insight as a sudden change in understanding should predict. And the poor performance of 3-year-olds in false belief and appearance/reality tasks may reflect the overall cognitive demands of the task rather than specifically a lack of insight into other minds, masking the continuity between 3- and 4-year-olds in terms of their insight into theory of mind.

The process of discovering other minds

- It's clear that social interactions play a vital role in the development of understanding of other minds. The more a child is exposed to social interactions in which people comment on others' feelings, intentions and beliefs, the faster and more effectively development progresses.

- Developmental change in cognitive processing power also plays a role in expanding the child's ability to represent alternative views of reality and perspectives other than his or her own.

- Given that an understanding of other minds is a universal feature of human beings, it seems likely that there is an innate neurological basis for this ability. Very recent research suggests that the likely factor here is the mirror neuron system: the neurons that would fire in our brains were we to move a hand or be pricked by a pin also fire when we merely watch someone else move or be pricked, mirroring or simulating their actions and reactions in our own minds.

- The probability is that we first discover other minds by simulating them. In babies such simulations may occur without awareness, through the reflexive activity of mirror neurons. As the baby becomes more aware of the distinction between self and other, the simulations generated by the mirror neuron system support a dawning awareness that the other has intentions and feelings and beliefs.

- Building on this intuitive basis, more deliberate simulations allow us to understand other minds by imputing to them the mental states we would experience in ourselves in a given situation.

- Mirror neurons and some capacity for understanding other minds are also found in chimpanzees, suggesting that the roots of insight into others are hard wired into us by evolution.

Empathy and sympathy

- The discovery of the mirror neuron system may well explain why it is that we do not just understand another person's feelings in a cold, detached way – we share them, empathically feeling with the other.

- Empathy with other minds is the essential prerequisite for sympathy (a concern to protect and help another in distress), but it is not sufficient to yield sympathy. Whereas an empathic response triggers sympathy and pro-social actions in some, it triggers only personal distress and withdrawal in others.

- Sympathy and personal distress are not related to age: either can occur in infants or in old age and at all points in between. Babies are certainly capable of sympathetic interventions by the age of 14 months. These reactions are related to anxiety: more anxious children find empathy noxious and react with personal distress where less anxious children react with sympathy.

- A tendency to be sympathetic develops when a child enjoys a secure attachment to the parent in infancy and a generally positive and supportive home through childhood and adolescence. Infants with insecure attachments and more negative homes are more likely to develop a tendency toward personal distress. It's probable that what the child learns about others (that they're kind and predictable/dangerous and unpredictable) plays a key role directly in biasing development toward sympathy or personal distress, and indirectly by affecting levels of social anxiety.

- Although there are gender differences in empathic and sympathetic behaviour, there is no evidence that these reflect any underlying biological differences in capacity for empathy and sympathy between the sexes. Social expectations and child-rearing practices may well account for the differences observed.

Autism and psychopathy

- Recent research suggests that both autism and psychopathy (antisocial personality disorder) involve genetic damage to the mirror neuron system.

- In both cases, there seems to be an absence of the intuitive empathy, the instinctive 'resonancing' between minds that the mirror neuron system provides in normal babies. However, the resulting clinical syndromes are very different, suggesting that there are differences in the nature of the neurological deficit and developmental process yet to be discovered.

- The individual with autism tends to have very poor conceptual insight into other minds (although the highly intelligent may develop effective theories of mind). Whether they have theories of mind or not, these individuals are typically not interested in other people, profoundly socially dysfunctional and withdrawn.

- The psychopath tends to have very good conceptual insight into other minds and is often sociable, charming and popular. But he (more rarely she) has no feeling for others, no conscience or compassion, and uses insight into other minds only to manipulate, exploit, bully or even torture.

10
personality
and identity

By the time they reach their second birthday toddlers are already complex individuals with an impressive repertoire of social skills and emotional understanding, and a degree of self-awareness (Chapter 4). They have formed important attachments (however secure or otherwise these may be) to key people (Chapter 4). They are beginning to have a degree of insight into other minds, to understand that other people have feelings and desires (Chapter 9), to empathize and show sympathy. The 2-year-old has made enormous progress over the reflexive social and emotional responses of the newborn baby. Nevertheless, by comparison with older children, adolescents and adults, the 2-year-old is still simple, unformed and naïve.

Where do adult personality and our adult sense of personal identity come from? How do these things relate to and develop from infant individuality? How do social and emotional skills and relationships expand and develop through childhood and adolescence? These are the questions explored in this chapter and the next.

The development of personality

Research on personality emphasizes the differences between individuals and the origins of these differences, whereas research on social and emotional development tends to focus on commonalities across children, emphasizing the developmental patterns of our growing understanding of emotions, our own subjectivity, the ways we relate to other people. You could be forgiven for thinking that these are separate topics, separate phenomena, from the lack of contact between research in one area and another! But of course, they are not. Our social and emotional responses are the means through which our personalities are expressed. Individual personality is social and emotional development in action. To understand social, personal and emotional development, we need to understand both the universal psychological processes that operate in this area and the specific factors that shape individuality, and how these things interact through childhood and adolescence. The concept of personality provides an excellent framework for starting to understand these issues.

Traits and types

The bulk of research on personality doesn't concern itself with development at all. Rather, it focuses specifically on identifying the ways in which adult social beings differ from one another. This, of course, is very relevant to developmental questions: it's as well to understand what is developing, before setting out to explore how that happens.

Studying the structure of personality

As in every area of research, there are serious methodological and theoretical problems in characterizing the ways in which people can differ from one another. Research with adults faces many of the same problems as research on infant temperament (Chapter 4). What should we be measuring? How should we measure it? How can we check the reliability of our measures, the validity of the dimensions of personality we identify?

Personality testing is 'big business'. Schools, careers advisors, employers, the military, psychologists all use personality tests. We seem to like taking personality tests – they pop up endlessly in magazines and self-help books. Perhaps surprisingly, given that important decisions that affect an individual's life are often made on the basis of the results, there is very little rigour in much of this testing. Many tests in magazines and self-help books are created by simply inventing questionnaires and scoring systems without the least effort at any sort of check on the reliability or validity of the test, still less any ethical consideration of the possible effects the results might have on the individual. Even many well-known and apparently 'official' tests turn out to lack any real evidence of reliability or validity (Paul, 2004), and are applied and interpreted by people who are untrained and naïve as to the limitations of such tests (Paul, 2004).

Untrained testers often make assumptions about the nature of personality that are simply untrue (Paul, 2004). For instance, they may assume that scores on a personality test will predict behaviour, when in reality (as we shall see), behaviour is actually always the product of complex interactions between personality and the details of the context in which the behaviour occurs (Caspi, 1998). They may over-emphasize specific traits, not realizing that the way any one trait functions is modified by others (an extravert high in neuroticism is not particularly similar to an extravert low in neuroticism). They may assume that the answers people give to the questions on a test are an accurate description of their actual traits, when (as we shall discuss later) the evidence suggests that in reality we tend to systematically misperceive ourselves in certain ways (Dunning, 2006).

All of the false assumptions that untrained testers tend to make have also been made by psychology researchers at one time or another. The issues these assumptions raise reflect genuine methodological problems. (If *you* don't perceive yourself accurately, should *I* be asking someone else to make an assessment of you? But then, how much time would they have to spend with you, in how many different situations, to assess you accurately? What effects would being observed have: would you suppress your temper, say, and exaggerate your propensity for sweetness to impress the observer, or become inhibited and distracted by being watched? Is it ethical to monitor someone in this way? Since researchers don't know what the effects of such surveillance might be, could you really give informed consent to being observed?). They also reflect fundamental conceptual issues about the very nature of personality. (Since behaviour is influenced by context, how useful is the basic idea of personality? Do we actually have a stable personality, or do we simply project consistent traits onto other people and ourselves where none actually exist? If behaviour is the result of complicated interactions between a whole pattern of traits plus situational factors, is it feasible, for either a researcher or in everyday life, to make predictions of any kind on the basis of an abstract description of someone's personality? And if not, why do we assume that we can?)

The history of research in any area is usually a story of wrong assumptions, unexpected complications and serendipitous discoveries that only gradually give way to any sort of clarity (Rabbitt, 2006). The history of research in personality is a prime example (Paul, 2004). What follows through the rest of this section is the general consensus among researchers: our current understanding of the best resolution of these problems.

Personality traits

The bulk of the research on adult personality has looked for the traits that describe how individuals differ. Just as with research on infant temperament, there has been a tendency for different researchers to come up with different answers: for example, Cattell argued that there are 16 core dimensions to personality (Cattell et al., 1970), whereas Eysenck argued that there are only three (Eysenck and Eysenck, 1985). These different answers reflected different assumptions about what should be measured and how the resulting data should be interpreted. The problem was to find a principled way of identifying all the dimensions along which adults vary.

The current answer to this problem is the *lexical hypothesis* (Goldberg, 1993): the idea that we can work back to the core dimensions of personality by looking at the words people use to describe individuality in an everyday natural language (such as English). It's assumed that we invent words for everything we need to describe, so that all the variation between individuals will be present in the adjectives used for this in a given language ('anxious', 'sly', 'boisterous', 'nosy' and so on). Furthermore, it's clear that the words we use to differentiate between people are not entirely independent of one another. Rather, they go together in patterns, with groups of related traits ('anxious', 'nervous', 'insecure' for example) subsumed under a higher order trait (in this example, neuroticism). By analysing the patterns of relationship between words and the way we use them, we can work back to the principal dimensions along which individuals vary.

The basic idea behind the lexical hypothesis is a very old one. It was at the root, for example, of some of the earliest efforts to develop personality tests (Allport, 1937). But it's only recently that the approach has been applied rigorously, and produced a general consensus on the traits that structure personality (Goldberg, 1993). This consensus is that there are five core dimensions of adult personality, known as the *Big Five* traits (Goldberg, 1993). These traits can be remembered by the mnemonic OCEAN: they are *Openness to experience* (which correlates with intelligence), *Conscientiousness, Extraversion, Agreeableness and Neuroticism*. Each of these broad traits subsumes a wide variety of more specific characteristics (Goldberg, 1993; John, 1990), as is summarized in Table 10.1. There is substantial evidence validating these Big Five traits as the core dimensions along which adult personality varies the world over (Caspi, 1998; McCrae and Costa, 2005). There are also tests with an established level of reliability in measuring these traits. However, it's worth noting that there are also many 'online' tests of the Big Five on the internet whose reliability is rather more questionable.

Types

A rather different approach to understanding personality involves looking for types rather than traits: in other words, looking at personality as a composite whole rather than decomposing it into separate traits. This holistic approach produces an even more abstract view of personality differences than does a trait-based account, standing back from the detail of behaviours ('I like parties') to look for the overall flavour of personality.

The most influential study taking this approach (Block, 1971) found three basic personality types. These were *ego resilients*, who were well adjusted and socially skilled; *vulnerable over-controllers* who were poorly adjusted and rigidly over-controlled; and *unsettled undercontrollers* who were also poorly adjusted, but impulsive and anti-social. Each of these types is at the top of a hierarchy subsuming a wide range of more specific characters or patterns of traits. Studies using a variety of different methods suggest that most adult personalities fall into one of Block's three main types (Pulkkinen, 1996), though other, rarer types are also occasionally found (York and John, 1992).

Traits, types and development

In adults, personality is often measured by using paper-and-pencil tests in which the individual reports the extent to which various statements table **10.1**   An overview of the Big Five personality factors

Big Five factor	Adjectives	Adult behaviour	Child behaviours
Extraversion	Active Assertive Enthusiastic Outgoing	Skilled in play, humour; facially, gesturally expressive; behaves assertively; gregarious	Emotionally expressive; a talkative child; makes social contact easily; not inhibited or constricted
Agreeableness	Generous Kind Sympathetic Trusting	Sympathetic, considerate; arouses liking; warm, compassionate; basically trustful	Warm and responsive; helpful and cooperative; develops genuine and close relationships; tends to give, lend, share
Conscientiousness	Organized Planful Reliable Responsible	Dependable, responsible; able to delay gratification; not self-indulgent; behaves ethically	Persistent in activities, does not give up easily; attentive and able to concentrate; planful, thinks ahead; reflective: thinks and deliberates before speaking or acting
Neuroticism	Anxious Self-pitying Tense Worrying	Thin-skinned; basically anxious; concerned with adequacy; fluctuating moods	Fearful and anxious; tends to go to pieces under stress; becomes rattled and disorganized; not self-reliant, not confident; appears to feel unworthy, thinks of self as 'bad'
Openness/intellect	Artistic Curious Imaginative Wide interests	Wide range of interests; introspective; values intellectual matters; aesthetically reactive	Curious and exploring; appears to have high intellectual capacity (whether or not actually achieved); creative in perception, thought, work or play; has an active fantasy life

Source: A. Caspi, Personality development across the life course. In N. Eisenberg (ed.), W. Damon (series ed.), *Handbook of Child Psychology*, vol.3: *Social, Emotional and Personality Development*. ©1998, New York: Wiley. Reproduced with permission from John Wiley and Sons.

apply to him or her. Obviously, this means of measuring personality would not be viable in infancy and early childhood, even if the questions typically validated for such measures applied to the very young ('I'd rather read a book than go to a party', and so on). In exploring personality in the very young we rely on observer ratings. How valid are the assessments of children's personalities made by observers? Here is yet another issue that combines the strictly methodological with the theoretical. If such ratings don't come up with consistent results, do we conclude that the raters aren't reliable or do we conclude that there isn't any consistency to be identified?

The data suggest that adult personality structures, whether traits or types, cannot be identified in the children below 3 years of age in any coherent way (Caspi, 1998). This is in marked contrast to observations of older children, adolescents and adults, where different raters between whom there is no possibility of collusion reliably produce strikingly similar descriptions of a given individual's personality characteristics (Kendrick and Funder, 1988). These descriptions are functional: that is to say, they validly describe an individual, differentiating him or her from others. The specific behaviours observed don't seem to matter. It seems, then, that raters are very effective in identifying personality traits and types. The failure to find these things in the very young strongly suggests that they aren't there.

The consensus is, then, that adult personality structures only begin to emerge at the very end of infancy. Only from 3 years of age onward can children's personalities be categorized in terms of Block's three adult personality types (Caspi and Silva, 1995; Hart et al., 1997; Robins et al., 1996; Van Lieshout et al., 1995). Equally, it is only at around 3 years of age that children's personalities begin to reflect the Big Five traits in any coherent way (John et al., 1994; Van Lieshout and Haselager, 1993). And even then, the structure of personality traits is not identical between children and adults. Through childhood and early adolescence observers identify two extra traits which are not seen in adults: these have been labelled *activity* and *irritability*. It seems that the structure of adult personality may begin to emerge at the end of infancy, but continues to develop through childhood and adolescence.

Infant temperament and adult personality

The general consensus of research is that individual differences in personality originate in the temperamental dispositions of early infancy (Goldsmith et al., 1987; McCrae and Costa, 2005). Right from birth, babies differ in how they respond to the world: one is upset by things which don't affect another at all; one is placid and sleepy, another active and alert; one is easy to soothe, another can't be consoled and screams until he or she (and everyone else) falls asleep exhausted. Up to six such dispositions have been identified (see Chapter 4). These temperamental dispositions are stable, innate characteristics of the individual which probably reflect the baby's neurological reactivity (Rothbart and Bates, 1998). They are the obvious place to look for the origins of adult traits.

The Big Five traits show a clear genetic influence (Caspi, 1998). Monozygotic twins who develop from a single egg and who therefore share exactly the same genes are more similar to one another on these traits than are dizygotic twins or non-twin siblings, who develop from different eggs and share fewer genes. Blood siblings who share the same parents are more similar to one another in personality than they are to siblings who have been adopted into the family and with whom they share no familial genes. This is true for all the Big Five traits, although there is some evidence suggesting that openness to experience may be more strongly influenced by genetics than the other four traits (Loehlin, 1992), possibly because openness to experience is closely associated with intelligence, which is itself heritable (see Chapter 8).

The obvious inference is that the stable dimensions of innate infant temperament provide the genetic component of personality traits. However, the relationship between infant temperament and adult traits is far from direct. For example, the individual differences in neurological reactivity that generate innate temperament seem to be stable through life (Rothbart and Bates, 1998). By contrast, personality changes: even monozygotic twins become less similar as they grow older (McCartney, Harris and Bernieri, 1990). The greater the differences in their experiences, the greater the divergence between their personalities (Rose et al., 1988). It's clear that experience plays a crucial part in the development of personality traits, whereas it plays no role in setting temperament. In fact, the evidence suggests that the importance of genetic factors in shaping personality declines markedly through development (Viken et al., 1994). Some researchers believe that by 20 years of age, personality is primarily a reflection of the particular experiences we've had, rather than of our innate temperaments (Baltes, Reese and Lipsitt, 1980).

Nor is there any straightforward mapping of the innate dimensions of infant temperament onto adult personality traits. That is to say, the dimensions of infant temperament don't match the 'Big Five' traits in any simple way, as **Figure 10.1** shows. The connections suggested in this figure are only speculative. We haven't got longitudinal studies which follow babies from birth to adulthood, relating their infant temperament to adult character. Even so, it seems likely that individual traits are influenced by a pattern of temperamental dispositions rather than being a 'mature' form of a given disposition.

And on closer inspection, there are good reasons that we shouldn't expect to see a direct line of descent between innate temperamental dispositions and adult personality traits: temperament and personality are fundamentally different things. Temperament is an unreflecting, reflexive bias to respond in certain ways: it's like the 'default' setting on a system. An individual is genetically disposed to be more or less reactive, for example – in other words, to have a stronger or weaker visceral reaction to experiences. All you need to have a temperamental disposition of this kind is a neural system innately set in a particular way (Rothbart and Bates, 1998). Personality isn't like that at all.

If you think about the Big Five personality traits, each one involves beliefs, attitudes and values. Extraverts *like* other people and social events, *expect* to be liked and have a good time, where introverts *prefer* their own company or at least, quieter social interactions, and *anticipate* awkward embarrassment, boredom or other forms of social misery. The neurotic fearfully *expect* to fail and to be failed, where this would never

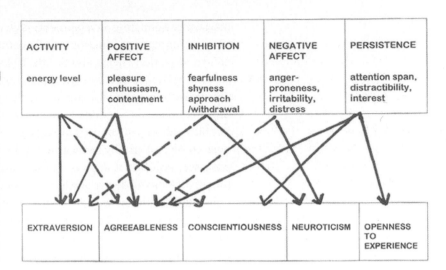

figure 10.1

Hypothesized links between the infant temperament and adult personality structure

Solid lines suggest positive correlations, dashed lines suggest negative correlations

Source: A. Caspi, 'Personality development across the life course', in N. Eisenberg (ed.), W. Damon (series ed.), *Handbook of Child Psychology*, vol. 3, *Social, Emotional and Personality Development*. © 1998, New York: Wiley. Reproduced with permission from John Wiley and Sons.

cross the mind of the more confident individual. The conscientious *value* responsibility and reliability, where the less conscientious don't – and so on. Personality traits can be seen as the story we tell ourselves about what we like and don't like; what we and other people are like and what to expect of them; who we are, and how much we matter. They have been described as the implicit theories about ourselves and the social world that we use to organize and regulate our own behaviour and experience (Westen, 1991).

From this perspective, the development of personality can be seen as a movement from reflexive (temperament-driven) reactions to conceptually driven ones (traits). This would explain why the structure of adult personality only begins to emerge in early childhood: the development of conceptually driven traits requires a degree of self-awareness and insight into other minds, and is almost certainly fuelled by the development of language: the mastery of words that can label and generalize experiences. These are the achievements of late infancy and early childhood (Kagan, 1984).

Some researchers have questioned the extent to which adult personality traits reflect conceptual theories rather than biological 'givens' (McCrae and Costa, 2005). Theories are, potentially, flexible and variable. So if the 'Big Five' reflect conceptual theories, why do they emerge the world over? Why aren't there cultures in which people vary in terms of an entirely different set of traits, reflecting entirely different sets of experiences? These researchers argue that, for all the differences between traits and temperamental dispositions, the universal nature of the Big Five *must* imply that they are the product of a maturing biological programme, in some way (McCrae and Costa, 2005).

But as we've seen in other chapters (Chapters 2 and 3), the existence of universal patterns need not mean that there is any sort of biological programme directing development: such effects can be explained in terms of the serendipitous functioning of a complex dynamic system formed by child and world (Thelen and Smith, 1994). There is no need to hypothesize the existence of a biological programme that predetermines the Big Five traits to explain why this particular structure of personality may be universal. The human mind is an extraordinarily skilled pattern-detector. We find patterns in almost everything. If there is a pattern there, we don't need to be biologically forewarned of its shape – our general conceptual processes will find it anyway. If there are patterns in how people differ, those patterns will determine how we conceptualize the variation between individuals, and how we conceptualize ourselves.

And of course, there *are* patterns in how people differ. The Big Five traits can be seen as capturing the essence of those patterns – of being what is 'out there' to discover (implicitly, in everyday life; explicitly, in formal research) as we try to make sense of the social world and our interactions with it (Buss, 1991). If people the world over differ in terms of these five traits, it is because these traits reflect the primary ways in which it is *possible* for human beings to differ. The point is most easily illustrated in connection with personality types. A key dimension of difference between Block's three types come down to people who react to events 'too much', 'too little' and 'just right': since these are the only real possibilities for variation, it's not surprising that these are what emerge.

The evidence strongly suggests that personality traits are conceptual constructions rather than the products of biological maturation (Roberts, Walton and Viechtbauer, 2006a). How then to explain the genetic component of traits, particularly in childhood and adolescence? The most plausible answer is that this genetic component is *indirect*: that it somehow reflects the influence of innate temperament on the particular way we come to construe ourselves and the social world as we develop (Caspi, 1998). To understand this we have to look at the *process* of development: the process through which the conceptual theories of self and others which define personality are constructed.

Developing a consistent personality

The way we behave has an enormous effect on how other people react to us, and vice versa. Leave work irritable and tense, for example, and there's a good chance you'll end up having a row with someone. Leave lively and happy, and a pleasant evening is more likely. We all know that it's easier to relate positively to someone who is positive, and all too easy to fall into hostility with someone who is behaving negatively.

This reaction–evocation cycle is at the root of all social experience for all of us, and is a major factor in the development of a consistent personality. In a very real sense our own behaviour creates the social world we live in: the affectionate, easy-going child evokes positive reactions and so experiences a positive and endorsing social world, and is therefore reinforced in a positive attitude and approach toward other people, whereas the irritable or hostile child evokes more negative reactions and rejection, a more negative and critical social world, which reinforces his or her suspicion and hostility.

Setting the tone of the reaction–evocation cycle

What determines whether a given child will experience a reaction–evocation cycle that is generally positive, or one that is negative? The answer lies in early infancy, and in the infant's earliest social experiences.

Given that personality is shaped by the reaction–evocation cycle and shows a clear genetic component, it seems probable that the overall tone of the particular reaction–evocation cycle that an infant experiences is influenced by his or her innate temperamental disposition. It's easy to see how this could happen. Babies and infants with 'difficult' dispositions, who are irritable and hard to soothe, are far less rewarding to interact with than 'easy-going' babies. Difficult babies are likely to experience more negative reactions than easy-going babies do, as a consequence. So right from birth, babies influence the way others react to them and what is there for them to learn about themselves and other people.

Exactly how big an impact a baby's innate temperament has on the reaction–evocation cycle he or she experiences in early infancy seems to vary. Studies of families where adult resources (economic and personal) are low and parenting skills poor have found evidence that the baby's temperament affects the quality of the attachment between parent and child, with 'difficult' babies experiencing poorer quality attachments (Van den Boom and Hoeksma, 1994). Other studies focusing on a broader and better resourced population find that the baby's tempera- ment has a negligible effect on this relationship (Roisman and Fraley, 2006). Skilled parenting can offset the effects of a difficult temperament and establish a good quality attachment relationship (Wachs, 1994).

Whether it is shaped more by the infant's own temperament or more by the parent's skills (or most likely, by an interaction between these things), the quality of the early attachment relationship has a funda- mental effect on the way the reaction–evocation cycle sets out. Secure attachment encourages generally positive social behaviour, insecure attachment encourages a more negative and hostile tendency. Once established, these patterns of behaviour extend beyond the attachment relationship to other contexts and relationships. Positive patterns of behaviour elicit positive reactions in new situations, and negative patterns elicit negative ones. The behaviours and expectations that the child takes into a situation are thus reinforced by the reactions of other people. A self-perpetuating cycle has been set up. By 3 years of age, this has produced the consistent behaviours and expectations that we call personality.

'Reality' and the power of the reaction–evocation cycle

The reaction–evocation cycle is immensely powerful, because once a particular way of reacting to events has been established, it's hard to break out of the social world that this evokes. This is because the social world doesn't provide 'reality checks' in quite the same way that the physical world does.

In the physical world, the laws of nature act as a firm constraint on development: we live in a physical environment with particular features (gravity, for example) that are impervious to our thoughts or behaviour. The infant taking his or her first wobbly steps gets objective feedback about what works or doesn't work in trying to balance a human body. Conceptual understanding of the physical world is also shaped by objective feedback: the 5-year-old playing with balance scales gets objective feedback on the accuracy or otherwise of his or her theories. But the social world doesn't provide objective information in this way, precisely because it is formed by, rather than impervious to, our own thoughts and behaviour.

Expect people to dislike you and they probably will, in response to the negativity your expectation generates in you; expect people to be kind and they probably will be. Because our behaviour evokes the social world we live in, the expectations that drive that behaviour will tend to be confirmed, making it more likely that we will go on behaving in the ways which elicit the very social world which will confirm our expectations. Whereas objective reality can offer corrective feedback in our efforts to understand the physical world, our beliefs about ourselves and social relationships have the quality of self-fulfilling prophecies.

The powerful self-fulfilling effects of the reaction–evocation cycle are clearly demonstrated in a study contrasting aggressive and depressive children (Quiggle et al., 1992). On past experience, the aggressive child believes that other people are generally hostile, out to do you down, and that the best way to deal with this is to respond in kind. With this mind-set, the child is on the lookout for the slightest cue that others have begun to be hostile, and over-interprets things, seeing hostility where none really exists. Reacting aggressively, the child now evokes real hostility from others, which confirms his or her world view and social strategy. The depressive child believes that he or she is inadequate and likely to fail, and that there's little to be done about this. This mind-set alerts the child to over-interpret the slightest sign that failure might be imminent, and cues the reaction of giving up when such 'evidence' is found, which means that failure does now become inevitable, reinforcing the child's poor self-image.

The same sort of process of getting what you expect goes on operating through adult life. For example, individuals with different orientations to the world (in other words, different personalities) experience exactly the same interaction with the stock market in very different ways: those with negative expectations having negative experiences and those with positive expectations having positive experiences, even though all had made exactly the same returns on their investment (Smith et al., 2006)!

The patterns of personality traits that emerge through the reaction–evocation cycle have far reaching consequences, influencing a great many aspects of life: success in school (Conard, 2006) and in adult career (Barrick and Mount, 1991) for instance; delinquency (Caspi et al., 1994; Manders et al., 2006), the tendency to make healthy or unhealthy lifestyle choices (Friedman, H. et al., 1995; Hampson et al., 2006), to become clinically depressed (Christensen and Kessing, 2006) – and many other things.

Working to maintain the familiar reaction–evocation cycle

It's easy to see how, once we have beliefs and expectations about ourselves and the social world, a characteristic style of reacting (personality) can become 'locked in' through the reaction–evocation cycle. But we are not simply the helpless victims of this cycle. The evidence suggests that we also deliberately (*proactively*) seek out situations and relationships that fit with our existing view of the world and of ourselves: situations that will inevitably reinforce our existing personalities (Caspi, 1998).

Why do we do this? It probably isn't a conscious choice, or even something we're really aware of. But the familiar, the world we understand generally seems safer than a world different from our expectations. In a familiar world, we know where we are, we know how to interpret things, what to expect, how to respond. Situations and people who react in familiar ways are therefore more attractive than those that threaten our understanding, so we actively seek out the familiar.

We choose friends who are like ourselves and who create the social world we are familiar with (Ennett and Bauman, 1994). We choose a marriage partner in the same way, preferring someone similar to ourselves (Epstein and Guttman, 1984), who will create a new family similar to the one we grew up in, even where that was unhappy (Buss, 1984, 1987; Caspi and Herbener, 1990). We'd rather feel safe knowing how things stand than risk the unfamiliar ('better the devil you know'). We also choose activities and careers that match our social expectations rather than exploring our full potential. For example, people who enjoy autonomy choose careers where autonomy can be exercised and reinforced, whereas those who fear autonomy choose work that is routine and without responsibility: in each case, choosing a career that strengthens their existing characteristics.

Proactive reinforcement of our personalities of this kind begins as soon as the child is old enough to make his or her own decisions, rather than living a life controlled by parents or carers. It becomes progressively more important through childhood and adolescence and on into adult life, shaping not just our personalities but the whole way a life can unfold. For example, set off on a negative reaction–evocation cycle by a combination of difficult temperament and poor parenting, the individual is progressively locked into negativity by the consecutive life-choices he or she proactively makes: choosing equally antisocial friends, dropping out of school, engaging in delinquency and so on.

Developmental processes in personality

Given the power of the reaction–evocation cycle and our tendency to proactively reinforce our own personalities, it's easy to see how early childhood experience might well create a set of traits which would persist through the whole of life. And in fact, the data suggest that there is a very considerable degree of stability in an individual's traits through childhood and adolescence, both in terms of the absolute level of a given trait, and in terms of the rank order of an individual's scores on a given trait relative to other people's scores (De Fruyt et al., 2006). This stability is lowest in early childhood, when traits are still forming, and increases in the period from childhood through adolescence and on into early adult life (Hampson and Goldberg, 2006), reaching a peak of stability at about 30 years of age (McCrae and Costa, 2005), although there is evidence for some degree of change continuing through middle and old age (Roberts, Walton and Viechtbauer, 2006b).

Stable traits, changing behaviour

Despite this basic stability, the characteristic behaviours that reflect our personalities show developmental changes through childhood and adolescence and even in adult life. A 2-year-old expresses aggression by throwing a tantrum, bashing things and other people. A 12-year-old may express aggression very differently: using words rather than physical violence, say, and subtlety rather than full frontal assault.

This kind of change in characteristic behaviour reflects the increasing sophistication of conceptual understanding and social skills, altering the way a given trait is expressed rather than a change in traits themselves. Such effects can continue through the whole of life: we (hopefully) know a thing or two about how to react to a recalcitrant colleague or difficult lover at 50 that we didn't know at 20, even if (sadly) our basic tendency to interpret events in a neurotic way and over-react hasn't changed a whit over the decades.

Changing roles and changing emphases

Furthermore, there are age-related changes in the social roles we occupy as we grow older: the progression from being baby of the family to older sibling, for example, or from preschooler to schoolchild, from schoolchild to college student, from student to employee, parent, retiree, grandparent. These successive roles bring new social expectations, activities and concerns which affect which aspects of our personalities are most relevant, and so most powerfully expressed or suppressed.

For example, the transition from the uncertainties of late adolescence (What shall I do for a career? Who shall I choose as a soulmate?) to the more stable circumstances and responsibilities of early adult life (got the job, got the mate) is developmentally associated with a fall in neuroticism and a rise in conscientiousness (Carmichael and McGue, 1994; Roberts et al., 2006b). Openness to experience rises in adolescence and falls in old age (Roberts et al., 2006b), reflecting the changing horizons of each age group: the expanding possibilities for the adolescent, the more proximate focus of the elderly.

Such effects reflect social roles rather than age as such: levels of conscientious responsibility are far higher in 8-year-olds in cultures where children of this age are expected to handle real responsibilities (guarding the cattle, looking after younger children) than they are in cultures such as our own where the average 8-year-old is not trusted with any important task at all (Rogoff, Gauvain and Ellis, 1984). Equally, at whatever age, becoming a mother is associated with a decline in levels of aggression and a corresponding rise in patience which seems essential to the survival and sanity of all concerned (Guttman, 1975), although the effect reverses when the children grow up and leave home (Wink and Helson, 1992).

Cultural processes in personality development

Not all the social roles we occupy are part of a developmental progression. For example, a key role we play throughout our lives is a gender role: being male or female. Society has generally had some pretty strong views as to how these roles should be played, and hasn't been particularly gentle with those bucking the system. This has clear effects on the way personality develops, probably both by providing the individual child with a 'script' for how to be male or female (which will be discussed further later in the chapter) and by moderating the reactions our behaviour evokes in others: a weeping girl is likely to receive sympathetic support where a weeping boy may well still be told to pull himself together.

Research from the 1960s illustrates the long-term impact of cultural gender expectations on personality development (Kagan and Moss, 1962). In this longitudinal study, the traits of passivity and dependency declined between childhood and adulthood in boys but not in girls, whereas aggressiveness declined in girls but not boys. In both cases, the development of personality reflected the gender stereotypes of the period.

It's worth noting that social stereotypes of gender (and many other social roles) vary enormously from one period of history to another, from one political and religious culture to another. Whatever particular cultural stereotype is in force influences the development of personality, so that political, religious and historical movements can affect the way characteristic behaviour and traits develop across whole populations, moderating the impact of innate dispositions. The middle-class 'ladette' is common in 21st-century Britain, but was unknown in the world of Jane Austen, for example.

The impact of gender stereotypes on the reaction–evocation cycle underlines the potential plasticity of personality development. The fact is that everyone we interact with comes with their own cultural as well as personal history, their own expectations, values, interpretations and characteristic reactions. My 'baggage' affects how I respond, just as yours affects how you respond. It's the interaction between us which creates the reaction–evocation cycle each of us experiences.

Many of the cultural expectations and stereotypes that affect the way others perceive and respond to us are active from the moment of birth, shaping the reaction–evocation cycle through which our personality traits are first formed in early childhood. This is true of gender expectations, for example, and for many other factors that define our lives, such as being born into a rich and powerful family or nation as opposed to a poor and powerless one, or being born into an ethnic majority or minority, or into a family structured around a patriarchal/matriarchal or egalitarian culture, a religion encouraging self-esteem or one emphasizing self-abasement. We are born into a world that has, in many ways, already decided who we're going to be, and which reacts to us through infancy and childhood in ways that tend to make sure we turn out as cultural stereotypes expect.

Change and consistency through the lifespan

As we've seen, there are powerful psychological, cultural and developmental forces shaping our personalities from infancy through to adult life. In general, the basic traits developed in childhood remain pretty stable over the course of our lives, a stability helped along by our own proactive choices, even if the expression of personality changes through the course of development. But the basic shape of personality isn't necessarily 'fixed' in childhood. This is evident from the fact that monozygotic twins become less alike in personality traits as they grow older and their life experiences diverge (McCartney et al., 1990; Rose et al., 1988).

There are some individuals who show quite remarkable changes in their whole approach to life (Saul of Tarsus – aka St Paul – on the road to Damascus, for instance), even if the majority of us don't. There would be very little point in psychologists investing their effort in therapies and training programmes designed to heal personality disorders (which are often exaggerated versions of normal personality characteristics) or to reduce delinquent recidivism and the like if we didn't believe that real change in the ways people habitually interpret and respond to life (in other words, changes in the implicit theories that underpin personality) were possible.

How can we understand the balance between consistency and change in personality through the course of life, and what determines whether an individual's personality will be consistent or change? One answer to this is to take a lifespan perspective (Sampson and Laub, 1993).

Life trajectories, transitions and turning points

The reaction–evocation cycle we inhabit, and the proactive choices that reinforce this cycle, create a basic *trajectory* for a life. Within this consistent trajectory, however, there are numerous *transitions*: specific changes in our circumstances and activities associated with starting school, for example, or finding a first job, getting married or divorced, promoted, fired, emigrating and so on. By exposing us to new roles and situations, new people whose reactions to us might be different from those of the people we've known so far, these transitions offer the possibility of breaking old patterns of behaviour and so disrupting and redirecting the reaction–evocation cycle, reshaping our characteristic reactions and even traits. The more transitions an individual experiences, and the more profound a change the transition involves, the greater the possibility of real change in personality and characteristic behaviour.

But in fact, the majority of transitions have relatively little effect on our characteristic behaviour, let alone our underlying traits. We simply import our old expectations and reactions into a new situation, modifying these only slightly (if at all), and so recreate the same old reaction–evocation cycle as before. Sometimes this happens because we ourselves have proactively chosen the specific transitions we experience, so that there is minimal challenge to our existing ways of being (choosing a job to match your personality, for example, or marrying someone 'just like Dad'). Sometimes transitions call forth a change in how we express our traits or in the relative importance of different traits (that is, a change in characteristic behaviour) that does not involve any fundamental change in underlying personality at all. (Developmental transitions are an example: everybody may become more subtle in expressing anger in middle childhood and less neurotic in late adolescence, but individual differences in the tendency to interpret the world angrily or neurotically remain the same.) Sometimes we simply throw away the possibility of breaking out of a particular cycle by being too fixed in our ways: the defensive child who habitually wards off the fear of being attacked by 'getting his retaliation in first' can alienate a new teacher or a new potential friend who might otherwise have provided the first supportive relationship of his life, for example. Personality traits really do have a tendency to remain remarkably consistent (McCrae and Costa, 2005).

And even when a transition *does* produce real change in how we typically react or view ourselves, the effect is often either transitory or limited to one particular context rather than generalized (Scarr and McCartney, 1983). For example, a diffident child who generally avoids all risk of failure by not trying might be led into effective effort and a degree of self-esteem by a sensitive and supportive science teacher, but be utterly unable to maintain this new approach in the face of parents who continue to devalue her efforts at home, or when confronted by the sarcasm of the geography teacher. (One of the notable and tiresome experiences of the transition between living at home and living at college is the helpless slide from the new, sophisticated persona who has emerged at college back to sulky adolescent when you go home for the holidays, brought on by parents who haven't stopped treating you like a child.)

Situation-specific transitions in how we behave are more common than is popularly supposed. At some level, we all know that a child who is lively and boisterous at home may be nervous and withdrawn in school, or that a man who is regarded by his colleagues at work as charming and gentle may be a bully to his wife. At one time such situational inconsistencies in characteristic behaviour led some researchers to doubt whether personality really had much effect on how we behave at all (Mischel, 1968). But the fact is that behaviour is never the product of personality alone: it is always the result of an interaction between our collection of traits as a whole, and factors in the situation in which it occurs (Funder, 2006). A child who is generally anxious but also extravert may feel safe enough to express her extraversion at home, but not in the more uncertain environment of the classroom. A man who is fundamentally aggressive and disagreeable may prudently mask these traits in playing his role as a doctor, but give them free rein in dealing with his more powerless family. Such situational variations in behaviour may reflect only the different ways traits are called forth or expressed in different situations, rather than necessarily involving variation or change in the underlying traits themselves.

However, there are some transitions that genuinely induce profound change in the implicit conceptual theories of self and other which define our personalities, and which hence create fundamental and general change in how we characteristically interpret and react to events across life as a whole (Roberts et al., 2006a, 2006b). Such transitions are called *turning points* (Elder, 1985). They can be precipitated by either radical changes in our physical circumstances (being adopted from poverty by a pop star, for example, or paralysed after a car crash), or radical changes in our social circumstances (marrying someone who thinks you're wonderful after a lifetime of being put down; discovering a new talent and gaining new respect in a new career; being publicly shamed and shunned after an ill-judged action, and so on), or by new ideas or insights that change how we conceptualize ourselves (the reason we read 'self-help' books or convert to religions). As these examples indicate, turning points can occur suddenly, or can arise from more gradual processes (Pickles and Rutter, 1991). What is critical to their effect is that something happens that radically challenges the very assumptions on which our interpretations of self and other, and our consequent behaviour, have been based.

Some people (maybe the majority) never encounter a turning point in life. They never make choices or experience events that take them out of the environment that maintains their basic life trajectory. This is particularly true in stable 'traditional' cultures where there is little variety of opportunity or experience, and where adult roles are not so very different from childhood ones. It's also likely in cultures where there are strong social expectations (stereotypes) about life trajectories which effectively hold the individual in place whatever he or she does. For example, an act of vandalism by a student at Oxford may be dismissed as a prank, leading to a reprimand that doesn't alter the positive trajectory of his or her life, whereas the same 'prank' by a delinquent is more likely to result in a prison sentence, reinforcing the negative trajectory of this life.

Some people are catapulted into turning points by cultural events: joining or being called up to the military in a war, for example, brings a radical discontinuity from past life which seems to be particularly potent in creating real turning points (Elder, 1985). Such experiences can radically shake up the social groups to which the individual is exposed (removing a delinquent from his delinquent peers, for example, or exposing an individual from a narrow social background to other ways of being), and can induce new activities, new challenges, new opportunities for reward and respect: in sum, new ways of seeing the self and others. The greater the opportunities for real change in activities and social contacts a culture provides, the greater the likelihood of individuals encountering turning points.

Often a turning point is triggered by events that we don't chose, and which don't reflect our existing personalities in any obvious way: being orphaned or widowed, say, or reduced to poverty by the failure of a crop, inflation, war or a natural disaster, or happening to meet a particular individual on the road (who turns out to be a charismatic guru/someone who offers you a job you'd never dreamed you could achieve/a homicidal maniac). Any event that radically disrupts the normal activities and experiences of life and forces us to re-evaluate ourselves and other people can make it impossible to continue to be the person we used to be, and so create a turning point. Chance events, as well as predictable ones, contribute to the progressive uniqueness of our individual personalities, our sense of who we are.

Developing a personal identity

Research on personality and its development provides a framework within which we can begin to see how the complexities of cultural expectations, social interactions and innate temperament combine to shape how we behave and how we think of ourselves and others. Central to this process is our sense of identity: our sense of who we are. The development of a sense of identity has been explored in more detail in a very different tradition of research, which focuses specifically on the way we construe ourselves.

Research in this vein relies primarily on the descriptions an individual gives of him or herself, and looks for patterns in how these descriptions develop through childhood and adolescence. As we've already noted, self-descriptions are not necessarily very accurate (Dunning, 2006). This is a source of difficulty for research in personality, which uses an individual's responses to questions describing the self as a means of establishing what his or her traits actually (objectively) are: misperceptions of the self introduce error into the measurement of traits, which may confound efforts to explore the influence of those traits on behaviour, say, or their stability over time.

But in studying personal identity, our focus is specifically on the individual's subjective experience of self. The accuracy (or otherwise) of that experience may throw interesting light on the way subjectivity develops, but it is not error variance: how you see yourself is how you see yourself, no matter how mistaken your perception seems to an outside observer! Thus even the inaccuracies of our self-perceptions are valid data in this context. (This is a useful example of the fact that there is, really, no such thing as error variance in research: there is only variance we are or aren't interested in, variance that is or isn't taken properly into account in a given research project or theory – see Chapter 1.)

The nature of personal identity

As we saw in Chapter 4, our sense of identity has two separate components (James, 1890, 1892): an *I-self*, which constitutes our self-awareness, our consciousness of having a continuous identity across different situations and through time; and a *me-self*, about whom I can gather information and knowledge. This me-self is multi-faceted: there is the *material self* (defined by my appearance, possessions, activities), the *social self* (or rather, many social selves brought into being by the various roles I play, the relationships I form, the interactions I have with others), and the *spiritual self*, which James considered to be the heart of self (the attitudes and values that provide continuity and meaning to our interactions with the world). James's analysis has, if anything, become more influential in research on the development of identity in the century since it was written (Lewis and Brooks-Gunn, 1979; Lewis, 1994).

The foundations of both the 'I-self' and the 'me-self' are laid down in infancy (see Chapter 4), through the child's experiences both as an individual and as part of a symbiotic attachment relationship. By the end of infancy babies know what they look like in mirrors and photographs

(Asendorpf, Warkentin and Baudonniere, 1996), and manifest a clear sense of their own agency (their ability to make things happen) and rights (as their temper tantrums when 'wronged' bear witness). But it is with the development of language that a sense of self really takes off: words allow us to articulate and interconnect our experiences, to create an *autobiographical narrative* – a story about who we are – in a way that simply isn't possible without language (Harter, 1998). It's this narrative that we mean when we refer to someone's sense of identity, their conception of self.

Like the implicit theories that underpin personality, then, our 'identity' narrative is a conceptual theory that makes sense of our social experiences. And like personality, identity is socially constructed (Cooley, 1925): that is to say, we discover who we are through making sense of how others react to us, just as we develop a consistent personality by developing expectations about how others will behave toward us. And in fact, there is a clear correlation between personality traits and the conceptions of self that constitute our sense of identity (Luyckx, Soenens and Goosens, 2006). But whereas the theories that underlie personality are generally implicit, unconscious and uncritical, the narrative that carries our identity story is more explicit, articulate and evaluative. And because we do not necessarily see ourselves very accurately (Dunning, 2006), the identity story we consciously articulate doesn't necessarily match the implicit assumptions about self that unconsciously shape how we actually behave. Thus it's perfectly possible for an individual to believe in their identity as a kind and sensitive friend while being (from the perspective of outside observers of personality) self-absorbed and unreliable. We all know people who don't really have much accurate self-knowledge; the trick, as Dunning (2006) puts it, is knowing when it's *me*.

Self-concepts in childhood and adolescence

The most influential research on the development of self-concepts in childhood is that of Susan Harter (1999). Harter recorded a great many children of different ages describing themselves, and created composite descriptions which capture the key features of self-concepts at different ages (see Box 10.1). A number of developmental themes emerge from a comparison of Harter's composite descriptions (Harter, 1999).

First, there is a clear developmental progression from very specific concrete descriptions of the self tied to particular characteristics or behaviours in early childhood ('I'm really strong, I can lift this chair') to more general statements covering a range of behaviours ('I'm pretty popular … because I'm nice to people and helpful and can keep secrets') in middle childhood, and then on to still higher-order or abstract descriptions embracing a whole style of being ('I'm an extrovert') in adolescence.

box 10.1

Composite examples of children's
self-descriptions

Source: S. Harter, *The Construction of the Self:
A developmental perspective.* © 1999, Guilford.
Reproduced with permission from Guilford Press.

Typical self-description aged 3 to 4 years:

I'm three years old and I live in a big house with my mother and father and my brother, Jason, and my sister, Lisa. I have blue eyes and a kitty that is orange and a television in my room. I know all my ABCs, listen: A,B,C,D,E,F,G,H, J,L, K,O,M,P,Q,X,Z. I can run real fast. I like pizza and I have a nice teacher at preschool. I can count up to 10, want to hear me? I love my dog Skipper. I can climb to the top of the jungle gym – I'm not scared! I'm never scared! I'm always happy ... I'm real strong, I can lift this chair, watch me!

Typical self-description aged 8 to 11 years:

I'm pretty popular, at least with the girls. That's because I'm nice to people and helpful and I can keep secrets. Mostly I am nice to my friends, although if I get in a bad mood I sometimes say something that can be a little mean .... At school, I'm feeling pretty smart in certain subjects like Language Arts and Social Studies .... But I'm feeling pretty dumb in Math and Science, especially when I see how well a lot of other kids are doing. Even though I'm not doing well in those subjects, I still like myself as a person, because Math and Science just aren't that important to me. How I look and how popular I am are more important. I also like myself because I know my parents like me and so do other kids. That helps you like yourself.

Typical self-description in early adolescence:

I'm an extrovert with my friends: I'm talkative, pretty rowdy and funny .... All in all, around people I know pretty well I'm awesome, at least I think my friends think I am. I'm usually cheerful when I'm with my friends, happy, excited to be doing things with them .... With my parents ... I feel sad as well as mad and also hopeless about ever pleasing them .... At school I'm pretty intelligent, I know that because I'm smart when it comes to how I do in classes, I'm curious about learning new things and I'm also creative when it comes to solving problems. My teacher says so .... I can be real introvert around people I don't know well – I'm shy, uncomfortable and nervous. Sometimes I'm simply an airhead, I act real dumb and say things that are just plain stupid ...

Typical self-description in mid-adolescence:

What am I like as a person? You're probably not going to understand. I'm complicated! With my really close friends, I am very tolerant, I mean I'm understanding and caring. With a group of friends I'm rowdier. I'm also usually friendly and cheerful but I can be pretty obnoxious and intolerant if I don't like how they're acting. I'd like to be friendly and tolerant all the time, that's the kind of person I want to be, and I'm disappointed in myself when I'm not. At school, I'm serious, even studious every now and then, but on the other hand, I'm a goof-off too, because if you're too studious you won't be popular .... I really don't understand how I can switch so fast from being cheerful with my friends, then coming home and feeling anxious, and then getting frustrated and sarcastic with my parents. Which one is the real me?

> Typical self-description in late adolescence/early adulthood:
>
> *I'd like to be an ethical person who treats other people fairly. That's the kind of lawyer I'd like to be, too. I don't always live up to that standard: that is, sometimes I do something that doesn't feel that ethical. When that happens I get a little depressed because I don't like myself as a person. But I tell myself that it's natural to make mistakes, so I don't really question the fact that deep down inside, the real me is a moral person. Basically, I like who I am .... Being athletic isn't that high on my own list of what is important, even though it is for a lot of the kids in our school. But I don't really care what they think anymore. I used to, but now what I think is what counts. After all, I have to live with myself as a person and to respect that person, which I do now, more than a few years ago.*

Alongside this shift from the concrete to the abstract is a progressive movement from descriptions emphasizing the material ('I have blue eyes ... and a television'; 'I live ... with my mother and father') in early childhood to descriptions more oriented to the psycho-social ('I'm pretty popular'; 'I'm awesome, at least I think my friends think I am') in middle childhood and early adolescence. In effect, the young child defines him or herself without reference to other people, as if his or her characteristics were absolutes. By contrast, later in childhood the self is defined very much with reference to others (Frey and Ruble, 1985), both in terms of how the individual relates to others ('Mostly I'm nice to my friends although if I get in a bad mood I ... can be a little mean') and by comparison with others ('I'm feeling pretty dumb in Math ... especially when I see how well a lot of other kids are doing').

Concern over social standing and relative competence deepens in early adolescence, becoming an ever more important focus of the self-concept. It also shifts ground, so that whereas children tend to emphasize *their own* perspective on comparisons of self and other, young adolescents become preoccupied by what *others* think of *them* (Elkind, 1967; Harter, 1999), imagining that everyone is looking at them, judging their appearance and behaviour all the time (Elkind, 1967). There is a marked tendency in adolescence not only to define the self in relation to others as children do, but also to deliberately edit the self to earn a good opinion ('I'm a goof-off too, because if you're too studious, you won't be popular'). Only in later adolescence and early adulthood does the social reference group become less important ('I don't really care what they think any more. I used to, but now what I think is what counts'). In late adolescence we internalize our own values (although these have been formed in interaction with others – see Chapter 12), and so become less directly dependent on other people's reactions to us for our sense of who we are and our self-evaluations.

There is a developmental change in how concerned we are with the consistency of the story we tell about ourselves. In early childhood there are often gross inconsistencies between self-descriptions and reality ('I know all my ABC's, listen: A,B,C,D,E,F,G,H,J,L,K,O,M,P,Q,X,Z,'), which seem not to disturb the child at all – probably because he or she is simply unaware of them. Through childhood children become more concerned with the accuracy of their descriptions, referring to 'benchmarks' (that is, external evidence or comparisons with others) to substantiate their claims about themselves ('I like myself because I know my parents like me and so do other kids. That helps you like yourself'; 'I'm creative ... my teacher says so').

But although they are concerned about the consistency of certain general attributions about the self (for example, how good at schoolwork they are relative to others, how likeable), 8- to 11-year-olds aren't bothered by apparent contradictions in their behaviour itself ('I am nice ... I can be ... mean'). By early adolescence, the teenager is more explicitly aware that he or she has a variety of selves that seem contradictory, a perception that has deepened and become problematic by mid-adolescence ('I'm complicated ...'; 'I can switch so fast from being cheerful with my friends, then coming home and feeling anxious ... and getting ... sarcastic with my parents. Which one is the real me?'). Only in late adolescence or early adulthood do we develop a more integrated sense of self, incorporating a more abstract and sophisticated overview of how our various different selves relate ('I'd like to be an ethical person ... I don't always live up to that standard').

Developmental processes in the evolution of self-concepts

Many aspects of the evolution of self-concepts through childhood reflect conceptual development as a whole. For example, the development of progressively more abstract and integrated accounts of the self parallels the general cognitive changes in the ability to conceptualize things in principled, abstract ways found in all areas of developing knowledge and reasoning (Chapter 6). Equally, the shift from the young child's egocentric view of self through to the older child's emphasis on their own perspective, the adolescent's acute awareness of what other people may be thinking of him or her, and finally the more independent self-judgments of late adolescence and early adulthood, reflects developmental changes in our ability to understand other people's perspectives, and to relate these to our own view or to more general standards (see **Box 10.2**).

But developmental changes in how we construe ourselves are not purely the product of growing cognitive skills and conceptual understanding. They also reflect systematic changes in the social roles we play and the situations we encounter through childhood and adolescence. The pre-school child lives in a fairly circumscribed world, often composed only of family and contacts in the immediate neighbourhood. Going to school opens up a whole new world, one in which suddenly, the

box **10.2**

Selman's stages of development in
social perspective taking in childhood
and adolescence

Infants and young children are notoriously poor at understanding what another person may be seeing or thinking in any context, as we've seen in Chapters 3, 4 and 9. By about 5 years of age, they have made substantial progress in this area: they can recognize that another person may know something different from what they know, for example, at least in simple, practical contexts (see Chapter 9). But the ability to understand other perspectives continues to develop throughout childhood and adolescence and even in adult life (Yeates and Selman, 1989), reflecting continuing developmental change in cognitive skill and conceptual understanding. This importantly affects the impact other people's opinions have on the child, and how children relate to others at different ages.

Selman (1981) identified five stages in the development of social perspective taking (the age at which each stage occurs is variable):

- **Stage 0: the egocentric stage** (ages 3 to 7) – the child is virtually unaware that others may have views different from his or her own.
- **Stage 1: informational perspective taking** (ages 4 to 9 years) – the child realizes that others may have a different view from their own, but assumes that this is simply a reflection of different information. In effect, the child believes that 'If you know what I know, you'll think what I think.' There is still only one legitimate perspective. The child is not yet aware of the possibility that others may have different values and so interpret the same information or events differently.
- **Stage 2: self-reflective perspective taking** (ages 6 to 12 years) – the child realizes that others do have different perspectives and is able to think about what those may be, and to reflect on his or her own views from the other's perspective (that is, considering how things might look to them). But the child is not yet adept at inter-relating their view and anyone else's, nor establishing the relative legitimacy of different views.
- **Stage 3: third-party perspective taking** (ages 10–15 years) – the adolescent can now reflect on his or her own view and someone else's as if from the perspective of an impartial observer, and can thus come to a more grounded and objective view of the relationship between different perceptions of events.
- **Stage 4: societal perspective taking** (ages 14 to adult) – the individual understands and evaluates their own and other people's perspectives on events by comparing them with the generalized perspective of the culture at large (the legal system, religious or moral principles, ethnic practice and so on).

ground-rules of living change: popularity and praise depend more on your actions, on how you behave relative to other people, making these things more salient than they have previously been in understanding your identity. The effect accelerates as the individual moves into adolescence. The greater autonomy allowed to adolescents is also demanded of them, so that success in the peer group, school and beyond becomes increasingly important, fostering adolescent preoccupation with other people's opinions of them and their relative standing in any activity. And as the social world expands through childhood and adolescence, the range and variety of situations and people we encounter grows, evoking a wider and wider variety of 'selves'. So it's not just that the adolescent is better placed (in other words, more cognitively able) than a young child to notice such apparent inconsistencies in his or her experience of self and worry about them. He or she also has more different selves to notice and be confused by.

In sum, although developmental changes in the way we conceptualize ourselves depend on the growth of cognitive skills, they are also propelled along by the changing structure of social experience through childhood and adolescence. The notion that the development of our understanding of ourselves is driven by a series of psycho-social challenges in this way has been most influentially articulated by Erik Erikson (1980; J. Erikson, 1997), who argued that human life presents us with a succession of very particular developmental problems, which form the focus of the questions we ask ourselves in working out who we are at different stages of life (see **Box 10.3**).

---

box **10.3**

Developing self-knowledge and identity through the lifespan – a psychoanalytic approach

The account of the development of personality and identity development given in the main body of the chapter derives from empirical analyses, but there have also been influential contributions to this area from psychoanalysis. For example, Sigmund Freud saw the development of social identity as the result of a succession of psycho-sexual challenges posed to the child by the physiological facts of gender and sexuality (see Chapter 1). More influential has been the work of another psychoanalyst, Erik Erikson, who argued that identity formation is driven by psycho-social crises rather than psycho-sexual ones as such. Though far from scientifically rigorous, Erikson's ideas have an intuitive appeal that adds another dimension to our approach to understanding what is going on as self concepts develop.

Erikson argued that the pattern of a human life throws up eight main psycho-social crises, each of which challenges us to resolve our identity in one direction or another. The crisis of infancy revolves around *trust versus mistrust* in the context of the attachment relationship. In early childhood, it revolves around *autonomy versus shame and doubt* as the child draws a clearer distinction between self and other and begins to feel responsibility for his or her actions. As childhood progresses and the child gains more independent agency, the focus shifts to the problems of *initiative versus guilt*. Schooling poses the challenge of *industry versus inferiority*. At puberty there is the crisis of *identity versus identity confusion*, which gives way in early adult life to the crisis of *intimacy versus isolation* as we search for sexual partnerships, friends and colleagues. In middle age, the challenge is one of *generativity versus stagnation* as we address the adult tasks of biological and sociological productivity. In old age it becomes one of *integrity versus despair*, associated with an autobiographical reintegration and evaluation. In his own old age Erikson added a ninth stage, suggesting that even in our 90s, when health and faculties may well be failing, we continue to face new challenges to our identity – in this case, the psycho-social crisis of response to death: *acceptance versus disgust*, with the optimal resolution being the achievement of a transcendental peace.

Continuities in self-concepts

There is substantial evidence supporting Harter's (1999) account of the ways in which our conceptions of self change through childhood. But these changes are tendencies. They are not, in any sense, developmental 'stages' that progress in a single direction and never revert (as was claimed for the cognitive stages proposed by Piaget: see Chapter 1). Elements of childish stages may be present in adult self-conceptions, and in the case of some adults, mature elements may be absent. In fact, various aspects of the ways 3-year-olds typically construe themselves are still evident in most adult self-concepts, even if they have been overlaid with a broader and more sophisticated range of emphases.

For example, our tendency to define our identities in terms of material things doesn't disappear in early childhood, even if other things become more salient (and perhaps more socially acceptable to focus on and mention). Money, possessions, physical appearance and the like continue to shape our self-image and the way we perceive others right through our lives. A beautifully groomed woman in an expensive dress stepping out of a Mercedes is always going to be perceived (by onlookers, and equally importantly, by herself) as having a very different identity from unkempt woman in a rumpled sweatshirt rummaging in the back of a small battered car. Even in adult life it seems that 'we are what we own' in important ways (Dittmar, 2004). The fact that various religions have tried for thousands of years (and failed) to get people to define their identity without reference to material possessions or bodily beauty testifies to the pervasiveness of this tendency throughout life.

Nor does our tendency to overestimate our abilities and charms fade in early childhood (Dunning, Heath and Suls, 2004; Dunning, 2006). Through adult life we tend to over-estimate the likelihood that we will do well in exams, maintain a successful relationship, perform acts of generosity, charity or civic duty, complete this essay in 2 hours flat and so on. And most of us tend to think that we're more able, idealistic, socially skilled, competent, efficient (and so on) than the average, which obviously (given the meaning of 'average') can't be true! It turns out that, even in adulthood, peer ratings are more accurate predictors of our actual behaviour than are our own self-descriptions, whether predicting our exam or career success (Bass and Yammarino, 1991; Risucci, Torolani, and Ward, 1989) or the outcome of our romantic relationships (MacDonald and Ross, 1999).

The fact that even adults don't have very accurate conceptions of self underlines just how hard it is to truly come to know yourself, and most of us probably never really do (Dunning, 2006). Often, we simply don't have all the right information to make accurate judgments about our own behaviour or abilities. For example, the 3-year-old who claims mastery of the 'ABCs' in Harter's composite evidently doesn't know what the right answer looks like, so how could he or she recognize that their own answer falls short? Even in adult life, *we don't know what we don't know*, so can't see the shortcomings of our efforts (Dunning, 2006). If you don't know that there is another, better way of being a friend, a parent, a lover (say), don't know a better way to write an essay, there is little basis for self-criticism and every reason to assume you're doing OK. Equally, if you don't know how other people react to a situation, or how observers evaluate how you react (our friends, relations and even colleagues tend to be fairly tactful on these issues, which is perhaps just as well) how can you know that you're impulsive, or overly emotional, or self absorbed?[1]

But the problem of self-knowledge is not simply the result of a lack of information at a given stage of life. The development of a coherent identity is a life-long challenge, as Erikson suggested (see Box 10.3). Although the various psycho-social challenges Erikson noted tend to first become salient, and so explored, at a given stage of life, they are in fact all pertinent to identity all the time. We are all as mortal as a 90-year-old, and many of us will face that problem well before 90, perhaps even in youth. Equally, even a 90-year-old may have as many issues of trust and mistrust as an infant (Erikson, 1997). Sometimes self-knowledge is only partial because we just haven't yet faced the kinds of psycho-social challenge that stimulate the development of a more profound self awareness (Erikson, 1997).

Adolescent identity formation

The issue of identity takes on a very particular importance in adolescence, at least in our culture (a point to which we shall return later). This is the period of life when the individual first begins to discover a variety of different selves, each one evoked by a different social group, and to wonder which is 'the real me?' (Harter, 1999). And with adulthood and independence just over the horizon, the need to answer this question, to work out who we are and what we are going to do in life becomes pressing. Resolving this conundrum is a multi-faceted thing: a matter of working out not merely what we are good at or enjoy, but where we stand in relation to a wide range of social, sexual, political and religious values. This is a process of narrowing down from all the possible choices to make commitments to particular ways of living and being.

Erikson (1968) identified the crisis of identity as the major issue facing adolescents (Box 10.3). To resolve this crisis successfully, the

---

[1] Dunning's advice on how to know yourself better is threefold. (1) Ask your peers to give feedback – and take what they say seriously, particularly if several people say the same thing. (2) 'Benchmark' more often: watch what other people do more closely and compare that with your own reactions. (3) Notice the inaccuracies in your predictions and expectations of yourself – and amend your expectations accordingly.

individual must construct a *coherent identity*: in other words, an integrated account of the self, of goals, aspirations, values and characteristics that can function in a stable way across time and different contexts. Failing to achieve this coherent resolution can leave the adolescent in a state of *identity confusion*, in which there is only an incoherent and uncertain sense of self: of not knowing who you 'really are', and not knowing what to do about that. Somewhat unsurprisingly, this can be a depressing experience, with feelings of isolation and of being 'lost'. Erikson believed that most adolescents[2] experience this state of identity confusion for at least a short while: it's this state that triggers the reflections which are needed to resolve the identity crisis. A few individuals never really escape from identity confusion, and are likely to suffer serious psychiatric disturbance as a consequence.

Resolving the problems of identity confusion is hard work, and it takes time. Erikson suggested that the healthy solution is for the adolescent to have a *psycho-social moratorium*:[3] a period in which he or she is free to try out a variety of different roles and personas, trying out new activities and new ways of being and hence exploring the range of possibilities, before making a mature commitment.

But for various reasons (ranging from personal insecurity to a familial situation that forbids or precludes it, as will be discussed below), not all individuals are able to work things through in this way. Erikson identified two other resolutions of the identity crisis, both less than optimal. Some individuals resolve their uncertainties by adopting an identity without really thinking it through. This *identity foreclosure* often involves accepting the identity offered by parents or school: becoming a farmer because that's what Dad wants, or going in for a scholarship in music because the teacher is excited about your talent, without taking personal responsibility for the choices or considering alternatives.

A second, still less desirable, solution is to adopt a *negative identity*, defining yourself simply as whatever your parents are not. This is another form of relatively unreflecting and premature commitment. It may not be too bad if you adopt the identity of a poet or a belly dancer in refutation of your parent's commitment to banking and accountancy, or even if you become an accountant when your family are creative and bohemian artists and intellectuals. But it can be very destructive: for example, when the daughter of a high court judge becomes a drug

---

2 Adults can re-experience this kind of identity confusion, if the structure of their lives collapses or undergoes a radical change, for example by losing a job or a career, or the end of a relationship around which life had revolved. Retirement and the 'empty nest' can trigger an identity crisis, as can being caught up in political or natural disasters. The transition from university to career is not without its moments, either.

3 'Moratorium' simply means a period of time during which a given activity (such as fixing on an identity) is either not required or not allowed.

pusher, or the son of a professor drops out of school and rejects any sort of career. (Erikson believed this is more likely to occur when the adolescent doesn't enjoy supportive attention from the parents, and that it is a form of attention seeking.)

Erikson's work on adolescent identity formation rests on his psychoanalytic insight, rather than on formal measures of 'identity status'. Other researchers have tried to measure the four identity states he describes in more formal ways: for example, through the use of questionnaires designed to identify whether or not an individual has firm *commitments to particular values*, and whether commitments that have been made reflect their own *exploration of choices* as opposed to values held by other people (Marcia, 1966, 1999). No commitments and no coherent exploration would indicate identity confusion (generally labelled 'diffusion'); commitments reflecting other people's values without exploration would indicate foreclosure; exploration without commitment indicates a moratorium status; commitment after exploration indicates coherent identity formation: 'identity achievement'.

Using such measures, it has been established that identity status affects both behaviour and psychological adjustment (Grotevant, 1998). Identity confusion is associated with apathy, restricted friendships and a higher than average propensity to take drugs; a moratorium brings higher self-esteem, active open-mindedness (which may include exploring sex and drugs) and the continuing anxiety of uncertainty; the achievement of coherent identity is associated with social maturity and a strong achievement orientation: ready for adult life. The majority of those in either identity confusion or moratorium go on to 'identity achievement'. By contrast, those who have accepted a foreclosed identity are generally authoritarian, passively looking to others to make decisions for them, and unsurprisingly, tend to remain in this state.

The percentage of individuals experiencing identity confusion falls steadily from 46 per cent in early adolescence to about 13 per cent at the end of the college years; identity achievement rises from 5 to 40 per cent over this period. At any one time, only a minority (about 12 per cent, peaking at 28 per cent in the early college years) are in moratorium; about a third have foreclosed identities (Waterman, 1985).

Moratorium and the successful identity achievement are strongly affected by family dynamics. Boys who are allowed to negotiate with their father, challenging his opinion and altering his decisions, and girls who are able to assert their point of view strongly, are more likely to engage in genuine identity explorations and achieve a coherent identity (Grotevant, 1998). Despite these slight gender differences, it seems that the crucial factor is that the family actively encourages the adolescent to have and express a distinct point of view (Grotevant, 1998).

Culture, class, ethnicity, race, gender and identity

The account of the development of self-concepts and adolescent identity given above very largely reflects research on white, Western individuals in industrialized societies (Sneed, Schwartz and Cross, 2006). This group represents a tiny fraction of the world population of children and adolescents. Do self-concepts and identity develop in the same way in other groups? For that matter, do self-concepts and identity develop in the same way in boys and girls, in either our own culture or anyone else's?

Over recent decades, there has been a certain amount of research specifically directed to understanding female identity formation, reflecting the more general interest in 'women's studies' sparked by the feminist movement. This has recently been joined by 'men's studies', exploring male identity formation (Phillips, 2006). But until recently there has been astonishingly little research on ethnic or racial identity in minority groups, or on the development of identity in cultures different from our own. Perhaps in the wake of the shock following '9/11' and the resulting increase in sensitivity to the issues of our 'multi-cultural' world and societies, there has been an explosion of research in this area since 2001. The importance of the topic, both theoretical and practical, is marked by the fact that the leading publication for developmental research (*Child Development*) presented a special issue dedicated to such research in 2006 (September/October issue: volume 77, part 5). Nonetheless, we still have remarkably little data about identity development in other cultures or subcultures.

Childhood

From a theoretical point of view, there are grounds for supposing that, at least in childhood, the basic patterns and processes that characterize the development of self-concepts are universal, even if the detailed content of the views of themselves that children end up with vary greatly between girls and boys, and between individuals from different social classes, ethnic and racial backgrounds and cultures.

Universal and specific processes in conceptualizing self

The tendency to try to make sense of things, to build conceptual theories about the world, ourselves and other people is universal, a part of what it means to be human whatever gender you may be and whatever culture or class you may grow up in. And although there may be very different information and experience to make sense of in different cultures, so that the theories a child constructs of what it means to be female (say) might be very different in rural Afghanistan under the Taliban and London in the year 2000, the basic cognitive equipment we use in generating our conceptual understanding is the same the world over. The proof of this is that babies adopted from one culture to another fit right in: a baby girl adopted from rural Afghanistan to an ordinary family in London would show the same pattern in developing a gender identity as her British-born peers, would develop the same theories of what it means to be female, no matter how different the theories she might have developed using that same cognitive equipment would have been had she remained in Afghanistan.

Equally, many of the social pressures which have been speculated to propel certain aspects of the development of the self-concept may be universal. For example, 8- to 10-year-olds in all societies must engage and impress a wider circle of people and shoulder greater responsibilities than 3-year-olds. Even the psycho-social crises identified by Erikson may be universal, at least in the first 10 years of life: the problems of trust, of growing distinction between self and other, and the progressive issues of independent autonomy, responsibility, and shame, doubt and guilt seem to be inevitable features of the progression from an infant identity symbiotically merged with the mother to an identity as a distinct agent.

From this point of view, we would predict that the world over, many aspects of the basic account of how self-descriptions change between the ages of 3 and 10 years given by Harter (1999) would be found in every culture, reflecting the universal features of cognitive development and the universal features of being a human child. That is to say, we'd expect to see the same developmental movement from the very concrete to more general statements in children's self-descriptions, for example, and the same developmental movement from a completely egocentric perspective to one that focuses more on interpersonal relationships and comparisons. Where we would expect to find differences would be in the specific detail of these descriptions, for example, in the possessions or skills the 3-year-old boasts of (a big house, a television in the bedroom, knowing the ABC in a white Western child, versus a plastic shelter, my own personal cup, knowing the best way to get to the front of a queue in a child in a refugee camp), or in the specific structure of social activities, relationships and comparisons of concern to 10-year-olds (a focus on popularity with peers and school success in a white Western 10-year-old, for example, versus a focus on relationships with a wider community and survival skills in an orphaned Brazilian street child). The structure of the self-descriptions in these examples is likely to be the same for both age groups. Only the content is bound to be different.

Culture and the content of children's self-concepts

Ultimately, every child's experience of life is unique, and so every child's self-concept is unique. There is no possibility that we could create a composite picture of the common *content* of children's self-concepts at different ages, even though we can create composites of the *structure* of their self-descriptions (Harter, 1999). This is true even within a given society, even within a given family. The diversity of experience around the world, and the diversity of content in children's descriptions of themselves and their lives, is almost beyond our imagination (for example, think of the diverse experiences of 3-year-olds eking out an existence on the edge of a rubbish dump in an African war zone, embedded in a traditional tribal life-style in the Arctic circle, in Pol Pot's Cambodia, tied to a cot in a Rumanian orphanage, festooned with toys in a house in London, and so on).

Nevertheless, it is possible to pick out common patterns in the content of children's self-concepts and in the ways this content develops. Every child is born into a complex cultural niche – a specific position within an entire *ecological system* (Bronfenbrenner, 1979) of interacting people, situations, social attitudes and values, religious, political, economic and legalistic practices (**Figure 10.2** gives a Western example). A child doesn't take part in all the layers of activity within a society, but he or she is nevertheless influenced and affected by them all. The things a child learns to accept as normal, the right way of doing things, and the experiences he or she has of self and other and the self-concept that develops as a result, are systematically affected by the exact niche he or she occupies within the social ecosystem. It's a very different thing to be a girl as opposed to a boy in any culture, for example. Equally, it is a very different thing to be born into a rich and powerful family or into a poor and marginalized one, into a racial or ethnic minority or into the dominant culture, into a minority religion or that endorsed by the state. We would expect these systematic influences on children's lives to create systematic patterns in the content of their self-concepts, patterns which developmental research can identify.

In many cases, systematic influences on children's experience and self-concepts interact in complex ways. For example, a study of the lives of 3-year-olds in Brazil, Kenya and the United States found that children's patterns of experience could not be explained simply by cultural group, race or socio-economic class, but were the product of a complex interaction between these things (Tudge et al., 2006). Developmental psychology has hardly begun to scratch the surface of documenting the range of practices across the world, let alone disentangling the effects of race, ethnicity, culture and class and the way these things interact. This is the focus of a major new initiative in research (Quintana et al., 2006). Only in the area of gender identity and (to a lesser extent) ethnic identity in minority communities have we made any real progress in understanding how the content of children's self-concepts is affected by cultural factors.

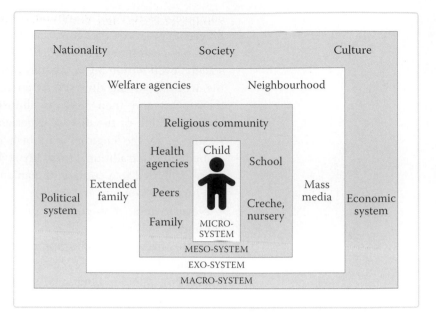

figure 10.2

An example of the ecosystem of a child's life

As this example shows, a baby exists in a series of nested environmental structures, from the micro-system that is the child's immediate environment through the meso-system, which presents a series of connected micro-systems, and on to the exo-system (social systems) and macro-system (general cultural context), with which the child doesn't engage directly but which shapes his or her life in various ways.

Source: after Bronfenbrenner (1979).

Gender and ethnic identity in childhood

In childhood, the world we live in is the one the adults around us have committed themselves to. It's presented to us as a 'fait accompli': children are almost never invited (or allowed) to question the way things are ('Because I say so!' could well be the commonest reaction most children get to asking 'Why …?'). They are seldom exposed to any alternative versions of reality. In any case, the under-10s lack the cognitive skills to challenge what they are told or to explore (what are necessarily hypothetical, given their restricted experience) alternatives to this way of doing things, this way of being. The result is that by and large, children conform to the expectations of their family and society (Rogoff et al., 1984), uncritically internalizing the cultural mores and social practices to which they are exposed and incorporating these into their self-concept.

At first, babies are unaware of any systematic features of identity. That is to say, they are not aware that they are male or female, or that they belong to a given ethnic group. By about 3 years of age, most children have identified themselves as male or female (Fagot and Leinbach, 1989), and begun to label themselves in this way ('I'm a girl'). Many children from ethnic minorities also label themselves ('I'm Indian') at this age (Bernal et al., 1993). Three-year-olds know that there are differences between boys and girls, and between members of an ethnic minority and the majority group, and may be able to articulate some of these. But their descriptions focus on superficial differences of appearance, clothing or behaviour. At this age, children don't have a principled grasp of what the difference between genders or ethnic groups really is, and don't realize that the difference is permanent. Typically, it's only between 7 and 9 years of age that children come to understand that gender, race or ethnicity are long-term features of self (Bennett and Sani, 2004; Ocampo, Bernal and Knight, 1993).

Bem (1989) provides a wonderful illustration of the confusions that a poor understanding of the nature of social categories such as gender can cause, in this illustration of the experiences of a small boy deciding to wear barrettes in his hair:

Several times that day, another little boy insisted that Jeremy must be a girl, because 'only girls wear barrettes'. After repeatedly asserting that 'wearing barrettes doesn't matter; being a boy means having a penis and testicles', Jeremy finally pulled down his pants as a way of making his point more convincingly. The boy was not impressed. He simply said, 'Everybody has a penis; only girls wear barrettes'.

The reason for the young child's difficulty in understanding that characteristics such as gender, race or ethnicity are permanent has been a matter of some debate. For example, Kohlberg (1966) argued that the achievement of 'gender constancy' was due to the development of Piagetian 'concrete operations' (see Chapters 1 and 6), which allow a child to have a general understanding that superficial changes don't alter substance (that the amount of water is not altered simply by pouring it from a tall thin glass to a short fat one, for example: a breakthrough that occurs at about the same age as gender constancy – Marcus and Overton, 1978).

However, more recent research suggests that this kind of conceptual change has less to do with the development of general cognitive structures of the kind Piaget described, and more to do with the specific knowledge the child has (see Chapter 6). For instance, at least in our society, most children under 7 simply haven't seen enough naked people to understand that gender is defined by genitals, which don't change. This discovery is a key element in the realization that gender is permanent (Bem, 1989). A child without the key insight that gender is a function of genitals would have no basis for defining the difference between male and female except the superficial features of appearance and activities. It's easy to see how such a child could become confused if a friend swapped from wearing and doing boy-things to wearing and doing girl-things, and why he or she might imagine gender was as changeable as a pair of trousers. Further evidence that it is specific knowledge rather than the development of any general cognitive structure that allows children to realize that gender, race or ethnicity are constants comes from the fact that exactly when children recognize the permanence of ethnic identity varies depending on the specific race or ethnicity of the child (Bennett and Sani, 2003). This should not be the case if understanding constancy in this area reflects general cognitive structures. The implication is that it is social experience and information that provide the crucial insight.

Discovering that there are different groups in society (gender groups, ethnic groups), and that you yourself belong to one or other of these groups is one thing. *Identifying* with that group membership, accepting it as part of your self-concept, is another. We know more about this process in relation to gender than in relation to ethnicity, though the processes may well turn our to be quite similar in many ways.

Kohlberg (1966) believed that it was the 7-year-old's realization that gender is permanent which spurred children to start actively engaging in gender-typed behaviours, and that their efforts to understand what those behaviours are inevitably involves over-simplified stereotypes (the classical example being a child who insisted that only men could be doctors, although his own mother was a doctor!). It's certainly the case that young children are often more fiercely sexist, more fiercely committed to the idea of fixed differences between the genders (differences that can be expressed as moral imperatives as much as pragmatic facts) than are their elders (Ruble and Martin, 1998). But the evidence is that this commitment to 'genderism' begins way before the child has realized that gender is constant and unchanging (Bem, 1989).

From about the age of 3 years (as soon as they realize that there are two genders and that they belong to one of them), children begin to show a clear motivation to behave as a member of their gender 'should'. This goes way beyond the gender-specific toy preferences (trucks versus dolls, for example) visible from early infancy, which may have some sort of biological basis (see Chapter 2). For example, offered two unfamiliar toys that don't have the characteristics associated with gender-specific toy preferences (in other words, two 'gender-neutral' toys), 4- to 9-year-olds preferred whichever one they were told was 'for' their own gender (Martin, Eisenbud and Rose, 1995).

Bem (1989) suggests that, having labelled the self as male or female, the young child begins to develop a *gender schema*: that is to say, a script specifying how to be male or female. He or she begins to observe members of his or her own (the 'in') gender more closely than members of the other (the 'out') gender, to remember more about what members of the 'in' gender do (Ruble and Martin, 1998) and to 'edit' memories to match their gender stereotypes: for example, 'remembering' that the child playing with a doll was a girl when it was actually a boy (Martin and Halverson, 1983). Gender schemas grow and develop through childhood as knowledge expands (Ruble and Martin, 1998).

Why does discovering that you are a member of a given gender motivate what appears to be a strong desire to behave in gender-appropriate ways? Discovering that other people see us as 'fat' doesn't inspire us to become fatter, nor do children enthusiastically embrace the label 'stupid'. Yet they throw themselves whole-heartedly into the role specified by a gender label, dressing to match it, choosing their preferred activities and friends on this basis, segregating themselves by gender and showing indifference or even hostility to the other gender (Ruble and Martin, 1998). So powerful is this 'genderism' that no efforts on the part of parents or progressive nurseries disrupt it.

In a very real sense, then, children socialize themselves into a gender identity – and at least in our culture, into one that is more stereotyped and sexist than the views of the surrounding society. Our best guess is that this commitment reflects a more general drive for conceptual coherence. There's a natural tendency to identify with and to prefer 'people like me'. So in identifying with and preferring members of our own assigned gender, in trying to behave more like 'people like me', we are, in effect, *becoming more ourselves* on a dimension that is, after all, of vast social significance.

This same tendency to identify with and imitate people like ourselves, and to draw clear distinctions between the 'in' group and the 'out' group, and to develop scripts or schemas for 'right' behaviour on this basis, probably operates in children's reactions to ethnic labels too. However, there are several factors that mitigate against the stark polarization and self-segregation of gender, in the case of ethnicity, at least during childhood. The first is that, while gender is inevitably a core dimension of social status (can you imagine a society in which this wouldn't be a key factor affecting how life will progress, short of banning all sexual activity and biological procreation?), the salience of ethnicity is a socio-political issue; there is no intrinsic need for ethnicity to be a salient factor, and in many children's home and school lives, it isn't. Furthermore, whereas girls and boys are both aware of the need to demarcate themselves from genderlessness, only one side of the ethnic 'divide' sees an issue. The majority culture regards itself as 'normal', without an ethnic identity at all (as is visible from our use of language: 'ethnic' is used to mean 'minority'). There's no need to demarcate yourself from 'normality'. Only children from an ethnic minority have any investment in 'marking' this identity as different or special. But this investment is ambiguous: the minority is the 'out' group with respect to the social institutions and assumptions of the mainstream culture, and may even be the target of overt or covert prejudice and discrimination. Very few of us would embrace an identity as part of an 'out' group with the enthusiasm we would give to membership of an 'in' group.

Adolescence

Whereas there are good grounds for predicting that the patterns and processes that characterize the development of self-concepts in childhood are universal, there are good grounds for supposing that the patterns and processes of identity formation in adolescence are not. The founder of research on adolescence, G. Stanley Hall (1904), described adolescence as a life-stage characterized by *Sturm und Drang* (storm and stress), at the heart of which is the crisis of identity (Erikson, 1968). Cross-cultural research, and even research over a broader range of groups in our own society, suggests that these features are far from universal, and that identity achievement follows a very different path in different cultures and subcultures.

Is the adolescent identity crisis a cultural artefact?

Paradoxically, the first effect of culture on adolescent identity formation is to determine whether or not there will actually be much of an identity crisis to resolve. In many parts of the world, there is no real issue over what an adolescent's future will be: the structure of society has predetermined that from the start. For example, in 'traditional' pre-industrial societies, virtually everybody does more or less exactly the same thing as everyone else: in fishing villages, the boys grow up to be fishermen, in farming communities they grow up to be farmers, in hunting tribes they grow up to be hunters. The girls grow up to a life with an equally predictable domesticity. Nor do such societies generally offer much variety in the matter of personal lifestyle or social activities. There's a homogeneity about the way things are done and a limited range of possibilities, so that adolescence involves little of the individual choice typical of our society, and uncertainty revolves only around people's adequacy in fulfilling the adult role they are expected to inhabit. In such societies, there may be little or none of the turmoil and confusion associated with adolescence in our own culture, but rather, a smooth and rapid transition from childhood to adulthood. This transition is made easier still by the fact that children participate in adult tasks (caring for the young, finding and preparing food, farming, fishing or hunting) from a very young age, so that there is considerable continuity between the activities and responsibilities of childhood and those of adult life (Mead, 1928).

Margaret Mead's research has had a dramatic impact on the study of adolescence as a whole. It obviously challenges Hall's assumption that the transition from childhood to adult life is necessarily a period of *Sturm und Drang.* Furthermore, Mead's report of a smooth and fairly rapid transition from childhood to adulthood led various researchers to wonder whether the whole phenomenon of adolescence itself might be a cultural artefact, the product of a particular cultural system (Aries, 1962). Surveys of a large number of pre-industrial societies have subsequently shown that virtually all had at least some notion of adolescence, of a special period of transition between childhood and adulthood (Schlegel and Barry, 1991). But as Mead's work shows, the nature of this transition varies importantly from one culture to another. Such cultural variations are important in their own right. They also throw new light on the factors that shape adolescence and adult identity formation in our own culture.

Culture and adolescent identity formation

In traditional, pre-industrial societies, adolescence is defined by the dramatic physiological changes of puberty, which convert childish bodies into mature sexuality. The transition from child to adult is handled through very explicit public rites of passage and ceremonies of initiation into the adult world marking these changes (Delaney, 1995). For example, in some societies, a girl's first menstruation (menarche) is marked by celebrations welcoming her to adult womanhood, and adolescent boys are awarded the status of manhood by braving the rigours of circumcision (without anaesthetic) in a ceremony secret to men. Adult identities are assumed at a far younger age than adult identities in Western society, including the new adult in the full range of sexual and economic pursuits. In such societies, as we have already noted, everybody has, in effect, a 'foreclosed' adult identity, simply stepping into the traditional ways of life on which the group depends (fishing, farming, etc.). But given the structure of such societies, the notion that this is necessarily a bad thing as Erikson suggested, or that a protracted period of identity moratorium reflecting on other ways of being adult would be healthier, seems inappropriate.

Modern industrial and technical societies don't manage adolescence in the same clear-cut way as do pre-industrialized societies. The period of adolescence in such societies is protracted by the need to formally educate the young to play their part in economic activities. The biological drives toward sexuality and reproduction brought on by puberty must be delayed to allow time for this education to be achieved, and to allow the individual to establish the means to support a new generation (a source of *Sturm und Drang* not present in traditional societies).[4] Very few are offered an immediate solution to this economic problem (few inherit a farm or a business, for example). The majority are faced with a vast range of possible careers, and alongside this, an even vaster range of possible lifestyles and values. It is the variety of choice that complex industrial cultures offer that sets the scene for adolescent identity crisis.

Is it right to refer to the uncertainties about their future identities that adolescents experience in industrial societies as a 'crisis'? Is adolescence necessarily a period of storm and stress in Western industrial societies, even if it isn't in more traditional cultures? The research is ambivalent on this issue. On the one hand, direct studies of stress among adolescents report that the majority experience few problems of this kind (Arnett, 1999). On the other hand, population statistics tell a different story: many thousands of adolescents run away from home and simply

---

4 The tensions around this delay are reflected in the outrage that Margaret Mead's account of the happy sexual freedom of teenage Samoan girls provoked in 1928: 'polite society' (including many researchers) simply wouldn't believe it!

disappear, from the family's point of view (in 2006, there were over 1500 16- to 17-year old runaways living rough on the streets in Britain, for example, a figure that rises to 25,000 by age 24 years); treatment for depression rises in adolescence, particularly in girls; and suicide rates are far higher in adolescents and young adults than in adults as a whole. These facts suggest that this is an unusually stressful period of life for many. Both suicide and running away from home are acts of extreme desperation, so that those who react in these ways almost certainly represent only the tip of the iceberg. There must be many others who experience stress, even severe stress in adolescence, who don't kill themselves or leave home but simply 'hack it'.

Why is there this discrepancy between adolescent stress levels reported by surveys and implied by population statistics? It could be that population statistics give a more accurate picture. Troubled adolescents often hide their distress (one of the most frequent reactions after a suicide is that no one, including family and close friends, had had any idea that the individual was suicidal: distress has been skilfully hidden). The distressed may 'fake' their responses if included in a survey, or simply fail to respond at all (or perhaps, are already unavailable for inclusion). Alternatively, it could be that the *Sturm und Drang* of adolescence is specific to particular sub-groups within the population, whereas the majority genuinely don't experience it.

Even within complex technical and industrial societies, there are marked differences between groups in social expectations about how adult identity should be (and so is) formed. For example, identity formation is affected by complex interactions between culture and socio-economic class, reflecting the pragmatic realities of families and individuals. The affluent can afford to support their offspring through a fairly lengthy period of identity moratorium, paying for 'grand tours' or 'gap years', supporting a college degree undertaken without real commitment to a particular follow-on career, and a period after graduation in which different careers can be started and dropped as the young adult explores possibilities before reaching 'identity achievement'. The poor can't afford this sort of thing, so that adolescents from poorer backgrounds may be forced by economic pressures to accept a foreclosed identity with regard to career and life-style, an identity chosen as much by circumstances as by the individual.

Equally, the possibility of enjoying identity moratorium varies with individual ability. The highly able have, and can imagine for themselves, a far wider range of possible careers, lifestyles and values than the less able. It's not merely a matter of education and qualifications: it's also the case that moratorium depends, fundamentally, on the ability to consider and evaluate hypothetical alternatives. This emerging ability is the main cognitive achievement of adolescence. It depends on formal education – it doesn't emerge in cultures where there is no such schooling, no literacy, no formal maths and algebra (Chapter 6). From this point of view, the basic ability, as well as the need, to experience moratorium is itself a product of technical, industrial culture. But even with formal schooling, not all individuals develop the ability to think in this way or to genuinely think through alternative values or ways of being, rather than foreclosing on an identity offered by family or society.

Is accepting a foreclosed identity such a bad thing, even in Western industrialized societies? There is little actual evidence to support Erikson's view that foreclosure is necessarily a negative outcome, from the point of view of the individual. It's true that foreclosed identity is associated with authoritarianism and a passive dependence on authority (Grotevant, 1998). But it's worth noting that these are only bad things from the perspective of a particular value system: one that admires individual autonomy and challenge to authority. Not all industrialized societies, nor all sectors within a society, share those liberal ideals.

For example, Chinese and Indian cultures tend to value obedience and loyalty to the family above personal autonomy, as do many white Western conservative groups. In such societies, there may be a general acceptance that the family, rather than the individual, will make important decisions about adult offspring's lives: arranging careers and marriages, demanding adherence to the particular values of a given religion or political system and so on. The degree to which an individual embedded within a given culture (industrialized or not) is expected (or allowed) to explore adult identities for him or herself as opposed to accepting a foreclosed identity varies enormously from culture to culture. For an individual who shares the values of a more authoritarian culture, accepting a foreclosed identity seems the functional and healthy option. Indeed, there may be many young people from liberal cultures who would (at least at times) envy the ordered simplicity of this, by contrast to their own struggles with uncertainty and individual responsibility.

Cross-cultural comparisons show that Erikson's account of adolescent identity crisis was far more 'culture specific' than he realized, rooted in liberal values of individualism and in the privileges (and pressures) of an economic and intellectual elite at a particular period in time. Even within our own culture, our attitudes to what constitutes a 'proper' identity formation have varied greatly through history (see **Box 10.4**).

There is no support for the notion that adolescence is necessarily a period of storm and stress. But there are groups for whom identity formation certainly does pose serious issues which might well lead to *Sturm and Drang*. These are the individuals who are exposed to *acculturation*: that is to say, the young who are exposed to more than one culture (either as a member of an ethnic minority within a larger culture or through exposure to other cultures through the mass media) and so are exposed to competing sets of values and lifestyles, rather than being embedded within a single culture.

Box 10.4

The self in history

There's a tendency to assume that the way we think about the self, or about our personal identity, is a reflection of something fixed and natural. In other words, we assume that the way we experience ourselves is nothing more than a reflection of the way we are. But in fact, our experience of self is a cultural artefact, shaped by the particular beliefs and practices in the culture we live in (Baumeister, 1987).

Baumeister points out that 600 years ago, our modern preoccupation with 'finding my real self', with developing a distinct individual identity ('doing it my way'), and with achieving 'self-actualization' would have struck our ancestors as incomprehensible or absurd. To them, embedded in a highly structured society and with the firm convictions of Catholicism, the questions we agonize over today would have been meaningless. You were born into a particular place in life (king or courtier, landowner or farmhand, blacksmith or soldier and so on), and that role, together with the specific relationships you had with others and your physical characteristics, defined who you were. 'Self' was simply a matter of those externals: there was no 'real inner self' to be discovered. Because you were embedded in a network of roles and relationships, identity was a collective matter: you identified with your community. Too much individuality would challenge the community. Life was generally hard. Salvation would come not here on earth ('this vale of tears') but in the next world: an earthly life lived in selfless obedience to God would ensure you a place in paradise.

Baumeister traces a number of factors which have combined to progressively change this view of self into our very much more complex modern views. For example:

- the changing relationship between man and God created through the Protestant Reformation, which brought in a new emphasis on individual rather than collective salvation and identity
- anxieties about appearance and reality, the possibility that other people might disguise themselves to deceive us (a major preoccupation for Shakespeare) fostered the concept that there is an inner 'real' self distinct from outer appearances
- the shift from a feudal society in which roles (the self) were fixed by accidents of birth to a more flexibly structured urban one where roles (identities) can (or must) be chosen brought in a new need to know the inner self, in order to make such choices appropriately
- the anxiety, greatly fanned by Freud's work on repression and denial, that our real self might be hidden, not only from others, but also from ourselves – so that self-knowledge is difficult, if not impossible
- the progressive decline in religious belief led to a waning interest in salvation after death, and a waxing interest in 'salvation' – i.e. individual self-fulfilment – in this life, raising questions as to what that would mean, making knowledge of the 'real inner self' even more vital.

A full description of Baumeister's analysis of the history of the self is beyond the scope of this book. But his work is worth reading: it casts a fascinating light on our modern preoccupations.

Is our current view of 'self' the end point in the development of this concept? It seems most unlikely that it is. Already there are signs of a new change, brought about by the astonishing advances in information technology, which have changed our world out of all recognition in the past decade or so.

Will our concept of what it means to be a person change as we achieve instant communication with anyone anywhere in the world, instant access to all human knowledge through the internet? Will the development of new technologies that embed computers, even the internet, in our brains (computer chips embedded in human brains are already a reality) affect our ideas of self? Will the possibility of 'living' in virtual worlds such as *Second Life* affect our personal and social development? Some researchers believe that information technology is already changing human nature in profound ways, and that this will pose new challenges for our concepts of individuality, personal identity and fulfilment as the 21st century progresses (Greenfield, 2003).

Identity formation in ethnic minorities

The issues associated with identity formation in groups facing acculturation become far more pressing in adolescence than they have been in childhood. Adolescents are generally more aware of, and more exposed to prejudice associated with their ethnicity than are children, and the problems of deciding how to live an adult life become more pressing. How to resolve the clashes between the lifestyles and values of the ethnic or religious group they have grown up in and the often very different values and lifestyles of the mainstream culture? Finding a way through to an adult identity in the context of such clashes is fraught with difficulty.

Reject too much of your family's ethnic background, adopt too much of the dominant culture's values, life-style and aspirations, and you risk rejection from family and peers. You may lose the support of your ethnic group, while not quite being allowed to be a full member of the majority culture, particularly when ethnicity is compounded by race (Parke and Buriel, 1998; Spencer and Markstrom-Adams, 1990). This creates a pressure to conform to ethnic origins and expectations which is often associated with premature identity foreclosure (Parke and Buriel, 1998; Spencer and Markstrom-Adams, 1990). Many African-Americans are reluctant to commit to success in school or career in the mainstream culture, embracing classic African-American identities for fear of peer rejection. Many Native Americans embrace their tribal traditions and lifestyles without exploring alternatives because the risk of isolation and loneliness if they leave the tribe to try to 'make it' in mainstream society is just too great (Parke and Buriel, 1998; Spencer and Markstrom-Adams, 1990). Similar effects occur among the ethnic minorities found in Britain and other European countries.

But although many adolescents from ethnic minorities avoid identity confusion and stress by foreclosing on the traditional values and identities offered by their family's culture of origin, others directly explore their ethnic identity and its implications. Such exploration seems often to be set off by a growing awareness of negative perceptions of their ethnicity, which have been picked up from the mainstream culture and internalized, creating unrest (Phinney and Kohatsu, 1997). This triggers a period of exploration, an explicit reflection on what it means to be a member of a particular racial, cultural or religious tradition, a fascination with the history and traditions associated with that, and a consideration of what the implications for the future within such an identity might be.

Some individuals, particularly those with strong family support (Umana-Taylor, Bhanot and Shin, 2006), resolve this moratorium period by adopting an *ethnic identity* involving a now conscious choice of commitment to, and pride in, that ethnic origin. This can create a renewal of optimism and self-esteem (Phinney, Cantu and Kurtz, 1997). Where family support is strong, this resolution is even viable when the parents come from very different ethnic backgrounds, so that embracing this dual cultural history involves forging a *multi-ethnic identity* (Jourdan, 2006).

But exploration of ethnic background doesn't necessarily lead to commitment to an ethnic identity. In a number of individuals it results in a reduced commitment to ethnic origins and groups. Some of these go the whole way and explicitly adopt a mainstream identity, while some develop a bicultural identity which fuses elements of both their original ethnic culture and the mainstream culture. This last resolution seems to be the optimal one: a bicultural identity is associated with better emotional and physical health than any other option (LaFramboise, Coleman and Gerton, 1993) – understandably, since it provides the individual with the best of both worlds. Of the other options, an ethnic identity deliberately chosen after a period of reflective moratorium is associated with greater well-being and personal integration than is a simply foreclosed ethnic identity which leaves the tensions associated with living as part of a minority within a larger society unaddressed (McLean and Pratt, 2006).

This view of how adult identity develops in ethnic minorities assumes that the individual is growing up in a relatively stable society: a society that may be in the throes of evolution in some way (perhaps as new adjustments are made between minorities and mainstream culture), and within which there may be prejudice and discrimination, but where there is no radical revolutionary or violent upheaval. Sadly, however, many children enter adolescence in societies torn apart by war, civil war or genocidal movements. And generally these things revolve around ethnic differences, real or supposed (Hitler's assault on the Jews and other 'non-Aryan' peoples; the 'troubles' between Catholics and Protestants in Northern Ireland; the racial and religious genocides and wars in Rwanda, Bosnia, between Hindu and Muslim in the Indian subcontinent, between Sunni and Shi'ite Moslems in Iraq and elsewhere, and so on).

How is identity formation affected by coming to adolescence in the middle of a vicious conflict? Such situations offer no realistic possibility of being allowed (by friend or foe) to adopt a bicultural or ethnically neutral identity. Even a moratorium period in which you reflect on whether or not to embrace your ethnic identity may be seen as an act of treachery in such situations (a dangerous position to risk). Safety lies in being included in a group, whether you are a member of the 'aggressor' or 'victim' group, since isolation may well (literally) be fatal. There is no option but to foreclose on the ethnic identity offered by your own group. And in the circumstances, this is easy to do: there's nothing like an attack on the people you love to trigger a passionate commitment to them, however you might have felt in easier times. The result is that, for the very best of motives, adolescents growing up in war zones of one sort or another show a very powerful emotional attachment to the ethnic identity of their familial group, foreclosing on this identity uncritically with little or no reflection or exploration of alternatives (Hjort and Frisen, 2006).

Sadly, this very natural reaction to the threat posed by attack on people's ethnic group fuels conflicts, maintaining them sometimes generation after generation (Hammack, 2006). The high emotions roused by attack, the passionate foreclosure in solidarity with your culture provide fertile breeding ground for a complete polarization between groups, and for the demonizing of the 'out' group. 'Being under attack' and the 'necessity' of retaliation can become fixed aspects of identity, not available for reconsideration. Typically, it's adolescents and young adults who carry such conflicts forward, providing the 'troops' for bombing missions of one sort or another, whipping up zeal. So far, efforts to break the destructive cycle by involving adolescents from opposing sides (for example, Palestinian and Israeli adolescents) in peace or co-existence programmes have had only very limited success (Hammack, 2006; Hjort and Frisen, 2006). The attitudes associated with the polarized, foreclosed identities common to such conflicts are too deeply entrenched.

Gender and sexual identity in adolescence

Another area in which Erikson's account of identity formation turns out to be very culture-specific is gender identity. Erikson believed that the course of identity formation was fundamentally different for male and female, since women could only achieve adult identity by marrying and having children (Erikson, 1968): in other words, that female identity is necessarily defined by a husband and family rather than by the woman as an individual! 1968 was not a good year to make this suggestion. By then, the cultural conditions in which Erikson's view might have applied had long passed, at least in Western societies.

In fact, the data strongly suggest that the processes of identity formation work in exactly the same way in male and female (Kroger, 1997). Certain cultures (such as the one Erikson grew up in) put more pressure on girls to accept a foreclosed identity than they do on boys: for example, in many Arab cultures, boys are free to choose between a range of careers and life-styles whilst women's lives are tightly restricted. Again, whether or not such imposed foreclosure is damaging depends on your values. Some girls share the value systems that underlie this imposition, and are presumably content. Many others do not, as subversive movements, from the British suffragettes to the secret schools for girls denied an education under the repressive regime of the Taliban demonstrate.

In childhood, gender identity focuses on the establishment of the self as a girl or as a boy. In adolescence we continue to build gender schemas, expanding them to cover an identity as an adult woman or man. In some cultures this has presented little problem: there is a script for masculinity and femininity, which society expects (insists) that everyone follows. The advent of the women's movement changed all that, so that within our society (and many others around the world) today there is at least a degree of ongoing debate about what it means to be male or female. In many ways, gender identity has been the chief issue of adolescent identity over the past 50 years. The range of identities open to women expanded enormously over the course of the 20th century, posing girls with real issues about what kind of women they would be. Changes in women's self-concepts and behaviour have created a 'crisis' in masculinity, forcing men to reconsider what it means to be male and spawning the new field of 'men's studies' (Phillips, 2006).

Not every individual successfully forms a gender identity within the gender to which they have been assigned. Some, for example, have a powerful feeling of being in the wrong body: of being a man trapped in a woman's body, or a woman trapped in a man's. These feelings often begin in childhood, but come to full force in adolescence. The power of the discomfort experienced by such transsexuals is evident from the lengths to which individuals will go to 'put things right', enduring numerous painful operations and often, the misunderstanding and rejection of family, friends and society at large.

There may be a strong biological element in the gender confusion of transsexuality, perhaps relating to abnormalities in hormonal levels in the fetus which can create not only the physical ambiguities of genitals known as 'intersex', but also the more subtle ambiguities of a brain sex that is different from genital sex (see Chapter 2). Support for this idea comes from the results of a terrible medical error, in which a baby's penis was accidentally burnt off during a botched circumcision. The child was given reconstructive surgery, but as a girl,[5] and was brought up entirely as a girl.

---

[5] As extraordinary as this seems now, the decision reflected the comparative difficulty of constructing male and female genitals at the time, and the strong belief in contemporary research – subsequently rejected – that there are no biologically founded differences between the genders other than sexual anatomy.

At first, this seemed successful, suggesting that gender identity is not biologically 'set' at all (Money and Ehrhardt, 1972). However, the child began to feel that he was 'in the wrong body', experiencing all the distress typically associated with transsexualism to the point of making several suicide attempts. Eventually as an adolescent he discovered the truth about the accident, and insisted on further surgery to return male genitals, He later married and lives successfully as a man (Diamond and Sigmundson, 1999). We don't know by what process 'brain gender' affects the development of gender identity, either in transsexuals or in the general population. It's unlikely to be the only factor: identity formation is influenced by complex interactions between many different things. But the implication of current research is that the resolution of identity in this area is not wholly a matter of conceptual choice.

Nor do we understand exactly how sexual identity develops: that is to say, the orientation to be heterosexual or homosexual/lesbian. By what mechanism do the majority of the population switch from the almost exclusive focus on their own gender in childhood to a heterosexual orientation? Given the biological facts of reproduction, a heterosexual orientation is fundamental to the survival of the species, so that it is very likely that there is a strong biological component to the adoption of a heterosexual identity in adolescence (probably mediated by rising sexual hormones). Furthermore, the 'gender schemas' we have been building throughout childhood and adolescence and which act as our script for how to 'be', generally include the presumption of heterosexuality, since that is what is predominantly presented by society and the media. But it is not clear that these factors are enough to explain the passion of heterosexual sexual feeling, or the psychological processes through which the same-sex relationships that have dominated our affections give way to an other-sex orientation.

Freud (see Chapter 1) believed that heterosexual passion reflected the emotional drama of the transfer of the strong but forbidden sexual feelings we have for the opposite-sex parent onto others outside the family. Other theorists argue that, because of our childhood same-sex bias, the other gender is relatively unfamiliar and seems both different, alien and exotic. This, coupled with our biological predispositions, is enough to create passion. As Bem (1996) put it, 'exotic becomes erotic'.

Not everyone develops a heterosexual identity: some become homosexual, lesbian or bisexual. In some societies, homosexual behaviour is tolerated, or even actively encouraged (for example, it was in certain societies in ancient Greece), although it's not necessarily the case that homosexual behaviour leads to a homosexual identity (Michael, 1994). But in many societies, adopting a homosexual identity is a risky thing.

Although it's likely that many factors influence the development of our sexual identities, there is increasing evidence that non-heterosexual orientations have a biological component, probably mediated by

Exercises

1. How would you design a research project to accurately assess levels of adolescent stress across a population as a whole, and in specific groups within that population? What practical and ethical problems would you anticipate?

2. You're the psychologist chosen by the international community, the United Nations, to make policy. Your first brief: what are the identity issues for adolescent survivors of a tsunami that has destroyed their family, home, neighbourhood, the infrastructure of their whole society? What do these adolescents need, and how could it be provided? What ethical issues might arise?

Suggested reading

For an overview of research on personality and personality testing aimed at a general audience read:

- A. Paul (2004) *The Cult of Personality: How personality tests are leading us to miseducate our children, mismanage our companies, and misunderstand ourselves.* London: Free Press.

For an overview of personality development read:

- A. Caspi (1998) Personality development across the lifecourse. In N. Eisenberg (ed.), W. Damon (series ed.), *Handbook of Child Psychology,* vol.3: *Social, Emotional and Personality Development.* New York: Wiley.

For a review of research on developing self concepts read:

- S. Harter (1998) The development of self representations. In N. Eisenberg (ed.), W. Damon (series ed.), *Handbook of Child Psychology,* vol.3: *Social, Emotional and Personality Development.* New York: Wiley.

For a review of identity in adolescence read:

- J. Kroger (2004) *Identity in Adolescence,* 3rd edn. London: Routledge.

For a variety of studies of racial and ethnic identity development see:

- *Child Development* vol. 77 no. 5: Special issue on Race, ethnicity, and culture in child development.

For a review of gender identity read:

- D. Ruble and C. Martin (1998) Gender development. In N. Eisenberg (ed.), W. Damon (series ed.), *Handbook of Child Psychology,* vol.3: *Social, Emotional and Personality Development.* New York: Wiley.

For an account of the development of concepts of self through history read:

- R. Baumeister (1987) How the self became a problem: a psychological review of historical research. *Journal of Personality and Social Psychology* 57, pp. 163–76.

Revision summary

The origins of personality

- Whereas infant temperament reflects innate dispositions, personality reflects conceptual understanding. It rests on the implicit theories about self and other that organize and regulate our behaviour and experience (Westen, 1991).

- These theories reflect the child's social experience: that is, what he or she learns about the self and others from the way others react to his or her behaviour.

- Babies who react positively to others evoke positive reactions and are reinforced in positive expectations of self and other; babies who react negatively evoke negative reactions and are reinforced in negative expectations.

- This self-perpetuating 'reaction–evocation' cycle acts to create the consistencies we call personality.

- Both genetic factors (innate temperament) and social factors (the level of parenting skill of the mother, cultural values) influence the tone of the reaction–evocation cycle set up in infancy: in other words, whether the cycle experienced by a given individual is generally positive or generally negative.

- Once this tone is set, it is hard to change. The way we behave creates the social world we live in. For example, aggressive children over-interpret events and see hostility where none exists. Their aggressive 'retaliation' creates real hostility in others, creating the very social world they expected and confirming the 'legitimacy' of those expectations. Because the social world is shaped by our expectations in this way, it can't provide objective feedback that would challenge those expectations in the way the physical world challenges wrong expectations (about gravity, say).

The structure of personality

- Personality can be described in terms of five core traits: Openness to experience, Conscientiousness, Extraversion, Agreeableness and Neuroticism (OCEAN for short). Although fairly stable from childhood to old age, the way these traits are expressed changes through development.

- Personality can also be described in terms of three core types: ego resilients (the well adjusted); vulnerable over-controllers (poorly adjusted and rigidly controlled); unsettled undercontrollers (poorly adjusted and lacking self control).

- The structure of adult personality traits and types is identifiable in children by 3 years of age.

Change and consistency

- The self-perpetuating reaction–evocation cycle can dominate the whole *trajectory* of a life, acting to maintain a consistent personality.

- Personality becomes more stable through childhood and adolescence up to about age 30. However, personality continues to evolve through the lifespan to some degree. Identical twins grow less alike as they grow older.

■ There are *transition points*, when we move from one role or situation to another, when new people and new activities offer the possibility of change. But generally, old reactions simply carry over into the new situation. Only when a transition fundamentally disrupts old ways of seeing self and other does it offer a *turning point* and real scope for change.

Identity

■ More explicit and conscious than the conceptual theories that underlie personality are the narratives we develop about who we are: our self-concepts.

■ The focus of self-concepts changes through the course of childhood and adolescence, for example shifting from material possessions to interpersonal relationships and comparisons; from an uncritical, concrete and fragmented view of self to a progressively more abstract, evaluative and integrated one; from a reliance on other's judgments to a reliance on our own internalized values

■ These changes reflect development in our general ability to think in abstract ways, and to understand other people's perspectives. But they also reflect social pressures toward greater responsibility for our actions and greater distinction from our parents: a succession of psycho-social crises, propelling self discovery.

■ The main crisis of identity comes in adolescence, as we become acutely aware of having a variety of selves each elicited in different contexts, and start wondering which is 'the real me'. It's also when we begin to anticipate entering adult life and searching for an adult identity. The identity confusion this generates can be depressing. Some adolescents deal with it by foreclosing on an adult identity chosen for them by family or society. Erikson viewed this as a negative solution. A healthier option is a period of identity moratorium in which the adolescent can explore different roles and values before committing to particular ones and so reaching a mature identity.

Culture, class, gender, ethnicity and identity

■ Although we have little data, there are good grounds for predicting that the developmental change in the focus of self-concepts is similar across cultures in childhood, reflecting universal cognitive and social factors, even though the content may be very different.

■ Children uncritically accept gender and ethnicity as facts of life, proactively working on understanding gender and ethnic differences and on becoming a 'good' member of their own group.

■ The development of identity shows very different patterns across different cultures in adolescence. Erikson's idealized notion of moratorium and individual autonomy in choosing an identity applies principally to Western liberal societies, and even here, to the privileged classes within those societies. Economic and political realities, more authoritarian cultures or pre-industrial societies where there is no real choice to be made all tend to produce foreclosed identities.

- Identity crisis is greatest in ethnic minorities, where clashing cultural values and expectations from the minority group and mainstream society are juxtaposed. Many in this situation foreclose on their ethnic identity rather than risk social exclusion. Those who do experience moratorium go on either to a conscious adoption of an ethnic identity, to the rejection of the ethnic identity, or (the healthiest option) to a bicultural identity.

- Adolescents growing up in war zones have little option but to foreclose on their ethnic identity, and often do so with an uncritical passion that can fuel conflicts across generations.

- The basic process of identity formation is the same in boys and girls, although many cultures pressure girls towards foreclosed identities more than boys.

- Adolescent gender identity is associated with sexual identity. Although they are not the only influence, biological factors (such as hormones) play a role in the emergence of both heterosexual and non-heterosexual identity.

11

The interactions we have with other people play a key part in shaping our personalities and identities, our sense of who we are and what we value, as we've seen in Chapter 10. Central to these interactions are the relationships we develop with our families and friends, and the romantic connections we later experience. How do these relationships develop and change through childhood and adolescence? How do we learn to form friendships, to fall in love, to treat one another (and ourselves) with compassion and respect? How does the deepening nature of our relationships affect our emotional development, our self-esteem, our understanding of self? These are the questions explored in this chapter.

Families and development

Throughout history, the family into which a child is born has been crucial both to physical survival and to the child's socialization, providing the basic tuition in skills, behaviour, attitudes and values needed for adult life. Whether or not a child physically thrives or even survives depends on the economic success of the family: the economic circumstances in which the family lives (African famine, the collapsed infrastructure of a war zone, Indian poverty, Western affluence …) and the ability of its adult members to manage effectively in those circumstances, which varies with intelligence, personality and luck. The particular skills, strategies, attitudes and values the family teaches its young will reflect what has worked for them, in those circumstances, and so will be enormously variable around the world. However, there are common patterns in family structures and dynamics, patterns that affect the way children develop.

Parenting styles, emotional development and self-esteem

Parenting styles have an enormous effect on a child's development in infancy, as we saw in Chapter 4. A sensitive and responsive mother[1] is likely to have a securely attached child who feels loved and worthy of love and who is confident and trusting. By contrast, a mother who is cold and unresponsive, or one who is inconsistent and ineffective, or worse yet, one who is herself emotionally disturbed or abusive, will have an insecurely attached child who feels neither loved nor worthy of love, and who has none of the trust in others or the self-esteem of the securely attached (Kochanska, Aksan and Carlson, 2005). It's the parenting style that is crucial to these effects, rather than the innate temperament of the baby (Chapter 4): for while a baby with a difficult temperament can discourage a mother to the point of reducing her willingness to be sensitively responsive, good parenting skills can cancel this effect – and such skills can be taught (Van den Boom and Hoeksma, 1994).

Experiences in early infancy set the tone for a child's basic orientation to self and others, a tone that can last a lifetime, as the child's own behaviour (driven by what he or she has learned to expect of others and believe about self in infancy) elicits the same pattern of reactions in others (and so reinforcing the child's expectations and beliefs still further) over and over again in an endless self-perpetuating cycle (see Chapter 10). Sigmund Freud (Chapter 1) believed that the attachment relationship of infancy forms the prototype for all future relationships, and there is some evidence to support this view, from the fact that the way we parent our children reflects the way we were parented ourselves (Fonagy, Steele and Steele, 1991; Levine et al., 1991) to the reflection of our infant attachment styles in our adult romantic relationships (Lamb, 2005; Roisman et al., 2005). Nonetheless, attachment relationships continue to grow and develop through childhood and adolescence, expanding to take in ever more members of the family (Stein, 2006). It's the quality of the current attachment that has greatest impact on a child's present adjustment and reactions (Thompson, 1998).

Parenting styles

Parenting styles for children and adolescents vary along two dimensions: *responsiveness* and *demandingness* (Baumrind, 1978). Responsiveness refers to the degree to which parents respond sensitively and nurturantly to a child's needs. Demandingness refers to the extent to which parents require their child to behave in certain ways. The intersection of these two dimensions creates four basic parenting styles (see **Table 11.1**):

- *Authoritative parents* are high on responsiveness and high on demandingness. They are warm and demonstratively loving, committed to providing nurturance and support for the child's development. They set clear and consistent standards for their child's behaviour, but at the same time, respect the child's developing need for autonomy. They handle disciplinary matters through dialogue rather than aggression, discussing the issues (for example, discussing why it is bad for a 5-year-old to steal someone else's toys, tell fibs or hit people; or what the implications of an adolescent having unsafe sex, binge drinking or taking drugs might be).

---

[1]   For various reasons the primary care giver is the mother in the overwhelming majority of cases, as is discussed further below.

- *Permissive parents* are also high on responsiveness, and show the same warmth and lovingness, the same commitment to nurturance and support. But they are low on demandingness, setting no standards for their children but rather, allowing them to act on their impulses and desires. They are accepting of these things, valuing the child's autonomy above discipline or conventionality. Such parents avoid punishing or reprimanding their children, or trying to shape particular behaviours or values.

- *Authoritarian parents* are low on responsiveness and high on demandingness. They make strong demands on the child to behave in certain ways, presenting a set of absolute values that are not available for discussion or negotiation. Typically, these are the conventional values of an authoritarian society: hard work, obedience to parents, respect for authority, for law and order, and for traditional ways of doing things. They are prepared to punitively enforce their views, even using violence or their power over a child's life to coerce compliance, restricting the development of autonomy rather than encouraging it. There is little respect for the child's individuality, little warmth or expression of love.

- *Neglectful parents* are low on both responsiveness and demandingness. They pay little attention to their children's lives and welfare, even to the point of abusive neglect in some cases. There is little warmth or love, little nurturance or support. Whereas the other three styles of parenting all involve a concern for the healthy development of the child (albeit a concern shaped by three completely different sets of values), neglectful parents are more concerned about themselves than they are about their offspring.

table **11.1**

Parental styles

	High demands	Low demands
Highly responsive	Authoritative parenting	Permissive parenting
Low responsiveness	Authoritarian parenting	Neglectful parenting

The impact of parenting styles on development

Unsurprisingly, the parental styles identified by Baumrind (1978) have a big impact on psycho-social development. Children with authoritative parents tend to be more socially competent, self-confident and self-controlled than those parented by any of the other three styles (Baumrind, 1978). They also tend to have higher self-esteem, to be more responsible, more independent, more creative and more successful in school, and in adolescence are less likely to be involved in anti-social behaviour, delinquency, experiments with drugs, alcohol or premature sex (Baumrind, 1991a; Steinberg et al., 1994).

By contrast, children and adolescents with authoritarian parents tend to lack social skills, to be low in confidence and self-esteem, to be passive, dependent, unhappy, unfriendly, to lack curiosity and to have relatively poor academic success (Baumrind, 1991b). Those with permissive parents tend to be impulsively lacking in self-discipline, to be low in responsibility and maturity, to be easily influenced by others, lower in school achievement and more likely to get involved in problems at school (Baumrind, 1991a, 1991b). Those with neglectful parents tend to be impulsive, and to have problems relating to other children (Parke and Buriel, 1998; Thompson, 1998), following on from poor attachment in infancy. In adolescence they are more likely than those parented in other styles to get involved in delinquent behaviour, to experiment with drugs, alcohol or unsafe sex. Their academic achievement and their self-esteem is typically very poor, and they are more vulnerable than most to depression and other emotional disorders (Steinberg et al., 1994).

It's easy to see how these different parenting styles would have their effect. By and large, children grow up to fulfil the social expectations presented to them, and to acquire the skills and values demanded by their social world (Rogoff, Gauvain and Ellis, 1984). Direct tuition and social interactions with adults are a vital part of mastering practical and cognitive skills, as we saw in Chapter 7. Direct tuition and shared activities with adults are also vital in acquiring values, in learning how to evaluate events, situations and behaviours, and in shaping emotions, reactions, and learning how to regulate these (see **Box 11.1**). And interactions with parents play a crucial role in the development of self-esteem (see **Box 11.2**). Authoritative parenting provides exactly the kind of adult support a child would need in developing a positive view of him or herself as an independent individual competent to take decisions and responsibility, to be successful both academically and in relating to others. It provides exactly the right support for the development of an independent adult identity through adolescence (see Chapter 10).

By contrast, the message of authoritarian parenting is that the child is not capable of autonomous action or decision, is not worthy of respect as an individual, is only a cog in a larger system – a message very likely to dampen the spirits and hamper the independent formation of an adult identity distinct from the parent's (see Chapter 10). Both neglectful and permissive parents provide very little (if any) of the structured input and shared activities a child needs to learn skills, values, or how to regulate and control their emotional reactions and impulses. Small wonder, then, that their children don't learn these things, and show less maturity and a greater tendency to disruptive behaviour, from attention deficit hyperactivity disorder, or ADHD, in childhood (McLaughlin and Harrison, 2006) to delinquency in adolescence. The age-old wisdom that 'children need standards' to develop pro-socially turns out to be true.

box **11.1**

Emotional development in childhood
and adolescence

Developing new emotions

Toddlers experience all the primary emotions (joy, sadness, fear, anger and so on), as we've seen in Chapter 4. But it's only as the infant begins to become self-aware, and aware of other people as separate individuals, that he or she can experience secondary emotions such as pride, embarrassment, shame and guilt (Lewis, 1998). These emotions begin to emerge between 18 months and 2 years of age (Zahn-Waxler and Robinson, 1995). Emotional range continues to develop through childhood and adolescence, reflecting the greater complexity of the child's conceptual understanding of the meaning and ambiguities of social situations. Adolescents can experience a bitter-sweet reaction that would be beyond the grasp of the more black-and-white views of the young child, for example. The precise range of emotions that develop also reflects the culture the child grows up in: for instance, the German language has the word *Schadenfreude* to describe an emotion that has no word in English; the old-fashioned 'stiff-upper-lip' stoicism of the British has no equivalent in many other cultures; the inner calm fostered in Buddhist cultures is not taught to the young in most Western societies. Secondary emotions are, in many ways cultural artefacts.

Patterns of emotional experience

What it is that elicits a given emotion changes with age. The younger the child, the less he or she will understand of the way a situation looks to someone else, or what other people's intentions may be. As a result, older children will sometimes experience an emotional reaction where younger ones do not: for example, a 15-year-old may be embarrassed in a situation where a 5-year-old understands too little to feel that way. And sometimes the younger child will experience an emotional reaction where the adolescent doesn't: for example, becoming angry when accidentally jostled, because he or she understands too little about intentions to know that this was an accident, as the older individual would. Furthermore, older individuals care about things that simply leave younger children cold, and vice versa: the young child makes little of adolescent angst over a romantic relationship, just as the adolescent finds the young child's passion for a collection of buttons incomprehensible.

The overall balance of positive and negative emotions changes with development. Negative emotions seem to reduce through childhood (Murphy et al., 1999), although they generally rise again in adolescence (Greene, 1990). These patterns seem to reflect the stresses and strains of different periods of life: adolescence presents many more challenges and the potential for more fundamental conflict with parents than childhood does. The same is true of gender differences in emotional experience: depression becomes more common in adolescence than it has been in childhood, markedly more so for girls than for boys (Nolen-Hoeksema and Girgus, 1994). Though this effect is found in many countries (Nolen-Hoeksema, 1990), it doesn't seem to reflect hormonal or genetic factors (Hankin and Abramson, 1999). Rather, adolescence may generally be more stressful for girls than for boys, for example, because of the obsession with appearance that afflicts girls more than boys in many cultures. There is also some evidence that girls brood on worries, and so incubate depression more than boys do (Nolen-Hoeksema, 2003).

Learning to regulate emotions

The ability to regulate your own emotions is vital for social competence (Rubin, Bukowski and Parker, 1998). Who wants to interact with someone who gives way to every impulse and mood? At first, parents take the primary responsibility for regulating our emotions: trying to protect us from distress, soothing and distracting us when negative emotions are inevitable, encouraging fun and the like. Progressively, through childhood and adolescence, we take over responsibility for regulating our own emotions.

Self-control begins to develop very early in life. Six-month-olds can soothe the pain of negative emotions by sucking a thumb, and can reduce the power of such feelings by looking away from the source of distress. These self-soothing and self-distracting skills develop through infancy and childhood (Bridges and Grolnick, 1995). As conceptual understanding and cognitive skills develop, the child's strategies for managing emotions expand. For example, the development of language allows a child to discuss distress with others, and to use less emotionally charged strategies to handle setbacks (debating the matter rather than throwing a tantrum). New cognitive skills allow a situation to be re-conceptualized in a more constructive and less distressing way. The sophistication of such self-regulating strategies continues to grow through childhood and adolescence, and even on into adult life, as we become more adept at understanding our (and other people's) emotions and selecting appropriate responses.

Individuals differ enormously in the way they control their emotions. Even in adult life some individuals have very poor control over their feelings. The uncontrolled impulse to anger is at the root of many crimes of violence, for example. In part, our emotional volatility reflects innate temperament (Rothbart and Bates, 1998). Far more, it reflects the way we have been socialized to experience and express emotions. (Is a public display of anger acceptable, for example, if someone upsets you, and should it be expressed by a caustic remark or a physical assault? Children in different social groups learn different things.) Most of our socialization in this area comes from our families, who provide both role models of what is or isn't appropriate, and (to a greater or lesser extent) direct tuition on the management of our emotions.

As we've seen, different parenting styles provide very different messages and very different levels of support in learning to control emotions. The neglected child gets virtually no help at all in these matters, and is typically very poor at controlling emotions. Equally, the child of permissive parents may be allowed to express every impulse without getting any help in developing self-control. Authoritarian parents certainly require self-control of their offspring, but may demand it without allowing the young to express or explore negative emotions (in effect demanding that they be repressed or denied rather than experienced and controlled), so that the young learn little about managing such feelings and may find them overwhelming when they arise. Authoritative parenting provides clear nurturant support for independent emotional development, and is most successful in producing young people who are in touch with their emotions and able to manage them appropriately.

Gender
There are gender differences in emotionality and in patterns of emotional experience (girls are more fearful, boys more aggressive). While there may be some biological basis for this, there is clearly a strong effect of social training, since some gender differences vary between cultures. For example, girls express more sadness than boys in America, boys express more sadness than girls in China (Ahadi and Rothbart, 1993). Parents generally allow girls to be more emotional than boys (Fuchs and Thelen, 1988), and boys to be more aggressive (Perry, Perry and Weiss, 1989). Mothers discuss emotions more with girls than with boys (Dunn, Bretherton and Munn, 1987).

box **11.2**

Self-esteem

The nature and origins of self-esteem
The concept of self-esteem is very closely related to personality and personal identity (Chapter 10). But whereas research on personality emphasizes the implicit expectations about the social world that shape our behaviour, and research on personal identity emphasizes our more explicit life narratives, research on self-esteem focuses on the *value* we place on ourselves (Ervin and Stryker, 2001): whether we judge ourselves to be competent or incompetent, whether we judge ourselves to be worthwhile or worthless, lovable or not. Like personality and identity, the foundations of our self-esteem are socially constructed: that is to say, how we judge ourselves is a reflection of how others judge us, or how we imagine they do. If others respect and praise our needs, efforts and contribution, we judge ourselves well (good self-esteem). If they don't, we internalize a more negative judgment of self. Our drive to achieve high self-esteem is therefore a drive toward social approval, generally defined by pro-social behaviour as our social group sees it (Owens, Stryker and Goodman, 2001).

In early childhood self-esteem depends almost entirely on the relationship to the primary care giver (mother), who dominates the infant's world. As children grow up, they engage in a broadening range of social roles (friend, pupil, employee, sports player, and so on). Each new situation provides new people, new judgments of self to internalize, judgments that may be contradictory (for example, negative at home, positive at school or vice versa) so that we may have different self-esteem in different specific contexts. But we also have an overall, global self-esteem. This is not produced by 'averaging' across judgments in different situations: rather, it reflects how we are judged in the roles that are most important to us: that matter most, or that dominate our lives (Owens et al., 2001). For example, parents have continuing power over the young, and their judgments may matter more in forming global esteem than those of peers or teachers.

The roles we play, the people we meet, and which of these matter most, change through a lifetime, so that what affects global esteem can go on changing from birth to old age, even being dramatically changed by new experiences (Owens et al., 2001). But like personality and personal identity, self-esteem plays a dynamic role in shaping our behaviour and experience, rather than being a passive reflection of those things (Gecas, 2001). We internalize a judgment of ourselves, and carry this forward to each new situation, often creating a self-perpetuating cycle. We can become impervious to feedback that ought to challenge our esteem.

Low self-esteem leads us to believe that all the bad outcomes are our own fault, and that good outcomes are a lucky fluke, locking us in a negative self-evaluation. By contrast, high self-esteem protects us, leading us to attribute success to our skill or charm and failure to the situation, a bad day, the other participants. We also tend to choose what to get involved in, in terms of what we expect of ourselves: think highly of your abilities and you'll aim high. Expect little and you'll aim low. There's a tendency to get what you expect: believe you 'can' and you'll try harder and be more successful than if you believe you 'can't' and invest little effort. Such effects may be stronger in childhood than in later life, since the younger the child, the fewer resources he or she will have to reflect on, question or change judgments of self, or to change the situations in which those judgments are maintained.

Self-esteem, success and happiness

Does self-esteem affect our success or happiness? Efforts to measure this have not always produced data supporting much of a connection. For example, studies of school achievement often suggest that self-esteem contributes only 4 per cent of the variance (Covington, 2001). This may well be because measures of self-esteem fail to separate out the two strands on which we judge ourselves (competence and worthiness), or to distinguish global and situation-specific self-esteem, and so produce under-estimates of the relationship of self-esteem to adjustment.

Success in specific tasks is primarily associated with how competent you judge yourself to be in that kind of task (Rosenberg et al., 1995), rather than reflecting either global self-esteem or self-worth. This makes intuitive sense: why should confidence in my general abilities as a scientist or in how generally lovable I am have any effect on my success in playing golf? It also explains why efforts to raise the self-esteem (and success) of children failing in academic skills by praising their talents in some other area (such as sport) have no effect (Scheirer and Kraut, 1979).

By contrast, happiness and depression are associated with global self-esteem, specifically with global worthiness rather than competence (Owens, 1994). Again, this makes obvious intuitive sense: there can be few things more depressing and debilitating than believing that you are worthless and unlovable, and few things more joyful than the conviction that you matter and are loved. Despite the materialistic obsession of our culture, there is no reason that worthiness should necessarily be connected to competence. Being bad at science doesn't make you a bad person.

Fostering self-esteem

We affect other people's self-esteem, particularly children's, all the time. Simple changes in what we say can have a huge effect. For example, compare these two reactions to a child's naughtiness: 'Robert! That's a silly thing to do, I'm surprised at you!' and 'Robert! Not again! You're such a bad boy.' The first criticizes the behaviour and indicates that it is separate from the child's worth; the second does the opposite, conveying a global message of worthlessness. Parenting and teaching styles that offer nurturant support can create global worthiness that allows more confidence in approaching specific tasks, a less stressed effort at competence and improved success, feeding back to boost self-esteem.

Low self-esteem is depressing, debilitating and destructive (Owens et al., 2001). Acting to boost low self-esteem is always worthwhile. However, encouraging excessively high self-esteem can be dangerous. A child who is given an inflated idea of his or her abilities is being set up for failure, and responds by devaluing the self rather than making more effort. A realistic view of the self that can be consistently lived up to is healthier than an unrealistic one, even if it means accepting a more modest view (Owens and King, 2001; Salmivalli, 2001). We can't all be outstanding, whatever the self-help books say – and actually, we don't have to be.

Moreover, uncritical self-satisfaction is not necessarily a healthy thing. A degree of dissatisfaction with self is a far stronger stimulus to self reflection and development (Simmons, 2001). The danger of fostering a smug complacency that works against personal growth is why campaigns aimed at giving all children high self-esteem regardless of their behaviour or achievement were dropped (California Task Force on Self-Esteem, 1990).

Culture and context

Self-esteem varies cross-culturally, reflecting cultural values. Western societies value individualism whereas more collectivist cultures (China, Taiwan, Native American tribes) value shared selves over individual ones. Singling an individual out for praise may boost his or her self-esteem in an individualistic culture but undermine it in a collectivist one (Owens et al., 2001). Self-esteem is, par excellence, socially defined.

Culture, parenting style and development

Most of the research on parenting styles and their effects has been done on White Western groups in Europe or America, where all four styles are observed across different families. Do the same styles and effects occur in other cultures? Baumrind's (1978) four categories capture the main ways in which it is possible for parenting styles to vary, so that it is no surprise that parenting can be described in terms of these general categories the world over. But cross-cultural research suggests that both the patterns of parental style and the impact of different styles on child development vary with culture, gender and circumstances in very complex ways.

For example, a study of families with adolescent children conducted in Egypt found that in rural communities the predominant style for parenting sons was authoritarian, but for daughters it was authoritative. By contrast, in urban communities, the predominant style was authoritarian for parenting both sons and daughters (Dwairy and Menshar, 2006). Furthermore, the authoritarian parenting style had less negative effect on development in this Egyptian sample than it typically has on European or American samples.

Dwairy and Menshar (2006) concluded that authoritarian parenting is not so harmful in the context of an authoritarian culture (such as that found in Egypt) as it is in the context of a liberal culture (such as is found in Western societies). This conclusion is supported by research on Asian adolescents growing up in an authoritarian culture, where the benefits of authoritative parenting reported in Caucasian populations are not always found (Ang and Goh, 2006). Ang and Goh suggest that this is because authoritarian parenting has a different cultural meaning in liberal and authoritarian cultures, and hence is experienced differently by the young in each society.

There is evidence to support this hypothesis in other societies, too. For example, as with the Egyptian and Asian samples, authoritarian parenting styles produce no negative effects among first-generation Chinese-American immigrants. Chinese culture is traditionally very authoritarian, placing strong emphasis on the child's obligation to obey parental commands even in adult life, and legitimating the use of scolding and punishment to ensure obedience. In this cultural context, scolding and even punishment may be interpreted as an evidence of the degree of a parent's commitment to and concern for your welfare – in other words, as a proof of love – rather than as evidence of rejection and distrust in your judgment, as they would be interpreted in a more liberal cultural context (Chao, 1994).

It's interesting that these cultural mores are apparently strong enough to mitigate the negative effects of an authoritarian parenting style in first-generation Chinese-Americans, but not in the second generation. Presumably this new generation has been more exposed (through school and the media) to the cultural values and meanings placed on authoritarian parenting in the more liberal mainstream culture of the United States, and so experiences it more negatively as the two cultures collide. Second-generation Chinese-Americans become progressively more like European-Americans between the ages of 12 and 17 (Huntsinger and Jose, 2006).

General cultural meanings are not the only influence on whether or not an authoritarian parenting style will be detrimental. In cultures or sub-cultures where there is real risk that a child will be 'led astray' by strong pressures from or temptations in the surrounding community, or where the child is under threat from circumstances in some way, an authoritarian parenting style actually has a protective function (Parke and Buriel, 1998). For example, among African-American adolescents, authoritarian parenting is associated with higher (rather than the usual lower) levels of academic success, and lower (rather than the usual higher) levels of delinquency (Lamborn, Dornbusch and Steinberg, 1996). It may be that the urban Egyptian families in Dwairy and Menshar's (2006) study felt a greater need to guide their daughters in their complex and potentially dangerous urban society than did their rural counterparts, and were more likely to adopt an authoritarian parenting style as a consequence. Where parental strictness is obviously aimed at protecting you, it has a very different and more positive meaning and impact than is the case when it appears to be out of step with the surrounding culture or circumstances.

But even if authoritarian parenting doesn't necessarily have negative effects on development in all cultural contexts, and indeed can be beneficial in some situations, it can go too far in any culture. Scolding and minor punishments are one thing, harsh punishment and parental violence is another. For example, even within the very authoritarian culture of the People's Republic of China, authoritarian parenting associated with harsh punishment has all the negative effects, including the low self-esteem, low social and low academic competence, found in Western samples (Chen, Dong and Zhou, 1997). And overall, the data suggest that, in any culture, an authoritative parental style yields the greatest benefits in social and academic competence, mental health and maturity (Dwairy and Menshar, 2006; Lamborn et al., 1991; Maccoby and Martin, 1983). Neglectful parenting is always detrimental, often amounting to abuse (see **Box 11.3**). Permissive parenting has a tendency to be ineffectual.

box **11.3**

Child abuse (NSPCC and government statistics)

There's much anxiety in our society about paedophiles who abduct and sexually attack children, even murder them. And indeed, 'stranger danger' is a real issue in some areas. But the greatest dangers to children are not quite what the public suppose them to be. The commonest abuser is not a stranger but a parent.

Stranger danger in perspective
The number of children abducted and murdered by strangers is tiny, and has not changed for a long time, despite parental fears that the risk is increasing. On average, no more than 11 children suffer this horrific fate each year in Britain – a figure that has been constant for 50 years.

Most 'stranger' child abduction attempts thankfully don't end in murder. In fact, most don't succeed at all: for example, in 2002/03, the police in England and Wales recorded 361 attempts by strangers to abduct children, of which all but 59 failed, and almost all of the victims of the successful abductions survived. The motive for such abductions may be sexual, but not all abductees are seriously assaulted.

It's hard to calibrate the risk to children from paedophiles. In 2003, there were 110,000 people in England and Wales who had been convicted of sexual offences against children (not all in that year). Not all of these had directly abused individual children: many were addicted to pornographic images on the internet. Others were social inadequates who had paid willing child collaborators to masturbate them or watch this in public toilets. Some were 16-year-old boys who had slept with their 14-year-old girlfriends (which is 'statutory rape' and enough to get you listed as a paedophile). Few paedophiles were 'strangers': over 80 per cent of assaults happen in the child's own home, perpetrated by a man known to the family. Typically, paedophiles take time to woo and seduce ('groom') their child victims into sexual relationships up to and including rape. The majority of victims (70 per cent) are female. But we don't know how many there are: not all such events are ever reported to the police, to parents, friends or anyone else. Seventy-two per cent of sexually abused children don't tell at the time. Nonetheless, over a quarter of the rapes reported to the police involve victims under 16 years of age.

Familiar abusers

For all the dangers posed by paedophiles, children are at far more risk of abuse from their own families than they are from strangers. Children are more at risk of being murdered in the first year of life than at any other age, and the killer is almost invariably a parent. The risk continues through early childhood: almost two-thirds of children murdered in England and Wales are under 5 years of age. On average, one or two children a week are killed by their parents: a total between 52 and 104 a year. In over 60 per cent of cases, at all ages, the *first* suspect in any child murder is a parent. And contrary to popular stereotypes, the killer is almost as likely to be the mother (47 per cent) as the father (53 per cent).

Four types of abuse are identified within families. *Sexual abuse* makes the headlines, but is the rarest reported. In the vast majority of cases, the perpetrator is male, usually a brother, step-brother, father or step-father. Statistics suggest that only about 1 per cent of children are sexually abused by a parent, and 3 per cent by another relative. Much more common is *physical abuse*. About a quarter of all children report at least one episode of physical abuse in childhood. This includes being hit with an instrument or a fist, shaken, thrown or knocked down, beaten up, partly strangled, burned or scalded on purpose, or threatened with a knife. Of these children, 78 per cent say the attacker was a family member, which could include siblings as well as parents. Such abuse is as likely to come from a mother as a father.

Rarer are *emotional abuse*, defined as excessive control and domination, humiliation or psychological attacks on self-esteem, withdrawal of affection/attention, hostility, terrorizing/threatening and the like, and *neglect*, defined as a lack of provision for the child's welfare: not providing adequate food, clean clothes, medical care, or leaving the child unsupervised and uncared for – for example, leaving a child under 10 years of age at home to fend for him/herself while the parent goes on holiday. About 6 per cent of children report serious emotional abuse, and 6 per cent report serious neglect, though milder forms are more common (about 20 per cent of children report mild or occasional abuse).

These figures are shocking. There is great debate over how accurate a picture they paint. Are they the tip of the iceberg, as children suppress assaults to protect the family (or themselves)? Or are they an over-estimate, reflecting the poor definition of what counts as abuse (which often includes both the trivial – 'he smacked my knee' – and the extreme, as in the case of Victoria Climbié, kept naked in a bath in an unheated bathroom, starved and beaten to death)? We don't really know. There are real methodological and ethical problems in finding out.

Causes of abuse by parents

Although abuse can happen in any family, it is far more likely in families that lack the psychological or economic resources to cope. All forms of abuse are more common where there is alcohol or drug abuse, poverty, or a violent relationship between the parents (Emery and Laumann-Billings, 1998). Abusive parents typically have little emotional control and low self-esteem, and tend to lack the social skills either to parent effectively or to seek social support in handling problems. Neglect may reflect little more than incompetence in parenting, though it can involve a more proactive hostility to the child. Mothers in particular may feel that the children are out of control, and may respond punitively as a reaction (Bugental and Johnson, 2000). The child's temperament may contribute to the problem: children with difficult temperaments are more often victims of neglect, physical and emotional abuse than are the easy-going (Cicchetti and Toth, 1998). Sexual abuse may involve a pathological inability to inhibit inappropriate desires, a psychopathic absence of concern with a child's welfare.

Effects of abuse

Children who suffer abuse typically do poorly in school and have difficulty forming friendships. They tend to be aggressive and anti-social, to lack sympathy for others, and may be withdrawn and dependent. In adolescence and adult life they are at risk of developing serious problems, from delinquency to drug or alcohol abuse, depression and psychiatric disorder (Cicchetti and Toth, 1998). Some, but by no means all, go on to become abusers themselves.

Sometimes the only way to protect a child from abuse is to remove him or her from the family. This solution is drastic: children in care are also notoriously vulnerable to abuse. That's a risk worth taking if a child's life is in danger. But often, less drastic interventions can keep a family intact. The sooner such interventions are made, the more likely they are to succeed.

It's obvious from the research reviewed here that conclusions about parenting styles drawn from research in one culture can't necessarily be applied to another. The predominant style of parenting reflects cultural values and circumstances, which vary enormously even between apparently very similar societies. For example, in 2006 European population statistics showed that French adolescents spent considerably more time in shared activities with their parents than British adolescents, who spent more time unsupervised and with their peers, with the result that (it was claimed) British teenagers had a far higher rate of binge drinking, sexually transmitted disease, drug abuse and general delinquency than their French counterparts. We are only just at the start of research exploring the reasons for this (and other) cultural differences, and things may be more complex than we've yet considered. For example, do the differences between French and British adolescents indicate that there are more permissive or more neglectful parents in Britain than in France? Or do they imply only that 'youth culture' is a more powerful force in compact and largely urban Britain than it is in more rural France? We don't yet know.

Parenting style and socio-economic class

The more affluent and better educated in liberal Western societies tend to adopt authoritative rather than authoritarian parenting styles, whereas less well-educated and poorer families tend to adopt authoritarian rather than authoritative styles (Hoff-Ginsberg and Tardif, 1995). Exactly why this is so is unclear. In part, it may reflect differences between social classes in child-rearing theories: maybe the better educated value and try to instil in their children the attributes (such as responsibility and autonomy) that are needed for the well-paid careers that they pursue, and hope that their children will also pursue – attributes largely irrelevant to those employed at the bottom of the socio-economic heap. In part it may be that the poor live in much more dangerous environments, where there is more need of an authoritarian parenting style to keep children safe (Parke and Buriel, 1998). Certainly, there is a world of difference between the gently ordered comfort of 'manicured' middle-class areas and the vandalism and dereliction, the omnipresent street crime, open drug pushing and prostitution found in some areas of high unemployment and low hope.

In part, the prevalence of authoritarian parenting styles in lower socio-economic classes may be a direct reflection of the sheer struggle of life when there is not quite enough money, not quite enough time, too much conflict between parents, so that adults are simply under too much stress to parent children patiently and tolerantly. Anyone can shout 'Because I say so!' – the authoritarian response – when at the end of their tether. The children most at risk not only from authoritarian parenting but also from abuse and neglect are those from families that have been struggling, economically, for a prolonged period of time (McLoyd, 1998).

Fathers, mothers and parenting

In some African cultures, fathers have little or no contact with their children (LeVine et al., 1996), leaving every aspect of the child's welfare to the mother. Even in liberal Western societies which pay at least lip-service to the concept of shared parenting, mothers still typically spend far more time with their offspring (even when they also go out to work) than fathers do, and this is true right through childhood and adolescence (Parke and Buriel, 1998). Typically, it's mothers who do the child care and look after the basic welfare of the young, teaching basic skills. In societies where fathers do spend time with their offspring, they are more likely to play than to attend to welfare, and to focus on outdoor games and rough-and-tumble. When mothers play, the game is more likely to be indoors, sedentary, and quite possibly educational: teaching the child to read, cook, paint, use scissors, complete jigsaws and the like (Parke and Buriel, 1998).

The reasons for these gender differences in parenting are complex. There are strong cultural traditions dictating that women should nurture the young while men focus on economic activity in virtually all human societies. There are practical reasons why the economic success of a family might be entrusted to the male parent rather than the female: males are physically stronger and don't need 'time out' from economic activity to produce a baby. Whether you're a farmer or a hunter, a corporate banker or a teacher, the strength and continuity males can give to economic activity can be a real factor in deciding the division of labour within a family.

But there are also strong biological reasons that could account for why mothers put more energy into child rearing than do fathers. In the first place, a mother puts considerably more effort into the production of a baby than a father does (9 months as opposed to a few minutes), and this greater parental investment alone has been argued to be enough to dispose a woman to continue to invest more in ensuring the welfare of an individual child (Trivers, 1972). Furthermore, a mother can have a high degree of certainty that the child she is nurturing is genetically her own, whereas a man can't be so sure of the paternity of a given child, and so can't be sure that the genes he is nurturing in that child are his own. Evolutionary biologists have estimated that about 10 per cent (or more) of babies are not the offspring of the man who thinks he's their father, although some believe this figure is too high.

Most intriguingly, new research in neuroscience is suggesting that, at least at the moment of birth, a mother's brain is already neurologically primed both to bond with her baby and to behave parentally, whereas a father's brain is not. For example, in rodents, virgin females are indifferent or hostile to infants; they may even kill them. Hormonal changes during pregnancy in effect 'reconfigure' their brains to create parenting behaviour (Bridges, 1990). There are good theoretical reasons for believing that a similar 'brain-wiring' for maternity also exists in primates, including human mothers (De Vries, 2004). Since fathers are never pregnant, such automatic biochemical rewiring can't happen, providing another reason why mothers might be more disposed to engage in parenting behaviour than fathers.

Very recent work with marmosets suggests that the male primate brain, too, can potentially be 'reconfigured' to be parental (Kozorovitskiy et al., 2006). This reconfiguration involves a marked increase in density in the front of the brain (the cortex), allowing the complex cognitive processing needed to cope with keeping track of and managing infants. (Mothers have always known that parenting involves a lot of intelligence and being able to do several things at once.) The reconfiguration of the male marmoset brain also involves a marked increase in the number of receptors for vasopressin, a hormone involved in bonding. Could male human brains potentially be reconfigured in this way to cope with parenting? We don't yet know. But any new and cognitively demanding task tends to produce increases in brain density and neural connectivity (De Vries, 2004), so that this seems perfectly possible. To get their rewiring, male marmosets put very considerable effort into parenting, doing an equal share with the female. Few human males come anywhere near this level of effort, so may miss out on the possibility of developing a brain as complex as a woman's.

Family structure and development

Families come in all sorts of shapes and sizes around the world. They may be monogamous (one husband, one wife) or polygamous (one husband, several wives) or even, in certain societies (Inuit societies, for example), polyandrous (one wife, several husbands). There are a growing number of families with two mothers or two fathers, as gay and lesbian couples rear children (see **Box 11.4**). And increasingly, in modern industrial societies, families may be led by a single parent (usually, but not always, a mother). Such single-parent families are also found in subsistence societies, where men must emigrate to find work, leaving their families at home (a pattern common in many areas of poverty particularly in Africa, Asia and Eastern Europe).

box **11.4**

Gay and lesbian parents

The issue of families headed by gay or lesbian couples has caused so much angst that it is worth considering in detail.

We live in a society that is only now emerging from a strong tradition of hostility toward all forms of homosexuality. For those living in liberal communities at the outset of the 21st century, it's hard to realize that homosexuality was once officially taken to be evidence of mental illness – an idea dropped only in the 1970s. Even today, certain Christian churches seem more obsessed with a fight against homosexuality than with standing up against the evils of corrupt and murderous political regimes, as Archbishop Desmond Tutu (2007) has pointed out. Many cultures, and even many sectors within our own liberal society, still maintain prejudices against homosexuality.

These prejudices raised serious questions for the courts and for government policy as homosexuality began to come out of the closet and demand human rights. Should gay or lesbian couples be allowed to adopt, or in the latter case, be helped to conceive by artificial insemination? Should parents leaving heterosexual liaisons for gay or lesbian ones be allowed custody, or even access to their children? There was considerable doubt, fuelled by traditional prejudiced stereotypes not only about gay and lesbian people but about men and women as a whole. These prejudices worried that two men could not 'mother' a child – and that lesbians lacked femininity and maternal tendencies too; that same-sex couples would therefore not be as effective in child rearing. Furthermore, they would not provide appropriate role models for the young, leading to gender and sexual confusions in their children; and the offspring of same-sex couples would be bullied and rejected by their peers and society at large, to the detriment of their general welfare and social development. Worse yet, it was widely believed that children in such families would be at higher risk of sexual abuse (an extension of the bizarre but common idea that non-heterosexuals are generally more predatory than heterosexuals). None of this is true (Allen and Burrell, 1996; Perrin, 2002).

In fact, the evidence suggests that there are very few differences in child-rearing practices between heterosexual families and gay or lesbian ones (Bos, van Balen and van den Boom, 2004). Some research suggests that parenting skills are actually higher in homosexual partnerships than heterosexual ones (Flaks et al., 1995). In part, this probably reflects the fact that most same-sex parents are lesbian couples, and the non-biological lesbian parent tends to be more involved with, and more sensitive, to her partner's child than the average biological father. But in both gay and lesbian couples the responsibilities of child rearing tend to be more evenly divided between the parents than is presently the case in heterosexual couples (Bos et al., 2004; Johnson and O'Connor, 2002). It may be that the mere fact of having two 'hands on' parents within a household also conveys some advantages, if only in reducing the pressures: a problem shared is a problem halved. Furthermore, gay and lesbian couples are less likely to spank, and more likely than heterosexual families to use discussion and reasoning to shape their children's behaviours (Johnson and O'Connor, 2002). In other words, gay and lesbian couples are more likely to adopt an authoritative parenting style, which conveys many developmental advantages, as we have seen in this chapter.

The fear that same-sex couples would be more likely to sexually abuse their children is entirely without foundation. There is not a single shred of evidence that gay men are any more likely than anyone else to sexually assault children. Sexual assault on a child led by (or even involving) a woman is vanishingly rare: children in the families of lesbian couples should be safer than those in heterosexual families, in this respect. And there is no evidence whatever to suggest that gay or lesbian couples are more neglectful, physically or emotionally abusive than heterosexual parents.

Nor is there any evidence that children suffer from growing up with same-sex parents. There is no evidence that their general welfare is harmed in any way (Patterson, 1997, 2000). The development of gender identity is not affected: that is to say, children raised by same-sex parents are as likely as anyone else to form a gender identity reflecting their anatomical sex, and to be happy with that identity (Golombok, Spencer and Rutter, 1983). Gender-related behaviour develops in the same way in children raised by heterosexual and same-sex couples (Brewaeys et al. 1997; Golombok et al., 1983). Children raised by same-sex couples are no more likely to become gay or lesbian than children from heterosexual families (Huggins, 1989). There is no evidence that children raised by same-sex couples have any greater difficulty in developing social relationships with either children or adults than those raised by heterosexual couples (Golombok et al., 1983).

Only two things have ever been identified that suggest children raised by same-sex parents may be developmentally disadvantaged in any way. The first relates to the timing of the discovery that your parents are gay or lesbian.

Pre-pubescent children take this easily in their stride, and in late adolescence we are ready to allow our parents their own reality (well, to a degree), and to accept their needs. But in early adolescence issues of sexual identity, sexual orientation, the whole business of transferring from a focus on same-sex friendships to other-sex eroticism is too raw. Discoveries about one's parent's sexual orientation which would pass without a flicker at 8 or 18 can cause serious confusion to the pubescent (Pennington, 1987).

The other issue is, of course, the reaction of society at large. Thirty years ago children raised by same-sex parents were often the butt of ridicule, bullying and rejection, reflecting the prejudices of the time. They either hid the family secret or suffered. At least in our Western society, surveys at the start of the 21st century suggest that children with same-sex parents seldom experience such punitive reactions, to the point where most are comfortable with others knowing about their families (Gartrell et al., 2005). But where children raised by same-sex couples encounter hostility against homosexuality or lesbianism, damage can be done. It's worth pointing out that such damage comes not from the parenting the child receives, nor from the fact that the parents are of one gender, but specifically from the reaction of the surrounding society to that fact.

Living arrangements vary: families may live in 'nuclear' units (parents and children) or in extended family groups with several generations (grandparents, parents, children, uncles and aunts) living together. And the division of labour in the family varies, too: in some, father goes out to work, mother runs the house and raises the children. In others, both parents work (either in equal careers, or in gender-specific ones, for example in African communities where women are subsistence farmers and men engage in economic activity beyond the family's land). Child care is provided either by the mother, alongside her economic work, or in industrial societies by a crèche, nursery, school or a paid employee; in other groups it's provided by grandparents, or by older children of the family. These different family structures have a major impact on a child's development (Whiting and Whiting, 1975; Rogoff et al., 1984).

The particular family structure within which a child grows up provides a basic model of what adult life and social structures at large are like. It provides a model of what it means to be male or female, what it means to be a family or a parent, what one has to do to 'make it' and survive. More subtly, it provides a model of the political, economic and moral world: a notion of *property* (whether things are owned by an individual or by the family group), of *power* (whether decisions can be made by an individual or democratically by the family as a whole, or authoritarianly by the head of a family), and most subtly of all, of *being* (whether people are growing up to replace older generations in a fixed cycle within the family, or growing up as an autonomous agent who will transcend and leave the family – and hence what their rights and obligations to others are).

The day-to-day dynamic of life within different family structures also has profound effects on the process of development itself. For example, it sets the 'agenda' for development by setting the expectations of what a child of a given age will have achieved. In many traditional societies children are expected to carry real responsibilities from a very early age. For example, by 7 or 8 years of age, girls are expected to take care of younger siblings and babies, and boys are expected to take on tasks such as herding cattle (which may be a family's main asset), without direct adult supervision (Rogoff et al., 1984). In modern Western societies children are not expected to be capable of carrying such responsibilities at such a young age (although we thought nothing of sending them to work 8-hour days in factories in Victorian times). In each case, children live up to the expectations of their society, so that genuinely responsible behaviour emerges at a far younger age in traditional societies than in modern Western industrial societies.

Is it a good thing that the young in some African (and other) societies become responsible and can be trusted with important tasks so very much younger than their Western contemporaries? Some American researchers have argued that loading young children with responsibilities as some cultures do, or even expecting teenagers to perform adult chores, from taking out the trash to babysitting, is a form of abuse which they call 'parentification' (Jurkovic, 1997). The premise of this idea is that there is an age at which the young are psychologically 'ready' to shoulder responsibilities, and to ask them to do this before they are ready is to impose a stunting burden on them. But this view rests on theoretical assumptions about the nature of development which do not fit with the data.

The stark cross-cultural differences in the age at which children develop important attributes such as responsibility strongly suggest that, to a far greater degree than we have supposed, the pace of development is socially constructed rather than reflecting the psychological status of the child (Rogoff et al., 1984). That is to say, the development of various core social and emotional abilities seems to be determined by the *opportunities* a family provides for development in these areas, and the *expectations* it has of the child's progress, rather than being determined by age-related processes. We mature when we are invited to, or when we must, rather than having to wait for some specific psychological 'readiness'. From this perspective, families who withhold opportunities for children to learn to engage in genuinely responsible tasks until late childhood or adolescence are as open to an accusation of distorting development (the abuse of 'babyfication', perhaps) as those who provide such opportunities early.

In many ways, the view we take about the 'rightness' of expecting children to be responsible or irresponsible at a given age is no more than a projection of our cultural values. We've already seen, in relation to parenting styles, that expecting too little by way of mature behaviour (as permissive or neglectful parents do) leads to immaturity and irresponsibility, and that high expectations provided by both authoritative and authoritarian parenting can be constructive unless enforced harshly or in ways out of keeping with the surrounding culture.

Perhaps what matters more than the timing of development is the degree to which different family structures support developmental progress. Some (for example, families where the child is home with mother or in well-staffed day care or school) lead children to spend a great deal of time with adults, living under close supervision and receiving a great deal of direct guidance and tuition from adults. In others (for example, families where the mother works the family's land and infants are looked after by young siblings), children may spend considerably less time with adults and receive considerably less direct tuition and guidance from adults, at least until they join the adult world (Whiting and Whiting, 1975).

Direct guidance and tuition are powerful processes in development, from the acquisition of practical and conceptual skills to the mastery of social and emotional skills (Rogoff, 1998). Adults make better tutors than children do (Radziszewska and Rogoff, 1991), so that we would expect children with greater exposure to adults to make swifter progress in mastering skills and developing conceptual understanding than those with less adult contact. Furthermore, adults are far more sophisticated, in every culture, than young children. They therefore have more to teach, which again may lead to differences in conceptual development between those whose tutors are 7 to 10 years old and those whose tutors are adult.

Siblings

Most children have one or more siblings. As we've seen, in some cultures siblings provide one another with a great deal of their day to day child care and tutoring. But even in Western societies, they are a more important influence on development than we previously supposed, playing an important part in the process of socialization for one another (Parke and Buriel, 1998). For example, through playing and sharing activities with older siblings children can learn more than they do playing alone or with a same-age friend, both through the opportunity to watch and copy, and through the direct tuition offered by the older child (Azmitia and Hesser, 1993). Games of 'let's pretend' shared with an older sibling play an important role in fostering a child's developing understanding of other minds (Perner, Ruffman and Leekam, 1994; Ruffman et al., 1998 – and see Chapter 9).

Relationships between siblings don't always flow as smoothly as this implies, however. A very young sibling's efforts to join in with his or her elders can be intensely annoying, and there is a tendency for the older child to either eject the younger or to take charge of the situation (Perez-Granados and Callanan, 1997), which reduces the younger child's scope for learning (Radziszewska and Rogoff, 1991). Only at around 8 years of age do older siblings start to make real allowances for younger ones; and only at around 4 years of age do younger sibs become more interesting playmates, able to hold their own (Brown and Dunn, 1991; Dunn and Shatz, 1989), although the older sib still tends to dominate the interactions (Abramovitch et al., 1986).

Nor are the things siblings learn from one another always wholly constructive. For example, siblings can encourage one another to defy parental authority, to engage in illicit behaviours and to become dishonest about this (Snyder, Bank and Burraston, 2005). Some research suggests that when families foster delinquent behaviour, it is not the parents who actively encourage this so much as the children: siblings often share delinquent adventures and egg one another on (Rowe, Rodgers and Meseck-Bushey, 1992). Equally, although parental behaviour does influence whether or not the young smoke, drink alcohol or use drugs, an adolescent's likelihood of engaging in these things is much more powerfully influenced by the behaviour of his or her siblings (Fagan and Najman, 2005).

As well as being friends and playmates, siblings are also often rivals, the relationship between them ambivalent and punctuated by considerable friction (Dunn, 1995). They are rivals for the parent's attention, a particular problem for the first-born, who must suddenly share the parent's attention with a newcomer. Such rivalry can be reduced by sensitive parenting, for example involving the first-born or other older children in activities with the new arrival, and later on by treating children equally rather than favouring one above another (Dunn, 1995). Rivalries are least common where every child feels loved and supported by the parents. Nevertheless, this is not always enough to secure amicable interactions between siblings: even one child with a 'difficult' temperament can cause friction and disruption (Munn and Dunn, 1989). Two with difficult temperaments will generate considerable friction, although with this one exception, siblings with similar temperaments tend to get along more easily than those who differ (Munn and Dunn, 1989). Conflict matters: siblings with high levels of conflict show far lower emotional well-being than those with low conflict (Sherman, Lansford and Volling, 2006).

There has been considerable debate over the years about whether a child's position in the family (only child, first-born, middle child, youngest) has long-lasting effects on personality or intelligence. Most lay people believe that it does, for example believing that only children are more selfish and more successful, that first-borns are more anxious and compliant, that middle children are likely to have more problems than other children since they lack the privileges of the oldest and the special status of the youngest (and so on). In fact, there is remarkably little evidence to support any of this (Dunn, 1995). There's little difference between only children and those with siblings in terms of their social skills and orientations (Falbo and Poston, 1993). Firstborns do tend to be a tad bossier (Beck, Burnet and Vosper, 2006) than younger children and to feel more responsible, just as you'd expect from their social position: parents often expect them to take responsibility over younger siblings. Younger siblings tend to be a tad more sociable (Beck et al., 2006), again just as you'd expect, given that they are born into a social group already containing peers and encouraged to interact with them, where first-borns and only children are not. But 'middle child' syndrome seems to be a myth.

Far more important an influence on a child's development than birth order is the relative health of a group of siblings. Many children today live with chronic illnesses, some of which are potentially fatal (asthma, cancer, cystic fibrosis, chronic arthritis, Crohn's disease, sickle cell anaemia, haemophilia, muscular dystrophy and many others), or with disabilities (blindness, deafness, physical disability, learning disability). Suffering a chronic illness or disability is a wretched thing for the child, with the potential for all sorts of disruption to normal development, through the disruption of normal life and activities. Such children are also, unsurprisingly, at greater risk of emotional distress, though very few actually develop symptoms of mental illness (Barlow and Ellard, 2006).

Inevitably, when a child is ill or in pain, distressed or at risk of dying, parents orient more to that child than to his or her siblings. When the disease is chronic, long-lasting and either continuous or recurrent, the sick child and his or her needs often come to dominate family life. This is particularly so when the chronic illness is genetic, so that parents feel a sense of guilt on top of everything else. The consequence is that the healthy siblings of the sick child can easily become marginalized, or can be drawn into the world of chronic illness. Many feel a sense of guilt (that they are healthy and going to survive), as well as a natural grief and anxiety on behalf of the sibling, and a powerlessness to help. The very young may have little understanding of either disease or death (see **Box 11.5**), and so may misinterpret the parent's behaviour in favouring the sick child, either becoming jealous and hostile or feeling withdrawn and rejected.

Paradoxically, the healthy siblings of a chronically ill child can be at as much, or even greater, risk of psycho-social damage than the child who is ill (Barlow and Ellard, 2006). For example, a month after their sibling had been diagnosed with cancer, many siblings experience a wide range of problems, including general stress and unhappiness, a decline in the ability to concentrate and complete cognitive tasks, even a decline in their physical coordination (Houtzager et al., 2006). The pressures and effects on siblings of children with such a disease can continue for months or years, escalating if the sick child begins a clear decline toward death. The need to counter this effect is well understood by the Children's Hospice Movement, part of whose efforts are directed to supporting the psycho-social development of these well siblings. This is a growing area of research (Barlow and Ellard, 2006; Stoneman, 2005).

box 11.5

Understanding illness and death

Illness is a complex concept with which even adults have problems. It has taken our species thousands of years to reach our present understanding of the mechanisms that underlie illnesses, the difference between infections, genetic disease and problems such as cancer, and many adults have only a hazy grasp on this knowledge. Small wonder, then, that children are often very confused.

Developing insight into illness

Young children typically have a very poor grasp on the causes of illness, as witness this exchange between a researcher and a young child: Researcher: 'How do people get colds?' Child: 'From trees' (Bibace and Walsh, 1981). Not understanding how disease arises, children up to 6 or 7 years of age tend to explain it as a punishment, blaming either the ill person or themselves for 'bad behaviour' that has brought this retribution (Kister and Patterson, 1980; Perrin and Gerrity, 1981). This kind of perception can induce profound and debilitating levels of guilt when a child falls ill, or when a sibling or parent is ill.

Understanding of the mechanisms that cause illness (germs, toxins, faulty cellular mechanisms) develops very slowly through the course of childhood. At one time, researchers believed that there were distinct developmental stages through which this understanding developed (Bibace and Walsh, 1981), reflecting the general conceptual changes described by Piaget (see Chapters 1 and 6), so that particular conceptions of illness would be tied to particular age groups. More recent research suggests that understanding develops as a reflection of the specific information available to the child, rather than through the development of general cognitive structures (see Chapter 6), so that development reflects knowledge rather than age. This view is supported by the fact that children's conceptions of illness are mediated by their general understanding of biology (Buchanan-Barrow, Barrett and Bati, 2003) – which reflects the acquisition of specific knowledge (Carey, 1985).

The notion that understanding illness depends on specific knowledge is supported by research that shows age alone is not enough to generate insight in this area. For example, a study by Veldman and colleagues (2000) found that 18-year-old heart patients had no more understanding of their disease than 7-year-olds (which some might view as a terrible indictment of the communication skills of the medics involved with those patients). Older children do have more conceptual resources for understanding illness than younger children, but they still need information. Direct experience of illness makes a major contribution to a child's understanding (Crisp, Ungerer and Goodnow, 1996), particularly where the situation is properly explained. But generally, through one source of information or another, most children have acquired enough knowledge to understand that illnesses can be caused in multiple ways and may have multiple outcomes by the time they enter adolescence (Perrin and Gerrity, 1981).

Understanding death

Understanding death presents further problems. Toddlers have no understanding of death. They can't anticipate the loss which death involves, and when the death of a sibling (or parent) occurs, experience a sense of loss and abandonment without comprehending the nature of the situation. Even in early childhood (3 to 6 years of age) children often believe that death is reversible, that it's like going to sleep, so you can always wake up (Grollman, 1990; Stambrook and Parker, 1987). If people disappear in death, it's a punishment. At this age, children may blame themselves for their loss. Somewhere between 6 (Grollman, 1990) and 8 (Stambrook and Parker, 1987) years of age, children begin to understand that death is permanent and irreversible, though this realization is not universal until about 10 years of age (Grollman, 1990). Only at around 13 do children consistently provide an adult conception of death as permanent, irreversible and applying to all living things.

Culture, illness and death

The accounts given above draw on research in Western industrialized societies, and are unlikely to apply to other cultures. The medical beliefs and practices of adults differ from culture to culture: for example, Western medical theories of pain and anaesthesia, diagnosis and treatment and the cause of different diseases are very different from those of traditional Chinese medicine. In other societies, adults adhere to magical approaches to illness, using witchcraft to secure health or cure disease. The 'knowledge' children have about illness is entirely a matter of cultural hearsay (unless you're a medical student, it's unlikely that you've ever actually seen a bacterium or virus). We believe what we're told in these matters, and children in different cultures will be told different things.

Children's understanding of death, too, may develop very differently in different cultures. Few children growing up in Western societies experience the death of anyone they know or care about, and insight may develop very differently in such societies than it does in societies where death from famine, disease, war or terrorism is endemic. A 3-year-old in a refugee camp during a famine will have seen far more death than a Western medical student, for example, and is likely to have a very much more realistic appraisal than far older children in Western societies.

Oversimplifying the phenomena

Even in our own culture we should be wary of assuming that the fact that children don't say that death is permanent, irreversible and final until early adolescence means that they don't understand this much earlier.

Death is a troubling thing. Many adults in our society engage in a kind of denial about the finality of death: not making wills, for example, or refusing to accept that a loved one is dying despite terrible illness, or using euphemisms to refer to death (fallen asleep, passed on) which have connotations of temporariness rather than permanence. Religion encourages a belief in death as a transition to life on a different plane rather than the termination of life, and many believers apparently expect to take on their human form in this afterlife. It may well be that many children get very mixed and confusing messages about the finality of death. But one cultural message is clear: this is a dangerous topic, and admitting that death is final is distressing. It may be that children far younger than we suppose are actually aware that death is final, but either share our adult propensity for denial, or hedge around the issue because of the social tension associated with this topic.

Divorce

Families have an important effect on the development of their children. But what when family life breaks down? Statistics recorded in 2002 suggest that 40 per cent of all marriages in European countries had ended in divorce. The figure for the United States was higher, at 55 per cent. And in all Western countries, divorce rates are steadily rising. A great many children are growing up in fractured families.[2]

How is development affected in families that disintegrate? There's never a good age for parents to divorce, from a child's perspective. Toddlers are not too young to experience the pain of separation from a loved parent. Even young adults can feel profoundly saddened and abandoned by the failure of their parents' marriage. This is not to say that there are no differences between the immediate reactions of children of different ages at the time of divorce: of course, there are.

Children's reactions to divorce

The immediate reaction of children to a divorce is one of abandonment, terror and loneliness. Babies may be the least affected by this since they have the least insight into what is going on, and may not yet have formed an attachment to the departing parent or any strong views of what 'normal' family life should be. Toddlers may believe that the whole horrible situation is their fault: lacking any understanding of the real dynamics of the relationship between the parents, they may conclude that this punishing experience wouldn't have happened if they had only been 'good'. School children, too, may have little insight into why mummy and daddy can't live together any more, and make desperate efforts to bring about a reconciliation. Adolescents may have more insight into their parents' relationship, but feel powerless and angry, resentfully forced to grow up and take on responsibilities to help the remaining parent. And for all their independence, young adults may feel a shifting of the foundations on which their world has been based, a sense of unease and anxiety.

---

[2] For the sake of brevity I shall use the word 'divorce' to cover all situations where parents who have shared a home with their children separate, whether they were legally married or not.

Divorce and development

Divorce produces a sense of shock in everyone. In children the ensuing insecurity and unhappiness are often associated with a regression to behaving in more childish ways: bed-wetting in small children who have long mastered continence, for example, or needing to be 'babied' in an older child, or childish behaviour in adolescents. This retreat back into childhood may take years to wholly vanish. Academic performance falls off: in fact, intelligence itself can show a marked decline, even in gifted children (Terman, 1954). A child may become difficult at school, withdrawn or aggressive, so that relationships with teachers and friends are affected. These effects can be very long-lasting: children who were between 2 and 6 years of age when their parents divorced have been found to be more likely than those from intact families to have experienced unsafe sex, drug and alcohol abuse by their mid-20s (Wallerstein and Lewis, 1998). They typically reach puberty earlier (see **Box 11.6**), are more likely to have a succession of unstable romantic relationships and to later divorce themselves, and they show a relatively poor commitment to parenting their own children (Bjorklund and Pellegrini, 2000).

box 11.6

Puberty

Physical changes at puberty

Puberty is defined by the maturation of the ability to reproduce. It's triggered by the release of growth hormones from the pituitary gland buried in the brain. This provokes a spurt in physical growth, over 2 or 3 years: legs lengthen first, then the trunk and arms, and the bones of the skull thicken, widening the head. A girl might grow 6 inches during this spurt, a boy might grow 9 inches, in each case achieving 98 per cent of final adult height. After this, growth continues ever more slowly. Bones finally lose their capacity to grow at around 25 years of age (Tanner, 1990).

During this growth spurt all the reproductive organs and functions develop. In boys, testicles and penis enlarge, semen is produced and ejaculation becomes possible. In girls, the breasts develop and the ovaries begin to release mature ova. Menstruation begins (the menarche). Alongside these primary sexual characteristics, secondary sexual characteristics develop: the growth of pubic and bodily hair, the changing distributions of fat and muscle, the alterations to voice that characterize male and female.

The timing of puberty

There are wide variations in when children reach puberty, so that a classroom of 14- to 15-year-olds might contain individuals for whom the transition has not begun and others who are fully mature. In part, the timing of puberty reflects genetic factors: for example, monozygotic twin girls who share the same genes tend to reach the menarche more closely in unison (within 2 months) than dizygotic twins (8 months apart on average) who share fewer genes (Marshall and Tanner, 1974). But it's clear that the major factors affecting the timing of puberty are environmental. Most research investigating such effects has focused on the menarche, which is a clear and obvious event. There's no parallel clear marker in boys.

In traditional hunter-gatherer tribes, menarche occurs in the late teens (Geary and Bjorklund, 2000). The same was true of European societies 150 years ago, when the average age of menarche was around 16 or 17 years of age (Katchadourian, 1977). However, menarche occurs much earlier in many countries today, at around 12 years of age. This change seems to be to do with nutrition: girls who are lean and fit (dancers and gymnasts, for example) reach menarche later than their chubbier peers (Warren et al., 1991), and menstruation is very delayed or stops in girls who are anorexic or suffer famine. In fact, it seems to be specifically fat that triggers the menarche, which occurs earlier where obesity is rife (the United States) than elsewhere (Katchadourian, 1977).

The timing of puberty is also affected by stress. For example, girls from divorced families or families in conflict reach menarche earlier than those from less stressed backgrounds (Graber, Brooks-Gunn and Warren, 1995). War and civil unrest seem to have a similar effect, lowering the age on menarche. It's believed that stress affects the hormones and that this triggers these earlier puberties. Exactly why this happens is unclear. Some researchers have suggested that such effects reflect evolutionary mechanisms (Bjorklund and Pellegrini, 2000). In evolutionary history (and in many circumstances today), the chances of living long enough to breed are lower in situations of stress and conflict, so that there is a reproductive advantage to earlier menarche.

Psychological impact of puberty

Adolescents' reactions to puberty depend very much on surrounding social attitudes. Girls who are prepared for menarche and boys prepared for a first nocturnal ejaculation have a more positive experience than those who are not prepared – provided their guide has a positive attitude to these events. For example, the level of discomfort a girl experiences in relation to menstruation is greater where the social attitudes she has been exposed to are negative than where they are positive (Brooks-Gunn and Reiter, 1990).

Puberty is often more stressful for girls than for boys. For boys, increased body mass is largely composed of muscle. For girls, it's predominantly fat. In our culture, which admires lean muscle and almost anorexic super-models, boys' body images generally remain positive through pubertal changes (unless they fail to develop masculine muscles), but girls generally become dissatisfied with their 'fat' (Brooks-Gunn and Reiter, 1990). This dissatisfaction is worst in families, peer groups or societies that reinforce the value of thinness (for example, North American and European cultures), and least in cultures (for example, many African or South American societies) that admire a larger or more femininely shaped body (Parker et al., 1995).

Dissatisfaction with body fat is a factor in triggering eating disorders such as anorexia nervosa (effectively, self-starvation) and bulimia nervosa (a cycle of starving, binge eating and self-induced vomiting). Anorexia is more common in girls from higher socio-economic groups, where it might affect up to 1 per cent (Hendren and Berenson, 1997), perhaps because these classes value slimness the most. Bulimia occurs in all classes, and may affect 5 per cent of girls in some societies to some degree. About 5 per cent of anorexics die of kidney or heart damage. Bulimia causes health problems, but fewer deaths. Although girls with the highest percentage of body fat as they enter puberty are at greatest risk of eating disorders, fat alone is not enough to trigger the problem. Depression and family conflict contribute importantly to the development of these problems.

Does the timing of puberty matter?

The evidence on this issue is contradictory. Reaching puberty markedly earlier than your peers is sometimes found to have positive effects in both sexes: early-maturing boys may gain respect through the greater strength and athletic success their mature bodies bring, and girls may enjoy respect for their sexual attractiveness. But early bodily changes can also be depressing and embarrassing as young people stand out from peers, and can have negative effects when they are expected to behave more maturely than peers simply because their body has matured: psychological maturity may well lag behind. Likewise, late puberty can have both positive and negative effects: it can allow time for psychological maturity to develop before bodily changes lead others to expect adult behaviours, but can also cause the embarrassment of having a childish body when everyone else at least looks adult. All we can be certain of is that the effects of early or late puberty are not absolute or universal: they depend entirely on the social meanings given to puberty in the particular social groups the adolescent inhabits, and the social expectations that puberty brings in those groups.

Boys and girls react differently to divorce. In boys, the relationship to both parents tends to be damaged, whereas in girls the relationship to the father is more damaged than the relationship to the mother, which may even become closer (Orbuch, Thornton and Cancio, 2000). The extent to which girls are depressed reflects the quality of their relationship with the mother and whether or not the mother herself is depressed, whereas boys tend to be depressed whatever the quality of this relationship or the mother's mood (Simons et al., 1999). It used to be thought that this differential reaction by boys and girls reflects the facts that normally, children live with the mother after a divorce, and that living with the same-sex parent is beneficial, particularly in adolescence. However, the data don't support this view (Guttman and Lazar, 1998). Which parent a child lives with matters far less than the quality of the relationship between parent and child.

Divorce and poverty

Some of the typical effects found after divorce are not to do with the breakdown of the family as such, or to do with now having only one parent. Rather, they reflect the circumstances of single mothers. For example, Clarke-Stewart and colleagues (2000) found that whilst children from intact families with two parents tended to be better adjusted and more socially and academically successful than those from single-parent families, these differences vanished when the income, education, child-rearing practices and depressiveness of the mothers was taken into account. It's low income, poor education, poor parenting skills and maternal depression that do the damage, not divorce itself.

Unfortunately, one practical consequence of divorce is that a mother's income tends to fall, sometimes drastically, and her tendency toward depression to rise – both factors associated with poorer parenting, as we've seen earlier in this chapter. Where these side-effects of divorce can be avoided, the damage to children's development is greatly reduced. This conclusion is underlined by studies that have shown that a child's physical and emotional health, social and academic development are markedly better when mothers receive good financial support after a divorce (Amato and Gilbreth, 1999). The provision of child support seems to have more impact on the child's welfare than the amount of contact with the father – although the data suggesting this are hard to interpret (Dunn, 2005).

Parental conflict

A second factor that damages children after a divorce is prolonged conflict between the parents, which creates stress and uncertainty, confusion and divided loyalties. It can affect a child's interactions with parents, siblings and friends. For example, boys whose divorced parents are in conflict have fewer friends and less rational interactions with others than their peers (Lindsey et al., 2006). And while adolescents may be able to take an independent view and make their own decisions as to whether mum/dad is in fact the devious, duplicitous, unreliable and utterly selfish monster described by the other parent (though their cynicism about human relationships may undergo a massive rise in the process), young children can't. Accusations of this sort by both parents about the other inevitably undermine a child's ability to trust anyone, or even to trust their own experience, a self-evidently depressing and damaging thing.

It's very hard to prevent conflict between divorcing parents. The very situation of divorce creates anxieties and practical problems that can easily fuel a feud. Legislative efforts to reduce this kind of problem haven't always been very successful. Mediation services of the kind introduced in Britain in the 1990s designed to secure joint responsibility for children have little effect, and the same result has been found in America (Dunne, Hudgins and Babcock, 2000). Only experiments in 'joint' custody (as opposed to awarding custody and control to one parent) have been shown to have beneficial effects (Gunnoe and Braver, 2001; Hawthorne, 2000), but this solution only works where parents are mature enough to cooperate.

The absent father

The fact is that custody and control of the children is normally given to the mother in a divorce. It's estimated that over 20 per cent of children in Britain are living apart from their fathers (Dunn, 2005), and similar figures must apply throughout Europe. Some researchers believe that this figure is nearer to 50 per cent in the United States, though this varies between ethnic groups (around 25 per cent for European Americans, 65 per cent for African-Americans). A great many fathers in this situation lose any meaningful contact with their children (Pruett and Pruett, 1998).

Fathers drift away from their children for various reasons. Sometimes, the mother actively blocks access and obstructs the child's relationship with the father. Even where this doesn't happen, it can be hard for a father to maintain a real relationship or genuine parental input after losing day-to-day contact with his child. Occasional visits can put both father and child under considerable strain, as is vividly illustrated by the reminiscences of children who lived through such experiences (Gillian Rose's moving account is an excellent example: Rose, 1997). It's hard for a parent who sees his child only intermittently to offer any sort of disciplinary input, and terribly tempting to simply shower the child in treats. Feelings of being marginalized can easily reduce a father's commitment to parenting (Braver and Griffin, 2000). Even the additional financial strain of a divided household can reduce a father's ability to maintain contact with his children (Simpson, Jessop and McCarthy, 2003); fathers at the lower end of the socio-economic scale more often lose contact with their children than those in better paid positions, as a result.

Occasionally, where the father was abusive and violent, his disappearance is to the child's advantage: a child develops more adaptively when an abusive father is cut out of his or her life than when he remains (Dunn, 2005). Equally, continuing contact with a father who is cold or rejecting is more damaging than losing contact altogether (Hazelton, Lancee and O'Neil, 1998). But few fathers are abusive or rejecting, and the vast majority of children would like to keep their relationship with their father after divorce. Many see the possibility of losing this contact as the worst aspect of the situation (Dunn, 2005). And where separated fathers can maintain a good quality of relationship with the child, one characterized by nurturant authoritative parenting, the evidence is that it is to the child's advantage to have continuing relationships with both parents (Shulman et al., 2001). For example, this greatly reduces children's feelings of anger and loss, which may otherwise persist for many years after the divorce.

Children without parents

The sad truth is that, around the world, millions of children are growing up without either parent. Some are orphaned by accidents, many by the

HIV-AIDS pandemic, others by natural disasters from tsunamis to earthquakes, floods or famines. Some are orphaned by war. Others are not so much orphaned as abandoned –sold into the sex trade or slave-labour factories, or simply tossed into the street by families too poor to cope – and some run away to escape abuse. The sheer scale of this problem worldwide is hard for those of us in affluent countries to absorb, as is the variability of the child's experience.

Some parentless children are taken in by grandparents or aunts and uncles, or raised by older siblings. Some are collected into orphanages, adopted or fostered. Some are simply abused and exploited. Others are left to fend for themselves. Children as young as 3 years of age (and quite possibly younger) live on the streets in India, Africa and South America, fending for themselves without adult support.

It's hard to generalize about the impact of any of this on an individual child's development. One grandparent (uncle or aunt, adoptive parent, foster parent) may be a wonderful parent, another not: these new families are as variable as any other. Equally, some orphanages produce lively, well-adjusted children, and others tie their charges to cots and leave them there unloved and uncared for, or offer them physical or sexual abuse on top of this emotional abuse and neglect. It's the quality of the child's experience that determines developmental outcomes in any of these situations.

What we can be sure of is that children subjected to severe neglect or abuse or left to fend for themselves in the streets are at very serious risk, not merely of failing to develop the academic and social skills normally imparted by the family (although these cognitive, social and emotional deficits can be severe), but also of serious malnutrition, disease and worse. Without adult protectors, these children are the natural prey of paedophiles, an easy recruiting ground for the child sex trade. In places, they are even deliberately 'culled' by the authorities to 'remove a nuisance': for example, thousands of homeless street children have been killed in certain countries, generally by the police. Rescuing these vulnerable children and finding ways to overcome the damage to their development is an urgent moral imperative.

Peer relationships

The development of social interactions

Right from birth, babies are interested in other people (see Chapter 4). Much of their attention is focused on adults. But even at 2 months of age, they are interested in their peers, gazing at one another, for example. By 6 to 10 months of age they show clear social interest in peers, make noises or gestures to attract another baby's attention, and interact by smiling, touching and so on (Hay, Nash and Pedersen, 1983; Jacobson, 1981), evidently deriving great pleasure in the process. By 12 months, infants are clearly more interested in an unfamiliar peer than in a strange adult, spending far more time looking at the other child than at either the strange adult or their own mother (Lewis et al., 1975). Their interactions with other infants extend to include imitating one another (Mueller and Brenner, 1977). But despite this clear social interest and developing responsiveness, infant interactions tend to be brief and are obviously quite limited. Neither partner has the social skills to keep things going for long.

From 12 months to 2 years of age, infants become progressively more mobile and more able to use words to communicate. Social skills develop, and interactions with peers become longer and more structured around activity. Mutual imitation increases (Ross, 1982), as does awareness of being imitated, factors that seem to lay the basis for cooperation and coordination with the playmate. But for all their remarkable progress in relating to one another, toddler interactions are very prone to ending in conflict (Hay and Ross, 1982).

Already, by late infancy, toddlers show preferences for one playmate over another (Vandell and Mueller, 1980), typically preferring outgoing companions over shy or aloof ones. It's hard to say whether these preferences represent 'friendships' or not. What does 'friendship' mean, to an 18-month-old? All we can say for sure is that toddlers of this age interact predictably with their playmates, positively with one, negatively with another, reflecting their past experiences with that individual (Ross et al., 1992).

Social relationships in preschool children

Social interactions change in striking ways through the preschool period. The classic description of this change was given by Parten (1932), who described a developmental sequence of six categories of social interaction (Table 11.2). For decades, Parten's six categories were taken to be stages of social development, each being replaced by a more sophisticated stage as conceptual and social skills grow. For example, the text-book view was that 3-year-olds engage mainly in solitary or parallel play, and 5-year-olds in associative or cooperative play. But recent research suggests that this is a gross over-simplification. All of Parten's categories are found at all ages from 2 to 5 years, 5-year-olds spend more time in solitary or parallel play than in associative or cooperative play, and parallel play is actually as common at 5 as it is at 3 (Rubin, Bukowski and Parker, 1998). And in fact, far from being simply an immature form of play, parallel play turns out to be the key element in a sophisticated strategy for easing your way into an ongoing game. Children who succeed in joining in with others in cooperative play typically begin by watching what's going on, drawing nearer to the game and playing alongside (parallel play) before beginning to interact with the other player or players (Rubin et al., 1998).

Parten's (1932) categories of social
interaction in infancy

Category	Description
Unoccupied	Not involved in any activity
Onlooker	Watching others, not joining in
Solitary play	Plays alone, away from others
Parallel play	Plays alongside others, engages similar activity but without interacting with others
Associative play	Interacts with others, contributing to the same activity and sharing toys
Cooperative play	Collaborative play that is well coordinated and involves a division of labour – one child's activities supporting another's

Over the past 20 years a different view of developmental change in preschooler's social interactions has emerged (Rubin et al., 1998). This subdivides Parten's six categories into different types of play (**Table 11.3**): functional, constructive and socio-dramatic play. While solitary play involving functional activities gets progressively rarer through the pre-school years, solitary play involving construction is as common at 5 as at 2. The only kind of social play that increases through the pre-school years is socio-dramatic play: shared games of 'let's pretend', structured by rules and agreements.

Socio-dramatic play is the most complex form of play, involving the need to negotiate ('Pretend he's hungry' – 'No, he's just tired'), to play reciprocal roles that complement and coordinate with other people's ('I'll be Batman, you can be Robin') and to agree rules ('You can't jump over the moon, only over the house'). In sum, socio-dramatic play involves sharing a fantasy world with a playmate, a world of symbols where things have new meanings quite outside their ordinary ones (an armchair becomes the Batmobile). Although even 3-year-olds can engage in this sort of play, the ability to do so develops through the pre-school years (Rubin et al., 1998), as children become more adept at

Types of play activity

Activity type°	Description
Functional play	Physical activities like bouncing a ball as an end in itself
Constructive play	Building things, drawing, colouring, making things
Socio-dramatic play	Games of 'let's pretend'

coordinating their interactions and negotiating a shared fantasy. This form of play (perhaps like every other form of play – see **Box 11.7**) is of enormous developmental significance, not only because it fosters children's understanding of other minds (see Chapter 9), but because it involves *knowingly* sharing a subjective world (an inner world) with a friend. This is a vital milestone on the path from peer relationships based on crude imitation in infancy, to friendships based on mutual understanding later in childhood.

box **11.7**

Play

What exactly do we mean by 'play'? At one level, this seems like a simple question to answer: we all know, more or less, what's play and what's not. A child building a castle in the sandpit is playing, a man building a house down the road is not. But pinning down an exact definition of play is surprisingly hard. Is it activity undertaken as an end in itself, serving no larger goal and engaged for the sheer pleasure of it, as some researchers have claimed? But this definition ignores the possibility that play serves real developmental purposes, and the fact that play can sometimes be a tense matter, a source of conflict and even rejection when games go wrong. Can we define play as a childish pastime? But even adults play. The truth is that 'play' is a somewhat fuzzy concept. We know it when we see it, but can't draw up a list of its defining features. (This doesn't make 'play' special or different from other words: even apparently simple concepts like 'lion' are actually quite fuzzy: for example, Leo would still be a lion even if he were bald, had lost his tail and one leg and was unable to roar.)

Babies begin to play in the first months of life, babbling and experimenting with sounds, waggling arms and legs, batting at cot toys. These activities serve no immediate end: babies babble away alone in their cots as often as they do in interactions with others, and wag their limbs whether or not this achieves anything. Nonetheless, these activities serve as important practice for later skills, from the development of speech to motor control and insight into cause and effect (I hit it, it rattles).

Social play, too, begins very early in infancy: within the first 6 months of life, babies begin to enjoy games of peek-a-boo, or taking turns at imitating simple facial expressions and being imitated in return, or being nuzzled, rocked or raised in the air. As they grow older, toddlers enjoy all sorts of social games, such as chanting nursery rhymes together or bouncing on a parent's knee to enact the story of such a rhyme ('This is the way the lady rides, clip clop, clip clop, clip clop', and so on). Again, though such games seem to have no direct purpose, they may well play an important part both in forging a bond between parent and child, and in setting the scene for later social skills and even for the development of language.

A great deal of play through the course of infancy involves construction: building things, making things, drawing things, painting things. At first such play would probably be better labelled 'destructive' play: parents or older siblings build a tower/draw a picture and the toddler bashes it down/scribbles over it. But progressively, coordination and understanding improve, and the toddler becomes constructive. Such play obviously contributes to the development of manual dexterity, but it also contributes to the child's discovery of the physical world: the facts of gravity, how one object can cover or occlude another, the physical properties of water, dry sand and their combination into mud, the differences between malleable plasticine/Playdoh and brittle plastic, the way paint colours mix to form new colours (or sludge), and so on. Constructive play continues through childhood, adolescence and even into adult life, albeit involving different projects.

Physical play also begins in infancy and persists to adult life. At first, such play is fairly formless, and consists (for example) of an infant tottering back and forth from A to B or hurling toys out of the pram to be retrieved and jettisoned again (a source of endless amusement to the very young). As children grow older, such play more clearly involves challenges of courage and coordination: climbing trees or other things, swinging, jumping over and across things and so on. As children grow older, physical play becomes rule governed, as, for example, in games of hide and seek, chasing games of 'tag' and the like. Even the rough and tumble typical particularly of young boys is rule-governed: there are manoeuvres that are 'fair' and others than are 'not fair'. Ultimately, physical play is formally organized into sports of one sort or another: football, netball and so on. Although it is always about the development of physical prowess and coordination, physical play involving others is also an important arena for developing skills of social integration.

The most striking phenomenon of childhood is 'pretend play' or socio-dramatic play. At around 18 months of age toddlers begin to pretend that one object is another: that a biscuit is a gun, or that the arm of a chair is a horse, and so on. By 3 years of age, pretend play has become far more elaborate, involving the construction of whole fantasy worlds in which complex stories are enacted. This socio-dramatic play is often social, involving two or more children. It's hugely popular right through childhood, but vanishes abruptly at around 10 years of age. Play of this kind serves the very obvious function of allowing children to explore adult roles and activities ('You be the doctor …'). It is also a rich environment in which children can discuss and discover things about other minds: motivations, feelings, thoughts ('Teddy wants to look in the box, he thinks his hat is in there' – 'No, he's too tired, he just wants to have supper'). And it's a context in which children can learn not only to collaborate in the physical construction of the game, but to negotiate a shared narrative of events. Some research suggests that this kind of play is vital, not only to discovering how human minds work (Chapter 9), but also to the development of the conceptual processes that are needed in constructing the personal narrative that we call consciousness (Singer and Singer, 2006).

Why does socio-dramatic play seem to disappear at the end of childhood? We don't know. In fact, it might be an exaggeration to say that it does. For example, many adolescents and young adults today play fantasy games on computers, some of which involve interactions with others. Such games improve certain cognitive skills (for example, planning, understanding cause and effect in different domains) and also contribute more generally to academic motivation and self-esteem. Others continue to engage in physical role-playing games of one sort or another: for example, dressing up and re-enacting medieval battles is popular among young adults down my way. To judge by the popularity of television programmes in which contestants live in fantasy worlds on 'desert islands', socio-dramatic play is still attractive even to adults. Perhaps we just don't have as much time to do it as young children do.

It seems that all forms of play actually contribute to development in one way or another, even if nobody plays *in order* to develop a skill. So what triggers children to play? It seems likely that the very young infant's play with sounds and limbs is a natural part of the exploration of the body and the world. Other forms of play, too, may develop as an extension and application of more general developmental processes. But to a surprising extent, play is taught, both by parents (Blundon and Schaefer, 2006) and by other children, both older siblings and peers.

Like infants, preschool children show marked preferences for some children over others, generally preferring someone like themselves (same age, similar activities and choices, same sex and similar traits). They behave very differently toward these friends than toward other familiar children, choosing to spend more time with friends, showing more positive social reactions and cooperative gestures. But friends also have more disagreements with one another than they do with other peers, probably because there is more opportunity to disagree with someone you spend more time with. However, disagreements with friends are resolved by negotiation to find a mutually acceptable solution, whereas disagreements with non-friends are not addressed this way. It's clear that preschoolers make a real distinction between 'friends' and 'others'.

Social relationships in middle childhood

Going to school greatly changes children's experience of peers: typically, they spend much more time with peers than before, and are exposed to a wider social circle than before, one less controlled and less selected by parents than in the preschool years. School children are less closely supervised than preschoolers, and so spend more time alone with peers than in the past, both in and out of school. Peer relationships take on a new importance at this stage of life.

While preschool children spend their time playing together, school children relate to one another in a broader range of contexts. By this age, children have very largely segregated themselves into social groups by gender, interacting and forming friendships only with members of their own sex. Throughout the school years, social interactions are dominated by shared school activities, the practicalities of getting to and from school and the like. Constructive and socio-dramatic play continue through the early school years, but begin to peter out as adolescence approaches (Baumeister and Senders, 1989), to be replaced by computer games, watching films and listening to music together, 'hanging out' in parks and shopping precincts and lengthy conversations on the phone.

Twenty years ago, the only difference between boys and girls in these activities was that girls were more likely to spend time talking to one another on the phone (Zarbatany, Hartmann and Rankin, 1990). It's doubtful whether this gender difference still exists, now that mobile phones are 'must-have' accessories covered in male-attracting gadgetry. Nor is there much difference between the genders in the ways that they approach friendships, at this or any other age, except that girls are less competitive with friends than boys are (Schneider et al., 2005), and marginally less aggressive in addressing conflicts (Shute and Charlton, 2006).

Middle childhood brings two new phenomena into social interactions: *bullying* and *victimization* (this is discussed later in the chapter: see Box 11.10), and *gossip*, which dominates exchanges between children (Parker and Gottman, 1989). Much of children's gossip is negative and defamatory, and this seems to play a role in raising the child's concern about his or her social standing and social acceptability: the desire to 'fit in' and avoid censure. Less pejorative explorations of social standing and relationships provide another strong strand of gossip, allowing the negotiation of a collective view of the shared activities, values and preferences that define who's 'in' or 'out' of a given group, and what the relationship between groups within a wider setting might be. (It may be that the fascination of exploring roles within this 'real' world makes earlier fantasy games of 'let's pretend' seem tame, contributing to their disappearance.)

Middle childhood is also the time when social life begins to revolve around groups or cliques rather than separate individual friends. Cliques are almost always made up of children from the same gender and ethnic group; they may have three to nine members (Kindermann, McCollom and Gibson, 1995). By 11 years of age, almost every child is a member of a clique (Crockett, Losoff and Peterson, 1984). An individual's status within such a clique becomes immensely important to him or her, a source of continuing concern and insecurity. This insecurity may reflect the fact that what's 'in' and what's 'out', who's 'hot' and who's not often varies from day to day within a clique, sometimes with a capricious cruelty, so that social standing is constantly shifting (Rubin et al., 1998). The majority of children fall painfully prey to this at some time or other (Kanner et al., 1987), which is probably why we can all remember the humiliation and rejection of being 'The one no one picked for their team'.

Children can most certainly form friendships from when they first enter school, markedly preferring some individuals over others and interacting very differently with these preferred individuals from the way they interact with others. But the conception of what friendship involves develops through middle childhood (see **Box 11.8**). The younger schoolchild has a fairly instrumental view of friendship: a 'best friend' is someone who is useful and reliable, who is rewarding to be with and imposes little cost on you. There is little concern for the needs of the other. By the end of childhood this has changed to a view of friendship more based on mutual affection, trust and understanding, and reciprocity: an awareness that the goodwill of friendship is voluntary, and that the friend's needs should matter as well as your own. Nevertheless, friendships are still relatively fragile: they last as long as each party pleases the other, and can end quite abruptly if one or other doesn't respond as required.

11.8

Selman's stages of the development of friendship in childhood and adolescence

What is a friend? What makes a 'best friend'? Answers to this question change through the course of childhood and adolescence, passing through a five-level developmental sequence (Selman, 1980, 1981) The age at which individuals reach a given level varies.

Level 0: ages 3 to 7 years
The very young make little distinction between the friend and the social activity they share: virtually any rewarding interaction with another child qualifies that child as a friend (Bigelow, 1977). A friend tends to be handy to meet up with, to have interesting toys and wants to do what you want to do. A typical answer at this level might be, 'Jack's my best friend. He lives next door and we play on his swing.'

Level 1: 4 to 9 years
As children begin to discover other minds – that is, that other people have intentions that are different from their own – their conceptions of friendship change. A friend is now defined as someone who chooses to 'do things with me' or 'play the games I want to play'. But this is a one-way street: the child is still concerned with his or her own self-interest, and feels no obligation to reciprocate the friend's kindness. A friend who stops choosing to do what you want becomes a non-friend.

Level 2: 6 to 12 years
The developing ability to take someone else's perspective, to see how things look to them, brings a new dimension to friendship. For the first time, the child becomes concerned about the friend's needs too, and begins to realize that friendships are reciprocal relationships in which both parties show consideration and affection to the other, both sharing toys and backing the other up. But despite valuing reciprocity, children are still focused on their own needs, and are 'fair weather friends': friendships last only as long as each party continues to please the other.

Level 3: 9 to 15 years
A deeper understanding of other people's thoughts, feelings and intentions in late childhood enriches the notion of friendship further. Friendships at this level are still based on mutual support, sharing and doing nice things for one another. But whereas at level 2 this reciprocity was confined to the superficial

(sharing toys, sweets, being courteous), at level 3 it also involves the exchange of intimacies: trusting a friend with your secret feelings and thoughts. And because they now understand one another better, friends no longer demand an immediate reciprocity from one another, and don't feel rejected if the other doesn't immediately want to do what they want to do. Both parties can take the other's perspective and realize that the other may have needs and feelings that preclude a collaborative activity just now. Friendships are more robust and durable as a result.

Level 4: 12 to adult

By now, adolescents are sophisticated in understanding other people's intentions, thoughts and feelings. They construe themselves and their friends as separate individuals with distinct personalities and perspectives, but at the same time as interdependent through their relationship. Friends know and understand one another, trust each other with their innermost thoughts and feelings, stand by and support one another through thick and thin – and are respectful of one another's individuality enough to be flexible in adapting to changing needs.

Selman's descriptions of children's changing conceptions of friendship have been widely replicated and are generally accepted. Selman (1980, 1981) argued that changing conceptions of friendship reflect the developing ability to understand other people's perspectives (see Chapter 10, Box 10.3). With virtually no such ability, the young child has nothing to relate to but superficial details and his or her own self-interest. Only as a child comes to recognize the existence, and later the content, of a friend's mind is he or she in a position to appreciate that friendship involves first mutual satisfaction, next intimacy, and finally respect for individuality.

Social relationships in adolescence

Adolescents spend even more of their time with peers than children do, and are even less closely supervised, free to explore a still wider range of social situations and types of friend. Peer influence is at its peak, as a consequence. The way peers judge you, your status and acceptance in the group is never more important than it is in adolescence. For the 13- to 15-year-old, social identity is fundamentally defined and protected by the clique to which he or she belongs (Cottrell, 1996). As in childhood, adolescent cliques are typically made up of three to nine individuals of the same gender, age and ethnic group who share judgments and preferences: in other words, people 'as much like me' as possible. *Belonging* really matters. It's the basis for psychological well-being, the ability to cope with the stresses of social life at large. The clique is held together by its shared values, attitudes and activities.

A new feature of the social world of the adolescent is that, in addition to the local clique of specific friends with whom he or she spends time and shares activities, there is a growing awareness that the clique itself is part of a wider social group, which has been called a 'crowd' (Brown, 1990). The exact identity of adolescent crowds varies over time and place (the 'Mods and Rockers' of Britain in the 1960s have long since been replaced by other factions, for example). But in almost every school there will be the 'sporty' crowd, or the academically committed crowd, or the crowd who pride themselves on their daringness or subversiveness – from outrageous clothes to partying, drinking, taking drugs, even vandalism and delinquency. In British towns and villages, there are also crowds defined by socio-economic factors, demarcating themselves by class and education. Doubtless in other parts of the world adolescents draw distinctions particular to the circumstances of their own society. In many cases, particularly where there is cultural conflict, religion or ethnicity may play the key role in such distinctions.

Birds of a feather flock together: and although individuals orient primarily to their particular clique, the clique as a whole defines itself in terms of the crowd whose values and lifestyle it shares, and strives to fit in with the appropriate image (Rubin et al., 1998). This is the age at which 'dressing the part' (in other words, dressing to look like a member of your clique and crowd) matters most, which is why whole populations of young people dress in what are almost uniforms of one sort or another (the dramatic black clothing of 'Goths', for example; the shaved heads, tight jeans and T-shirts of 'Skinheads'; the baseball caps and gaudy jewellery or 'bling' of the 'Chav'; the casual sweatshirt and deck shoes of the 'Rah'). This is also the age at which hostility between cliques and crowds is at its peak, spawning the development of derogatory labels and descriptions of 'out' groups (see www.urbandictionary.com for some hilarious but unprintable examples).

Perceptions of crowds change through adolescence. Younger teenagers focus more on the overt behaviour of different crowds, the signs and signals of membership, whereas older adolescents focus more on distinctions between values (Rubin et al., 1998). Younger adolescents also draw fewer distinctions than older ones, so naming a smaller and less subtly distinguished set of crowds. These changes seem to reflect general developmental change in the sophistication of social perceptions and social knowledge.

Commitment to crowds and cliques is at its peak in early adolescence, and decreases from 11 to 18 years of age (Shrum and Cheek, 1987). The hostility between cliques breaks down, and friendships across clique boundaries begin to emerge. A key feature of this process is that adolescents begin to move away from friendships exclusively with their own sex and start making friends with members of the other gender. It has been suggested that this move from a same-sex orientation to an openness to other-sex relationships plays a part in the collapse of cliques, but the evidence is equivocal (Rubin et al., 1998). This is discussed further below.

The conception of friendship continues to develop through adolescence (Box 11.8), first shifting from the rather superficial reciprocity (sharing toys, activities, sweets) of late childhood to a deeper mutuality based on sharing secrets and innermost thoughts, and later to a mutual respect for the independence and autonomy of the other. Friendships become more robust, through adolescence, first becoming able to survive temporary setbacks and let-downs as the partners realize that each has needs that may temporarily thwart the desires of the other. Later in adolescence friends come to accept and respect one another as autonomous individuals with distinct needs that may lead to more permanent divergences in their lives (for example, when one forms a romantic attachment, or goes to college in another town), and are able to adapt flexibly to this, so that friendships become very durable.

From platonic friendship to romance

We continue to treasure platonic friendships with others of our own gender all our lives. Some of the friendships forged in childhood or adolescence stay the course. Many new friendships of this kind are made along the way. But at some point in mid or late adolescence, a new form of relationship tends to emerge alongside these platonic friendships – the romantic relationship. Romantic relationships bring two new factors into play: sexuality, and (for the majority) the switch from relationships with our own gender to relationships with the opposite sex.

How does a platonic orientation to the need for intimacy and intersubjective connection become sexually charged? This question is, of course, related to the issue of the development of a sexual identity, whether heterosexual or not, which we have discussed in Chapter 10. But the focus here is at a different level, namely, what are the dynamics of the process through which adolescents make the transition from exclusively platonic relationships to an orientation to erotically charged romance? Psychology knows nothing about this process in a gay or lesbian context – we haven't done the research, so we are in no position to even to evaluate how typical or otherwise autobiographical accounts or psychiatric speculations may be. What follows is therefore confined to the dynamics of developing heterosexual relationships, on which there is considerable research.

Early ideas about the origins of heterosexual romance were dominated by the work of psychiatrists such as Sigmund Freud and John Bowlby. Both believed that the infant's early attachment to the mother formed 'the prototype of all later love relationships' as Freud (1940) put it, so that to understand the emergence of romantic affiliations, you had to look back into the individual's relationship with the mother. This idea dominated research for half a century (Hazan and Shaver, 1987). Although the idea owed more to clinical insight than to empirical evidence, there are data that suggest there's an element of truth in this view:

for example, both romantic relationships to lovers and parental relation-ships to our own offspring are influenced by the nature of our early relationship with our mother (Lamb, 2005; Roisman et al., 2005).

Infant attachment relationships and parenting styles play a powerful role in our social development, shaping how we see ourselves and others, how we interpret and respond to events, as we've seen in this and earlier chapters (Chapters 4 and 10). Our parents also provide us with a detailed close-up experience of a romantic relationship in action which may well serve as a model for our own future efforts. However, more recent research suggests that (at least in Western societies, which are the only ones studied so far) the emergence of erotic heterosexual romance, and the patterns of such romantic affiliations are importantly mediated and by the peer group (Brown, 1999; Connolly, Goldberg and Pepler, 1999; Furman and Wehner, 1997). The peer group has a far greater influ-ence on what we do, how we think at this stage in life, than does the family (Furman and Wehner, 1994).

Sexual behaviour emerges from the dynamic interaction between the biological phenomena of puberty and the complex dynamics of adoles-cent social groups dealing with those phenomena. The initial inclination toward 'romantic' contact with the opposite sex is stimulated by the hormonal surges of puberty (in other words, lust). Simply acting on this inclination would challenge the 'rules' of the same-sex cliques and friendships on which the adolescent depends: there is still a strong need to fit in and be accepted by those contacts. The reorientation to hetero-sexual romance must therefore be negotiated within the same-sex peer group, so that at first, lust provokes issues of identity rather than actual attempts at romantic contacts (Brown, 1999).

Luckily, everyone is in the same boat, Gradually, single-sex cliques begin to interact with other cliques of the opposite gender (Connolly et al., 1999; Dunphy, 1963). The original single-sex peer group exerts con-siderable influence over who it is permissible to find attractive and how romantic relationships should be handled, what you can and can't do (Brown, 1999; Connolly, Goldberg and Pepler, 1999). But the strict boundaries and control of the single-sex cliques begin to break down, so that these mixed-sex groups provide the young adolescent with a forum in which to begin to explore ways of relating to and communicating with the opposite sex. (These phenomena are entertainingly depicted in the film *Grease*.)

As adolescence progresses, the need for empathic intimacy and affec-tion grows, in terms of both same-sex friendships and romantic relationships. Whereas lust might have been the prime focus of earlier curiosity about the opposite sex, most 15-year-olds cite companionship and intimacy as the most important goals of dating (Feiring, 1996). Progressively, emotional intimacy is explored in the context of dating rather than with same-sex friends, so that by late adolescence, cliques have broken down as the major vehicle of social life, to be replaced by couples. At first, couples may orient to one another in highly romanticized ways. Progressively there is a greater pragmatism (Can I put up with his faults? Is she the kind of wife who will support my aspirations?) as individuals contemplate committing to a permanent bond with this partner (Brown, 1999). The result is either marriage (or its equivalent) or separation, to search again.

Culture and the development of peer relationships

The overwhelming majority of the research done on the development of peer relationships has focused on Western industrialized societies in America and Europe, and during a particular time in history. For this reason, we should be very cautious in assuming that all that has been described above applies in other societies.

Certain things are likely to be universal. For example, the tendency of children to segregate themselves into single-sex groups seems to occur in all societies studied. The need to reorient from this single-sex focus to opposite-sex relationships in adolescence must also occur to a degree, but even in this apparently basic developmental effect we must be cautious about over generalizing. For example, in some cultures, adult women are segregated in compounds, spending only brief periods of time with a husband whom they may share with several other wives. We would not expect either males or females in such a culture to have developed romantic relationships either in the way that the Western adolescents described above do, or of the kind that Western couples have.

Age-related change in how friendships are understood, which rests on general conceptual development in understanding other minds and in taking other people's perspective, might be expected to be universal, if the pattern of development of insight into other minds and perspectives is itself universal. We don't yet know to what extent that is the case. Certain aspects of the discovery of other minds are very likely to be universal: they rest on innate mechanisms, such as the mirror neuron system (see Chapter 9). But the speed of development in this area, and the level of development achieved, may be variable across cultures.

For example, socio-dramatic play speeds up and enriches children's insight into other minds (Chapter 9), but is not equally available, or equally encouraged, in all societies, so that we might predict social development will be slower in some cultures than others. Equally, different cultural mores may affect what social skills a child needs to learn or has the opportunity to learn, creating differences in the pattern of development across different societies. Some traditional cultures (in Kenya, for instance) actively discourage or even prohibit the young from interacting with people outside the extended family, so that children don't develop peer group relationships as other cultures do, but only relationships with their siblings. This might have important developmental effects: interacting with peers outside the family demands the development of different skills from those needed to maintain a relationship with siblings. Families expect siblings to interact, put pressure on them to behave constructively toward one another, referee conflicts between them and actively broker reconciliations. With peers, you're far more on your own, and must learn social skills to engage another child in an interaction, to maintain a voluntary relationship over time, and to manage and resolve conflicts and disputes. On the other hand, peers are on a level playing field: neither is 'the elder'. Peer relationships don't provide the same opportunities for learning to take responsibility or make allowances for a less sophisticated companion that sibling relationships do.

Furthermore, the higher levels of insight into other minds described as typical of late adolescence depend on forms of conceptual, cognitive and moral development that not all individuals achieve, even in our own society. These things reflect not only individual intelligence, but opportunities to engage in the kinds of activity that foster this development (principally formal schooling). Differences in such opportunities are stark, across different cultures.

Even the specific issues that define trust and friendship can vary from one culture to another. For example, among Russian adolescents, betraying a friend's secrets is the act most likely to end a friendship, whilst in the United States, friendships are more often ended by the failure of one partner to disclose a secret to the other (Sheets and Lugar, 2005). This difference is easy to understand, within the historic tradition of each culture. The United States has a long-standing liberal culture, endorsing freedom of speech and the legitimacy of political opposition. For half a century or more, Russian society prohibited freedom of thought or speech (often on pain of death). Sharing secrets, and risking another spilling those secrets had far different connotations in Russia and the United States. This fact was driven home for me after the breakdown of the Soviet system, when for the first time, academics from Russia began to attend scientific conferences in the West, and friendships across the 'iron curtain' became possible. It's hard to convey the sense of shock I experienced on realizing that a new Russian friend – so very like me in so many ways – had inhabited a world in which the wrong choice of friends could be (literally) fatal as opposed to a minor irritant, quickly shed, as in my world. Subject to censorship, Russian academics copied 'forbidden' books (sometimes in longhand), and shared them with friends by reading them aloud in 'kitchens' (the radio playing, the taps running to block eavesdropping devices). Who do you invite to your kitchen, to hear such a reading? Someone *you trust absolutely not to tell.* Where there is a possibility that a 'friend' might betray you to the secret police, trustworthiness in *keeping* secrets is rather more important a criterion of friendship than baring all.

The truth is that the way even apparently basic human fundamentals such as our relationships with friends and lovers develop is profoundly affected by cultural practices and images. We learn what a friend or lover is supposed to be as much from the stories we read, the films we watch, the attitudes and values of our culture and the activities it provides as from any individual development of insight into other minds. Cultural images vary, not only between one society and another, but within a single society over time and place. (Would Jane Austen view the courtship patterns of today's youth as normal? Would the stiff-upper-lip society of the Victorian era encourage young men to share their innermost feelings with their friends or wives?)

Social development is very much a reflection of the social context in which it occurs. Until recently, developmental psychology has paid only lip service to this idea, noting it in passing but not really taking the implications on board. We need to do so. Not only is it the case that what we describe in our own culture may not generalize to other societies, but, by failing to understand what does and what does not generalize across cultures, we cloud our understanding of what causes development in our own culture.

Information technology and friendships

In the past few years an entirely new phenomenon has developed in the area of friendship: increasing numbers of children in late childhood and adolescence are making contact and developing friendships over the internet, though chat rooms, personal blogs and social networking sites such as www.myspace.com. Mostly the adult world worries whether this will lead to unsuitable friendships – for example, with adult paedophiles posing as children in order to recruit victims – and sadly, that does happen. Research is only just starting to explore the nature of the friendships children make on the internet, and the implications these may have for social development overall (Cheng, Chan and Tong, 2006).

Who makes friends over the internet? What sort of friendships do they make? It seems that adolescents' motivations for forming online friendships, and the types of friendship they form vary. For extraverts, online friendships are an extension of their general sociability. Contacts are frequent and involve an easy self-disclosure. Overall, introverts have less contact with cyber friends. Their motivation in striking up such relationships may be to compensate for their relative lack of social confidence and competence in face-to-face interactions. The stronger the desire to overcome such problems, the more introverts interact over the net and the more they self-disclose (Peter, Valkenburg and Schouten, 2005).

Will the possibility of cyber-world friendship have an important effect on the development of friendship and social skills in the young? Insofar as the internet is creating a new culture with rules that transcend the norms of local communities, we can expect that it will. Some believe that the effects can only be beneficial: that exposure to a wider circle of contacts rather than a local clique of 'people just like me' can only expand horizons and enrich development (much the same idea that led to the encouragement of 'pen friends' in foreign countries in the days when there was only 'snail mail'). Others are concerned that, by retreating into a 'cyber-world' and forming friendships over the internet, children's contact with their own community, and even their willingness for and skill in face-to-face interactions may be eroded (Greenfield, 2003). It's too soon to say: the phenomenon is too new, and the research too sparse.

Some clues about the possible impact of the new information technologies on development come from an equally new phenomenon: text messaging. Today's young are in constant communication with others, parents as much as peers, in a way that no previous generation could have been (or could have imagined). Cellular mobile phones seem to offer some of the same opportunities as the internet: the possibility of developing a range of contacts and friendships beyond the immediate neighbourhood and beyond the control of parents, and thereby creating a greater scope for developing a distinct individual identity and lifestyle beyond local norms (Campbell, 2006). But the data suggest that adolescents don't in fact create more contacts or broaden their circle through phoning or texting. Rather, they use this technology to communicate with and strengthen ties to their local friendship circle (Bryant, Sanders-Jackson and Smallwood, 2006). And paradoxically, this technology has actually increased the extent to which adolescents are monitored by their parents. Parents encourage even the very young to carry cellular mobile phones as a safety measure, checking in regularly, and in our anxious and safety-conscious society, adolescents acknowledge the sense of this and comply (Campbell, 2006). The result is that even young adults living away from home at university are now in touch with their parents (and subject to comment) in a way that previous generations never were: the world was very different when a student had to queue for the only phone in a hall of residence to phone home.

Brains and adolescent behaviour

Until relatively recently, the phenomena of adolescence were interpreted as entirely due to the changing social circumstances of the adolescent, and in particular to the pressures of the peer group. But over the past few years there has been considerable interest in the discovery that there are marked developmental changes in the adolescent brain. Could these brain effects explain the phenomena of adolescence? The mass media (for example, Strauch, 2003) have leapt to the conclusion that they can. As Kuhn (2006) puts it, the newly discovered changes in adolescent brains have been taken 'as an explanation for just about everything about teens that adults have found perplexing, from sleep patterns to risk taking and mood swings'. We need to take a more critical view.

Is there good evidence for changes in the adolescent brain? The answer is, yes (Casey, Giedd and Thomas, 2000; Sisk and Zehr, 2005). Magnetic resonancing techniques have allowed us to identify two main changes. There is a steady increase in 'white matter' through progressive myelination – in other words, through the progressive growth of the insulating sheath around established neuronal connections. There is also a pattern of change in the 'grey matter' which is similar to that seen in infancy: first, a burst of new neural connections, and later a reduction of the grey matter as unused neural patterns are pruned out. This wave of new neural connections occurs in different areas of the adolescent brain at different times: it occurs first in areas associated with primary sensory functions, and later in areas associated with executive control and judgment. It is this pattern of change in grey matter which is of the greatest interest. The exact implications of enhanced myelination are unclear. This process is not special to adolescence: it has been progressing right through childhood in one area of the brain or another. Myelination does not necessarily imply any advantage in terms of intelligent processing (Johnson, 1998).

Are these changes in the brain at adolescence the cause of adolescent patterns of behaviour? For example, is the adolescent penchant for exploring the sensory experiences of sex, drugs, alcohol and the like caused by the growing neural circuits for sensory function? Is the adolescent's impulsive behaviour and poor judgment caused by the lag in the development of the cortical circuitry for critical judgment? Some commentators have suggested that this is so – going on to draw the inference that, since the necessary brain structures are 'immature', we should not expect adolescents to be able to inhibit risky sensual behaviours, nor expect them to be able to profit from adult counsels of caution or from educational programmes aiming to foster better risk analysis (Steinberg, 2007). Better not to waste time and money trying to teach adolescents to make better judgments, then? The mass media have taken this approach up with enthusiasm, as a short browse on the internet will show. But a more critical look suggests that this interpretation of the data is wholly misguided, if not downright dangerous. It flies in the face of recent trends in research as a whole.

The theory that changes in the brain are the *cause* of adolescent behaviours must assume that the changes in the brain *precede* changes in behaviour. The suggestion is that the brain changes themselves are biologically caused – and the most plausible biological influence over brain development at puberty is the rise in sexual hormones (Sisk and Zehr, 2005). It's true that, as hormone levels rise through puberty, male and female brains differentiate – developing in subtly different ways, ways associated with a range of behaviours from the sexual to spatial cognition (Sisk and Zehr, 2005). But do hormones work *directly* on the brain to produce such effects, or to trigger the changes in grey matter characteristic of puberty? Sisk and Zehr's careful review of neurological research found no evidence to support such a conclusion. It could as easily be that hormones affect the brain only *indirectly*. For example, the main impact of rising sexual hormones might be simply to alter various physiological aspects of the body: increasing sensory responsiveness in organs associated with sexuality, and altering physical appearance in ways which change how we view ourselves and how other people treat us. The changing behaviour produced by these effects would then be enough to modify brain structures (Sisk and Zehr, 2005), without the need for hormonal effects working directly on the brain. This second possibility is actually by far the more plausible.

The most important discovery about neural development of recent years is that the brain is fundamentally constructed by our behaviour and experience (De Vries, 2004; Kuhn, 2006). New neural connections of the kind observed in the growth of grey matter in infancy and adolescence don't pop into existence according to some maturing biological programme or chemical effect. Rather, they are specifically built up by our activities. This is as true in adult life as at any other time: take up a new skill and there will be a burst of neural growth reflecting the new neural pathways that this skill requires. The consensus of opinion now is that the traditional assumption that developments in the brain *precede* and *cause* changes in behaviour is simply wrong (Kuhn, 2006). Rather, the changes we see in adolescent brains are the *result* of changes in adolescent behaviour and experience – just as the changes in infant grey matter are the result of learning. That there should be an explosion of new neural connections specifically in infancy and adolescence should come as no surprise: the transition from womb to world opens up a vast new range of experiences and possibilities, triggering an explosion of new behaviours and experiences. The same is true for the transition from pre-pubescent child to adult sexual being.

How to interpret the lag in development between one area of the adolescent brain and another? There is no real mystery here. All skilled performances take time to master. As we saw in Chapters 6 and 7, the greater your expertise in any area, the better your executive control. The more you know about any skill or activity, the more experience you have with it, the better able you are to foresee the consequences of a given course of action, and so to plan and to make effective judgments. Being an adult is a skilled performance. The adolescent is a novice adult. And just as the novice chess player must begin by exploring the boundaries of the game, the possible moves, before he or she can begin to learn how to plan effectively, so the novice adult must begin by exploring the possibilities of this new stage of life (many of which involve sensory functions) before effective planning and executive control can begin to develop. If adolescents take risky decisions, it is not because their partly formed brains make more appropriate judgments impossible: it's because they haven't yet developed sufficient knowledge and expertise to allow them to plan more effectively. As this knowledge develops it creates the very neural connections needed for the job. From this point of view, the suggestion that educational programmes to develop such expertise are a waste of time in adolescence is a dangerous folly.

It's worth adding that the idea the adolescent is the helpless product of maturational changes in the brain is also refuted by cross-cultural data. Since adolescents the world over share the same biological systems as part of the defining inheritance which makes us human, any maturational changes in the brain that cause behavioural effects should be universal. But the behavioural phenomena that the mass media (and, until relatively recently, psychological researchers too) take to be universal features of adolescence are actually very situation-specific. As we saw in Chapter 10, there is enormous variability in the way adolescents behave, in their tendency to challenge adult authority, take risks, run wild, behave differently from adults, have identity crises (and so on) between one culture and another. There is also enormous variability in adolescent behaviour and experience between one social class and another within a culture, and even between one member of a family and another. No maturing biological change in the adolescent human brain could possibly account for the diversity of adolescent behaviour we observe. However, diversity of this kind is exactly what we would expect if adolescent behaviour is the result of the interaction between the many personal, familial, interpersonal and cultural factors that shape an individual's life and experience.

The consensus of research is still that social factors, and particularly peer groups, play the leading part in shaping the changing patterns of adolescent behaviour. New patterns of neural connections reflect the changing behaviours emerging from the interaction between many social and circumstantial influences. The early rise in such connections reflects the different behaviours the adolescent tries out in beginning to learn new things, and the subsequent pruning back reflects the rejection of the less successful efforts. The theoretical framework best suited to exploring the complexities of the processes involved here is dynamic systems theory (see Chapters 2 and 3) – an approach in flat contradiction to the idea that adolescent behaviour could be explained by a specific phenomenon in the brain.

Social status

Friendships play an important part in a child's life, so much so, that many children even invent imaginary friends (see **Box 11.9**). The companionship of friends provides one of the greatest pleasures of life. More than this, friendships provide a context in which the world can be more safely explored, in which social and other skills can be practised and honed, and in adolescence, identities tried out and refined. In extreme environments the friendship of peers even can be a matter of sheer survival. A gang of friends can protect one another from bullying. Homeless street children in Brazil gather together to support and protect one another. Such peer support can go far beyond the merely physical: for example, child survivors of the Nazi concentration camps of the Second World War tended to have great difficulty relating to adults after their rescue, but were found to have strong, supportive, affectionate and generally healthy relationships with the children with whom they had shared life in the camps (Freud and Dann, 1972). The peer group had provided some degree of protection for their psycho-social development, despite their horrific experiences at the hands of the adult world.

Not all children share equally in the benefits and pleasures of friendships. Put a number of children together, and you will find that a complex social structure develops, with some children dominating social networks and others marginalized. A child's position or status within the social community has important effects on their well-being and development.

box **11.9**

Imaginary friends

One of the more curious phenomena of childhood is the occurrence of 'imaginary friends'. Over 60 per cent of children aged 3 to 8 years have such friends (Taylor, 1999). I can remember one myself: a giant teddy bear called Sebastian, who went everywhere with me.

My Sebastian was unusual: most imaginary friends are ordinary children, just like the peer group the child experiences on a daily basis. But Sebastian the bear wasn't unique. Some children's imaginary friends are far more imaginative: dwarves and pixies, aliens, ancient creatures with weird personalities can be the invisible companions of childhood.

Children with imaginary friends often treat these friends as quasi-real: setting places for them at table, offering spoonfuls of food to imaginary mouths, consulting the invisible friend, blaming them for breakages and misdemeanours (all phenomena that can confuse and exasperate adults). Do children 'know' that these friends are fictional? The evidence suggests that they do. Nonetheless, imaginary friends can play an important part in development. For example, imaginary friendships are as emotionally supportive as real reciprocal relationships with other children (Gleason and Hohmann, 2006).

The phenomenon of imaginary friends is more common among only children, the first-born and the socially isolated, and in children who have a better insight into other minds than their peers (Singer and Singer, 1981; Taylor and Carlson, 1997). Imaginary friends are also more common in children with relatively restricted access to the multiple worlds of television.

Imaginary friends 'love you when you feel rejected by others, listen when you need to talk to someone' (Taylor, 1999). Who couldn't do with a friend like that?

Measuring social status

The usual method used to establish the structure of a social group and the status of particular individuals within it is to ask children (or adolescents) to nominate their best friends, or to identify the children they like most, and those they like least among the group (Coie, Dodge and Coppotelli, 1983). The information provided by children's answers can then be used to plot a *sociogram* (**Figure 11.1**), which graphically depicts the pattern of relationships and clusters of friends within the group. It can also be used to assess an individual's sociometric status, which is defined in terms of the relative distribution of nominations as most or least popular (**Table 11.4**). The four key status categories identified in this way are the *popular child*, who is well liked by many and disliked by few; the *rejected child* who most others dislike; the *neglected child* who is neither liked nor disliked, who may be marginalized or ignored; and the *controversial child* who you either like or loathe. In addition to these four categories there is the *average child*, who receives an average number of positive and negative nominations (Rubin et al., 1998; Rubin et al., 1999).

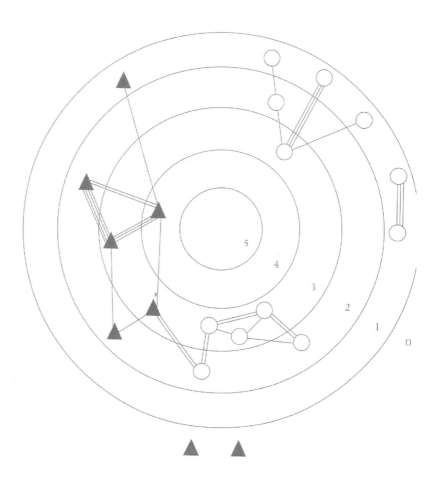

figure 11.1

An example of a sociogram

In this diagram, circles represent girls and triangles represent boys. The number of lines joining two children indicates the proportion of the time they spent together. The concentric circles indicate the number of playmates each child has. In this example, all but two boys are part of a single loose association pivoting around one particularly popular boy. The remaining two boys are socially isolated. The girls are divided into three separate groups. There is only one boy/girl connection.

Source: A. Clark, S. Wyon and M. Richards, 'Free play in nursery school', *Journal of Child Psychology and Psychiatry* vol. 10, pp. 205–16. © 1969. Reproduced with permission from Blackwell Press.

	Often nominated as 'most liked' by others	Rarely nominated as 'most liked' by others
Often nominated as 'least liked' by others	Controversial child	Rejected child
Rarely nominated as 'least liked' by others	Popular child	Neglected child

table **11.4**

Social status in terms of nominations by other children

What determines social status?

In childhood, for both boys and girls, popularity is strongly related to physical attractiveness (Boyatzis, Baloff and Durieux, 1998). Popular children are also highly socially competent, good at compromising and negotiating when conflict arises (Rose and Asher, 1999), and good at working out how to fit into a group they want to join (Rubin et al., 1999).

The commonest reason for a child being rejected by peers is that he or she is highly aggressive. Such children typically have poor social skills. They tend to over-interpret events, seeing hostility or attack where none was really intended. Worse still, they tend to impulsively respond in kind so that they are often in conflict with and unpleasant to others (Erdley and Asher, 1996; Newcomb, Bukowski and Pattee, 1993). But not all rejected children are aggressive: some are just painfully shy, lacking both the confidence and the social skill to join in and interact with others (Bierman, Smoot and Aumiller, 1993). Children rejected for shyness tend not to respond aggressively at all, not even when confronted aggressively by others (Erdley and Asher, 1996).

Controversial children tend to be highly aggressive, and may even be more aggressive than children rejected for aggressiveness. But whereas the aggressive-rejected child has poor social skills and cannot diffuse the negativity generated by their aggression, controversial children are adept at smoothing things over (Newcomb et al., 1993). Neglected children tend to be less sociable than their peers, but are neither particularly aggressive nor particularly shy.

Once a given social status has developed within a social group, the child's reputation with his or her peers can act to maintain it, even if the child's behaviour changes (Rubin et al., 1998). This makes it hard for children with a negative reputation to gain social acceptance, even if they substantially change their ways. For example, a child who has a reputation for being aggressive will be far less easily accepted into a new group than one who does not have this reputation, even if the actual level of social skill the two children use in trying to join in is the same. Preceded by his or her reputation, the aggressive child's behaviour is often interpreted as hostile when objectively it isn't, provoking renewed rejection (Hymel, Wagner and Butler, 1990). Only neglected children have much success in improving their popularity over time (Rubin et al., 1998).

Developmental outcomes, rejection and bullying

Popular children enjoy the maximum benefit of social endorsement and affection from their peers. Typically, they are more successful both academically and socially than the unpopular, and better adjusted in adult life (Bagwell, Newcomb and Bukowski, 1998). Is this the result of their popularity? Or is it that the traits that made them popular in the first place also ensure their later success and adjustment? It's hard to find data that would unravel this issue.

All that is clear is that having at least one best friend in childhood has beneficial effects. For example, children who have a friend in their class when they first start school make a better adjustment than those who don't (Ladd, 1990). Probably for this reason, children who are only of average popularity, neglected or controversial are not particularly distressed or disadvantaged by their status: most do have at least one 'best friend' most of the time. It's the rejected child who nobody likes who suffers the greatest loneliness and disadvantage (Parker and Asher, 1993). Not even a warm relationship with a sibling makes up for having no friends (Sherman et al., 2006), perhaps unsurprisingly. Through the school years, time spent with siblings is confined to holidays and after school, whereas children are with peers all day, every day. There can be few things more dispiriting than being forced to spend most of your time with people who don't like you.

Children who are generally rejected for their shyness and timidity tend to be acutely aware of their social isolation. They suffer considerable loneliness, anxiety and misery as a result, perceiving themselves as inadequate (Graham and Juvonen, 1998; Parker and Asher, 1993). Such children are not necessarily completely isolated: recent research suggests that they are as likely as anyone else to have one 'best friend' (Rubin et al., 2006). But this best friend is generally also painfully shy and lacking in social confidence or skills, so that the quality of the friendship is low. Withdrawn and shy, these children are vulnerable to further social problems. Insecure, unwilling or unable to stand up for themselves, without friends to do it for them (their best friend is as likely to be a victim as they are themselves), they are the natural prey of bullies (Boulton, 1999).

The effects of being bullied (**Box 11.10**) can be disastrous. Some children are driven to suicide. Virtually all are highly stressed and depressed, and perform poorly in schoolwork. The experience of being tormented and humiliated, on a daily basis, while everyone else just lets it happen (or worse, eggs the bully on) sends such children a very negative message about human nature and human relationships, undermining the capacity for trust, as well as creating destructive feelings of worthlessness. Research by the NSPCC (Cawson et al., 2000) found that a quarter of children bullied in school were still suffering harmful effects well into adult life.

Bullying is defined as persistent, systematic efforts to inflict pain and harm through physical or verbal attack, or through social humiliation and exclusion. Both boys and girls bully in all these ways, though boys are slightly more likely to use physical force and girls are slightly more likely to use verbal means (Lagerspetz and Bjorkquist, 1994). In the majority of cases, bullying involves a gang of children attacking the victim, rather than a single bully (Olweus, 1994).

The incidence of bullying

Since the intent is to inflict suffering, bullying requires some appreciation of the victim's feelings. Children first begin to develop sufficient insight into other minds to understand the impact of aggression at around 4 or 5 years of age, and this is when bullying begins. Although we think of bullying as primarily a problem of adolescence, in fact it's much more common in childhood (Olweus, 1993). It's hard to estimate just how prevalent bullying is. Teachers and parents are seldom aware of it, and rarely intervene (Olweus, 1993). Children themselves don't always report being bullied, still less confess to being bullies. Nevertheless, a survey of virtually all the children in school in Norway found that 7 per cent of children admitted to being bullies, and 3 per cent to being regularly bullied (Olweus, 1993). A British study found that 17 per cent of schoolchildren were regularly bullied and 13 per cent were bullies (Boulton and Underwood, 1992). Over 80 per cent of students in an American study admitted to at least some bullying activity (Bosworth, Espelage and Simon, 1999). Although the severity of these attacks undoubtedly varies, bullying is obviously a widespread problem.

Why do bullies bully?

Children who are high on aggression tend to attack when they believe themselves to be under attack, wronged or threatened. By contrast, bullies attack without provocation. It used to be thought that bullies lacked social skills, and there is some truth in this: children who are socially adept, who are neither weak nor gratuitously aggressive, will be popular, enjoy high status and influence and be envied by others. They have no need to bully to get into leadership positions in the group. Bullies do tend to be less socially adept than these popular children, but only marginally so (Crick and Dodge, 1999). Most are adept at understanding the social dynamics of the group well enough, for example, to both pick victims no one will stand up for, and to lure others to join in the attack. Bullying is about power and status. It's a way for a child who can't gain these things in more pro-social ways to become a gang leader. And in fact, bullies may become very popular through such tactics (Rodkin et al., 2000).

Children from all social classes and backgrounds bully. The phenomenon is found in all countries around the world. This is hardly surprising: picking out and attacking an 'enemy' has always been a powerful way of rallying others around you – as much in international politics as in the classroom. However, there is some research that suggests that children are more likely to bully when they themselves are under a degree of stress, for example, from poverty or parental conflict or divorce, or perhaps from themselves being subject to abuse at home. Such pressures may create a level of tension and aggression that undermine pro-social strategies, and make bullying the child's easiest route to social success.

Victims of bullying

Having lots of friends, or having a best friend who is popular in the group, protects a child from bullying (Fox and Boulton, 2006). Most of the victims of bullies are unpopular with their peers, 'rejected' children. But those rejected for their aggression are seldom picked on. They are too ready to fight back. Bullies tend to pick on the weak and vulnerable, children who won't stand up for themselves and have no friends who will stand up for them. Typically, victims are children who have been rejected by their peers for their extreme shyness and lack of social skills.

The victims of bullying don't always dislike their tormentor. This may reflect what is called 'Stockholm syndrome' in adults: a tendency to identify with the aggressor (in Stockholm, terrorist hostages came to identify with their captors).

The experience of being bullied is immensely distressing and damaging. Some children commit suicide to escape. Virtually all become even more insecure, withdrawn and anxious than they were before (the very characteristics that attracted the bully in the first place). Schoolwork falls off. Social confidence and self-esteem are grossly undermined. The experience of being regularly humiliated or wounded while others watch and laugh alters the victims' perception of self and others in very negative ways, reducing the capacity for trust. The damage done by bullying can persist for many years, even decades.

Disrupting bullying

The most coherent effort to disrupt bullying was begun in Norway in the 1980s (Olweus, 1993, 1994), after the suicide of two child victims. This was a national programme, backed by the government, through which teachers, parents and children combined to stop bullying. It was remarkably successful: levels of bullying in Norway fell substantially by comparison with other European countries, and have stayed low over 20 years. The lessons of this programme were that both the bully and the victim must be encouraged to act in different ways:

- *Bullies* as young as 4 years of age can be affected by discussions that focus on the effects of their behaviour. For all but the most disturbed child, it's psychologically easier to inflict 'just a little' pain than it is to really hurt, and that's what most bullies think they're doing. Making them understand how much their actions really hurt the victim often induces contrition and an end to the attacks. Adults need to understand the ringleader bully's motives. Is it to be popular? To be a leader? To 'act out' problems at home? Having established this, adults should help the bully to develop more pro-social ways of achieving his or her goal.
- *Victims* are often very lacking in assertiveness, and their supine behaviour invites attack. These children need to be taught how to stand up for themselves, how to be effectively assertive. A firm, loud riposte can often be enough to disrupt a bullying attack, and at the very least, may draw adult

attention and help. Victims often have no friends or allies to stand up for them. Teaching social skills can rectify this, and make them less vulnerable. Victims seldom 'tell' on their oppressors, both because there is generally a strong social prohibition against 'telling' and because they don't expect adults to help them. The only way round this is a proactive approach to bullying on the part of adults, and encouraging a culture of openness about bullying in the classroom as a whole.

By contrast, children who are rejected for their aggression tend to over-estimate their social adequacy and not to be aware of just how much their peers dislike and reject them (Parkhurst and Asher, 1992). At one level, this protects them from the pain of social isolation. At another, it makes things worse: their apparent self-satisfaction and imperviousness to their peers' dislike make them even more unpopular with others (Hughes, Cavell and Grossman, 1997). Excluded from social interactions, these aggressive children miss out on the normal 'give and take' exchanges through which the young learn to handle misunderstandings and conflicts, and to strike a balance between competition and cooperation: exactly the kinds of experience they need in order to overcome their aggression and become socially acceptable. Locked in their confrontational approach to life, these individuals are at risk of a lifetime of rejection and failed relationships with colleagues, spouses, their children.

In conclusion

The research reviewed in Chapter 10 reveals that the very essence of who we are, our personalities and our sense of identity, are fundamentally influenced by our social interactions with others. The way other people respond to us tells us about ourselves and about human nature, setting the implicit theories of self and other that define our personalities and direct our behaviour. Personal identity is a matter of internalizing messages from social experience and 'making them our own', and in the process taking responsibility for the values we embrace, the people we want to be. In the present chapter we've looked again in more detail at the various kinds of social interactions that shape our social and personal development: our interactions with parents and siblings, peers and friends. This research underlines just how profoundly human psycho-social development is socially constructed, reflecting the culture, the community and the family in which we grow up.

Thirty years ago almost all research on the effects of families and friendships on development was conducted in Western societies, very often focusing primarily on middle-class children. The patterns we saw were taken to reflect universal truths about human development (for example, that authoritarian parenting has negative effects). Today we are deeply aware that results from one culture, one social class, or even one social circumstance may not apply in another (in some cultures and situations, authoritarian parenting is beneficial, for instance). There is more diversity than we thought both between and within cultures in the way in which key factors (such as parenting style) contribute to developmental outcomes. There is an urgent need for more research on families and friendships across many different cultures, social classes and situations, to clarify these subtle effects. Research of this kind is growing rapidly.

Another recent development in research in this area is the use of dynamic systems theory to explore the detailed processes through which social relationships are formed, and through which these relationships structure and shape children's behaviour. Dynamic systems theory (see Chapters 2 and 3 for an introduction) asserts that all behaviour emerges from the interaction of many factors working together to form a dynamic, self-organizing system. Every social group or relationship can be viewed as such a system: for example, the family can be seen as a dynamic system comprised of all its members, their individual characteristics and the cultural assumptions they hold, the community they interact with, the social and economic circumstances that affect them. A child's development within the family can then be explored in terms of the dynamics of this system as a whole, rather than by looking at isolated factors (such as parenting style, or social class) one at a time as research has traditionally tended to do. This opens up important new areas of research which older approaches could not readily capture (Cox and Paley, 2003).

Self-organizing systems are dynamic in the sense that they are constantly in motion, constantly changing. Furthermore, the system is more than the sum of its parts: the interaction between the separate elements within a system produces effects that no one factor could yield or explain, but which emerge from the dynamics of the system as a whole. The methods of dynamic systems theory offer ways to conceptualize and explore these processes in action in a way we could not do before.

Dynamic systems theory is new, and there is as yet comparatively little work in this vein. But it is already clear that it will provide an important tool for exploring social and personal development at a greater level of detail than ever before, not only within the family but in peer groups (Martin et al., 2005) and in dyadic interactions between two children (Steenbeck and van Geert, 2005). Our understanding of the dynamics of social development looks set for important advance over the next decade.

Exercises

1. How would you design a study to explore the relative contributions of cultural, pragmatic and biological factors to the different contributions mothers and fathers make to parenting?

2. What are the ethical responsibilities of a developmental psychologist in advising legislators about the arrangements for children after divorce?

Suggested reading

For an account of sibling relationships read:

- J. Dunn and C. Kendrick (1982) *Siblings: Love, envy and understanding.* Boston, Mass.: Harvard University Press.

For emotional development read:

- A. Sroufe (1997) *Emotional Development: The organization of emotional life in the early years.* Cambridge, UK: Cambridge University Press.

For a review of research on self-esteem read:

- T. Owens, S. Stryker and N. Goodman (2001) *Extending Self-Esteem Theory and Research: Sociological and psychological currents.* Cambridge, UK: Cambridge University Press.

For an account of the development of friendship read:

- P. Erwin (1998) *Friendship in Childhood and Adolescence.* London: Routledge.

For an account of adolescent social development in social contexts read:

- J. Smetana, N. Campione-Barr and A. Metzger (2006) Adolescent development in interpersonal and societal contexts. *Annual Review of Psychology* 57, pp. 255–84.

Revision summary

Parenting style and development

- Parenting varies along two key dimensions: *responsiveness* (sensitivity to the child's needs and nurturance) and *demandingness* (whether certain standards of behaviour are demanded). The intersection of these dimensions creates four parenting styles, which have important effects on the development of emotional control, self-esteem and maturity.

- *Authoritative* parents are highly responsive and highly demanding. Warmly nurturant, they demand good behaviour, using explanation rather than punishment and orders to obtain it. Their children are confident, self-controlled, mature, high in self-esteem and low in delinquency.

- *Permissive* parents are also high on responsiveness, but low on demandingness, imposing little or no discipline. Their children are immature, impulsive, flout authority and do poorly in school.

- *Authoritarian* parents are low on responsiveness and high on demandingness. Their views are not negotiable; they enforce discipline through punishment.

There is little warmth or respect for the child's individuality. Their children lack self-esteem, confidence and curiosity.

■ *Neglectful* parents are low on responsiveness and low on demandingness. More concerned with themselves than the child, they're inattentive, offering neither nurturance nor discipline. Their children lack self-esteem, do poorly in school, and are more vulnerable to depression and delinquency.

Culture, class, parenting style and development

■ The benefits of authoritative parenting and negative effects of authoritarian parenting are greatest in liberal cultures that admire individual autonomy. Authoritarian parenting is both more common and less detrimental in authoritarian societies that admire discipline and obedience.

■ Immigrants from authoritarian to liberal societies may carry over the cultural meanings of authoritarian parenting and avoid negative effects for one, but not two, generations.

■ Authoritarian parenting can also be protective in liberal societies where it keeps the young away from dangers (such as delinquency) in the community.

■ In every culture, neglectful and authoritarian parenting and economic struggle are associated with a greater risk of child abuse.

Fathers and mothers

■ Mothers do more child care than fathers from birth through adolescence, in all cultures. There are biological as well as cultural reasons for this.

■ Family structures vary across cultures, from monogamous to polygamous to single-parent, and the division of labour within families varies. Family structure provides the child with a basic model of adulthood and basic notions of economics, politics and morality. It also affects child rearing practices – the degree of exposure to adults, the responsibilities and opportunities children experience – all of which have developmental consequences. Families determine what skills and characteristics must be learned as the child develops, and set the pace at which they expect this learning to occur. In effect, families set the agenda for development.

Siblings

■ Children learn a great deal from their siblings, from social and practical skills to conceptual insight into other minds – and sometimes delinquency.

■ High levels of conflict between siblings are associated with lower emotional well-being. Such conflict is most common where one or more siblings have 'difficult' temperaments or parents show favouritism.

■ Birth order/being an only child has little effect, although first-borns may be more responsible and later-borns more sociable, reflecting experiences.

■ 'Well' siblings of disabled, chronically ill or dying children are often marginalized. Despite developmental differences in understanding illness and death, even very young children suffer grief and anxiety. Schoolwork and emotional health tend to suffer.

Divorce

- Around 40 per cent of European marriages fail, and a higher proportion do in the United States. Offspring of all ages are distressed by this, from toddlers to young adults. The very young may blame themselves, whilst older children feel abandoned and forced to grow up and take responsibilities too early.

- Children may react to divorce by regression to more childish behaviour, emotional disturbance (withdrawal or aggression), drops in academic success and even IQ. Puberty may be earlier, and there is a greater risk of substance abuse, delinquency, early sexuality and unstable romances.

- Some of the negative effects of divorce reflect emotional trauma from the separation. Others reflect increased poverty (a common consequence) or continuing conflict between parents, and disappear if these are dealt with.

- Continued contact with the 'absent' parent (usually the father) reduces emotional pain and anger, provided the relationship is warm and nurturant.

Peers

- Our knowledge of peer relationships derives from Western societies. Some things may generalize to other cultures, some may not.

- Interactions with peers play a vital role in development, from the social play of childhood to the 'hanging out' typical of adolescents.

- Conceptions of friendship change with age, from the highly self-centred and instrumental view of the young child, to a view based on mutual concern and reciprocity in middle childhood, and on to an interdependence respecting individual autonomy in adolescence.

- Where children tend to have best friends and to form loose clusters of companions, adolescents form cliques. These exist within the larger context of 'crowds' or 'types' (for example sporty versus academic). Both cliques and crowds define identity, shaping behaviour, clothing and values.

- Children's friendships are generally 'same sex' until adolescence. Romantic relationships are shaped by peer group as much as parents.

The importance of friends and social status

- Easy-going, socially skilled, beautiful children are popular. Most children have at least one friend, but the very aggressive and very shy are rejected.

- Having no friends is distressing and lonely for the shy, although the aggressive are less affected. Shy, lonely, friendless children are prey to being bullied, which may cause long-lasting psychological damage.

12
prosocial and antisocial behaviour

Human beings are capable of acts of enormous compassion and kindness, acts which may even involve altruistic self-sacrifice of one kind or another. Even in everyday life we have a striking propensity to be supportive to others, to offer comfort and help, to shape our behaviour for the good of the community. But at least some members of our species also display the opposite tendency: a propensity for violence, vandalism and theft, for social disorder. A few are capable of acts of grotesque cruelty which amount to evil.

How do prosocial or antisocial behaviours develop? Are these things two sides of the same coin, forged by the same social processes, or are different processes involved? Why do some individuals become antisocial rather than prosocial? For that matter, why is a given individual sometimes prosocial, sometimes antisocial? These are the questions explored in this chapter.

Evolutionary theories

Many animals behave aggressively and uncooperatively. Rivals fight, inflicting terrible wounds and driving beaten foes off to gain access to mates or food, to dominate a group or a territory. Lions kill the cubs fathered by their ousted rivals when they take over a pride, to further the chances of rearing their own offspring. Chicks shove their weaker siblings out of the nest to secure greater access to food. Many creatures steal food or shelter from others.

None of this seems particularly surprising: the survival advantages of antisocial behaviour to the successful aggressors and their offspring seem obvious. In the 19th century, biologists saw such antisocial behaviour as the predictable outcome of the evolutionary process, needing no further explanation. It fitted with the idea of the 'survival of the fittest' (Spencer, 1864) and with a notion of 'Nature red in tooth and claw' (Tennyson, 1850).

The problem of prosocial behaviour

However, animals are not uniformly selfish. In fact, a great many species, from insects to birds, rodents, dogs and primates display quite marked prosocial, and even altruistic, behaviours. It therefore seems very likely that these behaviours too provide some sort of evolutionary advantage, and hence have some sort of innate basis – but what? Where is the advantage of sacrificing your own chance to live or breed to help others? Where is the advantage of sharing your spoils and pooling your efforts rather than focusing on your own survival? These things seemed not to fit with 'survival of the fittest', and so seemed to pose a challenge for an evolutionary view. This challenge resulted in a new and subtler understanding of evolutionary processes.

For example, the problem of altruism led to the insight that it is actually the survival of our genes that matters to evolution, rather than the survival of the individual (Hamilton, 1964). This explains the altruistic behaviour of many insects (such as bees), whose self-sacrifice is very specifically directed toward the survival of close relatives who share the same genes. But human beings are altruistic toward strangers in ways that could not possibly be to the advantage of their own genes (Kitcher, 1985). The consensus of research is that 'selfish gene' theory (Dawkins, 1976) doesn't explain human prosocial behaviour (see Chapter 1).

Many researchers today would agree that there must be some sort of evolutionary basis for prosocial and altruistic behaviour, but there is a continuing controversy over what this is. Are we innately equipped with neural mechanisms specifically geared to provide us with an instinctive sense of justice, for example by making us sensitive to social cheating, as some suggest (Cosmides and Tooby, 1992, 2005a)? Or does prosocial behaviour arise as a by-product of simpler neural processes with a broad social function rather than a specifically moral one? For example, could moral behaviour arise from the mirror neuron system (see Chapter 9) which underlies the newborn baby's social reflexes and provides a primitive empathy with others? The idea gains credence from the discovery that defects in this system seem to be implicated in the antisocial behaviour of the psychopath (Hare, 1999).

Beyond biology

Discovering the innate basis of prosocial and antisocial behaviour will be a major challenge for research in the 21st century. But whatever the answer, it is quite obvious that a description of innate mechanisms can only provide a part of the story of how these things develop. Prosocial and antisocial behaviours involve far more than instincts and reflexes. They are bound up in our social understanding, in our insight into what will help or hurt others. They reflect our intentions to help or hurt, and the moral reasoning that lies behind those intentions. They are at the heart of what William James (1890, 1892) called the *spiritual self*: the attitudes and values that form the core of identity, and which provide continuity and meaning to our interactions with the world.

The importance of empathy

To have the intention of helping others or comforting them, you must understand that they need help or comfort. From this point of view, we can infer that the development of prosocial behaviour must depend on the development of an empathic insight into other people's feelings (Eisenberg, 1992; Eisenberg and Fabes, 1998; Hoffman, 1982; Hoffman 2000). Hoffman (1982) suggested that a growing ability to empathize with others is not only *necessary* for prosocial development, it is *sufficient* to produce it: that 'feeling with' others provides the motivation to offer help as well as the insight that help is needed.

Hoffman's theory

Hoffman argued that the young baby is not capable of prosocial reactions because he or she has no insight into other minds, and so can feel no empathy. Young babies do react to other people's emotions, for example crying and becoming distressed if other babies cry (Martin and Clark, 1982; Dondi, Simion and Caltran, 1999). But this is purely a reflex: the baby has no idea that the other child has feelings, and is not even aware of the distinction between self and other. He or she simply experiences the imitated distress *as if* it were his or her own. This reflexive effect is known as 'emotional resonancing' (see Chapter 4).

According to Hoffman, reflexive emotional resonancing provides the crucial key to the development of prosocial concern for others. Gradually, from about 6 months of age on, the baby begins to differentiate between self and other (Chapter 4). As this happens, he or she is progressively able to realize that the distress experienced when imitating another child crying 'belongs' to someone else: to the other child and not the self. The natural desire for distress to be comforted transfers from seeking comfort for the self to wanting it for the person whose distress it is. This is the start of a prosocial concern for others. The tendency to cry when others cry diminishes (Hay, Nash and Pederson, 1981) and is replaced by a tendency to look at a distressed baby with an expression of concern (Zahn-Waxler et al., 1992). The tendency to actively offer comfort to others in distress increases from 12 to 18 months of age (Zahn-Waxler et al., 1992).

From this point on, the development of prosocial behaviour is shaped by the progressive sophistication of the child's empathic abilities (Hoffman, 1982). Toddlers' efforts to offer comfort are genuine but egocentric: their lack of understanding of other minds leads them to offer others what they themselves would find consoling – for example trying to comfort mother by giving her their own favourite comfort blanket (Zahn-Waxler and Radke-Yarrow, 1982). Between 3 and 5 years of age, children's growing insight into other minds allows them to begin to offer different forms of comfort to different people, although their efforts are still not always very well focused, reflecting continuing limitations of insight. At this age, children also begin to understand the circumstances that cause distress, and so can infer that someone needs comforting from the situation, rather than drawing this inference only if the other is actually exhibiting distress. In late childhood and adolescence these skills expand so that the comfort offered to others becomes progressively better suited to the recipient's needs, and the range of situations in which the child can infer that another person is distressed expands. By mid or late adolescence this range has grown to include abstract circumstances (such as poverty or famine) as well as concrete ones (no money for a coat, no supper) as was the case earlier. Empathic and prosocial reactions can now reflect the principles of social justice.

Does empathy explain prosocial behaviour?

Hoffman's theory seems very plausible. It seems almost self-evident that we can't want to help others unless we understand that they need help, and that our ability to understand who needs help and how to provide it depends on our ability to understand other minds, and most researchers would accept these conclusions (Eisenberg and Fabes, 1998). There is also a strong intuitive plausibility to the suggestion that empathically sharing someone else's distress triggers a powerful emotional urge to offer help. However, there are difficulties for this theory as an explanation of the development of prosocial behaviour.

Prosocial behaviour doesn't always reflect empathy

Hoffman's theory emphasizes a compassionate empathic reaction to another person's distress as the motivating force for prosocial behaviour. In many situations, this may be correct. But many forms of prosocial behaviour don't involve a response to distress. For example, a great deal of prosocial helping involves sharing tasks and goods where no one is distressed (often, quite the reverse). Two-year-olds engage in prosocial behaviour of this kind, voluntarily joining in and helping with chores (Rheingold, 1982), and spontaneously sharing toys with others (Rheingold, Hay and West, 1976). It's hard to see such behaviour as a reaction to any emotional state in another person. The implication is that there is more to prosocial behaviour than an emotional empathy with other people's feelings.

Exactly what motivates prosocial helping with chores and spontaneous sharing of toys is unclear. Could it be due to insight into other people's desires and intentions, a cognitive empathy rather than an emotional empathy with their feelings? Two-year-old helpers clearly understand the intentions of those they help with chores (Rheingold, 1982): they extrapolate from the goals they infer the adult to have, improvising to achieve those goals rather than simply copying what the adult does. There is also evidence that the inclination to help reflects insight into the other's intentions: for example, 18-month-olds will pick up and helpfully pass back an object a researcher drops by accident, but not one that has been dropped deliberately (Warneken and Tomasello, 2006).[1] But it's hard to see why understanding someone's intentions should be *enough* to motivate prosocial helping – and indeed it isn't. Neither children nor adults necessarily help others, no matter how clear the other's intentions might be. And if empathic insight into other people's intentions were enough to stimulate prosocial helping, we would expect enthusiasm for helping with the chores to increase with age, as conceptual understanding of social tasks and situations increases. But this is not the case: the spontaneous enthusiasm for helping with chores typical of 2-year-olds has all but disappeared by adolescence. It seems likely then that the 2-year-old's helpfulness with chores reflects something other than empathic insight into other people's minds.

Empathic ability is not enough to ensure prosocial behaviour

Despite their clear ability to experience emotional empathy with other people's distress, prosocial comforting is actually not very common in young children. Mothers' descriptions of their 2-year-olds suggest that there is only around a 50:50 chance of a 2-year-old reacting in this way (Zahn-Waxler et al., 1992). Direct observations of children suggest a much lower figure (perhaps as a result of observing children in a different context, perhaps because of the presence of an unfamiliar observer, but perhaps as a result of a less objective, more 'rose-tinted' view on the part of mothers compared with researchers). Howes and Farver (1987) observed that toddlers in distress were comforted by a peer in only about 20 percent of cases (the rest were ignored), and that only 40 percent of the children observed ever offered comforting support to others at all.

Studies of whether the frequency of prosocial behaviour increases through childhood and adolescence produce varying results. Some find that it does, some that it doesn't. Averaging across hundreds of studies, the data suggest that there is a tendency for prosocial behaviour to become more common through childhood and adolescence (Eisenberg and Fabes, 1998). Nevertheless, rates of prosocial behaviour are not necessarily high, even in adolescence, despite the marked increase in general empathic abilities.

In fact, there is direct evidence that neither the general ability to empathize nor the direct experience of emotional empathy is enough in itself to produce prosocial helping. For example, there are gender

---

[1] Interestingly, chimpanzees behave in exactly the same way, demonstrating that they too understand simple intentions and are prosocially helpful in relation to these.

differences in the tendency to act prosocially, but these seem to reflect social roles rather than any difference in either the general ability to experience empathy or the strength of emotional responses to other people's distress (see **Box 12.1**). There are also individual differences in whether or not strong emotional reactions to other people's distress elicit sympathetic behaviour. Some people (both adults and children) do react sympathetically, but others (again both adults and children) experience only personal distress (see Chapter 9), focusing on themselves and their own discomfort, and withdrawing self-protectively from the situation rather than offering help (Eisenberg et al., 1988). This difference between individuals does not reflect any difference in the strength of the emotional reaction of empathy: in fact, those who respond sympathetically may well be more effective in regulating their emotions and so more able to 'damp down' their reactions to a manageable level. Overwhelming emotions, even of empathy, may leave us unable to respond (Eisenberg and Fabes, 1998) or even to process information effectively (Thornton, Todd and Thornton, 1996).

box **12.1**

Gender differences in prosocial behaviour

Traditional gender stereotypes in our culture suggest that girls are more prosocial than boys: more caring and empathic, more helpful, less aggressive (Spence, Helmreich and Stapp, 1974). Is this true? It's remarkably hard to find out. For example, in a review of over 250 studies on this subject, Eisenberg and Fabes (1998) found a slight tendency for girls to be more prosocial than boys. But this was most clearly true when the data in a study relied on self-report – that is, on the individual's descriptions of their own behaviour. Studies using direct observations found much smaller gender differences. It may be that in self-report studies, girls describe an idealized self (the behaviour appropriate to living up to gender stereotypes) rather than their actual behaviour. This possibility is made more plausible by the fact that other people, too, seem to be affected by social stereotypes as much as by the facts in describing girls: parents, peers and teachers rate girls as more prosocial than they are either observed to be by researchers, or than they report themselves to be (Bernzweig, Eisenberg and Fabes, 1993)!

A further complication for research on gender effects comes from the fact that the types of prosocial behaviour typical of girls and boys are different. For example, girls are more likely to offer emotional help, whereas boys are more likely to offer practical help. Girls are more likely to help familiar people in familiar places, boys are more likely to help strangers in public places. It's easy to see how these differences reflect both social stereotypes and social realities: girls are socially encouraged in emotional gestures, where boys are discouraged. Girls are thought to be at more risk than boys (of assault or harassment) in approaching strangers in the street. Most surveys of sex differences use items more typical of female prosocial behaviour than male – which could explain the occurrence of the sex difference. Where more items biased toward masculine prosocial behaviours are used, boys may even come out as more prosocial than girls (Eisenberg and Fabes, 1998).

Evidence for behavioural differences

While issues of this kind complicate the situation, the consensus of opinion is that there really are slight differences between girls and boys in the tendency to behave prosocially (Eisenberg and Fabes, 1998), and these differences are found across many cultures (Whiting and Whiting, 1975) and increase with age (Eisenberg and Fabes, 1998). However, these gender differences are smaller than we popularly suppose, and less straightforward.

For example, from preschool to adolescence, girls are consistently less likely to be both physically (fighting, hitting) and verbally (overt rows) aggressive than boys (Coie and Dodge, 1998; Knight, Fabes and Higgins, 1996). However, girls are not less aggressive than boys in all areas. From preschool to adolescence, girls are consistently more likely to engage in 'relational aggression' (spreading vicious rumours about someone, shutting someone out of the group and so on) than boys (Crick, Casas and Ku, 1999). Do these differences reflect the differing biochemistry of male and female: the higher levels of testosterone in boys, for instance (Coie and Dodge, 1998)? Do they reflect the greater importance girls seem to place on intimate relationships, and the greater hurt that it is possible to inflict on a girl by social rejection, as a consequence (Galen and Underwood, 1997)? We don't yet know, although these are plausible speculations.

Differences in empathy?

Even the fact that girls do, on the whole, seem to behave more caringly to others, to be more helpful and to share more than boys (Eisenberg and Fabes, 1998) is not straightforward to interpret. Faced with a distressing scene (such as an injured child being teased), boys show exactly the same changes in heart rate and their faces express just as much distress as girls do (Eisenberg et al., 1989). In other words, the data suggest that boys are not different from girls in the degree of empathy they feel for others, but only in how likely they are to respond to that empathy by being prosocially helpful. We don't know what the origin of this difference in responding is. Does it reflect cultural mores, which project a more 'strong and silent' role for men and boys, a more 'warm and emotional' one for girls and women? Or do men and boys suppress or ignore their empathic impulses for some other reason?

Being selective with empathic concern

Even children who are generally disposed to be sympathetic are fairly selective in their willingness to offer comfort. For example, 2- to 4-year-olds are more likely to comfort the distress of people they know and like than they are to comfort strangers or people they don't like (Farver and Branstetter, 1994, Howes and Farver, 1987). Exactly the same thing is true of adults: for example, HIV-AIDS volunteers are more likely to be helpful to people they perceive as members of their in-group than to people from out-groups (Sturmer, Snyder and Omoto, 2005).

We withhold empathic concern in other contexts, too. For example, children who have themselves deliberately caused another person's distress are more likely to laugh and gloat, to stir things up even more, than to offer concern or help (Dunn, 1988). This phenomenon is so familiar that it is easy to miss its significance. Very young babies don't deliberately provoke others in this way: they simply haven't the empathic insight to know what will hurt or annoy. It's only at around 2 years of age, as this insight develops, that toddlers begin to be deliberately provocative (Dunn and Munn, 1985). The truth is that a degree of empathic insight is as much the prerequisite for deliberate cruelty as it is for prosocial helping (Olweus, 1993).

These data suggest that it is not the ability to experience empathic concern for others that determines whether or not we act prosocially. Rather, prosocial and antisocial behaviour reflect the *giving* or *withholding* of empathic concern. Evidence in support of this important conclusion comes from studies of rapists (see **Box 12.2**). It seems that rapists are as empathetic with the distress experienced by victims of rape as anyone else is, but that they withhold this empathy specifically from their own victims (Fernandez and Marshall, 2003).

What exactly is involved in withholding empathy? A commonsense view is that it involves somehow 'dehumanizing' others, and there is

---

Are rapists low in empathy?

Despite a widespread belief that rapists and other sex offenders must have lower empathy skills than other people (else how could they possibly inflict such harm?), the evidence is equivocal. Some studies report lower empathic skills in sex offenders, others find no difference between sex offenders and matched samples who don't commit such crimes. This is probably because different studies measure different facets of empathy (Thornton and Thornton, 1995).

Comparing the results from a large number of studies, Jolliffe and Farrington (2004) found that the major difference between those who commit violent or sexual offences and those who don't is in *cognitive empathy* (that is, event-related empathy, reflecting perspective-taking skills) rather than in *emotional empathy* (that is, participatory empathy, or sharing an emotional reaction with another). However, the lower cognitive empathy skills found in offenders reflects low intelligence and low socio-economic class. When these factors are controlled for by comparing offenders only with people of similar background and ability, the difference in empathy skills disappears: offenders are no less empathic than non-offenders.

In fact, the data suggest that rapists and child molesters may even show more emotional empathy with the victims of sexual assaults than either non-offenders (Beckett et al., 1994) or other types of violent offender (Fernandez and Marshall, 2003). Rapists certainly show as much general empathic insight into the distress of a rape victim as anyone else. It is only their own victim for whom they have no empathy (Fernandez and Marshall, 2003). The results from Fernandez and Marshall's study suggest that rapists actually switch off empathy for their victims, rather than being blind to it. Switching off empathy is a common human strategy: for example, it's common for soldiers to demonize or dehumanize their enemy, which may be a necessary preparation for attack. Social and political 'out-groups' are often treated in the same way.

some evidence to support this. For example, Harris and Fiske (2006) found that the areas of the cortex that normally become active when we think about ourselves or other people simply don't activate when we think about members of out-groups: the neural signature for social cognition simply isn't there. Rather, the brain patterns generated by out-groups are more like those generated by thinking about inanimate objects.

Understanding how and why human beings withhold empathy is an urgent project for research. Such withholding may be a major factor in antisocial behaviour at all levels, from the provocativeness of the young child to the thefts, vandalism and aggression of the adolescent delinquent. It may be a key element in many violent and racially motivated crimes. It is probably a key part of what allows ordinary people to go to war, to kill and commit the atrocities often associated with war or with terrorism. It is probably a key part of what allows whole communities to be swept along in the terrible brutalities of genocide.

An overview of the role of empathy

Few researchers today would dispute that empathy plays an important role in the development of prosocial behaviour (Eisenberg and Fabes, 1998). Hoffman may well be right in suggesting that empathic insight into other minds is the foundation for the emergence of prosocial concern for others, and that the quality and effectiveness of prosocial helping is limited by the degree of empathic insight into other minds.

But it is clear that the role of empathy in prosocial behaviour is far more complex than was supposed. Not all prosocial behaviour involves emotional empathy, and emotional empathy in itself is not enough to elicit prosocial behaviour. The strong emotional reactions involved in empathizing with others in distress sometimes elicit prosocial behaviour – and sometimes don't. Nor does the general cognitive ability to empathically understand other minds necessarily dispose us toward prosocial behaviour: it is also the prerequisite for effective bullying and cruelty. We can withhold empathic concern from those we wish to harm. In sum, however important it may be, there is much more to prosocial development than the development of empathy.

The development of moral reasoning

A very different approach to understanding prosocial development shares Hoffman's assumption that the ability to understand perspectives other than our own is vital to development in this area, but focuses on the cognitive, rather than the emotional, implications of the development of perspective taking (Kohlberg, 1976). Lawrence Kohlberg's work dominated research on moral development for many decades. He was strongly influenced by the ideas of Jean Piaget, who believed that young children have a profoundly egocentric view of the world, and that development involves a progressive awareness of alternative perspectives: an awareness made possible by the construction of new and more powerful cognitive operations (see Chapters 1 and 6).

Piaget's account of the development of morality

Piaget's work on morality came near the beginning of his research on cognitive development (Piaget, 1932). He studied children playing marbles, focusing on the rules they used for the competition and their understanding of where these rules come from. He also explored children's moral thinking by asking them questions (such as why it is wrong to lie or steal), and by asking them to judge the relative 'naughtiness' of children described in contrasting 'vignettes' or stories (for example, to say which was naughtier, a child who had broken lots of glasses while trying to be obedient or one who had broken a single glass while being disobedient). On the basis of his observations in these tasks, Piaget concluded that moral thinking develops through two main stages, beginning in middle childhood.

According to Piaget, very young children don't play games with rules at all, and have no moral understanding. For example, if 4-year-olds play with marbles they do as they like, making whatever patterns and effects please them without thinking of any particular 'point' to such play, or construing it as a structured competition. They can't offer any sort of explanation why lying or stealing (and so on) are bad: these things are 'just naughty'. But in middle childhood (from about 6 to 10 years of age) children begin to form theories about moral issues, and enter the first of Piaget's two stages, the *heteronomous*[2] stage.

The heteronomous stage begins (at about 6 years of age) with a dawning awareness of the existence of 'rules' both for playing games and for social behaviour. But there is no understanding of the social origin or negotiable nature of social rules. Rules are specified by authority figures (older children, parents, even God), and are absolute: not to be challenged or changed. It's as if the child makes no distinction between physical laws (such as the laws of gravity) and moral rules, or the rules of games such as marbles. At this stage, the child believes that you can no more change the rules of a game or the rules of social behaviour than you could change laws of gravity. **Box 12.3** illustrates children's thinking about this: 'invented' rules simply aren't 'real'.

This way of thinking leads the heteronomous child to interpret moral rules in a very absolutist way. Human intentions don't matter (any more than what you *meant* to do changes things, when you try to defy

---

[2] So called because 'hetero' means 'other', and the child at this age believes in the absolute authority of others.

gravity). The rules are the rules. According to Piaget, children at this stage define a lie simply as a factually inaccurate statement. It doesn't matter *why* a person said something untrue, doesn't matter whether they meant to deceive, or whether they themselves believed what they said. Lies are untruths, and that is that. The more factually inaccurate a statement is, the bigger (worse) the lie, so that a gross inaccuracy offered in good faith is a worse lie than a smaller inaccuracy offered with intent to deceive.

Equally, the 'badness' of behaviour is defined in terms of the degree of violation of what 'should' be. You shouldn't do damage; shouldn't break things, for example. The more damage you do, the more things you break, the 'naughtier' you are. So for children at this stage, breaking many glasses by accident in the course of an attempt at helpfulness is worse than breaking one glass in the course of disobedience.

Furthermore, children at this stage believe in immanent justice. Rules are absolute, and so are the consequences of transgression. Just as you can't defy the laws of gravity and escape unpunished, so you can't defy social rules without punishment. Defying social rules will lead to punishment just as surely as defying the rules of gravity by walking off a cliff will inevitably lead you to crash to your doom.[3]

Piaget argues that the absolutism of the heteronomous stage comes from the child's 'egocentric' inability to perceive more than one perspective on things. The child simply mistakes the one perspective he or she can see for the *only* perspective that there can be. But somewhere between 8 and 11 years of age, interactions with peers begin to expose flaws and problems with this approach. This, in interaction with new

box **12.3**	Piaget (1932, republished in 1965) quotes this example of a child at the heteronomous stage reasoning about the rules in a game of marbles. This 10-year-old child (Ben) had just been asked if it was possible to think up new rules, and had reluctantly suggested one.
Reasoning about rules	

> Piaget: *Then people could play that way?*
> Ben: *Oh no, because it would be cheating.*
> Piaget: *But all your friends would like to, wouldn't they?*
> Ben: *Yes, they all would.*
> Piaget: *Then why would it be cheating?*
> Ben: *Because I invented it: it isn't a rule! It's a wrong rule because it's outside of the rules. A fair rule is one that's in the game.*

---

[3] This account of how children think about moral transgression and punishment offers an interesting insight into why it is that children blame themselves for their parent's divorce, for being bullied or abused. Somewhere, we have all done 'something bad'. An absolutist belief in immanent justice can always, potentially, connect that to our present misery.

cognitive operations that allow the child to consider things from more than one perspective, leads to the development of the second stage of moral understanding: the *autonomous* stage.

Children at the autonomous stage can understand that there is more than one perspective on events. They can therefore realize that rules (whether for marbles or morality at large) are not 'God-given absolutes', but mutually agreed conventions fostering social interactions and serving goals. Rules are reconstrued as a social contract. You have to stick by the rules to play/successfully interact with other people, but changes in the rules can be negotiated by collective agreement. This new insight into the nature of rules reveals that intentions are profoundly important in the moral domain: since rules are mutually negotiable, transgressions involve a breaking of the implied social contract. Now, the child understands that even very gross misrepresentations of the facts are not lies, if the speaker believes the statement to be true and has no intent to deceive (in other words, is not breaking the social contract of honesty). Equally, even very damaging outcomes of an action (breaking lots of glasses) are understood not to be morally bad if the perpetrator had no intent to do damage. Far lesser damage (breaking only one glass) is more reprehensible, if it is the consequence of a rejection of mutual agreements (disobedience).

Piaget's account of children's thinking in this area is extraordinary, making sense of commonly observed reactions which otherwise might seem absurd. At a bare minimum, his work forces us to take the child's perspective seriously. But as with so many other areas of Piaget's work, more recent research suggests that his account is both over-simplified and inaccurate (Bussey, 1999). For example, Piaget's claim that children don't refer to intentions but only to factual accuracy in deciding whether a statement is a lie or not until they are about 11 years of age is not supported in other studies. Strichartz and Burton (1990) found that from 6 years of age onward, children identify lies not only in terms of the factual accuracy of the statement, but also in terms of whether or not the speaker knew the statement to be inaccurate, and whether or not he or she intended to deceive (as opposed to merely being sloppy). Furthermore, 5- to 10-year-olds are actually quite subtle in their appraisals of intentions in relation to lying, distinguishing between 'white lies' and self-serving lies (Peterson, Peterson and Seeto, 1983). Nevertheless, despite these problems Piaget's theory of moral development has had an enormous impact on research, completely changing how we think about moral understanding and sparking off a whole new field of study.

Kohlberg's stages of moral reasoning

Like Piaget, Kohlberg believed that moral reasoning develops through a number of stages, each one reflecting an increase in the individual's ability to understand different perspectives on the issues. Kohlberg studied moral reasoning through the lifespan, using vignettes to tell the story of a moral dilemma – the classic example, the 'Heinz' dilemma, is given in **Box 12.4**. Having told this story, Kohlberg asked people to say what Heinz or the judge ought to do, and why. The justifications for a course of action were then analysed, looking for qualitatively different ways of thinking about moral issues.

box 12.4

Kohlberg's 'Heinz' dilemma

Source: L. Kohlberg, The development of children's orientations toward a moral order: sequence in the development of moral thought. *Human Development* 6, pp. 11–33. © 1963 Krager. Reproduced with permission from Krager.

The most famous of the vignettes Kohlberg told the participants in his study goes as follows:

In Europe, a woman was near death from a special kind of cancer. There was one drug that the doctors thought might save her. It was a form of radium that a druggist in the same town had recently discovered. The drug was expensive to make, but the druggist was charging ten times what the drug cost him to make. He paid $200 for the radium and charged $2,000 for a small dose of the drug. The sick woman's husband, Heinz, went to everybody he knew to borrow the money, but he could get together only about $1,000, which was half what it cost. He told the druggist that his wife was dying and asked him to sell it cheaper or let him pay later. But the druggist said: 'No, I discovered the drug and I'm going to make money out of it.'

Kohlberg then asked the participants, 'Should Heinz steal the drug? Why/why not?'

After recording their answers, Kohlberg told the participants that Heinz had got desperate and had stolen the drug. He had then been caught, and sent to trial. Kohlberg asked, 'Should the judge send Heinz to jail? Why/why not?'

Using this methodology Kohlberg (1976) identified six different stages of moral reasoning. He later speculated that there would also be a seventh (Kohlberg and Power, 1981), which he described as a stage of 'transcendental morality' and which he believed would link the development of moral reasoning with the development of religious insight. Indeed, there are marked parallels between this hypothetical seventh stage of moral reasoning and the highest stage of religious reasoning (**Box 12.5**) identified by Fowler (1981, 1986). However, there is little if any empirical support for the existence of stages six or seven. Kohlberg argued that these stages didn't turn up in the data simply because they are extremely rare. Others suggested that it was because they don't exist. One way or the other, Kohlberg (1978) gave up scoring stage six as a separate stage, collapsing it into stage five. Research focuses therefore on the first five stages, which are well validated (**Box 12.6**).

Kohlberg's first stage of moral reasoning is very like Piaget's heteronomous stage. The individual believes that right and wrong are

box **12.5**

The development of religious belief

Contrary to all 'rationalist' expectations, religion is as important at the start of the 21st century as ever, affecting international politics as much as everyday life. We shouldn't be surprised. Our earliest human ancestors left signs of their religiosity, in their cave paintings and burials. Anything that survives through as many millennia of human history as 'organized religion' has done, in one tradition or another, is obviously serving a profound need and is unlikely to simply vanish.

Becoming religious

Faith may be born in the infant's absolute trust of the mother, which forms a model for the later sense of relatedness to the transcendental (Fowler and Dell, 2004). Families, schools and peers play a crucial role in fostering religious belief (Regnerus, Smith and Smith, 2004), teaching the creeds and values of a given faith, legitimating compliance with practice and facilitating the recognition and occurrence of 'transcendental experience'.

Becoming religious is a process of social learning and social inclusion: learning how to see, how to be. This is not to say that religious education is instrumental or cynical. The genius of our species lies in our capacity to find and experience meaning. Religious faith is as much about how we understand the meaning of our lives as it is about believing given 'facts', as much about emotional experience and identity as it is about reason. Religious education aims to share a transcendental meaning with the young.

Faith develops through six stages, reflecting developmental change in conceptual understanding and life experience (Fowler 1981, 1986):

- Stage 1: an intuitive, magical view of god, life and death, wrapped in fantasy. Typical of early childhood (over 3 years: infants have no idea of God).
- Stage 2: a literal belief in the stories and myths of religion. Belief in a reciprocal God: follow God's law and you will be rewarded, disobey and you'll be punished. Typical of mid-childhood, although many adults retain this simple faith.
- Stage 3: an uncritical acceptance of the values and attitudes of religion provides the foundation for social life and personal identity. Typical of adolescents, this is also common among adults.
- Stage 4: religious values are questioned rather than blindly accepted, and specific values are endorsed consciously, rather than conventionally. Faith is a matter of active commitment rather than conventional compliance. Commonly triggered by going to university, this stage is also induced by life-changes in adulthood: a changed career, failed romance and the like.
- Stage 5: the rational clarity of stage 4 fuses with the emotional power of early childhood stages. There's an openness to sources of spiritual insight beyond the conventional sources of the individual's religion: to Buddha alongside Jesus, for example. Paradoxes and contradictions are noted and tolerated. Few reach this stage before middle age.
- Stage 6: Religious experience is dominated by a vision of universal compassion, justice and love. The drive to *live* this vision puts personal welfare in second place, producing lives that observers view as mad – or saintly. The Buddha, Muhammad, Jesus would be examples, as would Mohandas Gandhi and Mother Theresa, Aung San Soo Kyi and the like. Very few individuals

reach this stage, though there are many 'unsung saints' of this type, besides the famous names.

Fowler's stages apply across all religions. Levels of spiritual insight are not a function of mastery of particular creeds or rituals, but a progression from a simple, self-centred and narrow view to a complex, multifaceted and altruistic view. Compassion, love and justice are at the core of all the world's great faiths.

No faith is static: theology evolves (Armstrong, 1999), as does individual insight (Rest et al., 1999), as human experience expands. But lower stages are not inferior to higher ones, according to Fowler (1981), who argues that each stage is capable of providing the believer with 'wholeness, grace and integrity', reflecting his or her present experience.

The effects of religious faith

Some view religion as wholly bad, fostering irrationality and violence that would be 'impossible' without it (famously, Dawkins, 2006). But Dawkins' is an outsider's view of religion that presumes all the faithful to be at stage 2, and ignores the fact that Hitler, Stalin, Pol Pot and the like did very well in leading people to acts of terrible and systematic evil entirely without the help of religion.

A more evidence-based approach to the effects of faith poses methodological challenges: *intrinsic* faith (that is, for its own sake) and *extrinsic* faith (that is, religion practised for social reasons) have different effects, but can be hard to distinguish (Milevsky and Levitt, 2004). Questionnaires designed to measure the depth of Protestant faith aren't valid measures for Catholics (Cohen et al., 2005), still less for Jews, Muslims or other faiths. Tests developed with samples from many religions and many different societies are beginning to solve these problems (Maiello, 2005).

Religious beliefs affect how families function, and the world view they provide to the young (Murrell, 2004). Depending on specific beliefs, religion may foster a more authoritarian or a more authoritative parenting style, a world view characterized by prejudice or by tolerance.

Overall, religious faith is associated with an increase in prosocial behaviour (Carlo, Hardy and Alberts, 2004, King, 2003), perhaps as much because religion provides a group identity that transcends self (Furrow, King and White, 2004; King, 2003; Mishra, 2005) as because it provides direct moral teaching, though that is increasingly rare elsewhere. Religious adolescents are less likely to engage in substance abuse (Marsiglia et al., 2005) and delinquency (Regnerus and Burdette, 2006), although only where parent and child share a faith: if they don't, delinquency rates may even be higher (Pearce and Haynie, 2004).

Faith also has beneficial effects on personal well-being (Carothers et al., 2005). Tillich (1958) argued that everyone needs faith in something for emotional health – although it needn't be in God. Certainly, it seems that faith helps us through difficult times, reducing levels of distress after divorce (Greeff and Van der Merwe, 2004), reducing suicide rates in the young (Eskin, 2004), and providing a buffer for loneliness (Arokach, 2006). There is also evidence that faith is associated with better recovery from both physical and mental illness (Koenig, McCullough and Larsen, 2001), perhaps because it teaches spiritual practices such as meditation that help the management of stress as much as for any specific belief.

box **12.6**

Kohlberg's levels and stages of moral reasoning

Pre-conventional moral reasoning:

Stage 1: 'Right' is defined as obeying authority, 'wrong' as disobeying. The reason for doing right is simply to avoid punishment.

- Heinz should steal the drug because if he doesn't, he might get into trouble for letting his wife die.
- Heinz should not steal the drug because he'll get caught and put in prison.

Stage 2: 'Right' is defined as what is in your own interest, or involves 'fair dos' or a 'tit for tat' reciprocity. If it's not in your own interest it's wrong. The reason for doing right is to serve your own interests.

- Heinz should steal the drug if he loves his wife and wants her to live, or if she'd steal it for him if he needed it.
- Heinz shouldn't steal the drug because it's not his fault his wife has cancer. Stealing it wouldn't do him much good if he gets sent to jail.

Conventional moral reasoning:

Stage 3: 'Right' is defined as what a good person would be expected to do in the relevant social role. 'Wrong' is failing to meet these social expectations. The reason for doing the right thing is to be (and be seen to be) a good person.

- Heinz should steal the drug because everyone will think he's a bad husband if he lets his wife die.
- Heinz shouldn't steal the drug because everyone will think he's a criminal if he does.

Stage 4: 'Right' is about doing one's duty as a citizen, supporting the whole community. The reason to do the right thing is to prevent the social system from breaking down.

- Heinz should steal the drug because it's a husband's responsibility to look after his wife. It's how marriage works.
- Heinz should not steal the drug because if everyone went around stealing, society would break down.

Post-conventional reasoning

Stage 5: 'Right' is defined in terms of universal ethical principles and human rights. The reason to do the right thing is simply because it is the right thing.

- Heinz should steal the drug because a human life matters more than mere money or profit. The right to life transcends the right to property.
- Heinz shouldn't steal the drug because that would put the needs of one woman above the needs of other, equally deserving people. He should campaign for the drug to be made available to everyone who needs it.

absolutes, defined by authority. It is morally right to obey the rules, and if you don't, you risk punishment. The only perspective the individual refers to in deciding whether to obey the rules or not is his or her own: what best fits *Heinz's* needs and desires? The risk of his going to prison makes it wrong to steal. There is no consideration of his wife's feelings or needs.

At the second stage, the individual shows more awareness of other people's feelings and desires, and is concerned with reciprocity, but his or her own perspective is still paramount. It might be right, for example, for Heinz to steal the drug if he loves his wife and doesn't want to lose her (although it would be wrong to steal it if he disliked her and wanted rid of her). Or it might be right to steal it if she would do that for him (although it would be wrong to steal if she wouldn't help him).

Despite the slight increase in perspective taking between them, stages one and two share a very self-centred approach to judging what course of action to follow in resolving moral dilemmas. You do what is in your own best interests, without reference to any broader consideration. For this reason, Kohlberg identified both stages as being at the *pre-conventional* level of reasoning about morality. By contrast, stages three and four both involve a consideration of a range of factors beyond the self, factors defined by society at large in one way or another. Kohlberg identified these two stages as the *conventional* level of moral reasoning.

At stage three, the individual is aware not only that other people have different perspectives to his or her own, but that others judge us. This ushers in a concern for how we look in other people's eyes, and the need to be seen as 'good'. Right and wrong are defined in terms of social conventions and sanctions: doing the right thing is a matter of doing what society expects you to do and will praise you for doing in a given situation, and doing the wrong thing is a matter of doing what transgresses against social expectation and will attract social criticism. So Heinz should steal the drug because a husband ought to look after his wife and people will think badly of him if he doesn't; or he shouldn't steal the drug because people would reject him as a criminal.

At stage four, the individual is aware not only of how other people look at him/her, but also of the wider perspective of society at large. Moral rules are understood not merely as social conventions, but as systems that hold society together. Moral behaviour is no longer a matter of doing what makes you look good in other people's eyes, but of doing what is right to support society as a whole. The individual refers to social institutions such as marriage or property rights to justify Heinz in stealing or not stealing, rather than to personal relationships.

Stage five transcends the conventional stages of reasoning in that it looks beyond the perspective of a given society to explore a more universal perspective on ethical principles. Whereas individuals at the conventional level accept the social conventions and legal systems of their own society, individuals at stage five view these as only one possible solution to the problem of morality. At this *post-conventional* level of reasoning, the individual refers to fundamental human rights (such as the right to life) and to fundamental principles of justice and fairness in justifying one course of action or another. From this perspective, Heinz should ignore social conventions and the law if these things violate fundamental human rights. Virtually every stage five argument thus favours

Heinz stealing the drug. It's worth noting that following universal ethical principles makes moral action an end in itself, rather than something done as a means to an end (whether self-centred or for conventional benefit). The post-conventional stage is thus the purest form of moral reasoning.

Kohlberg's theory is important, because it opened up a whole new way of looking at moral reasoning, and because there is some evidence that moral reasoning is associated with prosocial and antisocial behaviour, as will be discussed below. The five stages of moral reasoning Kohlberg identified are very robust, having been replicated by many researchers in many countries. There's no controversy about the existence of these stages, and many of Kohlberg's other results are easy to replicate, too.

However, Kohlberg's method of identifying the stage of an individual's reasoning by analysing interview material is difficult to use: scorers need an elaborate manual and considerable training to do it reliably. Much research nowadays relies on the easier to use 'Defining the Issues' (DTI) test (Rest, 1986), in which participants listen to a dilemma such as the Heinz dilemma, and then choose which of a series of fixed statements identify the most important issues (**Box 12.7**). The DTI is easy to use and reliable to score. It produces very similar results to those from Kohlberg's original method, although significantly more adolescents and adults choose statements reflecting post-conventional thinking on the DTI than spontaneously produce post-conventional reasoning in Kohlberg's interview (Rest et al., 1999). The key difference between the two tests is probably the difference between choosing and producing: Kohlberg's method requires the participant to generate a complex idea, where Rest's only requires that the idea be recognized, a far easier thing.

But despite the robustness of Kohlberg's findings, there has been considerable controversy about what these results mean, and how far his theory can actually explain the development of moral behaviour.

Kohlberg, gender and the ethic of care

In studies in the 1970s, it was regularly reported that girls lagged behind boys in moral reasoning. Specifically, the most common stage found among adolescent girls and women was stage three, whereas the most common stage found among adolescent boys and men was stage four (Haan, Langer and Kohlberg, 1976; Holstein, 1976). The 1970s was not a good time to suggest that women were in any way inferior to men! A serious challenge to Kohlberg's theory came from Carol Gilligan (1977, 1982), who argued that women only scored lower on Kohlberg's stages because the stages themselves were biased against feminine ways of reasoning.

Kohlberg had developed his stage model using data from interviews only with boys and men, and his stages place emphasis on the principles

box 12.7

The 'Defining the Issues' test

Source: J. Rest, *Moral Development: Advances in research and theory*, New York: Praeger/ Greenwood, © 1986. Reproduced with permission from Praeger/Greenwood.

In response to the 'Heinz' dilemma:

----- should steal   ----- can't decide   ----- should not steal

Importance:
Great / Much / Some/ Little/ No

1   Whether a community's laws are going to be upheld.
2   Isn't it only natural for a husband to care so much for his wife that he'd steal?
3   Is Heinz willing to risk getting shot as a burglar or going to jail for the chance that stealing the drug might help?
4   Whether Heinz is a professional wrestler, or has considerable influence with professional wrestlers.
5   Whether Heinz is stealing for himself, or doing this to help someone else.
6   Whether the druggist's rights to his invention have to be respected.
7   Whether the essence of living is more encompassing than the termination of dying, socially and individually.
8   What values are going to be the basis for governing how people act toward each other.
9   Whether the druggist is going to be allowed to hide behind a worthless law that only protects the rich anyway.
10 Whether the law in this case is getting in the way of the most basic claim of any member of society.
11 Whether the druggist deserves to be robbed for being so greedy and cruel.
12 Would stealing in such a case bring about more total good for the whole society or not?

From the list of questions above, select the four most important:

Most important...............................
Second most important...................
Third most important.....................
Fourth most important...................

of justice and rights. Gilligan argued that these principles are characteristic of male roles and male socialization, whereas female roles and female socialization place emphasis on principles of caring and responsibility. By failing to measure this feminine and compassionate dimension of ethics, Kohlberg's system produced a distorted picture of development.

Gilligan was right in pointing out that Kohlberg had under-estimated a whole dimension of ethical reasoning (the morality of care). It's quite clear now that people can and do draw on principles of care and responsibility in making moral judgments, and that compassion is an important dimension of ethics (Ryan, David and Reynolds, 2004). But this kind of reasoning doesn't seem to be a reflection of gender, as Gilligan thought. It's true that adolescent girls and women tend to focus more on principles of caring (Wark and Krebs, 1996), most notably when reasoning about their own personal moral issues (Jaffee and Hyde, 2000). And in fact, care-based reasoning is generally more appropriate, and more common, in resolving dilemmas when dealing with friends or an 'in-group' than it is when dealing with strangers, or an 'out-group' (Ryan et al., 2004). But males and females are equally likely to use care-based reasoning in dealing with friends and in-groups (Ryan et al., 2004), so any apparent differences between the genders in this area may reflect circumstances and situations rather than inherent gender biases in the bases of moral reasoning. This conclusion is made the more probable by the fact that recent research hasn't found much evidence to support the existence of any gender difference in levels of reasoning in Kohlberg's original dilemmas. Such gender differences as have been found are slight, and may even favour women (Turiel, 1998; Walker et al., 1995).

Kohlberg, culture and 'ethical imperialism'

Since cognitive development and perspective-taking are human universals, Kohlberg argued that moral reasoning should develop in the same way (in other words, through the same sequence of stages) in every culture. The content of moral attitudes and beliefs will vary between one culture and another, reflecting the social mores taught by that society (for example, Quakers encourage a pacificity and abhorrence for fighting which would have struck Genghis Khan and his band as incomprehensibly dangerous). Nevertheless, the structure of each stage of moral reasoning will be universal: for example, in both violent and pacifist cultures, children at stage three will justify their actions, whether fighting or not fighting, by referring to social approval and social expectation.

Kohlberg's stage system can be used to characterize the development of moral reasoning in all the cultures in which it has been tested (Nissan and Kohlberg, 1982; Snarey, 1985; Turiel, 1998). But there are very marked differences between cultures in the typical levels of development achieved in Kohlberg's task. For example, whereas stage four reasoning is common among American adolescents (Rest et al., 1999), it is rare in adolescents in either Turkey or Yucatan, where stage one reasoning is still the most common form even among 16-year-olds

(Kohlberg, 1969). In fact, the majority of studies show that very few adults living in traditional, non-industrialized societies progress beyond stage three reasoning, and (with the exception of leaders) they typically offer reasoning that is at stage one or stage two (Snarey, 1985; Teitjen and Walker, 1985). And even though adults often reach stages three or four in non-Western industrialized countries, stage five is very rarely found (Snarey, 1985).

Why do these cultural differences occur? Just as Gilligan (1977) argued that Kohlberg's system was biased in favour of male forms of reasoning and so misrepresented women's moral development, so other researchers have argued that Kohlberg's system is biased in assuming that Western liberal and egalitarian ethics are universal, and so misrepresents moral development in other cultures which may hold other, equally valid views (Simpson, 1973).

There are two separate issues to consider in relation to Simpson's criticism. The first is whether or not Kohlberg's stage system is actually shaped (distorted) by the assumption that the ethical principles he identified at stage five are universal; the second is whether or not there is a defensible rationale for that assumption. It is worth noting that Simpson (1973) provides no more evidence for the claim that the stage five ethical principles identified by Kohlberg are inappropriately culturally biased than Kohlberg does that they are not (Turiel, 1998).

In fact, the ethical principles which Kohlberg argues to be universal and which Simpson sees as culturally biased apply only at stage five (Schweder, 1982). Lower stages make no appeal to any sort of ethical principles at all. If there is any ideological bias in Kohlberg's system, it therefore affects the scoring only of stage five. But stage five is more or less irrelevant to cross-cultural studies of reasoning in Kohlberg's task, since it is so rarely found even in the Western liberal democracies based on its defining ethic. 'Ideological bias' cannot explain why there are cross-cultural differences in the frequency of the pre-conventional and conventional stages of reasoning among adults, which is what is generally reported.

It's true that in identifying stage five as drawing on universal ethical principles, Kohlberg is very firmly asserting that there are ethical principles that apply universally, and rejecting relativism (that is, the idea that moral codes are ultimately arbitrary, or that there are equally good alternative versions of ethical principles). Those who are studying philosophy alongside psychology will be aware that there has been a very long debate about whether there really are moral absolutes, as Kohlberg assumes (Blackburn, 2001 gives a fascinating and readable introduction). But this debate, and a tolerance (in principle) for relativism, is largely confined to a small group of Western intellectuals. The majority of people in Western industrialized societies and in all other cultures (particularly those where morality is based in religion or on an authoritarian tradition) reject relativism and accept the moral standards of their society as absolute (Turiel, 1998). This, of course, is characteristic of reasoning in all the pre-conventional and conventional stages.

Kohlberg's specific assumption about the nature of universal moral principles follows the work of the philosopher John Rawls (and the ideas were also held by people like Mohandas Gandhi and Martin Luther King). Rawls' basic claim is that universal ethical principles emerge when everybody's perspective is taken into account. His test for whether a system is morally 'just' or not is called the *veil of ignorance* (Rawls, 1971). That is to say, to see whether a system is ethical or not, you should step back from it and ask: if I could have seen this social system before I was born, would I have consented to be born into any role within it *without knowing* (in other words, through a veil of ignorance) which role that would be? Only if the answer is 'yes' is the system ethical. If the druggist in the Heinz story took this test he might find that he would not want to be in the wife's position, and that he too would accept that the right to life supersedes the right to profit.

According to Rawls, applying the 'veil of ignorance' across all societies would necessarily generate universal conclusions about fundamental ethical principles.[4] We simply don't have any evidence sufficient to test this hypothesis. But it's worth noting, in passing, that all the major religions, including Judaism, Christianity, Islam, Buddhism, Hinduism and so on, have come to pretty much the same conclusions on moral fundamentals, despite their very different cultural contexts (Armstrong, 1999). It's also worth noticing that these typically include both principles of social justice emphasized by Kohlberg, and the principles of caring or compassion emphasized by Gilligan.

To some extent, the heat has been taken out of the debate about the 'culture fairness' of Kohlberg's stages of moral development by the discovery that there are far smaller differences between cultures when moral reasoning is assessed by Rest's DTI questionnaire than when it is assessed by the full Kohlberg interview. Studies using the DTI suggest that a shift from conventional to post-conventional reasoning in adulthood is common in all cultures (Gielen and Markoulis, 1994), and that elements of stage five reasoning begin to appear in mid-adolescence. It may be that the higher levels of post-conventional reasoning produced by Western intellectuals in Kohlberg's interview reflect a specific advantage in the ability to produce post-conventional arguments, rather than in the ability to recognize their validity. We do not know what the implications of a cross-cultural difference in the ability to produce, as opposed to recognize, moral principles may be.

---

4   Although Rawls' veil of ignorance may produce universal ethical principles in many cases, it's not clear that it could easily resolve all moral dilemmas. For example, what about the problem of abortion?

Kohlberg, children, everyday dilemmas and distributive justice

Typically, young children produce reasoning at stage one in Kohlberg's moral interviews and older children produce reasoning at stage two. Conventional stages of reasoning do not appear until adolescence, and not always then (Colby et al., 1983; Rest, 1983). However, critics (Damon, 1977; Eisenberg, 1986) pointed out that the dilemmas used in Kohlberg's task are far removed from the young child's world, or even the young adolescent's experience. Moreover, Kohlberg's dilemmas present a choice between two bad acts: for example, letting someone die or stealing, in the Heinz dilemma. What would happen if children were asked to reason about dilemmas in more familiar situations, or given a choice between doing something prosocial or pursuing self-interest?

Eisenberg (1986, 1992) studied children's reasoning in tasks called *prosocial reasoning* tasks such as one in which a boy called Eric is on his way to a birthday party when he comes across a child who has fallen over and hurt his leg. What should Eric do? Why? Analysing children's responses, Eisenberg identified five stages of reasoning which closely correspond to the stages identified by Kohlberg, and which involve progressive increases in empathy and concern for social norms. Paralleling Kohlberg's results, she found that 5-year-olds' responses typically emphasize self-interest ('Eric should go to the party, he doesn't want to miss it') whereas older children are progressively more prosocial and empathic ('Eric should get help for the boy, he doesn't want him to get a broken leg or anything worse'). However, children across many cultures produce more sophisticated forms of reasoning at an earlier age in this kind of task than they do in Kohlberg's interview (Carlo et al., 1996; Eisenberg, 1986).

In a similar project, Damon (1977, 1980) explored children's notions of fairness in sharing things with others (often referred to as *distributive justice* tasks). He told children stories such as one in which a classroom of children spend the day drawing pictures, some drawing skilfully, others not; some working hard, others not. The drawings are sold at a school bazaar, to raise money for the school. But more money is raised than the school needs. How should the leftover money be distributed? In tasks like this, Damon found that children up to about 4 years of age simply assert their own desires ('I should get it because I want it'). Children from 4 to 5 years still assert their own desires, but dress these up a bit with a rationale ('I should have it, I'm the biggest'). Between 5 and 7 years of age, children shift to the belief that everyone deserves an equal share: only complete equality could be fair. At around 8 years of age, children start to focus on deservingness, believing that those who did the most (or the best) work merit a bigger share, or that those who are the most needy (poorest) deserve more, although they easily become bogged down in the problem of assessing the relative merits of these varying claims. Only after about 10 years of age are children able to weigh up competing issues in a coherent and coordinated way. Very similar results are found across a range of cultures (Damon, 1983).

Like Eisenberg, Damon's results broadly confirm that there is a pattern of developmental change in how children reason about moral issues, which closely parallels the pattern identified by Kohlberg. Like Eisenberg, Damon's results demonstrate that the reasoning children produce in relation to familiar issues is more morally sophisticated than the reasoning they produce in thinking about Kohlberg's more esoteric dilemmas. In fact, even Damon's tasks may under-estimate the sophistication of young children's moral reasoning, since children's understanding of money and economics is actually not very good (**Box 12.8**). In situations that are even more familiar (such as issues of social justice in classroom activities), children show a more sophisticated form of reasoning at a younger age than reported by Damon (Thorkildsen, 1989; Thorkildsen and Schmahl, 1997).

box **12.8**

Understanding economics

In one way or another, economic transactions govern all our lives. What do children understand about money? How does this understanding develop?

From an adult perspective, children often seem to have no idea about money. Below 3 years of age, this is literally true: infants are blissfully unaware even of the existence of money. From 3 years of age on, children know that you must give money to get goods. But many 8-year-olds seem to have very little comprehension of where money comes from, or why there isn't enough of it to buy exactly your heart's desire, regarding parental refusals as 'meanness' rather than based in realism.

Grasping the basics

Although young children have generally spotted that shopping involves passing over money, and that you can get money from the bank or cash machines, they often don't understand the nature of these transactions. For example, many 4-year-olds completely misunderstand the transaction involved in shopping. They see money handed over in exchange for goods, and money handed back by the shopkeeper (the change). Unaware of the relative value of notes and coins, they don't understand that money has been spent on the goods. The passing of money back and forth is just a ritual, like saying 'please' and 'thank you'. In fact, at this age, children often believe that a good way to get money is to go shopping (Berti and Bombi, 1988), because the shopkeeper will give you more! They have no idea that money must be *earned* by working, believing that banks just give it to you when you need it.

When do children begin to understand the value of coins and banknotes, or the idea that money must be earned rather than being freely supplied? The answer differs from one social group to another, reflecting the child's experience. For example, a study in Scotland found that, even at 11 years of age, children from relatively poor homes had little grasp on how banks work, whereas those from affluent homes (who had more experience of banking their pocket money) had a far more sophisticated view (Jahoda, 1984).

Wages and prices

Even after they have understood the value of notes and coins, the nature of the transaction involved in shopping and the sad fact that money must be earned by working, young children have a very poor grasp on wages and prices.

For example, they don't understand that some skills command higher wages than others. They generally believe that how much you're paid reflects how hard you work. This creates scant sympathy for the poor, who could easily get richer, in the child's view, by working harder. Equally, they don't understand prices, believing that there is a 'natural' price for everything and that the price you pay for a bar of chocolate (say) is the same price that the shopkeeper paid for it. There is no notion of overheads, profits and so on (Thompson and Siegler, 2000).

At what age do the young begin to understand the economic realities of wages and prices? Again, it depends on their individual experience and the specific information available to them. The fact is that children tend not to be exposed to the kind of information they need to make sense of economics. Few parents really discuss their financial situation (or finance at large) with their children, and economics is not taught in school to children under 11 – and only to the subset of adolescents who later choose that subject for advanced study.

All the evidence suggests that even the young schoolchild could understand the basics of an economic system, given the right information. Explicit discussion of the way money works improves understanding in 5- to 11-year-olds. Even more effective, particularly with 5- to 8-year-olds, is role play in which children play the various roles of the *shopkeeper*, who must both buy and sell goods and pay him/herself and any staff wages, the *shopper*, who must earn the money to buy the goods, and the *manufacturer*, who must pay the wages for the employees who make the goods for the shopkeeper to sell. In negotiating the prices to set and the wages to pay through such games, young children gain considerable insight into economic systems (Echeita, described in Berti and Bombi, 1988).

Mature understanding of economics

Studies in the United States show that children begin to elaborate an informal theory of economics somewhere between 7 and 9 years of age (Thompson and Siegler, 2000). The majority of 9-year-olds understand the point of seeking profits, being commercially competitive, 'buying low and selling high'. Increases in information processing skill seem to play a part in this development, but it's also likely that cultural factors are important (would you expect children in a communist or collectivist society to have the same grip on profit as those in a more market-driven society?).

It seems likely that the vast majority of adolescents have grasped the basics of the economic system and values governing their own society. Exactly how sophisticated this grasp is probably varies from culture to culture, reflecting the complexity of the system in question. In our own complex economic system, even highly educated adults (with the possible exception of professionally trained economists) often have only a rather hazy idea of exactly how the economic system works.

A stage model of moral reasoning?

Research over the past 30 years has broadly confirmed Kohlberg's description of a progressive qualitative change in the forms of reasoning individuals apply to moral dilemmas, even if the age at which given forms of reasoning emerge is not what Kohlberg thought. But does this moral reasoning develop through a succession of clear-cut stages, as Kohlberg's theory implies?

Kohlberg's expectation was that moral reasoning would develop through a succession of qualitatively different stages, each more sophisticated than the one before, each growing out of and superseding its predecessor. This was an extrapolation from Piaget's theory of conceptual development as a whole (see Chapter 6). Piaget claimed that all reasoning is generated by very abstract, general logico-mathematical structures of the mind which determine the quality of reasoning right across the board, and so create coherent and distinctive 'stages' of reasoning. However, the general implication of research over the past 30 years is that Piaget's view of the nature of cognitive development is fundamentally wrong.

There are no abstract, general logico-mathematical structures in the mind. Rather, we reason by drawing inferences from mental models representing what we know about the world (Chapter 6). The knowledge we need to reason is specific to the task in hand. Where we have sophisticated and subtle knowledge we can draw sophisticated and subtle inferences. Where we have hazy or incorrect knowledge our inferences will be much poorer. Knowledge develops patchily. So rather than expecting to see stage-like changes in reasoning (in other words, general changes in the way an individual reasons as a whole), we should expect to see a less coherent pattern of change in the quality of reasoning, reflecting the vagaries of the individual's knowledge and experience.

Studies of problem solving in general have shown that old, unsophisticated ways of reasoning are not swept aside when a new form of reasoning comes along, as Piaget's stage theory asserts. Rather, old strategies coexist alongside new ones, and may even be used more often for quite a while after the new strategy first emerges, reflecting the individual's past experience or the details of the situation (Siegler, 2000). Development is less a matter of discontinuous stage-like change, and more a matter of a gradual shift in the pattern of strategy choices the individual makes until a more sophisticated strategy becomes the dominant one (see Chapter 7). The same is true of moral reasoning. Studies with the DTI show that, at a given time, an individual might solve moral dilemmas predominantly by referring to arguments typical of a given stage (stage two, say) – but will also sometimes draw on arguments typical of both stage one and stage three. Over time reasoning at stage three will tend to become more dominant, but ideas from both of the lower stages are still used from time to time, and ideas from stage four begin to occur too (Rest et al., 1999).

In sum, it seems that moral reasoning develops in a far more fluid and dynamic way than Kohlberg's 'stage' theory assumed. The stages he described capture the quality of change in reasoning through the course of development, and are still useful at that descriptive level. But stages as conceptualized by Piaget are not useful ways of explaining the process of development.

Distinguishing moral and social rules

The notion that reasoning about moral dilemmas reflects specific knowledge of the situation in question rather than general logico-mathematical structures invites a broader view of what is going on in the development of moral thinking than Kohlberg's theory implies. This idea has been most systematically explored by Turiel, who pointed out that there are many different contexts in which children make decisions about whether or not rules should be obeyed, and that it may be a mistake to lump all of these together (as Piaget did) in trying to understand the development of moral reasoning.

Principally, Turiel argued that there is an important difference between the domain of *moral* rules and the domain of *social* rules. In the moral domain, violations of the rules tend to have an inherently bad impact on someone's welfare (hitting someone causes harm, for example), and so can be discovered to be *intrinsically* bad. In the social domain, violations of the rules have effects that are defined by fairly arbitrary social mores. (A streaker running naked through a shop may be shocking, but is not intrinsically harmful. In a nudist colony it would have no impact at all.) Violations of social rules must be discovered to be only *conventionally* bad. As a consequence of this difference, reasoning about moral and social rules focuses on quite different things. Moral reasoning focuses on the problem of understanding what is inherently harmful or not, fair or unfair, compassionate or uncaring. Social reasoning focuses on trying to understand the nature of social organization (see **Box 12.9**).

Children as young as 3 years of age already realize that there is a difference between moral and social rules, regarding transgressions against moral rules (such as hurting someone) as worse than transgressions against social rules (such as wearing inappropriate clothing). By 4 years of age they have understood that social rules are more a matter of negotiation than moral rules, so that a teacher or parent can legitimately waive a social rule, but not a moral one (Turiel, 1987). For example, 4-year-olds believe that it's legitimate for a teacher to allow children to strip on a hot day, although that is normally against the rules, but that it isn't ever legitimate for a teacher to say that it's OK to hit another child.

Moral dilemmas always come in a social context. As a result, in addressing a dilemma children may be activating conceptual understanding *both* in the moral domain *and* in the social domain at the same time, and trying to coordinate these (Turiel, 1998). Moreover, these are

box **12.9**

Understanding social rules

Turiel (1983) explored children's thinking about whether a boy could take on a career that was, at the time, almost exclusively a female occupation (nursing).

- Children of 5 to 8 years of age thought not: that would violate the 'natural order' of things, which shouldn't be changed.
- At around 8 or 9 years of age, children begin to realize that this social convention is in fact arbitrary: anyone can be a nurse, and it's a mistake to take the social convention too seriously.
- By 10 or 11 years, children realize that, although fundamentally arbitrary, social conventions play a useful role in regulating the way society works.
- By late adolescence, they view social conventions as the vital glue holding society together.

This developmental sequence seems to apply across a great many cultures (Turiel, 1998).

not the only domains of knowledge that may be activated in a given situation: purely personal domains of knowledge (I like parties/I don't like the boy who has fallen over) may also be relevant, and need to be coordinated with everything else. Turiel's point is that to understand the development of reasoning about dilemmas, we must understand far more than a child's moral framework.

Turiel believes that, by taking a broader view of the domains of knowledge that people bring to the task, we will also be better able to explain cultural differences in reasoning about moral dilemmas (Turiel, 1998). Different cultures draw the line between different domains in different places, some seeing as a social or personal issues what others take to be moral, and vice versa (Bersoff and Miller, 1993; Wainryb, 1995). An example is that traditional Roman Catholics regarded not eating meat on a Friday as a moral issue, where Protestants viewed it as a purely personal choice. By analysing what each culture regards as being in the moral, social or personal domains, we may be able to tease out a more subtle account of cultural similarities and differences. Turiel believes that the evidence from such analyses to date suggests that the pattern of moral development is the same across all cultures (Turiel, 1998).

Moral reasoning and moral behaviour

At first sight, there seems to be no obvious connection between an individual's level of moral reasoning and his or her likely behaviour. For example, at each of Kohlberg's five stages it's possible to find a reason to either steal or not to steal in the Heinz dilemma (Box 12.6). The development of moral reasoning seems to be more about how you justify what you do than about what you do. But this reflects the fact that Kohlberg's dilemmas involve a choice between two bad acts (letting someone die and stealing, in the Heinz dilemma). Everyday moral reasoning more often involves choices between a good act and a bad one, and has clearer implications for action.

Does what we do, faced with a moral dilemma, reflect our moral judgment? Subbotsky (1993) explored this issue by comparing children's moral judgments about a hypothetical dilemma with their actual behaviour when placed in the same situation. Children from 3 to 11 years of age were told about a boy who had to move ping-pong balls from a bucket to a jar using a shovel: he was not allowed to touch the balls with his hands. But the boy couldn't do it. Left alone with the task he cheated and used his hands, and lied about that when the experimenter came back. Asked what they would have done, virtually 100 per cent of children of all ages said that cheating and lying were wrong and that they would not have done it. But left alone to actually complete the task themselves (with a shovel subtly shaped so that the task was actually impossible), about 40 per cent of the younger children and 25 per cent of older children cheated and lied about that to the experimenter. The children then 'managed' (of course, this was arranged by the experimenter) to observe another child cheat, lie and get away with it, after which they had a second turn at the task themselves. The number of younger children who cheated and lied more than doubled on this second attempt, although about half the older children still behaved honestly and didn't cheat.

Subbotsky's results are strong evidence that moral reasoning does affect actual behaviour, even if the relationship between moral beliefs and behaviour is less than perfect. The results obtained after children had realized that cheating would not be detected or punished are particularly important. You would expect that younger children, whose pre-conventional reasoning focuses solely on self-interest and punishment, would be released by this news to cheat at will – and they were. But the developmental shift from a pre-conventional focus on self-interest to a conventional concern with right behaviour and social obligations for their own sake predicts that older children would be more likely to stick by their moral beliefs even if there is no risk of being caught – and that is what Subbotsky found. The higher the stage of moral reasoning, the more moral values are 'internalized', and so the more likely to be enacted.

Many studies have found that overall, the higher the stage of moral reasoning an individual displays, the more likely he or she is to behave in prosocial ways, and the less likely to behave antisocially. For example, adolescents who score at conventional or post-conventional levels of moral reasoning are more likely to perform altruistic acts and to help the distressed, and are less likely to cheat or to become involved in delinquency (Blasi, 1994; Rest, 1986; Turiel, 1990; Underwood and Moore, 1982). Levels of moral reasoning are also positively related to the development of political understanding and commitment to social justice (see **Box 12.10**).

box **12.10**

Political development

Children are apolitical creatures. They understand little about economic and social systems. What they do understand they take for granted as the 'way things are', the natural and inarguable order of things (see Box 12.9).

Studies in the United States and Europe have found a major change in reasoning about politics at around 14 years of age (Adelson, 1991). This change seems to reflect changes in the individual's factual knowledge about how economics (Box 12.8) and politics work, changes in the ability to take the perspective of other people, and changes in the ability to reason hypothetically (Chapter 6) and so to consider alternatives to the way things are right now.

Despite having considerably more knowledge and reasoning power than younger children, 13-year-olds tend to have a rather naïve view of social systems. For example, they tend to assume that poverty and homelessness are the result of laziness, and curable by hard work (Flanagan, 1995). They view social systems and laws uncritically and in very concrete terms: there is only one perspective – the one embodied in the child's society. Laws stop people stealing or committing murder and are absolutes, not to be challenged, changed or flouted – if people break the law, they should be punished severely. These young adolescents see the law as nothing to do with the individual, so nothing to do with themselves: it simply derives from 'authority' (Adelson, 1986). It's this view that makes the 13-year-old still apolitical.

By contrast, 16-year-olds have a more subtle and nuanced understanding of social systems. They typically understand, for example, that while individuals may contribute to their own poverty and homelessness, aspects of the broader society (such as economic recession) also play a role (Flanagan, 1995). They can take more than one perspective on the system, and so can evaluate it more critically. They understand that political and economic systems are not rigidly fixed, but change and evolve (Adelson, 1986), reflecting the way principles of social justice are understood in a given society. They can think abstractly about social systems, conceptualizing alternatives to the present system, and reflecting on the relative merits of one system or another. They understand that laws are made by people as part of a social contract, and that individuals not only can, but should, influence this process. It's this realization that allows the 16-year-old to become politically aware and politically involved.

Of course, individuals differ in the extent to which they become politically aware and involved. Many factors affect this. For example, individuals differ in the extent to which they develop the ability to think in abstract and hypothetical terms, reflecting both differences in intelligence and differences in education (Chapter 6). They differ in their level of moral development, in their ability to take perspectives and to understand the moral implications. And they differ in their experience of the economic and political system: things undoubtedly look very different to an adolescent growing up in an area of poverty, unemployment and political marginalization from the way they look to an adolescent growing up in middle-class security and bathed in the middle-class expectation of political influence.

Parental styles and the culture within which these are embedded may also affect the development of political awareness and action. *Authoritarian* parenting and communities are associated with a more authoritarian, less questioning approach to politics, and with conventional (stage three and four) moral reasoning. This tends to be associated with a conservative outlook and low involvement in political demonstrations. *Authoritative* parenting and liberal cultures are associated with the development of a more challenging and involved approach to politics, and with a greater probability of post-conventional reasoning, which tends to be more liberal.

Two worrying trends have recently provoked a renewed interest in understanding the development of political awareness and involvement. In the 1960s and 1970s, the young were highly politicized, so that student campuses from Berkeley to Sussex and Paris were bywords for demonstrations and marches. Student activity played a role in foreign policy (changing public attitudes to the Vietnam war, Apartheid and the like), and provided a constant and noisy commentary on the domestic politics of society. Of course, students do still protest in the 21st century, but not on the same scale. This is part or a general trend towards political apathy: in Britain, there is considerable concern about the low numbers of people under 25 years of age who even bother to vote, despite the importance of voting to our democracy. There's a growing need to understand this trend, and how to reverse it.

By contrast with this general apathy, the 21st century has seen an upsurge in the salience of political terrorism: the existence of young men and women prepared to kill and to die for a political point has become a focal issue in society. The phenomenon of terrorism isn't new. For example, Britain was subject for decades to a bombing campaign in connection with the 'troubles' in Northern Ireland, and terrorism by one group or another has been rife in various parts of the Middle East since the end of the Second World War (for that matter, the spark that set off the appalling destruction of the First World War was a terrorist assassination). Nor is terrorism the special province of religious or racial conflict: atheist gangs motivated by communism and drawn from the mainstream population (the Red Brigade in Italy, the Baader-Meinhof gang and Red Army Faction in Germany) have operated in Europe. Purely political terrorism has a long history: for example, it was a frequent tool in campaigns against European colonialism throughout the 20th century. (Britain was subject to such attacks from a great many quarters, including Aden, Malaya, India, and quite a lot of African countries.). What's new is the power of the weapons that terrorists might be willing and able to deploy, and the scale of the destruction they might cause.

The popular perception is that terrorists must be 'mad or bad'. The evidence suggests that they are neither (Horgan, 2005). In fact, they seem to be 'terrifyingly normal'. Willingness to murder for political ends is generally not associated with mental illness or more general criminality. Nor does it necessarily reflect a low level of moral development – for example, Pastor Dietrich Bonhoeffer, who was executed after a failed plot to kill Adolf Hitler, was clearly post-conventional in his reasoning – although it is hard to see how the higher forms of moral reasoning could justify terrorism aimed at killing random civilians.

People don't become terrorists overnight. There is a process through which such an identity develops (Horgan, 2005). The need to understand how this particular brand of politicization develops has never been greater. Although there has been an explosion of research in this area since 2001 (Eigen, 2006; Horgan, 2005), we have only scratched the surface of this problem.

Typically, juvenile delinquents who are involved in fighting, theft, vandalism and the like show a lower level of moral reasoning than their peers, although their empathy skills are much the same (Larden et al., 2006). Delinquents and criminals characteristically show pre-conventional moral reasoning, and specifically reasoning at Kohlberg's stage two (Trevethen and Walker, 1989): fear of punishment may hold the stage-one-thinker back from bad behaviour, but punishment has ceased to be the main consideration at stage two, when personal gratification is more salient. (Antisocial behaviour in the classroom, too, is associated with stage two rather than stage one reasoning – Richards et al., 1992.) There is also a tendency for delinquents to show 'moral distortions' in their reasoning, reacting as though things that are in the moral domain (such as beating people up) were transgressions against social conventions rather than moral rules (Leenders and Brugman, 2005).

That low levels of moral reasoning do play a role in 'enabling' delinquent behaviour is confirmed by the fact that improvements in the level of moral reasoning are associated with a decline in delinquency (Raaijmakers, Engels, and Van Hoof, 2005). Nevertheless, the overall relationship between moral reasoning and behaviour is not very strong (Blasi, 1994; Rest, 1986; Subbotsky, 1993; Turiel, 1990; Underwood and Moore, 1982). Even in adult life, we don't always do what we believe that we ought to do, or what we say we would do (Dunning, 2006; Radke-Yarrow, Zahn-Waxler and Chapman, 1983). We're more likely to behave well if someone is watching (Zarbatany, Hartmann and Gelfand, 1985), or if we're likely to be caught, as changes in our behaviour in the vicinity of police speed cameras testify. And the evidence is that even the higher levels of moral reasoning don't necessarily prevent us from behaving badly: conventional stages of moral reasoning may dispose us toward prosocial behaviour, but reasoning of this kind is not enough to prevent people from committing violent crimes (Stevenson, Hall and Innes, 2004). Sex offenders, for example, are no different from non-offenders in their levels of moral reasoning (Jolliffe and Farrington, 2004).

The fact is that moral reasoning in the abstract is a very different thing from moral reasoning in practice. In the abstract, we can focus purely on moral issues and identify the right course of action. In practice, moral issues are often muddled in with social and personal ones, and there are real cost/gains analyses to consider (Turiel, 1998). In real life we estimate not only what is right or wrong, but what the consequences of behaving morally (or immorally) will be, and how much these matter. In sum: like empathy, moral reasoning is only one facet in a complex process generating prosocial or antisocial behaviour.

Conscience and moral identity

Freud (1940) argued that the most important element in the development of moral behaviour was the development of the 'superego', which in effect internalizes the values and strictures of the parent and acts as a conscience, regulating behaviour. According to Freud, the child's motivation for internalizing the parent in this way was fear – specifically, fear of being castrated. To escape this fear the child identifies with (effectively, 'becomes') the same-sex parent. And since only boys fear castration, only boys develop a moral conscience in this way (see Chapter 1). Freud's views on the origins of conscience were never generally accepted. They were not based on empirical evidence, and have never been substantiated in that way. However, the basic idea that moral behaviour is regulated by individual conscience, and that the development of conscience involves the internalization of moral values, is generally accepted.

The origins of conscience in early childhood

Babies are born with an innate drive to form emotional bonds with their mothers,[5] and it is through this attachment that conscience first begins to develop (Kochanska, 1993, Kochanska and Aksan, 2006). At first, the baby's whole sense of identity is deeply embedded in a symbiotic relationship with the mother, forming what Emde (1988) calls a 'we-self' rather than a separate identity for the child. Through this relationship the child internalizes the mother's views of what is good or bad, fun or frightening and so on (see Chapter 4). Among the many things the child begins to learn through this relationship are his or her own personal worth (high if the mother is warmly responsive, low if she is not), and the appropriateness or otherwise of various behaviours. These things too are internalized, forming the basis of self-esteem and of the moral emotions of guilt, shame and pride. These emotions are the core of conscience.

The quality of the early relationship between mother and baby has important effects on the effectiveness of the development of conscience (Kochanska and Aksan, 2006). The warmer and more sensitively nurturant the mother is towards the child, the better the relationship and the stronger the child's identification with and internalization of the mother's values – in other words, the stronger the development of conscience will be. Maternal sensitivity is particularly important since children with different temperaments react to events in different ways. For example, neurotic, fearful babies can't cope with anything but very gentle remonstrances. More robust criticism may make such an infant

---

[5] There is no evidence or reason to suppose that babies could not just as easily bond to fathers (or any other principal care giver) or that the development of conscience could not as easily grow from those relationships as from a maternal one. But it happens that in our society, as in all others, mothers are the primary care givers for most babies. Only the mother–baby relationship has been studied in this context.

too anxious to learn, so that the development of conscience is undermined (Kochanska, 1993). By contrast, confident, fearless infants may pay too little attention to gentle reproofs and so learn nothing (Kochanska, 1995). All that matters for such children is that the parent gets their attention over issues of right and wrong: fearless babies are strongly motivated to please their mothers, so that all they need for the healthy development of conscience is a secure, cooperative attachment to the mother (Kochanska, 1997).

Two aspects of parenting contribute to the continuing strong development of conscience through childhood and adolescence. These are a warmly nurturant parenting style that encourages a continuing identification between parent and child long after the infant's symbiotic 'we-self' has been replaced by a separate identity (Kochanska and Aksan, 2006; Kochanska and Murray, 2000), and a parental approach that encourages clear values and moral standards through discussion rather than enforcing these in a dictatorial way (Kochanska, Padavich and Koenig, 1996). These are the attributes of the 'authoritative' parenting style (see Chapter 11).

Conscience and the development of moral emotions

The earliest sign of a developing conscience is the emergence of the moral emotions of pride, guilt and shame. These are the 'self-conscious' emotions, the ones that reflect our awareness of other people's evaluations of us. Though closely related, guilt and shame are not the same thing. Guilt involves some realization that one has done something wrong or caused a bad outcome. Shame implies a realization that events reflect badly on one's social standing or self-worth (Olthof et al., 2004). Very young babies don't show these moral emotions, perhaps because they don't yet have a sufficient sense of self (Lewis, 1998). But by about 18 months of age, infants begin to display *pride*: for example, smiling proudly when they achieve something. And at about the same time they also begin to display and differentiate between shame and guilt (Barrett, 2005; Kochanska and Aksan, 2006).

The development of shame and guilt have been studied in more detail than the development of pride, perhaps because we have tended, until recently, to be more interested in how children learn to inhibit bad behaviour than in the role of conscience in fostering good behaviour. The balance of these two emotions, and the situations in which a child experiences each one, have important repercussions for the effectiveness of conscience. This balance is again affected by parenting behaviours. For example, consider the difference between these two reactions to a 3-year-old who has angrily thrown his or her supper on the floor: 'That was a naughty thing to do!' or 'You're such a naughty child!' The first fosters a guilty interpretation of events, the idea of a wrong action that could have been inhibited. The second fosters a shameful interpretation and a general devaluing of the self, without suggesting that there is anything to be done about it.

Through this emphasis on 'wrong action' a guilt orientation conveys an empowering sense of agency, which is a strong foundation on which to build a conscience that can both recognize and control good and bad behaviour. A shame orientation is disempowering: if it is 'I' who am bad, what am I to do? This is a poor foundation for the development of an effective conscience, likely to induce low self-esteem rather than either knowledge of right and wrong or an effective self-control. Children are most likely to develop a constructive guilt interpretation where parents help them to understand the consequences of their actions and encourage them to make amends while communicating a continuing love, and most likely to develop a shame interpretation where they are humiliated, made to feel unworthy and unloved (Tangney and Dearing, 2002).

Although 2-year-olds plainly understand the basic notions of guilt and shame, understanding continues to develop through childhood. For example, 7-year-olds attribute both guilt and shame in situations where 12-year-olds and adults would attribute only guilt (Olthof et al., 2004). Furthermore, the range of situations in which either shame or guilt is experienced expands, as children and adolescents develop more coherent moral understanding and a better insight into how others may see them.

In early childhood, conscience is almost entirely dependent on an internalization of parental values. Progressively, as the child moves into the larger social world of school, the development of conscience is also shaped by the values of the community at large, the peer group, and particularly friends. And as the child's moral reasoning develops, he or she takes on a progressive personal responsibility for the values that the conscience will police.

Moral identity and moral behaviour

By definition, conscience is a mechanism for regulating good and bad behaviour. The moral emotions associated with conscience provide the basic motivation to behave well: pride is a seductive, life-enhancing emotion that is well worth working for. Shame and guilt can be extremely noxious and destructive, and most of us strive to avoid them. And indeed, there is evidence that the stronger a child's experience of these moral emotions the less likely he or she is to engage in antisocial behaviour (van Tijen et al., 2004).

But you and I know that virtually all human beings, child or adult, can and do allow ourselves to do things that go against our consciences, despite the ensuing guilt and shame. Sometimes this tendency seems to be associated with a lack of self-control, an impulsive action or an overwhelming temptation. Anyone might experience an episode of this sort, and have a momentary lapse, although children, adolescents and adults who are characteristically impulsive tend to engage in more antisocial behaviour than others (Caspi and Silva, 1995). But sometimes violations of conscience are quite deliberate and planful, so that an individual deliberately does something he or she will find shameful if it is discovered, and will experience guilt over whether it's discovered or not (having an extra-marital affair is a common adult example, or unfairly advancing our own interests above others in the promotion stakes; acting spitefully to a sibling or peer, or cheating on a test are common childhood examples). A surprising number of offenders in our prisons have also acted against their own conscience in getting there.

Why doesn't conscience act as a stronger control over our moral and immoral behaviour, biasing us more completely and consistently toward prosocial behaviour? One answer may lie in the conflicting demands of the different domains that govern social behaviour (Turiel, 1998): we are endlessly balancing the moral demands of conscience against those of personal interest and social convention. But in recent years there has been increasing interest in the possibility that, although most children and adolescents have *internalized* the moral values of their parents and community so that they can feel the moral emotions appropriately and can use these to regulate behaviour, only a few have *positively embraced* these values as part of their own personal identity in a way which gives them an overriding motivational force. To express this in Freudian terms, virtually all of us have developed a superego which monitors our behaviour and disrupts anything too bad. But only a few of us have whole-heartedly *become* the superego to the extent that this is our predominant mode of reacting.

Overall, adolescents who have achieved an integrated personal identity (see Chapter 10) are more likely to behave prosocially than those who have not yet done so (Hardy and Kisling, 2006). When this integrated identity is explicitly constructed around moral values, in other words, is specifically a moral identity, there is an even stronger commitment than normal to obeying the dictates of conscience and hence to prosocial behaviour (Hardy and Carlo, 2005). This makes good sense: human beings strive to find an integrated sense of self, of who I am. To experience the self as fragmented and inconsistent is noxious (see Chapter 10). If 'being a moral person' is a key part of your identity, then to go against the dictates of conscience becomes a threat to personal coherence. By contrast, if you haven't got an explicitly moral identity to protect, then the odd violation of conscience to serve other needs poses less threat to personal coherence.

As yet, there is relatively little research on the development of moral identity, or on its effects on behaviour. Many questions remain to be explored. But the suggestion that the formation of a moral identity extends the motivational power of conscience as a force for moral behaviour (Hardy and Carlo, 2005) offers an exciting new insight into development in this area.

'Saints' and 'moral exemplars'

Research on moral identity offers not only the possibility of a better understanding of how conscience gains more force in some individuals than in others, but also the possibility of understanding the moral motivation of exemplary people: the individuals conspicuous for their outstandingly caring behaviour, altruism or commitment to social justice. Is such 'saintliness' the product of a particular form of moral identity?

Of course, to truly answer this question we would need to directly study outstanding individuals, people like Mother Teresa, Martin Luther King, Nelson Mandela, those who have given their lives in one way or another to help others or oppose injustice. Such people are hard to study, not least because it's hard to gather a big enough sample to draw any general conclusions (but see Monroe, 2006).

However, there is a growing body of research that is directly looking at outstandingly prosocial individuals (called 'moral exemplars'), identified as those who are proactively involved in compassionate or social justice work for charities and other organizations, voluntary or otherwise. This work is so new that there are few results as yet. But it's already clear that moral exemplars typically have a more highly integrated representation of moral values than ordinary mortals (in other words, a more coherent moral understanding), and that this is central to their identity (Matsuba and Walker, 2004; Reimer and Wade-Stein, 2004).

Typically, moral identity is not a description of the present self in these exemplary individuals: that is to say, they don't have an idealized view of themselves. Rather, their moral values are their basic code of conduct for living, providing a powerful motivating force driving their behaviour. These values characteristically involve an active sense of personal responsibility for social justice and for the welfare of others. This responsibility is impartial, embracing strangers and out-groups rather than merely friends and neighbours, which suggests that it involves the very principled ethical stand characteristic of post-conventional moral reasoning.

One other intriguing discovery is worth mentioning in relation to outstanding prosocial behaviour. There is some research that suggests that the *compassionate love* for others and for humanity as a whole that is characteristic of outstandingly prosocial and altruistic individuals is separate from empathy (Sprecher and Fehr, 2005). This amounts to the suggestion that there is a whole dimension of moral emotion which hasn't yet been studied. The idea that compassionate love is 'something different' would have been no surprise to the ancient world: the Greeks had four different words for love, one of which, *agape*,[6] means an active, selfless and compassionate love for others. It is *agape* that is advocated by every major religion as the basis for a correct concern for the welfare of others and for social justice. It's interesting, from a developmental point of view, that religious leaders don't view this compassionate love as a warm, fuzzy emotion but as a spiritual discipline which is difficult to achieve and which must be worked for: something more infused with self-control than with spontaneity.

Individual differences in prosocial and antisocial tendencies

Why is it that one baby grows up to be an upright and responsible citizen and another grows up to be a crook or a violent and dangerous criminal? This is really the 'million dollar' question for research on the development of pro- and anti-social behaviour. The current consensus among researchers is that both the upright, responsible individual and the violent, delinquent one are shaped by the very same developmental processes. These are no less than the normal processes that shape our social, cognitive and emotional development as a whole, in other words, the sum of the developmental processes which have been described throughout this book, working together in one complex dynamic system.

One way to conceptualize the complex cascade of events through which babies grow up to be either responsibly prosocial (**Figure 12.1**) or delinquently antisocial (**Figure 12.2**) is to look at the overall trajectory of a life (Sampson and Laub, 1993). Both of the life trajectories depicted in these two figures are determined by genetics, by parenting practices and the circumstances of the family, by the child's experience of schooling, interaction with peers and community, by career and relationship histories. It's the differing detail in each of these factors that contributes to the contrasting outcomes.

Genetics

Twin studies suggest that both prosocial (Matthews et al, 1981) and antisocial (Coie and Dodge, 1998) behaviour have a genetic component. That is to say, identical (monozygotic) twins are more similar in their tendency to be prosocial or antisocial than non-identical (dizygotic) twins are. It is not that babies are born inherently 'good' or 'bad'. Rather, the particular pattern of the child's genetic legacy creates biases that can affect the overall trajectory of his or her life. Already, at the moment of

---

6   The other three are *eros*, which is sexual love; *storge*, which is the love shared between family members; and *philios*, which is the love you might have for knowledge, say, or for friends and companions.

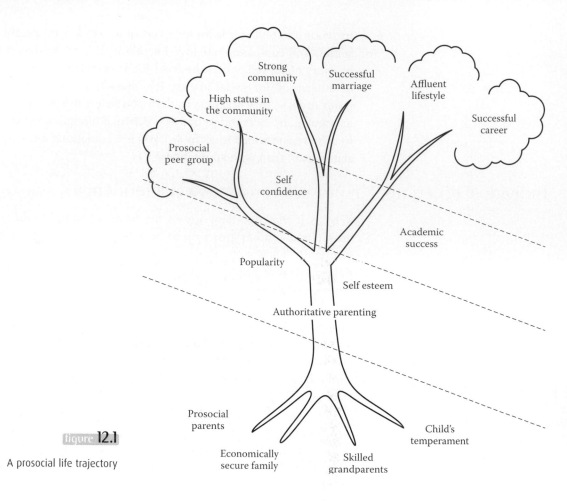

figure 12.1

A prosocial life trajectory

conception, the dice are stacked in favour of some individuals and against others.

The child's inheritance

Many genetic tendencies can affect the way a life develops. For example, physical attractiveness, the basic shape of your face and body, is strongly influenced by genes. The attractive tend to be more popular than the unattractive, and to enjoy a more positive social trajectory as a result (Boyatzis, Baloff and Durieux, 1998). Intelligence too is influenced by heredity, and is a factor in the child's school success, which will in turn determine the career paths open to the individual, the opportunities for economic success as well as the sophistication of both perspective taking and moral reasoning that is likely to be achieved. These things can affect the trajectory of a life for good or ill in a variety of ways.

However, the most important genetic legacy in relation to pro- or antisocial development is the child's innate temperamental disposition (see Chapter 4). New-born babies' temperaments differ on two over-arching dimensions: *reactivity* (in other words, how irritable or easily

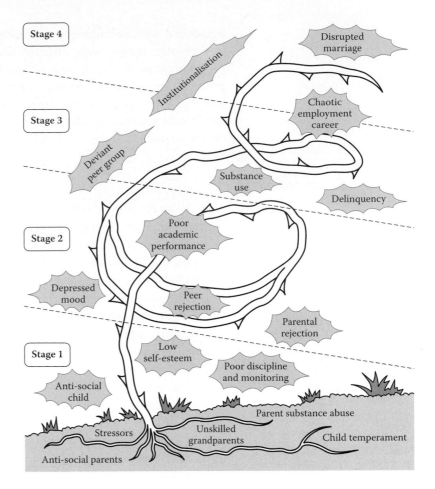

figure 12.2

An antisocial life trajectory
Source: G. Patterson, J. Reid and T. Dishion,
Antisocial Boys (Eugene, Oregon: Castilia Press).
© 1992. Reproduced with permission from
Castilia Press.

aroused the baby is) and *self-regulation* (in other words, how easily soothed the baby is). 'Difficult' babies who are highly irritable and hard to soothe are less likely to engage in prosocial behaviour in later life than 'easy-going' babies who are calm and easy to soothe (Eisenberg and Fabes, 1998), and they are more likely to grow up to engage in antisocial behaviour than are the easygoing (Rothbart and Bates, 1998).

'Difficult' babies who frequently express strong negative emotions (distress, anger) tend to be aggressive in infancy, and to continue to show this trait through childhood and adolescence (Bates et al., 1991; Olson et al., 2000; Rothbart and Bates, 1998). They are more likely to be involved in delinquency and fighting in late childhood and adolescence, and to be involved in aggression, violence and criminal behaviour in adult life (Caspi et al., 1995; Caspi and Silva, 1995).

A difficult temperament lays the groundwork for an antisocial life trajectory in various ways. Innate dispositions are stable through our lives (Rothbart and Bates, 1998), so that an individual who has a tendency to be irritable, impulsive and to lack self-control in infancy is likely to show the same tendencies in adolescence, and these dispositions are directly associated with delinquency and antisocial behaviour. Perhaps more importantly, babies with difficult dispositions are harder and less rewarding to parent. They are less likely than the easy-going to experience positive and secure attachment relationships with their parents in early infancy (Van den Boom and Hoeksma, 1994). The quality of this first attachment relationship plays a vital role in shaping the trajectory of the child's personality and social development as a whole (as will be discussed below).

Genes and families

As if the unfairness of different genetic legacies were not bad enough, the fact is that whatever genetic legacy the baby carries is also very likely also present in his or her parents. An attractive, intelligent and easy-going baby probably has attractive, intelligent and easy-going parents, and is likely to be born into a well-founded family which will foster his or her development in positive ways. An unattractive, not very bright and difficult baby may well have unattractive, not very bright and difficult parents, and is likely to be born into a family with economic, personal and social problems, all factors associated with poor parenting and poor developmental outcomes (Cicchetti and Toth, 1998; Emery and Laumann-Billings, 1998).

The extent to which babies' lives are already set on a trajectory toward antisocial behaviour and delinquency by their family background even before they are born is emphasized by a study aimed at identifying risk factors for delinquency and potential interventions to disrupt these risks (Sutton, Utting and Farrington, 2006). The findings of this study are summarized in Table 12.1. As this figure makes clear, the disadvantaged baby is also more likely than his or her more fortunate peer to be exposed to damaging substances while in the womb, from cigarette smoke to alcohol and drugs or high levels of stress hormones, all of which can damage fetal development (see Chapter 2). He or she is also more likely to suffer difficulties or damage at birth.

Parents and families

Even more vital than genetics to the general trajectory of a life is the quality of relationship the baby establishes with his or her parents, and the style of parenting the family adopts. Good parenting can mitigate the effects of a difficult temperament (Van den Boom and Hoeksma, 1994; Wachs, 1994), establishing a positive relationship with the infant and increasing the probability of a positive life trajectory. Poor parenting can derail the promise of the most easy-going of temperaments.

Early parenting and pro- or antisocial life trajectories

Parenting influences moral development in a number of fundamental ways, as we have begun to see through the course of this and earlier

table 12.1 A multi-factorial approach to an antisocial life trajectory
(Risk factors are shown in bold, protective factors in italics.)

Source: C. Sutton, D. Utting and D. Farrington (2006) Nipping criminality in the bud.
The Psychologist 19, pp. 470–5. Reproduced with permission from the BPS.

	Community/ school	Parenting	Personal experiences	Promising interventions
Pregnancy	**Neglected neighbourhood, low income, poor housing.**	**Stress, smoking in pregnancy.** *Having someone to confide in.*	**Prematurity or obstetric problems. Genetic disposition.** *Genetic disposition.*	*Active and ongoing support by a trained person in whom the mother can confide and trust.*
0–2 years	**Socio-economic stress.**	**Post-natal depression, harsh parenting style, rejection, hitting/frequent smacking, low level of stimulation.** *Bonding with child.*	**Infant's temperament, impaired attachment, ADHD – hyperactivity.** *Resilience. Strong attachment to at least one parent or carer.*	*Baby massage. Front pack baby carrier. Home visiting programme. Effective help with post natal depression.*
3–8 years	**Low achievement in primary school; behavioural problems/bullying; school disorganization.** *Strong school ethos.*	**Problems, inconsistency in managing child, mental ill health, hitting, much smacking.** *Authoritative parenting, opportunities/skills and praise for being 'helpful'.*	**Tantrums/aggressiveness, witnessing domestic violence, poor diet.** *Praise for good behaviour.*	*Parent management training. High-quality early childhood education.*
9–13 years	**Low informal school control, truancy.** *Opportunity for involvement in community issues.*	**Having a convicted parent at age 10.** *Firm supervision of child's whereabouts.*	**Many behaviour problems, physical/emotional/ sexual abuse, ADHD compounded by aggressive behaviour, antisocial peers, early initiation into offending.**	*Tutoring/whole class/school approaches. Functional family therapy. Cognitive-behavioural approaches.*
Circumstances of offending behaviour	**Unsupervised setting (eg poor street lighting, unlocked vehicle, previously burgled house).** *Close supervision.*		**Mood state (e.g. perception of rejection, resentful, angry). Cognitive and perceptual processes, cost–benefit analysis (e.g. perceived low risk of being caught).**	

chapters. The way our parents react to us provides us with our very first information about ourselves and others, and the way human beings are. This earliest social experience sets the tone for the expectations we have about self and other which come to guide our behaviour, creating the characteristic patterns which we call 'personality' (Chapter 10). Babies who are treated sensitively develop positive expectations, whereas those who are treated less kindly develop negative expectations. Positive expectations generate positive behaviours, which are generally rewarded by others – reinforcing the child's original positive expectations and tendency to behave positively. Negative expectations generate negative behaviours, which generally evoke negative responses from others – reinforcing the child's negative expectations and tendency to behave negatively. Thus in each case, the expectations about self and other set up in early infancy give rise to a self-perpetuating cycle (the 'reaction–evocation cycle': see Chapter 10), through which a given orientation to the world, positive or negative, is firmly established by about 3 years of age.

One key factor that disposes an infant to antisocial behaviour and delinquency later in life is a tendency to see hostility where none exists and to react with aggression where others would not have done so (Larden et al., 2006). Such *cognitive distortions* seem at first to be curious aberrations. But in fact, they are the natural product of the reaction–evocation cycle set up in early infancy. An infant who has experienced little kindness from parents, and maybe even a degree of violence and rejection, naturally learns to expect hostility from other people he or she meets. Expecting hostility, the child over-interprets small evidences and finds the aggression he or she is expecting. Believing hostility and aggression to be normal, the child naturally retaliates. The hostile reaction that this then provokes in other people confirms the child's expectations about human nature, reinforcing the cognitive distortion and entrenching the tendency to react aggressively in future (Quiggle et al., 1992). This explains why hitting, smacking, rejection and harsh parenting in the first 2 years of life can have a major impact in creating an antisocial trajectory for a child's whole life.

A good quality of attachment between infant and mother creates positive social expectations for the baby, and is a cornerstone of a prosocial life trajectory. It also lays the foundation for an effective conscience: warm attachments encourage infants to internalize the mother's views of right and wrong. Sensitive parenting shapes the moral emotions of pride, guilt and shame in functional ways that foster self-esteem and an empowering sense of agency (Kochanska and Aksan, 2006). Secure attachments help infants to learn to handle and regulate strong emotions, curbing the impulsiveness associated with antisocial behaviour and avoiding being overwhelmed by their feelings. It is this emotional control that fosters a prosocial sympathetic reaction to empathy with others in distress, rather than a self-protective personal distress (Zahn-Waxler, 1991; Mikulincer and Shaver, 2005).

By contrast, the infant exposed to insensitive or harsh parenting and a poor-quality attachment learns negative social expectations. He or she may discover a debilitating shame and helplessness rather than the bases for an effective conscience, and learn only that strong emotions are dangerous in other people and dangerous to experience yourself: associated with trouble. This is no basis for prosocial sympathy.

Moral development and parenting styles beyond infancy

Already, by the end of infancy, parenting styles have had a major effect in setting the overall tone of the infant's life trajectory. The impact of parenting styles continues through childhood and adolescence (see Chapter 11). Authoritative parents who are warmly nurturant, set clear moral standards and encourage these through explanation and debate, produce children who show strong development in all the factors disposing toward prosocial and against antisocial behaviour (Parke and Buriel, 1998; Thompson, 1998). The safe arena such parenting provides for the discussion of feelings and moral values encourages the development of both empathic insight and moral reasoning. The encouragement for autonomous thinking fosters the development of a strong personal responsibility, conscience and moral identity.

By contrast, parents who are authoritarian tend to crush the development of autonomy, personal responsibility and moral identity, even if they provide clear moral guidance. Permissive and neglectful parents provide little guidance for the child in developing either prosocial empathy or coherent moral reasoning. They do little to help children curb impulsiveness and develop emotional control. The serious lack of supervision provided by the neglectful parent is particularly associated with the development of delinquency (see Table 12.1).

Are there crimogenic families?

There is a tendency for antisocial behaviour to run in families. For example, one of the key risk factors for delinquency is whether or not a 10-year-old child has a parent with a criminal conviction (Sutton et al., 2006). Do families actively foster a criminal career?

There are many reasons that delinquency might occur in a family generation after generation, even though there is no deliberate encouragement for this. For example, the members of a family tend to share the same socio-economic niche, the same standards of housing, the same career opportunities (or lack of them), the same communities and social experiences. Poverty and deprivation are strongly associated with antisocial behaviour (Sutton et al., 2006). Simply 'being in the same place' in this way might be enough to ensure similar life trajectories in the members of a family, even if there is no active effort to engage a child in delinquency, or even active efforts to prevent this.

Socio-economic stress makes for bad parenting (Emery and Laumann-Billings, 1998), and bad parenting tends to be repeated in successive generations (Fonagy, Steele and Steele, 1991; Levine et al., 1991). Here is a second factor through which delinquency might inadvertently be fostered in successive generations of a family. Harsh and cold parenting tends to produce children who are aggressive, who have behavioural problems and who go on to become criminally delinquent in later life (Deater-Deckard and Dodge, 1997; DeKlyen et al., 1998; McCord, 1991; Rothbaum and Weisz, 1994), and who believe that aggression is an appropriate social strategy (Dodge et al., 1995).

Of course, parents do provide role models for what is or is not an appropriate life-style, so that criminal parents can provide a criminal model for their offspring. But it's not clear how much impact this has on the child's criminal behaviour. Those successfully engaged in crime tend to be rather discreet about it, so that the children of a burglar may not be aware of his activities. Those unsuccessful in crime tend to be imprisoned, scarcely presenting an attractive model to follow.

Direct studies suggest that the tendency to engage in antisocial and delinquent behaviour is more strongly influenced by siblings and peers than by parents (Fagan and Najman, 2005; Rowe, Rodgers and Meseck-Bushey, 1992; Snyder, Bank and Burraston, 2005). Siblings are often the first to initiate the young into subversive or delinquent behaviour (Fagan and Najman, 2005). But ultimately, it is the peer group that has the greatest effect.

Communities and peer groups

Standards of behaviour can vary enormously between different societies. For example, the traditional societies of the Papago tribe of North American Indians or the Aitutaki from Polynesia were characterized by striking levels of prosocial behaviour, while social behaviour in certain tribes in Uganda was (at least historically) strikingly nasty and antisocial (Eisenberg and Fabes, 1998). Equally large differences between societies are evident in the history of Europe in the 20th century, and in different parts of the world today.

These differences in the 'moral climate' of a culture probably reflect a great many factors, from the narratives and myths different cultures use to make sense of the world (for example, the religious, philosophical or scientific narratives about the origins and meaning of life) to the material circumstances of society. When times are hard, human beings focus more on the basic needs of survival and less on the 'higher' needs of morality (Bjorklund and Pellegrini, 2000; Maslow, 1970). Even geography can influence the way the moral values of a society develop (Padfield, 2000), for example by affecting whether survival depends more on collective obedience to a central authority (which fosters an authoritarian and often harsh moral climate) or more on independent initiative (which fosters liberal democracy and autonomy).

Whatever the cause, the fact that societies do have a distinctive moral climate is evidence enough that the prevailing expectations for prosocial and antisocial behaviour within a community must influence the way these things develop in individuals (Eisenberg and Fabes, 1998). The surrounding culture sets the tone for the moral, social and personal rules which families and communities teach to, and expect of children (Turiel, 1998).

'Just' and 'unjust' communities

In industrialized societies, antisocial behaviour and delinquency are concentrated in disadvantaged communities living on the margins of society: communities characterized by poor housing, high unemployment or low income, frank poverty, low levels of education and skill, alcohol and drug abuse (Sutton et al., 2004, 2006). Many of these factors have a direct effect on families, producing the kinds of poor parenting that would be likely to foster the development of antisocial behaviour in the young whatever community the family live in (Amato and Gilbreth, 1999). But some researchers believe that there is also an 'add-on' effect that comes directly from living in a community characterized by the low moral climate typical of such disadvantaged groups, over and above family and individual effects. For example, Kohlberg suggested that while living in a 'just' or morally positive community would foster high levels of prosocial behaviour, living in an 'unjust' community would discourage prosocial behaviour and encourage antisocial behaviour (Power, Higgins and Kohlberg, 1989).

Kohlberg explored his belief that living in a society with a positive moral climate would foster the development of moral reasoning and prosocial behaviour by setting up a series of programmes within schools to create 'just' communities. As predicted, exposure to such a community led to increased levels of prosocial behaviour (Power et al., 1989). Of course, it would be unethical to reverse this experiment and place young people in a community with a worse moral climate than their own to see if prosocial behaviour declined and antisocial behaviour increased, as the theory predicts. We can only test this second prediction by studying naturally existing communities.

To demonstrate that the moral climate of a community has an effect on the development of pro- and antisocial behaviour over and above the more direct effects of disadvantage, you must 'control' for disadvantage in some way. That is to say, you must compare the moral development of individuals from equally disadvantaged backgrounds. It is immediately apparent, when you do this, that not every child who grows up in a community characterized by an antisocial moral climate becomes antisocial or delinquent. The key difference between those who do and those who don't seems to lie in the family. In the most difficult of circumstances there are always some families who are prosocial, and who parent their children effectively. Such families typically protect their young from the surrounding community, providing strict discipline and close supervision (Lamborn, Dornbusch and Steinberg, 1996).

It is neglectful families that provide low levels of discipline and low levels of supervision whose offspring are most likely to become delinquent (Sutton et al., 2004, 2006). Is this delinquency simply the result of poor discipline and poor parenting, or does it also reflect greater exposure to an antisocial community?

One useful source of information about the effects of communities on pro- or anti-social behaviour comes from studies of imprisoned delinquents. Individuals who perceive the moral climate of the institution in which they were incarcerated to be low are more likely to behave in antisocial ways than those who perceive the moral climate to be high (Brugman and Aleva, 2004), whatever their personal level of moral development. This is clear evidence for an 'add-on' effect of the moral climate of a community, over and above family or personal factors, in creating antisocial behaviour.

There is some evidence that it is specifically the *degree* of exposure to antisocial behaviour in the community that affects the tendency for an individual to act in antisocial ways him or herself. For example, among adolescent boys from equally disadvantaged backgrounds, the more knife fights the individual has witnessed, the more likely he is to carry a knife and use it (Patchin et al., 2006). It is not just the local community that exposes the young to antisocial behaviour: television, too, allows the potential for children to witness a great deal of antisocial behaviour (**Box 12.11**). The more violent television children watch, the more likely they are to grow up to be violent themselves (Huesmann, 1986).

Peer groups

In adolescence, the peer group plays a more important part in shaping behaviour and identity than the surrounding community at large (Chapter 11), although that community may determine what kinds of peer group are available to join. Peer group membership is a vital element of adolescent development (Rubin, Bukowski and Parker, 1998).

Birds of a feather flock together: the members of a peer group are attracted to one another by their similarities of values, attitudes and behaviours. Individuals already set on a prosocial life trajectory will thus be attracted to peer groups of similarly prosocial friends, who will reinforce their positive values and prosocial behaviours. By contrast, individuals already set on an antisocial life trajectory will be attracted to peer groups of similarly hostile, negative and antisocial friends (Rubin et al. 1998). Shared attitudes and values then act to reinforce antisocial perceptions and activities (Coie and Dodge, 1998). Peers act as role models for one another. Individuals with antisocial friends are very much more likely to be involved in delinquent activities than those without. In particular, adolescents who join delinquent gangs tend to become increasingly delinquent (Lahey et al., 1999).

box **12.11**

Television and antisocial behaviour

There is a great deal of antisocial behaviour on television. It's been estimated that even before the 9 pm 'watershed', there are an average of three to five acts of violence and eight sexual interactions in every hour broadcast – and these categories often overlap, depicting acts of sexual violence. On average, children watch seven or more hours of television each week, much of it without adult supervision. Television is often used as a 'babysitter' while busy parents deal with domestic chores, and as the cost of electrical goods comes down, younger and younger children have their own televisions in their rooms and are free to choose any channel they like. And that means that, between the ages of 5 and 7, children have watched an average of 6000 sexual scenes and 3000 acts of violence – and if we counted acts of verbal assault, bullying and harassment it would be a great deal more.

The theoretical probability that behaviour is influenced by what is seen on television is strong. Studies in the 1970s showed that watching aggressive acts toward an inflatable doll disposed children to act more aggressively to the doll when given an opportunity to do so (Bandura, 1973). And in fact, longitudinal studies have found that the more violent television children watch, the more likely they are to grow up to be violent and delinquent themselves (Huesmann, 1986). Boys in particular are affected: those who had watched a lot of violent television by 8 years of age were four times as likely to be delinquent in their 20s than those who hadn't. Similar results have been found for children who play violent video games (Anderson and Bushman, 2001). Such data suggest that television is a potent provider of antisocial role models. It may even be the source of some of the more deviant desires of disturbed offenders.

Can some crimes be explained simply as a copycat of violence seen on television or film? This theory is often advanced in the media. For example, after the horrific abduction and murder of 2-year-old Jamie Bulger by two 10-year-olds (Venables and Thompson) in 1993, it was widely reported that the children had copied a murder on a violent video that they had watched that week. There were some parallels between the video and the murder, so that it might have played a role in their crime. But many other children have watched the same film without copying the crime, suggesting that the film is not sufficient in itself to trigger such violence. In fact, both Venables and Thompson came from very disadvantaged homes in which abuse and violence were common. It is likely that this background was a key factor in their disposition to delinquency and violence. Exposure to violent film was only one element in many.

Explaining evil

As we've seen, the ordinary processes of social development can act to produce either a prosocial or an antisocial life trajectory. The dice may be stacked against some individuals from the start, but as Table 12.1 shows, the risk factors for a delinquent life trajectory can potentially be addressed and turned around by appropriate interventions (Sutton et al., 2004, 2006). There seems to be nothing 'special' about antisocial behaviour: we need nothing outside the ordinary processes of development to explain it.

It's easy to accept this view when we are thinking of 'ordinary' delinquency and criminality: for example, of vandalism, theft, fighting and the like. But there are crimes of violence that seem so shocking that it's hard to accept that they are the product of ordinary developmental processes. Could ordinary developmental processes produce sadistic serial murderers such as Fred West, who tortured and murdered at least 12 girls and women in Britain in the 1980s and 1990s, or Jeffrey Dahmer, who murdered at least 17 boys and men in the United States between 1989 and 1991, committing sexual and cannibalistic acts? Can ordinary developmental processes explain the behaviour of medical professionals such as Dr Harold Shipman, who murdered dozens, possibly hundreds, of his patients, or various nurses who have serially murdered patients in their 'care'?

Ordinary people can do extraordinary and horrible things. The first to demonstrate this experimentally was Stanley Milgram (1974), who found that in certain circumstances, ordinary people will administer increasingly powerful electric shocks to others even though their victim (of course, it was really a stooge acting a part, although the participants in the study didn't know this) screamed and begged for mercy and eventually 'collapsed' and 'became unconscious'. Ordinary people can also 'dehumanize' others and withhold empathy from them (Harris and Fiske, 2006), which may explain why whole communities can sometimes behave in horrific ways to religious or racial 'out-groups'. Violent criminals such as rapists certainly withhold empathy from their victims in this way, although there seems to be nothing wrong with their general ability to empathize or their awareness that their actions are wrong (Fernandez and Marshall, 2003; Jolliffe and Farrington, 2004). And when very angry or afraid, desperate, exhausted, drunk or drugged, ordinary people can lose control and impulsively lash out in violence or take what isn't theirs. In the right circumstances (a war, say) most of us could probably execute acts of vandalism, theft, even abduction, torture and the murder of innocent children – although we might call these things 'sabotage', 'commandeering' 'capture', 'interrogation' and 'collateral damage'. The narratives we create about our actions play a crucial role in determining what we do, allowing ordinary people to do extraordinary things. Often, those who commit outrageous crimes have a narrative story which seems, at least to them, to justify their actions.

In sum, ordinary psychological processes can probably account for more of the kinds of antisocial behaviour which seem so shocking than we would like to think. But even so, there are things left to explain. Where does the idea of abducting, torturing and killing a complete stranger for sexual or other forms of gratification come from? What motivates some people who ruminate on such ideas to act out their fantasies while others merely write a novel or make a film about it? Where do the narratives which enable some people to act out cruel fantasies come from?

There aren't any easy answers to questions like these. There is some evidence that serious evil is associated with disorders such as antisocial personality disorder (psychopathy, see Chapter 9), or with mental illness or neurological damage. Such things undoubtedly do affect the way the individual reasons and behaves, making grossly deviant behaviour more likely. But such factors can only provide a partial explanation. Only a minority of those with neurological damage, mental illness or even anti-social personality disorder ever commit crimes of any sort. To explain why some do commit atrocious crimes, we still need to understand the cognitive and emotional processes that motivated and enabled their actions. As we understand more about the processes that generate behaviour as a whole, we may come to understand more about the general psychological processes involved in crimes of exceptional evil. But ultimately, we may never understand the unique workings of the minds of individual serial killers and the like.

A dynamic systems perspective

The research reviewed in this chapter reveals that the development of good – or bad – behaviour is a complex process. Empathy, moral reasoning, conscience and moral identity (or the lack of these things) all contribute to our propensity to behave prosocially (or antisocially). Our own individual dispositions, the family we grow up in, the peers we associate with, the community and circumstances in which we live, the socio-economic situation and the cultural messages we are exposed to all contribute to whether our overall life trajectory will develop along a prosocial or an antisocial path.

The way these multiple factors combine to produce good or bad behaviour is far from straightforward. Two individuals from the same family may grow up in very different ways – and it is notorious that policemen and the criminals they chase often come from the same social background, even the same social community. Furthermore, individuals are not 'all of a piece'. The classic example is the Nazi guard who callously shovels other people's children into a gas oven all week but who is a caring father and youth leader in his own community at weekends; and it has also been known for individuals renowned for their saintly compassion and adherence to high ethical principles to behave badly to their juniors.

How can we come to a better understanding of the processes through which prosocial and antisocial behaviour or life trajectories develop? Some researchers believe that the only approach capable of capturing all the complexities involved is dynamic systems theory (Lewis, 2004; see Chapters 2 and 3). As yet there are relatively few analyses applying this approach in the moral domain, and all focus specifically on the detail of how antisocial behaviour emerges from dynamic interactions within families, between peers and within communities (Granic and Dishion,

2003; Granic and Patterson, 2006; Lewis, 2004; Whaley, 2003). This research is intriguing, and is already altering how we phrase questions for research and where we look for answers. It's worth exploring the broader implications of a dynamic systems approach to research on moral development.

A dynamic systems approach presents a very different picture of the nature of moral development from that proposed by previous theories. Where most researchers through the 20th century looked for explanations of moral behaviour in terms of a single factor (empathy, say, or moral reasoning, or the development of conscience), and explored how individual factors (such as the family, or poverty, or the peer group) influenced the trajectory of a life, dynamic systems theory begins from the assumption that behaviour is never the product of a single factor, a single influence. Rather, behaviour is always the product of complex interactions between many different factors which coalesce to form a single dynamic system. This assumption has many important implications.

From a dynamic systems perspective, the system that generates moral development consists of the child in interaction with his or her social and physical environment. This system comprises all that characterizes the individual (ability, temperament, past history, desires, hopes, fears and so on) and all that characterizes his or her context (the specific social relationships, community, culture involved; the physical circumstances – the opportunities available, constraints on activities, whether resources are plentiful or scarce and so on). All of these factors combine to determine what psychological functions and behaviours will emerge at any one moment. The first implication of research in this vein is, then, that to understand how behaviour emerges we have to examine the whole context in which that behaviour is situated.

From this dynamic systems perspective we would not expect moral judgments (say) to determine moral behaviour. We would not even expect moral judgments to be consistent across time and situations. Rather, we would expect both judgment itself and the extent to which that judgment plays a leading part in determining behaviour to emerge from the complex dynamics of the situation in hand. Kohlberg predicted that an individual who had achieved a given level of development (stage five moral reasoning, say) would reason consistently at that level and would act on the principled ethic involved. A dynamic systems approach suggests instead that an individual who can produce and act on stage five moral reasoning when faced with a starkly moral dilemma, or when asked to speculate in principle, might well make judgements more typical of the 'tit for tat' of stage two in certain personal contexts (in deciding whether to make a small personal sacrifice to help an acquaintance, say), or might disregard a principled ethical judgment altogether if acting on it would endanger his or her own child. In each case, reactions are shaped by the dynamics of the situation as a whole, rather than simply by the individual's capacity for sophisticated moral reasoning.

Nor, from a dynamic systems perspective, would we expect the ability to empathically understand other minds to determine moral behaviour, or to consistently determine our own sympathy toward others, as Hoffman predicted that it would. The extent to which we feel with, want to help or actually do behave compassionately toward another person emerges from the dynamics of the situation as a whole. I may feel a vast sympathy and desire to help someone who has had a car crash, for example – although these sentiments might well evaporate if it turns out that the parked car they have carelessly crashed into is mine! Equally, even conscience is not predicted to consistently dictate moral behaviour from a dynamic systems perspective. Factors in the situation will determine the extent to which we even notice that issues of conscience may be relevant, and also the extent to which we are prepared to let those issues override other considerations of personal pleasure, safety or even convenience.

Overall, what we know about human beings fits better with a dynamic systems view than with the views of theorists such as Kohlberg or Hoffman. Moral behaviour (and for that matter social behaviour as a whole) is far more plastic, more fluid, far more variable from situation to situation than traditional theories focusing on one explanatory factor predict or can explain. By viewing all psychological functions and behaviours as intrinsically *situated* (in other words, tied to the context in which they occur), as a dynamic systems perspective does, we can begin to explore and understand the rich plasticity of human behaviour in ways other theories cannot.

Of course, in some situations, a single factor will play the leading part in determining behaviour. People have died for a moral principle, or because they refuse to go against the dictates of their conscience, or even by putting themselves in danger through overwhelming compassion for another's plight. But even here, the overall dynamics of the situation will have played a role: there are only certain circumstances in which such gestures are appropriate.

Moral judgment, empathy, conscience and moral behaviour emerge from the dynamics of the situation, assembled in the moment – but nonetheless, consistent patterns of responding emerge over time. These reflect consistencies and patterns in the dynamics of the individual's successive experiences: well-trodden paths are the easiest to follow, and systems tend to settle into familiar grooves. It is these consistencies of experience that shape the overall trajectory of a life, disposing it toward a prosocial or an antisocial path.

From a dynamic systems perspective, life trajectories are situated in the dynamic social context created by the family, the community and culture in which it exists, the peers, friendships, activities and opportunities that the social system affords. It is this social context that creates the consistencies of experience from which consistent patterns of responding emerge. This approach has several advantages over more traditional research which looks at factors (such as the family, or the peer group) in isolation. First and most obviously, the dynamic systems approach provides a framework within which the insights from different lines of traditional research can be integrated. And by looking at the dynamic interactions between different factors, a systems approach opens up the possibility of discovering effects quite invisible, or quite inexplicable to research examining only one factor at a time (such as that a given family dynamic – authoritarian parenting for instance – has different effects in different socio-economic circumstances).

In one sense the key message of a dynamic systems approach is that we shall understand more about moral behaviour and moral development by looking at these things in their whole context – in other words, by looking at the 'big picture' – than we ever can by examining fragments of the system in isolation. But paradoxically, dynamic systems theory also directs research toward a new level of detail. Traditional research tended to take 'snapshots' of this factor or that (identifying a family as authoritarian, for example, or neglectful), and to look for correlations between these 'snapshots' and fairly general factors (such as substance abuse, delinquency, violence, for example). Analyses at this level can never reveal the dynamic processes through which a given pattern of behaviour is generated. To do that, we must look in detail at the actual dynamics of the interactions between child and family. In other words, we need something more like a *microgenetic analysis* (see Chapters 1 and 7) of the moment-to-moment dynamics of social interactions.

Moving to this more 'microgenetic' level of analysis of the moment-to-moment dynamics of social behaviour is already yielding new insights about social processes as a whole, and about the genesis of anti-social behaviour. For example, we've long known that adolescents who engage in 'deviant talk' are more likely to later go on to be substance abusers, delinquent or violent. But how does deviant talk actually develop? Moment-to-moment analysis of the dynamics of social interactions between adolescents is beginning to identify how deviant talk emerges in some types of peer relationship, and how it becomes progressively absorbing for these groups (Granic and Dishion, 2003). This kind of research can provide insights at an entirely new level.

How radically will a dynamic systems approach alter our understanding of social and moral development? It's too soon to tell. We are only just beginning to explore these things from this perspective. But it is already clear that dynamic systems research will become increasingly prominent over the coming years.

In conclusion

Philosophers have been fascinated by moral development for thousands of years. Their main concern was with the question of 'true' human nature, by which they meant, is our species intrinsically bad or intrinsically good? Free of the civilizing influence of society, would children become *cruel* savages, as William Golding suggested in his novel *Lord of the Flies*? Or, free from the corrupting influence of society would they become *noble* savages, as Jean-Jacques Rousseau suggested in his early writings? The implication of current research in developmental psychology is that the quest to discover 'true' human nature as it would develop without social influence is misguided. Who we are, and whether we are disposed to behave well or to behave badly, is socially constructed: that is to say, it emerges from the dynamics of the social context in which we develop. Individuals are not born genetically pre-programmed to be 'saints' or 'sinners': such genetic influences as there are operate indirectly. The overall pattern of experiences plays a greater role in determining the path development will follow – for good or ill. As a species we have no inherent moral character. We are capable of either good or evil. Which emerges depends on the circumstances of our lives.

Moral development is a topic of more significance than most. It's not just that prosocial behaviour is of vital importance to society, and antisocial behaviour a dangerous problem – although that is true. Nor is it that in this one topic, every aspect of human development comes together, although that too is true: moral development involves conceptual understanding, the cognitive skills of reasoning and problem solving, our emotions and empathic skills, our social skills and strategies, our personalities, identities, the narratives and self judgements which form our conscience. Rather, the significance of research in this area is that it begins to address the most profound issues in human experience.

It is specifically through the development of moral values, motivations and conscience that we become aware of a potent responsibility for our actions, our fellows and our world. Some theorists believe that it is the clash between this perception of responsibility and the contrasting perception of our helplessness and fragile mortality that fuels the uniquely human search for what we call the 'meaning' of life, through the exploration of philosophical and religious ideas (Tillich, 1964). Certainly, it is the recognition of our moral responsibility that lifts our species above all others, laying the foundation for what William James regarded as the pinnacle of human identity: the spiritual self.

Exercises

1. Suppose we could confidently say that 80 per cent of young adolescents who showed a given rare personality profile would go on to commit sadistic serial murders. What practical and ethical issues would follow? Should we screen the whole population for this profile? Should we imprison or give compulsory treatment against their will to adolescents with this profile, even before they have committed a crime?

2. How could you design a research study to tease out the relative contribution of video/film violence and other factors, in the development of delinquent behaviour?

Suggested reading

For an evolutionary biology view of morality read:

- L. Cosmides and J. Tooby, J. (2005b) Neurocognitive adaptations designed for social exchange, pp. 584–627 in D. M. Buss (ed.), *The Handbook of Evolutionary Psychology*. Hoboken, N.J.: Wiley.

For a review of the development of prosocial behaviour read:

- N. Eisenberg and R. Fabes (1998) Prosocial development. In N. Eisenberg (ed.), W. Damon (series ed.), *Handbook of Child Psychology*, vol. 3: *Social, Emotional and Personality Development*. New York: Wiley.

For a review of the development of morality read:

- R. Turiel (1998) The development of morality. In N. Eisenberg (ed.), W. Damon (series ed.), *Handbook of Child Psychology*, vol. 3: *Social, Emotional and Personality Development*. New York: Wiley.

For an introduction to moral identity read:

- S. Hardy and G. Carlo (2005) Identity as a source of moral motivation. *Human Development* 48, pp. 232–56.

For a moving account of exemplary prosocial behaviour read:

- K. Monroe (2006) *The Hand of Compassion: Portraits of moral choice during the Holocaust*. Princeton, N.J.: Princeton University Press.

For an account of the development of antisocial behaviour read:

- C. Sutton, D. Utting and D. Farrington (2006) Nipping criminality in the bud. *The Psychologist* 19, pp. 470–5.

Revision summary

Evolutionary theories

- Most researchers would agree that the propensity for both antisocial and prosocial behaviour has an evolutionary basis.

- Antisocial behaviour often seems to need little explanation: it serves the survival needs of the individual and his or her offspring. But prosocial behaviour, and particularly altruism, seem not to be to the advantage of the individual at all, and so are harder to explain from an evolutionary perspective.

- There is continuing controversy as to the innate bases of prosocial behaviour. 'Selfish gene' theory doesn't fit the facts. Current debate revolves around whether we have innate neural mechanisms specifically designed to create prosocial behaviour, or whether prosocial behaviour stems from the innate reflexes that serve social development as a whole.

The importance of empathy

- Hoffman and others argue that empathy is essential for the development of prosocial behaviour. It is empathy that allows us to recognize other people's feelings and needs, and so to offer help and focus our efforts effectively.

- The evidence suggests that prosocial concern may well grow out of empathy, and that the extent to which we can help others in an appropriate way depends on the level of insight into other minds.

- However, the ability to feel empathy for others is not enough to ensure a prosocial response, as Hoffman implies. Both children and adults may react to another's distress by self-protectively withdrawing from the pain rather than sympathetically helping. And both children and adults can withhold empathic concern for members of 'out groups', or for the victims of their own bad behaviour.

- In fact, a certain amount of empathy is needed for causing hurt. The development of empathy is the prerequisite for bullying and deliberate cruelty as well as for prosocial helping.

Moral reasoning

- Building on Piaget's work, Kohlberg identified five stages of moral reasoning organized in three levels: the *pre-conventional* (typical of childhood; focused on self-interest); the *conventional* (adolescence and adulthood, focused on social reputations and systems); and the *post-conventional* (found in a minority of adults; focused on universal moral principles).

- Kohlberg's stages are found in a wide variety of different cultures, though there are some cultural differences in the typical stage of reasoning produced.

- Recent research asking children to reason about contexts more familiar to them than Kohlberg's original materials show that the ability to use more sophisticated forms of moral reasoning develops younger than Kohlberg supposed.

- There is a clear relationship between level of moral reasoning and behaviour, but it is not very strong. The higher stages of moral reasoning, and particularly post-conventional reasoning are associated with prosocial behaviour. Delinquents are more likely to reason at pre-conventional levels. However, conventional stage reasoning doesn't necessarily prevent violent crime. For example, rapists are not different from non-offenders in their moral reasoning.

Conscience and moral identity

- Through the symbiotic relationship with the mother, infants begin to internalize ideas of right and wrong. This internalization is marked by the emergence of the moral emotions of pride, shame and guilt, which form the basis for conscience, and which regulate our behaviour.

- Although conscience does affect our behaviour, it is not sufficient to wholly ensure prosocial behaviour. Children (and adults) want to look good, to attribute honesty and prosocial behaviour to themselves, but are prone to cheating if no one is looking, and more likely to behave well when they are observed.

- Recent research has begun to explore the development of 'moral identity', in which moral rules are not only internalized, but embraced as integral to personal identity. Moral identity provides a powerful motive for prosocial behaviour. A strong moral identity is associated with the personal responsibility for other's welfare and concern for social justice characteristic of individuals who are proactively prosocial (for example, charity volunteers).

Individual differences

- Individuals differ in the degree to which they develop empathic skills, moral reasoning, conscience or moral identity, and in the extent to which they are generally prosocial or antisocial. Many factors affect this. The processes of development can best be understood from a 'life trajectory' perspective.

- The tendency toward prosocial or antisocial behaviour reflects innate temperament, specifically how emotionally reactive an individual is and how able to regulate his or her emotions. Prosocial behaviour is associated with low reactivity and good self-regulation, antisocial behaviour with high reactivity and poor self-regulation.

- The development of prosocial and antisocial tendencies reflects parenting practices, the child's experience within the family, and the moral norms the parents model for the child to copy. The quality of parenting affects the development of empathy, self-control, moral reasoning, conscience and moral identity. Poor parenting fosters the hostility and poor impulse control associated with antisocial behaviour.

- Individual differences in moral development also reflect the influence of the peer group or the culture or subculture in which the individual lives.

- Although the ordinary processes of social development explain a great deal of the origins of prosocial or antisocial life trajectories, there are some crimes of exceptional evil that seem to need special explanations. As yet we have little insight into how a serial murderer (for example) develops.

A dynamic systems perspective

- Dynamic systems theory views moral reactions as situated in the context in which they occur. This suggests new insights into the relationship between moral reasoning, empathy, conscience, and prosocial or antisocial behaviour.

- Moral development as a whole is situated in the social relationships a child experiences. By understanding the dynamic detail of how such relationships function from moment to moment we can gain insight into how the moral tone of an overall life trajectory is established.

a final comment

13
toward a new view of development

Developmental psychology has come a long way in recent decades. Some of this progress has been brought about by new methods – for example, the techniques that have allowed us to study the living brain and to map the human genome, the methodologies for studying infant perceptions, and for studying the moment by moment dynamics of problem solving. Some new insights have come more or less by accident – the discovery of the mirror neuron system, for example. Often reality has intruded, producing results that we couldn't have predicted and can't explain, forcing us to adapt our methods and theories – Patrick Rabbitt (2006) provides a fascinating example of this kind of effect in a long-term research project. But it is the steady evolution of theoretical ideas through systematic research that plays the leading part in driving the boundaries of knowledge forward.

At the start of the 21st century there is a mounting interest in a new kind of theory in developmental psychology: dynamic systems theory. This approach presents a very different view of developmental processes from the views of the classical theories of 20th century psychology described in Chapter 1, as we have seen through the research reviewed in this book. Classical theories saw development in a one-dimensional way, focusing on one or another factor – viewing development as the result of social processes, for example, or as the result of information processing. By contrast, dynamic systems theory argues that development is always the product of multiple factors interacting to form a single, dynamic, self-organizing system. Where classical theories tended to draw a distinction between physiological and psychological processes, dynamic systems theory argues that behaviour, including conceptual and cognitive behaviour, is always embodied in the neurological and physiological systems that support perception, action, emotion. Where classical theories often studied psychological processes in isolation from any particular context, dynamic systems theory argues that all behaviour is 'situated': it emerges in the moment, in a particular context.

Many of the old questions that shaped research in the 20th century look very different from a dynamic systems perspective. For example, the claim that complex patterns of behaviour can emerge from the dynamics of a self-organizing system without there being any guiding plan or blueprint for the path development will follow cuts across the controversy over whether this or that aspect of development (from learning to crawl to mastering the grammar of language or developing a theory of mind) would only be possible if it were pre-programmed to occur.

A dynamic systems perspective also introduces new questions and challenges for research. For example, this approach predicts that individual children must improvize their way toward developmental milestones, reacting to the moment by moment circumstances of the situation and their own physiology. Different children will therefore follow subtly (or not so subtly) different paths, even if they all end up at the same milestones (such as walking or talking). Classical research had little or nothing to say about individual differences at this level, and did not look for them. But individual variability may be of practical as well as theoretical importance: perhaps some paths to a given milestone are more effective than others? Perhaps by understanding such effects we could identify interventions to correct less successful paths?

Then there is the issue of time: all behaviour emerges in the moment, reflecting the specific context in which it is situated, changing as the situation changes. And yet over longer periods of time behaviour settles into stable patterns, and even into a consistent life trajectory. Classical theories did not explore the process through which behaviour develops in sufficient detail to raise this problem. Dynamic systems theory throws new emphasis on the question of how effects occurring from second to second connect to effects occurring over longer periods of time. Can such effects be explained by studying the way neural systems learn – perhaps through using connectionist simulations (Munakata and McClelland, 2003; Spencer et al, 2006)?

In virtually every area of developmental psychology, research is moving toward the ideas of dynamic systems theory. From this perspective, the very same basic mechanisms of development can be applied to all topics from motor to social, cognitive and ethical development; the same developmental mechanisms can account for both the common milestones of development and individual differences; and through the application of non-linear dynamics, the same basic process accounts for both continuous and discontinuous change: in other words, both the steady growth and the striking qualitative changes we see in the course of development. From this point of view, dynamic systems theory is the most comprehensive approach to explaining development that we have ever had. It is a 'grand theory' of development. Some researchers believe that it will form a new paradigm for research in developmental psychology as a whole in the coming decades (Lewis, 2000; Spencer et al., 2006; Thelen and Smith, 1994).

Will dynamic systems theory fulfil its promise and provide us with a unified account of development as a whole? Not all researchers are yet ready to embrace the assumptions and methods of this approach. Changes in paradigm are always raggedy affairs, with some researchers leaping into the new approach and others hanging back more sceptically – and sometimes, wisely. Dynamic systems theory is not the first approach to be hailed as providing a framework for explaining everything in developmental psychology: the same claim was once made for behaviourism, and later for information-processing models. It is entirely possible that the dynamic systems approach will be found to have limitations – just as its predecessors did. Indeed, this approach faces serious challenges in finding ways to model the enormously complex, multi-factorial interactions from which behaviour emerges, and in finding ways to test its claim that the systems so modelled can both create and change themselves. Time will tell whether research can rise to these challenges. But there are already two reasons for taking the dynamic systems very seriously.

First, dynamic systems theory is special because its central claim, namely that the complex patterns of human development are emergent functions of the dynamics of a self-organizing system, is an extrapolation of ideas already well established in other branches of science, from biology to physics, from computer science to neuroscience, and captured in chaos mathematics or non-linear dynamics. The assumption that psychological systems parallel other systems in nature is elegantly simple. The mere fact that similar processes seem to occur across the domains of all the sciences makes it worthwhile to explore this approach in psychology.

But perhaps the most intriguing aspect of dynamic systems theory is its emphasis on the embodiment of psychological processes, its rejection of the idea that higher cognitive functions of the mind are separate from the physiological and neurological processes supporting perception, action and emotion. In conjunction with connectionist ideas about the way neural networks learn and develop, this approach is the nearest we've ever come to having an answer to the fundamental question for developmental research: how does intelligent self-awareness develop out of the physiological functioning of an organic entity?

Exercises

1. Why would it be an advantage to have a single paradigm embracing research on every aspect of human development?

2. Two researchers arrive on a new planet, to study the development of a particular behaviour in an alien species. One researcher has studied all the notes of all the previous experts who have addressed this puzzle. The other arrives with no knowledge of any of that history – only with what he or she regards as an 'open mind'. Commissioned to inform the Interplanetary Government, what would you see as the strengths and weaknesses of these two researchers?

Suggested further reading

For a fascinating account of how a research project unfolds over the years read:

- P. Rabbitt (2006) Tales of the unexpected: 25 years of cognitive gerontology. *The Psychologist* 19 (11), pp. 674–6.

For a review of dynamic systems theory and its implications for research in the 21st century read:

- M. Lewis (2000) The promise of dynamic systems approaches for an integrated account of human development. *Child Development* 71, pp. 36–43.

- J. Spencer, M. Clearfield, D. Corbetta, B. Ulrich, P. Buchanan and G. Schöner (2006) Moving toward a grand theory of development: in memory of Esther Thelen. *Child Development* 77, pp. 1521–38.

references

Abramovitch, R., Corter, C., Pepler, D. and Stanhope, L. (1986) 'Sibling and peer interaction: a final follow up and comparison', *Child Development* 57, 217–29.

Ackles, P. and Cook, K. (1998) 'Stimulus probability and event-related potentials of the brain in 6-month-old human infants', *International Journal of Psychophysiology* 29, 115–43.

Acredolo, C. (1978) 'The development of spatial orientation in infancy', *Developmental Psychology* 14, 224–34.

Acredolo, C. and Schmidt, J. (1981) 'The understanding of relative speeds, distances and durations of movement', *Developmental Psychology* 17, 490–3.

Adams, M. (1990) *Beginning to Read: Thinking and learning about print* (Cambridge, Mass.: MIT Press).

Adelson, J. (1986) *Inventing Adolescence: The political psychology of everyday schooling* (New Brunswick, N.J.: Transaction Books).

Adelson, J. (1991) 'Political development', in R. Lerner, A. Petersen and J. Brooks-Gunn (eds), *Encyclopaedia of Adolescence* (New York: Garland).

Adolph, K., Vereijken, B. and Denny, M. (1998) 'Learning to crawl', *Child Development* 69, 1299–312.

Ahadi, S. and Rothbart, M. (1993) 'Children's temperament in the US and China: similarities and differences', *European Journal of Personality* 7, 359–77.

Ainsworth, M. (1973) 'The development of mother–infant attachment', in B. Caldwell and H. Ricciutti (eds), *Review of Child Development Research* vol. 3 (Chicago: University of Chicago Press).

Ainsworth, M. (1974) 'Infant–mother attachment and social development: socialisation as a product of reciprocal responsiveness to signals', in M. Richards (ed.), *The Integration of the Child into the Social World* (London: Cambridge University Press).

Ainsworth, M., Blehar, M., Waters, E. and Wall, S. (1978) *Patterns of Attachment* (Hillsdale, N.J.: Erlbaum).

Alibali, M. (1999) 'How children change their minds: strategy change can be gradual or abrupt', *Developmental Psychology* 35, 127–45.

Allen, M. and Burrell, N. (1996) 'Comparing the impact of homosexual and heterosexual parents on children: meta-analysis of existing research', *Journal of Homosexuality* 32, 19–35.

Allport, G. (1937) *Personality: A psychological interpretation* (New York: Holt).

Amato, P. and Gilbreth, J. (1999) 'Nonresident fathers and children's wellbeing: a meta-analysis'. *Journal of Marriage and the Family* 61, 557–73.

Anastasi, A. and Urbina, S. (1997) *Psychological Testing* (Upper Saddle River, N.J.: Prentice-Hall).

Anderson, C. and Bushman, B. (2001) 'Effects of violent video games on aggressive behaviour, aggressive cognition, aggressive affect, physiological arousal and prosocial behaviour: a meta-analytic review of the scientific literature', *Psychological Science* 12, 353–9.

Anderson, M. (1992) *Intelligence and Cognitive Development* (Oxford: Blackwell).

Ang, R. and Goh, D. (2006) 'Authoritarian parenting style in Asian countries: a cluster-analytic investigation', *Contemporary Family Therapy* 28, 131–51.

Anglin, J. (1993) 'Vocabulary development: a morphological analysis', *Monographs of the Society for Research in Child Development* 58.

Anisfeld, M. (1984) *Language Development from Birth to Three* (Hillsdale, N.J.: Erlbaum).

Aries, P. (1962) *Centuries of Childhood* (New York: Knopf).

Armstrong, K. (1999) *A History of God* (London: Vintage Books).

Arnett, J. (1999) 'Adolescent storm and stress, a reconsideration', *American Psychologist* 54, 317–28.

Arokach, A. (2006) 'Alienation and domestic abuse: how abused women cope with loneliness', *Social Indicators Research* 78, 327–40.

Asendorpf, J., Warkentin, V. and Baudonniere, P. (1996) 'Self-awareness and other-awareness: mirror self-recognition, social contingency awareness and synchronic imitation', *Developmental Psychology* 32, 313–21.

Aslin, R., Juscyzk, P. and Pisoni, D. (1998) 'Speech and auditory processing during infancy: constraints on and precursors to language', in D. Kuhn and R. Siegler (eds), W. Damon (series ed.), *Handbook of Child Psychology,* vol. 2: *Cognition, Perception and Language* (New York: Wiley).

Aslin, R., Pisoni, D. and Jusczyk, P. (1983) 'Auditory development and speech perception in infancy', in M. Haith and J. Campos (eds), *Handbook of Child Psychology*, vol. 2: *Infancy and Developmental Psychology* (NewYork: Wiley).

Aslin, R., Saffran, J. and Newport, E. (1998) 'Computation of conditional probability statistics by 8-month-old infants', *Psychological Science* 9, 321–4.

Astington, J. (1993) *The Child's Discovery of Mind* (Cambridge, Mass.: Harvard University Press).

Astuti, R., Solomon, G. and Carey, S. (2004) 'Constraints on conceptual development', *Monographs for the Society for Research in Child Development* 69.

Atran, S. (1998) 'Folk biology and the anthropology of science: cognitive universals and cultural particulars', *Behavioral and Brain Sciences* 21, 547–609.

Atran, S., Medin, D., Lynch, E., Vapnarsky, V. and Sousa, P. (2001) 'Folkbiology doesn't come from folk psychology: evidence from Yukatek Maya in cross-cultural perspective', *Journal of Cognition and Culture* 1, 3–42.

Avenanti, A., Bueti, D., Galati, G. and Aglioti, S. (2005) 'Magnetic stimulation highlights the sensorimotor side of empathy for pain', *Nature Neuroscience* 8, 955–60.

Avis, J. and Harris. P. (1991) 'Belief–desire reasoning among Baka children: evidence for a universal conception of mind', *Child Development* 62, 460–7.

Azmitia, M. and Hesser, J. (1993) 'Why siblings are important agents of cognitive development: a comparison of siblings and peers', *Child Development* 64, 430–44.

Baddeley, A. (1976) *The Psychology of Memory* (New York: Harper & Row).

Bagwell, C., Newcomb, A. and Bukowski, W. (1998) 'Pre-adolescent friendship and peer rejection as predictors of adult adjustment', *Child Development* 69, 140–53.

Baillargeon, R. (1986) 'Representing the existence and the location of hidden object: object permanence in 6 to 8 month old infants', *Cognition* 23, 21–41.

Baillargeon, R. (1999) 'Young infants' expectations about hidden objects: a reply to three challenges', *Cognitive Development* 2, 375–92.

Baillargeon, R. and DeVos, J. (1991) 'Object permanence in young infants: further evidence', *Child Development* 62, 1227–46.

Baillargeon, R., Graber, M., DeVos, J. and Black, J. (1990) 'Why do infants fail to search for hidden objects?' *Cognition* 36, 255–84.

Baillargeon, R., Spelke, E. and Wasserman, S. (1985) 'Object permanence in 5 month old infants', *Cognition* 20, 191–208.

Baker-Ward, L., Ornstein, P. and Holden, D. (1984) *Influences on Human Development: A longitudinal perspective* (Boston: Kluwer Nijhoff).

Balacheff, N. (1988) 'Aspects of proof in pupils' practice of school mathematics', in D. Primm (ed.), *Mathematics, Teachers and Children* (London: Hodder & Stoughton).

Baldwin, J. (1895) *Mental Development of the Child and the Race: Methods and processes* (New York: Macmillan).

Baldwin, J. (1906) *Mental Development of the Child and the Race,* 3rd edn (New York: Kelley).

Baldwin, J. and Markman, E. (1989) 'Establishing word–object relations: a first step', *Child Development* 60, 381–98.

Baltes, P., Reese, H. and Lipsitt, L. (1980) 'Lifespan developmental psychology', *Annual Review of Psychology* 31, 65–110.

Bandura, A. (1973) *Aggression: A social learning analysis* (Englewood Cliffs, N.J.: Prentice-Hall).

Bandura, A. (1986) *Social Foundations of Thought and Action* (Upper Saddle River, N.J.: Prentice-Hall).

Bandura, A. (1990) 'Conclusion: reflections on nonability determinants of competence', in R. Sternberg and J. Kolligan (eds), *Competence Considered* (New Haven, Conn.: Yale University Press).

Banigan, R. and Mervis, C. (1988) 'Role of adult input in young children's category evolution: an experimental study', *Journal of Child Language* 15, 493–504.

Barlow, J. and Ellard, D. (2006) 'The psychosocial well-being of children with chronic disease, their parents and siblings', *Child: Care, Health and Development* 32, 19–31.

Baron-Cohen, S., Leslie, A. and Frith, U. (1985) 'Does the autistic child have a "theory of mind"?', *Cognition* 21, 37–46.

Baron-Cohen, S., Tager-Flusberg, H. and Cohen, D. (1993) *Understanding Other Minds: Perspectives from autism* (Oxford: Oxford University Press).

Barrett, K. (2005) 'The origins of social emotions and self–regulation in toddlerhood: new evidence', *Cognition and Emotion* 19, 953–79.

Barrett, K. and Campos, J. (1987) 'Perspectives on emotional development II: a functionalist approach to emotions', in J. Osofsky (ed.), *Handbook of Infant Development* (New York: Wiley).

Barrick, M. and Mount, M. (1991) 'The big five personality dimensions and job performance: a meta analysis', *Personnel Psychology* 44, 1–26.

Bartlett, F. (1932) *Remembering* (Cambridge, UK: Cambridge University Press).

Bartsch, K. and Wellman, H. (1995) *Children Talk about the Mind* (New York: Oxford University Press).

Bass, B. and Yammarino, F. (1991) 'Congruence of self and others' leadership ratings of naval officers for understanding successful performance', *Applied Psychology* 40, 437–54.

Bates, E. (1993) 'Comprehension and production in early language development', *Monographs of the Society for Research in Child Development* 58.

Bates, E. and MacWhinney, B. (1989) 'Functionalism and the competition model', in B. MacWhinney and E. Bates (eds), *The Crosslinguistic Study of Sentence Processing* (Cambridge, UK: Cambridge University Press).

Bates, E., O'Connell, B. and Shore, C. (1987) 'Language and communication in infancy', in J. Osofsky (ed.), *Handbook of Infant Development* (New York: Wiley).

Bates, J., Bayles, K., Bennett, D., Ridge, B. and Brown, M. (1991) 'Origins of externalizing behavior problems at eight years of age', pp. 93–120 in D. Pepler and K. Rubin (eds), *The Development and Treatment of Childhood Aggression* (Mahwah, N.J.: Lawrence Erlbaum Associates).

Bates, J. and Wach, T. (eds) (1994) *Temperament: Individual differences at the interface of biology and behaviour* (Washington, DC: American Psychological Association).

Baumeister, R. (1987) 'How the self became a problem: a psychological review of historical research', *Journal of Personality and Social Psychology* 57, 163–76.

Baumeister, R. and Senders, P. (1989) 'Identity development and the role of structure of children's games', *Journal of Genetic Psychology* 150, 19–37.

Baumrind, D. (1978) 'Parental disciplinary patterns and social competence in children', *Youth and Society* 9, 239–76.

Baumrind, D. (1991a) 'The influence of parenting style on adolescent competence and substance use', *Journal of Early Adolescence* 11, 56–95.

Baumrind, D. (1991b) 'Parenting styles and adolescent development', pp. 746–58 in R. Lerner, A. Petersen and J. Brooks-Gunn (eds), *Encyclopedia of Adolescence*, vol. 11 (New York: Garland).

Bayley, N. (1969) *Bayley Scales of Infant Development* (New York: Psychological Corporation).

Bayley, N. (1993) *Bayley Scales of Infant Development: Birth to two years* (San Antonio, Tex.: Psychological Corporation).

Beck, E., Burnet, K. and Vosper, J. (2006) 'Birth-order effects on facets of extraversion', *Personality and Individual Differences* 40, 953–9.

Beckett, R., Beech, A., Fisher, D. and Fordham, A. (1994) *Community Based Treatment for Sex Offenders: An evaluation of seven treatment programmes* (London: Home Office Publications Unit).

Bee, H. (1989) *The Developing Child* (New York: Harper & Row).

Bem, D. J. (1996) 'Exotic becomes erotic: a developmental theory of sexual orientation', *Psychological Review* 103, 320–35.

Bem, S. (1989) 'Genital knowledge and gender constancy in preschool children', *Child Development* 60, 649–62.

Benes, M. (1994) 'Development of the cortico-limbic system', in G. Dawson and K. Fischer (eds), *Human Behaviour and the Developing Brain* (New York: Guilford Press).

Bennett, M. and Sani, F (2004) *The Development of the Social Self* (Hove: Psychology Press).

Berger, S. (2004) 'Demands of finite cognitive capacity cause infant's perseverative errors', *Infancy* 5, 217–38.

Berko, J. (1958) 'The child's learning of English morphology', *Word* 14, 150–77.

Bernal, M., Knight, G., Ocampo, K., Garza, C. and Cota, M. (1993) 'Development of Mexican American identity', in M. Bernal and G. Knight (eds), *Ethnic Identity: Formation and transmission amongst Hispanics and other ethnic minorities* (Albany: State of New York Press).

Bernzweig, J., Eisenberg, N. and Fabes, R. (1993) 'Children's coping in self- and other-relevant contexts', *Journal of Experimental Child Psychology* 55, 208–26.

Bersoff, D. and Miller, J. (1993) 'Culture, context and the development of moral accountability judgements', *Developmental Psychology* 29, 664–76.

Bertenthal, B. (1993) 'Infant's perception of biochemical motions: intrinsic image and knowledge-based constraints', in C. Granrud (ed.), *Visual Perception and Cognition in Infancy* (Hillsdale, N.J.: Lawrence Erlbaum Associates).

Bertenthal, B. and Boker, S. (2004) 'The emergence of dynamic systems in development', *PsychCRITIQUES*, no pagination.

Bertenthal, B., Campos, J. and Kermoian, R. (1994) 'An epigenetic perspective on the development of self-produced locomotion and its consequences', *Current Directions in Psychological Science* 5, 140–5.

Bertenthal, B. and Fischer, K. (1978) 'Development of self-recognition in the infant', *Developmental Psychology* 14, 44–50.

Berti, A. and Bombi, A. (1988) *The Child's Construction of Economics* (Cambridge, UK: Cambridge University Press).

Bibace, R. and Walsh, M. (1981) *New Directions for Child Development: Children's conceptions of health, illness and bodily functions* 14 (San Francisco: Jossey-Bass).

Bierman, K., Smoot, D. and Aumiller, K. (1993) 'Characteristics of aggressive-rejected, aggressive (nonrejected), and rejected (nonaggressive) boys', *Child Development* 64, 139–51.

Bigelow, B. (1977) 'Children's friendship expectations: a cognitive developmental study', *Child Development* 48, 246–53.

Binet, A. and Simon, T. (1916) *The Development of Intelligence in Children* (Baltimore, Md.: William & Wilkins).

Bisanz, J. and Lefevre, J. (1990) 'Mathematical cognition: strategic processing as interactions among sources of knowledge', in D. Bjorkland (ed.), *Children's Strategies: Contemporary views of cognitive development* (Hillsdale, N.J.: Erlbaum).

Bjorklund, D., Miller, P., Coyle, T. and Slawinski, J. (1997) 'Instructing children to use memory strategies: evidence for utilization deficiencies in memory training studies', *Developmental Review* 17, 411–41.

Bjorklund, D. and Pellegrini, A. (2000) 'Child development and evolutionary psychology', *Child Development* 71, 1687–708.

Bjorklund, D. and Zeman, B. (1982) 'Children's organisation and meta memory awareness in their recall of familiar information', *Child Development* 53, 799–810.

Blackburn, S. (2001) *Being Good* (Oxford: Oxford University Press).

Blair, R. (1995) 'A cognitive developmental approach to morality: investigating the psychopath', *Cognition* 57, 1–29.

Blasi, A. (1994) 'Moral identity: its role in moral functioning', pp. 168–79 in W. Puka (ed.), *Fundamental Research in Moral Development (Moral Development: A compendium 2)*.

Block, J. (1971) *Lives through Time* (Berkeley, Calif.: Bancroft).

Block, R. and Harper, D. (1991) 'Overconfidence in estimation: testing the anchoring-and-adjustment hypothesis', *Organizational Behaviour and Human Decision Processes* 49, 88–207.

Bloom, L. (1998) 'Language acquisition in its developmental context', pp. 309–70 in D. Kuhn and R. Siegler (eds), W. Damon (series ed.), *Handbook of Child Psychology*, vol. 2: *Cognition, Perception and Language* (New York: Wiley).

Bloom, P. (2005) *How Children Learn the Meaning of Words* (Boston, Mass.: MIT Press).

Bloom, P. and Tinker, E. (2001) 'The intentionality model and language acquisition: engagement, effort and the essential tension in development', *Monographs of the Society for Research in Child Development* 66.

Blundon, J. and Schaefer, C. (2006) 'The role of parent–child play in children's development', *Psychology and Education* 43, 1–10.

Boden, M. (1990) *The Creative Mind: Myths and mechanisms* (London: Weidenfeld & Nicholson).

Bomba, P. (1984) 'The development of orientation categories between 2 and 4 months of age', *Journal of Experimental Child Psychology* 37, 609–36.

Bos, H., van Balen, F. and van den Boom, D. C. (2004) 'Experience of parenthood, couple relationship, social support, and child-rearing goals in planned lesbian mother families', *Journal of Child Psychology and Psychiatry* 45, 755–64.

Bosma, H. and Kunnen, E. (2001) *Identity and Emotion: Development through self organisation* (Cambridge, UK: Cambridge University Press).

Bosworth, K., Espelage, D. and Simon, T. (1999) 'Factors associated with bullying behavior in middle school students', *Journal of Early Adolescence* 19, 341–62.

Boulton, M. (1999) 'Concurrent and longitudinal relations between children's playground behavior and social preference, victimization and bullying', *Child Development* 70, 944–54.

Boulton, M. and Underwood, K. (1992) 'Bully/victim problems among middle school children', *British Journal of Educational Psychology* 62, 73–87.

Bower, B. (2005) 'Mirror cell's fading spark: empathy related neurons may turn off in autism', *Science* 168, 373.

Bower, T. and Wishart, J. (1972) 'The effects of motor skill on object permanence', *Cognition* 1, 165–72.

Bowlby, J. (1953) *Child Care and the Growth of Love* (Harmondsworth: Penguin).

Bowlby, J. (1969) *Attachment and Loss*, vol. 1: *Attachment* (London: Hogarth Press).

Boyatzis, C., Baloff, P. and Durieux, C. (1998) 'Effects of perceived attractiveness and academic success on early adolescent peer popularity', *Journal of Genetic Psychology* 159, 337–44.

Boysson-Bardies, B. de (1999) *How Language Comes to Children: From birth to two years* (trans. M. DeBoise), (Cambridge, Mass.: MIT Press).

Boysson-Bardies, B. de, Sagart, L. and Durant, C. (1984) 'Discernible differences in the babbling of infants according to target language', *Journal of Child Language* 11, 1–15.

Bradley, L. and Bryant, P. (1983) 'Categorising sounds and learning to read: a causal connection', *Nature* 301, 419–521.

Braine, M. (1971) 'The acquisition of language in the infant and child', in C. Reed (ed.), *The Learning of Language* (New York: Appleton Century Crofts).

Braine, M. (1994) 'Is nativism sufficient?' *Journal of Child Language* 21, 9–31.

Braver, S. and Griffin, W. (2000) 'Engaging fathers in the post-divorce family', *Marriage and Family Review* 29, 247–67.

Bremner, G. and Knowles, L. (1984) 'Piagetian stage IV errors with an object that is directly accessible both visually and manually', *Perception* 13, 307–14.

Bremner, J. G. (1997) 'From perception to cognition', in G. Bremner, A. Slater and G. Butterworth (eds), *Infant Development: Recent advances* (Hillsdale, N.J.: Psychology Press/Erlbaum, UK).

Bremner, J., Knowles, L. and Andreasen, G. (1994) 'Processes underlying young children's spatial orientation during movement', *Journal of Experimental Child Psychology* 57, 355–76.

Bretherton, I. (1991) 'Pouring new wine into old bottles: the social self as internal working model', in J. Osofsky (ed.), *Handbook of Infant Development* (New York: Wiley).

Brewaeys, A., Ponjaert, I., Van Hall, E. V. and Golombok, S. (1997) 'Donor insemination: child development and family functioning in lesbian mother families', *Human Reproduction* 12, 1349–59.

Bridges, L. and Grolnick, W. (1995) 'The development of emotional self-regulation in infancy and early childhood', in N. Eisenberg (ed.), *Social development: Review of personality and social psychology* (Thousand Oaks, Calif.: Sage).

Bridges, R. (1990) 'Endocrine regulation of parental behavior in rodents', in N. Krasnegor and R. Bridges (eds), *Mammalian Parenting: Biochemical, neurobiological, and behavioral determinants* (New York: Oxford University Press).

British Psychological Society (1991) *Code of Conduct, Ethical Principles and Guidelines* (Leicester: BPS).

Broad, C. (1953) *Religion, Philosophy and Psychical Research* (New York: Harcourt, Brace).

Bronfenbrenner, U. (1979) *The Ecology of Human Development* (Cambridge, Mass.: Harvard University Press).

Brooks-Gunn, J. and Reiter, E. (1990) 'The role of pubertal processes in the early adolescent transition', in S. Feldman and G. Elliot (eds), *At the Threshold: The developing adolescent* (Cambridge, Mass.: Harvard University Press).

Brown, A. (1975) 'The development of memory: knowing, knowing about knowing, and knowing how to know', in H. Reese (ed.), *Advances in Child Development and Behaviour*, vol. 10 (New York: Academic Press).

Brown, A. (1990) 'Domain-specific principles affect learning and transfer in children', *Cognitive Science* 14, 107–33.

Brown, A., Bransford, J., Ferrara, R. and Campione, J. (1983) 'Learning, remembering and understanding', in J. Flavell and E. Markman (eds), *The Handbook of Child Psychology*, vol. 3 (New York: Wiley).

Brown, A. and Campione, J. (1972) 'Recognition memory for perceptually similar pictures in preschool children', *Journal of Experimental Child Psychology* 95, 55–62.

Brown, A. and DeLoache, J. (1978) 'Skills, plans and self regulation', in R. Siegler (ed.), *Children's Thinking: What develops?* (Hillsdale, N.J.: Erlbaum).

Brown, A. and Scott, M. (1971) 'Recognition memory for pictures in preschool children', *Journal of Experimental Child Psychology* 11, 401–12.

Brown, B. (1999) 'Measuring the peer environment of American adolescents', in S. Friedman and T. Wachs (eds), *Measuring Environment across the Life Span* (Washington, DC: American Psychological Association).

Brown, J. and Dunn, J. (1991) '"You can cry mum": the social and developmental implications of talk about internal states', *British Journal of Developmental Psychology* 9, 237–56.

Brown, R. (1973) *A First Language: The early stages* (Cambridge, Mass.: Harvard University Press).

Brown, R. and Chiu, P. (2006) 'Neural correlates of memory development and learning combining neuroimaging and behavioural measures to understand cognitive developmental processes', *Developmental Neuropsychology* 29, 279–91.

Bruce, D. (1964) 'The analysis of word sounds', *British Journal of Educational Psychology* 34, 158–70.

Brugman, D. and Aleva, A. (2004) 'Developmental delay or regression in moral reasoning by juvenile delinquents?' *Journal of Moral Education* 33, 321–38.

Bruner, J. (1974) 'The organisation of early skilled action', in M. Richards (ed.), *The Integration of a Child into a Social World* (Cambridge, UK: Cambridge University Press).

Bruner, J. (1975a) 'The ontogenesis of speech acts', *Journal of Child Language* 2, 1–19.

Bruner, J. (1975b) 'From communication to language: a psychological perspective', *Cognition* 3, 255–87.

Bruner, J. (1975c) *Beyond the Information Given: Studies in the psychology of knowing* (New York: W. W. Norton).

Bruner, J. (1983) 'The acquisition of pragmatic commitments', in R. Golinkoff (ed.), *The Transition from Prelinguistic to Linguistic Communication* (Hillsdale, N.J.: Lawrence Erlbaum Associates).

Bruner, J. (1986) *Actual Minds* (Cambridge, Mass.: Harvard University Press).

Bruner, J. and Kenney, H. (1965) 'Representation and mathematical learning', *Monographs of the Society for Research in Child Development* 30, 50–9.

Bryant, J., Sanders-Jackson, A. and Smallwood, A. (2006) 'IMing, text messaging and adolescent social networks', *Journal of Computer-Mediated Communication* 11, 577–92.

Bryant, P. (1974) *Perception and Understanding in Young Children* (London: Methuen).

Bryant, P. (1993) 'Reading in development', in C. Pratt and A. Garton (eds), *Systems of Representation in Children* (Chichester: Wiley).

Bryant, P. and Trabasso, T. (1971) 'Transitive inferences and memory in young children', *Nature* 23(2), 456–8.

Buchanan-Barrow, E., Barrett, M. and Bati, M. (2003) 'Children's understanding of illness: the generalisation of illness according to exemplar', *Journal of Health Psychology* 8, 659–70.

Bugental, D. and Johnson, C. (2000) 'Parental and child cognitions in the context of the family', pp. 315–44 in S. Fiske, D. Shacter and C. Zahn-Waxler (eds), *Annual Review of Psychology* 51.

Bulmer, M. (1982) *Social Research Ethics* (London: Macmillan).

Bushnell, E. (1985) 'The decline of visually guided reaching in infancy', *Infant Behaviour and Development* 8, 139–55.

Bushnell, I., Sai, F. and Mullin, J. (1989) 'Neonatal recognition of the mother's face', *British Journal of Developmental Psychology* 7, 3–15.

Buss, D. (1984) 'Toward a psychology of person–environment correspondence: the role of spouse selection', *Journal of Personality and Social Psychology* 47, 361–77.

Buss, D. (1987) 'Selection, evocation and manipulation', *Journal of Personality and Social Psychology* 53, 1214–21.

Buss, D. (1991) 'Evolutionary personality psychology', *Annual Review of Psychology* 42, 459–91.

Bussey, K. (1999) 'Children's categorization and evaluation of different types of lies and truths', *Child Development* 70, 1338–47.

Butterworth, G. (1977) 'Object disappearance and error in Piaget's stage IV task.', *Journal of Experimental Child Psychology* 23, 391–401.

Butterworth, G. (1991) 'The ontogeny and phylogeny of joint visual attention', in A. Whiten (ed.), *Natural Theories of Mind: Evolution, development and simulation of everyday mindreading* (Oxford: Blackwell).

Butterworth, G. and Hopkins, B. (1988) 'Hand–mouth co-ordination in the newborn baby', *British Journal of Developmental Psychology* 6, 303–14.

Butterworth, G. and Jarrett, N. (1991) 'What minds have in common in space: spatial mechanisms serving joint visual attention in infancy', *British Journal of Developmental Psychology* 9, 55–72.

Byrne, R. and Whiten, A. (1988) 'Toward the next generation in data quality: a new survey of primate tactical deception', *Behavioural and Brain Science* 11, 267–83.

Byrne, R. and Whiten, A. (1991) 'Computation and mindreading in primate tactical deception', in A. Whiten (ed.), *Natural Theories of Mind: Evolution, development and simulation of everyday mindreading* (Oxford: Blackwell).

Cairns R. (1998) 'The making of developmental psychology', in R. Lerner (ed.), *Handbook of Child Psychology*, vol. 1: *Theoretical Models of Human Development* (New York: Wiley).

California Task Force to Promote Self-Esteem and Personal and Social Responsibility (1990) *Toward a State of Self-Esteem* (Sacramento: California State Department of Education).

Callanan, M. (1985) 'Object labels and young children's acquisition of categories', paper presented to the biennial conference of the Society for Research in Child Development, Toronto.

Camaioni, L. (1992) 'Mind knowledge in infancy: the emergence of intentional communication', *Early Development and Parenting* 1, 15–28.

Cameras, L, and Witherington, D. (2005) 'Dynamical systems approaches to emotional development', *Developmental Review* 25, 328–50.

Campbell, R. (2006) 'Teenage girls and cellular phones: discourses of independence, safety and "rebellion"', *Journal of Youth Studies* 9, 195–212.

Campos, J., Clapovitz, K., Lamb, M., Goldsmith, H. and Stenberg, C. (1983) 'Socioemotional development', in M. Haith and J. Campos (eds), *Handbook of Child Psychology*, vol. 2: *Infancy and Developmental Psychobiology* (New York: Wiley).

Cardoso-Martins, C. (1991) 'Awareness of phonemes and alphabetic literacy acquisition', *British Journal of Educational Psychology* 61, 164–73.

Carey, S. (1985) *Conceptual Change in Childhood* (Cambridge, Mass./London: MIT Press).

Carey, S. (1999) 'Sources of conceptual change', in E. Scholnick, K. Nelson, S. Gelman and P. Miller (eds), *Conceptual Development: Piaget's legacy* (Hillsdale, N.J.: Erlbaum).

Carey, S. and Gelman, R. (eds) (1991) *The Epigenesis of Mind: Essays on biology and cognition* (Hillsdale, N.J.: Erlbaum).

Carey, W. and McDevitt, S. (1978) 'Revision of the infant temperament questionnaire', *Pediatrics* 61, 735–9.

Carlo, G., Hardy, S. and Alberts, M. (2005) 'Moral exemplars', in L. Sherrod, C. Flanagan and R. Kassimir (eds), *Youth Activism: An international encyclopedia* (Westport, Conn.: Greenwood).

Carlo, G., Koller, S., Eisenberg, N., Da Silva, M. and Frohlich, C. (1996) 'A cross national study on the relations among prosocial moral reasoning, gender role orientations and prosocial behaviours', *Developmental Psychology* 32, 231–40.

Carlson, B. (1994) *Human Embryology and Developmental Biology* (St. Louis, Mo.: Mosby).

Carmichael, C. and McGue, M. (1994) 'A longitudinal family study of personality change and stability', *Journal of Personality* 62, 1–20.

Caron, R., Caron, A. and Myers, R. (1982) 'Abstraction of invariant face expressions in infancy', *Child Development* 59, 604–16.

Carothers, S., Borkowski, J., Lefever, J. and Whitman, T. (2005) 'Religiosity and the socioemotional adjustment of adolescent mothers and their children', *Journal of Family Psychology* 19, 263–75.

Carver, C. and Scheier, M. (2002) 'Control processes and self-organization as complementary principles underlying behaviour', *Personality and Social Psychology Review* 6, 304–15.

Case, R. (1984) 'The process of stage transition: a neo-Piagetian view', in R. Sternberg (ed.), *Mechanisms of Cognitive Development* (New York: Freeman).

Case, R. (1985) *Intellectual Development : Birth to adulthood* (New York: Academic Press).

Case, R. (1991) 'Stages in the development of the young child's first sense of self', *Developmental Review* 11, 210–30.

Casey, B., Giedd, J. and Thomas, K. (2000) 'Structural and functional brain development and its relation to cognitive development', *Biological Psychology* 54, 241–57.

Caspi, A. (1998) 'Personality development across the life course', in N. Eisenberg (ed.), W. Damon (series ed.), *Handbook of Child Psychology*, vol. 3: *Social, Emotional and Personality Development* (New York: Wiley).

Caspi, A., Henry, W., McGee, R., Moffitt, T. and Silva, P. (1995) 'Temperamental origins of child and adolescent behaviour problems: from age three to fifteen', *Child Development* 66, 55–68.

Caspi, A. and Herbener, E. (1990) 'Continuity and change: assortative marriage and the consistency of personality in adulthood', *Journal of Personality and Social Psychology* 58, 250–8.

Caspi, A., Moffitt, T., Silva, P., Stouthamer-Loeber, M., Krueger, R. and Schmutte, P. (1994) 'Are some people crime-prone? Replications of the personality–crime relationship across countries, genders, races, and methods', *Criminology* 32, 163–95.

Caspi, A. and Silva, P. (1995) 'Temperamental qualities at age 3 predict personality traits in young adulthood: longitudinal evidence from a birth cohort', *Child Development* 66, 486–98.

Cass, V. (1984) 'Homosexual identity formation: testing a theoretical model', *Journal of Sex Research* 20, 143–67.

Cassia, V., Turati, C. and Simion, F. (2004) 'Can a species-specific bias toward top heavy patterns explain newborn face preferences?' *Psychological Sciences* 15, 379–83.

Cassidy, J. (1990) 'Theoretical and methodological considerations in the study of attachment and the self in young children', in M. Greenberg, D. Cicchetti and E. Cummings (eds), *Attachment in the Preschool Years: Theory, research and intervention* (Chicago: University of Chicago Press).

Cassidy, J. (1994) 'Emotion regulation: influences of attachment relationships: biological and behavioural constraints', *Monographs of the Society for Research in Child Development* 59.

Cattell, R. (1963) 'The theory of fluid and crystallised intelligence: a critical experiment', *Journal of Educational Psychology* 54, 1–22.

Cattell, R., Eber, A. and Tatsuoka, A. (1970) *Handbook for the Sixteen Personality Factor Questionnaire (16PF) in Clinical, Educational, Industrial and Research Psychology, for Use with All Forms of the Test* (Champaign, Ill.: Institute for Personality and Ability Testing).

Cawson, P., Wattam, C., Brooker, S. and Kelly, G. (2000) *Child Maltreatment in the United Kingdom: A strong prevalence of child abuse and neglect* (London: NSPCC, 26).

Ceci, S. and Bruck, M. (1993) 'The suggestibility of the child witness: a historical review and synthesis', *Psychological Bulletin* 113, 403–39.

Ceci, S., Leichman, M. and White, T. (1999) 'Interviewing preschoolers: remembrance of things planted', in D. Peters (ed.), *The Child Witness in Context: Cognitive, social and legal perspectives* (Dordrecht, Netherlands: Kluwer).

Ceci, S. and Liker, J. (1986) 'A day at the races: a study of IQ, cognitive complexity and expertise', *Journal of Experimental Psychology: General* 115, 255–66.

Chalmers, A. (1999) *What is this Thing Called Science?* 3rd edn (Buckingham: Open University Press).

Chance, J. and Goldstein, A. (1984) 'Face recognition memory; implications for children's eye witness testimony', *Journal of Social Issues* 40, 6–85.

Chang, F., Dell, G. and Bock, K. (2006) 'Becoming syntactic', *Psychological Review* 113, 234–72.

Chao, R. (1994) 'Beyond parental control and authoritarian parenting style: understanding Chinese parenting through the cultural notion of training', *Child Development* 65, 1111–19.

Chazan, D. (1993) 'High school geometry students' justification for their views of empirical evidence and mathematical proof', *Educational Studies in Mathematics* 24, 359–87.

Chen, H. (2004) 'Arthrogryposis', EMedecine Specialities (online) http://www.emedicine.com/ped/topic142.htm.

Chen, X., Dong, Q. and Zhou, H. (1997) 'Authoritative and authoritarian parenting practices and social and school performance in Chinese children', *International Journal of Behavioral Development* 21, 855–73.

Chen, Z. and Siegler, R. (2000) 'Across the great divide: bridging the gap between understanding of toddlers' and older children's thinking', *Monographs for the Society for Research in Child Development* 65.

Cheng, G., Chan, D. and Tong, P. (2006) 'Qualities of online friendships with different gender compositions and durations', *CyberPsychology and Behavior* 9, 14–21.

Chi, M. (1978) 'Knowledge structures and memory development', in R. Siegler (ed.), *Children's Thinking: What develops?* (Hillsdale, N.J.: Erlbaum).

Chi, M. and Ceci, S. (1987) 'Content knowledge: its role, representation and restructuring in memory development', *Advances in Child Development and Behaviour* 20, 91–142.

Chi, M., Feltovich, P. and Glaser, R. (1981) 'Categorization and representation in physics problems by experts and novices', *Cognitive Science* 5, 121–52.

Chi, M., Glaser, R. and Rees, E. (1982) 'Expertise in problem solving', in R. Sternberg (ed.), *Advances in the Psychology of Human Intelligence* 1, 7–75.

Chomsky, N. (1957) *Syntactic Structures* (The Hague: Mouton).

Chomsky, N. (1979) 'Interview with Brian McGhee', in B. McGhee (ed.), *Men of Ideas* (London: BBC Publications).

Chomsky, N. (1980) 'On cognitive structures and their development: a reply to Piaget', in M. Piattelli-Palmarini (ed.), *Language and Learning: The debate between Jean Piaget and Noam Chomsky* (Cambridge, Mass.: Harvard University Press).

Christensen, M. and Kessing, L. (2006) 'Do personality traits predict first onset in depressive and bipolar disorder?' *Nordic Journal of Psychiatry* 60, 79–88.

Christian, R., Frick, P., Hill, N., Tyler, L. and Frazer, D. (1997) 'Psychopathy and conduct problems in children: II. Implications for subtyping children with conduct problems', *Journal of the American Academy of Child and Adolescent Psychiatry* 36, 233–41.

Chugani, H., Phelps, M. and Mazziotta, J. (1987) 'Positron emission tomography study of human brain functional development', *Annals of Neurology* 22, 487–97.

Cicchetti, D. and Toth, S. (1998) 'The development of depression in children and adolescents', *American Psychologist* 53, 221–41.

Clark, A., Wyon, S. and Richards, M. (1969) 'Free play in nursery school', *Journal of Child Psychology and Psychiatry* 10, 205–16.

Clarke-Stewart, K., Vandell, D., McCartney, K., Owen, M. and Booth, C. (2000) 'Effects of parental separation and divorce on very young children', *Journal of Family Psychology* 14, 304–26.

Clearfield, M. and Mix, K. (1999) 'Number vs contour length in infants' discrimination of small visual sets', *Psychological Science* 10, 408–11.

Cleckley, H. (2003) *The Mask of Sanity*, 5th edn (Textbook Publications).

Clifton, R., Muir, D., Ashmead, D. and Clarkson, M. (1993) 'Is visually guided reaching in early infancy a myth?' *Child Development* 64, 1099–110.

Cohen, A., Pierce, J., Chambers, J., Meade, R., Gorvine, B. and Koenig, H. (2005) 'Intrinsic and extrinsic religiosity, belief in the afterlife, death anxiety and life satisfaction in young Catholics and Protestants', *Journal of Research in Personality* 39, 307–24.

Cohen, B. (2004) 'Modelling the development of infant categorization', *Infancy* 5, 127–30.

Coie, J. and Dodge, K. (1998) 'Aggression and antisocial behaviour', pp. 779–862 in N. Eisenberg (ed.), W. Damon (series ed.), *Handbook of Child Psychology*, vol. 3: *Social, Emotional and Personality Development* (New York: Wiley).

Coie, J., Dodge, K. and Coppotelli, H. (1983) 'Dimensions and types of social status: a cross-age perspective: correction', *Developmental Psychology* 19, 224.

Colby, A., Kohlberg, L., Gibbs, J. and Lieberman, M. (1983) 'A longitudinal study of moral judgement', *Monographs of the Society for Research in Child Development* 48.

Cole, M. and Scribner, S. (1974) *Culture and Thought: A psychological introduction* (New York: Wiley).

Coleman, P. and Watson, A. (2000) 'Infant attachment as a dynamic system', *Human Development* 43, 295–313.

Coley, J. (2000) 'On the importance of comparative research: the case of folk biology', *Child Development* 71, 82–90.

Conard, M. (2006) 'Aptitude is not enough: how personality and behaviour predict academic performance', *Journal of Research in Personality* 40, 339–46.

Connolly, J., Goldberg, A. and Pepler, D. (1999) 'Conceptions of cross-sex friendships and romantic relationships in early adolescence', *Journal of Youth and Adolescence* 28, 481–94.

Conway, M. and Pleydell-Pearce, C. (2000) 'The construction of autobiographical memories in the self-memory system', *Psychological Review* 107, 261–88.

Cooley, C. (1925) *Human Nature and the Social Order* (New York: Schribner).

Cooper, R. and Aslin, R. (1994) 'Developmental differences in infant attention to the spectral properties of infant directed speech', *Child Development* 65, 1663–77.

Cosmides, L. and Tooby, J. (1992) 'Cognitive adaptations for social exchange', in J. Barkow, L. Cosmides and J. Tooby (eds), *The Adapted Mind: Evolutionary psychology and the generation of culture* (New York: Oxford University Press).

Cosmides, L. and Tooby, J. (2005a) 'Social exchange: the evolutionary design of a neurocognitive system', pp. 1295–308 in M. Gazzaniga (ed.), *The New Cognitive Neurosciences 111* (Cambridge, Mass.: MIT Press).

Cosmides, L. and Tooby, J. (2005b) 'Neurocognitive adaptations designed for social exchange', pp. 584–627 in D. M. Buss (ed.), *The Handbook of Evolutionary Psychology* (Hoboken, N.J.: Wiley).

Costa, F. and Izquierdo-Torres, E. (2006) Special issue on the dynamical systems approach to cognition, *Adaptive Behaviour* 14, 101–3.

Cottrell, J. (1996) *Social Networks and Social Influences in Adolescence* (London: Routledge).

Covington, M. (2001) 'The science and politics of self-esteem', in T. Owens, S. Stryker and N. Goodman (eds), *Extending Self-Esteem Theory and Research: Sociological and psychological currents* (Cambridge, UK: Cambridge University Press).

Cowan, N., Nugent, L., Elliot, E., Ponomarev, I. and Scott Saults, J. (1999) 'The role of attention in the development of short-term memory: age differences in verbal span apprehension', *Child Development* 70, 1082–97.

Cox, M. and Paley, B. (2003) 'Understanding families as systems', *Current Directions in Psychological Science* 12, 193–6.

Craik, F. and Lockhart, R. (1972) 'Levels of processing: a framework for memory research', *Journal of Verbal Learning and Verbal Behaviour* 11, 671–84.

Crano, W., Kenny, J. and Campbell, D. (1972) 'Does intelligence cause achievement? A cross-lagged panel analysis', *Journal of Educational Psychology* 63, 258–75.

Crick, N., Casas, J. and Ku, H. (1999) 'Relational and physical forms of peer victimization in preschool', *Developmental Psychology* 35, 376–85.

Crick, N. and Dodge, K. (1999) '"Superiority" is in the eye of the beholder: a comment on Sutton, Smith and Swettenham', *Social Development* 8, 128–31.

Crisp, J., Ungerer, J. and Goodnow, J. (1996) 'The impact of experience on children's understanding of illness', *Journal of Pediatric Psychology* 21, 57–72.

Crisafi, M. and Brown, A. (1986) 'Analogical transfer in very young children: combining two separately learned solutions to reach a goal', *Child Development* 57, 953–68.

Crockett, L., Losoff, M. and Peterson, A. (1984) 'Perceptions of the peer group and friendship in early adolescence', *Journal of Early Adolescence* 4, 155–81.

Csibra, G., Tucker, L. and Johnson, M. (1998) 'Neural correlates of saccade planning in infants: a high-density ERP study', *International Journal of Psychophysiology* 29, 201–15.

Damon, W. (1977) 'Measurement and social development', *Counseling Psychologist* 6, 13–15.

Damon, W. (1980) 'Patterns of change in children's prosocial reasoning: a two year longitudinal study', *Child Development* 51, 1010–17.

Damon, W. (1983) *Social and Personality Development: Infancy through adolescence* (New York: Norton).

D'Andrade, R. (1995) *The Development of Cognitive Anthropology* (Cambridge, UK: Cambridge University Press).

Dapretto, M., Davies, M., Pfeifer, J., Scott, A., Sigman, M., Bookheimer, S. and Iacoboni, M. (2006) 'Understanding emotions in others: mirror neuron dysfunction in children with autism spectrum disorders', *Nature Neuroscience* 9, 26–30.

Darwin, C. (1859/2003) *The Origin of Species by Means of Natural Selection* (Signet Classics).

Darwin, C. (1877) 'A biographical sketch of an infant', in A. Slater and D. Muir (eds) (1999) *The Blackwell Reader in Developmental Psychology* (Cambridge, Mass.: Blackwell).

Davies, P. (2006) *The Goldilocks Enigma: Why is the universe just right for life?* (London: Allen Lane).

Dawkins, R. (1976) *The Selfish Gene* (Oxford: Oxford University Press).

Dawkins, R. (2006) *The God Delusion* (London: Bantam).

Deater-Deckard, K. and Dodge, K. (1997) 'Externalizing behavior problems and discipline revisited: nonlinear effects and variation by culture, context and gender', *Psychological Enquiry* 8, 161–75.

De Fruyt, F., Bartels, M., van Leeuwen, K., De Clercq, B., Decuyper, M. and Mervielde, I. (2006) 'Five types of personality continuity in childhood and adolescence', *Journal of Personality and Social Psychology* 91, 538–52.

De Groot, A. (1965) *Thought and Choice in Chess* (The Hague: Mouton).

Deidrich, F., Highlands, T., Spahr, K., Thelen, E. and Smith, L. (2001) 'The role of target distinctiveness in infant perseverative reaching', *Journal of Experimental Child Psychology* 78, 263–90.

DeKlyen, M., Biernbaum, M., Speltz, M. and Greenberg, M. (1998) 'Fathers and preschool behaviour problems'. *Developmental Psychology* 34, 264–75.

Delaney, C. (1995) 'Rites of passage in adolescence', *Adolescence* 30, 891–7.

DeLoache, J. (2000) 'Dual representation and young children's use of scale models', *Child Development* 71, 329–38.

DeLoache, J., Cassidy, D. and Brown, A. (1985) 'Precursors of mnemonic strategies in very young children's memory', *Child Development* 56, 125–37.

DeLoache, J., Miller, K. and Pierroutsakos, S. (1998) 'Reasoning and problem solving', in D. Kuhn and R. Siegler (eds), W. Damon (series ed.), *The Handbook of Child Psychology*, vol. 2: *Cognition, Perception and Language* (New York: Wiley).

Dempster, F. (1985) 'Short term memory development in childhood and adolescence', in C. Brainerd and M. Pressley (eds), *Basic Processes in Memory Development: Progress in cognitive development research* (New York: Springer-Verlag).

Dennett, D. (1996) *Darwin's Dangerous Idea: Evolution and the meanings of life* (New York: Touchstone/Simon and Schuster).

Dennis, C. and Gallagher, R. (eds) (2002) *The Human Genome* (London: Palgrave Macmillan).

Descartes, R. (1637) *Discourse on Method* (Paris).

De Vries, G. (2004) 'Minireview: sex differences in adult and developing brains: compensation, compensation, compensation', *Endocrinology* 145, 1063–8.

De Vries, J., Visser, G. and Prechtl, H. (1984) 'Fetal motility in the first half of pregnancy', in H. Prechtl (ed.),

Continuity of Neural Function from Prenatal to Postnatal Life (London: Spastics International Medical Publications).

Diamond, A. and Doar, B. (1989) 'The performance of human infants on a measure of frontal cortex function, the delayed response task', *Developmental Psychology* 22, 271–94.

Diamond, M. and Sigmundson, H. (1999) 'Sex reassignment at birth', pp. 55–80 in S. Ceci and W. Williams (eds), *The Nature–Nurture Debate: Essential readings* (Cambridge, Mass./Oxford: Blackwell).

DiPietro, J. (1995) 'Fetal origins of neurobehavioural function and individual differences', paper presented at the meeting of the Society for Research in Child Development, Indianapolis.

DiPietro, J., Costigan, K., Shupe, A., Pressman, E. and Johnson, T. (1998) 'Fetal neurobehavioural development: associations with socioeconomic class and fetal sex', *Developmental Psychobiology* 33, 79–91.

DiPietro, J., Hodgson, D., Costigan, K., Hilton, S. and Johnson, T. (1996) 'Fetal neurobehavioural development', *Child Development* 67, 2553–67.

Dishion, T. and Snyder, J. (2004) 'An introduction to the special issue on advances in process and dynamic system analysis of social interaction and development of antisocial behaviour', *Journal of Abnormal Child Psychology* 32, 575–8.

Dittmar, H. (2004) 'Understanding and diagnosing compulsive buying', in R. Coombs (ed.), *Addictive Disorders: A practical handbook* (New York: Wiley).

Dodge, K., Pettit, G., Bates, J. and Valente, E. (1995) 'Social information processing patterns partially mediate the effect of early physical abuse on later conduct problems', *Journal of Abnormal Psychology* 104, 632–43.

Doise, W. (1978) *Groups and Individuals* (Cambridge, UK: Cambridge University Press).

Doise, W. and Hanselmann, C. (1991) 'Conflict and social marking in the acquisition of operational thinking', *Learning and Instruction* 1, 119–27.

Doise, W. and Mugny, G. (1984) *The Development of Social Intellect* (Oxford: Pergamon Press).

Donaldson, M. (1978) *Children's Minds* (London: Fontana).

Dondi, M., Simion, F., and Caltran, G. (1999) 'Can newborns discriminate between their own cry and the cry of another newborn infant?' *Developmental Psychology* 35, 323–34.

Donlan, C. (ed.) (1998) *The Development of Mathematical Skills* (Hove: Psychology Press/Taylor & Francis).

Dromi, E. (1987) *Early Lexical Development* (London: Cambridge University Press).

Dunn, J. (1988) *The Beginnings of Social Understanding* (Cambridge, Mass.: Harvard University Press).

Dunn, J. (1995) *From One Child to Two* (New York: Fawcett).

Dunn, J. (2005) 'Daddy doesn't live here any more', *Psychologist* 18, 28–31.

Dunn, J., Bretherton, I. and Munn, P. (1987) 'Conversations about feeling states between mothers and their young children', *Developmental Psychology* 23, 132–9.

Dunn, J., Brown, J. and Beardsall, L. (1991) 'Family talk about feeling states and children's later understanding of other's emotions', *Developmental Psychology* 27, 448–55.

Dunn, J., Brown, J., Slomkowski, C., Tesla, C. and Youngblade, L. (1991) 'Young children's understanding of other people's feelings and beliefs: individual differences and their antecedents', *Child Development* 62, 1352–66.

Dunn, J. and Kendrick, C. (1982) *Siblings: Love, envy and understanding* (Boston, Mass.: Harvard University Press).

Dunn, J. and Munn, P. (1985) 'Becoming a family member: family conflict and the development of social understanding in the second year', *Child Development* 56, 480–92.

Dunn, J. and Shatz, M. (1989) 'Becoming a conversationalist despite (or because of) having a sibling', *Child Development* 60, 399–410.

Dunne, J., Hudgins, E. and Babcock, J. (2000) 'Can changing the divorce law affect post-divorce adjustment?' *Journal of Divorce and Remarriage* 33, 35–54.

Dunning, D. (2006) 'Strangers to ourselves?' *The Psychologist* 19, 600–3.

Dunning, D., Heath, C. and Suls, J. (2004) 'Flawed self-assessment: implications for health, education and the workplace', *Psychology in the Public Interest* 5, 69–106.

Dunphy, D. (1963) 'The social structure of urban adolescence peer groups', *Sociometry* 26, 230–46.

Dwairy, M. and Menshar, K. (2006) 'Parenting style, individuation and mental health of Egyptian adolescents', *Journal of Adolescence* 29, 103–17.

Ebbinghaus, H. (1913) *A Contribution to Experimental Psychology* (New York: Teachers College, Columbia University).

Egan, V., Kavanagh, B. and Blair, M. (2005) 'Sexual offenders against children: the influence of personality and obsessionality on cognitive distortions', *Sexual Abuse* 17, 223–40.

Eibl-Eibesfeldt, I. (1971) *Love and Hate* (London: Methuen).

Eibl-Eibesfeldt, I. (1972) 'Similarities and differences between cultures in expressive movements', in R. Hinde (ed.), *Non-Verbal Communication* (Cambridge, UK: Cambridge University Press).

Eigen, M. (2006) 'Introduction to the special issue: Fundamentalism and terrorism', *Psychoanalytic Review* 93, 142–66.

Eimas, P., Siqueland, E., Juscyzk, P. and Vigorito, J. (1971) 'Speech perception in infants', *Science* 171, 303–6.

Eisenberg, N. (1986) *Altruistic Emotion, Cognition and Behavior* (Hillsdale, N.J.: Erlbaum).

Eisenberg, N. (1992) *The Caring Child* (Cambridge, Mass.: Harvard University Press).

Eisenberg, N. and Fabes, R. (1992) 'Emotion, regulation and the development of social competence', in M. Clark (ed.), *Emotion and Social Behaviour*, vol. 14: *Review of Personality and Social Development* (Newbury Park, Calif.: Sage).

Eisenberg, N. and Fabes, R. (1998) 'Prosocial development', in N. Eisenberg (ed.), W. Damon (series ed.), *Handbook of Child Psychology*, vol. 3: *Social, Emotional and Personality Development* (New York: Wiley).

Eisenberg, N., Fabes, R., Bustamente, D., Mathy, R., Miller, P. and Lindholm, E. (1988) 'Differentiation of vicariously induced emotional reactions in children', *Developmental Psychology* 24, 237–46.

Eisenberg, N., Fabes, R., Carlo, G. and Karbon, M. (1992) 'Emotional responsivity to others: behavioural correlates and socialisation antecedents', in N. Eisenberg and R. Fabes (eds), *New Directions in Child Development: Emotion and its regulation in early development*, vol. 5 (San Francisco: Jossey-Bass).

Eisenberg, N., Fabes, R., Carlo, G., Troyer, D., Speer, A., Karbon, M. and Switzer, G. (1992) 'The relations of maternal practices and characteristics to children's vicarious emotional responsiveness', *Child Development* 63, 583–602.

Eisenberg, N., Fabes, R., Schaller, M., Carlo, G. and Miller, P. (1991). 'The relations of parental characteristics and practices to children's vicarious emotional responding', *Child Development* 62, 1393–408.

Eisenberg, N., Fabes, R., Schaller, M. and Miller, P. (1989) 'Sympathy and personal distress: development, gender differences and interrelations of indexes', *New Directions for Child Development* 44, 107–26.

Eisenberg, N. and McNally, S. (1993) 'Socialisation and mother's and adolescent's empathy-related characteristics', *Journal of Research on Adolescence* 3, 171–91.

Eisenberg, N. and Miller, P. (1987) 'The relation of empathy to prosocial and related behaviours', *Psychological Bulletin* 101, 91–119.

Elder, G. (1985) 'Perspectives on the life course', pp. 23–49 in G. Elder (ed.), *Life Course Dynamics: Trajectories and transitions 1968–1980* (Ithaca, NY: Cornell University Press).

Elkind, D. (1967) 'Egocentrism in adolescence', *Child Development* 38, 1025–34.

Ellis, R. and Wells, G. (1980) 'Enabling factors in adult–child discourse', *First Language* 1, 46–62.

Emde, R. (1988) 'Development terminable and interminable: innate and motivational factors from infancy', *International Journal of Psychoanalysis* 69, 23–5.

Emery, R. and Laumann-Billings, L. (1998) 'An overview of the nature, causes and consequences of abusive family relationships: toward differentiating maltreatment and violence', *American Psychologist* 53, 121–35.

Ennett, S. and Bauman, K. (1994) 'The contribution of influence and selection to adolescent peer group homogeneity: the case of adolescent cigarette smoking', *Journal of Personality and Social Psychology* 67, 653–63.

Epstein, E. and Guttman, R. (1984) 'Mate selection in man: evidence, theory and outcome', *Social Biology* 31, 243–78.

Erdley, C, and Asher, S. (1996) 'Children's social goals and self-efficacy perceptions as influences on their responses to ambiguous provocation', *Child Development* 67, 1329–44.

Ericsson, K. and Simon, H. (1993) *Protocol Analysis: Verbal reports as data* (Cambridge, Mass.: MIT Press).

Erikson, E. (1968) *Identity, Youth and Crisis* (New York: Norton).

Erikson, E. (1980) extended by Erikson, J (1997) *The Life Cycle Completed* (New York: W.W. Norton).

Erikson, E. (1997) *The Life Cycle Completed* (extended version) (New York: W. W. Norton).

Ervin, L. and Stryker, S. (2001) 'Theorising the relationship between self-esteem and identity', in T. Owens, S. Stryker and N. Goodman (eds), *Extending Self-Esteem Theory and Research: Sociological and psychological currents* (Cambridge, UK: Cambridge University Press).

Erwin, P. (1998) *Friendship in Childhood and Adolescence* (London: Routledge).

Eskin, M. (2004) 'The effects of religious versus secular education on suicide ideation and suicidal attitudes in adolescents in Turkey', *Social Psychiatry and Psychiatric Epidemiology* 39, 536–42.

Evans, J. St. (1989) *Bias in Human Reasoning: Causes and consequences* (Hove: Erlbaum).

Evans, J. St., Barstow, J. and Pollard, P. (1983) 'On the conflict between logic and belief in syllogistic reasoning', *Memory and Cognition* 11, 295–306.

Evans, J. St., Newstead, S. and Byrne, R. (1993) *Human Reasoning: The psychology of deduction* (Hove: Erlbaum).

Evans, J. St. and Pollard, P. (1990) 'Belief bias and problem complexity in deductive reasoning', in J. Caverni, J. Fabre and M. Gonzales (eds), *Cognitive Biases* (Amsterdam: North Holland).

Eysenck, H. and Eysenck, M. (1985) *Personality and Individual Differences: A natural science approach* (New York: Plenum Press).

Fabricius, W. (1988) 'The development of forward search in preschoolers', *Child Development* 59, 1473–88.

Fabricius, W. and Wellman, H. (1983) 'Children's understanding of retrieval cue utilisation', *Developmental Psychology* 19, 15–21.

Fagan, A. and Najman, J. (2005) 'The relative contributions of parental and sibling substance use to adolescent tobacco, alcohol and other drug use', *Journal of Drug Issues* 35, 869–84.

Fagan, J. (1984) 'Infant memory: history, current trends and relations to cognitive psychology', in M. Moscovitch (ed.), *Infant Memory: Its relation to normal and pathological memory in humans and animals* (Hillsdale, N.J.: Erlbaum).

Fagot, B. and Leinbach, M. (1989) 'The young child's gender schema: environmental input, internal organization', *Child Development* 60, 663–72.

Falbo, T. and Poston, D. (1993) 'The academic, personality and physical outcomes of only children in Chinese children', *Journal of Biosocial Science* 21, 483–95.

Fantz, R. (1961) 'The origins of form perception', *Scientific American* 204, 66–72.

Farver, J. and Branstetter, W. (1994) 'Preschoolers prosocial responses to their peers distress', *Developmental Psychology* 30, 334–41.

Feigenson, L., Dehaene, S. and Spelke, E. (2004) 'Core systems of number', *Trends in Cognitive Science* 8, 307–14.

Feinman, S. (1982) 'Social referencing in infancy', *Merrill-Palmer Quarterly* 28, 445–70.

Feiring, C. (1996) 'Concepts of romance in 15-year-old adolescents', *Journal of Research in Adolescence* 6, 181–200.

Fenson, L., Dale, P., Reznick, J., Bates, E., Thal, D. and Pethick, S. (1994) 'Variability in early communicative development', *Monographs of the Society for Research in Child Development* 59.

Fernald, A. (1989) 'Intonation and communicative intent in mother's speech to infants: is the melody the message?' *Child Development* 60, 1497–510.

Fernald, A. and Morikawa, H. (1993) 'Common themes and cultural variations in Japanese and American mothers' speech to infants', *Child Development* 64, 637–56.

Fernandez, Y. and Marshall, W. (2003) 'Sexual abuse', *Journal of Research and Treatment* 15, 11–26.

Ferreiro, E. and Teberosky, A. (1983) *Literacy before Schooling* (Exeter, N.H.: Heinemann Educational).

Field, T., Woodson, R., Greenberg, R. and Cohen, C. (1982) 'Discrimination and imitation of facial expressions by neonates', *Science* 218, 179–81.

Fifer, W. and Moon, C. (1995) 'The effects of fetal experience with sound', in J. Lecanuet, P. Fifer, N. Kasnegor and W. Smotherman (eds), *Fetal Development: A psychobiological perspective* (Hillsdale, N.J.: Erlbaum).

Finlay, B., Darlington, R. and Nicastro, N. (2001) 'Developmental structure in brain evolution', *Behavioural and Brain Science* 24, 263–78.

Fischbein, E. (1975) *The Intuitive Sources of Probabilistic Thinking in Children* (Boston, Mass.: Riedel).

Fischoff, B. (1975) 'Hindsight is not equal to foresight: the effect of outcome knowledge on judgment under uncertainty', *Journal of Experimental Psychology: Human Perception and Performance* 1, 288–99.

Fisher, C. (2000) 'From form to meaning: a role for structural alignment in the acquisition of language', *Advances in Child Development and Behaviour* 27, 1–53.

Flaks, D., Fischer, I., Masterpasqua, F. and Joseph, G. (1995) 'Lesbians choosing motherhood: a comparative study of lesbian and heterosexual parents and their children', *Developmental Psychology* 31, 104–14.

Flanagan, C. (1995) 'Adolescents' explanations for poverty, unemployment, homelessness and wealth', paper presented at the biennial meetings of the Society for Research on Child Development, Indianapolis, Indiana.

Flavell, J. (1985) *Cognitive Development* (Englewood Cliffs, N.J.: Prentice-Hall).

Flavell, J., Flavell, E. and Green, F. (1983) 'Development of the appearance–reality distinction', *Cognitive Psychology* 15, 95–120.

Flavell, J., Green, F. and Flavell, E. (1995) 'Young children's knowledge about thinking', *Monographs of the Society for Research in Child Development* 60, 1–243.

Flavell, J. and Miller, P. (1998) 'Social cognition', in D. Kuhn and R. Siegler (eds), W. Damon (series ed.), *Handbook of Child Psychology*, vol. 2: *Cognition, Perception and Language* (New York: Wiley).

Flavell, J. and Wellman, H. (1977) 'Metamemory', in R. Kail and J. Hagen (eds), *Perspectives on the Development of Memory and Cognition* (Hillsdale, N.J.: Erlbaum).

Flom, R. and Pick, A. (2005) 'Experimenter affective expression and gaze following in 7-month-olds', *Infancy* 7, 207–18.

Fodor, J. (1983) *The Modularity of Mind* (Cambridge, Mass.: MIT Press).

Fodor, J. (1992) 'A theory of the child's theory of mind', *Cognition* 44, 283–96.

Fogel, A. and Thelen, E. (1987) 'Development of early expressive and communicative action: reinterpreting the evidence from a dynamic systems perspective', *Developmental Psychology* 23, 747–61.

Fonagy, P., Steele, H. and Steele, M. (1991) 'Maternal representations of attachment during pregnancy predict organization of infant–mother attachment at one year of age', *Child Development* 62, 891–905.

Ford, M. (2005) 'The game, the pieces, and the players: generative resources from two instructional portrayals of experimentation', *Journal of the Learning Sciences* 14, 449–87.

Forsyth, C., Frank, A., Watrous, B. and Bohn, A. (1994) 'The effect of coniine on the developing chick embryo', *Teratology* 49, 306–10.

Foster, S. (2006) 'A literature review: the effects of maternal stress in pregnancy on sensory integration in children', *Journal of Prenatal and Perinatal Psychology and Health* 21, 83–90.

Fowler, J. (1981) *Stages of Faith: The psychology of human development and the quest for meaning* (New York: Harper & Row).

Fowler, J. (1986) 'Faith and the structuring of meaning', in C. Dykstra and S. Parks (eds), *Faith Development and Fowler* (Birmingham, Ala.: Religious Education Press).

Fowler, J. and Dell, M. (2004) 'Stages of faith and identity: birth to teens', *Child and Adolescent Psychiatric Clinics of North America* 13, 17–33.

Fox, C. and Boulton, M. (2006) 'Friendship as a moderator of the relationship between social skills problems and peer victimisation', *Aggressive Behavior* 32, 110–21.

Fraisse, P. (1982) 'The adaptation of the child to time', in W. Friedman (ed.), *The Developmental Psychology of Time* (New York: Academic Press).

Freedman, D. and Freedman, N. (1969) 'Behavioral differences between Chinese-American and European-American newborns'. *Nature* 224, 1227.

Freud, A. (1973/1984) *Beyond the Best Interests of the Child* (New York: Free Press).

Freud, A. and Dann, S. (1972) 'An experiment in group upbringing', pp. 449–73 in U. Bronfenbrenner (ed.), *Influences on Human Development* (Hinsdale, Ill.: Dryden Press). Original work published 1951 in *The Psychoanalytic Study of the Child*, vol. 6, 127–68.

Freud, S. (1904/2002) *The Pathology of Everyday Life* (London: Penguin).

Freud, S. (1933/1964*) New Introductory Lectures on Psychoanalysis* (trans. J. Strachey) (New York: W.W. Norton).

Freud, S. (1940) 'An outline of psychoanalysis', in J. Strachey (ed.), *The Standard Edition of the Complete Works of Sigmund Freud* (London: Hogarth Press).

Frey, K. and Ruble, D. (1985) 'What children say when the teacher is not around: conflicting goals in comparison and performance assessment in the classroom', *Journal of Personality and Social Psychology* 48, 550–62.

Frick, P. and Hare, R. (1997) *The Psychopathy Screening Device* (Toronto: Multi-Health Systems).

Frick, P., O'Brien, B., Wooton, J. and McBurnett, K. (1994) 'Psychopathy and conduct problems in children', *Journal of Abnormal Psychology* 103, 700–7.

Friedman, H., Tucker, J., Schwartz, J., Tomlinson-Keasey, C., Martin, L., Wingard, D. and Criqui, M. (1995) 'Psychosocial and behavioral predictors of longevity', *American Psychologist* 50, 69–78.

Friedman, W. (1991) 'The development of children's memory for the time of past events', *Child Development* 62, 139–55.

Friedman, W., Gardner, A. and Zubin, N. (1995) 'Children's comparison of the recency of two events from the past year', *Child Development* 66, 970–83.

Frith, C. and Frith, U. (1996) 'A biological marker for dyslexia', *Nature* 382, 19–20.

Frith, U. (1989) *Autism: Explaining the enigma* (Oxford: Blackwell).

Frosch, C., Mangelsdorf, S. and McHale, J. (2000) 'Marital behaviour and the security of pre-schooler attachment relationships', *Journal of Family Psychology* 14, 144–61.

Frye, D. and Moore, C. (eds) (1991) *Children's Theories of Mind: Mental states and social understanding* (Hove: Erlbaum).

Frye, D., Zelazo, P., Brooks, P. and Samuels, M. (1996) 'Inference and action in early causal reasoning', *Developmental Psychology* 32, 120–31.

Fuchs, D. and Thelen, M. (1988) 'Children's expected interpersonal consequences of communicating their affective state and reported likelihood of expression', *Child Development* 58, 1314–22.

Funder, D. (2006) 'Towards a resolution of the personality triad: persons, situations and behaviors', *Journal of Research in Personality* 40, 21–34.

Furman, W. and Wehner, E. (1994) 'Romantic views: toward a theory of adolescent romantic relationships', in R. Montemayer, G. Adams and C. Fullotta (eds), *Personal Relationships during Adolescence* (Thousand Oaks, Calif.: Sage).

Furrow, T., King, P. and White, K. (2004) 'Religion and positive youth development: identity, meaning and prosocial concerns', *Applied Developmental Science* 8, 17–26.

Gagne, R. (1968) 'Contributions of learning to human development', *Psychological Review* 75, 177–91.

Galen, B. and Underwood, M. (1997) 'A developmental investigation of social aggression among children', *Developmental Psychology* 33, 589–600.

Gallese, V., Fadiga, L., Fogassi, L. and Rizzolatti, G (1996) 'Action recognition in the pre-motor cortex', *Brain* 119, 593–609.

Gallese, V. and Goldman, A. (1998) 'Mirror neurons and the simulation theory of mind reading', *Trends in the Cognitive Sciences* 2, 493–501.

Gallistel, C. (1990) *The Organization of Learning* (Cambridge, Mass.: MIT Press).

Galton, F. (1892) *Hereditary Genius* (London: Macmillan).

Ganchrow, J., Steiner, J. and Daher, M., (1983) 'Neonatal facial expressions in response to different qualities and intensities of gustatory stimuli', *Infant Behavior and Development* 6, 473–84.

Gandelman, R. (1992) *The Psychobiology of Behavioural Development* (Oxford: Oxford University Press).

Gardner, B. and Gardner, R. (1980) 'Two comparative psychologists look at language acquisition', in K. Nelson (ed.), *Children's Language,* vol. 2 (New York: Basic Books).

Gardner, H. (1983) *Frames of Mind: the Theory of Multiple Intelligences* (London: Heinemann).

Gardner, R. and Gardner, B. (1969) 'Teaching sign language to a chimpanzee', *Science,* 165, 664–72.

Gartrell, N., Deck, A., Rodas, C., Peyser, H. and Banks, A. (2005) 'The National Lesbian Family Study: 4. Interviews with the 10-year-old children', *American Journal of Orthopsychiatry* 75(4), 518–24.

Geary, D. (1998) *Male and Female: The evolution of human sex differences* (Washington, DC: American Psychological Association).

Geary, D. and Bjorklund, D. (2000) 'Evolutionary developmental psychology', *Child Development* 71, 57–65.

Gecas, V. (2001) 'The self as a social force', in T. Owens, S. Stryker and N. Goodman (eds), *Extending Self-Esteem Theory and Research: Sociological and psychological currents* (Cambridge, UK: Cambridge University Press).

Gelman, R. (1980) 'Cognitive development', *Annual Review of Psychology* 29, 297–332.

Gelman, R. (1982) 'Assessing one-to-one correspondence: still another paper about conservation', *British Journal of Developmental Psychology* 73, 209–20.

Gelman, R. and Brenneman, K. (1994) 'First principles can support both universal and culture-specific learning about number and music', in L. Hirschfeld and S. Gelman (eds), *Mapping the Mind: Domain specificity in cognition and culture* (New York: Cambridge University Press).

Gelman, R. and Meck, E. (1992) 'Early principles aid initial but not later conceptions of number', in J. Bideaud, C. Meljac and J. Fischer (eds), *Pathways to Number* (Hillsdale, N.J.: Erlbaum).

Gelman, R., Meck, F. and Merkin, S. (1986) 'Young children's numerical competence', *Cognitive Development* 1, 1–29.

Gelman, R. and Williams, E. (1998) 'Enabling constraints for cognitive development and learning: domain specificity and epigenisis', in D. Kuhn and R. Siegler (eds), W. Damon (series ed.), *Handbook of Child Psychology*, vol. 2: *Cognition, Perception and Language* (New York: Wiley).

Gelman, S. (2003) *The Essential Child: Origins of essentialism in everyday thought* (Oxford: Oxford University Press).

Gelman, S., Coley, J., Rosengren, K., Hartman, E. and Pappas, A. (1998) 'Beyond labelling: the role of maternal input in the acquisition of richly structured categories', *Monographs of the Society for Research in Child Development* 63.

Gelman, S. and Markman, E. (1986) 'Categories and induction in young children', *Cognition* 23, 183–209.

Gelman, S. and Markman, E. (1987) 'Young children's inductions from natural kinds: the role of categories and appearances', *Child Development* 58, 1532–41.

Gentner, D. (1982) 'Why nouns are learned before verbs: linguistic relativity versus natural partitioning', in S. Kuczaj II (ed.), *Language Development*, vol. 2: *Language, Thought and Culture* (Hillsdale N.J., Erlbaum).

Gentner, D. (1983) 'Structure mapping: a theoretical framework for analogy', *Cognitive Science* 7, 155–70.

Gerhardt, S. (2005) *Why Love Matters: How affection shapes a baby's brain* (Philadelphia: Routledge).

Gerken, L. (1994) 'Child phonology: past research, present questions, future directions', in M. Gernsbacher (ed.), *Handbook of Psycholinguistics* (New York: Academic Press).

Gershkoff-Stowe, L. and Thelen, E. (2004) 'U shaped changes in behaviour: a dynamic systems approach', *Journal of Cognition and Development* 5, 11–36.

Gesell, A. and Ames, L. (1940) 'The ontogenetic organization of prone behaviour in human infancy', *Journal of Genetic Psychology* 56, 247–63.

Ghim, H. (1990) 'Evidence for perceptual organization in infants: perception of subjective contours by young infants', *Infant Behaviour and Development* 13, 221–48.

Gholson, B., Dattel, A., Morgan, D. and Eymard, L. (1989) 'Problem solving, recall and mapping relations in isomorphic transfer and non-isomorphic transfer among preschoolers and elementary school children', *Child Development* 60, 1172–87.

Gibson, J. (1979) *The Ecological Approach to Visual Perception* (New York: Appleton Century Crofts).

Giedd, J., Blumenthal, J., Jeffries, N., Castellanos, F., Lui, H., Zijdenbos, A., Paus, T., Evans, A. and Rapaport, J. (1999) 'Brain development during childhood and adolescence: a longitudinal MRI study', *Nature Neuroscience* 2, 861–3.

Gielen, U. and Markoulis, D. (1994) 'Preference for principled moral reasoning: a developmental and cross-cultural perspective', pp. 73–87 in L. Adler and U. Loeb Gielen (eds), *Cross Cultural Topics in Psychology* (Praeger /Greenwood).

Gilligan, C. (1977) 'In a different voice: women's conceptions of the self and of morality', *Harvard Educational Review* 47, 481–517.

Gilligan, C. (1982) *In a Different Voice: Psychological theory and women's development* (Cambridge, Mass.: Harvard University Press).

Glachan, M. and Light, P. (1982) 'Peer interaction and learning: can two wrongs make a right?', in G. Butterworth and P. Light (eds), *Social Cognition* (Brighton: Harvester).

Gleason, T. and Hohmann, L. (2006) 'Concepts of real and imaginary friendships in early childhood', *Social Development* 15, 128–44.

Gleitman, L. (1990) 'The structural sources of verb meanings', *Language Acquisition* 1, 3–55.

Gleitman, L., Newport, E. and Gleitman, H. (1984) 'The current status of the motherese hypothesis', *Journal of Child Language* 11, 43–80.

Gnepp, J. and Hess, D. (1986) 'Children's understanding of verbal and facial display rules', *Developmental Psychology* 22, 103–8.

Goldberg, L. (1993) 'The structure of phenotypic personality traits', *American Psychologist* 48, 26–34.

Goldfield, B. and Reznick, J. (1990) 'Early lexical acquisition: rate, content and the vocabulary spurt', *Journal of Child Language* 17, 171–84.

Goldfield, E. (1994) 'Dynamical systems in development: action systems', in L. Smith and E. Thelen (eds), *A Dynamical Systems Approach to Development: Applications* (Cambridge, Mass.: MIT Press).

Golding, W. (1954) *Lord of the Flies* (Basingstoke: Palgrave).

Goldin-Meadow, S. and Feldman, H. (1979) 'The development of language-like communication without a language model', *Science* 197, 401–3.

Goldsmith, H. and Alansky, J. (1987) 'Maternal and infant temperamental predictors of attachment: a meta-analytic review', *Journal of Consulting and Clinical Psychology* 55, 805–16.

Goldsmith, H., Buss, A., Plomin, R., Rothbart, M., Thomas, A., Chess, S., Hinde, R. and McCall, R. (1987) 'Roundtable: what is a temperament? Four approaches', *Child Development* 58, 505–29.

Golinkoff, R., Alioto, A. and Hirsh-Pasek, K. (1996) 'Infant's word learning is facilitated when novel words are presented in infant-directed speech and in either sentence-medial or sentence-final position', in D. Cahana-Arnitay, L. Hughes, A. Stringfellow and A. Zukowske (eds), *Proceedings of the 20th Boston University Conference on Language Development* (Somerville, Mass.: Cascadilla Press).

Golombok, S., Spencer, A. and Rutter, M. (1983) 'Children in lesbian and single-parent households: psychosexual and psychiatric appraisal', *Journal of Child Psychology and Psychiatry* 24, 551–72.

Goodall, J. (1986) *The Chimpanzees of the Gombe* (Boston, Mass.: Houghton-Mifflin).

Goodglass, H. (1993) *Understanding Aphasia* (San Diego, Calif.: Academic Press).

Gopnik, A. (1993) 'How we know our minds: the illusion of first-person knowledge of intentionality', *Brain and Behavioural Sciences* 16, 1–14.

Gopnik, A. and Astington, J. (1988) 'Children's understanding of representational change and its relation to the understanding of false belief and the appearance–reality distinction', *Child Development* 59, 26–37.

Gopnik, A. and Choi, S. (1995) 'Names, relational words and cognitive development in English and Korean speakers: nouns are not always learned before verbs', in M. Tomasello and W. Merriman (eds), *Beyond Names for Things: Young children's acquisition of verbs* (Hillsdale, N.J.: Lawrence Erlbaum).

Gopnik, A. and Slaughter, V. (1991) 'Young children's understanding of changes in their mental states', *Child Development* 62, 98–110.

Goswami, U. (1986) 'Children's use of analogy in learning to read: a developmental study', *Journal of Experimental Child Psychology* 42, 73–83.

Goswami, U. (1992) *Analogical Reasoning in Children* (Hillsdale N.J.: Lawrence Erlbaum).

Goswami, U. (1995) 'Transitive relational mappings in 3- and 4-year olds: the analogy of Goldilocks and the three bears', *Child Development* 66, 877–92.

Goswami, U. and Brown, A. (1989) 'Melting chocolate and melting snowmen: analogical reasoning and causal relations', *Cognition* 35, 69–95.

Graber, J., Brooks-Gunn, J. and Warren, M. (1995) 'The antecedents of menarcheal age: heredity, family environment and stressful life events', *Child Development* 66, 346–59.

Graham, S. and Juvonen, J. (1998) 'Self blame and peer victimisation in middle school: an attributional analysis', *Developmental Psychology* 34, 587–99.

Grandin, T. and Scariano, M. (1986) *Emergence: Labelled autistic* (Novato, Calif.: Arena).

Granic, I. and Dishion, T (2003) 'Deviant talk in adolescent friendships: a step toward measuring a pathogenic attractor process', *Social Development* 12, 314–34.

Granic, I. and Patterson, G. (2006) 'Toward a comprehensive model of antisocial development: a dynamic systems approach', *Psychological Review* 113, 101–13.

Grant, R. (1996) *Backwards* (London: Penguin).

Greeff, A. and van der Merwe, S. (2004) 'Variables associated with resilience in divorced families.', *Social Indicators Research* 68, 59–75.

Greene, A. (1990) 'Patterns of affectivity in the transition to adolescence', *Journal of Experimental Child Psychology* 50, 340–56.

Greenfield, S. (2003) *Tomorrow's People: How 21st century technology is changing the way we think and feel* (London: Allen Lane).

Greeno, J., Riley, M. and Gelman, R. (1984) 'Conceptual competence and children's counting', *Cognitive Psychology* 16, 94–143.

Grimshaw, J. (1981) 'Form, function, and the language acquisition device', in C. Baker and J. McCarthy (eds), *The Logical Problem of Language Acquisition* (Cambridge, Mass.: MIT Press).

Grollman, E. (1990) *Talking about Death* (Boston, Mass.: Beacon Press).

Grossmann, K., Grossmann, K. E., Spangler, G., Suess, G. and Unzner, L. (1985) 'Maternal sensitivity and newborn's orientation responses as related to quality of attachment in North Germany', in I. Bretherton and E. Waters (eds), *Growing Points of Attachment Theory: Monographs of the Society for Research in Child Development* 50, 233–56.

Grotevant, H. (1998) 'Adolescent development in family contexts', pp. 1097–149 in N. Eisenberg (ed.), W. Damon (series ed,), *Handbook of Child Psychology*, vol. 3: *Social, Emotional and Personality Development* (New York: Wiley).

Guildford, J. (1967) *The Nature of Human Intelligence* (New York: McGraw Hill).

Guildford, J. (1988) 'Some changes in the structure-of-the-intellect model', *Educational and Psychological Measurement* 40, 1–4.

Gunnar, M. (1994) 'Psychoendocrine studies of temperament and stress in early childhood: expanding current models', in J. Bates and T. Wach (eds), *Temperament: Individual differences at the interface of biology and behaviour* (Washington, DC: American Psychological Association).

Gunnoe, M. and Braver, S. (2001) 'The effects of joint legal custody on mothers, fathers and children controlling for factors that predispose a sole maternal versus joint legal award', *Law and Human Behavior* 25, 25–43.

Guttman, D. (1975) 'Parenthood: key to the comparative psychology of the life cycle', pp.167–84 in N. Datan and L. Ginsberg (eds), *Life-Span Developmental Psychology: Normative life crises* (New York: Academic Press).

Guttman, J. and Lazar, A. (1998) 'Mother's or father's custody: does it matter for social adjustment?' *Educational Psychology* 18, 225–34.

Haan, N., Langer, J. and Kohlberg, L. (1976) 'Family patterns of moral reasoning', *Child Development* 47, 1204–1206.

Hadwin, J. and Perner, J. (1991) 'Pleased and surprised: children's cognitive theory of emotion', *British Journal of Developmental Psychology* 9, 215–234.

Haith, M. and Benson, J. (1998) 'Infant cognition', in D. Kuhn and R. Siegler (eds), W. Damon (series ed.), *Handbook of Child Psychology*, vol. 2: *Cognition, Perception and Language* (New York: Wiley).

Haith, M., Wentworth, N. and Canfield, R. (1993) 'The formation of expectations in infancy', in C. Rovee-Collier and L. Lipsitt (eds), *Advances in Infancy Research* (Norwood, N.J.: Ablex).

Halford, G. (1993) *Children's Understanding: The development of mental models* (Hillsdale, N.J.: Lawrence Erlbaum).

Halford, G. and Andrews, G. (2004) 'The development of deductive reasoning: how important is complexity?' *Thinking and Reasoning* 10, 123–45.

Hall, G. S. (1904) *Adolescence* (New York: Appleton).

Hamilton, C. (2000) 'Continuity and discontinuity of attachment from infancy through adolescence', *Child Development* 71, 690–4.

Hamilton, W. (1964) 'The genetical evolution of behaviour', *Journal of Theoretical Biology* 7, 1–52.

Hammack, P. (2006) 'Identity, conflict and coexistence: life stories of Israeli and Palestinian adolescents', *Journal of Adolescent Research* 21, 323–69.

Hampson, S. and Goldberg, L. (2006) 'A first large cohort study of personality trait stability over the 40 years between elementary school and midlife', *Journal of Personality and Social Psychology* 91, 763–79.

Hampson, S., Goldberg, L., Vogt, T. and Dubanoski, J. (2006) 'Forty years on: teachers assessments of children's personality traits predict self-reported health behaviors and outcomes at midlife', *Health Psychology* 25, 57–64.

Hankin, B. and Abramson, L. (1999) 'Development of gender differences in depression: description and possible explanations', *Annals of Medicine* 31, 372–9.

Hanson, R. and Morton-Bourgon, K. (2005) 'The characteristics of persistent sexual offenders: a meta-analysis of recidivism studies', *Journal of Consulting and Clinical Psychology* 73, 1154–63.

Happé, F. (1994) *Autism: An introduction to psychological theory* (London: UCL Press/Psychology Press).

Hardy, S. and Carlo, G. (2005) 'Identity as a source of moral motivation', *Human Development* 48, 232–56.

Hardy, S. and Kisling, J. (2006) 'Identity statuses and prosocial behaviors in young adulthood: a brief report', *Identity* 6, 363–9.

Hare, R. (1993, 1999) *Without Conscience: The disturbing world of the psychopaths among us* (New York: Pocket Books/Guilford Press).

Harlow, H. and Zimmerman, R. (1959) 'Affectional responses in the infant monkey', *Science* 130, 421–32.

Harris, L. and Fiske, S. (2006) 'Dehumanising the lowest of the low: neuroimaging responses to extreme outgroups', *Psychological Science* 17, 847–53.

Harris, M., Barlow-Brown, F. and Chasin, J. (1995) 'The emergence of referential understanding: pointing and the comprehension of object names', *First Language* 15, 19–34.

Harris, M., Barrett, M., Jones, D. and Brookes, S. (1988) 'Linguistic input and early word meaning', *Journal of Child Language* 15, 77–94.

Harris, P. (1974) 'Perseverative search at a visibly empty place by young infants', *Journal of Experimental Child Psychology* 18, 535–42.

Harris, P. (1991) 'The work of the imagination', in A. Whiten (ed.), *Natural Theories of Mind* (Oxford: Blackwell).

Harris, P. (1992) 'From simulation to folk psychology: the case for development', *Mind and Language* 7, 120–44.

Hart, D., Hofman, V., Edelstein, W. and Keller, M. (1997) 'The relation of childhood personality types to adolescents behavior and development: a longitudinal study of Icelandic children', *Developmental Psychology* 33, 195–205.

Hart, M. (1991) 'Input frequency and children's first words', *First Language* 11, 289–300.

Harter, S. (1998) 'The development of self representations', in N. Eisenberg (ed.), W. Damon (series ed.), *Handbook of Child Psychology*, vol. 3: *Social, Emotional and Personality Development* (New York: Wiley).

Harter, S. (1999) *The Construction of the Self: A developmental perspective* (New York: Guilford).

Hartley, R. (1986) 'Imagine you're clever', *Journal of Child Psychology and Psychiatry and Allied Disciplines* 27, 383–98.

Hartshorne, H. and May, M. (1928) *Studies in the Nature of Character: I. Studies in Deceit* (New York: Macmillan).

Hawkins, J., Pea, R., Glick, J. and Scribner, S. (1984) '"Merds that laugh don't like mushrooms": evidence for deductive reasoning by preschoolers', *Developmental Psychology* 20, 584–95.

Hawthorne, B. (2000) 'Split custody as a viable post-divorce option', *Journal of Divorce and Remarriage* 33, 1–19.

Hay, D., Nash, A. and Pederson, J. (1981) 'Responses of six-month-olds to the distress of their peers', *Child Development* 52, 1071–5.

Hay, D., Nash, A. and Pedersen, J. (1983) 'Interaction between six-month-old peers', *Child Development* 54, 557–62.

Hay, D. and Ross, H. (1982) 'The social nature of early conflict', *Child Development* 53, 105–13.

Hayes, K. and Hayes, C. (1951) 'The intellectual development of a home–raised chimpanzee', *Proceedings of the American Philosophical Society* 95, 105–9.

Hayes, L. and Watson, J. (1981) 'Neonatal imitation: fact or artefact?' *Developmental Psychology* 17, 655–60.

Hazan, C. and Shaver, P. (1987) 'Romantic love conceptualized as an attachment process', *Journal of Personality and Social Psychology* 52, 511–24.

Hazelton, R., Lancee, W. and O'Neil, M. (1998) 'The controversial long term effects of parental divorce: the role of early attachment', *Journal of Divorce and Remarriage* 29, 1–17.

Hebb, D. (1949) *The Organization of Behaviour* (New York: Wiley).

Hendren, R. and Berenson, C. (1997) 'Adolescent impulse control disorders: eating disorders and substance abuse', in L. Flaherty and R. Sarles (eds), *Handbook of Child and Adolescent Psychiatry*, vol. 3: *Adolescence: Development and Syndromes* (New York: Wiley).

Herrnstein, R. and Murray, C. (1994) *The Bell Curve* (New York: Free Press).

Hespos, S. and Baillargeon, R. (2001) 'Infants' knowledge about occlusion and containment events: a surprising discrepancy', *Psychological Science* 121, 141–7.

Hesse, E. (1999) 'The adult attachment interview: historical and current perspectives', in J. Cassidy and P. Shaver (eds), *Handbook of Attachment: Theory, research and clinical applications* (New York: Guilford).

Hines, M. (2004) *Brain Gender* (New York: Oxford University Press).

Hines, M., Ahmed, S. and Hughes, I. (2003) 'Psychological outcomes and gender related development in complete androgen insensitivity syndrome', *Archives of Sexual Behaviour* 32, 93–101.

Hines, M., Golombok, S., Rust, J., Johnson, K., Golding, J. and the ALSPAC study team (2002) 'Testosterone during pregnancy and childhood gender role behaviour: a longitudinal population study', *Child Development* 73, 1678–87.

Hinshaw, S. (1994) 'Conduct disorder in childhood: conceptualization, diagnosis, comorbidity and risk factor for antisocial functioning in childhood', in D. Fowles, P. Suket and S. Godman (eds), *Progress in Experimental Personality and Psychopathy Research* (New York: Springer).

Hirsh-Pasek, K. and Golinkoff, R. (1996) *The Origins of Grammar: Evidence from early language comprehension* (Cambridge, Mass.: MIT Press).

Hirsh-Pasek, K., Gleitman, H., Gleitman, L., Golinkoff, R. and Naigles, L. (1988) 'Syntactic bootstrapping: evidence from comprehension' (Boston language conference).

Hjort, H. and Frisen, A. (2006) 'Ethnic identity and reconciliation: two main tasks for the young in Bosnia-Herzegovina', *Adolescence* 41, 141–63.

Hobson, R. (1993) *Autism and the Development of Mind* (Hillsdale, N.J.: Erlbaum).

Hobson, R., Patrick, M., Crandell, L., Garcia-Perez, R. and Lee, A. (2005) 'Personal relatedness and attachment in infants of mothers with borderline personality disorder', *Development and Pathology* 17, 329–47.

Hoff-Ginsberg, E. and Tardif, T. (1995) 'Socioeconomic status and parenting', pp. 161–88 in M. Borenstein (ed.), *Handbook of Parenting: Biology and ecology of parenting*, vol. 2 (Mahwah N.J.: Marc H. Bornstein).

Hoffman, L. (1981) 'Is altruism part of human nature?' *Journal of Personality and Social Psychology* 40, 121–37.

Hoffman, L. (1982) 'Development of prosocial motivation: empathy and guilt', pp. 281–313 in N. Eisenberg (ed.), *The Development of Prosocial Behavior* (New York: Academic Press).

Hoffman, M. (2000) *Empathy and Moral Development: Implications for caring and social justice* (Cambridge, UK: Cambridge University Press).

Holloway, R. and Coste-Larey Mondie, M. (1982) 'Brain endocasts in pongoids and hominids: some preliminary findings'. *American Journal of Physical Anthropology* 58, 101–10.

Holmes, J. (2005) 'Disorganised attachment and borderline personality disorder: a clinical perspective', *Archives of Psychiatry and Psychotherapy* 7, 51–61.

Holstein, C. (1976) 'Development of moral judgement: a longitudinal study of males and females', *Child Development* 47, 51–61.

Holyoak, K., Junn, E. and Billman, D. (1984) 'Development of analogical problem solving skill', *Child Development* 55, 332–40.

Honzik, M. (1983) 'Measuring mental abilities in infancy: the value and limitations', in M. Lewis (ed.), *Origins of Intelligence: Infancy and early childhood* (New York: Plenum).

Honzik, M., Macfarlane, J. and Allen, L. (1948) 'The stability of mental test performance between two and eighteen years', *Journal of Experimental Education* 17, 309–24.

Hood, B. (2001) 'Combined electrophysiological and behavioural measurement in developmental cognitive neuroscience: some cautionary notes: comment', *Infancy* 2, 213–17.

Hood, B. and Willatts, P. (1986) 'Reaching in the dark to an object's remembered position: evidence for object permanence in 5-month-old infants', *British Journal of Developmental Psychology* 4, 57–65.

Hopkins, B. and Butterworth, G. (1997) 'Dynamical systems approaches to the development of action', in G. Bremner, A. Slater and G. Butterworth (eds), *Infant Development: Recent advances* (Hillsdale, N.J.: Psychology Press/Erlbaum, UK).

Horgan, J. (1996) *The End of Science* (London: Abacus).

Horgan, J. (2005) *The Psychology of Terrorism* (London: Routledge).

Houtzager, B., Grootenhuis, M., Hoekstra-Weebers, J. and Last, B. (2006) 'One month after diagnosis: quality of life, coping and previous functioning in siblings of children with cancer', *Child: Care, Health and Development* 31, 75–87.

Howe, M. (1989) 'Separate skills or general intelligence: the autonomy of human abilities', *British Journal of Educational Psychology* 59, 351–60.

Howe, M. and Courage, M. (1997) 'The emergence and early development of autobiographical memory', *Psychological Review* 104, 499–523.

Howes, C. and Farver, J. (1987) 'Toddlers' responses to the distress of their peers', *Journal of Applied Developmental Psychology* 8, 441–52.

Huesmann, L. (1986) 'Psychological processes promoting the relation between exposure to media violence and aggressive behaviour by the viewer', *Journal of Social Issues* 42, 125–39.

Huggins, S. L. (1989). A comparative study of self-esteem of adolescent children of divorced lesbian mothers and divorced heterosexual mothers', pp. 123–35 in F. W. Bozett (ed.), *Homosexuality and the Family* (New York: Harrington Park Press).

Hughes, C., Russell, J. and Robbins, T. (1994) 'Evidence for executive dysfunction in autism', *Neuropsychologica* 32, 477–92.

Hughes, J., Cavell, T. and Grossman, P. (1997) 'A positive view of self: risk or protection for aggressive children?' *Development and Psychopathology* 9, 75–94.

Huntsinger, C. and Jose, P. (2006) 'A longitudinal investigation of personality and social adjustment among Chinese American and European American adolescents', *Child Development* 77, 1309–24.

Hutchins, E. (1983) 'Understanding Micronesian navigation', in D. Gentner and L. Stevens (eds), *Mental Models* (Mahwah, N.J.: Erlbaum).

Huttenlocher, J., Haight, W., Bryk, A., Seltzer, M. and Lyons, T. (1991) 'Early vocabulary growth: relation to language input and gender', *Developmental Psychology* 27, 236–48.

Huttenlocher, J., Jordan, N. and Levine, S. (1994) 'A mental model for early arithmetic', *Journal of Experimental Psychology: General* 123, 284–96.

Huttenlocher, P. (1994) 'Synaptogenesis, synapse elimination, and neural plasticity in human cerebral cortex', in C. Nelson (ed.), *Threats to Optimal Development. The Minnesota Symposia on Child Psychology* 27, 35–54.

Huttunen, M. and Niskanen, P. (1978) 'Prenatal loss of father and psychiatric disorders', *Archives of General Psychiatry* 35, 429–31.

Hymel, S., Wagner, E. and Butler, L. (1990) 'Reputational bias: view from the peer group', in S. Asher and S. Coie (eds), *Peer Rejection in Childhood* (Cambridge, UK: Cambridge University Press).

Ingold, T. (2004) 'Conceptual development in Madagascar: a critical comment', *Monographs of the Society for Research in Child Development* 69.

Inhelder, B. and Piaget, J. (1958) *The Growth of Logical Thinking from Childhood to Adolescence* (New York: Basic Books).

Inhelder, B. and Piaget, J. (1964) *The Early Growth of Logic in the Child* (London: Routledge).

Istomina, Z. (1975) 'The development of voluntary memory in preschool age children', *Soviet Psychology* 13, 5–64.

Izard, C., Huebner, R., Risser, D., McGinnes, G. and Dougherty, L. (1980) 'The young infant's ability to produce discrete emotional expressions', *Developmental Psychology* 16, 132–40.

Jacobs, J. and Potenza, M. (1991) 'The use of judgment heuristics to make social and object decisions: a developmental perspective', *Child Development* 62, 16–178.

Jacobsen, T. and Hofmann, V. (1997) 'Children's attachment representations: longitudinal relations to school behaviour and academic competence in middle childhood and adolescence', *Developmental Psychology* 33, 703–10.

Jacobson, J. (1981) 'The role of inanimate objects in early peer interaction', *Child Development* 52, 618–26.

Jacobson, J., Boersma, D., Fields, R. and Olson, K. (1983) 'Paralinguistic features of adult speech to infants and small children', *Child Development* 54, 436–42.

Jaffee, S. and Hyde, J. (2000) 'Gender differences in moral orientation: a meta analysis', *Psychological Bulletin* 126, 703–26.

Jahoda, G., (1984) 'The development of thinking about socioeconomic systems', in H. Tajfel (ed.), *The Social Dimension*, vol. 1 (Cambridge, UK: Cambridge University Press).

James, D., Pillai, M. and Smoleniec, J. (1995) 'Neurobehavioural development in the human fetus', in J. Lecanuet, P. Fifer, N. Kasnegor and W. Smotherman (eds), *Fetal Development: A psychobiological perspective* (Hillsdale, N.J.: Erlbaum).

James, W. (1890) *The Principles of Psychology* (New York: Longmans Green).

James, W. (1892) *Psychology: The briefer course* (New York: Henry Holt).

Jenkins, J. and Astington, J. (1996) 'Cognitive factors and family structure associated with theory of mind development in young children', *Developmental Psychology* 32, 70–8.

Johanson, D. and Maitland, E. (1990) *Lucy: The beginning of mankind* (Tonbridge: Touchstone).

John, O. (1990) 'The "Big Five" factor taxonomy: dimensions of personality in the natural language and in questionnaires', pp. 66–100 in L. Pervin (ed.), *Handbook of Personality: Theory and Research* (New York: Guilford,.

John, O., Caspi, A., Robins, R., Moffitt, T. and Stouthamer-Loeber, M. (1994) 'The "Little five": exploring the five-factor model of personality in adolescent boys', *Child Development* 65, 160–78.

Johnson, J. and Newport, E. (1989) 'Critical period effects in second language learning: the influence of maturational state on the acquisition of English as a second language', *Cognitive Psychology* 21, 60–99.

Johnson, M. (1998) 'The neural basis of cognitive development', in D. Kuhn and R. Siegler (eds), W. Damon (series ed.), *Handbook of Child Psychology*, vol. 2, *Cognition, Perception and Language* (New York: Wiley).

Johnson, M., Dziurawiec, S., Ellis, H. and Morton, J. (1991) 'Newborns' preferential tracking of face-like stimuli and its subsequent decline', *Cognition* 40, 1–19.

Johnson, M. and Foley, M. (1984) 'Differentiating fact from fantasy: the reliability of children's memory', *Journal of Social Issues* 40, 33–50.

Johnson, M. and Morton, J. (1991) *Biology and Cognitive Development: The case for face recognition* (Oxford: Blackwell).

Johnson, S. and Nanez, J. (1995) 'Young infants' perception of object unity in two-dimensional displays', *Infant Behaviour and Development* 18, 133–43.

Johnson, S., and O'Connor, E. (2002) *The Gay Baby Boom: The psychology of gay parenthood* (New York: New York University Press).

Johnson, S. and Solomon, G. (1997) 'Why dogs have puppies and cats have kittens: the role of birth in children's understanding of biological origins', *Child Development* 68, 404–19.

Johnson-Laird, P. (1983) *Mental Models* (Cambridge, Mass.: Harvard University Press).

Johnson-Laird, P. (1993) *Human and Machine Thinking* (Hillsdale, N.J.: Erlbaum).

Johnson-Laird, P. and Byrne, R. (1991) *Deduction* (Hove: Erlbaum).

Johnson-Laird, P., Oakhill, J. and Bull, D. (1986) 'Children's syllogistic reasoning', *Quarterly Journal of Experimental Psychology* 38, 35–58.

Johnson-Laird, P. and Shafir, E. (1993) *Reasoning and Decision Making* (Amsterdam: Elsevier).

Jolliffe, D. and Farrington, D. (2004) 'Empathy and offending: a systematic review and meta-analysis', *Aggression and Violent Behavior* 9, 441–76.

Jones, R., Slatterlee, D. and Ryder, F. (1994) 'Fear of humans in Japanese quail selected for low or high adrenocortical response', *Physiology and Behavior* 56, 379–83.

Joseph, R. (2000) 'Fetal brain behaviour and cognitive development', *Developmental Review* 20, 81–98.

Jourdan, A. (2006) 'The impact of the family environment on the ethnic identity development of multiethnic college students', *Journal of Counseling and Development* 84, 328–40.

Juel, C. (1988) 'Learning to read and write: a longitudinal study of 54 children from first through fourth grades', *Journal of Educational Psychology* 80, 417–47.

Jurkovic, G. (1997) *Lost Childhoods: The plight of the parentified child* (London: Routledge).

Juscyzk, P. (1997) *The Discovery of Spoken Language* (Cambridge, Mass.: MIT Press).

Kagan, J. (1984) *The Nature of the Child* (New York: Basic Books).

Kagan, J. (1998) 'Biology and the child', in N. Eisenberg (ed.), W. Damon (series ed.), *Handbook of Child Psychology,* vol. 3: *Social, Emotional and Personality Development* (New York: Wiley).

Kagan, J., Kearsley, R. and Zelazo, P. (1978) *Infancy: Its place in human development* (Cambridge, Mass.: Harvard University Press).

Kagan, J. and Moss, H. (1962) *Birth to Maturity* (New York: Wiley).

Kahneman, D., Slovic, P. and Tversky, A. (eds) (1982) *Judgment under Uncertainty: Heuristics and biases* (Cambridge, UK: Cambridge University Press).

Kahneman, D. and Tversky, A. (1973) 'On the psychology of prediction', *Psychological Review* 80, 237–51.

Kail, R. (1990) *The Development of Memory in Children,* 3rd edn (San Francisco, Calif.: Freeman).

Kanner, A., Feldman, S., Weinberg, D. and Ford, M. (1987) 'Uplifts, hassles, and adaptational outcomes in early adolescents', *Journal of Early Adolescence* 7, 371–94.

Kanner, L. (1943) 'Autistic disturbances of affective contact'. *Nervous Child* 2, 217–50.

Kant, E. (1781/1929) *Critique of Pure Reason* (London: Macmillan).

Karmiloff, K. and Karmiloff-Smith, A. (2001) *Pathways to Language: From fetus to adolescent*, Developing Child Series (Cambridge, Mass: Harvard University Press).

Karmiloff-Smith, A. (1979) 'Macro and micro developmental changes in language acquisition and problem solving', *Cognitive Science* 3, 81–118.

Karmiloff-Smith, A. (1992) *Beyond Modularity: A developmental perspective on cognitive science* (Cambridge, Mass.: MIT Press).

Katchadourian, H. (1977) *The Biology of Adolescence* (San Francisco: W. H. Freeman).

Kauffman, S. (1995) *At Home in the Universe: The search for the laws of self organisation and complexity* (New York: Oxford University Press).

Kearins, J. (1981) 'Visual spatial memory in Australian aboriginal children of desert regions, *Cognitive Psychology* 13, 434–60.

Keating, D. (2004) 'Cognitive and brain development', pp. 45–84 in R. Lerner and L. Steinberg (eds), *Handbook of Adolescent Psychology* (Chichester: Wiley).

Keil, F. (1981) 'Constraints on knowledge and cognitive development', *Psychological Review* 88, 197–227.

Keil, F. (1990) 'Constraints on constraints: surveying the epigenetic landscape', *Cognitive Science* 14, 135–68.

Keller, C. and Keller, J. (1996) *Cognition and Tool Use*: *The blacksmith at work* (Cambridge, UK: Cambridge University Press).

Kellman, P. and Banks, S. (1998) 'Infant visual perception', in D. Kuhn and R. Siegler (eds), W. Damon (series ed.), *The Handbook of Child Psychology*, vol. 2: *Cognition, Perception and Language* (New York: Wiley).

Kellman, P., Spelke, E. and Short, K. (1986) 'Infant perception of object unity from translatory motion in depth and vertical translation', *Child Development* 57, 72–86.

Kendrick, D. and Funder, D. (1988) 'Profiting from controversy: lessons from the person–situation debate', *American Psychologist* 43, 23–34.

Kindermann, T., McCollom, T. and Gibson, E. (1995) 'Peer networks and students' classroom engagement during childhood and adolescence', in K. Wentzel and J. Juvonen (eds), *Social Motivation in Understanding Children's School Adjustment* (New York:: Cambridge University Press).

King, P. (2003) 'Religion and identity: the role of ideological, social and spiritual contexts', *Applied Developmental Science* 7, 197–204.

Kisilevsky, B., Fearon, I. and Muir, D. (1998) 'Fetuses differentiate vibroacoustic stimuli', *Infant Behaviour and Development* 21, 25–45.

Kister, M. and Patterson, C. (1980) 'Children's conceptions of the causes of illness: understanding contagion and the use of immanent justice', *Child Development* 51, 839–46.

Kitajima, Y., Kumoi, M. and Koike, T. (1998) *Japanese Journal of Physiological Psychology and Psychophysiology* 16, 93–100.

Kitcher, P. (1985). *Vaulting Ambition: Sociobiology and the quest for human nature* (Cambridge, Mass.: MIT Press).

Kitzinger, S. (1989) *The Complete Book of Pregnancy and Childbirth* (New York: Knopf).

Klaczynski, P., Schuneman, M. and Daniel, D. (2004) 'Theories of conditional reasoning: a developmental examination of competing hypotheses', *Developmental Psychology* 40, 559–71.

Klahr, D. (1984) 'Transition processes in quantitative development', in R. Sternberg (ed.), *Mechanisms of Cognitive Development* (New York: Freeman).

Klahr, D. (2000) *Exploring Science: The cognition and development of discovery processes* (Cambridge, Mass.: MIT Press).

Klahr, D. and MacWhinney, B. (1998) 'Information processing', in D. Kuhn and R. Siegler (eds), W. Damon (series ed.), *Handbook of Child Psychology*, vol. 2: *Cognition, Perception and Language* (New York: Wiley).

Klahr, D. and Robinson, M. (1981) 'Formal assessment of problem solving and planning processes in preschool children', *Cognitive Psychology* 13, 113–48

Klahr, D. and Wallace, J. (1976) *Cognitive Development: An information processing view* (Hillsdale, N.J.: Lawrence Erlbaum).

Klaus, M. and Kennell, J. (1976) *Maternal–Infant Bonding: The impact of early separation or loss on family development* (St. Louis: Mosby).

Kline, P. (1991) *Intelligence: The psychometric view* (London: Routledge).

Knight, G., Fabes, R. and Higgins, D. (1996) 'Concerns about drawing causal inferences from meta-analyses: an example in the study of gender differences in aggression', *Psychological Bulletin* 119, 410–21.

Kobasigawa, A., Ransom, C. and Holland, C. (1980) 'Children's knowledge about skimming', *Alberta Journal of Educational Research* 26, 169–82.

Kochanska, G. (1993) 'Toward a synthesis of parental socialisation and child temperament in early development of conscience', *Child Development* 64, 325–47.

Kochanska, G. (1995) 'Children's temperament, mother's discipline and security of attachment: multiple pathways to emerging internalisation', *Child Development* 66, 597–615.

Kochanska, G. (1997) 'Mutually responsive orientation between mothers and their young children: implications for early socialisation', *Child Development* 68, 94–112.

Kochanska, G. and Aksan, N. (2006) 'Children's conscience and self-regulation', *Journal of Personality* 74, 1587–617.

Kochanska, G., Aksan, N. and Carlson, J. (2005) 'Temperament, relationships and young children's cooperation with their parents', *Developmental Psychology* 41, 648–60.

Kochanska, G., Coy, K., Tjebkes, T. and Husarek, S. (1998) 'Individual differences in emotionality in infancy', *Child Development* 69, 375–90.

Kochanska, G. and DeVet, K. (1994) 'Maternal reports of conscience development and temperament in young children', *Child Development* 65, 852–68.

Kochanska, G. and Murray, K. (2000) 'Mother–child mutually responsive orientation and conscience development: from toddler to early school age', *Child Development* 71, 417–31.

Kochanska, G., Padavich, D. and Koenig, A. (1996) 'Children's narratives about hypothetical moral dilemmas and objective measures of their conscience: mutual relations and socialization antecedents', *Child Development* 67, 1420–36.

Koenig, H., McCullough, M. and Larsen, D. (2001) *Handbook of Religion and Health* (Oxford: Oxford University Press).

Koestner, R., Franz, C. and Weinberg, J. (1990) 'The family origins of empathic concern: a 26-year longitudinal study', *Journal of Personality and Social Psychology* 58, 709–17.

Koffa, K. (1935) *Principles of Gestalt Psychology* (New York: Harcourt Brace).

Kohlberg, L. (1963) 'The development of children's orientations toward a moral order: sequence in the development of moral thought', *Human Development* 6, 11–33.

Kohlberg, L. (1966) 'A cognitive-developmental analysis of children's sex role concepts and attitudes', in E. Maccoby (ed.), *The Development of Sex Difference* (Stanford, Calif.: Stanford University Press).

Kohlberg, L. (1969) 'Stage and sequence: the cognitive-developmental approach to socialization', in D. Goslin (ed.), *Handbook of Socialization Theory and Research* (Chicago: Rand McNally).

Kohlberg, L. (1976) 'Moral stage and moralization: the cognitive-developmental approach', pp. 84–107 in T. Lickona (ed.), *Moral Development and Behavior: Theory, research and social issues* (New York: Holt, Rinehart and Winston).

Kohlberg, L. (1978) 'Revisions in the theory and practice of moral development', *New Directions for Child Development* 2, 83–8.

Kohlberg, L. and Power, C. (1981) 'Moral development, religious thinking and the question of the seventh stage', *Journal of Religion and Science* 16, 203.

Komatsu, L. and Galotti, K. (1986) 'Children's reasoning about social, physical and logical regularities: a look at two worlds', *Child Development* 57, 413–20.

Kovas, Y., Hayiou-Thomas, M., Oliver, B. and Bishop, D. (2005) 'Genetic influences in different aspects of language development: the etiology of language skills in 4.5-year-old twins', *Child Development* 76, 632–51.

Kozorovitskiy, Y., Hughes, M., Lee, K. and Gould, E. (2006) 'Fatherhood affects dendritic spines and vasopressin V1a receptors in the primate prefrontal cortex', *Nature Neuroscience* 9, 1094–5.

Kreutzer, M., Leonard, C. and Flavell, J. (1975) 'An interview study of children's knowledge about memory', *Monographs for the Society for Research in Child Development* 40.

Kroger, J. (1997) 'Gender and identity: the intersection of structure, content and context', *Sex Roles* 36, 747–70.

Kroger, J. (2004) *Identity in Adolescence*, 3rd edn (London: Routledge).

Krouse, H. (1986) 'The use of decision frames by elementary school children', *Perceptual and Motor Skills* 63, 1107–12.

Kugiumutzakis, G. (1993) 'Intersubjective vocal imitation in early other–infant interaction', in J. Nadel and L. Camioni (eds), *New Perspectives in Early Communicative Development* (London/New York: Routledge).

Kugiumutzakis, G. (1999) 'Genesis and development of early infant mimesis to facial and vocal models', in J. Nadel and G. Butterworth (eds), *Imitation in Infancy* (Cambridge, UK: Cambridge University Press).

Kuhl, P., Andruski, J., Chistovich, I., Chistovich, L., Kozhevnikova, E., Ryskina, V., Stolyarova, E., Sundberg, U. and Lacerda, F. (1997) 'Cross-language analysis of phonetic units in language addressed to infants', *Science* 277, 684–6.

Kuhn, D. (1995) 'Microgenetic study of change: what has it told us?' *Psychological Science* 6, 133–9.

Kuhn, D. (2000) 'Does memory development belong on an endangered topic list?' *Child Development* 71, 21–5.

Kuhn, D. (2001) 'Why development does (and doesn't) occur: evidence from the domain of inductive reasoning', pp. 221–49 in R. Siegler and J. McClelland (eds), *Mechanisms of Cognitive Development: Neural and behavioral perspectives* (Mahwah, N.J.: Erlbaum).

Kuhn, D. (2006) 'Do cognitive changes accompany developments in the adolescent brain?' *Perspectives on Psychological Science* 1, 59–67.

Kuhn, D., Amsel, E. and O'Loughlin, M. (1988) *The Development of Scientific Thinking Skills* (San Diego, Calif.: Academic Press).

Kuhn, D. and Dean, D. (2005) 'Is developing scientific thinking all about learning to control variables?' *Psychological Science* 16, 866–70.

Kuhn, T. (1970) *The Structure of Scientific Revolutions* (Chicago: University of Chicago Press).

Kunzinger, E. (1985) 'A short term longitudinal study of memorial development during early grade school', *Developmental Psychology* 21, 642–6.

Kuyken, W. (2006) 'Digging deep into depression', *Psychologist* 19, 278–81.

Ladd, G. (1990) 'Having friends, keeping friends, making friends, and being liked by peers in the classroom: predictors of children's early adjustment?' *Child Development* 61, 1081–100.

LaFromboise, T., Coleman, H. and Gerton, J. (1993) 'Psychological impact of biculturalism: evidence and theory', *Psychological Bulletin* 125, 470–500.

Lagerspetz, K. and Bjorkquist, K. (1994) 'Sex differences in covert aggression among adults', in L. Rowell Huesmann (ed.), *Aggressive Behavior* (New York: Plenum Press).

Lahey, B., Gordon, R., Loeber, R., Stouthamer-Loeber, M. and Farrington, D. (1999) 'Boys who join gangs: a prospective study of predictors of first gang entry', *Journal of Abnormal Child Psychology* 27, 261–76.

Lamb, M. (1998) 'Non-parental child-care: context, quality, correlates and consequences', in I. Sigel and K. Renninger (eds), *Handbook of Child Psychology*, vol . 4: *Child Psychology in Practice* (New York: Wiley).

Lamb, M. (2005) 'Attachments, social networks and developmental contexts', *Human Development* 48, 108–12.

Lamb, M., Thompson, R., Gardner, W. and Charnov, E. (1985) *Infant–Mother Attachment: The origins and developmental significance of individual differences in strange situation behaviour* (Hillsdale, N.J.: Erlbaum).

Lamborn, S., Dornbusch, S. and Steinberg, L. (1996) 'Ethnicity and community context as moderators of the relations between family decision making and adolescent adjustment', *Child Development* 67, 283–301.

Lamborn, S., Mounts, N., Steinberg, L. and Dornbusch, S. (1991) 'Patterns of competence and adjustment among adolescents from authoritative, authoritarian, indulgent and neglectful families', *Child Development* 62, 1049–65.

Larden, M., Melin, L., Holst, U. and Langstrom, N. (2006) 'Moral judgement, cognitive distortions and empathy in incarcerated delinquent and community control adolescents', *Psychology, Crime and Law* 12, 453–62.

Larkin, J. (1983) 'The role of problem representation in physics', in D. Gnetner and A. Stevens (eds), *Mental Models* (Hillsdale, N.J.: Erlbaum).

Lave, J. and Wenger, E. (1991) *Situated Learning: Legitimate Peripheral Participation* (Cambridge, UK: Cambridge University Press).

Le, H. (2000) 'Never leave your little one alone: raising an Ifaluk child', in J. DeLoache and A. Gottlieb (eds), *A World of Babies: Imagined childcare guide for seven societies* (Cambridge, UK: Cambridge University Press).

Leakey, M. (1979) *Olduvai Gorge: My search for early man* (London: Collins).

Learmouth, A., Lamberth, R. and Rovee-Collier, C. (2004) 'Generalisation of deferred imitation during the 1st year of life', *Journal of Experimental Child Psychology* 88, 297–318.

Lecuyer, R. (2001) 'Are there good reasons to question early object permanence?' *Archives de Psychologie* 69, 270–71.

Lee, L. and Wheeler, D. (1989) 'The arithmetic connection', *Educational Studies in Mathematics* 20, 41–54.

Leenders, I. and Brugman, D. (2005) 'Moral/non-moral domain shift in young adolescents in relation to delinquent behaviour', *British Journal of Developmental Psychology* 23, 65–79.

Legerstee, M. (1992) 'A review of the animate–inanimate distinction in infancy: implications for models of social and cognitive knowing', *Early Development and Parenting* 1, 59–67.

Legerstee, M., Anderson, D. and Schaffer, A. (1998) 'Five and eight month old infants recognise their faces and voices as familiar and social stimuli', *Child Development* 69, 37–50.

Legrenzi, P., Girotto, V. and Johnson-Laird, P. (1993) 'Focusing in reasoning and decision making', in P. Johnson-Laird and E. Shafir (eds), *Reasoning and Decision Making* (Cambridge, Mass.: Blackwell).

Lemaire, P. and Siegler, R. (1995) 'Four aspects of strategic change: contributions to children's learning of multiplication', *Journal of Experimental Psychology: General* 124, 83–97.

Lempers, J., Flavell, E. and Flavell, J. (1977) 'The development in very young children of tacit knowledge concerning visual perception', *Genetic Psychology Monographs* 95, 3–53.

Leslie, A. (1987) 'Pretence and representation: the origins of "theory of mind"', *Psychological Review* 94, 412–26.

Leslie, A. (1994) 'ToMM, ToBy and agency: core architecture and domain specificity', in L. Hirschfield and S. Gelman (eds), *Mapping the Mind: Domain specificity in cognition and culture* (Cambridge, UK: Cambridge University Press).

Leslie, A. and Thaiss, L. (1992) 'Domain specificity in conceptual development: neuropsychological evidence from autism', *Cognition* 43, 225–51.

Levin, I. (1989) 'Principles underlying time measurement: the development of children's constraints on counting time', in I. Levin and D. Zakay (eds), *Time and Human Cognition: A life-span perspective* (Amsterdam: Elsevier).

LeVine, R. and Miller, P. (1990) 'Commentary', *Human Development* 33, 73–80.

LeVine, R., Dixon, S., LeVine, S., Richman, A., Leiderman, P., Keeferk, C. and Brazelton, B. (1996) *Child Care and Culture: Lessons from Africa* (New York: Cambridge University Press).

Levine, L., Tuber, S., Slade, H. and Ward, M. (1991) 'Mothers' mental representations and their relationship to mother–infant attachment', *Bulletin of the Menninger Clinic* 55, 454–69.

Lewis, C., Freeman, N., Kyriakidou, C. and Maridaki-Kassotaki, K. (1996) 'Social influences on false belief access: specific sibling influences or general apprenticeship', *Child Development* 67, 2930–47.

Lewis, M. (1994) 'Myself and me', in S. Parker, R. Mitchell, and M. Boccia (eds), *Self-Awareness in Animals and Humans: Developmental perspectives* (New York: Cambridge University Press).

Lewis, M. (1998) 'Emotional competence and development', pp. 27–36 in D. Pushkar, W. Bukowski, A. Schwartzman, D. Stack and D. R. White (eds), *Improving Competence across the Lifespan* (New York: Plenum Press).

Lewis, M. (1999) 'A new dynamic systems method for the analysis of early socioemotional development', *Developmental Science* 2, 457–75.

Lewis, M. (2000) 'The promise of dynamic systems approaches for an integrated account of human development', *Child Development* 71, 36–43.

Lewis, M. (2004) 'Trouble ahead: predicting antisocial trajectories with dynamic systems concepts', *Journal of Abnormal Child Psychology* 32, 665–71.

Lewis, M. (2005) 'The child and its family: the social network model', *Human Development* 48, 8–27.

Lewis, M. and Brooks-Gunn, J. (1979) *Social Cognition and the Acquisition of Self* (New York: Plenum Press).

Lewis, M. and Douglas, L. (1998) 'A dynamic systems approach to cognition: emotion in development', in M. Mascolo and S. Griffin, *What Develops in Emotional Development?* (New York: Plenum Press).

Lewis, M., Feiring, C. and Rosenthal, S. (2000) 'Attachment over time', *Child Development* 71, 707–20.

Lewis, M., Lamey, A. and Douglas, L. (1999) 'A new dynamic systems method for the analysis of early socio-emotional development', *Developmental Science* 2, 457–75.

Lewis, M. and Michalson, L. (1985) 'Faces as signs and symbols', in G. Zivin (ed.), *The Development of Expressive Behaviour* (New York: Academic Press).

Lewis, M., Young, G., Brooks, J. and Michalson, L. (1975) 'The beginning of friendship', pp. 27–65 in M. Lewis and L. Rosenblum (eds), *Friendship and Peer Relations* (New York: Wiley).

Liben, L. (1977) 'Memory in the context of cognitive development: the Piagetian approach', in R. Kail and J. Hagen (eds), *Perspectives on the Development of Memory and Cognition* (Hillsdale, N.J.: Erlbaum).

Liberman, I., Shankweiler, D., Fischer, F. and Carter, B. (1974) 'Explicit syllable and phoneme segmentation in the young child', *Journal of Experimental Child Psychology* 18, 201–12.

Liebermann, P. (1992) 'Human speech and language', in S. Jones, R. Martin and D. Pilbeam (eds), *The Cambridge Encyclopaedia of Human Evolution* (Cambridge, UK: Cambridge University Press).

Lieven, E. (1994) 'Crosslinguistic and crosscultural aspects of language addressed to children', in C. Gallaway and B. Richards (eds), *Input and Interaction in Language Acquisition* (Cambridge, UK: Cambridge University Press).

Lieven, E., Pine, J. and Baldwin, G. (1997) 'Positional learning and early grammatical development', *Journal of Child Language* 24, 187–219.

Light, P., Buckingham, N. and Robbins, A. (1979) 'The conservation task as an interactional setting', *British Journal of Educational Psychology* 49, 304–10.

Light, P. and Gilmour, A. (1983) 'Conservation of conversation? contextual facilitation of inappropriate conservation judgments', *Journal of Experimental Child Psychology* 36, 356–63.

Light, P. and Perret-Clermont, A. (1989) 'Social context effects in learning and testing', in A. Gellattly, D. Rogers and J. Sloboda (eds), *Cognition and Social Worlds* (Oxford: Clarendon Press).

Lindberg, M. (1980) 'Is knowledge base development a necessary and sufficient condition for memory development?' *Journal of Experimental Child Psychology* 30, 401–10.

Lindsey, E., Colwell, M., Frabutt, J., MacKinnon-Lewis, C. and Manusov, V. (2006) 'Family conflict in divorced and non-divorced families: potential consequences for boys' friendship status and friendship quality', *Journal of Social and Personal Relationships* 23, 45–63.

Linkletter, A. (1957) *Kids Say the Darndest Things* (Englewood Cliffs, N.J.: Prentice-Hall).

Lipton, J. and Spelke, E. (2004) 'Discrimination of large and small numerosities by human infants', *Infancy* 5, 271–290.

Locke, J. (1690/1913) *Some Thoughts Concerning Education* (London: Cambridge University Press).

Loehlin, J. (1992) *Genes and Environment in Personality Development* (Newbury Park, Calif.: Sage).

Lorenz, K. (1966) *On Aggression* (London: Methuen).

Lorenz, K. (1981) *The Foundations of Ethology* (Austria: Springer-Verlag).

McGarrigle, J. and Donaldson, M. (1975) 'Conservation accidents', *Cognition 3*, 341–350.

McGraw, M. (1945) *Neuromuscular Maturation of the Human Infant* (New York: Hafner).

McGuiness, D. (1987) *When Children Don't Learn: Understanding the biology and psychology of learning disabilities* (New York: Basic Books).

McLaughlin, D. and Harrison, C. (2006) 'Parenting styles of mothers of children with ADHD: the role of maternal and child factors', *Child and Adolescent Mental Health 11*, 82–88.

McLean, K. and Pratt, M. (2006) 'Life's little (and big) lessons: identity statuses and meaning-making in the turning point narratives of emerging adults', *Developmental Psychology 42*, 714–722.

McLoyd, V. (1998) 'Socioeconomic disadvantage and child development', *American Psychologist 53*, 185–204.

McNaughton, S. and Leyland, J. (1990) 'The shift in focus of maternal tutoring across different difficulty levels on a problem solving task', *British Journal of Developmental Psychology 8*, 147–55.

McNeill, D. (1970) *The Acquisition of Language* (New York: Harper & Row).

Mead, G. (1934) *Mind, Self and Society from the Standpoint of a Social Behaviourist* (Chicago: University of Chicago Press).

Mead, M. (1928) *Coming of Age in Samoa* (New York: Morrow).

Medin, D. and Atran, S. (2004) 'The native mind: biological categorization and reasoning in development across cultures', *Psychological Review 111*, 960–83.

Mehler, J. and Dupoux, E. (1994) *What Infants Know* (Oxford: Blackwell).

Mehler, J., Lambertz, G., Jusczyk, P. and Amiel-Tison, C. (1986) 'Discrimination de la langue maternelle par le nouveau-né' (Identification of the maternal language by the new born), *Comptes Rendes Academie des Sciences 303*, serie II: 637–40.

Meltzoff, A. (1981) 'Imitation, intermodal co-ordination and representation', pp. 85–114 in G. Butterworth (ed.), *Infancy and Epistemology: An evaluation of Piaget's theory* (London: Harvester Wheatsheaf).

Meltzoff, A. (1994) 'Representation of persons: a bridge between infant's understanding of people and things', International Conference on Infant Studies, Paris.

Meltzoff, A. (1995) 'Apprehending the intentions of others: re-enactment of intended acts by 18-month-old children', *Developmental Psychology 31*, 838–50.

Meltzoff, A. and Moore, K. (1994) 'Imitation, memory and representation of persons', *Infant Behaviour and Development 17*, 83–99.

Meltzoff, A. and Moore, M (1977) 'Imitation of facial and manual gestures by human neonates', *Science 198*, 75–8.

Meltzoff, A. and Moore, M. (1983) 'Newborn infants imitate adult facial gestures', *Child Development 54*, 702–9.

Mervis, C. (1987) 'Child-basic object categories and early lexical development', in U. Neisser (ed.), *Concepts and Conceptual Development: Ecological and intellectual factors in categorization* (Cambridge, UK: Cambridge University Press).

Messenger, D., Fogel, A. and Dickson, L. (1997) 'A dynamic systems approach to infant facial action', in J. Russell and J. Fernandez-Dols (eds), *New Directions in the Study of Facial Expressions* (New York: Cambridge University Press).

Meyer-Bahlburg, H., Ehrhardt, A., Rosen, L. and Gruen, R. (1995) 'Prenatal estrogens and the development of homosexual orientation', *Developmental Psychology 31*, 12–21.

Michael, R. (1994) *Sex in America: A definitive survey* (Boston: Little, Brown).

Mikulincer, M. and Shaver, P. (2005) 'Attachment security, compassion, and altruism', *Current Directions in Psychological Science 14*, 34–8.

Milevsky, A. and Levitt, M. (2004) 'Intrinsic and extrinsic religiosity in preadolescence and adolescence: effect on psychological adjustment', *Mental Health Religion and Culture* 7, 307–21.

Milgram, S. (1974) *Obedience to Authority: An experimental view* (London: Harper Collins).

Miller, G. (1956) 'The magical number seven plus or minus two: some limits on our capacity for processing information', *Psychological Review* 63, 81–97.

Miller, S., Seier, W. and Nassau, G. (1995) 'Children's understanding of logically necessary truths', paper presented at the biennial meeting of the Society for Research in Child Development, Indianapolis.

Mills, C. and Keil, F. (2005) 'The development of cynicism', *Psychological Science* 16, 385–90.

Mills, D., Coffey-Corina, S. and Neville, H. (1997) 'Language comprehension and cerebral specialisation from 13 to 20 months', *Developmental Neuropsychology* 13, 397–445.

Minton, H. and Schneider, F. (1980) *Differential Psychology* (Pacific Grove: Brooks/Cole).

Mischel, W. (1968) *Personality and Assessment* (New York: Wiley).

Mishra, S. (2005) 'Religious identity and ego strengths: a study of Hindu and Muslim boys and girls', *Psychological Studies* 50, 127–33.

Mitchell, P. (1997) *Introduction to Theory of Mind: Children, autism and apes* (London: Arnold).

Mitchell, P. and Lacohee, H. (1991) 'Children's early understanding of false beliefs', *Cognition* 39, 107–27.

Molfese, D. and Betz, J. (1988) 'Electrophysiological indices of the early development of lateralization for language and cognition, and their implications for predicting later development', in D. Molfese and S. Segalowitz (eds), *Brain Lateralization in Children: Developmental implications* (New York: Guilford).

Money, J. and Ehrhardt, A. (1972) *Man and Woman/Boy and Girl* (Baltimore, Md.: Johns Hopkins University Press).

Monroe, K. (2006) *The Hand of Compassion: Portraits of moral choice during the Holocaust* (Princeton, N.J.: Princeton University Press).

Moore, C. (1996) 'Evolution and the modularity of mind reading', *Cognitive Development* 11, 605–21.

Moore, C. and Corkum, V. (1994) 'Social understanding at the end of the first year of life', *Developmental Review* 14, 349–72.

Moore, C. and Frye, D. (1986) 'The effect of experimenter's intention on the child's understanding of conservation', *Cognition* 22, 283–98.

Morris, A. and Sloutsky, V. (1998) 'Understanding logical necessity: developmental antecedents and cognitive consequences', *Child Development* 69, 721–41.

Moshman, D. (1990) 'The development of metalogical understanding', in W. Overton (ed.), *Reasoning, Necessity and Logic: Developmental perspectives* (Hillsdale, N.J.: Erlbaum).

Mueller, E. and Brenner, J. (1977) 'The origin of social skills and interaction among playgroup toddlers', *Child Development* 48, 854–61.

Munakata, Y. (1998) 'Infant perseveration and implications for object permanence theories: a POP model of the AB task', *Developmental Science* 1, 161–84.

Munakata, Y. and McClelland, J. (2003) 'Connectionist models of development', *Developmental Science* 6, 413–29.

Munakata, Y. and Stedron, J. (2002) 'Modelling infant's perception of object unity: what have we learned?' *Developmental Science* 5, 176–8.

Mundy, P. and Markus, J. (1997) 'On the nature of communication and language impairment in autism', *Mental Retardation and Developmental Disabilities Research Reviews* 3, 343–9.

Munn, D. and Dunn, J. (1989) 'Temperament and the developing relationship between siblings.', *International Journal of Behavioral Development* 12, 433–51.

Murphy, B., Eisenberg, N., Fabes, R., Shepard, S. and Guthrie, I. (1999) 'Consistency and change in children's emotionality and regulation: a longitudinal study', *Merrill-Palmer Quarterly* 45, 413–44.

Murrell, K. (2004) 'The Catholic child, adolescent and family', *Child and Adolescent Psychiatric Clinics of North America* 13, 149–60.

Myers, J. (1984) 'Mother–infant bonding: the status of this critical-period hypothesis', *Developmental Review* 4, 240–74.

Myers, J., Juscyzk, P., Kemler-Nelson, D., Luce, J., Woodward, A. and Hirsh-Pasek, K. (1996) 'Infant's sensitivity to word boundaries in fluent speech', *Journal of Child language* 23, 1–30.

Naigles, L. (1990) 'Children use syntax to learn verb meanings', *Journal of Child Language* 17, 357–74.

Nakimichi, K. (2004) 'Young children's conditional reasoning on the four-cards selection task: the influence of context and experience', *Psychologica* 47, 238–49.

Namy, L. (2001) 'What's in a name when it isn't a word? 17-month-olds' mapping of nonverbal symbols to object categories', *Infancy* 2, 73–86.

Neisser, U. (1991) 'Two perceptually given aspects of the self and their development', *Developmental Review* 11, 197–209.

Nelson, C. (1987) 'The recognition of facial expressions in the first two years of life', *Child Development* 58, 889–909.

Nelson, C., Thomas, K., de Haan, M. and Wewerka, S. (1998) 'Delayed recognition memory in infants and adults as revealed by event-related potentials', *International Journal of Psychophysiology* 29, 145–65.

Nelson, K. (1973) 'Structure and strategy in learning to talk', *Monographs of the Society for Research in Child Development* 38.

Nelson, K. (1981) 'Individual differences in language development: implications for development of language', *Developmental Psychology* 17, 170–87.

Nelson, K. (1986) 'Event knowledge and cognitive development', in K. Nelson (ed.), *Event Knowledge: Structure and function in development* (Hillsdale, N.J.: Erlbaum).

Nelson, K. (1996) *Language in Cognitive Development: The emergence of the mediated mind* (New York: Cambridge University Press).

Nelson, K., Denninger, M., Bonvillian, J., Kaplan, B. and Baker, N. (1984) 'Maternal input adjustments and nonadjustments as related to children's linguistic advances and to language acquisition theories', in A. Pelligrini and T. Yawkey (eds), *The Development of Oral and Written Languages: Readings in developmental and applied linguistics* (New York: Ablex).

Nelson, K. and Kosslyn, S. (1976) 'Recognition of previously labelled or unlabelled pictures by 5-year-olds and adults', *Journal of Experimental Child Psychology* 21, 40–5.

Neville, A. and Bavalier, D. (1999) 'Specificity and plasticity in neurocognitive development in humans', pp. 83–98 in M.S. Gazzaniga (ed.), *The Cognitive Neurosciences*, 2nd edn (Cambridge, Mass.: MIT Press).

Newcomb, A., Bukowski, W. and Pattee, L. (1993) 'Children's peer relations: a meta-analytic review of popular, rejected, controversial and average sociometric status', *Psychological Bulletin* 113, 99–128.

Newcombe, N., Rogoff, B. and Kagan, J. (1977) 'Developmental changes in recognition memory for pictures of objects and scenes', *Developmental Psychology* 13, 337–41.

Newport, E. (1991) 'Contrasting concepts of the critical period for language', pp. 111–30 in S. Carey and R. Gelman (eds), *The Epigenesis of Mind: Essays on biology and cognition. Jean Piaget Symposium series* (Hillsdale, N.J.: Erlbaum).

Newport, E., Gleitman, H. and Gleitman, L. (1977) 'Mother, I'd rather do it myself: some effects and non-effects of maternal speech style', in C. Snow and C. Ferguson (eds), *Talking to Children: Language input and acquisition* (Cambridge, UK: Cambridge University Press).

Nissan, M. and Kohlberg, L. (1982) 'Universality and variation in moral judgement: a longitudinal and cross-sectional study in Turkey', *Child Development* 53, 865–76.

Nolen-Hoeksema, S. (1990) *Sex Differences in Depression* (Stanford, Calif.: Stanford University Press).

Nolen-Hoeksema, S. (2003) *Women Who Think Too Much* (London: Piatkus).

Nolen-Hoeksema, S. and Girgus, J. (1994) 'The emergence of gender differences in depression during adolescence', *Psychological Bulletin* 115, 424–43.

Novak, M. (1979) 'Social recovery in monkeys isolated for the first year of life: a long term assessment', *Developmental Psychology* 15, 50–61.

Nowak, A., Vallacher, R. and Zochowski, M. (2005) 'The emergence of personality: dynamic foundations for individual variation', *Developmental Review* 25, 351–85.

Nunes, T., Schliemann, A. and Carraher, D. (1993) *Street Mathematics and School Mathematics* (New York: Cambridge University Press).

Oakes, L. and Cohen, L. (1995) 'Infant causal perception', in C. Rovee-Collier and L. Lipsitt (eds), *Advances in Infancy Research* (Norwood, N.J.: Ablex).

Oakhill, J. and Johnson-Laird, P. (1985) 'The effect of belief on the spontaneous production of syllogistic conclusions', *Quarterly Journal of Experimental Psychology* 37A, 553–70.

Oakhill, J., Johnson-Laird, P. and Garnham, A. (1989) 'Believability and syllogistic reasoning', *Cognition* 31, 117–40.

Ocampo, K., Bernal, M. and Knight, G. (1993) 'Gender, race, and ethnicity: the sequencing of social constancies', in M. Bernal and G. Knight (eds) *Ethnic Identity: Formation and transmission among Hispanics and other minorities* (Albany: State University of New York Press).

O'Donnell, K. and O'Rourke, M. (2003) *Love, Sex, Intimacy and Friendship Between Men* (Basingstoke: Palgrave).

Oller, D. (1980) 'The emergence of speech sounds in infancy', in G. Yeni-Komshian, J. Kavanagh and C. Ferguson (eds), *Child Phonology*, vol.1: *Production* (New York: Academic Press).

Oller, D. and Eilers, R. (1988) 'The role of audition in infant babbling', *Child Development* 59, 441–9.

Olson, S., Bates, J., Sandy, J. and Lanthier, R. (2000) 'Early developmental precursors of externalizing behavior in middle childhood and adolescence', *Journal of Abnormal Child Psychology* 28, 119–33.

Olthof, T., Ferguson, T., Bloemers, E. and Deij, M. (2004) 'Morality- and identity-related antecedents of children's guilt and shame attributions in events involving physical illness', *Cognition and Emotion* 18, 383–404.

Olweus, D. (1993) *Bullying at School: What we know and what we can do* (Oxford: Blackwell).

Olweus, D. (1994) 'Bullying at school: basic facts and effects of a school based intervention program'., *Journal of Child Psychology and Psychiatry* 35, 1171–90.

Orbuch, T., Thornton, A. and Cancio, J. (2000) 'The impact of marital quality, divorce and remarriage on the relationships between parents and their children', *Marriage and Family Review* 29, 221–46.

Ornstein, P., Medlin, R., Stone, B. and Naus M. (1985) 'Retrieving for rehearsal: an analysis of active rehearsal in children's memory', *Developmental Psychology* 21, 633–41.

Ornstein, P., Naus, M. and Liberty, C. (1975) 'Rehearsal and organisational processes in children's memory', *Child Development* 46, 818–30.

Osherson, D. and Markman, E. (1975) 'Language and the ability to evaluate contradictions and tautologies', *Cognition* 3, 213–26.

Osmond, R. (2003) *Imagining the Soul: A history* (Stroud: Sutton).

Oster, H. (1981) '"Recognition" of emotional expression in infancy', in M. Lamb and L. Sherrod (eds), *Infant Social Cognition: Empirical and theoretical considerations* (Hillsdale, N.J.: Erlbaum).

Oster, H., Hegley, D. and Nagel, L. (1992) 'Adult judgments and fine-grained analysis of infant facial expressions: testing the validity of a priori coding formulas', *Developmental Psychology* 28, 1115–31.

Overman, W., Pate, B., Moore, K. and Peleuster, A. (1996) 'Ontogeny of place learning in children as measured in the radial arm maze, Morris search task and open field task', *Behavioural Neuroscience* 110, 1205–28.

Owens, T. (1994) 'Two dimensions of self-esteem: reciprocal effects of positive self-worth and self-depreciation on adolescent problems', *American Sociological Review* 59, 391–407.

Owens, T. and King, A. (2001) 'Measuring self-esteem: race, ethnicity and gender considered', in T. Owens, S. Stryker and N. Goodman (eds), *Extending Self-Esteem Theory and Research: Sociological and psychological currents* (Cambridge, UK: Cambridge University Press).

Owens, T., Stryker, S. and Goodman, N. (2001) *Extending Self-Esteem Theory and Research: Sociological and psychological currents* (Cambridge: Cambridge University Press).

Padfield, P. (2000) *Maritime Supremacy and the Opening of the Western Mind* (London: John Murray).

Parke, R. and Buriel, R. (1998) 'Socialisation in the family: ethnic and ecological perspectives', in N. Eisenberg (ed.), W. Damon (series ed.), *Handbook of Child Psychology*, vol. 3: *Social, Emotional and Personality Development* (New York: Wiley).

Parke, R., Ornstein, P., Reiser, J. and Zahn-Waxler, C. (eds) (1994) *A Century of Developmental Psychology* (Washington, DC: American Psychological Association).

Parker, J. and Asher, S. (1993) 'Beyond group acceptance: friendship and friendship quality as distinct dimensions of peer adjustment', in W. Jones and D. Perlman (eds), *Advances in Personal Relationships*, vol. 4 (London: Kingsley).

Parker, J. and Gottman, J. (1989) 'Social and emotional development in a relational context: friendship interactions from early childhood to adolescence', in T. Berndt and G. Ladd (eds), *Peer Relationships in Child Development* (New York: Wiley).

Parker, J., Nichter, M., Nichter, M., Vuckovic, N., Sims, C. and Ritenbaught, C. (1995) 'Body image and weight concerns among African American and White adolescent females: differences that make a difference', *Human Organization* 54, 103–14.

Parkhurst, J. and Asher, S. (1992) 'Peer rejection in middle school: subgroup differences in behaviour, loneliness and interpersonal concerns', *Developmental Psychology* 28, 231–41.

Parten, M. (1932) 'Social participation among preschool children', *Journal of Abnormal and Social Psychology* 27, 243–69.

Pascual-Leone, J. (1970) 'A mathematical model for the transition rule in Piaget's developmental stages', *Acta Psychologica* 32, 301–45.

Patchin, J., Huebner, B., McCluskey, J., Varano, S. and Bynum, T. (2006) 'Exposure to community violence and childhood delinquency', *Crime and Delinquency* 52, 307–32.

Patterson, C. J. (1997) 'Children of lesbian and gay parents', pp. 235–82 in T. Ollendick and R. Prinz (eds), *Advances in Clinical Child Psychology*, vol. 19 (New York: Plenum Press).

Patterson, C. J. (2000) 'Family relationships of lesbians and gay men', *Journal of Marriage and the Family* 62, 1052–69.

Patterson, F. and Linden, E. (1981) *The Education of Koko* (New York: Holt Rinehart & Winston).

Patterson, G, Reid, J. and Dishion, T. (1992) *Antisocial Boys* (Eugene, Oregon: Castillo Press).

Paul, A. (2004) *The Cult of Personality: How personality tests are leading us to miseducate our children, mismanage our companies and misunderstand ourselves* (London: Free Press).

Pavlov, I. (1927/2003) *Conditioned Reflexes* (New York: Dover).

Pearce, L. and Haynie, D. (2004) 'Intergenerational religious dynamics and adolescent delinquency', *Social Forces* 82, 1553–72.

Pearlman, E. (2005) 'Terror of desire: the aetiology of eating disorders from an attachment theory perspective', *Psychoanalytic Review* 92, 223–35.

Pease, A. and Pease, B. (2000) *Why Men Don't Listen and Women Can't Read Maps* (London: Orion).

Pelphrey, K., Reznick, J., Goldman, B., Sassoon, N., Morrow, J., Donahue, A. and Hodgson, K. (2004) 'Development of visuo-spatial short-term memory in the 2nd half of the 1st year', *Developmental Psychology* 40, 836–51.

Pennington, S. (1987) 'Children of lesbian mothers', pp. 58–74 in F. W. Bozett (ed.), *Gay and Lesbian Parents* (New York: Praeger).

Pennisi, E. and Roush, W. (1997) 'Developing a new view of evolution', *Science* 277, 24–31.

Perez-Granados, D. and Callanan, M. (1997) 'Parents and siblings as early resources for young children's learning in Mexican-descent families', *Hispanic Journal of Behavioral Sciences,* 3–33.

Perlmutter, M. (1986) 'A life-span view of memory', in P. Baltes, D. Featherman and R. Lerner (eds), *Lifespan Development and Behaviour,* vol. 7 (Hillsdale, N.J.: Erlbaum).

Perner, J. (1991) *Understanding the Representational Mind* (Cambridge, Mass.: MIT Press).

Perner, J., Leekam, S. and Wimmer, H. (1987) 'Three year olds' difficulty with false belief: the case for a conceptual deficit', *British Journal of Developmental Psychology* 5, 125–37.

Perner, J., Ruffman, T. and Leekam, S. (1994) 'Theory of mind is contagious: you catch it from your sibs', *Child Development* 65, 1228–38.

Perrin, E. and the Committee on Psychosocial Aspects of Child and Family Health (2002) 'Technical report: coparent or second-parent adoption by same-sex parents', *Pediatrics* 109, 341–4.

Perrin, E. and Gerrity, S. (1981) 'There's a demon in my belly: children's understanding of illness', *Pediatrics* 67, 841–9.

Perris, E., Myers, N. and Clifton, R. (1990) 'Long term memory for a single infancy experience', *Child Development* 61, 1796–1807.

Perry, D., Perry, L. and Weiss, R. (1989) 'Sex differences in the consequences that children anticipate for aggression', *Developmental Psychology* 25, 312–19.

Peter, J., Valkenburg, P. and Schouten, A. (2005) 'Developing a model of adolescent friendship formation on the internet', *CyberPsychology and Behavior* 8, 423–30.

Peterson, C., Peterson, J. and Seeto, D. (1983) 'Developmental changes in the ideas about lying', *Child Development* 54, 1529–35.

Peterson, C. and Siegal, M. (1998) 'Changing focus on the representational mind: deaf, autistic and normal children's concepts of false photos, false drawings and false beliefs', *British Journal of Developmental Psychology* 16, 301–20.

Petrill, S., Saudino, K., Cherny, S., Emde, R., Fulker, D., Hewitt, J. and Plomin, R. (1998) 'Exploring the genetic and environmental etiology of high general cognitive ability in fourteen to thirty-six-month-old twins', *Child Development* 69, 8–74.

Phillips, D. (2006) 'Masculinity, male development, gender and identity: modern and postmodern meanings', *Issues in Mental Health Nursing* 27, 403–23.

Phinney, J., Cantu, C. and Kurtz, D. (1997) 'Ethnic and American identity as predictors of self-esteem among African American, Latino and white adolescents', *Journal of Youth and Adolescence* 26, 165–85.

Phinney, J. and Kohatsu, E. (1997) 'Ethnic and racial identity development and mental health', pp. 420–43 in J. Schulenberg, J. Maggs and K. Hurrelmann (eds), *Health Risks and Developmental Transitions During Adolescence* (Cambridge, UK: Cambridge University Press).

Piaget, J. (1929) *The Child's Conception of the World* (New York: Harcourt, Brace, Jovanovich).

Rheingold, H., Hay, D. and West, M. (1976) 'Sharing in the second year of life', *Child Development* 47, 1148–58.

Richards, H., Bear, G., Stewart, A. and Norman, A. (1992) 'Moral reasoning and classroom conduct: evidence of a curvilinear relationship', *Merrill-Palmer Quarterly* 38, 176–90.

Richards, J. and Cronise, K. (2000) 'Extended visual fixation in the early preschool years: look duration, heart rate changes, and attentional inertia', *Child Development* 71, 602–20.

Risucci, D., Torolani, A. and Ward, R. (1989) 'Ratings of surgical residents by self, supervisors and peers', *Surgical Gynecology and Obstetrics* 169, 519–26.

Rizzolatti, G. and Craighero, L. (2004) 'The mirror neuron system', *Annual Review of Neuroscience* 27, 169–92.

Roberts, B., Walton, K. and Viechtbauer, W. (2006a) 'Personality traits change in adulthood: response to Costa and McCrae (2006)', *Psychological Bulletin* 132, 29–32.

Roberts, B., Walton, K. and Viechtbauer, W. (2006b) 'Patterns of mean-level change in personality traits across the life course: a meta-analysis of longitudinal studies', *Psychological Bulletin* 132, 1–25.

Robins, R., John, O., Caspi, A., Moffitt, T. and Stouthamer-Loeber, M. (1996) 'Resilient, overcontrolled and undercontrolled boys: three replicable personality types', *Journal of Personality and Social Psychology* 70, 157–71.

Robinson, A. and Pascalis, O. (2004) 'Development of flexible visual recognition memory in human infants', *Developmental Science* 7, 527–33.

Robson, C. (1993) *Real World Research: A resource for social scientists and practitioner-researchers* (Oxford: Blackwell).

Rochat, P. (1995) 'Early objectification of the self', in P. Rochat (ed.), *The Self in Infancy: Theory and research* (Amsterdam: North-Holland Elsevier).

Rochat, P. and Striano, T. (1999) 'Social-cognitive development in the first year', in P. Rochat and T. Striano (eds), *Early Social Cognition: Understanding others in the first months of life* (N.J.: Lawrence Erlbaum).

Rodkin, P., Farmer, T., Pearl, R. and Van Acker, R. (2000) 'Heterogeneity of popular boys: antisocial and prosocial configurations', *Developmental Psychology* 36, 14–24.

Rogoff, B. (1990) *Apprenticeship in Thinking: Cognitive development in social context* (New York: Oxford University Press).

Rogoff, B. (1998) 'Cognition as a collaborative process', in D. Kuhn and R. Siegler (eds), W. Damon (series ed.), *Handbook of Child Psychology,* vol. 2: *Cognition, Language and Perception* (New York: Wiley).

Rogoff, B., Gauvain, M. and Ellis, S. (1984) 'Development viewed in its cultural context', in M. Barrister and M. Lamb (eds), *Developmental Psychology: An advanced textbook* (Hillsdale, N.J.: Erlbaum).

Rogoff, B. and Lave, J. (eds) (1984) *Everyday Cognition* (Cambridge, UK: Cambridge University Press).

Roisman, G., Collins, A., Sroufe, L. and Egeland, B. (2005) 'Predictors of young adults' representations of and behaviour in their current romantic relationship: prospective tests of the prototype hypothesis', *Attachment and Human Development* 7, 105–21.

Roisman, G. and Fraley, R. (2006) 'The limits of genetic influence: a behavior-genetic analysis of infant–caregiver relationship quality and temperament', *Child Development* 77, 1656–67.

Ronnqvist, L. and von Hofsten, C. (1994) 'Neonatal finger and arm movements as determined by a social and an object context', *Early Development and Parenting* 3, 81–93.

Rosander, K. and Von Holsten, C. (2004) 'Infants' emerging ability to represent occluded objects', *Cognition* 91, 1–22.

Rosch, E. (1978) 'Principles of categorization', in E. Rosch and B. Lloyd, *Cognition and Categorization* (Hillsdale, N.J.: Erlbaum).

Rose, A. and Asher, S. (1999) 'Children's goals and strategies in response to conflicts within a friendship', *Developmental Psychology* 35, 69–79.

Rose, G. (1997) *Love's Work* (London: Vintage).

Rose, M. (1997) 'Toward an evolutionary demography', in K. Wachter and C. Finch (eds), *Between Zeus and the Salmon: The biodemography of longevity* (Washington, DC: National Academy Press).

Rose, R., Koskenvuo, M., Kaprio, J., Sarna, S. and Langinvainio, H. (1988) 'Shared genes, shared experiences and similarity of personality: data from 14,288 adult Finnish co-twins', *Journal of Personality and Social Psychology* 54, 161–71.

Rosenberg, M., Schooler, C., Schoenbach, C. and Rosenberg, F. (1995) 'Global self-esteem and specific self-esteem'. *American Sociological Review* 60, 141–56.

Rosengren, K. and Hickling, A. (1994) 'Seeing is believing: children's explorations of commonplace, magical and extraordinary transformations', *Child Development* 65, 1605–26.

Ross, H. (1982) 'The establishment of social games among toddlers', *Developmental Psychology* 18, 509–18.

Ross, H., Conant, C., Cheyne, J. and Alevisos, E. (1992) 'Relationships and alliances in the social interactions of kibbutz toddlers', *Social Development* 1, 1–17.

Ross, L. (1981) 'The "intuitive scientist" formulation and its developmental implications', in J. Flavell and L. Ros (eds), *Social Cognitive Development: Frontiers and possible futures* (Cambridge, UK: Cambridge University Press).

Ross, R., Begab, M., Dondis, E., Giampiccolo, J. and Meyers, C. (1985) *Lives of the Mentally Retarded: A forty year follow up study* (Stanford: Stanford University Press).

Rothbart, M. (1981) 'Measurement of temperament in infancy', *Child Development* 52, 569–78.

Rothbart, M. (1989a) 'Biological processes of temperament', in G. Kohnstamm, J. Bates and M. Robarth (eds), *Temperament in Childhood* (Chichester: Wiley).

Rothbart, M. (1989b) 'Temperament and development', in G. Kohnstamm, J. Bates and M. Robarth (eds), *Temperament in Childhood* (Chichester: Wiley).

Rothbart, M. and Bates, J. (1998) 'Temperament', in N. Eisenberg (ed.), W. Damon (series ed.), *Handbook of Child Psychology,* vol. 3: *Social, Emotional and Personality Development* (New York: Wiley).

Rothbaum, F. and Weisz, J. (1994) 'Parental caregiving and child externalizing behavior in nonclinical samples: a meta-analysis', *Psychological Bulletin* 116, 55–74.

Rousseau, J. (1763) *Émile* (Paris).

Rovee-Collier, C. (1984) 'The ontegeny of learning and memory in human infancy', in R. Kail and N. Spear (eds), *Comparative Perspectives on the Development of Memory* (Hillsdale, N.J.: Erlbaum).

Rovee-Collier, C. (1987) 'Learning and memory', in J. Osofsky (ed.), *Handbook of Infant Development* (New York: Wiley).

Rovee-Collier, C., Lipsitt, L. and Haynes, H. (eds) (2003) *Progress in Infancy Research*, vol. 1 (Hillsdale. N.J.: Lawrence Erlbaum Associates).

Rowe, D., Rodgers, J. and Meseck-Bushey, S. (1992) 'Sibling delinquency and the family environment: shared and unshared influences', *Child Development* 63, 59–67.

Rubin, K., Bukowski, W. and Parker, J. (1998) 'Peer interactions, relationships and groups', pp. 619–700 in N. Eisenberg (ed.), W. Damon (series ed.), *Handbook of Child Psychology,* vol. 3: *Social, Emotional and Personality Development* (New York: Wiley).

Rubin, K., Coplan, R., Nelson, L. and Cheah, C. (1999) 'Peer relationships in childhood', pp. 451–501 in M. Bornstein and M. Lamb (eds), *Developmental Psychology: An advanced textbook,* 4th edn (Mahwah N.J.: Erlbaum).

Rubin, K., Wojslawowicz, J., Rose-Krasnor, L., Booth-LaForce, C. and Burgess, K. (2006) 'The best friendships of shy/withdrawn children: prevalence, stability and relationship quality', *Journal of Abnormal Child Psychology* 34, 143–57.

Ruble, D. and Martin, C. (1998) 'Gender development', pp. 933–1016 in N. Eisenberg (ed.), W, Damon (series ed.), *Handbook of Child Development*, vol. 3: *Social, Emotional and Personality Development* (New York: Wiley).

Ruffman, T. (1999) 'Children's understanding of logical inconsistency', *Child Development* 70, 872–86.

Ruffman, T., Perner, J., Naito, M., Parkin, L. and Clements, W. (1998) 'Older (but not younger) siblings facilitate false belief understanding', *Developmental Psychology* 34, 161–74.

Ruffman, T., Perner, J., Olson, D. and Doherty, M. (1993) 'Reflecting on scientific thinking: children's understanding of the hypothesis–evidence relation', *Child Development* 64, 1617–36.

Ruiz, J. and Avant, K. (2005) 'Effects of maternal prenatal stress on infant outcomes: a synthesis of the literature', *Advances in Nursing Science* 28, 345–55.

Rumelhart, D. and McClelland, J. (1986) 'On learning the past tense of English verbs', in D. Rumelhart and J. McClelland (eds), *Parallel Distributed Processing: Exploring the microstructure of cognition*, vol. 1: *Foundations* (Cambridge Mass.: MIT Press).

Rushton, A. and Mayes, D. (2005) 'Research review: forming fresh attachments in childhood: a research update', *Child and Family Social Work* 2, 121–7.

Ryan, M., David, B. and Reynolds, K. (2004) 'Who cares? The effect of gender and context on the self and moral reasoning', *Psychology of Women Quarterly* 28, 246–55.

Russell, J., Mauther, N., Sharpe, S. and Tidswell, T. (1991) 'The "windows task" as a measure of strategic deception in preschoolers and autistic subjects', *British Journal of Developmental Psychology* 90, 331–50.

Saarni, C., Mumme, D. and Campos, J. (1998) 'Emotional development: action, communication and understanding', in N. Eisenberg (ed.), W. Damon (series ed.), *Handbook of Child Psychology*, vol. 3: *Social, Emotional and Personality Development* (New York: Wiley).

Sachs, J. and Devin, J. (1976) 'Young children's use of age appropriate speech styles in social interaction and role playing', *Journal of Child Language* 3, 81–98.

Saffran, J., Aslin, R. and Newport, E. (1996) 'Statistical learning by 8-month-old infants', *Science* 274, 1926–8.

Salmivalli, C. (2001) 'Feeling good about oneself, being bad to others? Remarks on self-esteem, hostility and aggressive behaviour', *Aggression and Violent Behaviour* 6: 375–93.

Saltmarsh, R., Mitchell, P. and Robinson, E. (1995) 'Realism and children's early grasp of mental representation: belief-based judgments in the state of change task', *Cognition* 57, 297–325.

Sampson, R. and Laub, J. (1993) *Crime in the Making: Pathways and turning points through life* (Cambridge, Mass.: Harvard University Press).

Sanson, A., Prior, M., Garino, E., Oberklaid, F. and Sewell, J. (1987) 'The structure of infant temperament: factor analysis of the Revised Infant Temperament Questionnaire', *Infant Behaviour and Development* 10, 97–104.

Sapir, E. (1929) 'The status of linguistics as a science', *Language* 5, 209.

Savage-Rumbaugh, E. (1986) *Ape Language: From conditioned response to symbols* (New York: Columbia University Press).

Savage-Rumbaugh, E., Murphy, J., Sevcik, R., Brakke, K., Williams, S. and Rumbaugh, D. (1993) 'Language comprehension in ape and child', *Monographs for the Society for Research in Child Development* 58.

Saxe, G. (1988) 'The mathematics of street vendors', *Child Development* 59, 1415–25.

Scarborough, H. (1990) 'Very early language deficits in dyslexic children', *Child Development* 59, 1415–25.

Scarr, S. and McCartney, K. (1983) 'How people make their own environments: a theory of genotype-environment effects', *Child Development* 54, 424–35.

Schaal, B., Marlier, L. and Soussignan, R. (2000) 'Human foetuses learn odours from their pregnant mother's diet', *Chemical Senses* 25, 729–37.

Schaal, B., Orgeur, P. and Rognon, C. (1995) 'Odor sensing in the human fetus: anatomical, functional and chemoecological bases', in J. Lecanuet, P. Fifer, N. Krasnegor and W. Smotherman (eds), *Fetal Development: A psychobiological perspective* (Hillsdale, N.J.: Erlbaum).

Schacter, D. (1996) *Searching for Memory: The brain, the mind and the past* (New York: Basic Books).

Schachter, S. (1965) 'A cognitive-physiological view of emotion', in O. Klineberg and R. Christie (eds), *Perspectives in Social Psychology* (New York: Holt, Rinehart & Winston).

Schafer, V., Shucard, D., Shucard, J. and Gerken, L. (1998) 'An electrophysiological study of infants' sensitivity to the sound patterns of English', *Journal of Speech, Language and Hearing Research* 41, 874–86.

Schaffer, H. (1984) *The Child's Entry into a Social World* (London: Academic Press).

Schank, R. and Abelson, R. (1977) *Scripts, Plans, Goals and Understanding* (Hillsdale, N.J.: Erlbaum).

Schauble, L. (1996) 'The development of scientific reasoning in knowledge rich contexts', *Developmental Psychology* 32, 102–19.

Scheirer, M. and Kraut, R. (1979) 'Increasing educational achievement via self–concept change', *Review of Educational Research* 49, 131–50.

Schieffelin, B. and Ochs, E. (eds) (1986) *Language Socialization across Cultures*. Studies in the Social and Cultural Foundations of Language no. 3 (New York: Cambridge University Press).

Schlegel, A. and Barry, H. (1991) *Adolescence: An anthropological enquiry* (New York: Free Press).

Schneider, B., Atkinson, L. and Tardif, C. (2001) 'Child–parent attachment and children's peer relations: a quantitative review', *Developmental Psychology* 37, 86–100.

Schneider, B., Woodburn, S., del Pilar Soteras del Torro, M. and Udvari, S. (2005) 'Cultural and gender differences in the implications of competition for early adolescent friendship', *Merrill-Palmer Quarterly* 51, 163–91.

Schneider, M. (1992) 'Prenatal stress exposure alters postnatal behavioral expression under conditions of novelty challenge in rhesus monkey infants', *Developmental Psychobiology* 25, 529–40.

Schneider, W. and Bjorklund, D. (1998) 'Memory', in D. Kuhn and R. Siegler (eds), W. Damon (series ed.), *Handbook of Child Psychology,* vol. 2: *Cognition, Language and Perception* (New York: Wiley).

Schneider, W. and Pressley, M. (1989) *Memory Development Between 2 and 20* (Berlin: Springer-Verlag).

Schneiderman, L. and Kaplan, R. (1992) 'Fear of dying of HIV infection vs hepatitis B infection', *American Journal of Public Health* 82, 584–6.

Schweder, R. (1982) 'Liberalism as destiny', *Contemporary Psychology* 27, 421–42.

Scott, J. and Fuller, S. (1965) *Genetics and the Social Behaviour of the Dog* (Chicago: University of Chicago Press).

Scribner, S. and Cole, M. (1981) *The Psychology of Literacy* (Cambridge, Mass.: Cambridge University Press).

Scullin, M. and Warren, H. (1999) 'Individual differences and responsiveness to suggestive interviewing techniques in children', poster presented to the Joint Meeting of the American Psychology/Law Society and the European Association of Psychology and Law. Dublin

Seifer, R., Schiller, M., Sameroff, A., Resnick, S. and Riordan, K. (1996) 'Attachment, maternal sensitivity and temperament during the first year of life', *Developmental Psychology* 32, 3–11.

Seligman, M. (1975) *Helplessness on Depression, Development and Death* (San Francisco, Calif.: Freeman).

Selman, R. (1980) *The Growth of Interpersonal Understanding* (New York: Academic Press).

Selman, R. (1981) 'The child as a friendship philosopher', in S. Asher and J. Gottman (eds), *The Development of Children's Friendships* (Cambridge: Cambridge University Press).

Seyfarth, R. and Cheney, D. (1993) 'Meaning, reference and intentionality in the natural vocalizations of monkeys', in H. Roitblat, L. Herman and P. Nachtigall (eds), *Language and Communication: Comparative perspectives* (Hillsdale, N.J.: Erlbaum).

Shanker, S. (2004) 'Autism and the dynamic developmental model of emotions', *Philosophy, Psychiatry and Psychology* 11, 219–33.

Shaw, D. and Vondra, J. (1995) 'Infant attachment security and maternal predictors of early behavior problems: a long-term study of low income families', *Journal of Child Psychology and Psychiatry* 35, 1109–22.

Sheets, V. and Lugar, R. (2005) 'Sources of conflict between friends in Russia and the United States', *Cross-Cultural Research* 39, 380–98.

Sheingold, K. and Tenney, Y. (1982) 'Memory for a salient childhood event', in U. Neisser (ed.), *Memory Observed: Remembering in natural contexts* (San Francisco: Freeman).

Shepard, R. (1967) 'Recognition memory for words, sentences and pictures.', *Journal of Verbal Learning and Verbal Behaviour* 6, 156–63.

Sherman, A., Lansford, J. and Volling, B. (2006) 'Sibling relationships and best friendships in young adulthood: warmth, conflict and well-being', *Personal Relationships* 13, 151–65.

Shinskey, J. (2002) 'Infant object search: effects of variable object visibility under constant means–end demands', *Journal of Cognition and Development* 3, 115–42.

Shoda, Y., LeeTientan, S. and Mischel, W. (2002) 'Personality as a dynamical system: emergence of stability and distinctiveness from intra- and inter-personal interactions', *Personality and Social Psychology Review* 6, 316–25.

Shrager, J. and Siegler, R. (1998) 'SCADS: A model of children's strategy choices and strategy discoveries', *Psychological Science* 9, 405–10.

Shulman, S., Scharf, M., Lumer, D. and Maurer, O. (2001) 'How young adults perceive divorce: the role of their relationships with their fathers and mothers', *Journal of Divorce and Remarriage* 34, 3–17.

Shultz, T. (1980) 'Development of the concept of intention', in W. Collins (ed.), *Minnesota Symposia on Child Psychology*, vol. 13: *Development of Cognition, Affect and Social Relations* (Hillsdale, N.J.: Erlbaum).

Shrum, W. and Cheek, N. (1987) 'Social structure during the school years: onset of the degrouping process', *American Sociological Review* 52, 218–23.

Shute, R. and Charlton, K. (2006) 'Anger or compromise? Adolescents' conflict resolution strategies in relation to gender and type of peer relationship', *International Journal of Adolescence and Youth* 13, 55–69.

Siegal, M. (1991) *Knowing Children: Experiments in conversation and cognition* (Hove: Erlbaum).

Siegal, M. and Beattie, K. (1991) 'Where to look first for children's knowledge of false beliefs', *Cognition* 38, 1–12.

Siegal, M. and Peterson, C. (1994) 'Children's theory of mind and the conversational territory of cognitive development', in C. Lewis and P. Mitchell (eds), *Children's Early Understanding of Mind: Origins and development* (Hillsdale, N.J.: Erlbaum).

Siegler, R. (1976) 'Three aspects of cognitive development', *Cognitive Psychology* 8, 481–520.

Siegler, R. (1981) 'Developmental sequences within and between concepts', *Monographs for the Society for Research in Child Development* 46, 1–84.

Siegler, R. (1986) 'Unities in strategy choices across domains', in M. Perlmutter (ed.), *Minnesota Symposium on Child Psychology* vol 19 (Mahwah, N.J.: Erlbaum).

Siegler, R. (1994) 'Cognitive variability: a key to understanding cognitive development', *Current Directions in Psychological Science* 3, 1–5.

Siegler, R. (1996) *Emerging Minds: The process of change in children's thinking* (New York: Oxford University Press).

Siegler, R. (1997) 'Beyond competence – towards development', *Cognitive Development* 12, 323–32.

Siegler, R. (2000) 'The rebirth of children's learning', *Child Development* 71, 26–36.

Siegler, R. (2004) 'U-shaped interest in U-shaped development – and what it means', *Journal of Cognition and Cognitive Development* 5, 1–10.

Siegler, R. and Chen, Z. (1998) 'Developmental differences in rule learning: a microgenetic analysis', *Cognitive Psychology* 36, 273–310.

Siegler, R. and Crowley, K. (1991) 'The microgenetic method: a direct means for studying cognitive development', *American Psychologist* 46, 606–20.

Siegler, R. and Jenkins, E. (1989) *How Children Discover New Strategies* (Hillsdale, N.J.: Erlbaum).

Siegler, R. and Shipley, C. (1995) 'Variation, selection and cognitive change', in T. Simon and G. Halford (eds), *Developing Cognitive Competence: New approaches to process modelling* (Hillsdale, N.J.: Erlbaum).

Siegler, R. and Shrager, J. (1984) 'Strategy choices in addition and subtraction + how do children know what to do?' in C. Sophian (ed.), *Origins of Cognitive Skills* (Hillsdale, N.J.: Erlbaum).

Siegler, R. and Stern, E. (1998) 'A microgenetic analysis of conscious and unconscious strategy discoveries', *Journal of Experimental Child Psychology: General* 127, 377–97.

Simion, F., Valenza, E., Umilta, C. and Barba, B. (1998) 'Preferential orienting to faces in newborns: a temporal–nasal asymmetry', *Journal of Experimental Psychology: Human Perception and Performance* 24, 1399–1405.

Simmons, R. (2001) 'Comfort with the self', in T. Owens, S. Stryker and N. Goodman (eds), *Extending Self-Esteem Theory and Research: Sociological and psychological currents* (Cambridge, UK: Cambridge University Press).

Simon, T., Hespos, S. and Rochat, P. (1995) 'Do infants understand simple arithmetic: a replication of Wynn', *Cognitive Development* 10, 253–69.

Simon, T. and Klahr, D. (1995) 'A computational theory of children's learning about number conservation', in T. Simon and G. Halford (eds), *Developing Cognitive Competence: New approaches to process modelling* (Hillsdale, N.J.: Erlbaum).

Simonoff, E., Bolton, P., Rutter, M. (1996) 'Mental retardation: genetic findings, clinical implications and research agenda', *Journal of Child Psychology and Psychiatry* 37, 259–80.

Simons, R., Lin, K., Gordon, L., Conger, R. and Lorenz, F. (1999) 'Explaining the higher incidence of adjustment problems among children of divorce compared with those in two-parent families', *Journal of Marriage and the Family* 61, 1020–33.

Simpson, B., Jessop, J. and McCarthy, P. (2003) 'Fathers after divorce', in A. Bainham, B. Lindley, M. Richards and L. Trinder (eds), *Children and Their Families: Contact, rights and welfare* (Oxford: Hart).

Simpson, E. (1973) 'Moral development research: a case study of scientific cultural bias', *Human Development* 17, 81–106.

Singer, J. and Singer, D. (1981) *Television, Imagination and Aggression: A study of preschoolers* (Mahwah, N.J.: Erlbaum).

Singer, J. and Singer, D. (2006) 'Preschoolers' imaginative play as precursor of narrative consciousness', *Imagination, Cognition and Personality* 25, 97–117.

Sisk, C. and Zehr, J. (2005) 'Pubertal hormones organize the adolescent brain and behaviour', *Frontiers in Neuroendocrinology* 26, 163–74.

Skinner, B. F. (1957/2002) *Verbal Behaviour* (B.F. Skinner Foundation).

Skinner, B. F. (1961) *Cumulative Record* (London: Methuen).

Skinner, B. F. (1974) *About Behaviourism* (London: Jonathan Cape).

Slater, A. (1997) 'Visual organisation in early infancy', in G. Bremner, A. Slater, and G. Butterworth (eds), *Infant Development: Recent advances* (Hillsdale, N.J.: Psychology Press/Erlbaum, UK.).

Slater, A. (2004) 'Novelty, familiarity and infant reasoning', *Infant and Child Development* 13, 353–5.

Slater, A., Bremner, G., Johnson, S., Sherwood, P., Hayes, R. and Brown, E. (2000) 'Newborn infants' preference for attractive faces: the role of internal and external facial features', *Infancy* 1, 265–74.

Slater, A. and Butterworth, G. (1997) 'Perception of social stimuli: face perception and imitation', in G. Bremner, A. Slater and G. Butterworth (eds), *Infant Development: Recent advances* (Hillsdale, N.J.: Psychology Press/Erlbaum, UK.).

Slater, A., Johnson, S., Brown, E. and Badenoch, M. (1996) 'Newborn infants' perception of partly occluded objects', *Infant Behaviour and Development* 19, 145–8.

Slater, A., Johnson, S., Kellman, P. and Spelke, E. (1994) 'The role of three dimensional depth cues in infant's perception of partly occluded objects', *Early Development and Parenting* 3, 187–91.

Slater, A., Mattock, A. and Brown, E. (1990) 'Size constancy at birth: newborn infants' responses to retinal and real size', *Journal of Experimental Psychology* 49, 314–22.

Slater, A., Mattock, A., Brown, E., Burnham, D. and Young, A. (1991) 'Visual processing of stimulus compounds in newborn babies', *Perception* 20, 29–33.

Slater, A. and Morison, V. (1985) 'Shape constancy and slant perception at birth', *Perception* 14, 337–44.

Slater, A., Morison, V. and Rose, D. (1983) 'Perception of shape by the newborn baby', *British Journal of Developmental Psychology* 1, 135–42.

Slater, A., Von der Schulenberg, C., Brown, E., Badenoch, M., Butterworth, G., Parsons, S. and Samuels, C. (1998) 'Newborn infants prefer attractive faces', *Infant Behaviour and Development* 21, 345–54.

Slobin, D. (1979) *Psycholinguistics* (Glenview, Ill.: Scott, Foresman).

Slobin, D. (ed.) (1985) *The Cross-Linguistic Study of Language Acquisition* (Hillsdale N.J.: Erlbaum).

Smetana, J., Campione-Barr, N. and Metzger, A. (2006) 'Adolescent development in interpersonal and societal contexts', *Annual Review of Psychology* 57, 255–84.

Smith, G., Williams, S., Cyders, M. and Kelley, S. (2006) 'Reactive personality–environment transitions and adult developmental trajectories', *Developmental Psychology* 42, 877–87.

Smith, L. (1989) 'In defence of perceptual similarity', paper presented to the biennial meeting of SRCD, Kansas City.

Smith, L. (1993) *Necessary Knowledge: Piagetian perspectives on constructivism* (Hove: Erlbaum).

Smith, L., Thelen, E., Titzer, R. and McLin, D. (1999) 'Knowing in the context of acting: the task dynamics of the A-not-B error', *Psychological Review* 106, 235–60.

Smith, N. and Tsimpli, I. (1996) 'Modules and quasi-modules: language and theory of mind in a polyglot savant', *UCL working papers in linguistics* 8 (full article available online).

Snarey, J. (1985) 'Cross cultural universality of social-moral development: a critical review of Kohlbergian research', *Psychological Bulletin* 97, 202–32.

Sneed, J., Schwartz, S. and Cross, W. (2006) 'A multicultural critique of identity status theory and research: a call for integration', *Identity* 6, 61–84.

Snow, C. (1999) 'Social perspectives on the emergence of language', in B. MacWhinney (ed.), *The Emergence of Language* (Mahwah, N.J.: Erlbaum).

Snyder, A., Bahramali, H., Hawker, T. and Mitchell, D. (2006) 'Savant-like numerosity skills revealed in normal people by magnetic pulses', *Perception* 35, 837–45.

Snyder, J., Bank, L. and Burraston, B. (2005) 'The consequences of antisocial behavior in older male siblings for younger brothers and sisters', *Journal of Family Psychology* 19, 643–53.

Society for Research in Child Development (SRCD) (2000) *Directory of Members*, pp. 283–4 (SRCD).

Sodian, B., Zaitchik, D. and Carey, S. (1991) 'Young children's differentiation of hypothetical beliefs from evidence', *Child Development* 62, 753–66.

Soken, N. and Pick, A. (1999) 'Infants' perception of dynamic affective expressions: do infants distinguish specific expressions?' *Child Development* 70 ,1275–82.

Somerville, S., Wellman, H. and Cultice, J. (1983) 'Young children's deliberate reminding', *Journal of Genetic Psychology* 143, 87–96.

Sophian, C. (1997) 'Beyond competence: the significance of performance for conceptual development', *Cognitive Development* 12, 281–303.

Sorce, J., Emde, R., Campos, J. and Klinnert, M. (1985) 'Maternal emotional signalling: its effects on the visual cliff behaviour of one year olds', *Developmental Psychology* 21, 195–200.

Sousa, P., Atran, S. and Medin, D. (2002) 'Essentialism and folk biology: evidence from Brazil', *Journal of Cognition and Culture* 2, 195–223.

Spear, N. (1984) 'Ecologically determined dispositions control the ontogeny of learning and memory', in R. Kail and N. Spear (eds), *Contemporary Perspectives on the Development of Memory* (Hillsdale, N.J.: Erlbaum).

Spearman, C. (1927) *The Abilities of Man* (New York: Macmillan).

Spelke, E. (1994) 'Initial knowledge: six suggestions', *Cognition* 50, 431–45.

Spelke, E., Breinlinger, K., Macomber, J. and Jacobson, K. (1992) 'Origins of knowledge', *Psychological Review* 99, 605–32.

Spence, J., Helmreich, R. and Stapp, J. (1974) 'Ratings of peers on sex role attributes and their relation to self-esteem and conceptions of masculinity and femininity', *Journal of Personality and Social Psychology* 32, 29–39.

Spencer, J., Clearfield, M., Corbetta, D., Ulrich, B., Buchanan, P. and Schoner, G. (2006) 'Moving toward a grand theory of development: in memory of Esther Thelen', *Child Development* 77, 1521–38.

Spencer, J., Smith, L. and Thelen, E. (2001) 'Tests of a dynamic systems account of the A not B error: the influence of prior experience on the spatial memory abilities of two-year-olds', *Child Development* 72, 1327–46.

Spencer, M. and Markstrom-Adams, C. (1990) 'Identity processes among racial and ethnic minority children in America', *Child Development* 61, 290–310.

Sprecher, S. and Fehr, B. (2005) 'Compassionate love for close others and humanity', *Journal of Social and Personal Relationships* 22, 629–51.

Springer, K. (1999) 'How a naïve theory of biology is acquired', in M. Siegel and C. Petersen (eds), *Children's Understanding of Biology and Health* (Cambridge, UK: Cambridge University Press).

Sroufe, A. (1997) *Emotional Development: The organization of emotional life in the early years* (Cambridge, UK: Cambridge University Press).

Sroufe, L. (1979) 'Socioemotional development', in J. Osofsky (ed.), *Handbook of Infant Development* (New York: Wiley).

Sroufe, L. and Sampson, M. (2000) 'Attachment theory and systems concepts', *Human Development* 43, 321–6.

Stambrook, M. and Parker, K. (1987) 'The development of the concept of death in childhood: a review of the literature', *Merrill-Palmer Quarterly* 33, 133–57.

Starkey, P. (1992) 'The early development of numerical reasoning', *Cognition* 43, 93–126.

Steenbeck, H. and van Geert, P. (2005) 'A dynamic systems model of dyadic interaction during play of two children', *European Journal of Developmental Psychology* 2, 105–45.

Stefan, K., Cohen, L., Duque, J., Mazzocchio, R., Celnik, P., Sawaki, L., Ungerleider, L. and Classen, J. (2005) 'Formation of a motor memory by action observation', *Journal of Neuroscience* 25, 9339–46.

Stein, H. (2006) 'Attachment from infancy to adulthood: the major longitudinal studies', *Psychological Medicine* 36, 569–71.

Stein, Z., Susser, M., Saenger, G. and Marolla, F. (1975) *Famine and Human Development: The Dutch winter of 1944–1945* (New York: Oxford University Press).

Steinberg, L. (2007) 'Risk taking in adolescence: new perspectives from brain and behavioural science', *Current Issues in Psychological Science* 16, 55–9.

Steinberg, L., Lamborn, S., Darling, N., Mounts, N. and Dornbusch, S. (1994) 'Over-time changes in adjustment and competence amongst adolescents from authoritative, authoritarian, indulgent and neglectful families', *Child Development* 65, 754–70.

Stern, D. (1985) *The Interpersonal World of the Infant* (New York: Basic Books).

Sternberg, R. (1977a) 'Component processes in analogical reasoning', *Psychological Review* 31, 356–78.

Sternberg, R. (1977b) *Intelligence, Information Processing and Analogical Reasoning: A componential analysis of intelligence* (Hillsdale N.J.: Lawrence Erlbaum Associates).

Sternberg, R. (1988) 'Intellectual development: psychometric and information processing approaches', in M. Bornstein and M. Lamb (eds), *Developmental Psychology: An advanced textbook* (Hillsdale, N.J.: Erlbaum).

Stevenson, S., Hall, G. and Innes, J. (2004). 'Rationalizing criminal behaviour: the influence of criminal sentiments on sociomoral development in violent offenders and nonoffenders', *International Journal of Offender Therapy and Comparative Criminology* 48, 161–74.

Stigler, J. and Hiebert, J. (1999) *The Teaching Gap: Best ideas from the world's teachers for improving education in the classroom* (New York: Free Press).

Stigler, J. and Perry, M. (1990) 'Mathematics learning in Japanese, Chinese and American classrooms', in J. Stigler, R. Shweder and G. Herdt (eds), *Cultural Psychology: Essays on comparative human development* (New York: Cambridge University Press).

Stoneman, Z. (2005) 'Siblings of children with disabilities: research themes', *Mental Retardation* 43, 339–50.

Strauch, B. (2003) *The Primal Teen: What the new discoveries about the teenage brain tell us about our kids* (New York: Doubleday).

Strayer, J. (1987) 'Affective and cognitive perspectives on empathy', in N. Eisenberg and J. Strayer (eds), *Empathy and its Development* (New York: Cambridge University Press).

Strayer, J. (1989) 'What children know and feel in response to witnessing', in C. Saarni and P. Harris (eds), *Children's Understanding of Emotion* (Cambridge: Cambridge University Press).

Strelau, J. (1983) *Temperament and Personality Activity* (New York: Academic Press).

Strichartz, A. and Burton, R. (1990) 'Lies and truth: a study in the development of the concept', *Child Development* 61, 211–20.

Stürmer, S., Snyder, M. and Omoto, A. (2005) 'Prosocial emotions and helping: the moderating role of group membership', *Journal of Personality and Social Psychology* 88, 532–46.

Subbotsky, E. (1993) *The Birth of Personality: The development of independent and moral behaviour in preschool children* (Hove: Harvester Wheatsheaf).

Sugita, Y. and Tani, J. (2005) 'Learning semantic combinatoriality from the interaction between linguistic and behavioural processes', *Adaptive Behaviour* 13, 33–52.

Sutton, C., Utting, D. and Farrington, D. (2004) *Support from the Start: Working with young children and their families to reduce the risks of crime and anti-social behaviour*, Research Report 524 (London: Department for Education and Skills).

Sutton, C., Utting, D. and Farrington, D. (2006) 'Nipping criminality in the bud', *The Psychologist* 19, 470–5.

Tangney, J. and Dearing, R. (2002) *Shame and Guilt* (New York: Guilford Press).

Tanner, J. (1990) *Fetus into Man: Physical growth from conception to maturity*, rev. edn (Cambridge Mass.: Harvard University Press).

Tardif, T. (1996) 'Nouns are not always learned before verbs: evidence from Mandarin speakers' early vocabularies', *Developmental Psychology* 32, 492–504.

Taylor, M. (1999) *Imaginary Companions and the Children Who Create Them* (New York: Oxford University Press).

Taylor, M. and Carlson, S. (1997) 'The relation between individual differences in fantasy and theory of mind', *Child Development* 68, 436–55.

Taylor, M. and Gelman, S. (1989) 'Incorporating new words into the lexicon: preliminary evidence for language hierarchies in two-year-old children', *Cognitive Development* 60, 625–36.

Teasdale, T. and Owen, D. (2005) 'A long-term rise and recent decline in intelligence test performance: the Flynn effect in reverse', *Personality and Individual Differences* 39, 837–43.

Teitjen, A. and Walker, L. (1985) 'Moral reasoning and leadership among men in a Papua New Guinea society', *Child Development* 21, 982–92.

Teo, T. (2005) *The Critique of Psychology: From Kant to postcolonial theory* (New York: Springer).

Terman, L. (1954) 'The discovery and encouragement of exceptional talent', *American Psychologist* 9, 221–38.

Teti, D. (2004) *Handbook of Research Methods in Developmental Psychology* (Oxford: Blackwell).

Thatcher, R. (1992) 'Cyclical cortical reorganisation during early childhood', *Brain and Cognition* 20, 24–50.

Thelen, E. (1986) 'Treadmill elicited stepping in seven-month-old infants', *Child Development* 57, 1498–1506.

Thelen, E. (1995) 'Motor development: a new synthesis', *American Psychologist* 50, 79–95.

Thelen, E. (2000) 'Motor development as foundation and future of developmental psychology', *International Journal of Behavioural Development* 24, 385–94.

Thelen, E. and Bates, E. (2003) 'Connectionism and dynamic systems: are they really different?' *Developmental Science* 6, 378–91.

Thelen, E. and Fisher, D. (1982) 'Newborn stepping: an explanation for the "disappearing reflex"', *Developmental Psychology* 18, 760–75.

Thelen, E., Fisher, D. and Ridley-Johnson, R. (1984) 'The relationship between physical growth and a newborn reflex', *Infant Behaviour and Development* 7, 479–93.

Thelen, E., Kelso, J. and Fogel, A. (1987) 'Self organising systems and infant motor development', *Developmental Review* 7, 39–65.

Thelen, E., Schöner, G., Scheier, C. and Smith, L. (2001) 'The dynamics of embodiment: a field theory of infant perseverative reaching', *Brain and Behavioural Sciences* 24, 1–86.

Thelen, E. and Smith, L. (1994) *A Dynamic Systems Approach to the Development of Cognition and Action* (Cambridge, Mass.: MIT Press).

Thelen, E. and Ulrich, B. (1991) 'Hidden skills: a dynamic systems analysis of treadmill stepping during the first year', *Monographs of the Society for Research in Child Development* 56 (1, serial no 223).

Thiessen, E., Hill, E. and Saffran, J. (2005) 'Infant-directed speech facilitates word segmentation', *Infancy* 7, 53–71.

Thomas, A. and Chess, S. (1977) *Temperament and Development* (New York: Brunner/Mazel).

Thompson, D. and Siegler, R. (2000) 'Buy low, sell high: the development of an informal theory of economics', *Child Development* 71, 660–77.

Thompson, G. and Nicholson, T. (eds) (1999) *Learning to Read: Beyond phonics and whole language* (New York: Teachers College Press).

Thompson, L., Fagan, J. and Fulker, D. (1991) 'Longitudinal prediction of specific cognitive abilities from infant novelty preference', *Child Development* 62, 530–8.

Thompson, R. (1990) 'Emotion and self-regulation', in R. Thompson (ed.), *Socioemotional Development*, Nebraska Symposium on Motivation 36 (Lincoln: University of Nebraska Press).

Thompson, R. (1998) 'Early sociopersonality development', in N. Eisenberg (ed.), W. Damon (series ed.), *Handbook of Child Psychology*, vol. 3: *Social, Emotional and Personal Development* (New York: Wiley).

Thorkildsen, T. (1989) 'Justice in the classroom: the student's view', *Child Development* 60, 323–34.

Thorkildsen, T. and Schmahl, C. (1997) 'Conceptions of fair learning practices among low income African American and Latin American children: acknowledging diversity', *Journal of Educational Psychology* 89, 719–27.

Thornton, S. (1982) 'Challenging early competence: a process-oriented approach to children's classifying', *Cognitive Science* 6, 77–100.

Thornton, S. (1995) *Children Solving Problems* (Cambridge, Mass.: Harvard University Press).

Thornton, S. (1996) 'Developmental change in the use of relevant recall as a basis for judgments', *British Journal of Psychology* 87, 417–29.

Thornton, S. (1999) 'Creating the conditions for cognitive change: the interaction between task structures and specific strategies', *Child Development* 70, 588–603.

Thornton, S. (2002) *Growing Minds* (Basingstoke: Palgrave Macmillan).

Thornton, S, and Thornton, D. (1995) 'Facets of empathy', *Personality and Individual Differences* 19, 765–7.

Thornton, S., Todd, B. and Thornton, D. (1996) 'Empathy and the recognition of abuse', *Legal and Criminological Psychology* 1, 147–53.

Thurstone, L. (1938) *Primary Mental Abilities* (Chicago: University of Chicago Press).

Tillich, P. (1958) *Dynamics of Faith* (New York: Harper and Row).

Tillich, P. (1964) *Theology of Culture* (New York: Oxford University Press).

Timbergen, N. (1951) *The Study of Instinct* (Oxford: Clarendon Press).

Tincoff, R. and Juscyzk, P. (1999) 'Some beginnings of word comprehension in 6-month-olds', *Psychological Science* 10, 172–5.

Todo, S., Fogel, A. and Kawai, M. (1990) 'Maternal speech to three-month-old infants in the United States and Japan', *Journal of Child Language* 17, 279–94.

Tollefsrud-Anderson, L., Campbell, R., Starkey, P. and Cooper, R. (1992) 'Number conservation: distinguishing quantifier from operator solutions', in J. Bideaud, C. Meljac and J. Fischer (eds), *Pathways to Number* (Hillsdale N.J.: Erlbaum).

Tomasello, M. (1992) 'The social bases of language acquisition', *Social Development* 1, 68–87.

Tomasello, M. (1992) *First Verbs: A case study of early grammatical development* (Cambridge, UK: Cambridge University Press).

Tomasello, M. (1994) 'Can an ape understand a sentence? A review of: *Language comprehension in ape and child* by E. Savage-Rumbaugh et al', *Language and Communication* 14, 377–90.

Tomasello, M. (1998) 'The return of constructions', *Journal of Child Language* 25, 431–42.

Tomasello, M. (1999) 'Social cognition before the revolution', in P. Rochat and T. Striano (eds), *Early Social Cognition: Understanding others in the first months of life* (Hillsdale, N.J.: Lawrence Erlbaum).

Tomasello, M., Strosberg, R. and Akhtar, N. (1996) 'Eighteen-month-old children learn words in non-ostensive contexts', *Journal of Child Language* 23, 157–76.

Trabasso, T. (1975) 'Representation, memory and reasoning: how do we make transitive inferences?' pp. 135–72 in A. Pick (ed.), *Minnesota Symposia on Child Psychology 9*.

Trabasso, T., Isen, A., Dolecki, P., McLanahan, A., Riley, C. and Tucker, T. (1978) 'How do children solve class inclusion problems?', in R. Siegler (ed.), *Children's Thinking: What develops?* (Hillsdale, N.J.: Erlbaum).

Trevarthen, C. (1993a) 'The functions of emotions in early infant communication and development', in J. Nadel and L. Camioni (eds), *New Perspectives in Early Communicative Development* (London and New York: Routledge).

Trevarthen, C. (1993b) 'The self born in intersubjectivity: the psychology of an infant communicating', in U. Neisser (ed.), *The Perceived Self: Ecological and interpersonal sources of self-knowledge* (New York: Cambridge University Press).

Trevarthen, C. (2005) 'First things first: infants make good use of the sympathetic rhythm of imitation, without reasoning or language', *Journal of Child Psychotherapy* 31, 91–113.

Trevarthen, C., Kokkinaki, T. and Fiamenghi, G. (1999) 'What infant's imitations communicate with mothers, fathers and peers', in J. Nadel and G. Butterworth (eds), *Imitation in Infancy* (Cambridge, UK: Cambridge University Press).

Trevethen, S. and Walker, L. (1989) 'Hypothetical versus real-life moral reasoning among psychopathic and delinquent youth', *Developmental Psychopathology* 1, 91–103.

Trivers, R. (1971) 'The evolution of reciprocal altruism', *Quarterly Review of Biology* 46, 35–57.

Trivers, R. (1972) 'Parental investment and sexual selection', pp. 136–79 in B. Campbell (ed.), *Sexual Selection and the Descent of Man 1871–1971* (New York: Aldine de Gruyter).

Troiden, R. (1993) 'The formation of homosexual identities', pp. 191–217 in L. Garnets and D. Kimmel (eds), *Psychological Perspectives on Lesbian and Gay Male Experiences* (New York: Columbia University).

Tryon, R. (1940) 'Genetic differences in maze learning in rats', *Yearbook of the National Society for Studies in Education* 39, 111–19.

Tudge, J., Doucet, F., Odero, D., Sperb, T., Piccinini, C. and Lopes, R. (2006) 'A window into different cultural worlds: young children's everyday activities in the United States, Brazil and Kenya', *Child Development* 77, 1446–69.

Turiel, E. (1983) *The Development of Social Knowledge: Morality and convention* (Cambridge, UK: Cambridge University Press).

Turiel, E. (1987) 'Potential relations between the development of social reasoning and childhood aggression', pp. 95–114 in D. Crowell, I. Evans, I. O'Donnell and R. Clifford (eds), *Childhood Aggression and Violence: Sources of influence, prevention and control. Applied clinical psychology* (New York: Plenum Press).

Turiel, E. (1990) 'Moral judgement, action and development', *New Directions for Child Development* 47, 31–49.

Turiel, E. (1998) 'The development of morality', in N. Eisenberg (ed.), W. Damon (series ed.), *Handbook of Child Psychology*, vol. 3: *Social, Emotional and Personality Development* (New York: Wiley).

Tversky, A. and Kahneman, D. (1973) 'Availability: a heuristic for judging frequency and probability', *Cognitive Psychology* 5, 207–32.

Udry, J., Morris, N. and Kovenock, J. (1995) 'Androgen effects on women's gendered behaviour', *Journal of Biosocial Sciences* 27, 359–68.

Uller, C. and Huntley-Fenner, G. (1995) 'Infant numerical representations', paper presented at the Society for Research in Child Development annual conference, Indianapolis.

Umana-Taylor, A., Bhanot, R. and Shin, N. (2006) 'Ethnic identity formation during adolescence: the critical role of families', *Journal of Family Issues* 27, 390–414.

Underwood, W. and Moore, A. (1982) 'Perspective taking and altruism', *Psychological Bulletin* 91, 143–73.

Vandell, D. and Mueller, E. (1980) 'Peer play and friendships during the first two years', in H. Foot, A. Chapman and J. Smith, *Friendship and social relations in children* (Brunswick, N.J.: Transaction Books).

Van den Bergh, B, Mulder, E, Mennes, M. and Glover, V. (2005) 'Antenatal maternal anxiety and stress and the neurobehavioural development of the fetus and child: links and possible mechanisms: a review', *Neuroscience and Biobehavioural Reviews* 29, 237–58.

Van den Boom, D. (1994) 'The influence of temperament and mothering on attachment and exploration: an experimental manipulation of sensitive responsiveness among lower-class mothers with irritable infants', *Child Development* 65, 1457–77.

Van den Boom, D. and Hoeksma, J. (1994) 'The effect of infant irritability on mother–infant interaction: a growth-curve analysis', *Developmental Psychology* 30, 581–90.

Van der Maas, H. and Jansen, B. (2003) 'What response times tell of children's behaviour on the balance task', *Journal of Experimental Child Psychology* 85, 141–77.

Van Geert, P. (1993) 'A dynamic systems model of cognitive growth: competition and support under limited resource conditions', in L. Smith and E. Thelen (eds), *A Dynamic Systems Approach to Development: Applications* (Cambridge, Mass.: MIT Press).

van Lieshout, C. and Haselager, G. (1993) 'The big five personality factors in Q-sort descriptions of children and adolescents', pp. 293–318 in C. Halverson, G. Kohnstamm and R. Martin (eds), *The Developing Structure of Temperament and Personality from Infancy to Adulthood* (Hillsdale N.J.: Erlbaum).

van Lieshout, C., Haselager, G., Risken-Walraven, J. and van Aken, M. (1995) 'Personality development in middle childhood', paper presented at the meeting of the Society for Research in Child Development, Indianapolis.

van Tijen, N., Stegge, H., Terwogt, M., and van Panhuis, N. (2004) 'Anger, shame and guilt in children with externalizing problems: an imbalance of affects?' *European Journal of Developmental Psychology* 1, 271–9.

van Vreeswijk, M. and de Wilde, E. (2004) 'Autobiographical memory specificity, psychopathology, depressed mood and the use of the Autobiographical Memory Test: a meta-analysis', *Behaviour Research and Therapy* 42, 731–43.

Van IJzendoorn, M. (1995) 'Adult attachment representations, parental responsiveness, and infant attachment: a meta-analysis on the predictive validity of the adult attachment interview', *Psychological Bulletin* 117, 387–403.

Vaughn, B. and Waters, E. (1990) 'Attachment behaviour at home and in the laboratory: Q sort observations and Strange Situation classifications of one-year-olds', *Child Development* 61, 1965–90.

Vaughn, B., Stevenson-Hinde, J., Waters, E., Kotsaftis, A., Lefever, G., Shouldice, A., Trudel, M. and Belsky, J. (1992) 'Attachment security and temperament in infancy and early childhood: some conceptual clarifications', *Developmental Psychology* 28, 463–73.

Vaughn, C. (1996) *How Life Begins* (New York: Times Books).

Veldman, G., Matley, S., Kendall, J., Quirk, J., Parsons, J. and Hewison, J. (2000) 'Illness understanding in children and adolescents with heart disease', *Heart* 84, 395–7.

Vellutino, F. and Scanlon, D. (1987) 'Phonological coding, phonological awareness and reading ability: evidence from a longitudinal and experimental study', *Reading Research Quarterly* 30, 854–75.

Vihman, M. (1992) 'Early syllables and the construction of phonology', in C. Ferguson, L. Menn and C. Stoel-Gammon (eds), *Phonological Development: Models, Research, Implications* (Timonium, Md.: New York Press).

Viken, R., Rose, R., Kaprio, J. and Koskenvuo, M. (1994) 'A developmental genetic analysis of adult personality: extraversion and neuroticism from 18 to 59 years of age', *Journal of Personality and Social Psychology* 66, 722–30.

Vintner, A. (1986) 'The role of movement in eliciting early imitation', *Child Development* 57, 66–71.

von Hofsten, C. and Spelke, E. (1985) 'Object perception and object--directed reaching in infancy', *Journal of Experimental Psychology: General* 114, 198–212.

Vygotsky, L. (1962) *Thought and Language* (Cambridge, Mass.: Harvard University Press).

Vygotsky, L. (1978) *Mind in Society: The development of higher psychological processes* (Cambridge, Mass.: Harvard University Press).

Wachs, T. (1994) 'Fit, context and the transition between temperament and personality', pp. 209–220 in C. Halverson, G. Kohnstamm and R. Martin (eds), *The Developing Structure of Temperament and Personality from Infancy to Adulthood* (Hillsdale, N.J.: Erlbaum).

Wadhwa, P. (1998) 'Prenatal stress and life-span development', pp. 265–80 in H. Friedman (ed.), *Encyclopedia of Mental Health 3* (San Diego: Academic Press).

Wadhwa, P. (2005) 'Psychoneuroendocrine processes in human pregnancy influence fetal development and health', *Psychoneuroendocrinology* 30, 724–42.

Waddington, C. H. (1966) *New Patterns in Genetics and Development* (New York: Columbia University Press).

Wahlsten, D. (1997) 'The malleability of intelligence is not constrained by heritability', in B. Devlin, S. Feiberg and K. Roeder, *Intelligence, Genes and Success: Scientists respond to the bell curve* (New York: Springer).

Wainryb, C. (1995) 'Reasoning about social conflicts in different cultures: Druze and Jewish children in Israel', *Child Development* 66, 390–401.

Wakely, A., Rivera, S. and Langer, J. (2000) 'Can young infants add and subtract?' *Child Development* 71, 1525–34.

Walker, L., Pitts, R., Henning, K. and Matsuba, M. (1995) 'Reasoning about morality and real-life moral problems', in M. Keller and D. Hart (eds), *Morality in Everyday Life* (Cambridge, UK: Developmental Perspectives).

Walker-Andrews, A. (1997) 'Infants' perception of expressive behaviours: differentiation of multimodal information', *Psychological Bulletin* 121, 437–56.

Wallerstein, J. and Lewis, J. (1998) 'The long term impact of divorce on children: a first report from a 25-year study', *Family and Conciliation Courts Review* 36, 368–83.

Wallis, C. (1994) 'Life in overdrive', *Time,* 18 July, 42–50.

Wallis, C. (2003) 'Computation and cognition', *Journal of Experimental and Theoretical Artificial Intelligence* 15, 177–93.

Wallman, J. (1992) *Aping Language* (Cambridge, UK: Cambridge University Press).

Walton, G., Bower, N. and Bower, T. (1992) 'Recognition of familiar faces by newborns', *Infant Behaviour and Development* 15, 265–9.

Wang, S., Baillargeon, R. and Brueckner, L. (2004) 'Young infants reasoning about hidden objects: evidence from violation of expectation tasks with test trials only.', *Cognition* 93, 167–98.

Wark, G. and Krebs, D. (1996) 'Gender and dilemma differences in real-life moral judgement', *Developmental Psychology* 32, 220–30.

Warneken, F. and Tomasello, M. (2006) 'Altruistic helping in human infants and young chimpanzees', *Science* 31, 1301–3.

Warren, M., Brooks-Gunn, J., Fox, R., Lancelot, C., Newman, D. and Hamilton, W. (1991) 'Lack of bone accretion and amenarchea in young dancers: evidence for a relative osteopenia in weight bearing bones', *Journal of Clinical Endocrinology and Metabolism* 72, 847–53.

Waterman, A. (1985) 'Identity in the context of adolescent psychology', in A. Waterman (ed.), *Identity in Adolescence: Progress and contents: (New Directions for Child Development 30)* (San Francisco, Calif.: Jossey-Bass).

Waters, E., Corcoran, D. and Anafarta, M. (2005) 'Attachment, other relationships, and the theory that All Good Things Go Together', *Human Development* 48, 80–4.

Watson, J. (1928) *Psychological Care of Infant and Child* (New York: Norton).

Watson, J. (1930) *Behaviourism,* 2nd edn (New York: Norton).

Watson, J. and Rayner, R. (1920) 'Conditioned emotional reactions', *Journal of Experimental Psychology* 3, 1–14.

Watson-Gegeo, K. and Gegeo, D. (1986) 'Calling out and repeating routines in Kwara'ae children's language socialisation', in B. Schieffelin and E. Ochs (eds), *Language Socialisation across Cultures. Studies in the social and cultural foundations of language,* no 3 (New York: Cambridge University Press).

Webb, C., Rose, F., Johnson, D. and Attree, A. (1996) 'Age and recovery from brain injury: clinical opinions and experimental evidence', *Brain Injury* 10, 303–10.

Wellman, H. (1993) 'Early understanding of mind: the normal case', in S. Baron-Cohen, H. Tager-Flusberg and D. Cohen (eds), *Understanding Other Minds: Perspectives from autism* (Oxford: Oxford University Press).

Wellman, H., Collins, J. and Glieberman, J. (1981) 'Understanding the combination of memory variables: developing conceptions of memory limitations', *Child Development* 52, 1313–17.

Wellman, H., Cross, D. and Bartsch, K. (1987) 'Infant search and object permanence: a meta-analysis of the A-not-B error', *Monographs of the Society for Research in Child Development* 51.

Wellman, H. and Gelman, S. (1998) 'Knowledge acquisition in foundational domains', in D. Kuhn and R. Siegler (eds), W. Damon (series ed.), *Handbook of Child Psychology,* vol. 2: *Cognition, Perception and Language* (New York: Wiley).

Werker, J. and Tees, R. (1984) 'Cross-language speech perception', *Child Development* 7, 49–63.

Werthheimer, M. (1945) *Productive Thinking* (New York: Harper).

Wertsch, J. (1979) 'From social interaction to higher psychological processes: a clarification and application of Vygotsky's theory', *Human Development* 22, 1–22.

Westen, D. (1991) 'Social cognition and object relations', *Psychological Bulletin* 109, 429–55.

Westermann, G. and Mareschal, D. (2004) 'From parts to wholes: mechanisms of development of infant visual object processing', *Infancy* 5, 131–51.

Whaley, A. (2003) 'Cognitive–cultural model of identity and violence prevention for African American youth', *Genetic, Social and General Psychology Monographs* 129, 101–51.

Whiting, B. and Whiting, J. (1975) *Children of Six Cultures: A psychocultural analysis* (Cambridge, Mass.: Harvard University Press).

Whorf, B. (1940/1956) *Language, Thoughts and Reality* (Cambridge, Mass.: MIT Press).

Whorf, B. (1952) 'Language, mind and reality', *Review of General Semantics* 9, 167–88.

Widaman, K., Carlson, J., Saetermoe, C. and Galbraith, G. (1993) 'The relationship of auditory evoked potentials to fluid and crystallized intelligence', *Personality and Individual Differences* 15, 205–17.

Wiebe, S., Cheatham, C., Lukowski, A., Haigh, J., Muehleck, A. and Bauer, P. (2006) 'Infants' ERP responses to novel and familiar stimuli change over time: implications for novelty detection and memory', *Infancy* 9, 21–44.

Willatts, P. (1984) 'Stages in the development of intentional search by young infants', *Developmental Psychology* 20, 39–396.

Willatts, P. (1989) 'Development of problem solving in infancy', in A. Slater and J. Bremner (eds), *Infant Development* (London: Erlbaum).

Willatts, P. (1997) 'Beyond the couch potato infant: how infants use their knowledge to regulate action, solve problems and achieve goals', in G. Bremner, A. Slater and G. Butterworth (eds), *Infant Development: Recent advances* (Hillsdale, N.J.: Psychology Press/Erlbaum, UK).

Willatts, P. (1999) 'Development of means–end behaviour in young infants: pulling a support to retrieve a distant object', *Developmental Psychology* 35, 652–67.

Willatts, P. and Rosie, K. (1989) 'Planning by 12-month-old infants', paper presented to SRCD biennial conference, Kansas.

Williams, J., Whiten, A., Suddendorf, T. and Perrett, D. (2001) 'Imitation, mirror neurons and autism', *Neuroscience and Biobehavioral Reviews* 25, 287–95.

Wilson, E. O. (1980) *Sociobiology: The new synthesis* (Cambridge Mass.: Harvard University Press).

Wimmer, H. and Hartl, M. (1991) 'Against the Cartesian view on mind: young children's difficulty with false beliefs', *British Journal of Developmental Psychology* 9, 125–39.

Wimmer, H. and Perner, J. (1983) 'Beliefs about beliefs: representation and constraining function of wrong beliefs in young children's understanding of deception', *Cognition* 13, 103–28.

Windle, M. and Lerner, R. (1986) 'Reassessing the dimensions of temperamental individuality across the life-span: the revised dimensions of temperament survey (DOTS-R)', *Journal of Adolescent Research* 1, 213–30.

Wink, P. and Helson, R. (1992) 'Personality change in women and their partners', *Journal of Personality and Social Psychology* 65, 597–605.

Wiser, M. and Carey, S. (1983) 'When heat and temperature were one', in D. Gentner and A. Stevens (eds), *Mental Models* (Hillsdale, N.J.: Erlbaum).

Wolff, P., Michel, G., Ovrut, M. and Drake, C. (1990) 'Rate and timing precision of motor coordination in developmental dyslexia', *Developmental Psychology* 26, 349–59.

Wolpert, L. (1991) *The Triumph of the Embryo* (Oxford: Oxford University Press).

Wood, D., Bruner, J. and Ross, G. (1976) 'The role of tutoring in problem solving', *Journal of Child Psychology and Psychiatry* 17, 89–100.

Wood, D., Wood, H. and Middleton, D. (1978) 'An experimental evaluation of four face to face teaching strategies', *International Journal of Behavioural Development* 1, 131–47.

Woodward, A. and Markman, E. (1998) 'Early word learning', in D. Kuhn and R. Siegler (eds), W. Damon (series ed.), *Handbook of Child Psychology*, vol. 2, *Cognition, Perception and Language* (New York: Wiley).

Woolley, J. (1997) 'Thinking about fantasy: are children fundamentally different thinkers and believers from adults?' *Child Development* 68, 991–1011.

Wynn, K. (1992a) 'Addition and subtraction by human infants', *Nature* 358, 749–50.

Wynn, K. (1992b) 'Children's acquisition of number words and the counting system', *Cognitive Psychology* 20, 220–51.

Wynn, K. (1995) 'Origins of numerical knowledge', *Mathematical Cognition* 1, 35–60.

Xu, F. and Pinker, S. (1995) 'Weird past tense forms', *Journal of Child Language* 22, 531–56.

Yeates, K. and Selman, R. (1989) 'Social competence in the schools: toward an integrative developmental model for intervention', *Developmental Review* 9, 64–100.

York, K. and John, O. (1992) 'The four faces of Eve: a typological analysis of women's personality at midlife', *Journal of Personality and Social Psychology* 63, 494–508.

Yuill, N. (1984) 'Young children's coordination of motive and outcome in judgments of satisfaction and morality', *British Journal of Developmental Psychology* 2, 73–81.

Zahn-Waxler, C. (1991) 'The case for empathy: a developmental review'. *Psychological Enquiry 2,* 155–158.

Zahn-Waxler, C., Cole, P. and Barrett, K. (1991) 'Guilt and empathy: sex differences and implications for the development of depression', in J. Garber and K. Dodge (eds), *The Development of Emotion Regulation and Dysregulation* (New York: Cambridge University Press).

Zahn-Waxler, C. and Radke-Yarrow, M. (1982) 'The development of altruism: alternative research strategies', in N. Eisenberg (ed.), *The Development of Prosocial Behavior* (New York: Academic Press).

Zahn-Waxler, C., Radke-Yarrow, M., Wagner, E. and Chapman, M. (1992) 'Development of concern for others', *Developmental Psychology* 28, 126–36.

Zahn-Waxler, C. and Robinson, J. (1995) 'Empathy and guilt: early origins of feelings of responsibility', in J. Tangney and K. Fischer (eds), *Self Conscious Emotions* (New York: Guilford Press).

Zahn-Waxler, C., Robinson, J. and Emde, R. (1992) 'The development of empathy in twins', *Developmental Psychology* 28, 1038–47.

Zarbatany, L., Hartmann, D. and Gelfand, D. (1985) 'Why does children's generosity increase with age: susceptibility to experimenter influence or altruism?' *Child Development* 56, 746–56.

Zarbatany, L., Hartmann, D. and Rankin, D. (1990) 'The psychological functions of preadolescent peer activities', *Child Development* 61, 1067–80.

Zelazo, P., Zelazo, N. and Kolb, S. (1972) '"Walking" in the newborn', *Science* 117, 1058–9.

name index

Short, K., 115
Shouldice, A., 166
Shrager, J., 284, 299, 303
Shrum, W., 485
Shulman, S., 475
Shultz, T., 362
Shupe, A., 162
Shute, R., 482
Siegal, M., 364, 365, 366
Siegler, R., 20, 24, 87, 214, 237–8, 255, 281–4, 295–304, 309, 316, 336, 340, 342, 364, 530, 531
Sigman, M., 144, 372, 379
Sigmundson, H., 439
Silva, P., 399, 405, 541, 545
Simion, F., 109, 136, 137, 508
Simmons, R., 454
Simon, T., 110, 229, 295, 333, 499
Simonoff, E., 348
Simons, R., 473
Simpson, B., 475
Simpson, E., 526
Sims, C., 472
Singer, D., 480, 495
Singer, J., 480, 495
Sisk, C., 492, 493
Skinner, B. F., 11, 12, 13, 24, 146, 193
Slade, H., 161, 447, 549
Slater, A., 103, 107, 109, 114, 115, 124, 127, 131, 137, 140, 188, 246, 250, 255, 266, 328
Slatterlee, D., 164
Slaughter, V., 359
Slawinski, J., 299
Slobin, D., 195, 203
Sloutsky, V., 234, 235, 239, 339
Slovic, P., 234, 242–4, 262, 339
Smallwood, A., 491
Smith, B., 519
Smith, C., 519
Smith, G., 405
Smith, L., 119, 123, 124, 127, 203, 258, 305, 315, 349, 402, 567
Smith, N., 348
Smoleniec, J., 71
Smoot, D., 497
Snarey, J., 525, 526
Sneed, J., 423
Snyder, A., 379, 466, 550
Snyder, J., 118
Snyder, M., 512
Sodian, B., 239
Soenens, B., 413
Soken, N., 145, 146
Soloman, J., 156
Solomon, G., 251
Somerville, S., 267
Sophian, C., 229, 301, 303, 304, 305, 315, 316, 342
Sorce, J., 147

Sousa, P., 251
Soussignan, R., 73
Spahr, K., 119
Spangler, G., 157
Spear, N., 274
Spearman, C., 324
Spelke, E., 112–13, 115–16, 232, 238, 250, 254
Speltz, M., 550
Spence, J., 56, 58, 86, 124, 511, 566–8
Spencer, A., 462
Spencer, H., 506
Spencer, M., 435,
Sperb, T., 425
Sprecher, S., 542
Springer, K., 251
Sroufe, A., 503
Sroufe, L., 143, 168, 447, 487
Stambrook, M., 469
Stanhope, L., 466
Stapp, J., 511
Starkey, P., 111, 228
Stedron, J., 123
Steele, H., 161, 447, 549
Steele, M., 161, 447, 549
Steenbeck, H., 502
Stefan, K., 144, 372
Stegge, H., 540
Stein, H., 447
Stein, Z., 77
Steinberg, L., 448, 449, 455, 456, 492, 551
Steiner, J., 141
Stenberg, C., 141
Stern, D., 150
Stern, E., 295, 301
Sternberg, R., 293, 336, 350–1
Stevenson, S., 537
Stevenson-Hinde, J., 166
Stewart, A., 537
Stigler, J., 238, 239
Stone, B., 276
Stoneman, Z., 468
Stouthamer-Loeber, M., 399, 405, 545, 552
Strauch, B., 491
Strayer, J., 381, 386
Strelau, J., 162
Striano, T., 131, 134, 171
Strichartz, A., 517
Strosberg, R., 189
Strupp, B., 77
Stryker, S., 452, 503
Stürmer, S., 512
Subbotsky, E., 534, 537
Suddendorf, T., 379–80
Suess, G., 157
Sugita, Y., 210
Suls, J., 419
Susser, M., 77

Vapnarsky, V., 251
Varano, S., 552
Varendi, H., 73
Vaughn, B., 66, 73, 158, 166
Veldman, G., 468
Vellutino, F., 236
Vereijken, B., 85
Viechtbauer, W., 402, 406
Vietze, D., 425
Vihman, M., 183
Viken, R., 400
Vintner, A., 132
Visser, G., 70
Vogt, T., 405
Volling, B., 466
Von der Schulenberg, C., 137
Von Hofsten, C., 132, 254
Von Holsten, C., 115
Vondra, J., 166
Vosper, J., 467
Vuckovic, N., 472
Vygotsky, L., 14, 15, 24, 41, 189, 193, 206, 252, 311, 312, 313, 339

W

Wach, T., 162
Wachs, T., 77, 403, 546
Waddington, C. H., 58n1
Wade-Stein, D., 542
Wadhwa, P., 79, 162
Wagner, E., 497
Wahlsten, D., 331
Wainryb, C., 533
Wakely, A., 111, 238
Walker, L., 525, 526, 537, 542
Walker-Andrews, A., 146
Wall, S., 155
Wallace, Alfred Russel, 342
Wallace, J., 20, 229, 284, 301
Wallerstein, J., 471
Wallis, C., 4, 315
Wallman, J., 180
Walsh, M., 468
Walton, G., 137, 250
Walton, K., 402, 406
Wang, S., 117
Ward, M., 161, 447, 549
Ward, R., 419
Wark, G., 525
Warkentin, V., 413
Warneken, F., 510
Warren, H., 273
Warren, M., 472
Wasserman, S., 113, 116, 232
Waterman, A., 422
Waters, E., 155, 158, 166
Watrous, B., 71

Watson, A., 169
Watson, John, 12, 24, 37, 132
Watson-Gegeo, K., 207
Wattam, C., 499
Webb, C., 82
Wehner, E., 487
Weinberg, D., 482
Weinberg, J., 384
Weiss, R., 452
Weisz, J., 550
Wellman, H., 118, 119, 124, 249, 260, 267, 274, 276, 277, 359, 362, 363, 364
Wells, G., 191, 192, 201
Wenger, E., 252
Wentworth, N., 250, 253
Werker, J., 183
Werthheimer, M., 292
Wertsch, J., 206, 312, 339
West, M., 509
Westen, D., 401, 443
Westermann, G., 107, 123
Whaley, A., 556
Wheeler, D., 234
White, S., 273
Whiten, A., 370, 379–80
Whiting, B., 463, 465, 512
Whiting, J., 463, 465, 512
Whitman, T., 520
Whorf, B., 193
Widaman, K., 329
Wiebe, S., 266
Willatts, P., 119, 120, 125, 285, 286–7, 288, 300
Williams, E., 111
Williams, J., 379–80
Williams, M., 243
Williams, S., 180, 214, 405
Wilson, E. O., 9, 24
Wimmer, H., 362, 363, 365
Winberg, J., 73
Windle, M., 163
Wingard, D., 405
Wink, P., 407
Wishart, J., 118, 120
Wojslawowics, J., 498
Wolfe, D., 87, 350, 373, 386, 391
Wolff, P., 346
Wolpert, L., 66, 67
Wood, D., 312, 313
Wood, H., 313
Woodburn, S., 482
Woodson, R., 132, 145
Woodward, A., 186, 188
Woolley, J., 220–1
Wynn, K., 110, 111, 112, 115, 238, 250, 301

X

Xu, F., 200

subject index

white coat syndrome, 27
witnesses to crime, 3–4
women
    defined by relationships to men, 437
    women's movement, 438
    see also gender, mothers
words
    confusion over nature of, 197
    learning, 185–90, 195–6, 215–16
    and the lexical hypothesis, 396–7
    and phonemic awareness, 236
    'verb expectation', 204
    see also language
work, hours of children's, 4

Z

zone of proximal development, 14, 313
zygote/zygotic stage of development, 64–5